This book is to be returned on or before
the last date stamped below.

UNIVERSAL GRAMMAR: 15 ESSAYS

CROOM HELM LINGUISTICS SERIES

Universal Grammar:
15 Essays

Edward L. Keenan

CROOM HELM
London • Sydney • Wolfeboro, New Hampshire

C

British Library Cataloguing in Publication Data
Universal grammar: 15 essays.—(Croom
    Helm linguistics series)
    1. Grammar, Comparative and general
    I. Keenan, Edward L.
    415   P151
    ISBN 0-7099-3109-3

Croom Helm, 27 South Main Street,
Wolfeboro, New Hampshire 03894-2069, USA

Library of Congress Cataloging in Publication Data

Universal grammar.
    Reprint. Originally published: Washington, D.C.:
Georgetown University Press, C1975.
    1. Grammar, comparative and general. I. Keenan,
Edward L., 1935–
P201.U55   1986   415   86-8848
ISBN 0-7099-3109-3

Typeset by Leaper & Gard Ltd, Bristol, England
Printed and bound in Great Britain by Mackays of Chatham Ltd, Kent

D
415
UNI

EDITORIAL STATEMENT

CROOM HELM LINGUISTICS SERIES

Chief Editor
Professor John Hawkins, University of Southern California

Consultant Editors
Professor Joseph Aoun, University of Southern California
Professor Bernard Comrie, University of Southern California
Professor Edward Finegan, University of Southern California
Dr Richard Hudson, University College London
Professor James Hurford, University of Edinburgh
Professor Douglas Pulleyblank, University of Southern
   California

The Croom Helm Linguistics Series does not specialise in any one area of language study, nor does it limit itself to any one theoretical approach. Synchronic and diachronic descriptive studies, either syntactic, semantic, phonological or morphological, are welcomed, as are more theoretical 'model-building' studies, and studies in sociolinguistics or psycholinguistics. The criterion for a work's acceptance is the quality of its contribution to the relevant field. All texts published must advance our understanding of the nature of language in areas of substantial interest to major sectors of the linguistic research community. Traditional scholarly standards, such as clarity of presentation, factual and logical soundness of argumentation, and a thorough and reasoned orientation to other relevant work, are also required. Within these indispensable limitations we welcome the submission of creative and original contributions to the study of language.

The editors and publisher wish to draw this series to the attention of scholars, who are invited to submit manuscripts or book-proposals to:

Professor John Hawkins, Department of Linguistics, University of Southern California, Los Angeles, CA 90089-1693, USA: *or to* Jonathan Price, Linguistics Editor, Croom Helm Publishers, Provident House, Burrell Row, Beckenham, Kent BR3 1AT, UK.

CONTENTS

REFERENCES FOR THE ARTICLES

1. 'Noun Phrase Accessibility and Universal Grammar' (with Bernard Comrie) in *Linguistic Inquiry* vol. 8 no. 1 (Winter, 1977). © 1977 MIT Press.
2. 'Variation in Universal Grammar' in R. Fasold and R. Shuy (eds.) *Analyzing Variation in English* Georgetown University Press, Washington D.C. © 1975 Georgetown University.
3. 'The Psychological Validity of the Accessibility Hierarchy' (with Sarah Hawkins) not before published. © 1986 Edward Keenan and Sarah Hawkins.
4. 'Towards a Universal Definition of "Subject of"' in C. Li (ed.) *Subject and Topic* Academic Press, 1976. © 1976 Edward Keenan.
5. 'On Collapsing Grammatical Relations in Universal Grammar' (with Judy Gary) in P. Cole and J. Sadock (eds.) *Syntax and Semantics*, vol. 8 *Grammatical Relations* Academic Press, 1977. © 1977 Edward Keenan and Judith Gary.
6. 'Semantic Correlates to the Ergative/Absolutive Distinction', *Linguistics* vol. 22 no. 2, 1984. © 1984 Edward Keenan.
7. 'Some Universals of Passive in Relational Grammar' in *Papers from the Twelfth Annual Meeting of the Chicago Linguistic Society*, Chicago Linguistic Society, Department of Linguistics, University of Chicago, Chicago, Illinois, 1975. © 1975 Edward Keenan.
8. 'Passive is Phrasal (not Sentential or Lexical)' in T. Hoekstra, H. van der Hulst, and M. Moortgat (eds.) *Lexical Grammar* Foris, Dordrecht, 1980. © 1980 Edward Keenan.
9. 'Parametric Variation in Universal Grammar' in R. Dirven and G. Radden (eds.) *Issues in the Theory of Universal Grammar*, Gunter Narr Verlag, 1982. © 1982 Edward Keenan.
10. 'Predicate Formation Rules' to appear in Michael Wescoat *et al.* (eds.) *Proceedings of the West Coast Conference on Formal Linguistics*, vol. 4, Stanford Linguistics Association, Department of Linguistics, Stanford University, Stanford, California, 1985. © 1985 Edward Keenan and Alan Timberlake.
11. 'The Logical Status of Deep Structures' in Luigi Heilmann (ed.) *Proceedings of the Eleventh International Congress of Linguists*, Società editrice il Mulino, Bologna, 1972. © 1972 Edward Keenan.
12. 'The Functional Principle' in *Papers from the Tenth Regional Meetings of the Chicago Linguistics Society*, Department of Linguistics, University of Chicago, 1974. © 1974 Edward Keenan.
13. 'On Surface Form and Logical Form' in *Studies in the Linguistic Sciences* vol. 8 no. 2, 1979, Department of Linguistics, University of Illinois. © 1979 Edward Keenan.
14. 'The Logical Diversity of Natural Languages' in S. Harnad, H. Steklis, and J. Lancaster (eds.), *Origins and Evolution of Language and Speech*, The New York Academy of Sciences vol. 280, 1976. © 1976 The New York Academy of Sciences.
15. 'Facing the Truth' in *Linguistics and Philosophy* 6, 1983, D. Reidel Pub. Co. Dordrecht. © 1983 D. Reidel Pub. Co.

Dédicace
A la marquise de Colmar, pour qui
le coeur et l'esprit ne font qu'un.

INTRODUCTION

The articles in this collection span a period of 14 years beginning with 'The Logical Status of Deep Structures' in 1972. They reflect my long-standing research interests in the comparative syntax of the languages of the world. I have included here two articles, 'Noun Phrase Accessibility and Universal Grammar' (with Bernard Comrie) and 'Towards a Universal Definition of "Subject of"' which are readily available elsewhere but which in many respects serve as a foundation for the themes presented in the other articles. The majority of the other articles appeared in sources not easily available to a large audience, and one, 'The Psychological Validity of the Accessibility Hierarchy' appears here for the first time.

I wish here to acknowledge my debt to John Hawkins for persuading me of the interest in bringing together a series of disparate publications on common themes, to Croom Helm Publishers for taking the initiative to publish this collection, and to the Max Planck Institut für Psycholinguistik, Nijmegen, for providing me with the environment needed to put this collection together and write the one new article it contains.

I should note that the articles appear in essentially the form in which they were originally published, though a few minor errors have been corrected and certain portions of commentaries published with the originals from conference proceedings have been eliminated.

PART ONE:
CROSS LANGUAGE VARIATION

This section includes one of the foundation articles mentioned in the Introduction, 'Noun Phrase Accessibility', written with Bernard Comrie in 1977. It introduces the Accessibility Hierarchy, which has proved to be of some utility in later studies in Universal Grammar, as well as in psycholinguistic and second-language-learning literature. The less well-known article here, 'Variation in Universal Grammar', is an extensive text study which supports the hypothesis that the Accessibility Hierarchy can be used as a measure of stylistic complexity. The remaining article in this section, 'The Psychological Validity of the Accessibility Hierarchy' (written with Sarah Hawkins), reports the results of a series of psycholinguistic experiments designed broadly to test the hypothesis that the Accessibility Hierarchy can be used as a measure of the cognitive complexity of relative clauses.

1 NOUN PHRASE ACCESSIBILITY AND UNIVERSAL GRAMMAR[1]

(Written with Bernard Comrie)

In section 1 we present the Accessibility Hierarchy, in terms of which we state three universal constraints on Relative Clause Formation. In addition, we present the data in support of these constraints and discuss certain partial counterexamples. In section 2 we propose a partial explanation for the hierarchy constraints and present further data from Relative Clause Formation supporting these explanations. Finally, in section 3 we refer briefly to other work suggesting that the distribution of advancement processes such as Passive can be described in terms of the Accessibility Hierarchy; these facts show that the proposed explanation for the Hierarchy needs to be generalised.

1. The Accessibility Hierarchy

1.1 Two Methodological Preliminaries

We are attempting to determine the universal properties of relative clauses (RCs) by comparing their syntactic form in a large number of languages. To do this it is necessary to have a largely syntax-free way of identifying RCs in an arbitrary language.

Our solution to this problem is to use an essentially semantically based definition of RC. We consider any syntactic object to be an RC if it specifies a set of objects (perhaps a one-member set) in two steps: a larger set is specified, called the *domain* of relativisation, and then restricted to some subset of which a certain sentence, the *restricting* sentence, is true.[2] The domain of relativisation is expressed in surface structure by the *head NP*, and the restricting sentence by the *restricting clause*, which may look more or less like a surface sentence depending on the language.

For example, in the relative clause *the girl (that) John likes* the domain of relativisation is the set of girls and the head NP is *girl.* The restricting sentence is *John likes her* and the restricting clause is *(that) John likes.* Clearly, for an object to be correctly referred

3

to by *the girl that John likes,* the object must be in the domain of relativisation and the restricting sentence must be true of it. We shall refer to the NP in the restricting sentence that is coreferential with the head NP as the NP relativised on (NP_{rel}); in our example, this is *her,* i.e. the direct object of *John likes her.*

Note that we only consider definite restrictive RCs in this study. The role of the determiner *the* is held constant and ignored, and the term *RC* is used to apply to the collocation of the head NP and the restricting clause.

Note further that our semantically based notion of RC justifies considering as RCs certain constructions that would perhaps not have been so considered in traditional grammar. Thus, in German, alongside the traditional RC in (1) we also count the participial construction in (2):

(1)   der Mann, der in seinem Büro arbeitet
      the man   who in his   study works
      'the man who is working in his study'
(2)   der in seinem Büro arbeitende Mann
      the in his   study working   man
      'the man who is working in his study'

As the German data above illustrate, not only do different languages vary with respect to the way RCs are formed, but also within a given language there is often more than one distinct type of RC. We shall refer to distinct ways of forming RCs as different relative-clause-forming *strategies.* Different strategies differ with regard to which NP positions they can relativise. Thus, the participial strategy in (2) above can only relativise subjects (that is, the head NP can only be understood to function as the subject of the main verb of the restricting clause), whereas the strategy in (1) above functions to relativise almost any major NP position in simplex sentences. Consequently, generalisations concerning the relativisability of different NPs must be made dependent on the strategies used. It will be critical therefore to provide some principled basis for deciding when two different RCs have been formed with different strategies.

There are many ways RCs differ at the surface, and hence many possible criteria for determining when two strategies are different. We have chosen two criteria that seem to us most directly related to our perception of how we understand the meaning of the RC —

that is, of how we understand what properties an object must have to be correctly referred to by the RC. The first concerns the way the head NP and the restricting clause are distinguished at the surface, and the second concerns how the position relativised is indicated.

In the first case we consider two RCs to be formed by different strategies if the relative position of the head NP and the restricting clause differs. There are three possibilities: the head occurs to the left of the restricting clause, as in (1) above (*postnominal* RC strategy); the head occurs to the right, as in (2) (*prenominal* RC strategy); or the head occurs within the restricting clause (*internal* RC strategy), as in (3) and (4), from Bambara (Bird 1966) and Digueño (Gorbet 1972), respectively:

(3) a. ne ye so ye.
      I Past horse see
      'I saw a horse.'

    b. ne ye so min ye
      I Past horse which see
      'the horse that I saw'

    c. tye ye ne ye so min ye san.
      man Past I Past horse which see buy
      'The man bought the horse that I saw.'

(4) a. tənay ʔəwa: + ɸ ʔəwu:w.
      yesterday house DO I-saw
      'I saw the house yesterday.'

    b. ʔəwa: + pu + Lʸ ʔciyawx.
      house Def in I-will-sing
      'I will sing in the house.'

    c. [$_{NP}$[$_S$ tənay ʔəwa:+ɸ ʔəwu:w]]+pu+Lʸ ʔciyawx.
         yesterday house DO I-saw Def in I-will-sing
      'I will sing in the house that I saw yesterday.'

In the second case we consider two RCs to be formed from different strategies if one presents a nominal element in the restricting clause that unequivocally expresses which NP position is being relativised, and thus we know exactly what the restricting clause is saying about the head NP (that is, we can recover the restricting sentence from surface) (+*case* RC strategy). For example, the English strategy that forms *the girl who John likes* is not case-coding since *who*, the only relevant particle in the restricting clause, can be used as well if the role of the head NP in the restricting clause is different, e.g. *the girl who likes John* (−*case* RC strategy). On the other hand, in comparable sentences is Russian, (5a) and (5b), the form of the relative pronoun does unequivocally tell us the role of the head NP, so that strategy in Russian is case-coding:

(5) a.   devuška, kotoruju   Džon ljubit
          girl   who (accusative) John likes
          'the girl who John likes'
     b.   devuška, kotoraja   ljubit Džona
          girl   who (nominative) likes John
          'the girl who likes John'

Note, however that RCs in English like *the chest in which John put the money* are considered case-coding, since the preposition *in*, which indicates the role of the head NP, is present in the restricting clause.

In addition to the use of relative pronouns, case can be coded in another way in the languages covered in our study. Namely, a personal pronoun can be present in the NP position relativised, as in Hebrew:

(6) ha- isha   she- Yon natan la   et   ha- sefer
     the woman that John gave to-her DO the book
     'the woman that John gave the book to'

1.2   The Accessibility Hierarchy and the Hierarchy Constraints

1.2.1 Statement of the Hierarchy and the Constraints.   On the basis of data from about fifty languages, we argue that languages vary with respect to which NP positions can be relativised, and that the variation is not random. Rather, the relativisability of certain positions is dependent on that of others, and these dependencies are, we claim, universal. The Accessibility Hierarchy (AH) below expresses the relative accessibility to relativisation of NP positions in simplex main clauses.

Accessibility Hierarchy (AH)
SU > DO > IO > OBL > GEN > OCOMP

Here, '>' means 'is more accessible than'; SU stands for 'subject', DO for 'direct object', IO for 'indirect object', OBL for 'major oblique case NP' (we intend here NPs that express arguments of the main predicate, as *the chest* in *John put the money in the chest* rather than ones having a more adverbial function like *Chicago* in *John lives in Chicago* or *that day* in *John left on that day*), GEN stands for 'genitive' (or 'possessor') NP, e.g. *the man* in *John took the man's hat,* and OCOMP stands for 'object of comparison', e.g. *the man* in *John is taller than the man.*

The positions on the AH are to be understood as specifying a set of possible grammatical distinctions that a language may make. We are not claiming that any given language necessarily distinguishes all these categories, either in terms of RC formation or in terms of other syntactic processes. For example, some languages (e.g. Hindi) treat objects of comparison like ordinary objects of prepositions or postpositions. In such cases we treat these NPs as ordinary OBLs, and the OCOMP position on the AH is unrealised. Similarly, in Gary and Keenan (1976) it is argued that the DO and IO positions are not syntactically distinguished in Kinyarwanda, a Bantu language. Further, it is possible that in some language RC formation might distinguish between two types of DOs. If this were so, we would like to expand the AH at that point and say that languages like English do not make the distinction. For the moment, however, we take the AH as specifying the set of possible grammatical distinctions to which RC formation (from simplex main clauses) may be sensitive, since our data do not appear to justify any further refinement in the categories.

In terms of the AH we now give the Hierarchy Constraints (HCs):

The Hierarchy Constraints (HCs)
1. A language must be able to relativise subjects.
2. Any RC-forming strategy must apply to a continuous segment of the AH.
3. Strategies that apply at one point of the AH may in principle cease to apply at any lower point.

The HCs define conditions that any grammar of a human language must meet. HC_1 says that the grammar must be designed to allow relativisation on subjects, the uppermost end of the AH. Thus, for example, no language can relativise only DOs, or only locatives. It is possible, however, for a language to allow relativisation only on subjects (and this possibility is in fact realised: see 1.3.1 for examples). HC_2 states that, as far as relativisation is concerned, a language is free to treat adjacent positions on the AH as the same, but it cannot 'skip' positions. Thus, if a given strategy can apply to both subjects and locatives, it can also apply to DOs and IOs. And HC_3 states that each point of the AH is a possible cut-off point for any strategy that applies to a higher point. This means that in designing the grammar for a possible human language, once we have given it a strategy that applies at some point on the AH, we are free to terminate its application at any lower point.

Note that it is HC_2 that justifies the actual ordering of terms in the AH. Further, HC_2 allows as a special case that a particular RC-forming strategy may apply to only a single position. Thus several languages (e.g. Javanese: see Table 1.1) have recourse to a case-coding strategy for positions low on the AH (e.g. genitives), whereas the strategy for major NPs is not case-coding. On the other hand, HC_3 states that each point on the AH is relevant. Thus, if no language could have an RC-forming strategy that applied to DOs but not to IOs, then the data would not justify making this distinction in the AH. In section 1.3 we substantiate the claim that each point on the AH is in fact a possible cut-off point by showing that for each point on the AH some language has a strategy that cuts off at that point.

1.2.2 The Primary Relativisation Constraint.   In 1.2.1 we stated that the AH determines, universally, the degree of accessibility to RC formation. But it is perhaps not obvious that the HCs actually make that intuition explicit. However, the Primary Relativisation Constraint (PRC) below does make that intuition more explicit, and it logically follows from the HCs. To state it we first define an RC-forming strategy in a given language to be a *primary strategy* (in that language) if it can be used to relativise subjects. The term *primary* is justified in that, by HC_1, a language must have a primary strategy but need have no other. Thus, of the various RC-forming strategies a language may have, only primary ones are necessary. We can now state:

The Primary Relativisation Constraint (PRC)
1. A language must have a primary RC-forming strategy.
2. If a primary strategy in a given language can apply to a low

position on the AH, then it can apply to all higher positions.
3. A primary strategy may cut off at any point on the AH.

Clearly, PRC_1 is just a restatement of HC_1. PRC_2 follows directly from HC_2 and the definition of *primary*, since a primary strategy that can relativise a low position on the AH is one that can relativise subjects (since it is primary) and a low position, and so by HC_2 it can relativise all intermediate positions. And PRC_3 is simply a special case of HC_3.

Thus the PRC states that, restricting our attention to primary RC-forming strategies, relativisability of a low position on the AH entails relativisability of all higher positions. And the converse fails. We may be able to relativise only subjects, both subjects and DOs, or subjects, DOs, and IOs, etc. So the possibility of relativising (with a primary strategy) decreases as we go down the AH, and in that sense the further we descend the AH the harder it is to relativise.

Note that there is a more obvious, and stronger, way to express the intuition that relativisability decreases as we descend the AH. namely, 'if a language can relativise any position low on the AH, then it can relativise all higher positions'. This claim says in effect that RC-forming strategies always distribute themselves so as to cover an initial segment of the AH. But this formulation is falsified by our data.

Thus Toba Batak (a Malayo-Polynesian language spoken in Sumatra) has a primary strategy, illustrated in (7), which is postnominal and −case:

(7) a. manussi   abit   boru-boru i.
         wash (active) clothes woman   the
         'The woman is washing clothes.'
     b. boru-boru na manussi abit   i
         woman   that wash   clothes the
         'the woman who is washing clothes'

(Note that the basic word order is VOS. See Silitonga (1973) for further substantiation of this point.)

However, direct objects cannot be relativised using this or any other strategy in Toba, as we see from (8a). The only way to achieve the semantic effect of (8a) is first to passivise the underlying sentence, (8b), and then relativise on the derived subject, (8c):

(8)   a.   *abit   na   manussi boru-boru i
               clothes that wash   woman   the
               'the clothes that the woman is washing'
       b.   disussi   ni boru-boru abit   i.
               wash (passive) by woman   clothes the
               'The clothes were washed by the woman.'
       c.   abit   na   nisussi ni boru-boru i
               clothes that washed by woman   the
               'the clothes that were washed by the woman'

(Note that the passive prefix *di-* becomes *ni-* in subordinate position.)

Thus Toba, like many Malayo-Polynesian languages (Keenan 1972b), cannot directly relativise NPs that can be promoted to subject. It must promote them and then relativise them as subjects. However, in distinction to Philippine languages and Malagasy, for instance, Toba has a rather limited promotion ('voicing') system. NPs governed by prepositions, including IOs, cannot be systematically promoted to subject. To relativise them, a second strategy, this time +case, can be used. The relativisation marker is different, and a personal pronoun is retained in the position relativised:

(9)   dakdanak i, ima-   na   nipaboa ni si Rotua turi-turian-i
                                                                              tu ibana
         child   the namely that told   by Art Rotua story   the
                                                                              to him
         'the child that Rotua told the story to'

Clearly, then, Toba has 'gapped' RC-forming strategies. One applies only to subjects, the other to IOs, OBLs, and GENS. The NPs in the 'gap', in this case the DO, must be promoted to subject to be relativised. All the languages in our sample that present gapped strategies (see Table 1.1) are similar to Toba in this respect. That is, unrelativisable NPs can be systematically promoted to higher positions on the AH, whence they can be relativised. The fact that NPs lying in strategy gaps can always be promoted to accessible positions does justify the following form of the strong constraint: if a language can relativise any position on the AH, then it can relativise any higher position either directly or by promoting it to a position that can itself be relativised directly.

We consider now, in section 1.3, the data that support the Hierarchy Constraints. In particular, we show that each point on the AH represents a cut-off point for some primary strategy. Then, in 1.4, we consider some of the problematic cases and possible counterexamples.

1.3 Justification of the Hierarchy Constraints

1.3.1 Subjects Only. In many Western Malayo-Polynesian languages, only subjects can be relativised; consider for instance Malagasy, which has basic word order V O X S and a developed system for promoting any major NP to subject position. RCs place the head NP to the left, followed optionally by an invariable relativiser *izay*, followed by the restricting clause with no pronoun in the NP_{rel} position (Keenan 1972b):

(10) a. Nahita ny vehivavy ny mpianatra.
         saw   the woman   the student
         'The student saw the woman.'
     b. ny mpianatra izay nahita ny vehivavy
         the student that saw   the woman
         'the student that saw the woman'
     c. *ny vehivavy izay nahita ny mpianatra
         the woman   that saw   the student
         'the woman that the student saw'
     d. Nohitan'   ny mpianatra ny vehivavy.
         seen (passive) the student the woman
         'The woman was seen by the student.'
     e. ny vehivavy izay nohitan'ny mpianatra
         the woman that seen the   student
         'the woman that was seen by the student'

Other Malayo-Polynesian languages in our sample that have primary strategies that apply only to subjects are Javanese, Iban, Minang-Kabau, and Toba Batak; also Tagalog, on the assumption that the 'focus' NP is the subject (see further 1.4.1.1). Finally, many European languages (e.g. German, Russian, and Polish) have participial RC-forming strategies that apply only to subjects; cf. (2) above.

1.3.2. Subjects — Direct Objects.   In Welsh, the primary strategy applies only to subjects and direct objects; it presents postnominal RCs introduced by the particle *a*, with deletion of NP_{rel}. Other positions are relativised by a different postnominal strategy, introduced by the particle *y* and with a personal pronoun in NP_{rel}:

(11) a.   y   bachgen a   oedd yn darllen
            the boy   who was   a' reading
            'the boy who was reading'
      b.   Dyma 'r llyfr y   darllenais y   stori ynddo.
            here-is the book that I-read   the story in-it
            'Here is the book in which I read the story.'

As a second case, one of the primary strategies in Finnish applies only to subjects and direct objects. This strategy places the relative clause prenominally, uses no relativisation marker, and puts the subordinate verb in a nonfinite form (different depending on whether the head NP functions as its subject or object). As this strategy is explicitly discussed in Karlsson (1972), we merely note here the illustrative examples:

(12) a.   Pöydällä tanssinut   poika oli sairas.
            on-table having-danced boy   was sick
            'The boy who had danced on the table was sick.'
      b.   Näkemäni   poika tanssi pöydällä.
            I-having-seen boy   danced on-table
            'The boy that I saw danced on the table.'

As a final case in this category, consider Malay. The primary strategy uses postnominal restricting clauses introduced by the invariable particle *yang* with no pronoun retained in the position relativised:[3]

(13) Ali bunoh ayam   yang Aminah sedang memakan.
      Ali kill   chicken that Aminah Prog   eat
      'Ali killed the chicken that Aminah is eating.'

But this strategy applies only to subjects and direct objects. Thus from (14a) we cannot form (14b) or (14c), either stranding or moving the preposition:

(14) a. Ali beri ubi kentang itu kapada perempuan itu.
      Ali give potato   the to   woman   the
      'Ali gave the potato to the woman.'
    b. *perempuan yang Ali beri ubi kentang itu kapada
      woman   that Ali give potato   the to
    c. *perempuan kapada yang Ali beri ubi kentang itu
      woman   to   who Ali give potato   that

The only systematically elicitable possibility was (15):

(15) perempuan kapada siapa Ali beri ubi kentang itu
      woman   to   who Ali give potato   the
      'the woman to whom Ali gave the potato'

Here, the interrogative pronoun *siapa* preceded by the preposition is used to introduce the relative clause. Clearly, the use of the interrogative pronoun, which can take prepositions (i.e. +case), is a different strategy from that using the invariable particle *yang*. In fact, this use of the interrogative pronoun was elicited only under pressure, and was felt to be bookish and clumsy. The preferred alternative was (16), in which the original sentence has been reorganised lexically so that the position relativised is the subject:

(16) perempuan yang menerima ubi kentang itu daripada Ali
      woman   that received   potato   the from   Ali
      'the woman that received the potato from Ali'

1.3.3 Subject — Indirect Object. The indirect object position is perhaps the most subtle one on the AH. For purposes of relative clause formation, it appears that many languages either assimilate indirect objects to the other oblique cases (e.g. English, Malay) or to direct objects (e.g. Shona, Luganda). Nonetheless, Basque does appear to discriminate indirect object from both its immediate neighbours on the AH.

In Basque, subject, direct object, and indirect object are represented in the verb by verbal affixes (Lafitte 1962, 193-4). Relativisation on any of these positions is effected naturally by deleting the position relativised, putting the restricting clause in prenominal position, and marking the juncture with an invariable marker − *n*. Thus, from (17a) we can generate any of the three relative clauses (17b)-(17d):

(17) a. Gizon-a -k   emakume-a -ri liburu-a   eman dio.
        man the SU woman   the IO book the give has
        'The man has given the book to the woman.'

   b. emakume-a -ri liburu-a   eman dio-n   gizon-a
       woman   the IO book the give   has Rel man   the
       'the man who has given the book to the woman'

   c. gizon-a -k   emakume-a -ri eman dio-n   liburu-a
       man the SU woman   the IO give   has Rel book   the
       'the book that the man has given to the woman'

   d. gizon-a -k   liburu-a   eman dio-n   emakume-a
       man the SU book the give   has Rel woman   the
       'the woman that the man has given the book to'

However, once we attempt to relativise on positions that are not explicitly coded in the verb, a variety of difficulties arise. For speakers of what de Rijk (1972) has called the restricted dialect, no further relativisation is possible. For other speakers a somewhat greater variety of positions may be relativised, but often a different strategy is used. For instance, a pronoun may be retained in the position relativised and the relative clause may occur post-nominally. Consequently, for speakers of the restricted dialect, as well as for certain other speakers, the primary strategy works only on the subject, direct object, and indirect object.

Another language in this category is Tamil, a Dravidian language of southern India and Sri Lanka (Ceylon). One RC-forming strategy puts the restricting clause in prenominal position, with the participial (nonfinite) ending -*a* on its verb, and no indication in the restricting clause of the syntactic function of NP_{rel}. This strategy applies to subjects, direct objects, and indirect objects:

(18) a. Jān pātu-kir -a   penmani(y)-ai kan-t   -ān.
       John sing Pres Part woman   DO see Past Sg-3rd-Masc
       'John saw the woman who is singing.'

   b. Anta manitan ati-tt -a   penmani(y)-ai jān kan-t
                               -ān.
       that man   hit Past Part woman   DO John see Past
                                Sg-3rd-Masc
       'John saw the woman that that man hit.'

c. Jāṉ puttakatt-ai(k) koṭi-tt -a peṉmaṉi(y)-ai nāṉ
                                    kaṉ-ṭ -ēṉ.
   John book   DO give Past Part woman   DO I
                                    see Past Sg-1st
   'I saw the woman to whom John gave the book.'

It does not work on other positions, e.g. instrumentals, where a different RC-forming strategy is required, retaining NP_{rel} in the restricting clause:

(19) Eṉṉa(k) katti(y)-āl̤   koṟi(y)-ai   anta maṉitaṉ
     which   knife   with chicken DO that man
     kolaippi-tt -āṉ   anta katti(y)-ai jāṉ kaṉ-ṭ -āṉ.
     kill   Past Sg-3rd-Masc that knife   DO John see Past
                                    Sg-3rd- Masc
     'John saw the knife with which the man killed the chicken'
     (literally: with which knife the man killed the chicken, John saw that knife).

Roviana, a Melanesian language spoken in New Georgia, Solomon Islands, also provides some support for discriminating the indirect object position. There, in simplex sentences, indirect objects are treated like other oblique case NPs in that they are preceded by a preposition, whereas direct objects are not:

(20) Ele ponia Jone koe Mere sa buka.
     Past give John to Mary the book
     'John gave the book to Mary.'
(21) Vekoa Jone sa bereti pa tevelo.
     put   John the bread at table
     'John put the bread on (the) table.'

On the other hand, in relative clauses indirect objects are relativised just like direct objects and subjects — a postnominal strategy, in which the case of the relativised position is not marked, as the relativisation marker *sapu* is morphologically invariable and no pronoun is retained in the position relativised. But in the oblique cases the function of NP_{rel} is coded, either in the form of a stranded adverb or in the variable form of the relativisation marker:

(22) a. sa buka sapu ele ponia Jone koe Mere
         the book that Past give John to Mary
         'the book that John gave to Mary'

b.   sa barikalege sapu ele   ponia buka Jone
     the woman   that Past give   book John
     'the woman that John gave the book to'
(23)   sa tevelo vasina vekonia   Jone sa bereti
       the table   where put (by?) John the bread
       'the table where John put the bread'

1.3.4 Subject — Oblique.   The primary strategy in Korean
(Tagashira 1972) places the restricting clause to the left of the
head NP, separated from it by the suffix -$(i)n$, -nin. NP$_{rel}$ is simply
deleted for all NPs on the AH down to and including obliques:

(24) hyənsik -i ki lä -lil ttäli-n   maktäki
     Hyensik SU the dog DO beat Rel stick
     'the stick with which Hyensik beat the dog'

However, where genitives are relativised, a pronoun must be
retained:

(25) chaki-ij lä -ka chongmyəngha-n   ki salam
     he   of dog SU smart   Rel the man
     'the man whose dog is smart'

In fact, many languages besides Korean change RC-forming strategies at the genitive position by presenting a pronominal element in
the position relativised; see Table 1.2 in section 2.2.2.
   Further support for distinguishing genitives on the AH comes
from languages like Catalan and North Frisian (Fering dialect),
where genitives (and objects of comparison) are simply not relativisable at all, although all NPs higher on the AH than genitives
are relativisable, e.g. North Frisian:

(26) a.   John kland det wuf's henk.
          'John stole the woman's chicken.'
     b.   det henk wat kland John
          'the chicken that John stole'
     c.   *det wuf wat's henk John kland
          'the woman whose chicken John stole'

1.3.5 Subject — Genitive.   A great many well-known languages
have primary strategies that permit relativisation on all the

positions on the AH except that of objects of comparison. Thus in French we cannot relativise *le jeune homme* in (27a):

(27) a.   Marie est plus grande que le jeune homme.
           'Marie is bigger than the young man.'
     b.   *le jeune homme que que Marie est plus grande
           'the young man than whom Marie is bigger'

The same situation holds in Spanish, German, and Romanian (nonparticipial strategy, in each case).

1.3.6 Subject — Object of Comparison.   Few languages that distinguish objects of comparison from direct objects or oblique NPs permit them to be relativised. In English we do have phrases like (28), though some find them rather uncomfortable:

(28)   the man who Mary is taller than

And in Urhobo, whose primary strategy is postnominal, and pronoun-retaining for all positions on the AH, we have:

(29)   oshale na l- i Mary rho n-   o
       man   the that Mary big than him
       'the man that Mary is bigger than'

This completes the argument that primary RC-forming strategies can discriminate all the positions on the AH. Thus, the PRC is established, and we may conclude generally that the Accessibility Hierarchy determines the relative ease of relative clause formation from unmarked simplex sentences across languages.

Table 1.1 summarises our data concerning the relativising power of the RC-forming strategies we considered in the languages in our sample. A key to the entries in the row—column intersections is given at the end of the table. Needless to say, such a summary cannot adequately represent all the language-particular problems involved in determining the nature of an RC-forming strategy.

1.4 Problems and Possible Counterexamples

We shall consider here two types of difficulties with the analysis we have proposed. The first concern methodological problems involved in identifying subjects and relative clauses (RCs). The second concern specific counterexamples to the Hierarchy Constraints.

1.4.1 Methodological Problems

1.4.1.1 Identifying Subjects. We are using a largely traditional notion of subject. An attempt to make explicit the large number of specific properties that comprise this notion is given in Keenan (1976b) and will not be discussed here. It is clear from that investigation, however, that the NPs we call subjects in some languages are more subject-like than those of other languages. That is, they possess a greater number of the properties that are characteristic of subjects in general. A language in which the subject properties were systematically distributed across two or more NPs then might arguably be said not to have a single category of subject. In such a case the AH for that language would lack the subject position, much as the AH applied to other languages may lack an OCOMP position (see 1.2.1), and the predictions made by the HCs would be reduced and further principles would have to be found to account for the degree of relativisability of NPs not on the AH.

Fortunately, many languages do appear to present NPs that conform fairly well to the traditional concept of subject. Nonetheless, three categories of possibly subjectless languages have been recently discussed in the literature: Tagalog and Philippine languages generally (Schachter 1976), 'topic' oriented languages like Lisu and other Sino-Tibetan languages (Li and Thompson 1974; 1976), and ergative languages (Tchekhoff 1973) (see 1.4.2).

Of these categories, Schachter's claim that the 'focus' NP in Tagalog cannot be regarded as a subject is the most damaging to our claim, since Tagalog was one of the languages that justified HC_1 and HC_3 (a language may relativise only subjects). However, it has been shown in Keenan (1976a) that others of the Western Malayo-Polynesian languages, notably Malagasy, do not present the evidence that supports Schachter's claims for Tagalog, and consequently there are still sufficient data to support HC_1.

The evidence Li and Thompson present from Sino-Tibetan is less damaging, since the NPs that are most subject-like do not present any Hierarchy violations. What they argue, however, is that the syntactic category 'subject' has a very low functional load in these languages in that few if any syntactic processes need to be

Table 1.1

Language Relative clause forming strategy	Relativisable positions					
	Subj	DObj	IObj	Obl	Gen	OComp
Aoban (North-East)						
1. postnom, −case	+	−	−	−	−	−
2. postnom, +case	−	+	+	+	+	+
Arabic (Classical)						
1. postnom, −case	+	−	−	−	−	−
2. postnom, +case	−	+	+	+	+	+
Basque						
1. prenom, −case	+	+	+	−	−	−
Batak (Toba)						
1. postnom, −case	+	−	−	−	−	
2. postnom, +case	−	−	+	+	+	
Catalan						
1. postnom, −case	+	+	+	−	−	−
2. postnom, +case	−	−	−	+	−	−
Chinese (spoken Pekingese)						
1. prenom, −case	+	+	−	−	−	−
2. prenom, +case	−	+	+	+	+	+
Czech (colloquial)						
1. postnom, +case	+	+	+	+	+	+?
Dutch						
1. postnom, −case	+	+	−	−	−	−
2. postnom, +case	−	−	+	+	+	−
English						
1. postnom, −case	+	+	−	−	−	−
2. postnom, +case	−	−	+	+	+	+
Finnish						
1. postnom, +case	+	+	+	+	+	−/*
2. prenom, −case	+	+	−	−	−	−/*
French						
1. postnom, +case	+	+	+	+	+	−
North Frisian (Fering dialect)						
1. postnom, −case	+	+	+	−	−	−
2. postnom, +case	−	−	−(?)	+	−	−
Fulani (Gombe dialect)						
1. postnom, −case	+	+	*	−	−	
2. postnom, +case	−	−	*	+	+	
Genoese (Zeneyze)						
1. postnom, −case	+	+	−	−	−	−
2. postnom, +case	−	+	+	+	+	+
German						
1. postnom, +case	+	+	+	+	+	−
2. prenom, −case	+	−	−	−	−	−
Gilbertese						
1. postnom, −case	+	−	−	−	−	*
2. postnom, +case	−	+	+	+	+	*
Greek (Modern)						
1. postnom, −case	+	+	−	−	−	−
2. postnom, +case	−	−	+	+	+	+

Table 1.1 continued

Language Relative clause forming strategy	Relativisable positions					
	Subj	DObj	IObj	Obl	Gen	OComp
Hausa						
1. postnom, −case	+	+	−	−	−	
2. postnom, +case	−	−	+	+	+	
Hebrew						
1. postnom, −case	+	+	−	−	−	−/*
2. postnom, +case	−	+	+	+	+	+/*
Hindi						
1. postnom, +case	+	+	+	+	+	*
2. internal, +case	+	+	+	+	+	*
Iban (Sea Dayak)						
1. postnom, −case	+	−	−	−	−	−
2. postnom, +case	−	−	−	+/−	−	−
Italian						
1. postnom, −case	+	+	−	−	−	−/*
2. postnom, +case	−	−	+	+	+	−/*
Japanese						
1. prenom, −case	+	+	+	+/−	+/−	−?
2. prenom, +case	−	−	−	−	+/−	−?
Javanese						
1. postnom, −case	+	−	−	−	−	
2. postnom, +case	−	−	−	−	+	
Kera						
1. postnom, −case	+	−	−	−	−	*
2. postnom, +case	−	+	+	+	+	*
Korean						
1. prenom, −case	+	+	+	+	−	−
2. prenom, +case	−	−	−	−	+	−
Luganda						
1. postnom, +case	+	+	*	−	−	*
Malagasy						
1. postnom, −case	+	−	−	−	−	−
Malay						
1. postnom, −case	+	+/−	−	−	−	*
2. postnom, +case	−	−	+	+	+	*
Maori						
1. postnom, −case	+	−	−	−		
Minang-Kabau						
1. postnom, −case	+	−	−	−	−	*
2. postnom, +case	−	−	−	+	+	*
Persian						
1. postnom, −case	+	+	−	−	−	*
2. postnom, +case	−	+	+	+	+	*
Polish						
1. postnom, +case	+	+	+	+	+	*/−
Romanian						
1. postnom, +case	+	+	+	+	+	*

Roviana						
1. postnom, −case	+	+	+	−	−	−
2. postnom, +case	−	−	−	+	+	−
Russian						
1. postnom, +case	+	+	+	+	+	−/*
Sinhala						
1. prenom, −case	+	+/+?	+?	+/−	−	−
Shona						
1. postnom, −case	+	+?	+?	−	−	*
2. postnom, +case	−	−	−	+	+	*
Slovenian						
1. postnom, +case	+	+	+	+	+	+
Spanish						
1. postnom, −case	+	+	+	−	−	−
2. postnom, +case	−	−	−	+	+	−
Swedish						
1. postnom, +case	−	−	+	+	+?	−?
2. postnom, −case	+	+	−	−	−	−
Tagalog						
1. postnom, −case	+	−	−	−	−	−
2. prenom, −case	+	−	−	−	−	−
Tamil						
1. prenom, −case	+	+	+	−	−	*
2. internal, +case	+	+	+	+	+	+
Tongan						
1. postnom, −case	+	+	−	−	−	
2. postnom, +case	+	−	+	+	+	
Turkish						
1. prenom, −case	+	+	+	+	−	−
2. prenom, +case	−	−	−	−	+	+?
Urhobo						
1. postnom, +case	+	+	+	+	+	+
Welsh						
1. postnom, −case	+	+	−	−	−	−
2. postnom, +case	−	−	+	+	+	+
Yoruba						
1. postnom, −case	+	+	*	*	−	*
2. postnom, +case	−	−	*	*	+	*
Zurich German						
1. postnom, −case	+	+	−	−	−	−
2. postnom, +case	−	−	+?	+	+	+??

Key: + means that the strategy generally applies to that NP position; − means that it does not. +? means it applies, but with loss of acceptability and perhaps some informant disagreement. −? means it does not apply, although the result is not judged too bad by informants. An entry of the form *x/y* means that for certain of the NPs in that position *x*(?) means that our data are not entirely unequivocal, but our best judgement is that *x* is the appropriate entry. * means that that NP position does not exist as such, but rather is treated as some other position: e.g. objects of comparison are often either direct objects of verbs like *exceed* as in Shona or oblique case NPs governed by pre- or postpositions as in Hebrew and Hindi. A blank means that we lack the relevant data.

made sensitive to the NP that is the subject. Further research in those languages might then reveal that categories other than those on the AH, e.g. topic, are relevant in determining RC-forming possibilities.

With the possible exception of Dyirbal (and perhaps Eskimo; see Woodbury 1975) (see section 1.4.2.1), the claim that ergative languages lack subjects has been refuted by Anderson (1976), who shows that with respect to many major syntactic processes transitive subjects (the ergative NP) and intransitive subjects behave alike, in distinction to DOs, thus establishing the fact that there is a category of subject in those languages.

1.4.1.2 Identifying Relative Clauses. We have been considering an RC to be any syntactic structure that designates an object (or set of objects) in a certain way, namely, by first specifying a larger domain of objects and then restricting it to a subset, perhaps a one-member subset, of which a certain sentence, the *restricting* sentence, is true. However, many languages present sentence types that appear to designate objects in this way but in which there is no surface constituent with which we can associate the designating properties. One such example concerns extraposed RCs, as in (30a) below:

(30) a. The student finally arrived who we had been waiting all morning for.
     b. the student who we had been waiting all morning for

Clearly, to evaluate the truth of (30a) it is necessary to determine that the main predicate holds of an object that is, first a student, and second, is such that the sentence *we had been waiting all morning for him* is true of him. That is, the object in question is clearly the one designated by the RC in (30b), and in this sense the logical structure of (30a) contains the RC in (30b). But (30a) itself does not present in surface a constituent that has the referential properties of (30b) and so does not contain an RC.

In this case, however, it is easy to argue that at a fairly shallow level of underlying structure (30b) does occur in the syntactic structure of (30a), and that a late rule of RC Extraposition moves the restricting clause around the main verb. Thus the syntactic structure of (30a), considered as the sequence of phrase markers representing its derivation, does contain an RC, and it is clear, then, that our definition of RC does not require that, in surface, the head NP and the restricting clause be a constituent.

It is clear, furthermore, that the most ordinary type of RC in English is expressed by structures like (30b), those in (30a) being more marked and of more restricted distribution. But in many languages the usual translations of English sentences containing RCs do not present the head NP and the restricting clause as a constituent. (31) from Hindi and (32) from Walbiri (Hale n.d.) illustrate this type:

(31) Mai us aurat   ko janta hoon jis- ko Ram ne kitab diya.
    I   that woman DO know   who IO Ram Erg book gave
    'I know the woman that Ram gave the book to.'

(32) ŋatjulu-ḷu   ɸ-ṇa yankiri pantu-ṇu, kutja-lpa ŋapa ŋa-
                                                        ṇu.
    I   Erg Aux emu   spear Past CompAux water drink
                                                       Past
    'I speared the emu that was drinking water/while it was drinking water.'

In these cases it is not clear that what corresponds to the restricting clause in English ever occurs as a constituent with the head NP in underlying structure. Both Hale (n.d.) and Andrews (1975) argue that it does not.

However, languages with this type of construction very regularly exhibit a related type of construction in which there is a constituent that meets our semantic conditions of relative clause-hood. The corresponding versions of the Hindi (31) and Walbiri (32) are given below in (33) and (34), respectively:

(33) [Ram ne jis   aurat   ko kitab diya] us (aurat) ko mai
                                                   janta hoon.
    Ram Erg which woman IO book gave that woman DO I
                                              know
    'I know the woman that Ram gave the book to.'

(34) [yankiri-ḷi̇ kutja-lpa ŋapa ŋa- ṇu] ula   pantu-ṇu
                                                     ŋatjulu-ḷu.
    emu   Erg CompAux water drink past that-one spear Past
                                                I   Erg
    'I speared the emu that was drinking water.'

It is not clear that the bracketed constituents above should be considered NPs. Certainly they present the normal syntax of full sentences, except that they contain the markers *jis* and *kutja*. Whatever the grammatical category of these constituents, however, it does appear that they meet our definition of RC — they specify a domain of objects, those marked by *jis* and *kutja*, and they give the restricting clause, the one determined by the entire clause in which they occur. Thus, like the examples (3) from Bambara and (4) from Digueño mentioned earlier, they illustrate an RC-forming strategy in which the head NP occurs within the restricting clause. Our definition of RC then does not require that an RC be an NP, nor does it require that the head NP command the restricting clause (a use of 'head' that differs from the usual one in the linguistic literature).

The RC-forming strategies illustrated above in Walbiri are perhaps responsible for the claim sometimes heard that, in violation of HC_1 (which states that subjects are universally relativisable), Australian languages do not have RCs. Walbiri at least clearly does not present embedded RCs in which the head NP commands the restricting clause and in which the two form an NP constituent. But it certainly does present constituents that meet our semantically-based criteria for what constitutes an RC, so HC_1 is not violated here.

1.4.2 Some Possible Counterexamples

1.4.2.1 Possible Counterevidence to HC_1.   We consider first the best documented counterexample to HC_1 (subjects are always relativisable). The counterevidence comes from Dyirbal (Dixon 1969; 1972), an Australian language. Dyirbal appears ergative in the standard sense that full NP subjects of intransitive sentences and full NP DOs of transitive sentences are case-marked in the same way (zero, in this case), whereas subjects of transitive sentences carry a special marker, the ergative. In the analysis to follow we shall refer to intransitive subjects and transitive DOs collectively as *absolutives*. Examples are from Dixon (1972, 100-1).

(35) bayi   yaṛa   banagaɲu.
     Det-Abs man-Abs return
     'The man is returning.'

(36) bayi   yuɽi   baŋgul yaɽaŋgu bagan.
     Det-Abs kangaroo-Abs Det-Erg man-Erg spear
     'The man speared a kangaroo.'

Dixon demonstrates that absolutives can be relativised from both transitive and intransitive sentences, but the ergative NP cannot be relativised. To talk about *the man who speared a kangaroo*, it is necessary to apply a transformation that promotes the ergative NP to absolutive status (37a), whence it can be relativised (37b):

(37) a. bayi   yaɽa   bagalŋaɲu bagul   yuɽigu.
         Det-Abs man-Abs spear-'Pass' Det-Instr kangaroo-
                                                          Instr
         'The man speared the kangaroo.'
     b. [$_{NP}$bayi   yaɽa   bagal-ŋa -ŋu bagul
         Det-Abs man-Abs spear 'Pass' Rel Det-Instr
         yuɽigu]   banagaɲu.
         kangaroo-Instr return
         'The man who speared the kangaroo is returning.'

On the basis of the Dyirbal data, Johnson (1974a) has suggested that the upper segment of the AH is inapplicable to ergative languages generally, and that an Ergative Hierarchy (EH), ABS > ERG > IO > OBL, etc. more adequately describes the accessibility to RC formation in those languages. The EH differs significantly from the AH only in that it predicts the possibility of RC-forming strategies that relativise only absolutives, such as in Dyirbal. But general support from ergative languages for this prediction is lacking. The majority of ergative languages known to us permit both ergative and absolute NPs to relativise. We have already illustrated relativisation on ergatives in Basque (17b) and Walbiri (34). Examples (38)-(42) illustrate relativisation on ergatives from a few other languages.

Hindi
(38) Ram us   larki ko pasand kartahe, jis- ne kapre   dhoye.
     Ram that girl   DO likes   Rel Erg clothes washed
     'Ram likes the girl who washed clothes.'

Tongan (Anderson 1975)

(39) te mo fetaulaki mo e   tangata 'oku ne fua   'a   e
                                              sipoki vai.
     Fut 2Du meet   with Art man   Pres 3Sg carry Part Art
                                              jug water
     'You will meet a man who is carrying a jug of water.'

Gahuku (Deibler 1973)

(40) izegipa get -a ve
     child begot 3Sg man
     'the man who had begotten the child.'

Greenlandic Eskimo (Woodbury 1975)

(42) qimmi-ɸ   -a   tuquk-kiga nalu   Nil- saNa.
     dog   Abs-Sg Poss-3S kill   Trans ignorant Neg Indic-3Sg-
                                              1Sg
     'He knows about me, who killed his dog.'

Jacaltec (Craig 1974)

(41) x- ɸ-   w-   'il [naj x- ɸ-   watx'e-n hun ti']
     Asp him-Abs I-Erg see man Asp him-Abs make Rel one this
     'I saw the man who made this.'

Woodbury (1975) does argue, however, that absolutives are more relativisable in Greenlandic than are ergatives, on the grounds that (1) RCs formed on ergatives are somewhat more restricted in the distribution in matrix clauses (p. 21) than are those formed on absolutives, and (2) for certain verb classes ergatives cannot be relativised out of the active participle (p. 27). To relativise that NP from an active participle, the ergative must first be promoted to an absolutive via Antipassive. Nonetheless, it is the case that ergatives can in general be relativised, even if not quite so freely as absolutives, and so the AH does appear to apply, although more work would need to be done to distinguish according to our criteria what the different RC-forming strategies in Greenlandic are.

The general claim, then, that in ergative languages absolutives are more relativisable than ergatives receives little support. This in turn suggests that the Dyirbal data might be analysed differently. One reanalysis that would have the effect of making Dyirbal conform to the AH would be simply to regard the absolutive NP in transitive sentences (as well as in intransitive ones) as in the subject. Such an analysis again calls into question the defining criteria for subjecthood and would require much independent support. Perhaps surprisingly, however, Dyirbal does provide such support. Below we summarise this evidence, citing page numbers from Dixon (1972) for the supporting data.

1. Absolutives are the most essential NP in the sentence. Thus an unspecified agent (ergative) may simply be eliminated from a sentence, much like unspecified agents of passive sentences in English. But unspecified absolutives cannot be so eliminated. If we want to eliminate an unspecified patient, we must first 'passivise' the sentence so that the ergative becomes a surface absolutive and the former absolutive becomes oblique, whence it can be deleted when nonspecific (p. 70).

2. Absolutives are the only target of advancement rules. Dyirbal has several rules, rather like Passive in English, that promote e.g. ergatives and instrumentals to the absolutive position of underlying transitive sentences, as we illustrated in (37a).

3. Absolutives normally precede ergatives in simplex sentences (p. 291).

4. Only absolutives can be coreferentially deleted by operations like Equi and Conjunction Reduction (pp. 73, 67). To coreferentially delete an ergative NP, it must first be advanced to an absolutive.

5. It appears that certain demonstratives, always definite and presupposing reference — a characteristic property of subjects — are restricted to absolutive positions (p. 218).

6. In the few cases where we can tell, absolutives appear to control reflexives. Usually reflexivisation is done by verbal affixing, so the derived verb is intransitive and the subject is absolutive on independent grounds. However, in a few examples the object is an inalienable body part and is expressed in surface structure even though the verb is reflexivised. And in these cases the controller is absolutive (p. 153):

(43) bayi   yaṛa   mala   ḍaŋgaymariɲu.
     Det-Abs man-Abs hand-Abs eat-Refl-Pres/Past
     'The man chewed his finger.'

If we adopt the analysis of Dyirbal in which absolutives in transitive sentences are the subjects, then Dyirbal will be typologically anomalous in only one major respect: namely, in the least marked type of transitive sentence the NP with the referential or topic properties of subjects does not express the agent. And since the predominance of topic properties over agency properties in this case is quite large (very few transformations mention ergatives, but very many mention absolutives), it turns out that the most subject-like NP in basic transitive sentences is the absolutive and does not express the agent.

This analysis at least has the (metalinguistic) advantage of isolating at a single point the anomaly of Dyirbal — namely, transitive subjects in basic sentences are not agents. The ergative analysis on the other hand makes Dyirbal anomalous in a great many respects: the word order is OSV; DOs are the most essential constituent of transitive sentences, subjects being freely deletable when unspecified; etc. Furthermore, it is possible that when the lexicons of more languages have been analysed in detail, it will be seen that many languages have classes of verbs that select goal subjects but allow agents present in oblique cases. Biggs (1974) has recently argued, for instance, that Fijian has one large class of verbs that select goal rather than agent subjects, whereas another class selects agent subjects, as is more usual. Perhaps Dyirbal will then be seen to be merely near the end of a continuum in that most of its transitive verbs select nonagent subjects.

1.4.2.2 Apparent Exceptions to HC$_2$. A second type of counterexample we consider are apparent exceptions to HC$_2$, that a given RC-forming strategy must apply to a continuous segment of the AH. Hausa (Abrahams 1959; Schachter 1973) and Yoruba appear to use RC strategies that apply to discontinuous segments of the RC.   Thus Hausa seems to use a +case strategy to relativise subjects, since a personal pronoun seems present in the position relativised:

(44) dokin da ya mutu
    horse Rel it died
    'the horse that died.'

Relativisation on DOs, however, does not permit retention of a pronoun in the position relativised, and as no other nominal particle is present to code the case of the relativised NP (the relativiser *da* is invariable), RC formation on DOs appears to be effected by a −case strategy:

(45) mutumin da na gani (*shi)
    person   Rel I saw   him
    'the person that I saw'

However, when we relativise on OBLs in Hausa, a pronoun is again present. (In relativising on IOs, the presence of a pronoun is optional.)

(46) yaron da suka gaya {wa/masa}
     child Rel they said   to to-him
     'the child whom they told'
(47) wuqad da ya kashe ta da· ita
     knife   Rel he killed her with it
     'the knife with which he killed her'

It appears, then, that the postnominal, +case strategy in Hausa does not apply to a continuous segment of the AH, in violation of HC_2.

On examining further the pronoun that appears in the RC when a subject is relativised, however, we note that this same pronoun is also required in simplex sentences with a subject NP:

(48) a. Yusufu ya zo.
         Joseph he came
         'Joseph came.'
     b. *Yusufu zo.

Quite generally in Hausa, full subject NPs must be accompanied by clitic pronouns. This suggests a different line of analysis for such pronouns. Instead of regarding them as constituent parts of a +case strategy, we may regard them as an instance of verb agreement. In many languages verb-agreement affixes are known to derive from (clitic) pronouns (Givón 1976), and it is often difficult to draw a precise dividing-line between clitic pronouns and agreement affixes. We are therefore suggesting that where the presence of a pronoun is required by the presence of a full NP, then the pronoun be regarded as an instance of verb agreement, and not as an instance of NP case marking. In Hausa, such 'internal pronouns' (for this terminology, see Keenan 1972a, 447-50) occur only with subjects: with DOs, etc., we have (49a) and (49c) for instance, but not (49b) and (49d):

(49) a. Na gani mutumin.
     b. *Na gani shi mutumin.
         'I saw the person.'

    c. Ya kashe ta da wuqad.
    d. *Ya kashe ta da ita da wuqad.
        'He killed her with the knife.'

Another similar possible counterexample, from Tongan (pointed out in Anderson 1975), is not so easily disposed of, however. Here it appears that pronouns may, and in some cases must, be retained when subjects are relativised. (39) already illustrates this. Similarly, relativisation on IOs, OBLs, and GENs obligatorily leaves behind a pronominal trace (examples from Anderson 1975, Chung — personal communication):

(50) ko e   'eiki eni na'e langa mo'ona 'a   e   fale   lahi.
     Part Art chief this Past build for-3Sg Part Art house big
     'This is the chief for whom the big house was built.'
(51) fakahā mai   kiata au 'a   e   tamasi'i na'e
     show   towards to-Pers me Abs Art child   Past
     ngalo   'ene polosi fulunifo.
     disappear his brush toothbrush
     'Show me the boy whose toothbrush disappeared.'

However, it is not possible to present pronominal traces when DOs are relativised:

(52) 'oku 'ikai 'ilo   'e   ha taha 'a e   tangata na'a ku taa'i
                                               (*ia).
     Pres not know Erg any one Abs Art man   Past I hit him
     'Nobody knows the man who I hit.'

Furthermore, the type of explanation used above for Hausa and Yoruba does not in general seem applicable. The subject pronouns present when subjects are relativised do not in general function as agreement particles, although the pronoun present in the RC is the clitic one, not the independent one. Thus it occurs preverbally, whereas the independent pronouns and full NPs functioning as subjects normally occur postverbally (Tongan is VSO).

(53) na'e 'ave 'e   Sione ho'o telefone.
     Past take Erg John your telephone
     'John took away your telephone.'
(54)*na'a ne 'ave 'e   Sione ho'o telefone.
     Past he take Erg John your telephone

Furthermore, the clitic pronouns can be present when the subject is an independent pronoun, although the meaning here is emphatic:

(55) na'a ne taa'i 'e   ia pē   ia.
     Past he hit Erg he Emph him
     'He hit himself.'

This use of the clitic could conceivably develop so that the clitic would cooccur with full NPs in subject position without the emphatic meaning. This at least would be a normal way for an agreement to arise (see Givón 1976 for justification of this claim). But this would be to anticipate the development of Tongan and cannot be used to justify its current status as a counterexample to HC_2.

Perhaps the best explanation we can offer for the pattern of RC-forming strategies in Tongan is a historical one. As we have mentioned, Tongan is an ergative language in which the ergative marker *'e* is cognate with the passive agent marker in related Polynesian languages. Hohepa (1969) has presented evidence that the ergative paradigm present in Tongan and the closely related Niuean has evolved from an original nominative-accusative paradigm in which the productive distinction between active and passive verb forms was lost and the passive morphology retained on the major NPs. Thus, historically speaking, the ergative subject of Tongan is a passive agent, and the absolutive DO in Tongan is historically the subject. We suggest here that the evolution of the agent NP to subject status in Tongan is not quite complete. While Anderson (1976) has shown that it does possess many general properties of subjects, it may retain a few traces of its original oblique case status. For example, in simple active sentences the ergative NP can be omitted when unspecified, like the ergative NP in Dyirbal and the passive agent in English, as illustrated in (56) and (57) below (both from Churchward 1953):

(56) na'e tamate'i 'e   Tevita 'a   Koliate.
     Past kill   Erg David Abs Goliath
     'David killed Goliath.'
(57) na'e tamate'i 'a   Koliate.
     Past kill   Abs Goliath
     'Goliath was killed.'

Now, since OBLs in general in Tongan require retention of a clitic pronoun when relativised (in one case a nonclitic pronoun can be retained, but this is quite exceptional), the ergative NP in Tongan is behaving like the other OBLs in this respect. On the other hand, the DO does not allow a pronoun to be retained under relativisation. But, as we show in 2.2.2, this is characteristic of subjects in general. That is, even in languages like Hebrew in which pronoun retention is normal under relativisation, subject pronouns are normally not retained. So, in this way, the DO in Tongan is behaving like a subject. In these very minor respects, then, perhaps the ergative and absolutive in Tongan betray their earlier status as passive agent and subject, respectively.

2. Towards an Explanation of the Hierarchy Constraints

2.1 The AH as a Psychologically Valid Entity

Given that the HCs do make correct predictions about RC formation in a wide range of languages, it is natural to wonder why this should be so. We propose the following explanation: *the AH directly reflects the psychological ease of comprehension.* That is, the lower a position is on the AH, the harder it is to understand RCs formed on that position.

If the AH does reflect the psychological accessibility of NPs to RC formation, then we can use this fact, in conjunction with certain other assumptions, to explain the HCs in the following way. First, it would be natural that a way of relativising a certain position might not be applicable at the next lower position (HC$_3$) on the general assumption that syntactic processes are ways of encoding meanings; and, if one meaning is inherently more difficult to encode than another, then a strategy for encoding the first need not apply to the second. By the same token, a strategy that applies to one position but fails to apply to the next lower position would not be expected to apply to a still lower position (HC$_2$). For, if a given strategy is used to encode a fairly easy meaning and that strategy is 'strong' enough to encode a rather difficult meaning, then it is surely strong enough to encode the meanings of intermediate difficulty. However, this rather informal line of reasoning can be slightly extended to yield an argument that languages should not have 'gapped' RC-forming strategies. Thus, if speakers can in general encode a meaning of a certain difficulty in some way, then they should certainly be able to encode meanings of lesser difficulty (possibly in a different way). Yet we have seen that Toba Batak, for example, can relativise directly subjects using one strategy, and IOs, OBLs, and GENs using another. But DOs cannot be directly relativised using any strategy. As we mentioned, however, in all cases in our sample in which languages present gapped strategies, the NPs that occur in the gap can always be promoted to positions that can be directly relativised via operations like Passive. In these cases, then, we would like some independent evidence that it is psychologically easier, in those languages, to for instance promote a DO to subject and then relativise it rather than to relativise it as a DO. We have no direct psychological evidence of the right sort. It is worth noting, however, that in those languages that promote an NP to a higher position on the AH in order to relativise it, the promotion system (e.g. the ways of converting NPs low on the AH to ones higher on the AH) is usually well developed, very commonly used, and has a wide syntactic distribution, in distinction for instance to Passive in English, which is, by comparison, a less usual, more marked form. In fact, in Hawkins and Keenan (1974) it is reported that on certain types of repetition tasks, English-speaking children (10-12 years) do significantly less well on RCs like *the boy who was seen by Mary* than they do on ones like *the boy who Mary saw*. Thus, promoting to relativise is certainly not universally easier than relativising directly.

Finally, note that this psychological interpretation of the AH cannot fully account for HC_1, that subjects must, in general, be relativisable. It only justifies the claim that subjects are easier to relativise than any other position on the AH, but it would allow in principle that, in some language, no position on the AH be relativisable.

2.2 Evidence in Support of the Psychological Validity of the Accessibility Hierarchy

Several recent experimental studies do provide partial support for the claim that the AH does represent the psychological accessibility to RC formation. Thus, in Legum (1975) it is shown that English-speaking children, aged 6-8, comprehend RCs formed on subjects better than ones formed on DOs. Similar results were achieved by Brown (1971) for children aged 3-5 years. Hatch (1971) shows that young children respond more rapidly to RCs formed on subjects than on objects, and Cook (forthcoming) has shown that children and adults recognise with fewer errors instances of head NPs bearing the subject to the subordinate verb in RCs than instances of the head bearing the object relation to the verb. And Valli *et al.* (1972), in a production test, show that French children at the level of 6^e (approx. 12 years of age) produce RCs formed on subjects much more readily than on objects, and RCs on possessor NPs are much rarer still and in the majority of instances incorrectly formed.

It should be noted that the purpose of these studies was not specifically to validate the AH. Variables other than the position on the AH of the NP relativised were in general shown to be relevant (e.g. whether the RC was embedded or not, whether the function of the RC in the matrix was the same as that of the head in the RC (Sheldon 1974); see Legum (1975) for some discussion of these other parameters).

On the other hand, Hawkins and Keenan (1974) report a study specifically designed to test the psychological validity of the AH. Children, aged 10-12, were given repetition tests involving RCs formed on all the positions on the AH. Correctness of recall correlated significantly ($< .05$) with the AH. In fact, the recall hierarchy established in that study was:

$$SU > DO > IO > OBL, OCOMP > GEN$$

Thus, RCs formed on subjects were recalled with fewer errors than those formed on DOs, which were better than ones formed on IOs, which were better than those formed on either OBLs or OCOMPs, which were better than ones formed on possessor NPs. Clearly the only position out of place on the recall hierarchy is the OCOMP position, which was treated by the children as the same in accessibility as the OBL position. All RCs on OBLs left the preposition stranded, e.g. *the boy who Johnny took the toy from.* Apparently stranding the comparative article, e.g. *the boy who Johnny is taller than,* was interpreted as being similar to preposition stranding.

While it would certainly be premature, on the basis of these few studies, to conclude that the AH does establish a hierarchy of psychological accessibility, it does appear that the available evidence points in that direction. If further research along these lines justifies the psychological interpretation of the AH, then we will have an explanation for two further facts from our own study.

Alternatively, these facts can be considered further support for the psychological interpretation of the AH. The first concerns a pattern of judgements of relative accessibility of RCs from languages in which most positions on the AH can be grammatically relativised. The second concerns the distribution of personal pronouns retained in the RC.

2.2.1 Intralanguage Relative Accessibility Judgements. One natural way to extend the HCs would be to interpret them not only as a cross-language ordering of grammaticality, as we have done, but to consider them as an acceptability ordering within each language. Thus one might expect that in general, within a given language, RCs formed on the high end of the AH would be judged more acceptable than RCs formed on the low end. And in the extreme cases this appears to be correct.

RCs formed on subjects are always among the most acceptable in any given language, and those formed on objects of comparison, where possible at all, are often judged to be only marginally acceptable. For instance, many informants in English are uncomfortable with *the man who Mary is taller than.* Similar judgements of relative acceptability obtained for our Hebrew informants. Thus, even in languages in which objects of comparison can be relativised, there will be a preference to express the RC as one formed from a semantically equivalent sentence in which the semantic object of comparison is presented as a subject. That is, the preferred way to express the idea of *the man who Mary is taller than* will be, in general, *the man who is shorter than Mary.*

A somewhat more subtle performance preference is illustrated by the genitive position on the AH. Although a majority of languages in our sample possessed some way of relativising genitives, there was often some awkwardness in doing so, and not infrequently, in specific cases, a preferred alternative was offered — one that relativises a position higher on the AH. For example, (58) is perfectly grammatical in French:

(58) la femme dont le manteau a été volé
the woman whose the coat   has been stolen
'the woman whose coat was stolen'

But in practice people will tend to say:

(59) la femme qui s'   est fait   voler   le manteau
     the woman who herself is caused to-steal the coat

(59) is literally 'the woman who got her coat stolen', although there is no necessary implication of her having engineered the theft; relativisation is on the subject, rather than the genitive. The translations above indicate that a similar alternative to genitive relativisation exists in English. A like situation holds in Swedish, where the (b) alternative in each pair is preferred:

(60) a. kvinnan, vars   kappa blev stulen
        woman   whose coat   was stolen
    b. kvinnan, som fick sin kappa stulen
        woman   who got her coat   stolen
(61) a. kvinnan, vars   man   är på sjukhuset
        woman   whose husband is in hospital
    b. kvinnan, som har sin man   på sjukhuset
        woman   who has her husband in hospital

In Yoruba, inalienable possessives/genitives can often be paraphrased by other constructions, and even with simple sentences these paraphrases are preferred:

(62) a. John lu   ese okunrin naa.
        John strike leg man   the
        'John struck the man's leg.'
    b. John lu   okunrin naa l' ese.
        John strike man   the on leg
        'John struck the man on his leg.'

Under relativisation, the preference is even more strongly marked, and our informant was very hesitant about admitting (63a) below:

(63) a ?*Mo ri okunrin ti   John lu   ese re.
       I   see man   that John strike leg his
       'I see the man whose leg John struck.'
    b. Mo ri okunrin ti   John lu   l' ese.
       I   see man   that John strike on leg
       'I see the man that John struck on the leg.'

Bamgbose (1966, 158-9) claims that the relation between sentences like (63a) and (63b) is transformational.

2.2.2 Pronoun Rentention. A less obvious patterning determined in part by the HCs concerns the distribution of personal pronouns in relativised positions. (We exclude pronouns that are instances of verb agreement; see section 1.4.2.1). We have already noted that Semitic languages 'characteristically' present such pronouns, e.g. Hebrew:

(64) ha- isha   she- David natan la   et   ha- sefer
    the woman that David gave to-her DO the book
    'the woman that David gave the book to'

Further, it has been argued in Keenan (1972a, 1975a) that such RC-forming strategies present in surface structure more of the logical structure of the RC than do languages like English that do not present such pronouns. The reason, in brief, is that in the pronoun-retaining strategies the restricting clause in surface is a sentence — one that expresses exactly the restricting sentence of logical structure. That is, it is just the sentence that must be true of the referent of the RC. So a possible referent of (64) above must be a woman of whom the sentence *David gave the book to her* is true. And the translation of that sentence in Hebrew is precisely *David natan la et ha-sefer* — the surface restricting clause. Note that the corresponding clause in English, *David gave the book to* or *to whom David gave the book*, is not a surface structure sentence, and so is not immediately perceived as the sort of linguistic entity that is true of objects.

It has been shown elsewhere (Keenan 1972a, and especially 1975a) that the RC-forming strategies that retain pronouns are applicable to a greater range of otherwise 'difficult' environments (e.g. it is often, but not always, possible in these languages to relativise into coordinate NPs, other relative clauses, indirect questions, and even sentence complements of NPs). The reason is that the logically more explicit strategies still successfully express the basic meaning of the RC in contexts where the meaning is otherwise difficult to perceive. Consequently, we are led to predict that, as we descend the AH, languages will exhibit a greater tendency to use pronoun-retaining RC-forming strategies. Table 1.2 dramatically supports this prediction. Languages that do not normally retain pronouns in any position are not included in the table; nor is the use of pronouns as markers of verb agreement (see 1.4.2.2).

It should be clear from Table 1.2 that not only does the tendency to present pronouns in positions relativised increase as we descend the AH, but also that once a language begins to retain pronouns it must do so for as long as relativisation is possible at all. This is a natural consequence of the hypothesis that pronoun retention will be used in proportion to the difficulty of the position

Table 1.2

| Language | Pattern of pronoun retention in relative clauses | | | | | |
	Subj	DO	IO	Obl	Gen	OComp
Aoban (North-East)	(+)	+	+	+	+	+
Arabic	−	+	+	+	+	+
Batak	−	0	+	+	+	
Chinese (Pekingese)	−	+/−	+	+	+	+
Czech (colloquial)	−	+/−	+	+	+	+
Fulani (Gombe)	−	−	*	+	+	
Genoese	−	(+)	+	+	+	
Gilbertese	−	+	+	+	+	+
Greek (Modern)	−	−	+(?)	+(?)	+	+
Hausa	−	−	(+)	+	+	
Hebrew	−	+	+	+	+	+
Japanese	−	−	−	−	+/−	
Javanese	−	−	−	−	+	
Kera	−	+	+	+	+	*
Korean	−	−	−	−	+	0
Malay	−	−	−	−	+	*
Minang-Kabau	−	−	−	−/+	+	*
Persian	−	(+)	+	+	+	+
Roviana	−	−	−	−	+	0
Shona	−	−	−	(+)	+(?)	*
Slovenian	−	+	+	+	+	+
Turkish	−	−	−	−	+	+
Urhobo	+	+	+	+	+	+
Welsh	−	−	+	+	+	+
Yoruba	−	−	*	*	+	*
Zurich German	−	−	+	+	+	+

Key: + means that personal pronouns are normally present in that position when it is relativised, using that RC-forming strategy which admits of pronoun retention. (+) means optional retention. +/− means that in some cases the pronoun is retained and in others it is not. − means that pronouns are usually not retained. * means that that NP position does not naturally exist in that language. 0 means that that position is not relativisable, and a blank means that we lack the relevant data. An entry of the form *x*(?) means that our data are uncertain but *x* is our best guess.

being relativised, though the critical point of difficulty is different for different languages.

2.2.3 Explaining the Psychological Validity of the AH. To some extent, explaining the HCs by interpreting the AH as a psychological hierarchy merely pushes back the problem of explanation one step. We would still want to know why it is psychologically easier to relativise subjects than objects, etc. We have two speculations to make here.

2.2.3.1 A Recognition Strategy. Impressionistically, the initial portion of the AH appears to coincide with the degree to which NPs are required to appear in simple sentences. Thus, lexical predicates almost always require a subject. Many require DOs, some require IOs, and a few (e.g. *put*) require OBLs. Furthermore, a few verbs (R. Stockwell, P. Schachter, personal communication) such as *gnash (one's teeth)*, *blink (one's eyes)*, and *water (his eyes watered)* appear to require that their arguments be possessed body parts, similar to the more idiomatic constructions *lose one's nerve, blow one's cool*, etc. Finally, no lexical predicate in English requires that it be construed in a comparative construction.

Perhaps, then, there is a kind of universal recognition strategy of the sort: 'If an NP plays a role in another clause, interpret it as a subject unless there are indications to the contrary, otherwise try the DO slot, etc.' Needless to say, such a general recognition strategy would require a more precise formation and much experimental research before it could constitute a serious explanation of the AH.

2.2.3.2 Independent Reference. Another explanation, which pertains only to the relative accessibility of subjects over other NPs, was offered in Keenan (1974). There it was argued that heads of RCs share a logical property with subjects of sentences but do not share this property with nonsubjects. Thus, more of what we need to know to understand the meaning of a RC formed on subjects is already contained in the meaning of simple sentences than is the case when the RC is formed on a nonsubject. In more 'transformational' terms, RC formation on subjects distorts the meaning of the underlying sentence less than RCs formed on objects.

The logical property shared by heads and subjects is that of *independent reference.* Thus, in simple sentences we cannot generally make the reference of the subject NP dependent on that of some other NP in the sentence. For instance, if subject and object are marked as coreferential, it must be the object which is marked (if anything is), by for instance a reflexive pronoun. Thus, the reference of object phrases can be made dependent on that of subjects, but not conversely. But it is in the inherent nature of subjects to be independently referring. (For a weakening, but not abandonment, of this principle for more complex cases, see Keenan 1974.)

Similarly, to understand the meaning of an RC such as *the girl that John likes,* we must be able to understand what set is designated by the head NP independently of the reference of the NPs in the restricting clause. For instance, the head NP can never be coreferentially pronominalised by an NP in the restricting clause, even if, as in many languages, the restricting clause precedes the head. But of course NPs within the restricting clause can be stipulated as, for instance, being identical in reference to the head, as in (1), repeated below:

(65)   der in seinem$_i$ Büro arbeitende Mann$_i$
       the in his   study working   man
       'the man who is working in his study'

Consequently, if we relativise on a nonsubject, the resulting structure will contain two necessary independently referring expressions, the head of the RC and the subject of the restricting clause. This explains, for instance, why the pronoun in *the man who he hit* cannot be understood as being necessarily coreferential with the head.[4] But if we relativise on a subject, there is only one necessarily independently referring expression. In this sense, then, subject relatives are psychologically simpler than nonsubject relatives.

3. Further Prospects

In this article, we have restricted ourselves by and large to the particular data area that originally led us to propose the Accessibility Hierarchy, namely, restrictions on relative clause formation. We wish here to indicate briefly two other areas where recent work has shown the possible relevance of the same Accessibility Hierarchy.

In Comrie (1974), it is shown that the AH is useful in the syntactic description of causative constructions, in particular synthetic causative formations, in a variety of languages. Summarising the argument presented in the cited work, we may say that the syntactic position used to encode the causee of a causative construction (i.e. the individual caused to carry out some action) will be the highest position on the AH that is not already occupied. The following French examples illustrate the general trend of the data:

(66) J'ai fait courir Henriette.
     'I made Henriette run.'

In (66), the causee is presented as a DO (*Henriette*); note that the construction already has a subject.

(67) J'ai fait manger les gâteaux à Henriette.
     'I made Henriette eat the cakes.'

Here, the causee is presented as an IO (*à Henriette*); the construction already has a subject (*je*) and a DO (*les gâteaux*).

(68) J'ai fait écrire une lettre au directeur par Henriette.
     'I made Henriette write a letter to the director.'

In (68), the causee is an OBL (*par Henriette*); there is already a subject (*je*), a DO (*une lettre*), and an IO (*au directeur*).

A second extension of the range of applicability of the AH is in determining cross-language restrictions on advancement processes (Keenan and Comrie 1972; Perlmutter and Postal 1974; Johnson 1974b; Keenan 1975b; Trithart 1975). By an 'advancement process' we shall mean a productive syntactic process that converts sentences containing NPs on a low position on the AH into roughly synonymous sentences containing that NP on a higher position on the AH. An obvious example would be Passive, which in many languages serves to advance direct objects to subject position. The work cited above leads us to posit two Advancement Conditions:

(AC1)   *The Target Condition*
The higher an NP is on the AH, the more accessible it is, in general, as a target of an advancement.

(AC2)   *The Distance Condition*
The farther X is from a fixed position Y higher than X, the more difficult it is, in general, to advance X to Y.

(The qualification 'in general' is required because many such advancement processes, though productive, are subject to idiosyncratic government by individual lexical items.) The Target Condition would claim, for instance, that if a language has a rule advancing non-DOs to DO, then it must also have a rule advancing non-Subjects to Subject; that is, since DO is a target for such processes, there must also be processes with Subject as their target. Indonesian (Chung 1976) is an instance of a language with advancement of IO to DO, and, as predicted by AC_1, it also has advancement of DO to Subject. The Distance Condition would claim, for instance, that if a language has a rule advancing OBL to Subject, then it must also have a rule advancing DO to Subject: that is, since OBL is farther away from Subject than DO is. OBL is a less likely candidate for advancement than DO. Malagasy (Keenan 1972b) has a rule advancing OBLs (and also IOs) to Subject, and also has a rule, as predicted, advancing DO to Subject. For further examples and detailed justification, the works cited above should be referred to.

In conclusion, this article has aimed to demonstrate that the Accessibility Hierarchy correctly characterises the relative accessibility of different syntactic positions to relative clause formation; other work indicates that the Accessibility Hierarchy may play a more general role in determining the accessibility of noun phrases as candidates and targets for syntactic processes, although the precise delimitation of the area of relevance of the Accessibility Hierarchy remains a task for future research.

Notes

1. This article is a developed version of Keenan and Comrie (1972). We attempt in this version to account for several objections to the earlier formulation that have since been brought to our attention.

We would like to acknowledge the following sources for significant help with this article:

(i) One *Linguistic Inquiry* reviewer for constructive criticisms of an earlier draft;

(ii) Support from an NSF postdoctoral research grant and two Wenner-Gren grants, 2384 and 2944, for work on the Malayo-Polynesian languages reported herein; for support of the psycholinguistic work on the Accessibility Hierarchy we are indebted to a grant from the Nuffield Foundation;

(iii) The willing and substantive help from the following linguists concerning languages they have worked with: G. Brettschneider (Basque), P. Brown (Tzeltal), M. Butar-Butar (Toba Batak), S. Chung (Indonesian, Tongan), O. Dahl and J. Allwood (Swedish), K. Ebert (North Frisian, Kera), J. Hawkins (German, Slovenian), A. Janhunen (Finnish), M. Perera (Catalan), H. van Riemsdijk (Zurich German), J. de Rooij (Dutch), A. Salmond (Maori), P. Sgall (Czech), R. Tanaka (Japanese), B. Vattuone (Genoese), N. Vincent (Italian);

(iv) The willing and substantive help of our informants.

2. A more formal statement of this semantic notion in which the logical structure of an RC is represented as a pair, a common noun phrase and an open formula, can be found in Keenan (1972a).

3. Our two informants were from Malaya. MacDonald and Soenjono (1967) present a slightly more restricted strategy for Indonesian.

4. Similar facts obtain in languages in which the RC precedes the head. Thus in Japanese and Basque, for instance, in the equivalent of '(the) he hit man' (= 'the man that he hit'), the subject pronoun of the main verb in the RC cannot be understood as being coreferential with the head. See Keenan (1974) for examples. Thus the Crossover Principle (Postal 1971) is not the correct explanation for these cases.

References

Abrahams, R.C. (1959) *The Language of the Hausa People*, University of London Press, London.

Anderson, S.R. (1975) 'Tongan', unpublished manuscript.

—— (1976) 'On the Notion of Subject in Ergative Languages' in C. Li, (ed.), (1976).

Andrews, A. (1975) *Studies in the Syntax of Relative and Comparative Clauses*, unpublished doctoral dissertation, MIT, Cambridge, Massachusetts.

Bamgbose, A. (1966) *A Grammar of Yoruba*, Cambridge University Press, Cambridge.

Biggs, B. (1974) 'Some Problems of Polynesian Grammar', *Journal of the Polynesian Society* 83, 401-26.

Bird, C. (1966) 'Relative Clauses in Bambara', *Journal of West African Languages* 5, 35-47.

Brown, H.D. (1971) 'Children's Comprehension of Relativised English Sentences', Child Development 42, 1923-36.

Chung, S. (1976) 'An Object-Creating Rule in Indonesian', *Linguistic Inquiry* 7, 41-87.

Churchward, C. (1953) *Tongan Grammar*, Oxford University Press, London.

Cole, P. and J. Sadock (eds.) (1976) *Syntax and Semantics: Grammatical Relations*, Academic Press, New York.

Comrie, B. (1974) 'Causatives and Universal Grammar', *Transactions of the Philological Society*, 1974.

Cook, V.J. (forthcoming) 'Strategies in the Comprehension of Relative Clauses', *Language and Speech*.

Craig, C.G. (1974) 'A Wrong Cyclical Rule in Jacaltec?' in M.W. LaGaly, R. Fox, and A. Bruck (eds.) (1974).

Deibler, E. (1973) *Gahuku Verb Structure*, unpublished doctoral dissertation, University of Michigan, Ann Arbor, Michigan.

Dixon, R.M.W. (1969) 'Relative Clauses and Possessive Phrases in Two Australian Languages', *Language* 45, 35-44.

—— (1972) *The Dyirbal Language of North Queensland*, Cambridge University Press, Cambridge.

Gary, J.O. and E.L. Keenan (1977) 'On Collapsing Grammatical Relations in Universal Grammar', in P. Cole and J. Sadock (eds.) (1976).

Givón, T. (1972) 'Complex NPs in Word Order and Resumptive Pronouns in Hebrew', in *You Take the High Node and I'll Take the Low Node*, Chicago Linguistic Society, University of Chicago, Chicago, Illinois.

—— (1976) 'Topic, Pronoun, and Grammatical Agreement', in C. Li (ed.) (1976).

Gorbet, L. (1972) 'How to Tell a Head When You See One: Disambiguation in Digueño Relative Clauses', unpublished manuscript.

Grossman, R.E., L.J. San, and T.J. Vance (eds.) (1975) *Papers from the Eleventh Regional Meeting of the Chicago Linguistic Society*, University of Chicago, Chicago, Illinois.

Hale, K. (n.d.) 'The Adjoined Relative Clause in Australia', mimeo, MIT, Cambridge, Massachusetts.

Hatch, E. (1971) 'The Young Child's Comprehension of Relative Clauses', *Technical Note* 2-71-16, Southwest Regonal Laboratory, Los Alamitos, California.

Hawkins, S. and E.L. Keenan (1974) 'The Psychological Validity of the Accessibility Hierarchy', Summer Meeting, Linguistic Society of America.

Hohepa, P. (1969) 'The Accusative to Ergative Drift in Polynesian Languages', *Journal of the Polynesian Society* 78, 259-329.

Johnson, D.E. (1974a) 'On the Role of Grammatical Relations in Linguistic Theory', in M.W. LaGaly, R. Fox, and A. Bruck (eds.) (1974) 269-83.

—— (1974b) 'Prepaper on Relational Constraints on Grammar', unpublished paper, Mathematical Sciences Department, IBM Thomas J. Watson Research Center, Yorktown Heights, New York.

Karlsson, F. (1972) 'Relative Clauses in Finnish', in P.M. Peranteau, J.N. Levi, and G.C. Phares (eds.) (1972).

Keenan, E.L. (1972a) 'On Semantically Based Grammar', *Linguistic Inquiry* 3, 4, 413-61.

—— (1972b) 'Relative Clause Formation in Malagasy (and some related and not so related) Languages', in P.M. Peranteau, J.N. Levi, and G.C. Phares (eds.) (1972).

—— (1974) 'The Functional Principle: Generalising the Notion of Subject-of', in M.W. LaGaly, R. Fox, and A. Bruck (eds.) (1974) 298-309.

—— (1975a) 'Logical Expressive Power and Syntactic Variation in Natural Language', in E.L. Keenan (ed.) *Formal Semantics of Natural Language*, Cambridge University Press, Cambridge.

—— (1975b) 'Some Universals of Passive in Relational Grammar', in R.E. Grossman, L.J. San, and T.J. Vance (eds.) (1975) 340-52.

—— (1976a) 'Remarkable Subjects in Malagasy', in C. Li (ed.) (1976).

—— (1976b) 'Towards a Universal Definition of "Subject of"', in C. Li (ed.) (1976).

—— and B. Comrie (1972) 'Noun Phrase Accessibility and Universal Grammar', Winter Meeting, Linguistic Society of America.

Lafitte, P. (1962) *Grammaire Basque*, Editions des 'Amis du Musée Basque' et 'Ikas', Bayonne.

LaGaly, M.W., R. Fox, and A. Bruck (eds.) (1974) *Papers from the Tenth Regional Meeting of the Chicago Linguistic Society*, University of Chicago, Chicago, Illinois.

Legum, S. (1975) 'Strategies in the Acquisition of Relative Clauses', *Technical Note* 2-77-10, Southwest Regional Laboratory, Los Alamitos, California.

Li, C. (ed.) (1976) *Subject and Topic*, Academic Press, New York.

—— and S. Thompson (1974) 'Subject and Topic: A New Typology of Language', Winter Meeting, Linguistic Society of America.

—— and S. Thompson (1976) 'Evidence Against Topicalisation in Topic Prominent Languages' in C. Li (ed.) (1976).

MacDonald, R. and D. Soenjono (1967) *Indonesian Reference Grammar*, Georgetown University Press, Washington, D.C.

Peranteau, P.M., J.N. Levi, and G.C. Phares (eds.) (1972) *The Chicago Which Hunt*, Chicago Linguistic Society, Chicago, Illinois.

Perlmutter, D.M. and P.M. Postal (1974) *Linguistic Institute Lectures*, unpublished manuscript.

Postal, P.M. (1971) *Crossover Phenomena*, Holt, Rinehart and Winston, New York.

de Rijk, R.P.G. (1972) 'Relative Clauses in Basque — a Guided Tour', in P.M. Peranteau, J.N. Levi, and G.C. Phares (eds.) (1972).

Schachter, P. (1973) 'Focus and Relativisation', *Language* 49, 19-46.

—— (1976) 'The Subject in Philippine Languages: Topic, Actor, Actor-Topic, or None of the Above', in C. Li (ed.) (1976).

Sheldon, A. (1974) 'The Role of Parallel Function in the Acquisition of Relative Clauses in English', *Journal of Verbal Learning and Verbal Behavior* 13, 272-81.

Silitonga, M. (1973) *Some Rules Reordering Constituents and their Constraints in Batak*, unpublished doctoral dissertation, University of Illinois, Urbana, Illinois.

Tagashira, Y. (1972) 'Relative Clauses in Korean', in P.M. Peranteau, J.N. Levi, and G.C. Phares (eds.) (1972).

Tchekhoff, C. (1973) 'Some Verbal Patterns in Tongan', *Journal of the Polynesian Society* 82, 281-92.

Trithart, L. (1975) 'Relational Grammar and Chicewa Subjectivisation Rules', in R.E. Grossman, L.J. San, and T.J. Vance (eds.) (1975) 615-24.

Valli, H., N. Hernandez, M. Archard-Baule, and M.F. Beretti (1972) *Compte-rendu d'une expérience réalisée dans une classe de 6ᵉ2, dont le but était d'étudier les mécanismes de la production des relatives chez l'enfant*, Institut de Didactique et Pédagogie, Université de Provence.

Woodbury, A. (1975) *Ergativity of Grammatical Processes: A Study of Greenlandic Eskimo*, unpublished M.A. essay, Department of Linguistics, University of Chicago, Chicago, Illinois.

2 VARIATION IN UNIVERSAL GRAMMAR

If the study of universal grammar (UG) is conceived of loosely as the study of those properties which all natural languages (NLs) have, then it would appear that properties which vary from one NL to another are precisely those which cannot constitute universals. And narrowly construed this thesis is surely true. Yet I shall argue in this paper that the study of variation *can* provide universal generalisations about NLs — often, in fact, ones that could not be established on the basis of data from any single language.

In this paper I shall propose two such generalisations. The first is basically a syntactic constraint which any rule of relative clause formation (RCF) in any NL must obey. As an earlier form of this generalisation was reported on in Keenan and Comrie (1972) I shall only summarise here the conclusions of that work without discussing in detail the evidence which supports it. The second generalisation, whose discussion constitutes the major part of this paper, is a performance one based on, but independent of, the first generalisation.

1. A Syntactic Constraint on Relative Clause Formation (RCF)

In Keenan and Comrie (1972) the possibilities of relativising on various noun phrase (NP) positions in a large range of NLs was investigated. It was found that NLs varied considerably with regard to which NPs could be relativised. But the variation was not random, as the relativisability of certain NP positions was not independent of that of others. Restricting ourselves to major or near major NP positions of main verbs, we can express these dependencies in the Case Hierarchy below:

Case Hierarchy (CH)
Subjects $\geq$ Dir Obj $\geq$ Ind Obj $\geq$ Oblique $\geq$ Genitive $\geq$ Obj of Comparison

To understand the interpretation of the CH let me point out that I am using a liberal, and semantically based, notion of relative clause (RC). Roughly I am thinking of a RC as a syntactic means a language uses to restrict the referents of a NP to those objects of which some sentence is true (the sentence being expressed by the 'subordinate clause' in surface). Thus a RC in English like *the boy who stole the pig* can refer to any object which, one, is a boy, and two, is such that the sentence *he stole the pig* is true of him. Clearly many NLs will have two or more formally distinct means of forming RCs. I shall refer to such distinct means as relative clause forming (RCF) *strategies*. For example, German has both a post-nominal and a prenominal RCF strategy. We can say *the man who is working in his study* either by *der Mann, der in seinem Büro arbeitet* or *der in seinem Büro arbeitende Mann*.

Now suppose a NL has a RCF strategy that works on subjects of main verbs, as in e.g. *the boy who stole the pig*, where *boy* is the subject of *steal*. Well that strategy may or may not also work on direct objects. If it *doesn't* then it will also fail to work on any of the positions lower on the CH than the direct object position. And indeed some NLs (e.g. Tagalog, Malagasy) can relativise only on subjects. On the other hand, if that RCF strategy works on subjects and direct objects then, once again, it either may or may not work on indirect objects. If not, then it also fails to work on any of the NP positions lower than Ind Obj on the CH. And again, there are NLs with RCF strategies that work only on subjects and direct objects (Shona, Finnish (prenominal strategy)). And similarly, for each of the other positions on the CH we have found NLs which can relativise continuously from subjects through that position but no farther using the same strategy.

These facts can be generalised (Bernard Comrie, personal communication) to establish the following universal constraint on RCF:

The Case Ordering Constraint (COC)
Any RCF strategy in any NL must operate on continuous segments of the CH.

Thus, if a given RCF strategy works on two NP positions in the CH it necessarily works on all intermediate positions. So, e.g. no NL has a RCF strategy that works only on subjects and oblique case NP (e.g. objects of prepositions in English). If it works on these it must also work on direct and indirect objects.

Notice now that the COC is a constraint which the grammars of each NL obey, yet no one NL affords sufficient data to determine the COC as we have given it. For any given NL the data are usually compatible with several different ways of ordering the six

NP positions listed in the CH. In many dialects of English for example all the NP positions are relativisable, so any of the six factorial = 720 possible combinations of the six NP elements would be compatible with the data. For dialects in which objects of comparison are not relativisable (e.g. *the boy Mary is taller than*) we still have 120 possible orderings compatible with the data. Even languages like German with two RCF strategies which both cut off before the end (the prenominal strategy works only on subjects, the standard strategy works on all positions except objects of comparison) still admit of 48 possible orderings compatible with the data (viz. any ordering which presents Dir Obj, Ind Obj, Oblique, and Genitive positions as a continuous segment and which places the Subject either before or after the sequence).

Consequently, it is only the data from cross language variation which can correctly determine the most general, that is, the most universally applicable, form of the constraint on relative clause formation.

2. A Performance Constraint on Relative Clause Formation

In addition to the ordering expressed in the CH, there is a sense in which the Subjects end of the CH expresses the 'easiest' or most 'natural' positions to relativise. Thus all NLs possess at least one strategy that works on subjects. But this claim fails for all the other positions. This suggests the idea that, even in NLs where all, or most, of the NP positions on the CH can be relativised, there may be some sense in which it is 'easier' or more 'natural' to form RCs on the Subjects (or higher) end of the CH than on the lower end.

One way to attempt to directly verify this intuition would be to elicit judgements of relative acceptability on RCs formed on the various positions. Thus if English speakers generally agreed that RCs formed on subjects were more acceptable than those formed on objects, etc., then we would have direct evidence in favour of the hypothesis that RCF is more natural on the upper end of the CH. Now indeed there is some, but insufficient, direct evidence of this sort. Thus most speakers agree that it is more acceptable to relativise on the subject of a comparative construction than on the object. Thus *the boy who is taller than Mary* is more acceptable than *the boy that Mary is shorter than*. Further, in some NLs such as Swedish and Dutch, colloquial speech clearly prefers subject relatives over genitive relatives. Thus while Swedish offers in fact two genitive relative pronouns, *vars* and *vilkens*, and so can directly express e.g. *the woman whose coat was stolen* (= *kvinnan, vars kappa blev stulen*) it prefers to use a semantically equivalent construction in which RCF has taken place on the subject position e.g. *kvinnan, som fick son kappa stulen* (= *the woman that got her coat stolen*), in which the head NP *woman* (= *kvinnen*) functions as the subject of the verb *get* (= *fick*).

In fact it was these judgements of relative acceptability which led me to think that the CH, established on the basis of cross language data, might have intralinguistic validity as well. Nonetheless, it must be admitted that the judgements of relative acceptability for all NP positions on the CH are neither reliable nor public enough to constitute the data of a serious scientific claim. This is particularly true when the NP positions considered are adjacent on the CH. Thus there is simply no reliably elicitable judgement that the acceptability of *the farmer whose pig John stole* (a Genitive RC) is less than or equal to that of *the farmer that John stole the pig from* (an Oblique RC). So to verify our hypothesis that RCF is more natural on the higher end of the CH than on the lower end we shall have to have recourse to indirect evidence. That is, let us assume that hypothesis and attempt to directly verify various of its consequences. Below we give three performance-based predictions which are entailed or at least naturally suggested by the hypothesis. We substantiate the predictions and consequently present confirmation (partial only of course) of the hypothesis.

3.

3.1 First Prediction (P-1)

The frequency with which people relativise in discourse conforms to the CH, subjects being the most frequent, then direct objects, etc.

To substantiate P-1 we have collected over 2,200 RCs from a variety of written materials (whose choice will be discussed shortly). In Figure 2.1 we present the distribution of the RC with respect to the relativised NP positions which occur in the CH. Note that we have collapsed the Indirect Object position with the

Oblique case NPs since for purposes of RCF in English it behaves in just the same way — a preposition (*to*) must be retained, and is either stranded, or fronted with the relative pronoun. Hence, when applied to English, the CH has only five, not six, positions. We note also here that the Genitive position includes relativisation into *of* complements of NPs e.g. *the gate the hinges of which were rusty, the gate of which the hinges were rusty*, etc.

We note furthermore that these results are in substantial agreement with those obtained by Block (1973), who considered a RC sample similar in size to ours for early Scots English (c. 1400).

Unfortunately these figures constitute only weak confirmation of our hypothesis, since there is an alternative (but undemonstrated) hypothesis which would explain them. Namely, that RCF in English applies randomly with respect to NP positions that are relativisable at all, and the observed distribution in Figure 2.1 is due to the general distribution of NPs in discourse i.e. NPs occur most frequently as subjects, then as direct objects etc. This latter hypothesis has not been demonstrated, although it is consistent with some very small sample checks performed. Thus, while the frequency distributions in Figure 2.1 support our hypothesis they are insufficient to establish it. For more conclusive support, we must

Figure 2.1

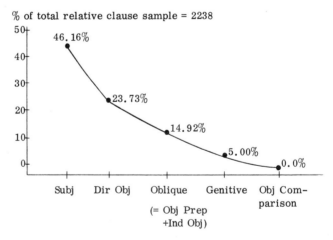

(Positions not represented on the chart include *locatives* i.e. *the place where* ... which represent 4.87% of the total; temporals i.e. *the time when* ... which represent 3.31% of the total, and a miscellaneous category which represents 1.79% of the total.)

turn to a closer analysis of our data and somewhat finer predictions.[1]

3.2 Second Prediction (P-2)

Authors who are reliably judged to use syntactically simple sentences will present a greater proportion of RCs near the high end of the CH than authors independently judged to use syntactically complex sentences.

Note that P-2 is certainly reasonable. For if an author generally uses complex sentence structures we would not expect him to eschew the more 'difficult' or less 'natural' end of the CH when he forms RCs. Authors who restrict themselves to simple sentence structures however would naturally be expected to restrict themselves to the 'easy' or more 'natural' end of the CH.

To substantiate P-2 we have taken RCs from two sources judged to be 'simple' and compared them with two sources judged to be 'complex'. (By '*simple*' and '*complex*' we refer here only to internal sentence structure, of course, not e.g. to the structure of the entire discourse in which the sentences may occur.) Our first source of simple structures consisted of all the relative clauses (there were 421 such) found on pages 1 and 2 of a collection of issues of the *Sun* and the *Daily Mirror*. (These are among the most popular newspapers in Europe. They are in tabloid form, have lots of pictures, large headlines, short sentences, frequent paragraphs, and are obviously designed for 'snapshot' reading.) Clearly they are to be judged, pre-theoretically, as sententially simple. Any formal simplicity metric which judged them complex would simply be an inadequate metric.

Our second source of simple structures were all the RCs found in George Orwell's *Animal Farm* (there were 344 such). Again there is very general agreement that Orwell's sentences (which often present the world as seen through the eyes of the 'lower animals') are syntactically simple. A not atypical sample would be (p. 87):

The very next morning the attack came. The animals were at breakfast when the look-outs came racing in with the news that Frederick and his followers had already come through the five-barred gate. Boldly enough the animals sallied forth to meet them, but this time they did not have the easy victory that they had in the Battle of the Cowshed. There were fifteen men, with half a dozen guns between them, and they opened fire as soon as they got within fifty yards. The animals could not face the terrible explosions and the stinging pellets, and in spite of the efforts of Napoleon and Boxer to rally them, they were soon driven back. A number of them were already wounded. They took refuge in the farm buildings and peeped cautiously out from chinks and knot-holes. The whole of the big pasture, including the windmill, was in the hands of the enemy. For the moment even Napoleon seemed at a loss. He paced up and down without a word, his tail rigid and twitching. Wistful glances were sent in the direction of Foxwood. If Pilkington and his men would help them, the day might yet be won. But at this moment the four pigeons, who had been sent out on the day before, returned, one of them bearing a scrap of paper from Pilkington. On it was pencilled the words: 'Serves you right'.

Similarly, we considered two sources of complex sentence structures: first all the RCs (there were 675 such) in Virginia Woolf's *To the Lighthouse.* And second, all the relative clauses (there were 798 such) found in a collection of P.F. Strawson's works[2]. These authors are clearly sententially complex (although in stylistically quite different ways). Even Ph.D.s in linguistics often have to read their sentences several times to understand them — whereas one never has this difficulty with Orwell or with the *Sun* or *Daily Mirror.*

Figure 2.2 opposite presents in summary form the distribution of RCs (with respect to the CH applied to English) for the simple group, and Figure 2.3 for the complex group.

Clearly RCs from the complex sources are far less frequent on subjects (40.1%) than is the case for those from simple sources (57.8%). (The difference is significant well past the .00005734 level, i.e. the probability of producing such a difference by chance is much less than 1 in a million. In general all differences we explicitly discuss have been checked for statistical significance and are usually several degrees of magnitude more significant than is required in the literature.) On the other hand, RCs from complex sources occur significantly more frequently on Dir Objs, Obliques, and Genitives than do RCs from simple sources. (We should also note that Temporal relatives occurred with a frequency of 6.0% in the simple group, and only 1.9% in the complex group, again a very significant difference.) These figures clearly support P-2, so

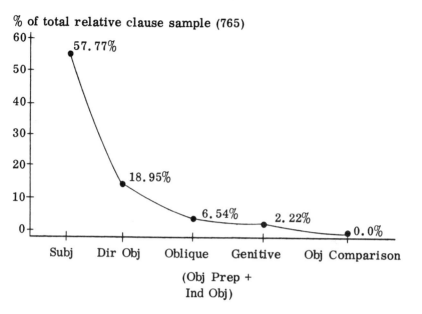

Figure 2.2 'Simple' sources: G. Orwell and *Sun/Mirror*

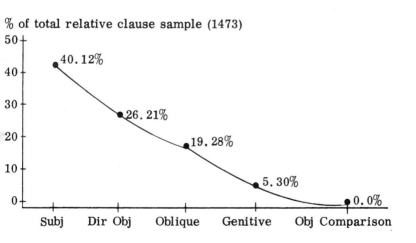

Figure 2.3 'Complex' sources: V. Woolf and P.F. Strawson

our hypothesis is (partially) confirmed.

Having established that RC distribution with respect to the CH can discriminate syntactically complex authors from syntactically simpler ones, we can now use the criterion to distinguish cases which are not so clear on impressionistic grounds.

Consider first the difference between the members of the simple group: Orwell's *Animal Farm* on the one hand and the issues of the *Sun* and *Daily Mirror* on the other. Impressionistically one feels that Orwell's sentences are somewhat more complex syntactically than those of the *Sun* and *Daily Mirror*, although our judgements here carry much less conviction than they did when we compared the simple group as a whole with the complex group.

Applying our complexity criterion however we can see, Figure 2.4, that Orwell is somewhat more complex than the *Sun* and *Daily Mirror*.

Figure 2.4

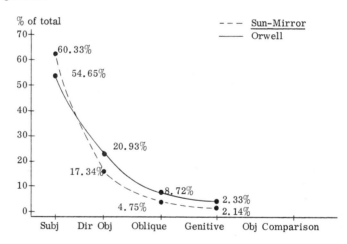

Orwell relativises significantly less frequently on subjects than do the *Sun* and *Daily Mirror* and relatively more in the Oblique NP position. The differences between the other positions on the CH are not significant.

Even more interesting perhaps is the comparison between the members of the more complex group — Woolf and Strawson. Impressionistically both are complex but in quite different ways. Woolf's style is clearly more flowing — it is easy to get caught up in the rhythm, or better, the momentum that her sentences impart. Strawson, on the other hand, is less overwhelming, more *obviously* thought out, and impressionistically, his sentences are more highly structured. Compare in this respect the beginning of V. Woolf's *To the Lighthouse* with the introductory paragraphs of Strawson's *Individuals*:

'Yes, of course, if it's fine tomorrow,' said Mrs Ramsay. 'But you'll have to be up with the lark,' she added.

To her son these words conveyed an extraordinary joy, as if it were settled the expedition were bound to take place, and the wonder to which he had looked forward, for years and years it seemed, was, after a night's darkness and a day's sail, within touch. Since he belonged, even at the age of six, to that great clan which cannot keep this feeling separate from that, but must let future prospects, with their joys and sorrows, cloud what is actually at hand, since to such people even in earliest childhood any turn in the wheel of sensation has the power to crystallize and transfix the moment upon which its gloom or radiance rests, James Ramsay, sitting on the floor cutting out pictures from the illustrated catalogue of the Army and Navy Stores, endowed the picture of a refrigerator as his mother spoke with heavenly bliss. It was fringed with joy. The wheel-barrow, the lawn-mower, the sound of poplar trees, leaves whitening before rain, rooks cawing, brooms knocking, dresses rustling — all these were so coloured and distinguished in his mind that he had already his private code, his secret language, though he appeared the image of stark and uncompromising severity, with his high forehead and his fierce blue eyes, impeccably candid and pure, frowning slightly at the sight of human frailty, so that his mother, watching him guide his scissors neatly round the refrigerator, imagined him all red and ermine on the Bench or directing a stern and momentous enterprise in some crisis of public affairs.

(V. Woolf. *To the Lighthouse*, P.5)

BODIES

I. The Identification of Particulars

[1] We think of the world as containing particular things some of which are independent of ourselves; we think of the

world's history as made up of particular episodes in which we may or may not have a part; and we think of these particular things and events as included in the topics of our common discourse, as things about which we can talk to each other. These are remarks recognisably philosophical, though no clearer, way of expressing them would be to say that our ontology comprises objective particulars. It may comprise much else besides.

Part of my aim is to exhibit some general and structural features of the conceptual scheme in terms of which we think about particular things. I shall speak, to begin with, of the identification of particulars ...

(P.F. Strawson, *Individuals*, P.15)

Figure 2.5 summarises the differences in RC patterning between Strawson and Woolf.

Figure 2.5

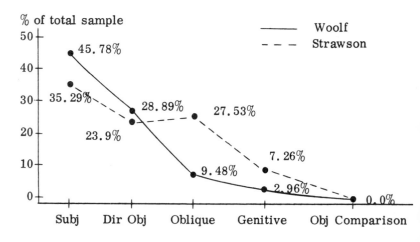

Clearly Strawson relativises significantly less on both subjects and direct objects than does Woolf, but relatively more on oblique case NPs and genitives. Note in fact that Strawson relativises much more frequently on objects of prepositions than he does on direct objects. Thus the complexity ordering of our four text determined by RC distribution on the CH is: *Sun* and *Daily Mirror* the least difficult; then Orwell, then V. Woolf, and finally P.F. Strawson, the most difficult. This ordering accords well with our pretheoretical intuitions and so not only supports P-2 but provides a diagnostic for syntactic complexity useful in cases where our pretheoretical judgements are less than overwhelming.

3.3 Prediction Three (P-3)

There is a tendency in 'simple' authors to move underlying direct objects into superficial subject position (e.g. by PASSIVE) under relativisation.

P-3 is reasonable in that if it is really grammatically more natural to relativise subjects than objects it is natural that authors should move objects into subject position, as PASSIVE would do, in order to relativise the NP from the easiest position. We would expect this particularly in authors who are the more constrained to present their RCs high on the CH anyway.

So far we have only attempted to confirm this prediction in Orwell but there the results are very encouraging, and perhaps sufficient to establish the 'tendency' referred to in P-3. To confirm P-3 we first computed the total number of underlying direct objects present in the text as a whole (there were 1,846 such). Of these, 480 occurred as derived subjects. That is, in the text as a whole, one has a 26.00% chance of presenting an underlying direct object as a superficial subject. Now, restricting ourselves to underlying direct objects that were relativised, we would predict that a greater percentage occurred as superficial subjects i.e. that Orwell moved them into subject position 'in order' to relativise them. And this is correct. Of a total of 116 underlying direct objects that appeared as head NPs of RCs 44 were in fact superficial subjects of the subordinate verb. That is, there was a 33.93% chance of presenting an underlying direct object as a superficial subject if you were going to relativise it. (And again, given our large sample size, this difference is highly significant.)

3.4 Some Additional Predictions

In addition to P-1—P-3, several other performance tests of our basic hypothesis suggest themselves. One very interesting one, not so applicable to English as to certain other languages, has in fact been validated by Block (1973) for early Scots English. Namely, in languages which have a word order norm but which admit of variations on it with only very minor (or no) differences in meaning we would expect that word order freedom would decrease so as to approach the norm in RCs formed on the low end of the CH. That is, the more difficult the position relativised the greater the tendency to present the rest of the material in the most unmarked way, that is, the easiest way, possible.

Further the basic idea behind this hypothesis has also been validated in Givón (1973) who has shown that word order freedom in Hebrew relative clauses decreases according as the NP relativised is the less accessible (but the NP positions Givón considered were even more difficult than those represented in the CH).

A second prediction suggested by the CH is that RC comprehension is a function of the CH. Thus we predict that, on recall tests, native speakers will do less well if the basic information were presented in RCs formed low on the CH than in one formed high on the CH. We are currently testing this hypothesis in a series of tests given to school children of different ages, but we have as yet no concrete results to report.

4. Conclusion

We have shown that cross language variation in syntactic structures can serve not only as the basis of universal constraints on the grammars of languages, but can determine performance constraints within languages. This rather suggests that competence and performance are merely two ends of a scale, rather than exclusive categories.

Notes

1.   The statistical differences between the figures for adjacent NP positions on the CH are in all cases highly significant, using the standard tests discussed in Hayes (1966) and Reed (1949). In fact, no matter what pair of adjacent positions on the CH we pick, the chances that the difference in frequency would arise on a random basis is much less than .00005734%. That is, much less than one in a million.

2.   The works were the first two chapters of *Individuals*, Methuen, London (1959), and the articles 'Identifying reference and truth-values' in *Thoeria*, Vol. 30, Part 2, (1964) pp. 96-118, and 'Singular terms and predication', in *Journal of Philosophy*, Vol. 58, No. 15 (1961), pp. 393-412.

References

Block, D. (1973) 'Relativisation in Early Middle Scots', to be read at the meetings of the Midwest Modern Language Association, Chicago.

Givón, T. (1973) 'Complex NPs, Word Order and Resumptive Pronouns in Hebrew', in *Supplement to Chicago Linguistic Society*, University of Chicago, Chicago, Illinois.

Hayes, C.W. (1966) 'A Study in Prose Styles: Edward Gibbon and Ernest Hemingway', in Donald C. Freeman (ed.) *Linguistics and Literary Style*, Holt, Rinehart and Winston (1970).

Keenan, E. and B. Comrie, (1972) 'Noun Phrase Accessibility and Universal Grammar', paper presented at the Linguistic Society of America Meetings, Winter, 1972 and the Linguistic Association Meetings, Hull, 1973.

Reed, D.W. (1949) 'A Statistical Approach to Quantitative Linguistic Analysis', *Word*, V 235-47.

3 THE PSYCHOLOGICAL VALIDITY OF THE ACCESSIBILITY HIERARCHY[1]

(Written with Sarah Hawkins[2])

1. Abstract

The present experiment was designed to test the hypothesis that mastery of relative clauses correlates with the position of the relative clause on the Accessibility Hierarchy of Keenan and Comrie (1977). In a repetition task (which tests both comprehension and production), forty young adults and forty ten to eleven-year-old children heard a sentence containing a relative clause, followed by a number of spoken digits. They attempted to reproduce the digits and then the sentence in writing. Our results support the conclusion that errors in reproducing the sentence increase as the type of relative clause decreases in position on the Accessibility Hierarchy. As expected, overall accuracy on the repetition task improved with age, and with the intelligence or educational level of the subject. Ten-year-old girls were more accurate than boys, but adult men and women did not differ in accuracy on the test. Within each of these subject groups, however, the pattern of errors was the same and followed the Accessibility Hierarchy. Furthermore, in 74% to 80% of cases in which the syntactic class of the stimulus relative clause differed from the one that was reproduced, the erroneous relative clause was higher on the Accessibility Hierarchy than was the stimulus relative clause.

2. Introduction

2.1 The Accessibility Hierarchy and Psycholinguistic Studies of Relative Clauses

The past fifteen years have seen a large number of psycholinguistic studies of relative clauses. All of those studies differ in several respects from each other (and from the one reported here), making direct comparison difficult. Despite their many differences, however, a surprisingly large range of this literature has produced results which are broadly consistent with the general claim that the Accessibility Hierarchy of Keenan and Comrie (1977) (described in other papers in this volume) serves as a predictor of psycho-linguistic complexity as measured by errors in imitation, other modes of production, or acting-out experiments. We might cite here, with no pretence at exhaustiveness, Gass (1979), Gass and Ard (1980), Hyltenstam (1981, 1983), and Tarallo and Myhill (1983), all concerned with second-language acquisition; and Brown (1971), Noizet *et al.* (1972), Smith (1974), de Villiers *et al.* (1979), Slobin (1982), and Herzberg (1984), concerned with first-language production and/or comprehension.

Although the results reported in these papers are broadly (sometimes quite strikingly) consistent with the predictions derived from the Accessibility Hierarchy, in many of the above studies the crucial variables tested were ones not directly related to the Accessibility Hierarchy. Several studies were primarily concerned with second-language acquisition, many were primarily concerned with comprehension as opposed to production. Most have been concerned solely with children. Many have focused on properties such as centre-embedding or relatives and/or parallel function (in which the position relativised has the same grammatical function as that played by the entire relative clause in the matrix). Most importantly, the majority of studies considered only a subset of the positions on the Accessibility Hierarchy. The psychological validity of the Accessibility Hierarchy has, therefore, not been directly examined.

2.2 Rationale for the Experimental Design Used

The present study was intended to test the hypothesis that mastery of relative clauses correlates with the position of the relative clause on the Accessibility Hierarchy. To fulfil this purpose, we needed a test which included relative clauses on all the positions of the Accessibility Hierarchy, and we needed to show that adults as well as children have progressively greater difficulty in processing rela-tive clauses as the clause's place in the hierarchy decreases. Ideally, the experiment would address both comprehension and pro-duction. If the Accessibility Hierarchy is in fact universal and correlates with the relative complexity of psychological processes, then the number of factors should have no effect on relative per-formance (between relative clauses), although these factors could affect the absolute level of success on such a test. Specifically, while the overall level of test performance should be affected by differences in factors such as the age, sex, intelligence, or educational level of the individual, the hierarchy itself should be independent of these factors.

A repetition test was chosen as most suitable for the requirements of the study. Subjects were presented with a stimulus sentence followed by a certain number of digits and asked, first, to write down the digits, and then to write down the stimulus sentence. Each stimulus sentence contained a relative clause formed on one of a variety of positions, including all those in the Accessibility Hierarchy.

The rationale behind repetition tasks of the type used in this experiment is as follows. If the subject does not understand the sentence, then the primary limitation on accuracy of repetition is memory span, and therefore sentence length. If the test sentence exceeds memory span, then errors in the form of omissions and substitutions will occur, presumably in proportion to the length of the sentence. If, on the other hand, the subject understands the sentence, memory span will be vastly increased since the sentence will be 'chunked' into semantic units. The primary limitation to accuracy in this case is structural complexity, and errors will occur in proportion to the degree of complexity.

Experiments indicate that repetition tasks are in fact a sensitive indicator of an individual's command of a linguistic structure. The results of repetition tests appear to reflect with some fidelity the use of that structure in spontaneous speech, with a tendency for greater ease in the repetition situation (Menyuk 1969, 112-25). Since errors generally involve the substitution of grammatically simpler structures, we hoped that an error analysis would further test the Accessibility Hierarchy by showing that relative clauses low on the Accessibility Hierarchy were replaced by ones higher on the hierarchy.

Repetition tests also have a number of practical advantages. The procedure tests production as well as comprehension, and, in the case of the present experiment, forces subjects to attempt to produce relative clauses on all desired positions. Essentially the same test can be given to individuals of a wide range of ages and abilities, memory load being varied by changing the amount of irrelevant material, in our case the digit sequences. Finally, the test is relatively quick and easy to administer, and so is particularly suitable for children.

2.3 Relative Clause Positions Tested

Nine types of relative clauses were presented. They differed with regard to the grammatical function (Subject, Direct Object, etc.) of the head noun in the restricting clause. We list below the types of relative clauses used, together with mnemonics for their grammatical functions.

(1) S (Subject):   the boy who told the story
     DO (Direct Object):   the letter which Dick wrote
                                      yesterday
     IO (Indirect Object):   the man who Ann gave the
                                      present to
     OBL (Oblique NP):   the box which Pat brought
                                      the apples in
     GenS (Genitive Subject):   the girl whose friends bought
                                      the cake
     GenO (Genitive Direct   the man whose house
     Object):   Patrick bought
     OCOMP (Object of   the boy who Mike writes
     Comparison):   better than
     DS (Derived Subject   the dog which was taught by
     = Subject of Passive):   John
     GenDS (Genitive Derived   the boy whose brother was
     Subject):   taught by Sandra

The original Accessibility Hierarchy in Keenan and Comrie (1977) was: S > DO > IO > OBL > GEN > OCOMP. In this experiment, then, we tested several positions that are not on the hierarchy, and we distinguished between Genitive Subject and Genitive Object. Additionally, the OCOMP position may justifiably be excluded from the hierarchy, since, unlike the other positions, OCOMP may occur in a number of different ways across languages. In some languages the comparative particle (*than, as,* in English) is just an ordinary preposition or postposition, so that position in those languages is not distinct from OBL. In other languages, objects of comparison are presented as DOs in serial verb constructions ('John big exceed Bill' for 'John is bigger than Bill') so here OCOMPs look like DOs in otherwise more complex sentence types. Finally, in several languages, objects of comparison are presented as Subjects in two-clause constructions: 'John big, Bill small'. We do not feel then that OCOMP is a grammatically identifiable position in the same way as the relative clauses that are higher than OCOMP on the original Accessibility Hierarchy.

3. Experimental Method

3.1 Stimulus Sentences

A total of 36 relative clauses were formed, four for each of the grammatical functions being studied, as in (1) above. From these relative clauses, sentences were constructed in which the relative clause always functioned as the Subject of an intransitive verb phrase (sometimes referred to below as the *final frame*). The resulting sentences were embedded in one of the four (initial) frames, *They had forgotten that —*, *The fact that —*, *I know that —*, and *He remembered that —*. A complete list of the 36 stimulus sentences is given below.

S (Subject)
They had forgotten that the boy who told the story was so young.
The fact that the girl who paid for the tickets is very poor doesn't matter.
I know that the girl who got the answer right is clever.
He remembered that the man who sold the house left the town.

DO (Direct Object)
They had forgotten that the letter which Dick wrote yesterday was so long.
The fact that the cat which David showed to the man likes eggs is strange.
I know that the dog which Penny bought today is very gentle.
He remembered that the sweets which Dave gave Sally were a treat.

IO (Indirect Object)
They had forgotten that the man who Ann gave the present to was old.
The fact that the boy who Paul sold the book to hates reading is strange.

I know that the man who Stephen explained the accident to is kind.

He remembered that the dog which Mary taught the trick to was clever.

OBL (Oblique Noun Phrase)
They had forgotten that the box which Pat brought with apples in was lost.

The fact that the girl who Sue wrote the story with is proud doesn't matter.

I know that the ship which my uncle took Joe on was interesting.

He remembered that the food which Chris paid the bill for was cheap.

GenS (Genitive Subject)
They had forgotten that the girl whose friend bought the cake was waiting.

The fact that the boy whose brother tells lies is always honest surprised us.

I know that the boy whose father sold the dog is very sad.

He remembered that the girl whose mother sent the clothes came too late.

GenO (Genitive Direct Object)
They had forgotten that the man whose house Patrick bought was so ill.

The fact that the sailor whose ship Jim took had one leg is important.

I know that the woman whose car Jenny sold was very angry.

He remembered that the girl whose picture Clare showed us was pretty.

OCOMP (Object of Comparison)
They had forgotten that the boy who Mike writes better than was listening.

The fact that the man who Neil is as rich as gave less is important.

I know that the girl who Maureen is as pretty as teaches English.

He remembered that the girl who Jane is older than could read.

DS (Derived Subject = Subject of Passive Predicate)

They had forgotten that the dog which was taught by John was hungry.

The fact that the coat which was bought by Janet was so cheap surprised us.

I know that the story which was told by Jill wasn't true.

He remembered that the game which was suggested by Peter was fun.

GenDS (Genitive Derived Subject)

They had forgotten that the boy whose brother was taught by Sandra was ill.

The fact that the girl whose pen was taken by Angela wasn't angry surprised us.

I know that the boy whose name was suggested by Ian was proud.

He remembered that the girl whose books were bought by Andrew was poor.

The stimulus sentences contained only words graded A or AA on the Thorndike-Lorgc G count and greater than 100 on their J count (Thorndike and Lorge 1968). The average sentence length was 13.28 words, with a range of 12.75 (for GenO) to 13.75 words (for IO, OBL, and GenDS). Within a given frame, sentences differed in length by not more than one word. All nine stimulus sentences beginning with *They had forgotten that* had either 13 or 14 words; all those beginning with *The fact that* had 14 or 15 words; and all those sentences beginning with *I know that* and *He remembered that* had 12 or 13 words.

All relative clauses in the test sentences used the determiner *the*. Relative clauses formed on IO, OBL, and OCOMP always stranded the preposition or particle. All relative clauses contained between six and eight words. All verbs in the relative clauses could take both direct and indirect objects. The only relative pronouns used were *who* and *which*. No verb, and no final sentence frame (intransitive verb phrase) occurred more than once within each type of relative clause.

3.2 Design

So that both adults and children could hear the same sentences while floor and ceiling effects in repetition accuracy were avoided, each sentence was followed by a number of digits which subjects were required to remember in addition to remembering the sentence. Adults heard sequences of eight digits whereas the children heard either the first or last three digits from each sequence of eight. The lengths of digit sequences were determined during pilot studies. Digits were spoken at a rate of one per 0.66 sec, and each digit had a falling (list final) intonation. Digit order in each sequence was random, save that no obviously memorable sequence such as 123 or 642 was allowed. Only one digit could be repeated per block of eight, and no digits could be repeated in a block of three. Each sentence was followed by a unique digit sequence.

The stimulus sentences were randomised in four (sentence frames) blocks of nine (relative clauses) with the restriction that no sentence frame would be followed by itself and that each frame should occur twice in each block. The order of sentences (but not of associated digits) was counterbalanced across blocks. Test items were tape recorded at 19 cm/sec in a woman's voice, with normal intonation that was unmarked for all sentences except those beginning with *The fact that.* Sentences with this frame were more difficult and a more marked intonation pattern was used that pilot work had shown facilitated their comprehension.

3.3 Subjects

Forty children and forty adults, all native speakers of British English, were divided into eight groups of ten by sex and by Stanford-Binet IQ scores (children) or educational attainment (adults). Thus there were four groups of ten children, high-IQ girls, low-IQ girls, high-IQ boys, and low-IQ boys; and four groups of ten adults, women with long education, women with short education, men with long education, and men with short education.

The children were ten and eleven years old, and all were in the same year at the same school. The high-IQ girls had a mean IQ of 131.6, range 120-144. Low-IQ girls had a mean IQ of 109.7, range 96-118. Mean IQ for the high-IQ boys was 127.3, range 112-151, and the low-IQ boys had a mean IQ of 101.3 with a range of 91-111.

The twenty adults with long education were Masters or Ph.D. students at the University of Essex, with equal numbers of each sex chosen from the arts and sciences. The adult subjects with short education included ten male naval ratings with no formal academic education beyond the age of 15 years and either no or only minimal academic qualifications, and ten women of similar educational experience. The mean age of the women with long education was 22.7 years, range 21-27. Women with short education had a mean age of 21.1 years, range 17-27. Men with long education had a mean age of 24.3 years, range 21-28, and men with short education had a mean age of 20.1 years, range 17-24.

3.4 Procedure

Before presentation of a test item, subjects heard a warning tone, followed by three seconds of silence. Then came the test sentence, followed by 0.5 seconds of silence, and then the digit sequence. Subjects then had four seconds in which to write down the digit sequence, after which the word 'Recall' was heard as the signal to write the sentence. No time limit was imposed on the latter task. The entire test was preceded by ten practice stimuli. Subjects were told that the purpose of the experiment was to test how well people recall different kinds of material, sentences and numbers.

Subjects were tested in groups in a quiet room at their school (children), at the Cambridge MRC Applied Psychology Unit (naval ratings), or at the University of Essex (other adults). Half of each of the eight groups heard the sentences in one order, the other half hearing them in the reverse order. Adults were tested in one session with two breaks, totalling about an hour. Children were tested in three or four sessions with one break per session.

4. Results of the Experiment

4.1 Scoring the Data

When response errors can take many different forms, as in this experiment, there is always a variety of methods by which the data can be scored. Two scoring methods were used in this experiment. One method was considerably more complicated than the other, in an attempt to reflect subtle differences in error pattern. The two methods gave very similar results, so only analyses from the simplest method of scoring are reported here.

Using this simpler method, a sentence could be assigned a score of 2, 1, or 0, a higher score representing more accurate repetition. A sentence was assigned a score of 2 if it was recalled essentially perfectly, the only errors allowed being a grammatically permissible change in or deletion of a relative pronoun (e.g. *that* for *which,* or *the box Pat brought* for *the box which Pat brought*). A sentence was assigned a score of 1 if it contained any, some, or all of the following minor errors: a tense change, verb particle omission, omission or incorrect addition of a noun modifier, lexical substitution with the meaning retained (e.g. *doesn't like* for *hates*), substitution of one proper noun for another, substitution of one of the other initial frames, incorrect recall of the final transitive verb phrase. The sentence was given a score of 0 if it contained any other error.

4.2 Analysis

Scores derived as described above were submitted to a 2 (sexes) × 2 (educational or intelligence level) × 9 (relative clause types) × 4 (sentence frames) analysis of variance. Measures on relative clause types and sentence frames were repeated over subjects, and frames were treated as a random variable, the others being fixed. Separate analyses of variance were conducted on the scores for adults and children, since we were primarily interested in the pattern of results *within* each age group, and in any case the testing conditions between the two groups differed. Other analyses were conducted on certain aspects of the data, as described below.

4.3 Accuracy of Responses

The results of the analyses of variance were encouragingly consistent between groups of subjects, and in general supported the psychological validity of the Accessibility Hierarchy in that errors increased in frequency and severity as the stimulus relative clauses decreased on the Accessibility Hierarchy. A number of significant interactions between variables in both children's and adults' analyses indicated that certain factors had a greater influence on response errors under some conditions than under others. In each of these cases, the interaction term acquired statistical significance for the same reason: factors that hindered response accuracy had little effect on scores for relative clauses high in the Accessibility Hierarchy (Subject, Direct Object, and Indirect Object), but had an increasingly deleterious effect on accuracy as positions decreased in the Accessibility Hierarchy. In particular, errors to relativisations involving possessives (GenS, GenO, and GenDS) increased disproportionately under all conditions that reduced response accuracy. None of these significant interactions contributes relevant information that is not also found in the various main effects, so, for clarity, no further mention of the interactions will be made.[3]

The relative ordering of the nine relative clauses in terms of response accuracy was very much the same for all groups of subjects, although the groups did differ in absolute accuracy, particularly for relative clauses that generated a lot of response errors.

Table 3.1 shows that, for both adults and children, the observed order of response accuracy correlates essentially perfectly with the predicted order, that of the Accessibility Hierarchy. It correlates completely perfectly if Genitive is (justifiably) treated as one category by taking the average of GenS and GenO. Furthermore, except for DS, response accuracy for relative clauses not on the Accessibility Hierarchy is quite poor.

The Accessibility Hierarchy is not only supported in that the observed and predicted orders of relative clause positions closely correspond. In addition, some relative clauses are processed and reproduced significantly more accurately than others. The difference in response accuracy across the different types of relative clause is significant for both adults ($F''(9,43) = 5.22$, $p < 0.001$) and children ($F''(9,29) = 5,62$, $p < 0.001$). Adults and children scored equally on the Subject relatives, but children's scores began to drop off at the DO level, and fell faster than adults' as we progress down the hierarchy, resulting in a much larger range of scores for children than for adults. We conclude that greater experience

Table 3.1: Repetition Accuracy for Sentences Containing a Relative Clause

| | \multicolumn{9}{c}{Relative Clause} | | | | | | | | |
	S	DO	IO	OBL	GenS	GenO	OComp	DS	GenDS
Adults	204	200	181	167	100	114	120	152	111
Children	202	164	161	112	67	57	115	139	84

Scores reflecting the accuracy with which the stimulus sentences were reproduced by adult and child groups, for each of the nine relative clause types. The higher the score, the more accurate the response (see text for details). The maximum score per sentence was 2. There were 40 subjects in each group, and four stimulus sentences for each relative clause type. The maximum score possible for each cell is therefore 320.

with the relative clauses lower on the hierarchy, or, perhaps, factors associated with maturation, encourages greater accuracy for adults than for children.

The individual's ability to process these different types of relative clause is affected by a number of factors other than age, however. Each of the additional variables built into this experiment influenced subjects' response accuracy, though not the overall tendency for the order of the Accessibility Hierarchy to be followed, and there are probably other influences that have not been examined. The influence of sex and of length of education on the adults' performance is shown in Figure 3.1, while Figure 3.2 shows the influence of sex and measured intelligence level on the children's performance. Adults who had received long formal education, represented by solid lines in Figure 3.1, made fewer response errors than adults who had left school at 15 years of age, represented by dashed lines in Figure 3.1 ($F(1,36) = 35.8$, $p < 0.001$). Similarly, comparing solid with dashed lines in Figure 3.2 shows that children with high IQs made fewer errors than children with low IQs ($F(1,36) = 17.8$, $p < 0.001$).

The influence of the subject's sex on response accuracy was less consistent than that of length of education or intelligence. Comparing circles (females) with crosses (males) in Figure 3.2, we see that girls were more accurate in their responses than were boys ($F(1,36) = 9.07$, $p < 0.01$). The same comparison for adults (Figure 3.1) shows that this sex-based difference in accuracy does not continue into adulthood ($F(1,36) = 0.99$, not significant), largely due to the high level of accuracy achieved by the men with lengthy educations.

Notice that for all these comparisons, the overall pattern of results does not differ between subject groups for relative clauses on the hierarchy. Except for the two best-performing groups, men with long education and girls with high IQs, the pattern also does not differ between groups for the relative clauses that are not on the hierarchy.

The final comparison is between sentence frames. Response accuracy varied significantly with the sentence frame for both adults ($F(3,117) = 17.59$, $p < 0.001$) and children ($F(3,117) = 39.16$, $p. < 0.001$), and in fact both groups had significant interactions between frames and clauses, as described in Note 3. The differences are neither surprising nor particularly interesting within the framework of this research, but it is worth noting that both

Figure 3.1: The Influence of Sex and of Length of Education on Response Accuracy

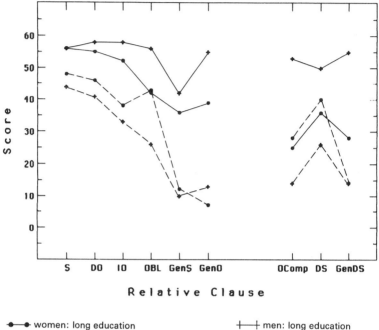

Scores achieved by four groups of adults for each of the types of relative clause tested. A higher score represents greater accuracy of response, as described in the text. The curves at the left of the figure are for relative clauses on the Accessibility Hierarchy. Scores for these relative clauses were predicted to decrease from left to right. The curves at the right of the figure are for relative clauses not included in the hierarchy. No formal predictions were made about response accuracy for these constructions. The maximum possible score for each group on a single relative clause is 80 = 4 sentence frames × 10 subjects × 2 points for a correct response.

adults and children were one-and-a-half times to twice as accurate for sentences beginning with *I know that* (the most accurate) compared with sentences beginning with *The fact that* (the least accurate).

4.4 *Errors in Reproducing the Correct Relative Clause*

We turn now from considering the number of errors made to the

Figure 3.2: The Influence of Sex and of IQ Level on Response
Accuracy

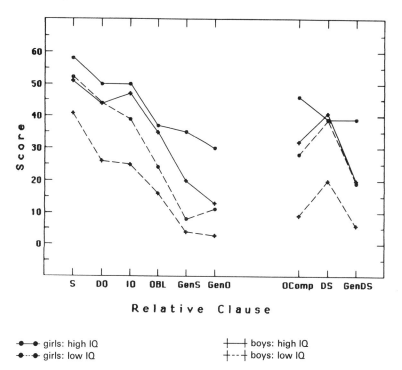

Relative Clause

●——● girls: high IQ   +——+ boys: high IQ
●--●girls: low IQ   +--+ boys: low IQ

Scores achieved by four groups of children for each of the types of relative clause
tested. Details as in Figure 3.1.

stimulus sentences, to the types of errors made. Several interesting
patterns are observable. We discuss here only the children's data,[4]
and only those errors that involved a change in the type of relative
clause — that is, children's responses that received a score of zero.
Table 3.2 is a Confusion matrix showing, for each stimulus relative
clause, the distribution of responses in terms of the same and other
types of relative clause. Each row represents responses to one
stimulus relative clause which is named in the left-hand column.
The types of relative clause produced in response to each stimulus
are named along the top of the matrix. Each cell shows the number
of times a relative clause of the type named in the top row was produced in response to a relative clause of the type named in the

Table 3.2: Confusion Matrix of Children's Errors in Type of Relative Clause Produced

Type presented	Type of relative clause in the response									
	S	DO	IO	OBL	GenS	GenO	OComp	DS	GenDS	Other
S	155	1	3							2
DO	4	140						6		10
IO	13	15	125	2				1		4
OBL	17	30		103				5		5
GenS	72	2	1	2	64			4	1	14
GenO	17	60	8	6		40		3	5	21
OComp	53	3		1			86	1		16
DS		58	1	1				91		9
GenDS	12	24	1	4		9		43	50	17

appropriate row of the left-hand column. Thus cells on the diagonal are correct responses; cells to the left of the diagonal are errors that involved a relative clause of a position higher on the Accessibility Hierarchy than that of the stimulus; and cells to the right of the diagonal represent errors that involved a relative clause of a lower position in the hierarchy than that of the stimulus. See the text for an example. The column marked 'Other' represents errors in which the stimulus relative clause was incorrectly reproduced, but was not identifiable as any other type of relative clause. Data are for 40 children aged 10 to 11 years.

The confusion matrix in Table 3.2 shows the pattern of errors for all nine relative clauses in the test. For each grammatical function, there were four test sentences, so the total number of responses (and hence possible errors) for the forty children was 160. To read the matrix, let us take as an example the row marked OBL. It tells us that of the 160 responses to OBL relatives, 17 were relative clauses formed on the Subject position, 30 were relative clauses formed on the Direct Object position, none were relative clauses formed on the Indirect Object position, 103 were relative clauses formed (correctly) on the Oblique position, five were relative clauses formed on Subjects of passive predicates (DS), and five responses were not classifiable as being relative clauses formed on any of the positions investigated.

The vast majority of responses that received a score of zero nevertheless contained well-formed relative clauses — ones whose heads however did not match the function of the head in the relative clause of the stimulus sentence. Very few of the responses were meaningless, in fact.[5] Perhaps the most striking pattern is that most of the incorrect responses were relative clauses formed on positions higher in the Accessibility Hierarchy than those of the stimulus relative clauses — usually the Subject or Direct Object. In other words, accepting the conclusions of the above analyses that relative clauses formed on positions low on the Accessibility Hierarchy are more difficult to process than ones formed on higher positions, we see that errors tended strongly to be in the direction of grammatical simplification, as expected in tests of this type.

These conclusions are highlighted in Table 3.3, which condenses some of the data of Table 3.2. The left-hand column of numbers shows the total number of responses containing an incorrect type of relative clause, for each type of relativisation in the Accessibility Hierarchy. The right-hand column of numbers represents the percentage of these incorrect relative clauses that were formed on positions higher on the Accessibility Hierarchy than the stimulus relative clause. (Responses that resulted in relative clauses of the types OComp, DS, or GenDS are all omitted from this table.) Thus, for example, in the row marked OBL, the responses included 57 incorrect relative clauses, 83% (or 47) of which were relative clauses formed on a position higher than OBL on the hierarchy — namely on Subject, Direct Object or Indirect Object.

As expected, as we descend the Accessibility Hierarchy, (ranking GenS higher than GenO, or instead taking their average), the

Table 3.3: Children's Response Errors in Type of Relative Clause (rc)

function of stimulus rc	number of errors in rc type	percentage of errors containing an rc that is higher on the accessibility hierarchy
S	5	0
DO	20	20
IO	35	80
OBL	57	83
GenS	96	80
GenO	120	76

The left-hand column of numbers shows the total number of responses containing an incorrect type of relative clause, for each position on the Accessibility Hierarchy. The right-hand column shows the percentage of these incorrect relative clauses that were formed on positions higher on the Accessibility Hierarchy than that of the stimulus relative. Data are for 40 children aged 10 to 11 years.

number of incorrect relative clauses increases dramatically, and indeed perfectly preserves the predicted ordering based on the ordering of relative clauses in the Accessibility Hierarchy. The most striking fact about Table 3.3, however, is that of the total 333 incorrect relative clauses, fully 74% (or 247) were formed on higher positions in the Accessibility Hierarchy than the stimulus relative clause. This number rises to 80% (a total of 266) if the response errors that were formed on Subjects of passive predicates (DS) are lumped with Subjects of active predicates. Both theoretical considerations and the responses of subjects in this experiment encourage pooling the two types of Subject relative clauses, or at least placing DS in the region of DO and IO in terms of accuracy of processing. It is of course true that errors in relative clause type made as responses to positions low on the hierarchy can only result in types that are higher on the hierarchy, (or in nonsense). But this point does not account entirely for the fact that most erroneous clauses were formed on positions higher in the Accessibility Hierarchy. The percentage of erroneous relative clauses that rose in the Accessibility Hierarchy relative to the position of the stimulus relative clause was of the order of 80% for all positions except the two highest, Subject and Direct Object.

Referring again to Table 3.2, we see that the same error pattern is true for OComp and GenDS, under the reasonable assumptions that all relative clauses in the Accessibility Hierarchy proper, together with DS, should be counted as higher than OComp and GenDS. The situation is a little more complex for DS, since there is no independent evidence telling us where to place it in the Accessibility Hierarchy. It does not seem surprising, however, that of the 69 erroneous relative clauses made to DS stimuli, almost all (84%) were formed on the Direct Object. The response relative, in fact, was often a paraphrase on the stimulus one (e.g. *the dog that John taught* for *the dog which was taught by John*). These types of error provide good evidence that subjects understood the stimulus relative clause and tended to make systematic errors that were grammatically simpler but preserved the original meaning.

An unanticipated pattern is that responses to relative clauses formed on possessors of a given position (the Genitives) tend to assimilate to relative clauses formed on that same position but without the genitive. Specifically, Table 3.2 shows that of the 96 errors in relative clause that were produced in response to relative clauses formed on GenS, possessors of active subjects, fully 76 (or

79%) were relative clauses formed directly on Subjects, either active or passive. Of the 120 errors in relative clause that were produced in response to relative clauses formed on GenO, possessors of Direct Objects, 60 (or 50%) were relative clauses formed on Direct Objects. And of the 110 errors in relative clause produced in response to relative clauses formed on GenDS, possessors of Subjects of passive predicates, 55 (or 50%) were formed on Subjects, 43 of these being on passive subjects, and 12 on active subjects. Moreover, these particular errors were by far the most common category for each of the three genitive constructions. These data suggest that the possessive (Genitive) construction is an isolatable part of what subjects were asked to comprehend and produce, and that in a large proportion of cases, the children simply omitted the possessive construction in attempting to reproduce the stimulus relative.

It is particularly tantalising to speculate on the pattern of errors in response to relative clauses formed on GenDS, possessors of subjects of passive predicates. Four different types of response error are logically possible, and indeed Table 3.2 shows that the great majority of errors to GenDS that change the type of relative clause (but yet are still meaningful) falls into one of these categories. We have just noted that the genitive (possessive) structure is often omitted while the rest of the structure is preserved. In the case of GenDS, simply omitting the genitive results in a relativisation on the subject of a passive predicate, and as pointed out above, DS is the relative clause most commonly substituted for GenDS (39% of 110 errors). We have also noted, however, that the passive may be omitted while still preserving semantic function. If only the passive is omitted from a GenDS relative and the semantic function is otherwise preserved, then the error would result in a GenO, that is, a relative clause formed on the possessor of a Direct Object. Only nine (or 8%) of the 110 incorrect responses were of this sort. If, on the other hand, both the genitive and the passive structures were omitted, either of two things might happen, depending on the order in which the omissions occurred. If, so to speak, the genitive were omitted first, then the passive would be omitted from an (erroneous) DS formed from the GenDS, and we would be left with a relative clause formed on a Direct Object. This is the second largest category of error to GenDS in Table 3.2, with 24 (or 22%) of the 110 errors in relative clause type. Omitting the passive operation first would result in a GenS structure, that is, the possessor of a Subject. If the possessive structure were then omitted, the resulting relative would be formed directly on a Subject. With 12 (or 11%) of the response errors of this sort, this, like the omission of the passive structure alone that would result in GenO, does not appear to be a very common process. Nevertheless, these four types of omissions together account for 88 (or 80%) of the 110 incorrect relative clauses produced in response to GenDS. Of the remaining 22 incorrect relativisations, 17 (about 16% of the total) were not recognisable as relative clauses formed on any of the positions tested.

Of these four categories of error, by far the strongest influence appears to be the omission of the Genitive, since this accounts for 61% of the total 110 errors in relative clause, and 76% of the 88 errors attributable to the four categories alone. What this means in terms of psycholinguistic processes remains to be seen. While it is clear that additional experiments would have to be done to determine whether 'Passive' and 'Possessive' function as units in some sense, and whether there is any testable sense in which one can be omitted 'before' the other, the above analysis does show that errors are far from random and that to a large extent subjects appeared to understand the stimulus items.

4.5 Summary of the Results

1. Accuracy of performance on the repetition test correlated significantly with the order of relative clauses on the Accessibility Hierarchy, for all groups tested. Specifically, errors increased as the stimulus relative clause decreased on the Accessibility Hierarchy: S > DO > IO > OBL > GEN. The number of errors to relative clauses in adjacent positions on the Accessibility Hierarchy were not always significantly different from each other, especially for adults, but the overall difference between the most accurately and least accurately reproduced relative clauses was significant for both groups.

2. Adults as a group responded more accurately than children, but only on relative clauses lower in the Accessibility Hierarchy, and the children who responded most accurately tended to do better than the least accurate adults.

3. Children with higher IQ scores were more accurate than those with lower IQ scores, and adults who had lengthy educations were more accurate than those with shorter educations.

4. Girls were more accurate than boys, but men and women did not differ significantly in accuracy.

5. The accuracy with which a sentence was reproduced depended partly on the particular frame that began it.

6. The lower the position of the relative clause in the Accessibility Hierarchy, the greater the effect of any factor that tended to reduce response accuracy (namely age, sex, IQ, length of education, and sentence frame).

7. Genitive constructions were particularly poorly reproduced. These relative clauses tended to be replaced by relativisations on the same position except without the genitive aspect (GenS as S, GenO as DO, and GenDS as DS).

8. When one type of relative clause was substituted for another, (a) the substituted relative clause generally retained some of the grammatical function characteristics of the stimulus relative clause, and (b) in 74%-80% of cases, the substituted relative clause's position in the Accessibility Hierarchy was higher than that of the stimulus sentence.

5. Discussion

Our results support the initial hypothesis that difficulty in comprehending and producing relative clauses is in direct proportion to their position on the Accessibility Hierarchy. Not unexpectedly, mastery of all possible relative clauses in English is not attained before puberty. Order of acquisition appears to follow the Accessibility Hierarchy, with Subject being mastered before full mastery of Object (Direct and Indirect) relative clauses, and Obliques and Genitives coming later if at all. Mastery of the entire set of relative clauses does not appear to be a purely maturational phenomenon eventually achieved by everyone (as suggested, for example, by Borer and Wexler (1984) for full versus agentless passives), since adults with low educational levels do not exhibit mastery of relative clauses formed on genitives. Furthermore, intelligence and length of education significantly affect performance on most relative clause positions in the Accessibility Hierarchy.

We do not know why length of education and intelligence (and the sex of children) should affect accuracy of performance. The differences in accuracy between groups may indeed reflect a dif-

ference in linguistic ability *per se*, but they could also reflect differences in exposure to less common constructions (perhaps
through reading) or differences in memory capacity. If the latter is
the case, the effect should lie in the individuals' *strategies* for
remembering rather than in simple memory span, since the length
of the sentences and the requirement to remember the digits
ensured that the task far exceeded short-term memory span.
Linguistic ability is presumably a major determinant of the
sophistication of strategies for remembering in this type of task.
(The more highly educated adults and the more intelligent children
were generally also more successful than the other groups at reproducing the digits that followed each sentence. We cannot therefore
attribute their better reproduction of the sentences to their 'seeing
through' the purpose of the experiment and ignoring the digits.)

Not all results of other research on relative clauses are consistent with ours, though the large differences in the types of test
employed and the characteristics of the experimental subjects
require that further directly comparable experiments be conducted
to determine the significance of these inconsistencies. For example,
in contrast with our study, de Villiers *et al.* (1979) report no sex
bias. However, they used acting-out experiments with children
aged three to five years, whereas we used a repetition task with
children aged ten to eleven years.

One potentially more damaging result is the parallel function
work by Sheldon (1974). She found that comprehension, as
measured by acting-out procedures with young children, was facilitated by parallel function — the function of the entire relative
clause in the matrix and the position relativised being the same. In
our study, the function of the relative clause in the matrix was held
constant: always Subject. Thus in our study, relative clauses
formed on Subject position exhibited parallel function whereas no
other relative clause we tested exhibited parallel function. Possibly,
then, this biased our results in favour of Subject relatives. Further
work is needed to test for this bias.

There are, however, several reasons why such a parallel function
bias for Subject relatives may not have been significant in our
experiment. In the first place, the studies cited above also show
that fewer errors are made to Subject relatives than to non-Subject
relatives. Disparities with the predictions based on the Accessibility Hierarchy tend more to occur between the IO and OBL
positions (Tarallo and Myhill 1983) or between OBL and GEN

positions (Gass 1979). Second, several studies have yielded results incompatible with the parallel function hypothesis (Brown 1971; de Villiers *et al.*, 1979; Smith 1974; Ioup and Kruse 1977; and Gass and Ard 1980). And third, there seems to us to be serious reason to doubt that the acting-out procedure used by Sheldon and several other researchers (e.g. de Villiers *et al.*) really do test that the child has comprehended a relative clause at all.

In acting-out procedures, a display of toy animals is presented to the child, and after suitable familiarisation, she is asked to use the toys to act out the action expressed in spoken sentences such as

(2)   The horse that jumped over the pig kicked the dog.

A correct response to the above sentence would be one in which the child picked up the horse, had it jump over the pig, and then kick the dog. Note that (in contrast to the sounder testing procedure of Herzberg, 1984), there is usually only one horse in the display, and that in consequence the child does not need the information in the relative clause *that jumped over the pig* to identify the horse. Had there been several horses, one of which jumped over a pig and the others of which did other things, the child would have needed this information in the relative clause in order to identify the horse she was to move. In order to produce a correct response when there is only one horse in the display, the child does not need to know that the relative clause *that jumped over the pig* modifies *horse*, and she does not need to assign a meaning to the expression *The horse that jumped over the pig*. Nor does she have to interpret this expression as a syntactic unit. In terms of correct response, then, the stimulus sentence above is not significantly different from *The horse jumped over the pig (and) kicked the dog*.

By contrast, we feel that repetition tasks of the sort used in the present study provide more assurance that correct responses only occur when the child has interpreted the relative clauses as syntactic and semantic units. The reason is that the vast majority of incorrect responses did in fact contain a relative clause, moreover one which bore a sensible cognitive relation to the stimulus relative. It was usually higher than the stimulus relative on the Accessibility Hierarchy, and frequently differed from the stimulus relative by simply omitting part of its structure, for example the possessive or the passive structure, or both. Our error patterns then support the claim that the child did interpret the stimulus relative clause as a syntactic and semantic unit, production errors being due to the complexity of the stimulus.

With the exception of the speculations concerning error patterns, we have attempted no explanation of the regularities our experiment documents. We do not suppose, of course, that the linguistic and psycholinguistic regularities are pure coincidence. But exactly what their relationship is remains to be explained. We cannot claim that the (linguistic) Accessibility Hierarchy explains the psycholinguistic data, nor can we claim the opposite. It certainly could be the case that both types of regularity are characterisable more precisely in terms other than 'Subject', 'Direct Object', etc. Such functional notions might be better characterised as combinations of semantic properties (e.g. Agent, Patient), and surface syntactic properties (e.g. word order, centre embedding, verb agreement, case marking). Keenan (1976) discusses this point.

The performance of subjects on OCOMP relative to other relative clauses seems to support a surface-syntactic characterisation rather than a 'deep' one in terms of grammatical functions and syntactic relations. Both adults and children perform better on relative clauses formed on objects of comparison than on ones formed on genitives. In the case of the children, response accuracy for OCOMP was the same as for OBL, and considerably better than for the genitives. In the adult case, OCOMP was reproduced only about as accurately as the genitives, and considerably less accurately than OBL.

Since genitives were the least accurately responded types of relative clause, the data suggest that children find it relatively easier to form relative clauses on objects of comparison. Moreover, in contrast with adults, children reproduce equally accurately relative clauses formed on objects of comparison and on objects of prepositions. It is plausible that children understand less well than adults the syntactic and semantic differences between prepositions on the one hand and comparative particles (*than, as*) on the other. In consequence, they might tend to treat comparative particles as if they were prepositions in the relative clauses presented, based on the surface similarity between OBL and OCOMP relatives. The two sorts of relative clauses are in fact very much alike. Compare, for example, *the box which Pat brought the apples in* with *the boy who Mike writes better than*. Both relative clauses end with a stranded 'particle' — either a preposition (*in*) in OBL or a comparative particle (*than*) in OCOMP, which we have hypothesised as being non-distinct for the child but not for the adult.

Explanations of our findings in terms of confusions due to surface similarities do not fit all the data equally well, and they are in any case only speculative. We stress: it remains unexplained just why relative clauses should be more difficult to comprehend/ produce as they are formed on positions lower on the Accessibility Hierarchy.

A final conclusion from this work is that cross-linguistic patterns of variation may profitably suggest patterns of (psycho)linguistic behaviour. Thus our experimental work provides some documentation of psycholinguistic regularities for speakers of a single language that parallel the descriptive, cross-linguistic ones established in the original Accessibility Hierarchy generalisation by Keenan and Comrie (1977). Equally, psycholinguistic patterns observed for speakers of a single language could be indicative of cross-linguistic regularities.

In summary, the Accessibility Hierarchy, established from linguistic analysis of many languages, appears to be reflected in the psychological processing of relative clauses in that repetition errors increase as the position of the relative clause on the hierarchy decreases. Furthermore, errors of relative clause type generally result in relativisations on a position higher in the hierarchy, and individuals' characteristics tend to affect the absolute but not relative degree of mastery of relative clauses in the Accessibility Hierarchy. There is some evidence that the Accessibility Hierarchy also reflects the order of acquisition of relative clauses: relative to their mastery of other types of relative clause, children deal with Subjects better than adults do, and adults with minimal educational experience may never master the Genitive positions. In so far as comparisons are possible, these data are broadly consistent with the literature, but the cause of these psycholinguistic and linguistic correspondences has yet to be found.

Notes

1. The experimental work reported here was conducted in England by Sarah Hawkins in 1974. The initial results of the work (with children) were reported at the summer LSA meeting of that year. We would like to acknowledge a strong debt to the teachers and children of the Wivenhoe Primary School, Wivenhoe, Essex, the Medical Research Council Applied Psychology Unit, Cambridge, the

University of Essex, and the Max Planck Institut für Psycholinguistik, for their various contributions in bringing this work to fruition.

2. Sarah Hawkins teaches in the Department of Linguistics, University of Cambridge.

3. The significant interactions for the adults were as follows. (1) Sex $\times$ education ($F(1,36) = 8.11$, $p < 0.01$): education distinguished more between males than between females, males with long education being the most accurate of the four groups of adults, and males with short education being the least accurate. (2) Relative clauses $\times$ sentence frames ($F(24,864) = 2.07$, $p < 0.01$): response accuracy to the frame *I know that* varied less across relative clauses than did the other frames (3) Sex $\times$ education $\times$ relative clauses ($F''(22,95) = 1,80$, $p = 0.05$): the same effect as the sex $\times$ education interaction, with the additional fact that males with short education were particularly inaccurate on the possessives, GenS, GenO, and GenDS.

The children's analysis showed the following significant interactions. (1) Sex $\times$ relative clauses ($F''(57,74) = 1.75$, $p < 0.05$): the greater accuracy of girls than boys was more evident for relative clauses on positions low in the Accessibility Hierarchy and for the positions that are not in the hierarchy than it was for the higher positions. (2) Relative clauses $\times$ sentence frames ($F(24,864) = 4.12$, $p < 0.001$): response accuracy to the four frames varied considerably across clauses. Responses to *The fact that* were consistently low, while those to *I know that* were good but nevertheless variable across clauses; responses to *He remembered that* and *He had forgotten that* were also variable but generally intermediate in accuracy. (3) Sex $\times$ intelligence $\times$ relative clauses ($F''(27,77) = 2.46$, $p < 0.01$): high-IQ boys tended to be as accurate as the high-IQ girls in reproducing relative clauses from the upper end of the Accessibility Hierarchy, but their response accuracy to GenDS and to most positions that are low on the hierarchy grouped them with the low-IQ girls and/or low-IQ boys.

4. Error analysis on the adult data was not performed at the time of the original experiment and those data are not available to the authors at the present time (1985).

5. Of the total of 1,440 children's responses, 586 contained incorrect relative clauses. Only 97 (about 17...%) of these were not recognisable as relative clauses formed on any of the nine positions tested.

References

Borer, H. and K. Wexler (1984) 'The Maturation of Syntax', manuscript, Program in Cognitive Science, University of California at Irvine.

Brown, H.D. (1971) 'Children's Comprehension of Relativised English Sentences', *Child Development* 42, 1923-36.

Gass, S. (1979) 'Language Transfer and Universal Grammatical Relations' *Language Learning* 29, 2, 327-44.

—— and J. Ard (1980) 'L2 Data: Their Relevance for Language Universals', *TESOL Quarterly* 14, 4.

Herzberg, O. (1984) 'Relative Clauses in the Usage of Hebrew-speaking Children', manuscript, Tel Aviv University, Department of Linguistics.

Hyltenstam, K. (1981) 'The Use of Typological Markedness Conditions as Predictors in Second Language Acquisition: The Case of Pronominal Copies in Relative Clauses', to appear in R. Andersen (ed.) *Second Languages*, Rowley, Massachusetts, Newbury House.

—— (1983) 'Data Types and Second Language Variability', in Hakan Ringbom (ed.) *Psycholinguistics and Foreign Language Learning,* Research Institute of the ABO AKADEMI Foundation.

Ioup, G. and A. Kruse (1977) 'Interference Versus Structural Complexity as a Predictor of Second Language Relative Clause Acquisition', in C. Henning (ed.) *Proceedings of the Second Language Research Forum* Los Angeles, UCLA.

Keenan, E.L. (1976) 'Towards a Universal Definition of "Subject of"' in C. Li (ed.) *Subject and Topic* Academic Press, New York.

—— and B. Comrie (1977) 'Noun Phrase Accessibility and Universal Grammar', *Linguistic Inquiry* 8, 1.

Menyuk, P. (1969) *Sentences Children Use,* MIT Press, Cambridge, Massachusetts.

Noizet, G., F. Deyts, and J.P. Deyts, (1972) 'Producing Complex Sentences by Applying Relative Transformation', *Linguistics* 89, 49-68.

Sheldon, A. (1974) 'The Role of Parallel Function in the Acquisition of Relative Clauses in English', *Journal of Verbal Learning and Verbal Behavior* 13: 272-81.

Slobin, D. (1981) 'Developmental Psycholinguistics' in W.O. Dingwall (ed.) *A Survey of Linguistic Science,* Linguistic Program, University of Maryland.

—— (1982) 'The Acquisition and Use of Relative Clause in Turkic and Indo-European languages', to appear in K. Zimmer and D. Slobin (eds.) *Studies in Turkish Linguistics.*

Smith, M. (1974) 'Relative Clause Formation Between 29-36 months: a Preliminary Report', *Papers and Reports on Child Language Development* 8, 104-10, Committee on Linguistics, Stanford University.

Tarallo, F. and J. Myhill (1983) 'Interference and Natural Language Processing in Second Language Acquisition', *Language Learning* 33, 1, 55-76.

Thorndike, E.L., and I. Lorge (1968) *The Teacher's Word Book of 30,000 Words,* Teachers' College Press, New York.

de Villiers, J.G., H.B. Tager Flusberg, K. Hakuta, and M. Cohen (1979) 'Children's Comprehension of Relative Clauses', *Journal of Psycholinguistic Research* 8, 5.

PART TWO:
GRAMMATICAL RELATIONS

The articles in this section concern themselves with language-independent characterisations of grammatical relations, as used for example in the work on the Accessibility Hierarchy in the previous section. The article 'Towards a Universal Definition of "Subject of"' was a first broad-brush attempt on my part to abstract away from language-particular properties of Subjects. The article notes a variety of properties, some far from obvious, which Subjects characteristically present, but concludes nonetheless that no simple set of these will suffice as a set of necessary and sufficient conditions for an NP in an arbitrary sentence in an arbitrary language to be a Subject. The article with Judith Olmsted Gary 'On Collapsing Grammatical Relations' was stimulated by work in Relational Grammar. It argues on the basis of a detailed analysis of one language, Kinyarwanda, that more than one NP in a given sentence may present those properties which are characteristic of Direct Objects. The more recent article on Ergatives and Absolutives shows that there is a body of properties, mostly semantic in nature, which unites Subjects of intransitive verbs and Direct Objects of transitive ones to the exclusion of Subjects of transitive ones.

4 TOWARDS A UNIVERSAL DEFINITION OF 'SUBJECT OF'

1. The Problem

In this paper[1] I will attempt to provide a definition of the notion 'subject of' which will enable us to identify the subject phrase(s), if any, of any sentence in any language.

Such a definition is needed in universal grammar in order for the many universal generalisations which use this notion to be well defined. For example:

(1) *Accessibility Hierarchy* (Keenan and Comrie 1972): NPs on the upper end of the AH, given below, are universally easier to relativise than those on the lower end. Thus some languages (Ls) have relative clause forming strategies which apply only to subjects; other Ls have strategies which apply only to subjects and direct objects, others have ones which apply only to the top three positions on the AH, etc.

Subj > Dir Obj > Ind Obj > Obl > Gen > Obj of Comp

(2) *Functional Succession Principle* (Perlmutter and Postal 1974): if one NP can be raised out of another then it assumes the grammatical relation (subject of, direct object of, etc.) previously borne by the other.

(3) *Advancement Continuity Principle* (Johnson 1974; Trithart 1975; Keenan 1975a): if a L can advance (e.g., via operations like Passive) NPs low on the AH to subject then it can advance all intermediate positions to subject. Thus if a L has a locative voice (e.g., *the school was seen Mary at by John*) then it necessarily has a direct object (= Passive) voice.

Clearly generalisations like (1)-(3) determine constraints on the form, and substance, of possible human languages. But to verify them and determine their universality it is necessary to be able to identify subjects, direct objects, etc., in a principled way across Ls. If we use different criteria to identify subjects in different Ls then 'subject' is simply not a universal category and apparently universal generalisations stated in terms of that notion are not generalisations at all. In addition, absence of identifying criteria for subjects, etc. makes verification of putative universals like (1)-(3) difficult. Counter-examples can be rationalised away by merely saying that an offending NP is not 'really' a subject, etc. Finally the claim that we have primitive intuitions concerning which NPs are subjects founders, like all arguments from intuition, when the intuitions of different individuals do not agree. For example, it would appear that George (1974) and Keenan and Comrie (1977) have different intuitions concerning which NPs are subjects of simple transitive sentences in Dyirbal (Dixon 1972).

2. Defining 'Subject of'

We are not free to define a notion like 'subject' in any way that suits our purposes. There is a large body of lore concerning the notion, and any proposed definition must at least largely agree with the traditional, and to some extent, pretheoretical usage of the term. Our approach then will be to collect a large and diverse set of cases from different Ls in which our pretheoretical judgements of subjecthood are clear. Then we shall attempt to abstract from this set a set of properties which will be jointly necessary and sufficient to pick out the subject of an arbitrary sentence in an arbitrary L in a way that is in conformity, of course, with our pretheoretical intuitions in the clear cases.

However, even a cursory examination of subjects across Ls reveals that in many Ls subject NPs are characterised by properties which are not only *not* universally valid, they are peculiar to the particular L in question. For example, in Latin, subject NPs carry a characteristic case marking (the nominative). But that particular ending probably occurs as a nominative marker in no other L; there is no universal nominative case marker. And in Malagasy (Malayo-Polynesian; Madagascar) subjects characteristically occur clause finally, whereas in most Ls subject NPs precede the other major NPs within clauses. Nonetheless, we do want to say that the prima facie evidence that an NP is the subject of some sentence in Latin is that it is nominative, and in Malagasy that it is clause final. Consequently we want to phrase a universal definition of 'subject' in such a way as to allow that different Ls may use language specific means to mark subject NPs. This we shall do in the following way:

First, universal means of distinguishing a privileged subset of sentences in any L will be given. These sentences will be called the *semantically basic sentences* (henceforth *b-sentences*) and their subjects will be called *basic subjects* (henceforth *b-subjects*). Then we shall attempt to provide universally valid criteria for identifying subjects of b-sentences in any L. Once the b-subjects have been identified in any particular L then the full set of properties characteristic of b-subjects in that L can be determined. So in some Ls b-subjects may have a certain case marker, or position, or they may exhibit a very specific type of transformational behaviour, or even have semantically specific properties. Finally, once the full complement of b-subject properties has been determined for a given L, subjects of non-basic sentences will be defined to be those NPs, if any, which present a clear preponderance of the properties characteristic of b-subjects. Thus in any given L, subjects of non-basic sentences may present very few of the universal properties in that L since they possess very many of the language specific properties of b-subjects in that L.

Note further, that on this type of definition, subjects of certain sentences, and more generally of certain sentence types, will be more subject-like than the subjects of others. The reason is that they will exhibit more of the complement of properties which characterise b-subjects in general. Thus the subjecthood of an NP (in a sentence) is a matter of degree.

In addition, it seems to me that subjects in some Ls will be more subject-like than those of other Ls in the sense that they will in general, present a fuller complement of the properties which universally characterise b-subjects. Very possibly, for example, European Ls are more subject oriented than those Sino-Tibetan Ls discussed by Li and Thompson (1976).

2.1 The Definition of Basic Sentence in a Language

(4)   For any Language L,

    a.   a syntactic structure x is *semantically more basic than* a syntactic structure y if, and only if, the meaning of y depends on that of x. That is, to understand the meaning of y it is necessary to understand the meaning of x;

b. a sentence in L is a basic sentence (in L) if, and only if, no (other) complete sentence in L is more basic than it.

Concerning (4a), there is no simple way of determining whether some sentence e.g. is more basic than another since such a determination requires that we understand the meaning of the two sentences. So some cases will surely be problematic. But many cases we feel are quite clear. E.g., *John is a linguist* is clearly semantically more basic than *Fred thinks that John is a linguist* since we cannot understand the meaning of the latter without understanding that of the former. If we didn't know what *John is a linguist* meant, we wouldn't know what Fred is thinking. Further, each of the following structures is semantically more basic than all of those which follow it: *John sang, John sang off-key, John didn't sing off-key, the fact that John didn't sing off-key, some newspaper reported the fact that John didn't sing off-key, some newspaper which reported the fact that John didn't sing off-key*, etc. The relation *more basic than* (henceforth *MBT*) is transitive. If x MBT y, and y MBT z, then x MBT z. For if we need to know the meaning of x in order to know that of y, and that of y is required in order to know that of z, then clearly we can't understand the meaning of z without understanding that of x. Note however that the meanings of two different structures may simply be independent, so neither need be more basic than the other.[2] E.g., the meaning of *John's leaving surprised everyone* neither depends on nor is dependent upon the meaning of *if anyone screams Mary will faint*.

Concerning (4b), the b-sentences in any L are defined to be the maximally basic structures having the category 'sentence' although we do require that a sentence be in the set of b-sentences if the only other sentences more basic than it are 'too context dependent' for their meaning (that is, they do not express a 'complete thought'). The intent here is to rule out cases where the only NPs occurring in b-sentences would be pronouns. Thus in many Ls, if not in English, it is arguably the case (Keenan 1972) that pronominal sentences like *he hit him* are more basic than ones like *John hit Bill.* Compare e.g. (5a) and (5b) from Swahili.

(5) a. a-   li-   m-   piga
         3sg past-3sg hit
         human   human
         subj   obj
         'he hit him'

b. Juma a- li- m- piga Faru
Juma he-past-him-hit Faru
'Juma hit Faru'

Sentence (5b) differs in meaning from (5a) solely in that the reference of the pronominal elements in (5a) is made more specific. To determine e.g. the truth of (5b) we must first determine the reference of the pronominal elements in Juma and Faru, and then determine that (5a) is true. So we can't really understand the meaning of (5b) without being able to understand that of (5a), so (5a) is plausibly more basic than (5b). Nonetheless (5a) is 'incomplete' in that it does not really tell us who is being talked about. Plausibly then no complete sentence in Swahili is more basic than (5b), or (5a), so both of these are among the b-sentences in Swahili (although the basicness of the tense marking in the example would have to be further considered).

2.2 Some General Properties of Basic Sentences

While there is no mechanical procedure for identifying the set of b-sentences in a L, the set will generally have several characteristic properties, which makes the identification of a fairly large set of relatively basic sentences reasonably easy.

Thus, in general, if the meaning of one structure depends on that of another, then the form of that structure also depends on the form of the other. In general then we expect that b-sentences will exhibit the greatest morphological and syntactic potential of the sentences in a L. Thus they will present the greatest range of tense, mood, aspect, mode, and voice distinctions. They will have the greatest privileges of occurrence: they will accept the greatest range of verbal and sentential modifiers; they will be the easiest to embed and adjoin to other sentences, the easiest to nominalise and internally reorder, the easiest to relativise, question and topicalise out of, the easiest to pronominalise and delete into, etc. In other words, the b-sentences are roughly the 'simplest' sentences syntactically. For example, (6a) is clearly more basic than (6b).

(6) a. Mary doesn't like John any more.
b. As for John, Mary doesn't like him any more.

For clearly, to understand (6b) we need to know what *Mary doesn't like him any more* means, where *him* is understood to refer to John. But this is exactly what we need to know to understand (6a). The syntactic test for b-sentencehood then predicts that (6a) has more potential than (6b), which is clearly correct. E.g., we can nominalise (6a), *Mary's not liking John any more*, but not (6b); we can cleft on *Mary* in (6a), *It is Mary who doesn't like John any more*, but not in (6b), etc.

Semantically speaking as well, b-sentences can be expected to have certain characteristic properties. They will e.g. generally be structurally unambiguous. The reason is that in general the operations which form less basic structures from more basic ones affect only part of the meaning of the less basic one. And since b-sentences in general have fewer 'parts' than non-basic ones they present fewer possibilities for the interpretation of which parts are understood to be affected by the operation.

Consider for example passives in English. Although the case is less clear than the ones considered earlier, we consider passives to be, in general, less basic than the corresponding actives. For what we must understand about the relations between the participants and the action in a passive sentence is basically the same as that of the active. But in addition, in the passive we require that the referent of the object NP be identifiable independently of that of the agent (see Section 2.3 for more discussion), that is, loosely, the patient is more of a topic in the passive than the active sentence. Assuming then that actives are more basic than passives we would expect from our argument above that at least some ways of forming complex structures from simpler ones would engender more ambiguities when applied to passives than to actives. And this seems to be the case. Consider e.g. the addition of adverbials like *willingly* in (7). (See Lasnik and Fiengo 1974, for some discussion.)

(7) a. The police arrested John willingly
     b. John was arrested by the police willingly

In (7a) no indication that John was a willing participant in the act is given. But (7b) is ambiguous according as it was John or the police who acted willingly. A further instance, more problematic in some respects, concerns pairs like

(8) a. Every boy kissed a girl.
     b. A girl was kissed by every boy.

Sentence (8b) seems to me more clearly ambiguous according as it was necessarily the same girl or not. But (8a) seems to me to have only the reading on which it is not necessarily the same girl (though it might be). Not everyone agrees with these judgements, however, and in the (remarkable) absence of a clear pretheoretical intuition concerning what it means to say that a structure is ambiguous the case is hard to argue.

In addition to the general absence of structural ambiguity b-sentences may be expected to have other semantic properties which more directly depend on the fact that they are the semantically primitive sentences. Thus they will in general be declarative and affirmative. Further in many cases non-basic sentences seem semantically richer than the more basic ones whose meaning they depend on. It is tempting to think that the b-sentences of a L will always be among the least informative sentences of the L (Talmy Givón, personal communication). But while this is often so, I think it not always the case. Thus there is a class of non-basic sentence forming operators whose semantic effect is precisely to attenuate to some degree the more specific meaning of the more basic sentences. Thus I would want to say that *John left* is more basic than *John didn't leave, John might have left*, and *It is possible that John left*. Yet all the latter sentences, in some intuitive sense, tell us less about how the world is than does the more basic *John left*.

Another measure of the semantic 'simplicity' of b-sentences concerns their relative freedom from presupposition. Thus many of the clear examples of presuppositional structures (see e.g. Keenan 1970) involve embedded sentences (e.g. relative clauses, factive complements of verbs like *realise, surprise*, etc.). And generally if a sentence contains an embedded sentence then its meaning depends on that of the embedded one and so it is not basic. Unfortunately, however, b-sentences are not presupposition-free. The use of proper names and demonstrative NPs in b-sentences normally carries the presupposition that the NP has a referent. It seems to me likely however that aside from lexically specific presuppositions of basic predicates the presuppositions of b-sentences can be limited to existence claims.

A final characteristic of b-sentences: it is not necessarily the case that a b-sentence of one L will translate as a b-sentence of another L. The basic predicates of different Ls codify somewhat different concepts. So e.g. *the president resigned* receives no b-sentence translation in Ls spoken only by people who do not have the sort of political institutions referenced by terms like *president* and *resign*. A more interesting question perhaps is whether the syntactic *types* of b-sentences are the same across Ls. The question is an empirical one and the answer is not obvious. E.g. while passive sentences may be non-basic in English they are at least much more basic (see Note 2 for this more generalised use of 'basic') in many Malayo-Polynesian Ls such as Maori, Tagalog, Malagasy. In particular the privileges of occurrence of passives in those Ls are much greater than in English. Further, syntactic properties which are obligatory in some Ls may only be optional in others, and possibly then not present in the b-sentences of those Ls. E.g. in English all sentences, and therefore the b-sentences, are marked for tense/aspect. But in Indonesian such marking is optional. Sentences lacking such marking occur frequently in discourse (and in isolation, in translation). Plausibly then the b-sentences in Indonesian express 'naked propositions' whose meaning is made more specific by the addition of tense/aspect adverbs in non b-sentences.

2.3 Characteristic Properties of Basic Subjects

Below we present a list of 30 odd properties which subjects characteristically possess (if any NP in the L does). The properties are organised into groups and sub-groups according to their relationships. Plausibly in many cases properties in the same sub-group are not independent (although they can be verified independently) but we cannot at the moment show this, in general.

Furthermore, we have not been able to isolate any combination of the b-subject properties which is both necessary and sufficient for an NP in any sentence in any L to be the subject of that sentence. Certainly no one of the properties is both necessary and sufficient, and in our statement we point out counter examples both ways for properties which might have been thought fully general.

Consequently we must have recourse to a somewhat weaker notion of definition. We shall say that an NP in a b-sentence (in any L) is a subject of that sentence *to the extent that* it has the properties in the properties list below. If one NP in the sentence has a clear preponderance of the subject properties then it will be called *the* subject of the sentence. On this type of definition then subjects of some b-sentences can be more subject-like than the subjects of others in the sense that they present a fuller complement of the subject properties.

Note further that on this type of definition 'subject' does not represent a single dimension of linguistic reality. It is rather a cluster concept, or as we shall say, a *multi-factor* concept. Many basic concepts in social science are multi-factor concepts. Thus one's *intelligence* is a combination of abilities (Thurstone 1956): verbal comprehension, immediate recall, numerical manipulation, visualising flat objects in three dimensions, and deductive reasoning. So one can be intelligent in different ways and to different degrees. And being a subject is, we claim, more like being intelligent than, for instance, like being a prime number. The factors which compose the concept of subject might coincide with our groupings of properties, though in the worst of cases each of the 30 odd properties would be an independent factor.

2.3.1 The Subject Properties List (SPL)   We present four major categories of b-subject properties. The first, Autonomy Properties, is by far the largest.

A. AUTONOMY PROPERTIES

1. Independent Existence. The entity that a b-subject refers to (if any) exists independently of the action or property expressed by the predicate. This is less true for non-subjects. Thus in *a student wrote a poem* the existence of the poem is not independent of the act of writing, whereas the existence of the student is. Other examples: *someone committed a booboo, defined a term, proved a theorem*, etc.

2. Indispensability. A non-subject may often simply be eliminated from a sentence with the result still being a complete sentence. But this is usually not true of b-subjects. E.g. *John hunts lions (for a living), John hunts (for a living), *hunts lions (for a living)*.

Several ergative Ls however do appear to permit unspecified subject deletion, notably Tongan, Eskimo, and Tibetan.

Tongan (Churchward 1953)
(9)   a.   Na'e tamate'i 'e   Tevita 'a Koliate
           killed   subj David obj Goliath
           'David killed Goliath'

b.   Na'e tamate'i 'a   Koliate
    killed   obj Goliath
    'Goliath was killed'
(NB: *'a* marks both transitive objects and intransitive subjects.)

3. Autonomous Reference. The reference of a b-subject must be determinable by the addressee at the moment of utterance. It cannot be made to depend on the reference of other NPs which follow it. Thus if two NPs in a b-sentence are to be stipulated as being the same in reference it will either be the non-subject which gets marked (perhaps deleted) or the rightmost NP. Thus in English we could never say *He-self admires John*$_i$ for *John*$_i$ *admires himself*, for in the first sentence the reference of the subject cannot be determined independently of that of a following NP, so the subject would not be autonomous in reference. Note however that in Ls in which b-subjects can follow other NPs it is sometimes (but not always) possible for a leftmost NP to control the reference of the subject. The subject's reference is still determinable at the moment of utterance since it is stipulated as being co-referential to an NP whose reference has already been established.

Tagalog
(10) a.   sinampal ng   lalake ang   babae
        +pass
        hit-by   Agt man subj   woman
        'the woman was hit by a/the man'
    b.   sinampal ng   lalake ang kaniyang sarili
        hit-by   Agt man subj his   self
        'the man hit himself'

Here subject NPs i.e. *ang* phrases (see Schachter 1976 for some problems with the notion of 'subject' in Philippine languages) normally may precede or follow objects, as long as both follow the verb. But when objects are definite as they are if specified as being co-referential to a definite subject — and subjects are always definite in Tagalog — they must be presented as surface subjects. And in this case, contrary to the usual pattern, the subject must follow the agent phrase. Thus its reference is determinable at the moment of utterance.

Samoan (example from Chapin 1970)
(11) a. sa sogi e   ioane ia lava
         past cut Agt John he emph
         'John cut himself'
     b. sa sogi ioane ie ia lava
         past cut John Agt he emph
         'John cut himself'

Here again the NP whose reference is dependent on that of another occurs second. In (11a) that NP is plausibly a subject if that sentence is passive. If Samoan is ergative in this case then *John* is the subject and it is the object that is pronominalised. But then in (11b) it would be the ergative subject whose reference was not independent. But on either analysis the reference of the b-subject is always determinable at the moment of utterance. In fact, we know of no clear counter-examples to this property, so *autonomous reference* is plausibly a universal necessary condition on b-subjecthood.

But this property does seem to understate the facts a bit. Thus in many Ls in which the subject may follow the objects, such as Malagasy, Gilbertese, and Tzeltal (see Keenan 1974), the reference of the subject cannot be made to depend on that of the object, even though the object precedes and so the property of autonomous reference would not be violated. E.g.

Malagasy
(12) a. manaja tena Rabe
         respect self Rabe
         'Rabe respects himself'
     b. *manaja an-dRabe tena/ ny tena-ny
         respect acc-Rabe self   the self-his
         'He-self respects Rabe'

There are several other properties of subjects that plausibly are related, more or less closely, to the property of autonomous reference.
3.1 b-subjects are always (in general, not necessarily in every sentence) among the possible controllers of stipulated co-reference, either positive or negative (see Keenan, 1975a for discussion). Thus,
3.1.1 b-subjects in general can control reflexive pronouns. And

in some Ls control of reflexives within clauses is largely restricted to b-subjects. E.g. in Malagasy, Japanese, and German.

3.1.2 b-subjects are among the possible controllers of co-referential deletions and pronominalisations. Note:

(13) a.   John$_i$ talked to Bill$_j$ for a while and then he$_{i,j}$ left.
     b.   John$_i$ talked to Bill$_j$ for a while and then Ø$_{i,*j}$ left.

3.1.3 The possible controllers of backwards pronominalisation and deletions include b-subjects. E.g.

(14) a.   When he$_{i,?j}$ got home, John$_i$ talked to Bill$_j$.
     b.   On Ø$_{i,*j}$ arriving home, John$_i$ talked with Bill$_j$.

3.2 The NPs which control 'switch reference' indicators include b-subjects. Thus in the Eastern Highlands Ls of New Guinea as well as among many groups of American Indian Ls, subordinate verbs will carry either one of two affixes according as their subject is co-referential or *not* co-referential with the *subject* of some other clause. E.g.

Hopi (example from Pam Munro, personal communication)

(15) pam navoti:ta pam mo:titani $\left\{ \begin{array}{l} \text{-q} \\ \text{-qa}^2\text{e} \end{array} \right.$

he   thinks   he   win $\left\{ \begin{array}{l} \text{-diff. subj.} \\ \text{-same subj.} \end{array} \right.$

'He thinks that he will win'

Thus if the suffix -*q* is chosen on the subordinate verb the person who is being thought about is necessarily different from the one doing the thinking, whereas they are the same if the suffix *qa²e* is chosen. For further discussion see Keenan, 1975a; Jacobsen, 1967, Munro, 1974a. Our point here is only that control of switch reference is largely limited to subjects. We note however that switch location markers rather than switch subject markers are reported for Angaataha (Huisman 1973) in New Guinea.

3.3 The NPs which control verb agreement, if any, include b-subjects. (For an argument that verb agreement is, at least historically, pronominalisation, see Givón, 1976). We further note that verb agreement across clauses appears restricted to subjects, though this is only attested to our knowledge for the Ls of the E. New Guinea Highlands. See Keenan, 1975a for examples.

Since verb agreement is one of the properties which people have considered definitional of subjects, it is worth noting that it fails to be a necessary condition on b-subjecthood since in very many Ls verbs agree with no NP, e.g. Swedish, Sinhalese, Afrikaans, Thai, Vietnamese, Chinese, Japanese, Maori, Malagasy, etc. Similarly verb agreement fails to be a sufficient condition on b-subjecthood since in many Ls verbs agree with NPs in addition to subjects, e.g. Basque, Chinook, Arosi (Melanesian), Jacaltec (Mayan), Kapampangan (Philippine), Hungarian, Georgian, Blackfoot, Machiguenga (Arawak; Peru), etc. Note further that in a very few cases verbs may agree with objects but not with subjects. E.g. Avar (Caucasian), Mabuiag (Australia), and, very partially, Hindi.

3.4 b-subjects are the easiest NPs to stipulate the co-reference of across clause boundaries.

3.4.1 If reflexive (i.e. essentially anaphoric) pronouns in sentence complements of verbs of thinking can be bound by NPs in the matrix clause then these pronouns can always occur in subject position in the complement clause.

Yoruba
(16) Ojo$_i$ ro   po on$_i$/ò$_j$ mu sasa
     Ojo$_i$ thinks that he$_i$/he$_j$ is clever
     'Ojo thinks that he is clever'

3.4.2 NPs which can be co-referentially deleted in sentence complements when co-referential with matrix NPs always include subjects.

Malagasy
(17) Nihevitra Rabe$_i$ fa   notadiavin-   dRasoa Ø$_i$/izy$_j$
     thought   Rabe$_i$ that was looked-for-by Rasoa Ø$_i$/he$_j$
     'Rabe thought that (he) was being looked for by Rasoa'

Similarly the most likely NPs to undergo Equi-NP deletion include b-subjects.

(18) a.   John$_i$ wants Ø$_i$ to help Fred.
     b.   *John$_i$ wants Fred$_j$ to help Ø$_i$.

3.4.3 The NPs which can be co-referentially deleted across co-ordinate conjunctions include b-subjects.

(19) a.   John$_i$ went up to Fred$_j$ and Ø$_i$ insulted him$_j$
     b.   *John$_i$ went up to Fred$_j$ and he$_j$ insulted Ø$_i$
     c.   *John$_i$ went up to Fred$_j$ and he$_i$ insulted Ø$_j$

3.4.4 The NPs which can be co-referentially deleted under verb serialisation generally include b-subjects.

Akan (example from Schachter 1974a)
(20) Kofi de   aburew$_i$ Ø$_i$ gu   nsum
     Kofi takes corn   flows water-in
     'Kofe pours corn into the water'

3.5 Absolute Reference. In the overwhelming majority of cases, if a b-sentence is true then we understand that there is an entity (concrete or abstract) which is referred to, or has the property expressed by, the b-subject. Thus *John worships the Sun Goddess*, if true, requires that there be someone referenced by 'John' but does not require that there exist a Sun Goddess, in distinction to *The Sun Goddess worships John*, where *Sun Goddess* is a subject. Other examples of this sort: *John bought a present for the prime minister, cursed Santa Claus, is talking about the perfect woman*, etc.

Even if the subject of a basic (or at least fairly basic) sentence is 'indefinite' we still normally understand that there must be an object with that property, whereas this is often not the case for indefinite object phrases. Thus *a student owes John a report*, if true, does imply the existence of a student but not of a report. Other examples of not necessarily referential objects: *John ordered a beer, painted a pony, resembles an elephant, imitates alchemists*, etc.

However if weather expressions are basic, and they appear to be, then absolute reference is not a necessary condition on b-subjecthood, since weather expressions may have 'dummy' i.e. non-referential subjects. E.g. *it is raining*, etc. Most b-sentences distinguish between an object spoken about and some property it has or some activity it is involved in. But in simple statements about the weather there appears to be little distinction between the activity (the raining) and the object involved (the rain). So in general, if a weather sentence has a subject-predicate form (they may consist of just a single verb) then either the subject will be semantically weak or the predicate will (e.g. Russian *rain goes*).

3.6 Presupposed Reference. Certain operations like negation, questioning, and conditionalisation (below) have the effect of suspending the reference of normally referential NPs. The reference of a b-subject however is harder to suspend under these operations. Thus (from Donellan 1966) *De Gaulle was the king of France* implies the existence of a king, but *De Gaulle wasn't the king of France* need not have this implication. It can be used simply to deny that De Gaulle had a certain title or office. On the other hand, *The king of France wasn't de Gaulle*, where *the king of France* is subject, still does imply the existence of a king. Analogous claims hold for the pair *Was de Gaulle the king of France?* and *Was the king of France de Gaulle?*. Conditionalisation of the following sort (Larry Horn, personal communication) seems to work the same way. Thus *if the coup had succeeded de Gaulle would have been the king of France* does not imply the existence of a king of France, whereas *if the coup had succeeded the king of France would have been de Gaulle* does, and the difference between the two sentences is merely that in one *the king of France* is a subject and in the other it isn't.

Note of course that if b-sentences may have indefinite subjects, e.g. *a student attacked John*, then under the most natural form of denial, *no student attacked John*, the existence implication of the subject is not preserved. It is not clear to me at the moment whether we want to consider such sentences as basic English or not (see 3.8). Arguably understanding such a sentence requires that we understand *there exists a student*, or perhaps *students exist*, and so sentences with indefinite subjects are perhaps not basic.

3.7 Metaphoric Idioms. These often suspend the reference or existence implication of NPs. And again, b-subjects are the most reluctant of the major NPs to abandon their reference. Thus in *the man took the bull by the horns, let the cat out of the bag, has an ace up his sleeve, is looking for a needle in a haystack*, etc. only *man* has its literal referent. Normally if the reference of a b-subject is suspended in an idiom then so also is the reference of the other major NPs. E.g. *the fat's in the fire, the early bird gets the worm*, etc.

3.8 Topic. b-subjects are normally the topic of the b-sentence, i.e. they identify what the speaker is talking about. The object they refer to is normally known to both speaker and addressee, and so is, in that sense, old information. If a L has special topic or old information markers (Japanese, Korean) they will most naturally be used on subjects.

3.9 'Highly Referential' NPs, e.g. personal pronou is, proper nouns, and demonstratives can always occur as subjects. In some Ls, e.g. Malagasy, Tagalog and Philippine Ls generally, Kinyarwanda (by and large) and probably much of Bantu generally, subjects of b-sentences must be definite. And in Tagalog, direct objects must be indefinite. So if a NP position cannot be filled by definites that is evidence that it is not a subject, and if it cannot be filled by indefinites that is evidence that it is a subject.

3.10 Subjects are the most natural targets of 'advancement' (Perlmutter and Postal 1974) transformations. That is, roughly, if a L can assign to one NP in a clause the position, case marking and verb agreements appropriate to another NP in the clause then it can assign the position, case marking, and verb agreements of subject NPs to non-subjects (and we say that that NP has been advanced to subject). E.g. Passive in English advances direct object to subject. Many Ls, e.g. Bantu generally (see Keenan 1975a), can advance NPs to object. But all such Ls can also advance NPs to subject, whereas the converse fails. So subjects are the most accessible targets of advancement processes. (See Johnson 1974 for discussion.)

3.11 Basic, or relatively basic, subjects have wider scope, logically speaking, than non-subjects. (See Keenan, 1974 for justification of why this is related to the autonomous reference property of subjects.) Thus suppose we are given a sentence in some L containing the main verb *kiss* and two quantified NPs, *every man* and *a woman*. If the truth of the sentence most naturally allows that the choice of woman can vary with the choice of man, as in *every man kissed a woman*, then that is evidence that *every man* occurs as a subject. But if, on preference, the choice of woman must be made independently of that of the man, as in *a woman was kissed by every man*, then that is evidence that *a woman* is subject.

3.12 b-subjects are normally the leftmost occurring NP in b-sentences. Note, however, that in a few cases Ls have fairly fixed word order in which the subject follows one or more objects. E.g. Malagasy, Tzeltal (Mayan), Mezquital Otomi (Oto-Manguean; Hess 1968), Gilbertese (Micronesian). Note also Ls like Walbiri (Hale 1967) in which basic word order appears totally free, and Ls like Tagalog in which NPs in b-sentences occur in any order as long as they are all after the verb.

3.13 The NPs which can be relativised, questioned, and cleft include b-subjects. In some Ls, e.g. Malagasy, only subjects can be relativised.

3.14 The NPs whose possessors can be relativised, questioned, and cleft include b-subjects. E.g. in Tagalog, it appears, possessors of objects cannot be questioned, but possessors of subjects can.

3.15 A personal pronoun is rarely present in a position relativised if that position is a b-subject one. So even if a L, like Arabic, Fijian, or Welsh, normally presents such pronouns, as in *the girl that John give the book to her* it will not normally say *the girl that she gave the book to John* but only *the girl that gave the book to John*.

3.16 b-subjects are always among the NPs in a L which can undergo raising. E.g.,

(21) a.   John believed Fred to have struck the gatekeeper.
      b.   *John believed the gatekeeper Fred to have struck.

3.17 Subjects can always be expressed by morphologically independent, possibly emphatic, pronouns. These pronouns can be conjoined with full NPs.

3.18 NPs which 'launch' floating quantifiers (e.g. *all the boys left/the boys all left*) include subjects (Perlmutter and Postal 1974).

B. CASE MARKING PROPERTIES

1. b-subjects of intransitive sentences are usually not case marked if any of the NPs in the L are not case marked (Greenberg 1966). Exceptions: in Motu (Malayo-Polynesian, New Guinea; Capell 1969) both transitive and intransitive subjects are marked (different markers) but transitive objects are not marked. Similarly in several Yuman Ls, e.g. Mojave (Munro 1974a) direct objects are unmarked but transitive and intransitive subjects are marked (same marker).

2. The NPs which change their case marking under causativisation include b-subjects.

Malagasy
(22) a.   manasa lamba Rasoa
                 +acc +nom
          wash   clothes Rasoa
          'Rasoa is washing clothes'
     b.   mampa-nasa lamba   an-dRasia Rabe
                      +acc   +acc   +nom
          cause-wash clothes   Rasoa   Rabe
          'Rabe is making Rasoa wash clothes'

3. The NPs which change their case marking action nominalisations include b-subjects. Usually a b-subject changes to a possessor case or the non-subject agent case. E.g.,

(23) a.   John swept the floor.
     b.   John's sweeping (of) the floor
     c.   the sweeping (of) the floor by John

C. SEMANTIC ROLE

1. The semantic role (Agent, Experiencer, etc.) of the referent of a b-subject is predictable from the form of the main verb (Li and Thompson 1976). Some semantic category information, e.g. animacy, is usually also predictable, but semantic restrictions on objects are usually more specific than those on subjects (Edith Moravscik, personal communication).

2.1 b-subjects normally express the agent of the action, if there is one. Note that this property cannot be used to identify subjects of sentences in which there is no agent, and sentences of that sort will be numerous among the b-sentences in a L. E.g. *John is tall, is in Chicago, is a plumber*, etc. Note further that in Dyirbal (Australia; Dixon 1972) the NP in b-sentences which has most of the Reference properties cited in B.3 above does not express the agent. See Keenan and Comrie (1972) for justification of this point. Thus expressing the agent, if there is one, does not seem even a sufficient condition on b-subjecthood.

2.2 Subjects normally express the addressee phrase of imperatives. But note that in many Malayo-Polynesian Ls, e.g. Maori and Malagasy, imperatives are frequently in non-active forms, and the addressee phrase, if present, appears as a passive (or other type of non-active) agent phrase. E.g.,

Maori (example from Hale 1968)
(24) tua- ina   te raakau raa   (ke te toki)
     fell-passive the tree   yonder (with this axe)
     'be chopped down (by you) the tree there (with this axe)'
     ='chop down the tree there (with this axe)'

2.3 b-subjects normally exhibit the same position, case marking, and verb agreements as does the causer NP in the most basic type of causative sentence. Again we note however that Maori and Malagasy causatives are very easily passivised, so the agent there is not a surface subject.

Malagasy
(25) a. mampianatra angilisy an-dRabe aho
         cause-learn   English acc-Rabe I
         'I am teaching Rabe English'
     b. ampianara-ko   angilisy Rabe
         cause-learn-by me English Rabe
         'Rabe is taught English by me'

D. IMMEDIATE DOMINANCE

The b-subject is immediately dominated by the root node S. This is the type of definition given in *Aspects* (Chomsky 1965) and may represent a necessary condition on b-subjecthood. It is difficult to tell, since, as far as I know, there is no simple test to determine whether or not a subpart of a sentence is a constituent.

For example, in many Ls person/number particles or tense/aspect particles form a higher level constituent with the main verb. By parity of reasoning then they should form higher level constituents with the subject in those Ls in which they are bound to the subject. If so, then the subject would not be immediately dominated by the root node S. Thus in *Fred's the one*, or *Fred'll go*, only *Fred* is the subject, not *Fred'll* or *Fred's*. In the English cases, however, such sentences are arguably not basic. But in Luiseño (Uto-Aztecan) or Walbiri they arguably are.

Luiseño (example from Hyde 1971)
(26) Xwaan-po   wiiwish   naachaxan-an
     Juan -2 or 3 sg acorn mush eat   +future
           +future
     'Juan will eat acorn mush'

Further, it is quite clear that being immediately dominated by
the root S is not a sufficient condition for b-subjecthood. We note
three categories of cases where more than one NP is arguably
immediately dominated by the root S.

1. Ls whose unmarked word order is VSO. While these are a
minority type across Ls, they probably constitute between 5 to 10
per cent of the world's Ls. Thus, Malayo-Polynesian: Maori,
Samoan, Tongan. Semitic: Classical Arabic. Celtic: Welsh, Breton,
Scots Gaelic. Nilo Saharan: Maasai. American Indian: Chinook
(Penutian), Jacaltec (Mayan), Zapotec (Oto-Manguean).

2. In some Ls the relative position of subject and object is completely free. E.g. Walbiri (Australia), Tagalog (Philippines).

3. In many Ls cited as SOV there is little evidence for a VP
constituent. E.g. in Turkish, Hindi, and Persian wh-interrogative
words are naturally placed in the object slot, even if they question
the subject NP. In Tibetan this placement seems obligatory. For
arguments that Japanese lacks a VP constituent see Hinds (1974).
For arguments that VP constituency is limited to SVO Ls see
Schwartz (1972).

3. The Utility of a Multi-Factor Concept of 'Subject'

Using the Subjects Properties List (SPL) one can, we claim, identify the b-subjects in any L. Then the full set of properties characteristic of b-subjects in any given L can be determined, and then
subject NPs of non-basic sentences can be identified. While complex, this means of identifying subjects does permit us to verify the
universal generalisations stated in terms of 'subject' at the beginning of this paper.

This concept of subject has, however, another use: it suggests
that we look for cross-L generalisations which express relations
between the properties in the SPL. One such generalisation, which
seems to us to be valid, is the following: in general, non-basic sub-

jects are never more subject-like than basic subjects. In other words, in any given L, subjects of non-basic sentences frequently do not have quite as full a complement of the subject properties as do subjects of b-sentences. One reason for this is that syntactically derived subjects are, by our tests, usually somewhat less subject-like than b-subjects. To consider just the case of passive sentences in English, note that the subject does not express the agent, need not have the property of autonomous existence (e.g. *a beer was ordered by John* does not imply the existence of beer), and controls reflexives less easily than b-subjects (*?*John was insulted by himself*). This suggests that operations which create derived subjects may do so to a greater or lesser extent.

Thus perhaps some properties of subjects are harder to pass on to underlying non-subjects than are others, and conversely some properties will be harder for NPs which have lost their subject status to lose. If the subject properties can be ordered in terms of how hard they are to pass on to other NPs then we would have another universal generalisation. Namely, if an operation which derives a complex sentence from a simpler one passes on one of the subject properties to another NP in the derived sentence then it necessarily passes on all the properties higher on the ordering than the given property. Further, if certain transformations were actually defined as subject-creating ones (e.g. Perlmutter and Postal 1974 would define Passive as an operation which converts an object to a subject) then each such transformation could simply be marked according to how far down the ordering of subject properties it could extend in assigning subject properties to another NP. So some operations would be more subjectivising than others.

An attempt to empirically support any particular ordering of the 30 odd subject properties, however, would go beyond the bounds of this paper. So we shall here simply suggest a hypothesis concerning a partial ordering of the properties, and then present some evidence in support of that hypothesis, acknowledging that more evidence would be needed for our conclusions to be definitive.

3.1 The Promotion to Subject Hierarchy (PSH)

Coding Properties	>	Behaviour and Control Properties	>	Semantic Properties
position > case marking > verb agreement		deletion, movement, case changing properties, control of cross-reference properties, etc.		Agency, autonomous existence, selectional restrictions, etc.

The claim made by the PSH is that if an NP in a derived sentence is assigned any of the three categories of subject properties then it is assigned all the higher categories. And within the category of coding properties, if an NP acquires the verb agreements characteristic of subjects then it must also acquire the case marking and position; and if it acquires the case marking then it must acquire the position. So the characteristic position of subjects is the easiest property to assign to a derived subject. Further, the PSH also claims that the subject properties assigned to a derived subject may be any initial sequence of those on the PSH. So a derived subject may e.g. present the coding and behavioural properties of b-subjects but not the semantic properties (which is very frequently the case. We know of no clear cases in which derived subjects become e.g. agents. However, the direct and inverse theme markers in Algonkian need to be further investigated in this regard. See Frantz 1971 for some discussion.) Or a derived subject may present only the coding properties of b-subjects. Thus derived subjects may look like subjects without behaving like them, but if they behave like subjects then they look like subjects.

We should stress here that the relation we postulate between coding and behavioural properties represents merely a hypothesis. It states that while a derived subject may have the position and morphological characteristics of b-subjects, it is possible that they do not raise, or delete, or relativise, or control co-reference, etc. in the way characteristic of b-subjects. E.g. Maori has a transformation which moves certain types of possessives, namely pronouns, preverbally. But it applies only to active subjects, not to subjects of passive sentences. In Jacaltec (Craig 1975) certain types of Equi apply only to active (i.e. basic) subjects, and do not apply to subjects of passive sentences. And so on. But our evidence in support of the hypothesis is only impressionistic, and not systematic. (See Timberlake 1976 for more systematic support for this claim from N. Russian.)

We have, however, more evidence in support of the ordering of the coding properties, which we shall refer to as the Coding Hierarchy (CH).

3.2 The Coding Hierarchy

The first prediction made by the CH is that some derived 'subjects' in some Ls would take on the characteristic position of b-subjects in those Ls but not acquire the characteristic case marking and verb agreements.

Some support for this claim comes from Biblical Hebrew in which subjects characteristically occur after the verb, are not case marked, and trigger verb agreement. In passive sentences, however, two major patterns appear (Richard Steiner, personal communication). Either the derived subject has the full complement of coding properties, as in (27a), or it has only the position, retaining its former case marking, and the verb going into a 3rd Sg, masc. form, so not agreeing with anything, as illustrated in (27b).

(27) a. lɔ-'ellɛ tehɔleq   hɔ- 'ɔrɛṣ (Numbers 26:53)
        to-these shall-be-divided the-land
                fem. 3sg, pass.   fem, 3sg.

   b. bĕ-ɣorɔl yehɔleq   'ɛθ hɔ- 'ɔrɛṣ
        by-lottery shall-be-divided acc the-land
                masc. 3sg pass.   fem. 3sg. (Numbers 26:55)

A second piece of supporting evidence comes from Kimbundu (Bantu, spoken in Angola. Data from Talmy Givón. See also Chatelain 1888). The basic word order in Kimbundu is SVO. NP subjects and objects are not case marked, and verbs agree with subjects only. In the passive, however, the derived subject moves to subject position, but does not trigger the expected subject agreement. Rather that is filled by the 3pl human prefix (regardless of the person and number of the derived subject). The verb does, however, take the direct object pronoun which does agree with the derived subject. The clear inference here is that this type of passive developed from an 'impersonal' active of the sort *they saw John*, then a topicalisation of the object yielding, *John, they saw him*, and finally the possibility of reintroducing the agent, *John they saw him by me*. Sentences (28a)-(28d) illustrate the relevant data.

(28) a.   nga-mono Nzua
          I   -saw   John
     b.   nga-mu- mono
          I   -him-saw
          'I saw him'
     c.   Peter na Dick a-   mono Nzua
          Peter and Dick they-saw John
          'Peter and Dick saw John'
     d.   Nzua a-   mu- mono kwa meme
          John they-him-saw   by me
          'John was seen by me'

This type of passive may be characteristic of a group of West
Bantu Ls (it occurs as well in Luvale; see Horton 1949) and is
distinct from the suffixal passive characteristic of Swahili, Shona,
Luganda, etc.

A third piece of very interesting support for the prediction
comes from Maasai (Nilo-Saharan. All data from Tucker and
Mpaayei 1955). The basic word order is VSO, and in passives the
old object occurs in the immediate postverbal position, as
predicted.

(29) e-nyer Tinkoi nkishu
      3-love Tinkoi cattle
      'Tinkoi loves cattle'
(30) e-rik-i   nkishu aainei lmurran
      3-led-pass cattle by   young-men
      'my cows will be led by the young men'

Further, full NPs are case marked, by tone!

(31) a.   e-dol embártá
          3-see horse (acc)
          'he sees the horse'
     b.   e-dol embartá
          3-see horse (nom)
          'the horse sees him'

And in passive sentences the derived subject retains the accusative
tone. (We mark tone only where it is relevant to our discussion.)

(32) e-isis- i   Sirónkà
   3-praise-pass Sironka (acc)
   'Sironka is praised'

Compare:

(33) a- dol   Sirónkà
   1sg-see Sironka
   'I see Sironka'

Note as well that passive sentences in Maasai are intransitive in that no NP other than the derived subject is needed for the sentence to be complete.

As regards agreement, verbs normally only agree with subjects. (Note that the prefixal e- indicates either 3sg or 3pl subject agreement.) However, when the direct object is first or second person singular, the agreement prefix changes. Compare:

(34) a.   áa-   dol (nánú)
        3sg subj   (acc) 1sg
        1sg obj
        'he sees me'
    b.   á-   dol (nanú)
        1sg subj see (1sg, nom)
        'I see him'

Thus we can tell by the verb marking whether a first or second person singular functions as a subject or an object. And in passives, when the derived subject is first or second person singular, it triggers the verb prefix appropriate to 3 person subject and 1sg or 2sg object!

(35) áa-   rik-   i
   3sg subj nauseate-pass
   1sg obj
   'I am nauseated'

Thus it appears that in Maasai the passive verb always has a 3 person subject agreement marker, reminiscent of the Kimbundu passive in this respect, and that where the passive verb agrees with the derived subject, namely when it is 1sg or 2sg, it agrees with it as though it were an object. Thus the derived subject retains its object case marking and verb agreements, acquiring only the position of subject.

Final, but in some ways less convincing, evidence for our claim comes from Ls like Latin and German. Here when passive advances accusative direct objects to subjects they acquire the full complement of coding properties. However, a few verbs in both Ls take their direct objects in the dative case. And in these cases one could argue that when the verbs are passivised the dative NP takes on the subject position but retains its dative case marker and does not trigger verb agreement, the verb reverting to a 3sg form. (Examples from Gildersleeve and Lodge 1913.)

(36) mihi invidetur (ab aliquo)
      1sg envied   (by someone)
      dat +pass
      'I am envied'

The problem with these data for our analysis, as Paul Postal (personal communication) pointed out, is whether there is any real sense in which the underlying object has acquired the subject position (it very clearly has not taken subject case or subject verb agreement). This is perhaps better analysed as in impersonal passive in which the old subject gets demoted to oblique status and the verb becomes passive, but nothing gets promoted to subject position, the other NPs merely remaining where they were. (See Keenan 1975b for some discussion of impersonal passives.)

The PSH might also be interpreted to mean that we could expect to find Ls in which subjects demoted by operations like Passive lost only their characteristic position but not their case marking or verb agreements. That is the subject properties that are the hardest to acquire are also the hardest to give up. At the moment we have relatively little evidence for this, although the Maasai data, if further analysed, might support it. Further, the following example from Luiseño (Munro 1974a) is suggestive.

(37) ?ivi no-naawu-ki no-yo   po-lo?xa
      this my-dress-poss my-mother her-make
      'this dress was made by my mother'

Now Luiseño is dominantly SOV, with objects case marked, usually. Subjects trigger a kind of agreement which may tack onto the end of the first word in the sentence or, in more complex sentence types, show up as a possessive-type affix on the verb. Now, as the passive above illustrates, the demoted subject loses its sentence initial position, but remains nominative and appears to trigger a kind of possessive agreement on the verb. Historically speaking this is natural, since it would appear that passives in Luiseño, at least this type, are similar to those in Chemehuevi (Munro 1974b), which look like *this dress is what my mother made*, where *mother* would be expected to remain nominative and trigger verb agreement.

3.3

A second prediction made by the Coding Hierarchy is that derived subjects in some Ls would acquire the position and case of b-subjects, but not trigger the verb agreements characteristic of b-subjects. We have less evidence for this, but some none the less which is suggestive.

Thus in Welsh, active (=basic) sentences present VSO order. Verbs agree only in person with subjects (although they also agree in number with pronominal subjects). Neither full NP subject nor object are case marked but pronominal constructions for subjects and objects are different. In passives, the old object now occurs in the expected subject position, and uses the nominative pronominal construction, and so to that extent, acquires the case of b-subjects. But the derived subject does not trigger verb agreement. The verb becomes morphologically invariable. (Examples below from Bowen and Jones 1960.)

(38) a. gwelir fi
is-seen I
'I am seen'
  b. gwelir di
is-seen you
'you are seen'
  c. dysgir Cymraeg gan yr athro
is-taught Welsh   by the teacher
'Welsh is taught by the teacher'

A second example which supports this point in the CH concerns cases where a demoted subject loses its position and case marking, but does not lose its ability to trigger verb agreement. Kapampangan (Philippines; all data from Mirikitani 1972) is illustrative here. Kapampangan is verb initial in basic word order and seems to permit a fair degree of freedom of word order of full NPs after

the verb, although this cannot be judged with certainty on the basis
of the data in Mirikitani. Surface subjects take the pre-position *ing*
and other NPs have other prepositions. Verbs agree with subjects
in b-sentence types.

(39) sumulat ya ng poesia ing lalaki
      write   he obj poetry subj boy
      'the boy will write a poem'

In passive sentences the former object gets assigned the subject
pre-position and appears to take the subject position (but position
may not really be criterial of subjects), and it acquires the capacity
to trigger verb agreement. The old subject, while losing its position
and most important its pre-position, still retains the possibility of
triggering verb agreement. Thus the derived verb now agrees with
two NPs, the derived subject and the former subject.

(40) isulat   na ya (=ne) ning lalaki ing   poesia
     be-written it he   agent boy   subj poem
     'the poem was written by the boy'

Another example of a L in which demoted subjects still trigger
verb agreement is Achenese (Lawler 1975).

3.4 Some Possible Counter Examples

One interesting class of possible counter example to the claims in
the CH is presented by the possibility of promoting to subject various types of locatives in Bantu Ls. Consider (41a) and (41b) from
Chicewa. (See Trithart 1975 for discussion.)

(41) a.   John a- nathamang-ir- a   ku sukulu
          John he- ran   dir-indic to school
          'John ran to school'
     b.   ku sukulu ku- nathamang-idw- ir- a-   ko ndi John
          to school loc- ran   -pass-dir-indic loc by John
          'School was run to by John'

It appears in (41b) that the derived subject triggers verb agreement
and acquires the subject position but retains its locative case
marking. If so, this clearly violates the claim of the CH. Note, however, that the subject agreement it triggers is not one of the normal

noun class markers, as is the case for b-subjects. Rather, it is the locative marker itself. This suggests that the original locative phrase *ku sukulu* 'to school' has been reanalysed as a mere NP, the old locative *ku* now being interpreted as the noun class marker. Then the verb agreement is regular, and the subject no longer carries an oblique case marker, and the CH is not violated. Further work is needed to determine whether this analysis receives any independent motivation.

A second counter example comes from Biblical Hebrew (again supplied by Richard Steiner, personal communication). While the general pattern for passives is as cited in section 3.1 above (either the derived subject takes the position, case, and agreements of b-subjects, or else it ony takes the position, retaining its case and the verb becoming 3sg), there are a very few cases in which a derived subject remains accusative but does trigger verb agreement.

(42) wĕ 'ɛθ hɔ- 'ɔh   lĕfɔnɔw   mĕvo'ɔrɛθ
 and-acc the-brazier in front of him was-kindled
           fem 3sg   fem 3sg pass

It would appear then that Hebrew, at this stage, was in the midst of analysing subjects of passive sentences as real objects. Sometimes all the surface, i.e. coding, properties are assigned to subjects, and sometimes not. In a large majority of cases where not all the coding properties are assigned to derived subjects the properties that are assigned are in accordance with the CH, but in a few cases this is not so. (Note incidentally, that the accusative NP which triggers verb agreement in (42) also occurs clause initially, plausibly not the subject position in Biblical Hebrew.)

This type of historical shift may also serve to rationalise a final counter example to the CH pointed out by Butler (personal communication) in which the evolution of impersonal constructions in Old and Middle English is discussed. Such constructions had a major NP which was dative/accusative and did not trigger verb agreement — the verb being fixed as 3sg. Such constructions survive in frozen expressions until somewhat later, e.g. *me-thinks*, *if you please*, etc. Now one of the ways the impersonal constructions were lost is that the surface dative/accusative was reanalysed as a subject, becomes nominative and triggers verb agreement. Butler points out, however, that during the reanalysis, 'Constructions like the following occasionally turn up with *think*, *seem*, and *ail*: *Me-seem my head doth swim*. (1571. Damon and Pythias. 79.) ...' It appears then that during an historical transition in the reanalysis of a subject NP we can have NPs with subject position and verb agreement but which do not have subject case marking. Judging from Butler's use of 'occasionally' however, we may infer that, like Hebrew, this violation of the CH was not the norm, but merely the reflection of an instability of surface pattern. Nonetheless the instability does lead to 'occasional' violations of the CH and cannot be dismissed.

4. Conclusion

We have attempted to provide a definition of the notion 'subject of' which would be universally valid in the sense that it would allow us to identify subjects of arbitrary sentences from arbitrary languages. The definition we proposed, while cumbersome, does none the less allow us to verify many universal generalisations stated in terms of that notion. And in addition it has suggested further generalisations concerning universal properties of subjectivising transformations.

Postscript: The information on the evolution of impersonal constructions in Old and Middle English communicated to me by Butler is contained in an unpublished paper by Milton C. Butler, titled, 'The re-analysis of impersonal constructions in Middle English'.

Notes

1. Research for this paper was supported by a grant (# 2994) from the Wenner-Gren Foundation and a grant from the Social Science Research Council in Britain.

2. We might note, however, that in general the meaning of a non-basic structure will depend on the meaning of only finitely many other structures. We might take this number to determine the degree of basicness of the structure. Then any two structures can be compared with regard to basicness using the normal 'greater than or equal to' relation. Thus the basicness of a structure x would be greater than or equal to that of y. In this way the relation *more basic than* can be extended to apply to all the structures in a L.

References

Bowen, J.T. and T.J. Rhys Jones (1960) *Welsh*, Teach Yourself Books, English Universities Press, London.

Capell, Arthur (1969) *A Survey of New Guinea Languages*, Sydney University Press, Sydney, Australia.

Chapin, Paul (1970) 'Samoan pronominalization', *Language*, 46, 366-78.

Chatelain, H. (1888) 'Grammatica Elementar do Kimbundu', Genera, reprinted in Gregg.

Chomsky, N. (1965) *Aspects of the Theory of Syntax*, MIT Press, Cambridge, Massachusetts.

Churchward, C. (1953) *Tongan Grammar*, Oxford University Press, London.

Craig, C (1975) *Jacaltec Syntax: A Study of Complete Sentences*, unpublished doctoral dissertation, Harvard University, Cambridge, Massachusetts.

Dixon, R.M.W. (1972) *The Dyirbal Language of North Queensland*, Cambridge University Press, Cambridge.

Donellan, K. (1966) 'Reference and definite descriptions' in *Philosophic Review*, LXXV, No. 3, 281-304.

Frantz, D. (1971) *Toward a generative grammar of Blackfoot*, Publication of the Summer Institute of Linguistics.

George, L. (1974) 'Ergativity and relational grammar' in *Papers from the 5th Meeting of the New England Linguistic Society*.

Gildersleeve, B.L. and G. Lodge (1913) *Latin Grammar* (3rd edn.)

Givón, T. (1976) 'Topic, Pronoun, and Grammatical Agreement', in C. Li (ed.) *Subject and Topic*, Academic Press, New York.

Greenberg, Joseph (1966) 'Some Universals of Grammar with Particular Reference to the Order of Meaningful Elements, *Universals of Language*, ed. by J.H. Greenberg, 73-111, MIT Press, Cambridge, Mass.

Hale, K. (1967) *Preliminary Remarks on Walbiri Grammar*, MIT Press, Cambridge, Massachusetts.

—— (1968) 'Review of P.W. Hohepa, Profile-generative grammar of Maori', *Journal of the Polynesian Society*, 77: 83-99.

Hess, H. (1968) *The Syntactic Structure of Mesquital-Otomi*, Mouton, The Hague.

Hinds, J. (1974) *On the Status of the VP Node in Japanese*, Indiana University Linguistics Club, Bloomington, Indiana.

Horton, A.E. (1949) *A Grammar of Luvale*, Witwatersrand University Press, Johannesburg, South Africa.

Huisman, R.D. (1973) 'Angaataha Verb Morphology', *Linguistics* 110:43, 54.

Hyde, V. (1971) *An Introduction to the Luiseño Language*, Malki Museum Press.

Jacobsen, W.H. (1967) 'Switch-reference in Hokan-Coahuiltecan', in D. Hymes, *Studies in Southwestern Ethnolinguistics*, Mouton, The Hague.

Johnson, David (1974) 'Prepaper on Relational Constraints on Grammar', unpublished manuscript. Mathematical Sciences Department, T.J. Watson Research Center, IBM, Yorktown Heights, N.Y.

Keenan, E.L. (1970) 'Two Kinds of Presupposition in Natural Language' *Studies in Linguistic Semantics*, C.J. Fillmore and D.T. Langdendoen (eds.) Holt, Rinehart and Winston.

—— (1972) 'On Semantically Based Grammar', *Linguistic Inquiry*, III, 4, 413-61.

—— (1974) 'The Functional Principle: Generalising the Notion of "Subject-of"', in M.W. Lagaly, R. Fox, and A. Bruck (eds.) *Papers from the Tenth Regional Meetings of the Chicago Linguistic Society*, University of Chicago, Chicago, Illinois, pp. 298-310.

—— (1975a) 'The Logical Diversity of Natural Languages'. Paper presented to the Conference on the Origins and Evolution of Language and Speech. To appear in the Annals of the New York Academy of Sciences.

—— (1975b) 'Some Universals of Passive in Relational Grammar', *Papers from the XIth Regional Meeting of the Chicago Linguistic Society.*

—— and B. Comrie (1972) 'Noun Phrase Accessibility and Universal Grammar', presented at the Winter Meeting of the Linguistic Society of America.

—— (1977) 'Noun Phrase Accessibility and Universal Grammar', *Linguistic Inquiry* 8, 1.

Lasnik, H and R. Fiengo (1974) 'Complement Object Deletion', *Linguistic Inquiry.* V. 4, 535-573.

Lawler, J. (1975) 'On Coming to Terms in Achenese: The Function of Verbal Dis-Agreement' in R.E. Grossman, L.J. Sam, and T.J. Vance (eds.) *Papers from the Parasession on Functionalism*, Chicago Linguistic Society, University of Chicago, Chicago, Illinois.

Li, C. and S. Thompson (1976) 'Evidence Against Topicalisation in Topic Prominent Languages' in C. Li (ed.) *Subject and Topic*, Academic Press, New York.

Mirikitani, L. (1972) 'Kapampangan Syntax', *Oceanic Linguistics* No. 10.

Munro, P. (1974a) 'Topics in Mojave syntax', Ph.D. dissertation, University of California, San Diego.

—— (1974b) 'Imperatives, passives and perfectives in Chemenuevi', paper presented at the American Anthropological Association Meeting, Mexico City, Mexico.

Perlmutter, D.M. and P.M. Postal (1974) *Linguistic Institute Lectures*, unpublished manuscript.

Schachter, P. (1976) 'The Subject in Philippine Languages: Topic, Actor, Actor-Topic, or None of the Above', in C. Li (ed.) *Subject and Topic*, Academic Press, New York.

Schwartz, Arthur (1972) 'The VP-constituent of SVO Languages', *Syntax and Semantics*, vol. 1, ed. by J. Kimball, 213-35. New York: Academic Press.

Thurstone, Thelma G. (1956) 'The Test of Memory Mental Abilities', *Personnel and Guidance Journal*, 35.

Timberlake, A. (1976) 'Subject Properties in the North Russian Passive' in C. Li (ed.) *Subject and Topic*, Academic Press, New York.

Trithart, L. (1975) 'Relational Grammar and Chicewa Subjectivisation Rules', in R.E. Grossman, L.J. Sam, and T.J. Vance (eds.) *Papers from the Eleventh Regional Meeting of the Chicago Linguistic Society*, University of Chicago, Chicago, Illinois.

Tucker, A.N. and J. Tomp. Ole Mpaayei (1955) *A Maasai Grammar. Publications of the African Institute of Leydon*, No. 11. London: Longmans, Green & Co.

ON COLLAPSING GRAMMATICAL RELATIONS
IN UNIVERSAL GRAMMAR

(Written with Judith Olmsted Gary)

The purpose of this study is to contribute to our understanding of
the Relational Hierarchy (RH) — *Subject (SU)* > *Direct Object
(DO)* > *Indirect Object (IO)* > *Oblique (Obl)* — in universal
grammar. First, in Section 1 we summarise some of the facts which
justify including the RH in the statement of universal grammar.
We present two contrasting views concerning the relation between
the RH and the grammars of particular languages: a COMPARA-
TIVE view versus a GENERATIVE view. We find that the generative view is the stronger of the two in that it provides some justification for the generalisations which the comparative view permits
us to make. In Section 2 we give a detailed analysis of Kinyarwanda (a Bantu language spoken in Rwanda and Burundi), which
is shown to support the comparative view but not the generative
view as stated. We then, in Section 3, consider what revisions
might be made in the generative view to make it compatible with
the Kinyarwanda data and still permit the type of strong predictions it makes about the nature of human language. We conclude
with a consideration of an alternate hypothesis.

The Relational Hierarchy

The Comparative View

The basic data which support the existence of the Relational Hierarchy in universal grammar come from the comparison of particular syntactic processes across languages. E.g. in Keenan and
Comrie (1972 and 1977) it was argued that the distribution of
relative clause types follows the Accessibility Hierarchy (AH) —
Su > *DO* > *IO* > *Obl* > *Possessors* > *Object of Comparison* —
in the following sense: first, Su is the easiest position to relativise,
i.e. if a language can form relative clauses (RCs) at all it can form
them on Su. Second, any particular RC-forming strategy which
applies to Su may, in principle, apply continuously down the AH,

cutting off at any point. Thus a human language may have (and some do have) RC-forming strategies that apply only to Su; others, RC-forming strategies which apply to Su and DO, but nothing else; still others, RC-forming strategies which apply to Su, DO, and IO, but nothing else, and so forth. And, more generally, any RC-forming strategy must apply to a continuous segment of the AH. Thus, for example, no possible language could relativise DOs and Obls in the same way unless it also relativised IOs in that way.

Another hierarchy generalisation has been proposed in Johnson (1974a) and modified somewhat in Trithart (1975). There it is argued that, among other things, operations which promote NPs low on the RH to higher positions (as Passive promotes DOs to Su) distribute according to the RH. Thus if a language can promote locatives to Su (e.g. *the forest was seen-in a lion by John*) then it can necessarily promote IOs and DOs to Su (e.g. *Mary was shown the picture by John*).

Note that justifying the particular ordering of elements in the RH or the AH depends on comparative data from several languages. No one language, for example, has enough distinct ways of forming RCs to justify the particular ordering of the six elements in the AH. In Malagasy, for example, only subjects are relativisable (Keenan 1972), and on the basis of the Malagasy data alone there is no reason to think that DOs are in any sense more relativisable than are Obls.

Further, such comparative generalisations can be stated using only very weak assumptions concerning the relation between the RH and the grammar of an arbitrary language. We present two such assumptions, which will distinguish the comparative from the generative view of the RH.

The Metalinguistic Assumption.   The RH — and more generally the AH — merely specify an ordered set of possible distinctions a language can make. But no one language need avail itself of all the distinctions. Within limits which will have to be determined empirically, languages are free to choose which distinctions they will use. Suppose, for example, that a language does not utilise a distinct category of IO, and that, further, objects of comparison are treated in all respects like objects of pre- or postpositions. Then the AH in that language will simply have this form: $Su > DO > Obl > Genitive$. But the hierarchy generalisations which are expressed in terms of the AH will remain unchanged in their application to that language. It will still be the case that any given RC-forming strategy must operate on a continuous segment of the (reduced) hierarchy, and that, if elements low on the hierarchy can be promoted to subject, then so can all intermediate elements. In fact, in Keenan and Comrie (1977) it was stated, but not argued, that some languages do in fact collapse the Object of Comparison position with the Obl position, and that other languages collapse Obls with DO.[1] Further, it will be one of the major claims of this paper that Kinyarwanda does not realise the IO slot in the RH.

We should note here that, in our opinion, it is a defect of all work on both the AH and the RH that no explicit, universal definition of the positions in the hierarchies has been given. (For an attempt at a universal definition of Su see Keenan 1975b.) Thus the universality of the positions in the hierarchies and the generalisations stated in terms of these positions remain in doubt. Nonetheless, linguists will agree for many sentence types in many languages which NPs are to be called Su, which are to be called DO, etc. And, by beginning with the distinguishing properties of these categories in the relatively clear cases, we can at least construct noncircular arguments that the putatively universal hierarchy generalisations fail in some particular case, or that no class of NPs in some language exhibits the properties which normally distinguish IOs from DOs, for example.

The Nonuniqueness Assumption.   The hierarchy generalisations allow in principle that a given position on the hierarchy be manifested by more than one NP in a given sentence. This is clearly the case for Obliques. Thus *The pudding was put in a bowl with a spoon by John* presents three oblique NPs. Further, the hierarchy generalisations will have to be made sensitive to subclasses within a given hierarchy position. E.g. Trithart (1975) has argued that in Chicewa (a Bantu language of Malawi) only certain subclasses of locatives can be promoted to DO, while others cannot. Similarly, in English certain subclasses of DOs cannot be passivised to Su. E.g. the DOs of highly stative verbs like *resemble, fit* (*The dress fits Mary, *Mary is fitted by the dress*), *suit, have, cost* (*That cost me my job, *I was cost my job by that*), *strike* (*John struck me as clever, *I was struck as clever by John*), etc., do not passivise. In addition, although many would claim there is a Dative rule which converts IOs to DOs in English (*John gave the toy to Mary → John* *gave Mary the toy*), only a small subclass of IOs undergo this rule — those of common verbs like *give, tell, show,* and *teach.* But in very many sentences containing IOs the IOs cannot be promoted to DOs: *add* (*John added a book to the pile,* *John added the pile a book*), *describe, contribute, praise, entrust, introduce, dedicate, talk/sing* (*Mary sang to the children,* *Mary sang the children*), *refer* (*John referred Bill to the special services department,* *John referred the special services department Bill*), etc.

It seems clear, then, that more exact statements of hierarchy generalisations than we have given to date will require us to distinguish subtypes of NPs which occupy the same position on the hierarchy. But the generalisations do not place any restrictions on the number of NPs of any given hierarchy category or subcategory which may be present in a simplex sentence. (A sentence like *John was born in Wyoming in a log cabin* illustrates the cooccurrence of two NPs from the same locative subcategory.) Of course, if there are universally valid restrictions of this sort, then that is a further constraint on the form of possible human languages that we can give in terms of the hierarchy. Perhaps, for instance, no language can present basic sentences having more than one IO. Perhaps. But the question is an empirical one and cannot be decided *a priori.* For example, many languages in general treat IOs and Benefactives in the same way. In such languages then we might expect the translation of *John wrote a letter to the president for Mary* to present two IOs.

In the paper we argue explicitly that in Kinyarwanda (KR) the category DO allows more than one exponent in a given sentence, and thus is like the category Oblique in English.

The Generative View

The generative view of the RH which we present here is based on lectures by David Perlmutter and Paul Postal at the 1974 Linguistics Institute, University of Massachusetts, Amherst (hereinafter Perlmutter and Postal, 1974). The inferences we draw from their work, however, may not be in accordance with their views. The essential property of the generative view, in the respects which concern us, is that the categories in the RH are among the primitive categories in the generative grammar of each language. These categories are interpreted as relations which NPs bear to their verbs. The first three relations on the RH — Su, DO, and IO — are called GRAMMATICAL RELATIONS, and NPs which bear those relations to a verb are called the TERMS (of those relations). Relations like INSTRUMENT, GOAL-LOCATIVE, etc., which oblique NPs bear to their verbs are not GRAMMATICAL relations; such NPs are called NONTERMS.

The transformations which generate complex structures from simpler ones reference these relations explicitly. Thus Passive is defined, in essence, as an operation which promotes DOs to Su status; Dative promotes IOs to DO status; and still further operations (prominent in many Bantu languages) can promote Instrumentals, Locatives, etc., to DO or to Su.

In common with other work in generative grammar, a major motivation of this approach is to define 'possible grammar of a natural language' in such a way as to permit the statement of constraints on the form of possible human languages. Some such constraints (called 'laws' by Perlmutter and Postal, 1974), with which we shall be concerned in what follows, are:

CYCLICITY LAW: *Operations which alter the termhood status of NPs are cyclic.*

RELATIONAL ANNIHILATION LAW: *NPs whose grammatical relations have been taken over by another (as in Passive, when an underlying DO takes over the Su relation of the active subject) cease to bear any grammatical relation to their verb. That is, they are* DEMOTED *to nonterm status.*

Certain operations like controlling verb agreement, controlling reflexivisation, controlling coreferential NP deletions, and being the NP slot to which other NPs can be raised are universally restricted to terms.

In keeping with the spirit of these laws (i.e. to constrain the form of possible human languages) it is natural to assume, pending evidence to the contrary, (i) that no more than one NP in any given sentence in any language can bear a given grammatical relation to a given verb, and (ii) that the grammar of each language distinguishes all three grammatical relations: Su, DO, and IO. The alternate assumptions in each case would allow for a larger class of possible human languages. We argue in this paper that both of these assumptions are in fact violated in Kinyarwanda, and thus that the generative view (as we present it) is incorrect. We consider it important, however, to modify the generative view to handle the

Kinyarwanda data, since this view provides a basis for explaining the hierarchy generalisations we want to make on the comparative view. That is, if categories like Su and DO figure in the operations which define the class of human languages, then it is natural that we can make cross-language generalisations in terms of them. But, if such notions do not figure in the grammar of any particular language, then it remains mysterious why cross-language generalisations should be statable in terms of them. To take one such example, why should the cross-language distribution of relative clause types or voicing rules be sensitive to categories which are irrelevant to the grammar of each language?

The Relational Hierarchy in Kinyarwanda

Below we present the properties characteristic of DOs in Kinyarwanda, indicating those properties which differentiate DOs from the clear cases of nonterms (pp. 126-9). We then consider the properties of NPs which express the semantic role of IOs and Benefactives in languages for which such categories are attested and show that, on the surface, they do not differ in syntactically significant ways from DOs (pp. 129-33). On p. 147 we contrast our analysis of KR, which supports the metalinguistic assumption and the nonuniqueness assumption, with the generative view inherent in Perlmutter and Postal (1974). We argue that our proposal is both simpler and capable of capturing more generalisations than is that of Perlmutter and Postal (1974). As necessary background, we include discussion on the formal nature of derivations within RG.

Properties of DOs in Kinyarwanda

VERB AGREEMENT   A verb agrees only with a Su, not with a DO or an Oblique (nonterm):

(1)   *Yohani y- Ø- iish-e   impysisi mw-ishyamba.*
      John   he-past-kill-asp hyena   in- forest
      'John killed a hyena in the forest.'

POSITION   The Su precedes the verb; the DO and Obl follow. The DO precedes the Obls:

(2)   *Yohani y- Ø-   iish-e   mw-ishyamba impysisi.*
    John   he-past kill-asp in- forest   hyena

CASE MARKING   Su and Do are not case-marked or constructed with a preposition, whereas Obls do take prepositions.

PRONOMINALISATION   The subject agreement prefix functions as the unmarked subject proform. DOs are pronominalised by an infix which immediately precedes the verb root and agrees in noun class with the controller:

(3)   a.   *Yohani y- a-   kubis-e   abagore.*
           John   he-past-strike-asp women
           'John struck the women.'
     b.   *Y- a-   ba-   kubis-e.*
           he-past-them-strike-asp
           'He struck them.'

Oblique NPs cannot be pronominalised in this way. In some cases they can be pronominalised by the use of an independent form of the pronoun following the preposition:

(4)   a.   *Yohani yanditse ibaruwa n-   ikaramu.*
           John   wrote   letter   with pen
           'John wrote a letter with the pen.'
     b.   *Yohani yanditse ibaruwa na   yo.*
           John   wrote   letter   with it
           'John wrote a letter with it.'

Further, locative NPs like 'forest' in (1) cannot be directly pronominalised (although they can be promoted to object status and then pronominalised, a process we discuss on p. 000):

(5)   *Yohani yishe impysisi mw-.*
      John   killed hyena   in-it
      'John killed a hyena in it.'

REFLEXIVISATION   DOs are reflexivised by inserting an invariant -*i*- in the DO pronominal slot in the verb:

(6)   *Yohani y- Ø-   i- kubis-e.*
      John   he-past-refl-strike-asp
      'John struck himself.'

Obls cannot be reflexivised directly, even in those few cases where this might seem semantically possible, because there is no independent reflexive pronoun:

(7)   a.   *Yohani yashyize ibiryo mu bana.*
           John   put   food in child
           'John put food in the child.'
      b.   *Yohani yashyize ibiryo muri we.*
           John   put   food in   him
           'John put food in him.'

In (7b) the pronoun *we* 'him' cannot be understood to be co-referential with the subject *Yohani*.

PASSIVISATION   DOs passive to Su in a 'usual' way. The old DO moves to a preverbal position, and triggers subject agreement. The old Su is demoted to oblique (nonterm) status. Its occurrence is optional, and, if present, it is constructed with a preposition in postverbal position and does not trigger any agreement on the verb. The verb takes a passive nonfinal suffix *-w-*:

(8)   a.   *Yohani y- a- kubis-e   abagore.*
           John   he-past-strike-asp women
           'John struck the women.'
      b.   *Abagore ba- a- kubis-w- e   (na Yohani).*
           women   they-past-strike-pass-asp (by John)
           'The women were struck by John.'

Nonterms do not passivise:[2]

(9)   **Isyamba ry-Ø- iish-w- e impysisi (mu) (na Yohani).*
      forest   it-past-kill-pass-asp hyena (in) (by John)
      'The forest was killed a hyena in by John.'

RELATIVISATION   Both Su and DO relativise. RCs formed on subjects place a high tone on the verb root and, for Class 1 nouns only, the subject agreement prefix has a special form:

(10) *N-a- bon-ye umugabo w- a-   kubis-e   abagore.*
     I- past-see-asp man   rel-past-strike-asp women
     'I see the man who struck the women.'

RCs formed on DOs mark the verb root with a high tone, but do not otherwise change the verb morphology:

(11) *N-a- bon-ye abagore Yohani y- a-   kubis-e.*
     I- past-see-asp women   John   he-past-strike-asp
     'I saw the women who John struck.'

Oblique NPs cannot be relativised directly.[3]

(12) **ikaramu Yohani y- andika ibaruwa [na (yo)].*
     pen   John   he-write letter   [with (it)]
     'the pen that John wrote the letter [with (it)]'

There is also a class of cleft constructions in KR which discriminates Su and DO from the nonterms in the same way as do RCs. For further discussion of clefts in KR see Kimenyi (in preparation).

The Categories IO and Benefactive in Kinyarwanda

In this section we will show that suface NPs which we expect to be IOs or Benefactives present the characteristic properties of DOs in KR. We further show that a given sentence may present more than one NP with the DO properties. In Section 2.4 we argue that this surface-based analysis also represents the basic or underlying sentence pattern.

The paradigm case of IOs, in languages which have this category, is represented by the recipient NP in active sentences whose main verbs are verbs like *give, send, show,* and *tell.* We use the term RECIPIENT (R) to designate the SEMANTIC relation which such NPs bear to the verb. Similarly, the term BENEFAC-TIVE (B) designates the semantic relation which *for*-NPs bear to their verb in sentences like *Mary danced for the children, Mary cut the meat for Harry,* etc. It is clear that these semantic relations are distinct. The R and B NPs in sentences like *John sent the letter to Mary (R) for Bill (B), who was ill* clearly are semantically related to the action expressed by the verb in different ways.

PROPERTIES OF RECIPIENT NPs

Coding Properties: Verb Agreement, Case Marking, Position.
Like DOs, R's occur in postverbal position, without a case marker
(or preposition); they do not trigger verb agreement:

(13) a.   *Yohani y- oher-er-eje Maria ibaruwa.*
      John   he-send-R-asp Mary letter
      'John sent a letter to Mary.'

There is a clear preference for the R to precede the DO, but the
alternate order is possible:

(13) b.   *Yohani y- oher-er-eje ibaruwa Maria.*
      John   he-sent-R-asp letter   Mary
      'John sent a letter to Mary.'

If both the DO and the R are animate, however, the R must
precede the DO:

(14) *Umuhungu y- a-   oher-er-eje umwana umugore.*
     boy   he-past-send-R-asp child   woman
     'The boy sent the woman to the child.'
     *'The boy sent the child to the woman.'

   Note further that the verb obligatorily carries a nonfinal suffix
which is underlying /ir/ and which may be realised by phonologically conditioned variants — [ir], [i], [er] (as above), or [e]. These
suffixes as used above indicate that there is a R present in the
clause.

Pronominalisation.   Like DOs, the postverbal R pronominalises
with an infix between the tense marker and the verb root. Both the
R and the DO can be pronominalised in this way in the same
sentence:

(15) a.   *Yohani y- a-   mw-oher-er-eje ibaruwa.*
      John   he-past-her-send-R-asp letter
      'John sent her the letter.'
   b.   *Yohani y- a-   y-oher-er-eje Maria.*
      John   he-past-it-send-R-asp Mary
      'John sent it to Mary.'

    c.   *Yohani y- a-   yi-mw-oher-er-eje.*
        John   he-past-it-her-send-R-asp
        'John sent it to her.'

Note that both of the infixed pronouns can also represent animate class objects:

(16) *Yohani y- a-   mu- mw-oher-er-eje.*
      John   he-past-him-him-send-R-asp
      'John sent him to him.'

Further, the order of the pronominal forms within the verb is fixed, the (nonreflexive) DO pronoun preceding the (nonreflexive) R pronoun, although the morphological shape of the pronouns is not distinct. Sentences which contain one full NP unmarked after the verb and an infix pronoun are structurally ambiguous:

(17) *Yohani y- a-   mw-oher-er-eje umugore.*
      John   he-past-her-send-R-asp woman
      'John sent her to the woman.' or 'John sent the woman to her.'

Reflexivisation.   R's reflexivise in the same way as DOs:

(18) *Yohani y- a-   yi- oher er-eje ibaruwa.*
      John   he-past-refl-send-R-asp letter
      'John sent himself a letter.'

Further, it is possible to have both a reflexive form and a DO pronoun infixed in the verb together:

(19) *Yohani y- a-   yi- y-oher-er-eje.*
      John   he-past-refl-it-send-R-asp
      'John sent it to himself.'

Passivisation.   Both the DO and the R passivise in the same way:

(20) a.   *Yohani y- Ø-   oher-er-eje Maria ibaruwa.*
         John   he-past-send-R-asp Mary letter
         'John sent a letter to Mary.'

    b. *Ibaruwa y-Ø- oher-er-ej- w- e   Maria(na Yohani).*
        letter   it-past-send-R-asp-pass-asp Mary (by John)
        'The letter was sent to Mary by John.'
    c. *Maria y- Ø oher-er-ej- w- e   ibaruwa(na Yohani).*
        Mary she-past-send-R-asp-pass-asp letter   (by John)
        'Mary was sent a letter by John.'

We note that Passive cannot apply twice to the same verb. Once we have passivised on the DO, for example, we cannot then again passivise on the R, and vice versa. Note further that the R suffix -*ir*- remains on the verb under passivisation.

Relativisation.   Finally, Rs relativise in the same way as DOs, and in a given sentence both the DO and the R relativise:

(21) a. *N-a- bon-ye ibaruwa Yohani yohér-er-eje Maria.*
        I- past-see-asp letter   John   sent- R-asp Mary
        'I saw the letter that John sent to Mary.'
    b. *N-a- bon-ye Maria Yohani yohér-er-eje ibaruwa.*
        I- past-see-asp Mary John   sent- R-asp letter
        'I saw Mary to whom John sent a letter.'

(If the R is a common noun, Relativisation applies in the same way.)
    On the surface, then, Rs exhibit the full range of syntactic properties of DOs. The only difference — to be discussed in the next section — is the obligatory presence of the -*ir*- suffix on a verb which has an R NP among its arguments.

PROPERTIES OF BENEFACTIVES

Coding Properties.   With regard to verb agreement, case marking, and position, Benefactive NPs follow the paradigm of Recipients exactly.

(22) *Maria y- a- tek- e-ye abana   inkoko.*
     Mary she-past-cook-B-asp children chicken
     'Mary cooked a chicken for the children.'

Thus Bs do not trigger verb agreement. They do occur postverbally without a preposition. Most commonly they precede the DO, but, as with R's, the alternate order is possible. Note that the suffix *-e-* is the same suffix which occurs when an R is present. A verb may not take two such suffixes and, in fact, cannot be constructed with both an R and a B NP:

(23) **Yohani y- Ø-   oher-er-er-eje Bill Maria ibaruwa.*
       John   he-past-send-R-B-asp Bill Mary letter
       'John sent a letter to Mary for Bill.'

A simple sentence like (24) is ambiguous (or vague) according to whether *Mary* is understood to be a B or an R:

(24) *Yohani y- Ø-   oher-er-   eje Maria ibaruwa.*
       John   he-past-send-R/B-asp Mary letter
       'John sent a letter to/for Mary.'

Note further that Bs occur easily with verbs which are otherwise intransitive:

(25) a.   *Maria y- a-   byin- ye.*
            Mary she-past-dance-asp
            'Mary danced.'
      b.   *Maria y- a-   byin- i- ye   umugabo.*
            Mary she-past-dance-B-asp man
            'Mary danced for the man.'

In regard to the other DO-like properties of Bs, they passivise, pronominalise, reflexivise, and relativise exactly like Rs. Below we illustrate Passive, but dispense with repetition of the other properties:

(26) a.   *Inkoko y-a- tek- e-w- e   abana   (na Maria).*
            chicken it-past-cook-B-pass-asp children (by Mary)
            'The chicken was cooked for the children by Mary.'
      b.   *Abana ba- a-   tek- e-w- e   inkoko (na Maria).*
            children they-past-cook-B-pass-asp chicken (by Mary)
            'The children were cooked a chicken (for) by Mary.'

Generating the Double Object Constructions in KR

In this section we sketch some basic properties of derivations of sentences within a Relational Grammar (RG) framework, in order to present our analysis of KR and to contrast it with the view in Perlmutter and Postal (1974). We shall be particularly concerned with the relation between grammatical categories and coding rules — case marking, verb agreement, and linear ordering — since part of our analysis of KR involves case marking. To our knowledge this relation has not been explicitly studied within RG.

Our formulation of underlying structures and the transformations which operate on them derives largely from Perlmutter and Postal (1974), but also draws on Johnson (1974b). Our proposals differ from those of Perlmutter and Postal and of Johnson in several respects concerning formalism and the basic nature of underlying structures. This difference is motivated, in part but not entirely, by the need to make explicit in underlying structure the information needed by case-marking rules. (Here and elsewhere we use CASE MARKING to refer to the morphological means used to indicate the grammatical or semantical relation between surface NPs and their verbs.)

DERIVATIONS IN RELATIONAL GRAMMAR   The underlying structure of a sentence in RG will be called a RELATIONAL STRUCTURE (RS). It is to RSs that transformations apply initially, and so RSs are the equivalent in this theory of base phrase markers in e.g. the Standard Theory. A relational structure *RS* consists of a DOMAIN, *D*, of objects, and of two sets of RELATIONS, R_g and R_s, defined on *D*. *D* is a finite set consisting of exactly one active verb and of one or more (occurrences of) noun phrases. The unique verb in any domain *D* will be referred to as V_D, the MAIN VERB of *D*.[4] R_g is a set containing the grammatical relations[5] which NPs in the domain *D* bear to V_D. Thus R_g will have members like '$Su(x, V_D)$', '$DO(y, V_D)$' etc., indicating that the noun phrase *x* bears the subject relation to the verb, etc. The only relations which may be mentioned here are Su, DO, and IO. Finally, R_s will be the set of nongrammatical relations which NPs in the domain bear to V_D. It will thus include elements like $INST(z, V_D)$ and $GOAL\text{-}LOC(w, V_D)$. It is important to include such relations in the underlying structures of a RG because many transformations will be sensitive to them — e.g. in many Bantu languages there will be rules promoting instrumentals or locatives to DO or Su status. The rules must be able to distinguish among the NPs which do not bear a grammatical relation to the verb, for only one particular NP can undergo the rule that promotes instrumentals to DO, etc. Similarly, case-marking rules (including the insertion of pre- and postpositions) will obviously be sensitive to what types of nonterm an NP is.

Note that the nongrammatical relations are semantically specific. To know that an NP in a given simple sentence is an instrumental, a goal-locative, etc., is to know how that NP is semantically related to the verb. Thus R_s is the set of SEMANTIC relations which NPs in D bear to V_D. Note further that the NPs which bear grammatical relations to the verb also bear semantic relations to them, but that the semantic relation is not unique for any given grammatical relation. Thus a subject may be an AGENT, or an EXPERIENCER, or simply some sort of NEUTRAL, as in *John is fat*. As we shall illustrate shortly, however, the semantic relation a subject or DO bears to its verb must also be referenced in the statement of various transformations; thus that information will also be included in the underlying relational structures. It will be required that every NP in the domain bear some semantic relation to the verb of the domain. Further, in general this semantic relation will not change throughout the course of a derivation (unless, perhaps, the NP is deleted — a topic we do not discuss here), although the grammatical relation the NP bears to the verb may change.

We note that the inclusion of this set of semantic relations among the primitive elements in the underlying structures for sentences, and allowing that some NPs can bear both grammatical relations and semantic relations to their verb, is not part of the original proposal by Perlmutter and Postal (1974).

We shall now exemplify our definition by means of a simple English sentence (ignoring a great many problems such as the representation of tense and aspect, cross-reference, and quantification). We then propose a relational definition of the Passive transformation and illustrate how it would operate in the simple case.

(27) A relational structure *RS* for *John cut the meat with a knife*
is a set $\{D, R_g, R_s\}$, where:
$D = \{cut_V, John_N, meat_N, knife_N\}$
+act
(Clearly the V_D = 'cut' in this case)
+act
$R_g = \{Su(John, V_D), DO(meat, V_D)\}$
$R_s = \{Agent(John, V_D), Patient(meat, V_D), Inst(knife, V_D)\}$

In this view, Passive is an operation which converts one relational structure, $\{D, R_g, R_s\}$, to another, $\{D', R'_g, R'_s\}$. The input relational structure must meet three conditions: first, its verb, V_D, must be marked +active; second, some noun phrase in the domain D must bear the DO relation to V_D; and, third, a distinct noun phrase must bear the Su relation to V_D. The derived relational structure differs from the input structure in the following ways: first, its domain, D', is identical to D except that $V_{D'}$ is marked as +passive rather than +active; second, the noun phrase which bore the DO relation to V_D now bears the Su relation to $V_{D'}$; and, third, the noun phrase which bore the Su relation to V_D bears no grammatical relation to $V_{D'}$. The semantic relations in the derived structure are identical to those of the input structure.

Somewhat more formally, we might represent Passive as follows:

(28) PASSIVE: $\{D, R_g, R_s\} \rightarrow \{D', R'_g, R'_s\}$ where

D: $\{V, n_1, n_2, \ldots, n_k\} \rightarrow \{V, n_1, n_2, \ldots, n_k\}$
$\quad$ +act $\qquad\qquad\qquad$ +pass

R_g: $\{\text{Su}(n_i, V_D), \text{DO}(n_j, V_D), X\} \rightarrow \{\text{Su}(n_j, V_D), X\}$
R_s: $\{Y_1, Y_2, \ldots, Y_m\} \rightarrow \{Y_1, Y_2, \ldots, Y_m\}$
CONDITION: $n_i \neq n_j$

Remarks on the definition of Passive:

1. The statement of the rule could be simplified by taking advantage of the Relational Annihilation Law (RAL), which guarantees that the subject NP in the input structure will not bear any grammatical relation to the verb in the output structure. Thus this information would not have to be included explicitly in the statement of the transformation. (But, as we show below, the Kinyarwanda data will force a reconsideration of the RAL.)

2. The Passive rule as we have given it is intended to be universal. It is the same transformation in every language which has a passive. Of course, language-particular rules will assign the appropriate passive morphology on the verb, thereby eliminating the feature +passive. Similarly, language-particular rules will assign the appropriate case marking and position to the demoted subject. Note that an advantage of taking semantic relations as basic in relational structures is that we can, in effect, define DEMOTED SUBJECT (of an activity verb — and similar definitions would

work for other subclasses of verb) to be a NP which bears the AGENT relation to the derived verb but does not bear the Su relation to it. It is this phrase which will be marked with *by* in English. We do not need then a special category for demoted terms (CHÔMEURS, in the terminology of Perlmutter and Postal 1974), nor do we need any special nongrammatical relations which demoted terms would have to bear to their verbs (as used in Johnson 1974b). Similarly, a demoted DO can be defined, in the paradigm case, as an NP which bears the Patient relation but not the DO relation to the verb. Note that the positioning and marking of demoted DOs in English is different from those of demoted Sus (e.g. only the latter take a preposition; and there are order restrictions, e.g. *Mary was given the stamp by John, *Mary was given by John the stamp*).

3. Languages will, of course, vary considerably in regard to the contexts in which Passive can apply. In Tagalog and Malagasy, for example, Passive may not apply if the DO is indefinite (and in Tagalog it must apply if the DO is definite). It is to be expected that taking semantic relations as basic in relational structures will allow us to state, on a language-particular basis, at least certain fairly general restrictions on Passive. E.g. if the Su is not an agent, and the DO is not a patient, it is often the case that Passive will not apply. (Recall the list of verbs (*suit, resemble,* etc.) in English which do not passivise. They are all verbs whose subjects are not agents and whose DOs are not patients.)

The one condition we have stated in the rule is designed to prevent Passive from applying to the structure underlying e.g. *John cut himself*, which appears correct since *John was cut* does not have that meaning. This condition on Passive appears extremely general, but even here is perhaps not universal. Thus in Modern Greek, in addition to an active sentence type with an overt reflexive pronoun, truncated Passives are used to indicate a reflexive (but somewhat accidental) action — a usage which presumably goes back to the use of the 'middle' voice in Classical Greek:

(29) a.   *O Yianis xtipise ton anθropo.*
   art John   struck the man

  b.   *O Yianis xtipise ton eaftó tu.*
   art John struck the self his
   'John struck himself (intentionally).'

(30) a.   *O Yianis xtipiθike apo ton anθra.*
      art John   +pass   by   the man
               strike
      'John was struck by the man.'
   b.   *O Yianis xtipiθike.*
      art John   +pass
               strike
      'John struck himself (accidentally).'

CONSTRAINTS ON DERIVATIONS IN RG

Constraints on Underlying Structures.   In addition to the constraints on the form of relational structures inherent in the definition, certain other 'meta' constraints will have to be given. For example, we want to require that each NP in a domain (of a simplex sentence) bear some semantic relation to the verb. Further, on the strong generative view we have been characterising we would have to require that no more than one NP bear a given grammatical relation to its verb. And we might want to require that one NP always bear the Su relation to its verb, etc.

Constraints on Transformations.   The transformations which apply to relational structures are not externally ordered, with one exception: those transformations which alter the termhood status of NPs are required to operate cyclically. In addition, certain other transformations — such as Reflexivisation and perhaps Relative Clause Formation — are held to be universally cyclic. (The latter transformation, of course, will operate on a cycle higher than that determined by the verb whose NP is relativised.)

Note further that RG will need rules to introduce the CODING PROPERTIES — linear ordering, case marking, and verb agreement — as none of these is present in the initial stage of a relational structure. The ordering of these rules relative to the cyclic ones poses some problems, and is not universally statable. Example in Achenese (Lawler 1975) passive verbs agree only with the underlying subject, not the derived subject. Thus in that language verb agreement must apply, presumably, before term-changing rules (or else agreement is subject to a global constraint), not after them. In Kapampangan (Mirikitani 1972), on the other hand, passive verbs agree with both the underlying and the derived subject, so presumably agreement applies both before and after the term-changing rules, but in such a way that cycle-initial agreement (with the active subject) is not lost when subject agreement applies again after Passive. In Chicewa, on the other hand, active verbs agree with subjects and, optionally, with DOs. In passive sentences, however, the verb subject agrees with the derived subject, but optionally retains its object agreement, and so agrees twice with the same surface NP:

(31)[6] a. *John o- ma- (chi)-lim- a   chi-manga.*
             John he-habit-it   -farm-indic corn
             'John farms corn.'

      b. *chi-manga chi-ma- (chi)-lim- idw- a   (ndi John).*
             corn   it- habit-it- farm-pass-indic by John
             'Corn is farmed by John.'

Thus in Chicewa it appears that object agreement applies before Passive — and is not lost afterwards — and that subject agreement applies after Passive.

In Palauan (Foley 1975) active verbs agree only with DOs. (This is the case in the perfective. In the imperfective active verbs agree with nothing.) Passive verbs, however, still OBJECT-agree with the patient, even though it is a derived subject, and, further, they now also agree with the demoted subject!:

(32) a. *A ngalek a s- il- seb- iy_i a $blai_i$.*
           art child   perf-past-burn-it_i art $house_i$
           'The child had burned down the house.'

      b. *A $blai_i$ a le_j- s- il- seb- iy_i a $ngalek_j$.*
           art $house_i$ pass perf-past-burn-it_i art $child_j$
                       3 sg_j-
           'The house had been burned down by the child.'

Presumably verb agreement in Palauan must apply both before and after term-changing rules, and the later application is subject to a global condition. (Perhaps both subject and object agreement apply precyclically, and some late rule deletes the subject-verb agreement in actives. But the existence of such a rule would have to be motivated.)

In the languages with which we are concerned here, English and KR, it seems most natural to require that verb agreement, as well as linear ordering and case-marking rules, apply after the term-changing rules: it is clear that they must apply after term-changing rules in any event (since verbs agree only with derived subjects, for example), and, if they were to also apply before the term-changing rules, then the later application would have to be made more complex so as to assure that the effect of the earlier application was lost (in distinction e.g. to the Kapampangan and Palauan cases).

In the literature on RG with which we are familiar, we have not seen an explicit formulation of the rules which introduce the coding properties (position, verb agreement, and case marking). Because our analysis of KR will require that these rules have certain properties, however, here we wish to establish, on universal grounds, certain general relations between coding properties — specifically case marking — and grammatical relations in order that our particular analysis of KR be seen to reflect the general case and not appear peculiar to KR.

SOME GENERAL RELATIONS BETWEEN GRAMMATICAL RELATIONS AND CODING PROPERTIES IN PARTICULAR CASE MARKING   Very generally speaking, there is an extremely poor correlation between the coding properties and grammatical relations. For example, it is almost never the case that an NP takes a certain case marking if, and only if, it bears a certain grammatical relation to its verb. Thus:

Fact 1.   In many languages, NPs which bear different relations to their verbs are case marked in the same way. Several patterns of this sort recur in many languages and thus are not accidental.

CASE 1.   Many languages, such as Hindi and Spanish, case mark IOs and certain definite DOs in the same way. (We are not claiming here or in what follows to give a thorough description of the case-marking conditions in any particular language.) Here are examples from Hindi (Saeed Ali and Boyd Mikailovsky, personal communication):

(33) a.   *Rām-ne rādha-ko chiṭhī bhējī.*
      Ram-erg Rada-dat letter sent
      'Ram sent Radha a letter.'

   b.   *Rām-ne murgī- ko mārā.*
      Ram-erg chicken-acc kill
      'Ram killed the chicken.'

CASE 2.   In many ergative languages subjects of transitive verbs are marked in the same way as are instrumentals, e.g. Gugu-Yalanji (Hershberger 1964), or even as are genitives, e.g. Eskimo (Woodbury 1975).

CASE 3.   In many languages, such as English, IOs and goal-locatives are marked in the same way (*to*).

CASE 4.   In many languages agent NPs in passive sentences are marked like instrumentals (Russian) or locatives (English, French). For further discussion of this property of case marking see Starosta (1973).

Fact 2.   NPs which bear the same relation to their verbs in sentences of somewhat different structural types may be case marked in different ways. One of the most widespread cases is that of ergative languages, in which subjects of transitive sentences take one case marker (the ergative) and those of intransitive sentences take another (often zero). Such languages are widely represented in several of the major language families of the world (Australian, Caucasian, and Amerindian). For illustrative purposes compare (34a) and (34b) below from Hindi:

(34) a.   *Wah   ro rahā   thā.*
        he (nom) cry be (past, imperfective)
        'He was crying.'
    b.   *Us-   ne aurat- ko   mārā.*
        he (oblique)-erg woman-acc/dat hit
        'He hit the woman.'

Hindi illustrates a second type of variation. For the subject to take the ergative marker, not only must the sentence be transitive, but it must also be perfective. Compare:

(35) a.   *Wah   kitāb likh rahā   thā.*
        he (nom) book write be (past, imperfective)
        'He was writing a book.'
    b.   *Us-   ne kitāb likhī.*
        he (oblique)-erg book wrote (perfective)
        'He wrote a book.'

(Note that in (35b) the verb agrees with the DO *kitab* 'book', whereas in (35a) it agrees with the subject *wah* 'he'.) In fact, many languages are ergative only in certain tenses or aspects. Georgian, for example, is ergative only in the aorist.

Other types of examples here would include languages like Russian and certain other Slavic languages in which DOs are marked accusative in affirmative sentences but genitive in negative sentences; and languages like Mojave (Munro 1974) and Wappo (Li and Thompson 1975), in which the subject case marking present in main clauses is lost in certain types of subordinate clauses. Below are examples from Wappo (Sandra Thompson, personal communication):

(36) a. *Ce kew- i   ew toh- ta?.*
        that man-subj fish catch-past
        'That man caught a fish.'
    b. *Ah ce   kew ew toh- ta? hatiskhi?.*
        I   that man fish catch-past know
        'I know that that man caught a fish.'

We might note that facts 1 and 2 above are paralleled by similar facts concerning verb agreement. Thus, in some languages, NPs bearing different relations to the verb will trigger the same agreements, and NPs bearing the same relation to verbs in different sentences may have different verb agreements. Both cases are illustrated by languages like Abaza and Jacaltec, in which subjects of transitive verbs trigger one type of verb agreement and subjects of intransitives and DOs of transitive verbs trigger another type. Examples from Jacaltec (Craig 1975) follow:

(37) a. *X- Ø$_i$-cam no'   cheh.*
        asp-it-die class. horse
        'The horse died.'
    b. *X- Ø$_i$-s$_j$- watx'e na$_j$ te'   ngah.*
        asp-it-he-make he$_j$ class. house$_i$
        'He made a house.'

Fact 3.   The case marker that an NP carries may also depend on its underlying semantic relation to the verb or on its inherent semantic features. As we have already seen, subjects of transitive perfective sentences in Hindi may take an ergative marker *-ne*

(example 34). But they take this marker only if they are semantically AGENTS. If they are experiencers, as in (38) below, they
are not marked as ergative, but rather are unmarked:[7]

(38) *Ram (*-ne) Radha-ko   bhula.*
     Ram   (-erg) Rada-acc/dat forgot
     'Ram forgot Rada.'

   Similarly, in many languages (e.g. Hindi, Spanish, Hebrew
(Givón 1975), and Malagasy (Keenan 1975a)) definite animate
DOs are case marked differently from indefinite inanimate DOs.
(The relative importance of definiteness versus animacy is not
exactly the same in these languages.):

(39) a. *Rām-ne murgī-Ø mari.*
        Ram-erg chicken killed
        'Ram killed a chicken.'
     b. *Rām-ne murgī ko   mārā.*
        Ram-erg chicken-dat/acc killed
        'Ram killed the chicken.'

Animacy is more clearly a factor in Gugu-Yalanji (Hershberger
1964), in which transitive subjects take one case marking if
animate and another (the instrumental) if inanimate:

(40) a. *Dingkar-angka   kaya kunin.*
        man-   erg animate dog   hit
        'The man hit the dog.'
     b. *Kalka-bu   kaya kunin.*
        spear- erg inanimate dog   hit
                 (= instrument)
        'The spear hit the dog.'

   A third type of case concerns case marking on DOs in Finnish.
A given DO may be marked in the partitive case if it is only
partially affected by the action of the verb, but may be marked in
another case if it is affected more totally (example from Raimo
Anttila, personal communication):

(41) a. *Vien poja-t   kouluun.*
      take-I boy-nom/-pl school
           acc
      'I am taking the boys to school.'
   b. *Vien poiki-a   kouluun.*
      take-I boy- part-pl school
      'I am taking some of the boys to school.'

In general, then, case marking in surface structure may depend on (i) the surface grammatical relation the NP bears to its verb, (ii) the underlying semantic relation that it bears to its verb, and (iii) its inherent semantic properties. Note further:

Fact 4.   Case marking may affect the verb. Given that one of the major parameters expressed by case marking concerns the syntactic-semantic relation an NP bears to its verb, it would not be surprising if case marking were marked both on the verb and on the noun, or even on the verb alone. In fact, there are instances of both situations.

CASE 1.   In the examples below from Hungarian (Katalin Radics, personal communication), the locative postposition on the noun is matched by the locative prefix on the verb; clearly, case is marked on both the verb and the noun:

(42) a. *Janos ra-Ø-te- tt- e   a   kalap-ot az asztal-ra.*
      John on-it-put-past-3sg 3sg the hat- acc the table- on
      'John put the hat on the table.'
   b. *Janos ala- Ø-te- tt- e   a   kenyeret az asztal-ala.*
      John under-it-put-past-3sg 3sg the bread   the table-
                                     under
      'John put the bread under the table'.

Similarly, in Homeric Greek, although we have not found instances of a case marker occurring simultaneously on both the verb and the NP, we do find markers which occur sometimes on the noun and sometimes on the verb. E.g. the particle *en/eni* may occur as a preposition (43a), as a postposition (43b), or as a verbal prefix. In all uses it governs the dative case of the noun:

(43)[8] a.   *en spéssi*
      in caves (dat)

    b. *elēmō*   *éni trôōn*
       populace (dat) in of-Trojans
       'among the Trojans'

    c. *paidos gar mŷtʰon pepnyménon én-tʰeto   tʰymô̂.*
       of-child for word   thought-out **in-** placed spirit (dat)
       'for the thoughtful word of her son lodged in her mind'

CASE 2. In the examples below from Machiguenga (Snell and Wise 1963) the semantic relation that the major NPs bear to their verb is marked only on the verb (where it is marked at all):

(44) *I- kʸisa- ši-   ta- ka- ro no- šinto   hoa.*
    he-be angry with   vb-refl-her my-daughter John
               ref. to
    'John was angry with my daughter.'

(45) *I- kʸisa- ko   ta- ka- ro no- šinto   hoa.*
    he-be angry-because of vb-refl-her my-daughter John
    'John was angry because of my daughter.'

(46) a. *I-tog-an- ta- iga-ka- ro_i ača_i camairinci.*

    a. *I-tog-an- ta- iga-ka- ro$_i$ ača$_i$ camairinci.*
       3-cut-inst-vb-pl- refl-it axe field
       'They cut the field with an axe.'

    b. *O- pašit- an- ta- kʸe- na-   ro$_i$ no- šinto$_i$ o-*
                                          bašikaro.
       she-cover-inst-vb-nrefl-for me-her my-daughter her-
                                          blanket
       'She covered my daughter with her blanket for me.'

    c. *I- tog-an- ta- kʸe- ne- ri   no- ačane i-   camaire.*
       he-cut-inst-vb-nrefl-ben-him my-axe   his-field
       'He cut his field for him with my axe.'

In general, then, full NPs carry no marking in Machiguenga. Among the approximately 150 sentences cited in Snell and Wise (1963), only one noun marker is recorded: a generalised locative postposition *-k* (remarkable, because Machiguenga is a verb-initial language, and such languages are usually prepositional). The normal way to indicate semantically specific relations that NPs bear to verbs is to mark the verb, as in our examples. It is worth noting that these markers are present whenever there is a NP in the sentence which bears the semantically specific relation to the verb, regardless of the surface grammatical relation it bears. Thus, when semantically instrumental NPs are passivised to subject, and so trigger the prefixal agreement, the instrumental marker *-an-* is still present. Compare:

(47) a.   *No-kamarang-an- ta- ka seri.*
       I-   vomit-   inst-vb-refl tobacco
       'I vomit by means of tobacco.'
   b.   *O-kamarang-an- t- a- gani seri.*
       it-vomit-   inst-vb-refl-pass tobacco
       'Tobacco is an emetic.' (more literally, 'Tobacco is vomited by oneself.')

We further note that instrumental NPs (the NPs discussed most extensively in Snell and Wise 1963, which we might expect to be nonterms) do not seem to differ much in their behaviour from P(atient) NPs. Note that while the Inst triggers the suffixal agreement on the verb in (46a), it is the P which triggers it in (46b). The Inst is still present, however, and still requires the instrumental case marker on the verb. In (46c) neither the P nor the Inst triggers the suffixal agreement, as benefactives usurp that slot (in the third person). Similarly, we have already noted that Insts may passivise to subject; so also may Ps, in which case the Inst is still unmarked and the case marker is still present on the verb:

(48) *O-tog-an- t- a- gani camairinci ača.*
     it$_i$-cut-inst-vb-refl-pass field$_i$ axe
     'The field was cut down with an axe.'

Snell and Wise cite further examples which show that the Causee in causative sentences can trigger the suffixal agreement, and that Causees and Recipients, as well as Ps and Insts, can passivise to subject. These data provide prima facie evidence that Machiguenga tolerates more than one (Direct) Object in surface, although more data than present in Snell and Wise would be needed to substantiate this claim.

Machiguenga does appear to illustrate more fully than our other examples a type of case-marking typology that we shall call VERB CODING. The extreme form such a typology would take would be a language in which the case of NPs is never marked on the NP, but only on the verb. Machiguenga fails to realise this typology in the most extreme form since certain locative NPs may carry case marking.

We shall now argue that Kinyarwanda illustrates a verb-coding typology, although to a somewhat lesser extent than Machiguenga in the sense that fewer NPs can have the 'case' marked only on the verb.

Two Proposals for a Relationally Based Analysis of Kinyarwanda

We are concerned here with the derivation of sentences in KR like (13a), repeated from above, which appear to have two DOs on the surface:

(13) a.   *Yohani n- oher-er-eje Maria ibaruwa.*
      John   he-send-R-asp Mary letter
      'John sent Mary a letter.'

On what we shall call the Promotional Analysis (PA), represented in Perlmutter and Postal (1974), the underlying structure of (13a) would be as follows: the domain would consist of the verb 'send' (here and elsewhere, for ease of reference, we use English rather than KR morphemes), and three NPs — 'John', 'Mary', and 'letter'. In the set of grammatical relations, R_g, they would bear the Su, DO, and IO relations, respectively, to 'send'. In the set of semantic relations, R_s, they would bear the AGENT (A), PATIENT, and RECIPIENT relations to 'send'. (13a) would be derived by a Dative transformation in which 'Mary' comes to bear the DO relation to 'send' and 'letter' ceases to bear any grammatical relation to 'send'. The -*ir*- marker on the verb would be a surface reflex of the fact that Dative had applied, just as the -*w*- suffix on the verb is a reflex of Passive.

On the analysis we propose, which we shall call the Two Objects Analysis (TOA), the underlying structure of (13a) would be as in the PA, except that both 'Mary' and 'letter' would stand in the DO relation to 'send' and no NP will bear the IO relation to 'send'. No Dative rule is needed to generate (13a). Coding rules, of course, are needed in both approaches. In ours they will position DOs indifferently in immediate postverbal position, subject to the constraint that if there are two animate DOs the R will precede the P. This is a semantic or role-based constraint of the sort that we have already seen is necessary to impose on coding rules in general.

The two analyses, the PA and the TOA, make rather different

predictions about KR. We shall outline these differences and argue that TOA is superior both in terms of overall simplicity and in terms of capturing generalisations about KR:

1. PA is prima facie more complicated than TOA in that it requires distinguishing three grammatical relations rather than just two, and in that it requires that KR have a Dative rule. There is no evidence, however, that KR has a Dative rule. The primary motivation for such a rule in English (or in any other language for which there is asserted to be a Dative rule) is that the language presents pairs of sentences like *John gave Mary the book* and *John gave the book to Mary* in which the corresponding NPs present the same semantic relations to the verb and in which similar distributional and selectional restrictions are exhibited. The Dative rule represents those generalisations. If both the dative and the non-dativised sentences were generated independently, then the similarity in privileges of occurrence and selectional restrictions would be accidental.

In KR, however, there are no 'undativised' sentences. It is not possible on the surface to present an R as an object of a preposition. This is perhaps surprising, since in some related Bantu languages (see Trithart 1975 for examples from Chicewa) R's can be introduced by the goal-locative preposition *ku*. But in KR, an NP, even if animate, must be interpreted as goal-locative when it follows *ku*. Thus in (49) below the phrase *kwa Maria* must be interpreted to mean 'Mary's place' and not simply 'Mary' herself.

(49) *Yohani y- ohere-je   ibaruwa kwa Maria.*
     John   he-send- asp letter   to   Mary
     'John sent a letter to Mary's house.'

The primary generalisations that Dative is designed to capture in English, then, simply do not exist in KR. Analogous claims hold for Benefactives. That is, it is not possible to construe a B with a preposition in KR. The closest preposition is *kubera*, which most accurately translates as 'because of'. Thus (50) does not mean that the action was done FOR Mary, but only BECAUSE of her — that is, Mary is some sort of indirect cause:

(50) *Yohani a- ra- andik-a kubera Maria.*
     John   he-pres-write-asp because Mary
     'John is writing the letter because of Mary.'

There is, however, another possible, if unobvious, source for benefactive DOs — namely, as possessor NPs. Thus (51) below has, in addition to the expected meaning, a benefactive reading:

(51) *Yohani y- a- buz-e   inzu ya Maria.*
     John   he-past-buy-asp house of Mary
     'John bought Mary's house.' **or** 'John bought a house for
                                     Mary.'

Furthermore, there is a transformation which promotes possessors of DOs to DO status; this transformation does introduce the *-ir-* affix on the verb:

(52) *Yohani y- a-   gur-i- ye Maria inzu.*
     John   he-past-buy-R-asp Mary house
     'John bought Mary's house.' **or** 'John bought Mary a house.'

Possessor-Promotion cannot be a general source for benefactives DOs, however, since the sentences it generates necessarily contain three NPs (the Su, the derived DO, and the old head of the possessive construction). Thus this transformation cannot generate derived DOs in sentences which are otherwise intransitive, as in (25b), repeated below:

(25) b. *Maria y- a-   byin- i- ye   umugabo.*
       Mary she-past-dance-B-asp man
       'Mary danced for the man.'

On the TOA, however, such sentences pose no problem. Their underlying structures simply contain a NP which bears the DO relation to the verb and also bears the (semantic) BENE-FACTIVE relation to the verb. (Recall that it is a general property of terms that a given term, like Su, may express many different semantic relations (AGENT, EXPERIENCER, etc.) to the verb in different sentences.

Also, note that in sentences generated by Posessor-Promotion the former possessed NP does not behave like a DO. That is, it cannot passivise to subject, relativise, etc. Thus from (52) we cannot form (53) or (54) and preserve the possessive reading. ((53) and (54) are acceptable, however, on the benefactive reading.)

(53) *Inzu Yohani y- a-   gúr- i- ye Maria
     house John   he-past-buy-B-asp Mary
     'the house of Mary's that John bought'
(54) *Inzu y-a-   gúr- i- w-   e   Maria(na Yohani).
     house it-past-buy-B-pass-asp Mary (by John)
     'The house of Mary's was bought by John.'

Thus Possessor-Promotion does not generate sentences with two apparent DOs and so is not the source for the benefactive DOs in sentences like (13a).

So far, then, TOA is to be preferred to PA on the grounds that PA requires the existence of two transformations for which the primary motivation is lacking.

2. PA and TOA differ in a second respect in regard to the analysis of (13a) ('John sent Mary a letter'). Namely, PA claims that, in the output of Dative, 'letter' bears no grammatical relation to the derived verb. Thus it should not have any of the properties characteristic of DOs in general. But, as we have seen on pp. 129-33, both the unmarked NPs after the verb appear to have all the properties characteristic of DOs in simple cases: both relativise, passivise, reflexivise, etc. It would appear, then, that 'letter' still does bear a DO relation to the verb and that, on the PA, the Relational Annihilation Law is violated, since the DO 'letter' was not demoted after Dative promoted the IO 'Mary' to DO status.

Some, but not all, of these data, however, can be expressed without relinquishing the PA, although only at the cost of considerable complication in the grammar. Consider for illustrative purposes the fact that both 'Mary' and 'letter' can passivise. We repeat the relevant examples for convenience of reference:

(13) a.   *Yohani yoher-er-eje Maria ibaruwa.*
     John   send- R-asp Mary letter
     'John sent the letter to Mary.'
(20) b.   *Ibaruwa yoher-er-ej- w-   e   Maria(na Yohani).*
     letter   sent- R-asp-pass-asp Mary (by John)
     'The letter was sent to Mary by John.'
    c.   *Maria yoher-er-ej- w-   e   ibaruwa(na Yohani).*
     Mary sent- R-asp-pass-asp letter   (by John)
     'Mary was sent the letter by John.'

(20c) can be easily generated on the PA by the simple application of Passive to the output of Dative. And (20b) can be generated by applying Passive first to 'letter', when it is still a DO, and then applying Dative, endowing the passive verb with a derived DO. Since the transformations in the cycle are unordered, both orders of application are possible.

But there are strong objections to this approach: first, recall that only terms in KR can relativise. But we do get relative clauses in which the P(atient) NP has been relativised and the R(ecipient) NP is present in surface as a DO:

(21) a.   *Nabonye ibaruwa Yohani yohér-er-eje Maria.*
       I-saw   letter   John   sent- R-asp Mary
       'I saw the letter that John sent Mary.'

To account for this fact (preserving the generalisation that only terms relativise) in the same way that the Passive facts above were accounted for, the PA would have to claim that 'letter' in (21a) was relativised when it was a DO, and then that Dative was applied. But 'letter' is relativised on a cycle higher than that determined by 'send'. Thus promotion of the supposed IO to DO could not be a strictly cyclic rule in violation of the cyclicity assumption. (See p. 00.)

PA could simply abandon the generalisation that only terms relativise, and say that only terms or demoted terms relativise. But this latter generalisation is also not correct; e.g. demoted subjects do not relativise:

(55) **umugabo abagore ba- a-   kúbis- w- e   (NA)*
       man   women they-past-strike- pass-asp (by)
       'the man whom the women were struck by'

Furthermore, there are object-creating rules in the language which do force the demotion of the old object, and that old object does not relativise (nor does it have any of the other properties of DOs). E.g. there is a rule which we call LOC which promotes locatives to DO status as in (56a-b) below, where they relativise, passivise, and otherwise behave as DOs should in KR:

(56) a.   *Yohani y- Ø- iish-e   impyisi mw-ishyamba.*
       John   he-past-kill-asp hyena in- forest   **Loc** ⇒
       'John killed a hyena in the forest.'

   b. *Yohani y- Ø- iish-e- mo ishyamba impyisi.*
       John   he-past-kill-asp-loc forest   hyena   **Pass** ⇒
       'John killed-in the forest a hyena.'
   c. *Ishyamba ry-Ø- iish-w- e- mo impyisi (na Yohani).*
       forest   it-past-kill-pass-asp-loc hyena (by John)
       'The forest was killed-in a hyena by John.'
   d. *Ishyamba Yohani y- Ø- iish-e- mo impysis.*
       forest   John   he-past-kill-asp-loc hyena
       'The forest that John killed-in a hyena.'

However, once the locative has been promoted to DO, as in (56b), the former DO becomes a nonterm, and can, for example, no longer relativise or passivise:

(57) a. **Nabonye impiyisi Yohani y- Ø- iish-e- mo ishyamba.*
        I-saw   hyena   John   he-past-kill-asp-loc forest
        'I saw the hyena that John killed-in the forest.'
    b. **Impyisi y-Ø- iish-w- e- mo ishyamba (na Yohani).*
        hyena   it-past-kill-pass-asp-loc forest   (by John)
        'The hyena was killed-in the forest by John.'

Thus on this approach the conditions of relativisation would have to specify that not only terms, but certain former terms created in certain ways (e.g. by Dative) but not in others (e.g. by Passive or Loc), can relativise. In our opinion, this unnecessarily complicates the statement of the conditions on relativisation. In the TOA both the P and the R in (13a) are DOs and so relativisation applies without problems. In (56b) the locative is a derived DO and the former DO, 'hyena', simply bears no grammatical relation to the verb and so does not undergo relativisation. And the generalisation that only terms relativise is preserved.

    Second, PA cannot adequately account for Object Pronoun Incorporation (OPI). Recall that nonterms do not take their pronouns infixed in the verb. But it is easy to have a patient pronoun infixed and a full NP recipient present:

(58) *Yohani y- a- y-oher-er-eje Maria.*
      John   he-past-it-send-R-asp Mary
      'John sent it to Mary.'

Surely the infixed pronoun -*y*- still bears the DO relation to the verb. And clearly 'Mary' is present, on the PA, as a derived DO. So, again the sentence appears to present two DOs and the Relational Annihilation Law would appear to have failed.

PA could perhaps argue here that once OPI has applied the verb somehow becomes intransitive and does not really have a DO. (This is the case that would be made for Reflexivisation.) Then another NP (e.g. the supposed IO in the underlying structure for (58)) would be free to be promoted to DO status. But this analysis is objectionable on several grounds (quite aside from the fact that we find no basis for saying that pronominal DOs are not 'really' DOs). For one thing, OPI cannot take place on the cycle determined by the verb of the clause in which the NPs to be pronominalised occur, for the controller of the pronominalisation will be specified on a higher cycle. Thus if the promotion of the putative IO occurs after OPI then, again, this process must not be strictly cyclic. Further, this approach creates problems in the generation of sentences like 'John sent it to her' (15c) — cases where the controller of the R is reached before the controller of the P. This will yield an intermediate stage at which we have (correctly) 'John sent her the letter'. But at this stage, initially, 'letter' is a nonterm since it has been demoted by Dative. It must now be repromoted to DO status! In other words, we have a DO which is demoted and then repromoted to DO, but we have no evidence of the stage at which it was a nonterm. Such a rule is totally opaque, and seems motivated solely by the desire to preserve the 'no more than one DO at a time' hypothesis. It is certainly difficult to see how children would acquire such a rule (but then again it's difficult to see how children acquire any rules).

Note further that the repromotion problem is not limited to the case concerning OPI. Even to generate a relative clause like 'the letter that Mary was sent', as in (59) below, we must either relativise 'letter':

(59) *ibaruwa Maria y- Ø- ohér-er-ej- w- e*
     letter   Mary   she-past-send-B-asp-pass-asp
     'the letter that Mary was sent'

when it is an original DO (assuming the generalisation that only terms relativise), in which case Dative and Passive must apply on the lower cycle after relativisation has applied on the higher cycle (a gross violation of strict cyclicity), or we must allow that 'letter' in 'Mary was sent the letter' be repromoted from nonterm status to DO again.

So far then, it seems to us that the comparison of the PA and the TOA weighs heavily in favour of TOA, for none of the problems cited above arise in the TOA. For instance, Passive applies exactly as we originally defined it. It selects any NP bearing the DO relation to the verb, makes it a Su in the derived sentence, and makes the former subject cease to bear any grammatical relation to the verb. The conditions of Relative Clause Formation are not problematic. The only condition we need (of concern here) is that whenever the structural description is met, the lower (see Note 4) NP must be a term (i.e. Su or DO). The cyclicity of the promotion rules is not endangered since, because we have multiple DOs in any case, there is no need to fiddle the derivation so that the right NP is a DO at the right time. And OPI is not problematic, since any NP which is a DO may undergo it. And since sentences may have more than one DO there is no problem saying that an object pronoun is still a DO.

3. There is a third point of comparison between the two approaches, however, which, on the basis of data so far presented, would appear to favour the PA over the TOA. In the TOA we need two ways to get the / ir/ marking on the verb. On the one hand, it arises by a kind of case-marking rule (to be discussed below), and, on the other hand it is introduced transformationally during Possessor-Promotion. In the PA, however, the verb is marked /ir/ only if an NP has been promoted to DO. Thus PA appears to give a uniform analysis of the source of /ir/ marking.

Unfortunately, further data show that there is no uniform source for /ir/ marking. Thus, in addition to signalling the presence of an underlying recipient or benefactive, /ir/ also signals optionally the presence of locatives. And these locatives need not be present as surface DOs. They may occur obliquely, carrying a preposition and not triggering any of the operations which are sensitive to DO-hood:

(60) *Umugabo a- ra- andik-ir-a ku meeza.*
     man   he-pres-write- L-asp on table
     'The man is writing on the table.'

On either approach we need two sources for *-ir-* marking, and in this respect neither approach is to be preferred to the other. We would like to stress, however, that regarding *-ir-* marking as a kind of case marking is natural in the sense that its properties resemble those of coding properties in other languages. Thus we want to say that a verb in underlying structure gets marked *-ir-* obligatorily when it has a R or a B NP, and optionally when it has a locative. In marking case partially or wholly on the verb, then, KR resembles Homeric Greek, Hungarian, and Machiguenga. In using the same case marker for different semantic roles KR resembles most, if not all, languages. In making case marking dependent on underlying semantic role KR resembles Hindi, Gugu-Yalanji, and Finnish. (See pp. 143-4.) In the marking of verb agreement KR resembles Kapampangan, in which verbs agree with underlying agents regardless of whether they are surface subjects, and Palauan (example 32), in which verbs agree with underlying patients, regardless of whether they are surface DOs. And finally, in sometimes case marking for DOs and sometimes not, KR resembles Hindi, Spanish, Hebrew (Givón 1975), and Malagasy (Keenan 1975a), in which DOs are sometimes marked and sometimes not.

4. A final point of comparison between PA and TOA concerns a very general constraint on promotion transformations, first enunciated in Perlmutter and Postal (1974). We will show that, on the PA but not on the TOA, KR violates this otherwise well-motivated constraint. The constraint, called the Advancee Tenure Law (ATL) in Perlmutter and Postal (1974), applies only to ADVANCEMENT rules. Advancement rules are promotions which affect only NPs in the domain of a given verb. Thus rules which promote DOs, IOs, and Obls to Su are advancement rules. So also are rules which promote IOs and Obls to DO. On the other hand, Possessor-Promotion, mentioned earlier, is not an advancement rule. (This rule, recall, converts sentences like *John took Mary's clothes* to *John took Mary the clothes*, promoting an underlying possessor to DO. But the underlying possessor is not in the domain of *took*. The only NPs in its domain are *John* and *Mary's clothes.*)

The ATL states, in effect, that a term derived by an advancement rule cannot be demoted by any other advancement rule (on any cycle). In fact, to the best of our knowledge, the ATL can be generalised as follows: *No derived term of any sort can be demoted by an advancement rule.*

The ATL receives very substantial support from many languages. E.g. in Tagalog and in Malagasy (Keenan 1972 and 1975a) basically any major NP in a clause can be advanced to subject. But once one NP has been so advanced no others can be.

On both the PA and the TOA, KR possesses several advancement to DO rules. We have already mentioned Loc, which converts locatives to DO. Another rule, Inst, which converts instrumental NPs to DOs, is illustrated below:

(61) a. *Yohani yandit-se ibaruwa n- ikaramu.*
        John   wrote- asp letter   with-pen
        'John wrote the letter with the pen.'
     b. *Yohani yandik-ish- ije ikaramu ibaruwa.*
        John   wrote- inst-asp pen   letter
        'John wrote-with the pen the letter.'

Further, the derived DO clearly behaves as a DO should in KR, e.g. it passivises and relativises:

(62) *Ikaramu y-andik-ish- ij- w- e   ibaruwa (na Yohani).*
     pen   it-write- inst-asp-pass-asp letter   (by John)
     'The pen was written-with a letter by John.'
(63) *Nabonye ikaramu Yohani y- Ø- andik-ish- ije ibaruwa.*
     I-saw   pen   John   he-past-write- inst-asp letter
     'I saw the pen that John wrote-with a letter.'

In addition, on the PA, but not on the TOA, there is a rule which converts IOs to DOs. On the PA, the ATL clearly predicts that no two of these rules can apply on the same cycle, for such a rule would necessarily demote a DO that was derived by an advancement rule (assuming the Relational Annihilation Law). The TOA does not necessarily make this prediction, since it allows multiple DOs and therefore does not require that a derived DO be demoted when something else has been promoted to DO status. And in fact, although there are severe constraints on the permissible combinations of derived DOs (see Kimenyi, in preparation, for discussion), it is possible to get sentences in which more than one DO has been derived.

(64) a. *Yohani y- a- andits-e ku meza n- ikaramu.*
        John   he-past-write- asp on table with-pen   ⇒ **Loc**
        'John wrote on the table with the pen.'

b. *Yohani y- a-   andits-e- ho ameza n-   ikaramu.*
   John he-past-write- asp-loc table with-pen   ⇒ **Inst**
   'John wrote on the table with the pen.'

c. *Yohani y- a-   andik-iish-ije- ho ameza ikaramu.*
   John he-past-write- inst-asp-loc table pen
   'John wrote on the table with the pen.'

We note that (64c), like its English translation, is ambiguous according to whether 'table' is merely the locus of the action or actually receives the writing, as in the sence of INSCRIBE. The sentences which have undergone Loc above (64b and 64c) have only the inscribe sense.

Consequences for Universal Grammar

The facts cited in the previous section argue, persuasively, we feel, in favour of the TOA over the PA. And this in turn supports our original suggestion that the Relational Hierarchy — $Su > DO > IO > nonterm$ — merely stipulates a set of possible grammatical relations out of which a language may choose. But a language is not obliged to opt for all of these relations; in particular, IO may be lacking, as in KR. Further, we have supported the nonuniqueness claim that a language may present more than one NP in a given grammatical relation, e.g. the DO relation, to its verb.

Thus in a RG for any language we will require a specification of which particular grammatical relations it uses and what the minimum and maximum number of permissible NPs of any given relation are in an arbitrary sentence. Indeed, these two facts can be incorporated in a single statement. Thus the min-max pairs for English would be: $Su(1, 1)$; $DO(0, 1)$; $IO(0, 1)$; $OBL(0, \infty)$.[9] That is, any sentence (in underlying structure) must have at least one Su and at most one Su; possibly zero DOs and at most one, etc. The min-max pairs for KR might be: $Su(1, 1)$; $DO(0, 2)$; $IO(0, 0)$; $OBL(0, \infty)$. (We discuss the status of two as the max number for DOs in KR below.)

Accepting our case as proven for the moment, the consequences of allowing more than one NP to bear the same grammatical relation to a verb are perhaps less severe than expected. Although we have not investigated all the constraints imposed on RG in Perlmutter and Postal (1974), the principle consequence of the nonuniqueness hypothesis seems to affect only the Relational Annihilation Law. Thus, if a language allows more than one DO and it promotes an NP to DO in a sentence containing only one DO, does the original DO necessarily get demoted or not? It seems to us that the RAL simply has no prediction to make here. Perhaps the original DO's relation is taken over, in which case there is a demotion to nonterm status, or perhaps it is the available DO relation which is now filled. Note that even in Perlmutter and Postal (1974) it is necessary to allow that an advancement to DO does not create a nonterm in cases where the original sentence did not have a DO to begin with. Thus the application of Inst in (65a) could not create a nonterm:

(65) a. *Yohani y- a- hiin- ze n- isuka.*
         John   he-past-cultivate-asp with-hoe
         'John cultivated with the hoe.'
    b. *Yohani y- a- hiing- iish-ije isuka.*
         John   he-past-cultivate-inst-asp hoe
         'John cultivates-with the hoe.'

Further, it appears that KR illustrates both possibilities. We have already shown that when Loc applies to an already transitive sentence the old DO becomes a nonterm. When Inst applies to a transitive sentence, however, the promoted NP acquires the DO properties, as already exhibited in (61)-(63), and the former DO retains its DO properties. Thus from (66a), generated by Inst, we can passivise and relativise the old DO:

(66) a. *Yohani yandik-ish- ije ikaramu ibaruwa.*
         John   wrote- inst-asp pen   letter
         'John wrote-with a pen a letter.'
    b. *Ibaruwa y-andik-ish- ij- w- e ikaramu (na Yohani).*
         letter   it-write- inst-asp-pass-asp pen   (by John)
         'The letter was written-with a pen by John.'
    c. *Nabonye ibaruwa Yohani y- andik-ish- ije ikaramu.*
         I-saw   letter   John   he-wrote-inst-asp pen
         'I saw the letter that John wrote-with a pen.'

We might then have to abandon the RAL in light of the KR facts. This would mean that for each promotion rule we would have to specify whether or not an NP gets demoted. However, abandoning the RAL totally does not seem warranted, i.e., even in KR it still applies unequivocally to advancement to subject rules. We would like to suggest, as an hypothesis for further research, a weaker version of the RAL — the Weak Relational Annihilation Law (WRAL). To state it we will first define the VALENCE of a grammatical relation X to be the maximum number of full NPs which can simultaneously bear the relation X to a given verb in a RELATIONALLY PRIMITIVE sentence. A sentence is relationally primitive just in case no term-changing rules are involved in its derivation.

The Weak Relational Annihilation Law

If, in a given language, L, application of a promotion to X rule exceeds the valence of X in L, then one of the Xs is demoted to non-term status.

The WRAL, still requires, then, that promotion to subject rules in KR demote the old subject, since the valence of Su is one, and if the old subject were not demoted then the derived sentence would have two subjects. On the other hand, promotion to DO rules in KR need not demote old DOs, since these rules need not result in exceeding the valence of DO, which is two. In this sense the WRAL is a kind of weak structure-preserving constraint, a point made in Kimenyi (in preparation). An advancement to DO rule can result in two DOs only if the language independently allows two DOs. The WRAL is clearly much weaker than the RAL, however, since it allows that a promotion to X rule demote an old X even if the valence of X is not exceeded. This is in fact what Loc does in KR.

The WRAL seems to us largely correct for KR. Of the many ways we might expect to be able to generate a sentence with more than two full NP DOs (and KR has at least two more promotion to DO rules than we have considered here), all are generally blocked in one way or another. Note, however, that most of the expected derivations satisfy WRAL vacuously. That is, if a sentence like (67a) below already has two DOs, then it is now generally the case that a promotion to DO rule applies demoting one of the former DOs:

(67) a. *Y- a- andik-i- ye Maria ibaruwa n- ikaramu.*
       he-past-write- R-asp Mary letter   with-pen
       'He wrote a letter to Mary with the pen.'

b.   * *Y- a-   andik-ish- ir-ije ikaramu Maria ibaruwa.*
      he-past-write-inst-R-asp pen   Mary letter
      'He wrote-with the pen a letter to Mary.'

Rather, some constraint prevents the promotion rule from applying. The WRAL (and the RAL) in no wise rule out such constraints. In fact, the Advancee Tenure Law is one presumably universal such constraint. Thus, to take a simple case, if the input structure to an advancement to Su rule were met, but the current Su were derived, then the advancement rule would be prevented from applying.

Furthermore, even acknowledging that we have not pursued in depth the various ways in which more than two DOs might be created, we must note one case that may violate even the WRAL. Namely, if some of the NPs bearing the DO relation to the verb are pronominal then we easily get more than two DOs. Note the following example, taken from Kimenyi (in preparation):

(68) *Y- a-   yi-ki-bi-ba-   andik-iish-ir-ije- ho.*
       he-past-it- it- it- them-write-inst-B-asp-loc
       'He wrote it on it with it for them.'

Such a sentence has clearly had two underlying DOs; it evidences two promotions to DO, namely, Inst and Loc. A considerably more detailed investigation of the constraints on such multiple promotion to object rules is being undertaken in Kimenyi (in preparation), and we refer the reader to that source for further consideration of these problems.

Conclusion, and an Alternate Hypothesis

We have argued that unmarked Patient and Recipient-Benefactive NPs in Kinyarwanda share an overwhelming number of syntactic properties and hence should not be considered to bear distinct grammatical relations to the verb, but rather should be viewed as subtypes of the same grammatical relation. If P and R-B NPs do not bear distinct grammatical relations to the verb, then the Promotional Analysis is *a fortiori* incorrect. And, we have argued, the Two Objects Analysis is preferable.

However, as Peter Cole (personal communication) has pointed

out, there is an alternative to the TOA which is also prima facie plausible. Namely, we regard unmarked P and R-B NPs as bearing DO and IO relations to the verb, respectively and simply note that in KR their transformational properties are almost identical. But there are, of course, two differences. The IO shows a strong preference for preceding the DO and it triggers the *-ir-* marking on the verb. The *-ir-* marking can be regarded as a dative or an IO case marker, but on the verb, not on the NP.

Concerning case marking, however, we cannot regard the *-ir-* marker as coding the grammatical relation of IO. We have already seen (example 62) that *-ir-* may signal the presence of a locative which is not a DO. Furthermore, Alessandro Duranti (personal communication) has pointed out to us some cases of verbs — e.g. 'want', 'like', and 'win' — which lexically select R-B subjects, as in (69):

(69) *Yohani y- a-   tsiind-i-   ye   igiheembo.*
     John   he-past-win-   R-B-asp   award
     'John won the award.'

This is clear evidence that *-ir-* does not code grammatical relations but only semantic relations: if an R-B is present, regardless of its grammatical role, mark the verb with *-ir-*.

Note further that sentences like (69) passivise, as in (70):

(70) *Igiheembo cy-a-   tsiind-i-   w-   e   na Yohani.*
     award   it- past-win-   R-B past-asp by John
     'The award was won by John.'

Thus, if the R-B subject in (69) were derived by an advancement rule (70) would be a further violation of the Advancee Tenure Law. And since the ATL is well-motivated we have further support that *-ir-* is not a reflex of an advancement to subject rule.

Consequently, the putative DO and IO on the alternate hypothesis do not differ with regard to grammatical case marking, and part of the apparent support for that hypothesis is nonexistent. The grammatical case marking of the two NPs is identical, namely, zero. Thus we are left with only the word-order difference in basic sentences to distinguish DOs and IOs on the alternate hypothesis. And, in the face of the overwhelming syntactic similarity of P and R-B NPs, this difference is not great enough to warrant making a distinction in grammatical category. A minor difference in coding properties (position, verb agreements, and case marking) can be naturally attributed to subcategory differences between NPs bearing the same grammatical relation to the verb. We have already indicated that in Hindi, for example, different subclasses of subject NPs differ in case marking (ergative versus unmarked) and in control of verb agreement (ergative NPs do not trigger subject agreement on the verb, while unmarked subjects normally do). Further examples where subcategories of a given grammatical relation bear different positions are not hard to find. For example, in Hungarian (Katalin Radics, personal communication) definite DOs follow the verb and trigger object agreement. Indefinite nonspecific DOs precede the verb and do not trigger object agreement:

(71) a. *a férfi ver-i   az asszony-t.*
         the man hit-3sg 3sg the woman-acc
         'The man is hitting the woman.'
     b. *a férfi néhány asszony-t ver-Ø.*
         the man some   woman-acc hit-3sg
         'The man is hitting some woman.'

Thus linearisation rules which place different subcategories of NPs bearing the same grammatical relation to the verb in different positions are not unnatural, and the alternate hypothesis is largely unsupported relative to the Two Objects Analysis which we have proposed.

Acknowledgement

We wish to thank Alexandre Kimenyi, not only for having served as our informant, but for substantive contributions concerning the theoretical claims we have made. We also thank him for having made available his unpublished papers on Kinyarwanda.

Notes

1. We refer to languages which exhibit serial verb constructions, such as Akan and many other West African languages, as well as Thai, Vietnamese, and a number of other languages of South Asia. In such languages *John killed the chicken with a knife* might be rendered as *John use knife kill chicken*, and *John brought the book to Bill* as *John take book go Bill.* The apparently simplex

sentence presents two verbs, both of which occur independently in that form as single verbs of main clauses. For some discussion of the analysis of such constructions within a 'classical' transformational framework see Schachter (1974).

2. We should note, however, that there is a very restricted class of locatives that can passivise more or less directly. In all examples the verb is otherwise intransitive. The promoted locative retains its locative marking and the subject-verb agreement becomes impersonal, taking *ha-*, which is morphologically invariant (examples from Kimenyi, in preparation):

(i) *Umukoobwa y- iica-ye kuu ntebe.*
girl   she-sit- asp on chair
'The girl is sitting on the chair.'

(ii) *Kuu ntebe h- iica-w- e n- umukoobwa.*
on chair imp-sit- pass-asp by-girl
'The chair is sat on by the girl.'

3. In Note 2 we mentioned a small class of locatives which undergo a kind of partial passivisation (locative marker retained on NP, verb impersonal). These NPs may also directly relativise, although the analysis is problematic, because a locative suffix is optionally present on the verb. This could be interpreted as indicating that the locative has first been promoted to DO status, an operation that is independently justified in the language (see p. 151) and then relativised, which would somehow allow that the promotion to object marker could be deleted. As in the passive case, the 'promoted' NP retains its locative marking, but here the verb retains its normal agreement with its subject (examples from Kimenyi, in preparation):

(i) *Umugore a- ryaam-ye mu gitaanda.*
woman   she-lie-   asp in bed
'The woman is lying in bed.'

(ii) *Mu gitaanda umugore a- ryaam-ye-(mo).*
in bed   woman she-lie-   asp-(loc)
'the bed in which the woman is lying'

4. It is allowed that the NPs in a domain *D* be themselves relational structures, although we shall not discuss such structures explicitly in this article. E.g. the RS underlying *John thinks that Fred left* would have *thinks* as its V_D and two NPs in its domain — *John* and the RS of *Fred left*. Like other NPs, as we discuss immediately above, sentential NPs may bear both grammatical and semantic relations to the V_D. Thus the NP (*that*) *Fred left* above would be a grammatical DO of *think*. Semantically it might be in, say, the CONTENT relation to *think*, indicating that it expresses the content of the thought.

Using this formalism, then, we have natural definitions of CLAUSEMATE and BE IN A HIGHER CLAUSE THAN. Thus two NPs are CLAUSEMATES just in case they are members of the same domain. And *X* IS IN AN IMMEDIATELY HIGHER CLAUSE THAN *Y* just in case *Y* is in the domain of some NP — *Z* — and *Z* and *X* are clausemates. Clearly, then, a notion equivalent to COMMAND can be defined on the underlying structures in RG. Note, however, that the formalism would have to be extended to represent structures for sentences containing two verbs, like *John came early and left late*, as well as for sentences containing the series verb constructions discussed above.

5. The term grammatical RELATION is perhaps slightly inaccurate in the framework of Perlmutter and Postal (1974), since they require that an NP bearing such a relation to a given verb be unique (if there is any at all). Such 'relations',

then, are more accurately referred to as (partial) FUNCTIONS defined on the set of domains. The term relation is more accurate in our proposals, however, since we allow in principle that more than one NP may bear a given relation to the verb of a given domain.
    6. Examples from Lee Trithart (Personal communication).
    7. Boyd Mikailovsky (personal communication) points out to us, however, that the class of such verbs is very small, perhaps being restricted to 'forget'. Most verbs which would take experiencer subjects, like *jānnā* 'to know', cannot be constructed in the perfective, and since perfectivity is another prerequisite for ergativity, would not be present in an ergative format in any case.
    8. Examples from E.J.W. Barber (personal communication).
    9. '∞' means 'unbounded'.

References

Craig, C. (1975) *Jacaltec Syntax: A Study of Complex Sentences*, unpublished doctoral dissertation, Harvard University, Cambridge, Massachusetts.

Foley, B. (1975) 'Comparative Austronesian Syntax and Linguistic Theory', presented at Linguistics Colloquium, University of California, Los Angeles, California.

Givón, T. (1975) 'Promotion, Accessibility and the Typology of Case Marking', unpublished paper, preliminary draft, University of California, Los Angeles, California, and Stanford University, Stanford, California.

Hershberger, H. (1964) 'Case-Marking Affixes in Gugu-Yalanji', in R. Pittman and H. Kerr, (eds.) *Papers on the Languages of the Australian Aborigines*, Australian Institute of Aboriginal Studies, Canberra.

Johnson, D. (1974a) 'Prepaper on Relational Constraints on Grammars', unpublished paper, Mathematical Sciences Department, IBM Thomas J. Watson Research Center, Yorktown Heights, New York.

—— (1974b) 'On Relational Constraints on Grammars', unpublished paper, IBM Thomas J. Watson Research Centre, Yorktown Heights, New York.

Keenan, E.L. (1972) 'Relative Clause Formation in Malagasy (and some related and some not so related) Languages', in P. Peranteau, J.N. Levi, and G.C. Phares (eds.) *The Chicago Which Hunt* Chicago Linguistic Society, University of Chicago, Illinois.

—— (1975a) 'Remarkable Subjects in Malagasy', in C. Li (ed.) *Subject and Topic*, Academic Press, New York, pp. 247-303.

—— (1975b) 'Towards a Universal Definition of "Subject of"' in C. Li (ed.) *Subject and Topic*, Academic Press, New York.

—— and B. Comrie (1972 and 1977) 'Noun-Phrase Accessibility and Universal Grammar', presented to the 1972 Annual Meeting, Linguistic Society of America; also in *Linguistic Inquiry*, 8, 1.

Kimenyi, A. (in preparation) *Topics in the Relational Grammar of Kinyarwanda*, chs. 1-3, doctoral dissertation, University of California, Los Angeles, California.

Lawler, J. (1975) 'On Coming to Terms in Achenese: The Function of Verbal Dis-Agreement' in R.E. Grossman, L.J. Sam, and T.J. Vance (eds.) *Papers from the Parasession on Functionalism*, Chicago Linguistic Society, University of Chicago, Chicago, Illinois.

Li, C. and S. Thompson (1975) 'Subject and Word Order in Wappo', unpublished paper, University of California, Los Angeles, California.

Mirikitani, L. (1972) 'Kapampangan Syntax', *Oceanic Linguistics* No. 10.

Munro, P. (1974) *Topics in Mojave Syntax*, unpublished doctoral dissertation, University of California, San Diego, California.

Schachter, P. (1974) 'A Non-Transformational Account of Serial Verbs', *Studies in African Linguistics*, Supplement 5.

Snell, B. and R. Wise (1963) 'Noncontingent Declarative Clauses in Machiguenga (Arawak)', *Studies in Peruvian Indian Languages* 1, 103-45, Summer Institute of Linguistics, University of Oklahoma, Norman, Oklahoma.

Starosta, S. (1973) 'The Faces of Case', *Language Sciences* 25, 1-14, Research Center for the Language Sciences, Indiana University, Bloomington, Indiana.

Trithart, L. (1975) 'Relational Grammar and Chicewa Subjectivisation Rules', in R.E. Crossman, L.J. Sam, and T.J. Vance (eds.) *Papers from the Eleventh Regional Meeting of the Chicago Linguistic Society*, University of Chicago, Chicago, Illinois.

Woodbury, A. (1975) *Ergativity of Grammatical Processes: A Study of Greenlandic Eskimo*, unpublished Master's essay, University of Chicago, Chicago, Illinois.

6 SEMANTIC CORRELATES OF THE ERGATIVE/ ABSOLUTIVE DISTINCTION[1]

I present below a battery of semantic properties which *absolutives* (subjects of intransitive verbs and direct objects of transitive ones) have in common to the exclusion of subjects of transitive verbs. These properties are broadly characterised in terms of *bondedness to the verb, thematic role*, and *control phenomena*. In consequence we may regard languages in which case marking and verb agreement operate on an ergative/absolutive basis as codifying these semantic properties in surface.

Following (by now) standard usage we shall say that a linguistic phenomenon is *ergative* (or *ergative/absolutive*) if it treats subjects of intransitive predicates and direct objects of transitive ones in the same way to the distinction of subjects of transitive predicates. For example, a case marking system is ergative if subjects of intransitive predicates, which we denote by S_i, and direct objects (DOs) of transitive predicates are marked in the same way *and* the subject S_t of transitive predicates is case marked differently. We use the term *absolutive* to refer to S_i and DO collectively. Ergative phenomena contrast with *nominative* (or *nominative/accusative*) ones in which subjects, both S_i and S_t, are treated identically to the distinction of DO. Thus a typical nominative/accusative case marking system will mark S_i and S_t identically and use a distinct marker for DO.

Ergative phenomena, in particular case marking, were once thought (ethnocentrically) to be rare and exotic. However, given the extensive descriptive work in recent years, we now know that ergative case marking systems as well as ergative verb agreement systems enjoy a wide distribution across the world's languages, both in terms of areal and of genetic distribution. See the extensive discussion in Plank (1979) and references cited there for corroboration of this point.

A plausible explanation for the distribution of ergative phenomena comes from S.R. Anderson (1976, 1977a). He observes first that ergative phenomena are largely limited to ones, such as case marking and verb agreement, which are reflected in the surface morphology of languages. While there are some non-accidental exceptions to this claim — see Dixon (1979) and Larson and Norman (1979) — Anderson's own data and those of later researchers (Blake 1979; Li and Lang 1979; and E. Moravcsik, 1978) support the general correctness of the claim. Anderson further observes that surface marking patterns of an ergative/ absolutive sort, especially case marking, are generally limited to verb peripheral languages — ones which place the verb either initially or finally in the least marked sentence types of the language.

He suggests then that case marking paradigms have a perceptual function in that they enable speakers to discriminate the two major actants in a transitive clause. If S_t receives a marker we will have an ergative system (DO remaining unmarked, and S_i not needing any particular mark as it is the only major actant in simple intransitive sentences). If DO gets marked we have a nominative/accusative system with S_i and S_t being unmarked. We note that Comrie (1981, 119-20) also supports this line of explanation.

This reasoning seems to me plausible. In particular it gives an account of several of the distributional facts concerning ergative phenomena. It accounts for their prominence in verb peripheral languages and their relative absence in verb medial ones as follows: in verb medial languages (SVO being the most wide-spread type here) the position of S_t and DO relative to the verb in basic sentences is distinctive, and the distinctness is preserved under major perturbations such as NP fronting and deletion. Deleting either S_t or DO yields a surface form which lacks either a preverbal or a postverbal NP so we may reconstruct which NP was deleted. Similarly with fronting. If the S_t is fronted we remain with an SVO order. If the DO is fronted the derived form lacks again a postverbal NP, so it must have been the DO which was fronted.

On the other hand, in verb peripheral languages, position relative to the verb does not enable us to determine which NP was deleted or fronted. If we delete either S_t or DO from an SOV structure we are in each case left with a structure of the form NP+V, so in the absence of distinctive case marking on the NPs it is difficult to reconstruct unambiguously which of S_t or DO was deleted. Similarly, if we front the DO we are still left with a structure of the form NP+NP+V so mere position relative to the verb does not even enable us to tell whether fronting has occurred or not. The initial NP might be S_t, if no fronting occurred, or it might be DO if fronting occurred. An analogous analysis holds for verb initial languages. Deleting either S_t or DO leaves the same surface string: V+NP. And fronting of either NP in both cases yields the same surface string NP+V+NP. So once again distinctive case marking of S_t and DO enables one to reconstruct the identity of subjects and objects under the common perturbations of basic word order.

Furthermore, the arbitrariness of choosing S_t or DO to mark in transitive structures accounts for the most widespread type of ergative/absolutive marking systems: the one in which S_t receives an overt mark and both S_i and DO are unmarked. There is on this view no perceptual advantage in marking S_i since we do not need to distinguish it from any other major NP.

On the other hand, something more must be said here about what appears to me to be the most common type of nominative/accusative case marking system (a more extensive investigation is needed here): S_i and S_t are overtly marked (the same) and DO is overtly marked (differently). The reasoning analogous to the previous case would predict merely that DO had an overt mark and S_i and S_t were unmarked (a reasoning which Comrie (1981) accepts).

Additional rationale for overtly marking both S_i and S_t is not hard to find. In Keenan (1976) it is shown that subjects, whether S_i or S_t, present a large battery of syntactic and semantic properties in common. Overtly marking these NPs then would be a surface coding of those properties. It would thus enable language users to better retrieve the antecedents or controllers of reflexives and other anaphors, coreferential deletions, etc. We refer the reader to that work for detailed discussion.

Our concern in this paper is to determine whether there is a comparable battery of properties for absolutives (S_i and DO) — properties which they have in distinction to transitive subjects, and which then can be understood as coded in surface by uniform case marking. We argue here that there is such a battery of properties. Unsurprisingly, given Anderson's observation concerning the surfacy nature of ergative/absolutive phenomena, these properties are largely semantic in nature.[2] We will note, however, a few cases where the surface manifestation of these properties is more extensive than the discussion of case marking above would lead us to expect.

For mnemonic reasons we present these semantic properties under three headings: 1 *Bondedness to the Verb*, 2 *Thematic Role*, and 3 *Control Phenomena*. These categories are not intended as either exhaustive or exclusive. Several examples we cite illustrate points from more than one category.

1. Bondedness to the Verb

1.1 Existence Dependency

The referent of a transitive subject S_t normally exists independently of the activity expressed by the predicate. But this is often not the case for absolutive NPs, where the activity expressed by the predicate may express the coming into existence of a referent for such NPs. (1)-(3) illustrate this for S_is.

(1) a. A puddle formed on the floor.
     b. A crowd gathered around John.
(2) a. A fire broke out in the West wing of Haines Hall yesterday.
     b. A breeze sprang up and fanned the flames.[3]
(3) a. A tragic accident took place/happened/occurred yesterday on the corner of 4th and Main.

In (1) the existence of the puddle and the crowd is not independent of the act of forming or gathering. Similarly the fire and the breeze in (2) do not exist independently of the action of breaking out or springing up. The point is even more obvious in (3).

The sentences in (4) illustrate that the referent of a DO may not exist independently of the activity expressed by the transitive verb:

(4) a. A student lit a fire in the basement.
     b. He committed a crime/made a mistake.
     c. He took a walk/gave a lecture/hummed a little ditty/ told a lie.

Again, the fire does not exist independently of the lighting (but the student, S_t, does). Nor does the crime exist independently of the committing, or the mistake of the making, or the ditty of the humming, or the lie of the telling.

What examples (1)-(4) have in common is that the predicates are semantically weak, saying little more than that an event took place, though sometimes incorporating some notion of the manner in which the event took place. It is the absolute NP in these examples which in some sense actually gives the content of the predication. But such content sharing by and large does not seem to extend from transitive verbs to their S_t subjects, as noted above for (4a).

I am not claiming of course that absolutives always designate referents which come into existence as a function of the activity expressed by the predicate, but only that this is a possibility for absolutives in a way in which it is not for transitive subjects. It thus indicates one way in which absolutive arguments form a closer unit with the predicate than do S_ts.

1.2 Multiple Senses

It is very common that the 'sense' of a predicate varies with the semantic nature of the referent of an absolutive argument, but much less common to find such variation with S_ts.

More specifically, we find, for common everyday predicates, that exactly what is predicated of an absolutive argument varies with the semantic nature of that argument. This sort of variation appears to occur only infrequently with transitive subjects. (5) below illustrates this for S_i:

(5)   a.   John/the horse is still running.
      b.   The car motor/my watch is still running.
      c.   The tap/my nose is still running.
      d.   My Fair Lady/the Braque exhibition is still running.

In (5a) *run* predicates both external movement of the S_i, that is, change of location, however momentary, relative to things which are not John or the horse, as well as internal movement, that is, movement of the parts of the S_i. In (5b) no predication of external movement is made. At best one of internal movement is. In (5c) no movement of any sort is predicated of the referent of the S_i itself, but only of some other object of an appropriate sort whose existence can be inferred from the nature of (the referent of) the S_i. And in (5d) no notion of physical movement is present at all. *run* there means something like 'be available for public enjoyment'.

Note that it does not seem appropriate here to say that *run* is four (further senses are not hard to find) ways ambiguous. The difference in the interpretation of *run* in these examples is conditioned by the nature of the object it is being predicated of. It is like a numerical function f whose value at x is x^2 if x is even and x^3 if x is odd. There is just one function, but it assigns values differently according to the nature of the argument.

To see that a similar sort of interpretative dependency obtains between transitive predicates and DOs consider:

(6)   a.   John cut his arm/his foot.
      b.   John cut his nails/his hair/the lawn.
      c.   John cut his cake/the roast.
      d.   John cut a path (through the field)/a tunnel (through the mountain).
      e.   John cuts his whisky with water/his marijuana with tea.
      f.   The company cut production quotas/prices.

If the DO of *cut* is an animal or a largish body part *cut* means something like 'make an incision in the surface of'. The integrity of the object cut is understood to be preserved — it still exists. No notion of intentionality is implied — John can cut Mary either intentionally or accidentally and in each case the adverb adds new, non-contradictory information. On the other hand, if the DO of *cut* denotes 'filamentous' objects, such as hair, grass, etc. as in (6b), we do understand, in distinction to the sense of *cut* in (6a), that the object was cut all the way through, not just made an incision in the surface of. Integrity is still preserved, but some notion of purpose is implied. *cut* in this sense means something like 'trim', 'cut for the purpose of beautifying'.

If the DO of *cut* is a prepared foodstuff, like a cake or a roast as in (6c), we find a sense of purpose, as with the sense in (6b), as *cut* here means something like 'divide into portions for purposes of serving'. But no sense of 'beautifying' is present. Moreover, in distinction to both the earlier senses, the integrity of the object cut is by and large destroyed. Once you have cut the roast you cannot, by and large, cut it again. Nor of course can you be said to have cut the roast if you only made an incision in the surface of it. So the sense of *cut* in (6c) is different from those used in (6a) and (6b).

In (6d) we see that the DO of *cut*, the path or the tunnel, is in no sense itself dismembered. Rather what is cut is something else (the field or the mountain). The path, etc. is *created by cutting* (cf 1.1). In (6e) the DO of *cut* is a mass object which is ingestible, and the sense of *cut* is something like 'decrease the potency of by admixing a physically comparable substance'. The sense here is obviously different from the previous ones. For example the instruments that can be used for cutting in (6a) to (6d) are quite different in nature from the 'instrument' (water, tea) in (6e). Finally, we note that the sense of *cut* used in (6f) is something like 'reduce the value of along a (more or less) continuous dimension', the DO of course denoting something which can be measured or evaluated in such a way.

In short, we adjust our interpretation of *cut* to the nature of the object we are cutting. Examples of this sort are discussed more extensively and for a broader range of categories in Keenan (1979). Here we merely note that the sort of sense dependency discussed only seems to arise (for the cases of interest to us) between predicates and absolutive arguments. The reader may try choosing a transitive verb plus object and varying the subject to test for alternate sense, but in the many cases I have tried relatively little variation showed up.[4] By contrast dictionaries commonly list very many senses for common verbs such as *run* and *cut* where the sense varies with the nature of the absolutive argument.

Once again then we have a close interpretative bond between predicates and absolutives but relative independence of interpretation between predicates and S_is.

1.3 Selectional Restrictions and Verbal Classifiers

As noted by Moravcsik (1978) predicates in a language may impose highly specific selectional restrictions on absolutive arguments but typically only impose weak and rather general restrictions such as humanness, animacy or concreteness on S_is. Moreover the restrictions imposed on S_i and DOs are highly similar. Perhaps this is at least part of the reason so many verbs in English can be used both intransitively and transitively.

For example, the sorts of things which can spill (intransitive) are the sorts of things which someone can spill (transitive). At a guess they are limited to liquids and quantities of relatively small granular objects such as coffee grounds. But I know of no transitive verb whose subjects must denote in that class. The sorts of things one can peel$_{tr}$ easily and that can peel$_{intr}$ easily must have some sort of tegument. But we know of no transitive verb which requires that its subject have a tegument. Similarly the sorts of things that can shatter$_{intr}$ and that one can shatter$_{tr}$ must have a rather specific physical character — one not to my knowledge required by any transitive verb of its subject.

Checking different pairs of verbs we may note that the kinds of things that can stink are the kinds you can smell, the kinds that flutter are the kinds you can wave, the kinds that explode are the kinds you can blow up, etc. Again in each case we know of no transitive verb that requires its subject to be one that emits an odour, or is wavable, or explodable, etc.

It seems clear then that given an arbitrary predicate in English we may infer more about the semantic nature of its absolutive arguments than we can about its S_t (if the predicate is transitive). So once again we have a case for a tighter link between predicates and absolutives than between predicates and transitive subjects.

A phenomenon semantically similar to selectional restrictions but morphologically more regular is evidenced by the 'object' classifiers on verbs in various Amerindian languages. These are verbal affixes which require that various arguments of the verb satisfy one or another semantic condition. For example, Navaho (Hoijer 1964, cited in Moravcsik 1978) has six such affixes which, when applied to transitive roots, indicate that the DO is a round solid object, a long slender object, a wool-like mass, a mud-like mass, etc. Similarly when applied to intransitive roots they indicate that the referent of the S_i has these properties. It appears however that they do not function to classify properties of S_ts. Larson and Norman (1979) cite Mayan languages quite generally as possessing such classifiers, again restricted to absolutives. They further cite Hoijer (1946) to the effect that Cherokee and Chipewyan (Athabascan) also present such classifiers similarly restricted. Finally Klamath (Mary Louise Kean, personal communication) also presents such classifiers, again restricted to absolutives.

Clearly then these languages overtly codify the notion absolutive in their morphology.

1.4 Noun Incorporation

Noun incorporation is a process whereby a noun phrase is physically incorporated within the verbal structure. (7a,b) from Kitonemuk, taken from Mardirussian (1975), is illustrative:

(7) a. a- kəm a- ho- j
         he make he hole DO
         'He digs his hole'
     b. a- ho- kəm
         he-hole- make
         'He hole-digs'

Typically the incorporated noun is understood as non-referential, lacks determiners, is not a proper noun, and participates in whatever phonological properties, e.g. vowel harmony, may affect complex words. We refer the reader to Mardirussian (1975) for a more detailed survey of the properties of incorporation.

What is of interest for our purposes is that the verb + incorporated noun seems to form a single semantic unit. We note in this regard that if the verb was transitive and it was the DO that was incorporated, the derived verb is intransitive. So e.g. if the language is ergative/absolutive in case marking, the subject of the verb in such a case will be absolutive not ergative (Comrie 1973). We might expect then that of the various NP arguments of predicates it would be absolutives that would be the easiest to incorporate as they already form a closer unit with the verb than do transitive subjects. Mardirussian explicitly supports that claim and gives examples of incorporation of S_i and DO but not of S_t. We note that the most often cited examples of noun incorporation involve DOs. So further work is necessary to determine whether S_is are fairly generally accessible to incorporation to the exclusion of S_ts. Still, the survey in Mardirussian covers a reasonable number of languages, so we may conclude on the basis of our knowledge to date that the incorporation facts support the claim that absolutives are more closely bonded to their predicates than transitive subjects. (I note as well that while Mardirussian does not cite the basic word order of the languages he illustrates incorporation with, the examples of his with which I am independently familiar are all verb terminal' e.g. Sora and Turkish are verb final, Fijian and Malagasy are verb initial. If this correlation turns out to be correct it would further support a link between incorporation and ergative/ absolutive phenomena.)

2. Thematic Role Properties

By thematic role we understand relations such as Agent, Patient, Recipient, Beneficiary, etc. which NP arguments of predicates may bear to the action or state expressed by the predicate. We use the term loosely enough to cover the use of *theme* as developed in Gruber (1956, 1976) and utilised in Jackendoff (1972) and Anderson (1977b).

2.1 Patient

Absolutives, both S_i and DO, are commonly Patients in the sense that their existence state is understood to be affected by the action expressed by the predicate. S_t is rarely if ever a Patient in this sense. The examples in (8) illustrate cases where the referent of the S_i has its existence state so affected. In particular it goes out of existence or moves in that direction.

(8)   a.   The car exploded/broke down.
      b.   The milk evaporated/spilled.
      c.   The wheat withered and blew away.
      d.   John disappeared/vanished/perished/died in Butan.
      e.   Fred's argument collapsed/fell apart.
      f.   The house is decaying/rotting away.

That DOs may function as Patients is of course well known. (See Hopper and Thompson 1980 for an extensive discussion). We cite the examples below to illustrate cases where the referent of the DO goes out of existence or moves in that direction and thus which are similar in this sense to those in (8) above:

(9)   John blew up the car/drank the milk/ate the cheese/killed the cat/broke the vase/destroyed Fred's argument/removed the stain.

Again, we find it difficult to find transitive verbs whose subjects undergo a loss of existence in virtue of the activity presented by the predicate.[5] More typically subjects of transitive verbs are thematically Agents, Instruments, or Experiencers and somewhat less frequently Locatives, Temporals, and Possessors, but not Patients. The point is the more significant given that English seems quite generous with respect to which semantic roles it allows subjects to have. See Hawkins (1981) and Rohdenburg (1974) for justification of this claim.

Furthermore, the degree of existence affectedness may be morphologically reflected in the case marking paradigms of a language. Thus Moravcsik (1978) cites languages such as Russian, Lithuanian, and Finnish (all nominative/accusative in case marking) where various NPs may take different case markers (holding the verb constant) according as their referents are understood to be totally or only partially (including not at all) affected by the action. For example, in Russian the meaning difference between *pour the coffee* and *pour some more coffee* may be reflected in the choice of accusative case for *coffee* in the first instance and the genitive case in the second. Equally Russian may discriminate the meanings of *the kasha remained on the table* and *some kasha remained on the table* according as *kasha* is case marked nominative or genitive respectively.

The relevance of these examples for our claim, as Moravcsik points out, is that the alternative case paradigms are available only for absolutives.

We may note as well that Anderson (1971) points out that somewhat comparable distinctions exist with respect to DOs in English. Thus in the pairs below the unmarked DO is understood to be more totally affected than when it carries a preposition.

(10) a. John shot/struck Bill.
        John shot at Bill/struck at Bill.
    b. John dug/hoed the garden.
        John dug in the garden/hoed in the garden.
    c. John visited/toured France.
        John visited in France/toured in France.

Note that this phenomenon in English is less regular than the cases cited by Moravcsik in that the choice of preposition varies and the difference in degree of affectedness varies from one example to another.[6]

Moreover, it is not obvious that this 'irregular' pattern in English extends to S_is. But the examples in (11) are supportive, noting that English requires a surface subject and will not accept oblique NPs (PPs) as subjects.

(11) a. Chicago is windy/rainy.
    b. It is windy/rainy in Chicago.
    a. The room/the roof is hot.
    b. It is hot in the room/on the roof.
    a. The afternoon was rainy/cold.
    b. It was rainy/cold in/during the afternoon.

Clearly in these examples the property determined by the adjective is understood to hold more extensively, exhaustively, or thoroughly of the S_i, in the a-sentences than of the corresponding oblique NP in the b-sentences.

Moreover, it appears that we do not find such alternations with respect to transitive subjects, even ones expressing location or duration:

(12) a. New York overwhelmed Mary.
   b. *It overwhelmed Mary in New York.
   a. The evening cooled the building.
   b. *It cooled the building in/during the evening.
   a. This article claims that ergativity is beautiful.
   b. *It claims in this article that ergativity is beautiful.

(For certain cases in (12) the starred sentences are acceptable if *it* is understood to refer to some object or event previously mentioned rather than used in the impersonal sense intended.)

Finally, let us note a very surfacy coding of affectee in German (pointed out to me by W. Klein): it appears that the unmarked nuclear stress in simple transitive sentences, especially ones with modals or auxiliaries, falls on the DO. Thus in *er hat den Vater gesehen*, literally: 'he has the father seen' stress most naturally falls on *Vater*. There is more variability in sentences with intransitive predicates but it appears that with agentive intransitives nuclear stress most naturally falls on the verb, whereas with more Patient-like S_is it falls on the S_i. Thus in answer to the question, What is all that noise? the answer *Der Vater singt*, 'Father is singing', it is *singt* which takes the stress, whereas in an answer like *Das Radio läuft*, 'The radio is on', it is *radio* which takes the stress. This difference can even be productively used, as in sentences like *Die Kirche fällt ein*, literally: 'The church fell in', stress on *Kirche* prompts the Patient reading with 'fell in' understood as *collapse*. But with final stress, on *ein*, we get a more agentive reading translated by something like 'The church goers joined in.' We leave this observation for further speculation, having no idea whether such use of stress or intonation contour has any cross language application.

2.2 Theme

Absolutive arguments are always among those whose path of movement is specified by Goal and Source locatives with verbs of motion. S_t arguments are only so specified if the DO argument is also so specified.

We note that Gruber (1956, 1976) and Jackendoff (1972) use *theme* for 'object which moves', and then extend that notion to a great many more abstract cases. Here we limit ourselves to verbs of physical motion and Goal locatives to PPs with *into* and Source locatives to ones with *from*.

The examples in (13) show that the Goal locative *into the kitchen*, etc. specifies the endpoint of the motion of the absolutive (S_i).

(13) a.   John went/ran/crawled into the kitchen.
　　 b.   John fell/dived/slipped into the pool.
　　 c.   The ball rolled/bounced/fell into the pool.

The examples in (14) below show that the Goal locative specifies the endpoint of the motion of the absolutive argument (the DO) and not that of the transitive subject, which is not necessarily understood to change location.

(14) a.   Bill pushed/pulled/yanked Bill into the kitchen.
　　 b.   Bill dropped/threw/slid the log into the pool.
　　 c.   Bill rolled/dropped/lobbed the ball into the pool.

I can find no transitive verbs of motion where the Goal locative specifies a movement path solely for the S_t. Note, however, that in (15) the referent of the S is understood to move and its path is (more or less depending on the example) specified by the Goal locative in virtue of the fact that the S must accompany, at greater or lesser distance, the DO whose path is directly specified by the Goal locative.

(15) a.   John brought/carried/wheeled the patient into the
　　　　　 room.
　　 b.   John accompanied/escorted Mary into the room.
　　 c.   John followed/pursued/chased Mary into the kitchen.

Note that *carry, wheel, accompany,* and *escort* imply close physical contact between the referents of the S_t and the DO, so if the latter moves the former must follow the same path; *follow* and *chase* allow that the distance be greater. In fact, with *chase* (15c) does not entail that John entered the room, so the path of the S_t is not precisely specified by the Goal locative.

Note also that there are intransitive verbs with Goal locatives which do not overtly present any NP whose referent changes location, though the nature of the predicate is such that we infer easily just what it was that moved. Some examples are given below with 'bodily release' verbs:

(16) a. John spat/vomited/urinated into the sink.
     b. John breathed/exhaled/burped into the flask.

Note that where such verbs permit a DO it is clearly its referent which moves:

(17) John spat blood/vomited his lunch into the sink.

Turning now to the second part of the generalisation in 2.2 consider Source locatives with *from* PPs. Such locatives may predicate mere location rather than change of location, like *in* as opposed to *into*, but with verbs of motion they are usually understood as predicating change of location. (18) below shows that for intransitive verbs it is clearly the referent of S_i which changes location, beginning at the one specified by the *from* PP.

(18) John fell/slipped/jumped/leapt from the roof.

Similarly the most natural reading of (19) below is the one on which the referent of the DO changes location:

(19) a. John yanked/threw/lifted/dragged Bill from the roof/
        the bus.
     b. John took/pulled/removed/withdrew the clothes from
        the tub.

Again it is difficult to find transitive verbs of motion where the Source locative directly predicates change of location of the referent of the S_t. However, the following complicating factors should be noted:

First, a *from* PP does predicate (mere) location of an S_t (or an S_i) if the verb is not one of motion. Thus (20a) below entails (20b) and not (20c).

(20) a. John pinched Bill from the bus.
     b. John was on/in the bus.
     c. Bill was on/in the bus.

Unsurprisingly then many sentences of the form illustrated in (19) above are ambiguous according as the Source locative *from the roof* etc. predicates change of location of the DO or mere location of the S_t. The ambiguity is perhaps clearer in:

(21) a. John grabbed/pushed Bill from the bus.
     b. John shot/speared Bill from the roof.

The point of these examples which is supportive of our claim in 2.2 is that if the Source locative is understood as predicating of the referent of the DO then, as claimed, we understand that it changes location. But if it is predicated of the S_t it merely specifies location. We do not infer that the referent of the S_t changed location.

Note that the verbs of motion in (21b) are somewhat analogous to the (mainly intransitive) bodily release verbs like *spit* in (16). Something moves (the bullet, the spear) which is not overtly expressed in the sentence. Note further that if the DO in (21) is presented as an oblique, that is, with a preposition and thus indicating less than total affectedness, as in (22) below, we get only the reading where the *from* phrase predicates location of the S_t.

(22) a. John grabbed/pushed at Bill from the bus.
     b. John shot at Bill from the roof.

Second, the sort of analysis for the accompaniment verbs of motion in (15) for Goal locatives applies to Source locatives as well. Thus in (23) John is understood to accompany Bill/the book and thus changes location because they do.

(23) a. John carried Bill from the car.
     b. John brought the book from the car.

Finally, let us note that we might like to strengthen the generalisation in 2.2 to the claim that in distinction to absolutes, S_ts are never themes, that is, are not understood as changing location. The stronger claim, however, is falsified by examples such as those in (24) below as well as those in (15) and (23):

(24) a.   John entered/left the room at 6 p.m.
b.   John crossed the highway/swam the English Channel/ fled the battle/jumped the fence/cleared the high bar.
c.   John pursued/tailgated/drove Mary to Chicago.

3. Control Phenomena

We are concerned here with expressions such as adjectives and infinitival phrases which occur within predicates and are understood to predicate something of the NP arguments of the main predicate. Not all the cases we consider would be called 'control' in current theories of generative grammar, but the term as we use it has no particular theoretical significance. We use it simply as a cover term for a class of phenomena we want to draw attention to, much as 'bondedness' and 'thematic role' were used.

3.1   Control of Predicated Adjectives

Adjectives within predicates are normally understood to predicate of absolute arguments and only exceptionally of transitive subjects.

In examples (25) and (26) the entire predicate is intransitive, taking only one NP argument S_i. The adjective within the predicate straightforwardly asserts a property of the referent of S_i. The adjectives in (25) express a (possibly momentary) state that S_i is understood to be in, with varying degrees of certitude. The examples in (26) are change of state predicates, indicating that S_i has acquired the property expressed by the adjective.

(25) a.   John is/seems/looks smart/angry/lazy.
b.   John remained/stayed/died young/honest/penniless.
c.   The table felt sticky/smooth.
d.   The milk tasted sour/bitter.
e.   The meeting sounds noisy/calm.
f.   John arrived angry/happy.
(26) a.   John got/became angry/lazy/fat.
b.   The milk turned sour/green.
c.   John grew old/stubborn.
d.   John waxed loquacious.
e.   The door flew/swung open/slammed shut.

In the examples below the main verb is transitive, taking two NP arguments, and the predicate adjective is understood to express a property of the DO, not of the S_t. (27) are 'state' predications as in (25) above, and (28) are change of state ones, as in (26):

(27) a. John saw/found Bill angry/despondent.
     b. John considers/esteems Bill smart/clever.
     c. John keeps his room clean/The medicine keeps him healthy.
     d. John likes/wants/needs Bill happy/prosperous.
     e. John ate/packaged the meat raw/dirty.
(28) a. John made Bill angry/happy.
     b. The sun turned the milk sour/bitter.
     c. The medicine rendered Bill anaemic/lethargic.
     d. John drove Bill insane/crazy.
     e. John washed/scrubbed/steamed the clams clean/spotless.
     f. John painted the wagon red/hammered the ring flat/shot Bill dead.
     g. John swung the door open/slammed the door shut.

There seem to be no examples of structures like those in (27) and (28) with a bare underived adjective understood to predicate of the transitive subject. Recall, however, the oft cited examples *John struck/impressed Bill as (being) clever.* These violate the spirit of 3.1 since *clever* is understood to predicate of John, not Bill. But they seem to me the exceptional case, the productive paradigm being that in (27) and (28). Note that even with an *as* complement, itself somewhat unusual, the more productive paradigm seems to be the object control case, as indicated in (29):

(29) a. John regarded/described/characterised Bill as clever.
     b. The panel dismissed/ignored the remark as irrelevant/unworthy.
     c. The rebels presented/promoted their cause as just/righteous.
     d. John praised/lauded/touted Bill as exceptional.
     e. John acknowledged the case as unusual.
     f. They rejected the candidate as inept.

3.2 Control of Predicate Infinitives

It is overwhelmingly absolutives rather than transitive subjects which control the subject position of infinitives within predicates (*within* here is intended to rule out purpose clauses).

The examples in (30) below illustrate this with respect to S₁ for several standard and a few not so standard cases.

(30) a. John wants/hopes/needs to arrive on time.
  b. John decided/refused/agreed to review the proposal.
  c. John began/started/ceased to study law.
  d. John tried/managed/got to leave early.
  e. John forgot/remembered/didn't think to lock the door.
  f. John meant/intended/planned to leave early.
  h. John asked/pleaded/demanded to leave the room.

The examples in (31) illustrate again some standard and a few not so standard cases of DO control:

(31) a. John asked/begged/beseeched/enjoined/encouraged Bill to review the proposal.
  b. John allowed/permitted Bill to leave early.
  c. John advised/warned Bill to lock his door.
  d. John ordered/told Bill to lock his door.
  e. John got/obliged/forced Bill to review the proposal.
  f. The incident caused/decided/taught Bill to lock his door at night.

As is well known of course *John promised Bill to leave early* is a counterexample to our claim, but again it seems to be the exception, the rule here being exemplified in (31).

The examples we have adduced so far to illustrate 3.2 cover the classical Equi NP Deletion cases (and perhaps a little more). But equally the classical Raising to Subject and Raising to Object generate surface paradigms with similar control properties. In any event it is only surface absolutives which function as the understood subjects of such predicate infinitives. (32) illustrates the classical Raising to Subject, (33) Raising to Object.

(32) a. John appears/seems to be honest.
  b. John is likely/certain to arrive late.
(33) John believes/expects Fred to be a genius.

We should note here that control of infinitives of the sort illustrated above was represented in 'classical' generative grammar by
cyclic rules — thus syntactic rules *par excellence.* Have we not then
gone beyond the claims of Anderson that ergative/absolutive
phenomena are surface ones? Perhaps we have to some extent, but
I think not to the extent that the 'classical' generative treatment
would suggest. Specifically, the control cases cited above are in
some reasonable sense determined as a function of the predicate,
and on current syntactic views would be represented as part of the
lexical entry of the predicate. It is in fact reasonable to consider
that the infinitives in question are arguments of the predicate. In
this way they differ significantly from properly cross clausal
deletions — *John struck Mary and cried* — where in most languages it is the subject of the initial verb, whether transitive or
intransitive, which controls the subject position of the second verb.
It is principally this sort of control which is cited in Keenan (1976)
as being a property of subjects. Control into arguments, however,
as we have seen above, is more properly a property of absolutives.

4. Summary, and a Note on Explanatory Adequacy

Reflecting on the distinctive properties of absolutives discussed in
1-3, it seems fair to observe that they are 'deeper' and more extensive than has been noted in the literature. There is then reason to
believe that ergative case marking and verb agreement systems do
codify, or signal in surface, a coherent semantic bundle of properties, in addition to the perceptual value they have in discriminating subjects from objects. Let us emphasise further that the
absolutive properties we have discussed are somewhat artificially
divided into the three mnemonic categories we used. In fact, the
existence dependence property cited in 1.1 is easily seen as of a
piece with an appropriately generalised notion of Patient: an NP
whose referent exhibits a change in existence state as a function of
the activity expressed by the predicate. Equally this generalised
notion covers the use of theme discussed in 2.2, as a theme undergoes a change in existence state, namely its location. Moreover the
control properties discussed in 3 overlap at least with the
discussion of Goal and Source locatives. It was in fact rather arbitrary to decide that absolutives 'control' predicate adjectives but

behave as themes with regard to predicate PPs. They could equally well have been said to control the PP in the sense of denoting the object which the PP predicates something of.

It is then reasonable to expect that the absolutive/ergative distinction is one which other linguistic phenomena would be sensitive to, or alternatively, which speakers would be sensitive to in interpreting expressions of their language. This would in fact seem to be the case. We shall illustrate it with a discussion of ways of deriving one place predicates (P_1s) from two place ones (P_2s) and conversely. As we use these terms, a P_1 may be syntactically simple (*walk*) or syntactically complex (*walk slowly, walk slowly and whistle rapidly*, etc.). What is criterial here is that a P_1 requires just one argument expression to form a sentence (P_0). An argument expression may be of category NP, Š, or a nominalised predicate. Similarly a P_2 requires two argument expressions to form a sentence.

4.1 Deriving One Place Predicates from Two Place Ones

Languages present productive means of deriving P_1s from P_2s which *respect absolutives*. We say that a way of deriving a P_1 from a P_2 *respects absolutives* if the absolutive argument (S_i) of the derived predicate has the absolutive properties (as presented in sections 1-3) of the absolutive argument (DO) of the P_2 it is derived from. It may of course have additional properties determined by the meaning of the derivational operation.

The examples in (34) illustrate that Passive respects absolutives. (We treat Passive here as a way of deriving P_1s from P_2s, e.g. *be kissed* from *kiss*, etc.)

(34) a.   A fire was lit in the basement.
       A crime was committed yesterday.
   b.   John's arm was cut.
       John's nails were cut.
       The cake was cut.
       A path was cut through the field.
       Production quotas were cut.
   c.   The car was blown up.
       The cat was killed/Fred's argument destroyed/the stain removed.
   d.   Bill was pushed/yanked/thrown/dropped into the pool.

    e.   Bill was made happy/rendered anaemic/scrubbed clean/shot dead.

    f.   Bill was asked/allowed/advised/told/forced/taught to lock his door.

    g.   Fred was believed/expected to be a genius.

The predicates in the examples above are passives of various of the transitive predicates used earlier to illustrate one or another properties that absolutives typically have in distinction to transitive subjects. The NP which functioned as the absolutive (the DO) of the transitive predicate now functions as the absolutive (S_i) of the derived intransitive predicates *was lit in the basement, was cut,* etc. And indeed the reader may check that the derived absolutive (S_i) presents the properties of the absolutive of the underived predicate. E.g. the existence of the fire in (34a) is still not independent of the activity of lighting (being lit). The passive predicates in (34b) still exhibit the different senses of their underived transitive sources. The selectional restrictions which the passive predicate imposes on its absolutive argument include those which the underived P_2 imposes on its absolutive argument. The existence of the car in (34c) is still affected in the same way as when that NP functions as the absolutive argument of the underived *blow up*. The absolutive argument in (34d) still has its movement path specified by the *into* PP as in the corresponding transitive. And the absolutive NPs in (34e,f,g) still control the subjects of the adjectives and infinitives as in the corresponding transitive forms.

As noted, a derivational operation has its own meaning and may impose additional syntactic and interpretative constraints on what it affects. For example, not all P_2s have natural passives, and the subject of the passive may have stronger selectional restriction and thematic role requirements than those imposed by the underived P_2 on its DO. E.g. we sometimes find that subjects of passives are understood to be more affected by the action than when they function as DOs of transitive predicates.

(35) a. John supports the Obstructionist Party.
          The Obstructionist Party is supported by John.

      b. John changed his job.
          John's job was changed.

    c.   John was watching Bill's house.
         Bill's house was being watched.
    d.   John saw Mary entering the building.
         Mary was seen entering the building.

(35a) is naturally interpretable as a mere statement of John's political allegiance, but its passive rather suggests that the Obstructionist Party depends in an important way for its existence on John's support. In (35b) we may naturally infer that John got a new job and that his old one itself remains unchanged (same duties and responsibilities, etc.). It is more natural to interpret the passive, however, in such a way that the nature of the job itself was changed. (35c) is naturally a mere statement describing a possibly aimless activity of John's, whereas its passive suggests possibly ominous consequences for Bill or his house. Similarly the passive in (35d) carries a faint suggestion that Mary will experience negative consequences for her act, while the active carries no such suggestion.

We may then conclude that Passive respects absolutives. Note that we are not claiming that a formal definition of Passive must mention the theoretical term absolutive. We are only making the interpretative claim that subjects of passives are understood to have the absolutive properties of DOs of the verb the passive one was derived from.

Further, these semantic claims seem to me to have a natural explanatory role of a psycholinguistic sort: the language learner faced with forms like *cut* and *be cut*, *kiss* and *be kissed*, etc. may fairly infer on general principles (Compositionality) that the more complex forms are semantically related in a more or less regular way to the forms they are built up from. But to learn just what that relation is he surely must learn what properties of the more basic form carry over to the derived one and what properties are peculiar to the derived one. And from what we have argued above he may infer that the absolutive properties of the two place predicate carry over to the absolutive of the derived one place one. Once a few cases have been learned then the pattern may be extended to novel cases.

In addition to Passive it seems to me that Reflexive and Middle are also derivational operations which respect absolutives (though my analysis here rests on considerably less cross-linguistic data than in the case of Passive).

As is well known, many languages (e.g. Russian) may form intransitive reflexive predicates by affixing transitive ones. The French example below will serve as an illustration:

(36) a.   Jean a tué Pierre.
          John has killed Pierre.
          'John killed Pierre.'
     b.   Jean s'-est tué.
          John self-is killed
          'John killed himself.'

Taking the predicate *se tuer* in (36b) as intransitive, note that its absolutive, *Jean*, preserves the Patient property, going out of existence, that it would have as the DO absolutive of the transitive predicate *tuer* 'to kill'. In addition of course it acquires agent properties, which is the principle way in which such reflexives differ in meaning from their corresponding passives *Jean a été tué* 'John has been killed/was killed'. Equally subjects of reflexive predicates control predicate adjectives, PPs, and infinitives, as illustrated below:

(37) a.   Jean se croit intelligent.
          John self believes intelligent
          'John believes himself to be intelligent.'
     b.   Jean se permet d'-aller en vacances six fois par an.
          John self allows to-go on vacation six times per year.
          'John allows himself to go on vacation six times a year.'
     c.   John s'- est jeté dans la bagarre.
          John self-is thrown in the fight.
          'John threw himself into the fight.'

(Note in (37c) that we are only claiming that the locative PP *dans la bagarre* 'in the fight' specifies the trajectory of John.)

Finally it also seems to me that Middles, illustrated by (38) from French as well as its English translation, also respect absolutives. In distinction to both Passives and Reflexives, all notion of Agenthood is absent.

(38) La porte s'- est fermée.
     the door mid-is closed.
     'The door is closed.'

Note in particular that existence affecting properties are preserved. Thus in *un accident s'est produit* 'An accident took place (literally: produced itself)' the existence of the accident is not independent of the action of 'producing'. Similarly in *le vaisseau s'est effondré* 'the boat sank' the existence state of the boat is as affected in the same way as if someone sank it.

While it is clear that more work from this perspective needs to be done concerning the relation between Passives, Reflexives, and Middles it seems clear enough that in many basic cases we can infer that these derivational operations respect absolutives.

We may not, of course, infer that all ways of deriving P_1s from P_2s respect absolutives. For example Unspecified Object Deletion (UOD), morphologically productive in some languages of the Uto-Aztecan family for example, would derive the verb of (39b) below from that of (39a) by affixing the latter.

(39) a.   John is sewing shirts.
     b.   John is sewing.

Clearly the absolutive (*John*) of (39b) does not have the absolutive properties of the absolutive (*shirts*) of (39a). Here rather we want to say that UOD respects *subject* properties not absolutive properties. Similarly *Anti-passive* is a derivational process which preserves subject properties, not absolutives. See van Valin (1980) for some discussion.

Overall my strong impression is that the P_1 derivational process Passive/Reflexive/Middle (they often use the same or overlapping derivational affixes, e.g. Russian, French, Quechua) are considerably more widespread than anti-passive and (overtly marked) unspecified object deletion. But a systematic study is needed to ascertain that (recall the ethnocentric bias in early studies of ergativity). If further work bears out my impression then we will have a stronger generalisation: *the* major intransitivising operations in languages respect absolutives. But for the moment it is sufficient to acknowledge that several obviously major intransitivising operations respect absolutives. Moreover, somewhat comparable claims can be made for major transitivising operations in languages.

4.2 *Deriving Transitive Predicates from Intransitive Ones*

Languages commonly present ways of deriving P_2s from P_1s which respect absolutives.

Probably the most widespread valency increasing operator is Causative. See Shibatani (1976) for detailed discussion. Thus many languages, e.g. Turkish, Palauan, Kinyarwanda, may form P_2s with meanings like *cause-to-cry* from P_1s like *cry*. (40a) below from French is illustrative.

(40) a.   Jean fait pleurer les enfants.
           John makes cry the children
           'John is making the children cry.'
      b.   Les enfants pleurent.
           the children cry
           'The children are crying.'

As (40a) entails (40b) it is clear that the absolutive, *les enfants* 'the children' in (40a) has the absolutive properties of the S_i of (40b). E.g. the absolutive of *faire pleurer* 'make cry' must satisfy the selectional restrictions of *pleurer* 'to cry' (and perhaps must satisfy even stronger selectional restrictions). If the existence state of the absolutive of *pleurer* is affected to some extent then the existence state of the absolutive of *faire pleurer* is affected to at least that extent (and often more) etc. Similarly Goal locatives specify the movement path of the absolutive of causative predicates as they do for the uncausativised one they are derived from:

(41) a.   Jean est entré dans la pièce.
           John entered into the room
      b.   Pierre a fait entrer Jean dans la pièce.
           Pierre made enter John into the room

Clearly in both cases John moves from a point outside the room to a point inside the room. We note that without further investigation it seems difficult to check that absolutives of causativised predicates control predicate adjectives and infinitives, as the simple cases we considered in English do not seem to causativise naturally in French. Even so, however, it appears clear that causativisation respects absolutives to a significant extent.

Of course, as with P_1 derivational processes, not all ways of extending the valency of a predicate respect absolutives. Moreover, these processes seem fairly productive across languages, though probably not as productive as Causative. An interesting one, which I have elsewhere called *verbal case marking*, is evidenced by languages as diverse as Totonac (Penutian, Mexico), Kinyarwanda (Bantu), Latin and Greek. For the Kinyarwanda data see Gary and Keenan (1977). As for Latin, recall that verbs may be prefixed with expressions which independently function as prepositions, yielding a verb with a valency increased by one, the derived verb requiring an NP that could have been introduced independently in the corresponding PP. For example, from the P_2 *ferre* 'to carry', we may form P_3s such as *trans+ferre* 'to carry across', *in+ferre* 'to carry into', *ex+ferre* (= *efferre*) 'to carry from' etc. And of course from P_1s such as *ire* 'to go' we may form P_2s such as *ad+ire* 'to go to, approach', *ante+ire* 'to go before, precede', etc.

Clearly verbal case marking respects subject properties, however, not absolutes. The subject of the derived predicate inherits the thematic role, selectional restrictions, etc., of the subject of the underived verb.

4.3 Lexical Relations: A Psycholinguistic Problem

From the many examples we have given of P_1s and P_2s in English it is clear that many verbs have uses both as P_1s and P_2s. Of course in some languages we would have two forms, one basic and one derived for e.g. transitive and intransitive *break*, transitive and intransitive *sew*, etc. But equally it is common to find a given lexical item functioning both as a transitive and an intransitive predicate.

Does our analysis of absolutes have anything of interest to say about such pairs? I think it does. Let us pose the question psycholinguistically. How does the language learner/user learn or comprehend the meaning relation between the two *breaks*, the two *sews*, etc.? *Modulo* idioms he can expect that the meanings of the two are not randomly related. Transitive *sew* will not be expected to mean *describe, employ*, etc. He may reasonably expect that one of the two arguments of the transitive use will have the same sort of semantic properties that the single argument of the intransitive use has. But which?

It would be elegant if we could say that the DO of the transitive use always has approximately the same semantic properties as the S_i in the intransitive use. But examples like *sew/sew a dress, smoke/smoke a cigar, paint/paint a portrait*, etc. show this to be false. Nor can we assume that the S_t argument of the transitive use is semantically similar to that of the S_i in the intransitive use. Examples like *the window shattered/John shattered the window, the water boiled/John boiled the water,* etc. show this to be false. Still there seems to me at least one generalisation which can be made:

(42) For verbs with both transitive and intransitive uses, if the absolutive argument on the intransitive use has many of the properties we have characterised as absolutive in 1-3 above then it will function as the absolutive argument (DO) of the transitive use.

We may infer from (42) that if a language has intransitive verbs translating those in (43) below then their subjects will function as DOs of those verbs on any transitive uses which may exist.

(43) form, gather, break out, occur, start, spread, explode, spill, wither, die, collapse, rot, evaporate

It would be nice to be able to strengthen the *if* claim in (42) to an *if and only if* one, but in the absence of a more refined analysis we cannot do so. For the *only if* part would allow us to infer that a P_2 whose DO had many absolutive properties would assign those properties to its S_i on an intransitive use. But this is incorrect, since the DOs in (44a) are arguably Patient-like, as their existence is affected or they undergo some change in state. But the subjects of those verbs in the intransitive use of (44b) are clearly Agent-like, not Patient-like.

(44) a.   John walked the dog/ran the students around the park/ marched the troops up the hill.
     b.   The dog walked/the students ran around the park/the troops marched up the hill.

But even without the strengthened generalisation, the one in (42) is still empirically significant and does provide a basis for a language learner to creatively use intransitive verbs as transitive once a few instances have apprised him of the relation in (42).

Notes

1. The author would like to thank the Max-Planck-Institut für Psycholinguistik for having supported this research and UCLA for having provided the necessary leave time. The author would also like to thank John Hawkins, Mary Louise Kean, and Wolfgang Klein for helpful suggestions on an earlier version of this paper.
2. We do not rule out of course that the ergative/absolutive distinction may be relevant at a level of pragmatic or discourse analysis. See Du Bois (1984) for some discussion along these lines.
3. Examples of this sort were given to me by Wayles Browne, years ago, citing Jan Firbas as the source.
4. Note that a clear counterexample to our claim here must be one where the sense of the verb varies just with the interpretation of S_t. So to check we must hold the transitive verb + DO constant. The best candidates for counterexamples that I have found are ones like those in (i)-(iii) below:

   (i)   a. The soldiers cross the river here.
         b. The bridge crosses the river here.
   (ii) a. The police surrounded the house.
         b. A moat surrounded the house.
   (iii) a. Leaves covered the drain.
         b. John covered the drain (with leaves).

So we may want to acknowledge that the sense of transitive verbs can vary with general properties such as animacy and (potential) Agenthood of their S arguments, but such differences seem rather systematic, rather than the *ad hoc* adaptation of sense we saw in the case of absolutives.
5. The examples in (8) and (9) may be compared to those in (1)-(4) which indicate the coming into existence of the referent of an absolutive. Similarly we may note absolutives whose referent expands their existence state:

   (i)   a. The disease spread.
         b. The rabbits multiplied.
         c. Prices doubled/went up.
         d. The corn grew.
   (ii) a. The travellers spread the disease.
         b. John copied/distributed/reprinted the article.
         c. The company increased its production/doubled its prices.

6. Wolfgang Klein (personal communication) draws to my attention however that this variation is somewhat more systematic in German, where a variety of predicates may prefix *be-* allowing an otherwise oblique NP to appear as accusative without a preposition and with a greater affectedness reading:

   (i)   a. Wir sprachen über das Problem.
             We spoke about the problem.
         b. Wir besprachen das Problem.
             We discussed/talked out? the problem.
   (ii) a. Er klagt über das schlechte Wetter.
             He complained about the bad weather.
         b. Er beklagt das schlechte Wetter.
             He 'was very sorry about/regretted' the bad weather.

References

Anderson, S.R. (1971) 'On the Role of Deep Structure in Semantic Interpretation', *Foundations of Language*, 7, 387-96.

—— (1976) 'On the Notion of Subject in Ergative Languages' in C.N. Li (ed.), *Subject and Topic*, Academic Press, New York, pp. 1-23.

—— (1977a) 'On Mechanisms by which Languages become Ergative' in C. Li (ed.), *Mechanisms of Syntactic Change*, University of Texas Press, Austin, pp. 317-63.

—— (1977b) 'Comments on the Paper by Wasow (same volume)' in P. Culicover, T. Wasow, and A. Akmajian (eds.), *Formal Syntax*, Academic Press, New York.

Blake, B.J. (1979) 'Degrees of Ergativity in Australia', in F. Plank (ed.).

Comrie, B. (1973) 'The Ergative: Variations on a Theme' *Lingua*, 32, 239-53.

—— (1981) *Language Universals and Linguistic Typology*, University of Chicago Press, Chicago, Illinois.

Dixon, R.M.W. (1979) 'Ergativity', *Language*, 55, 59-138.

Du Bois, J. (1984) 'Competing Motivations', to appear in J. Haiman (ed.) *Iconicity in Syntax*, Benjamins, Amsterdam.

Gary, J.O. and E.L. Keenan (1976) 'On Collapsing Grammatical Relations in Universal Grammar', in P. Cole and J. Sadock (eds.) *Syntax and Semantics: Grammatical Relations*, Vol. 8 Academic Press, New York.

Gruber, J. (1956, 1976) *Lexical Structures in Syntax and Semantics*, MIT PhD dissertation, North Holland.

Hawkins, J. (1981) 'The Semantic Diversity of Basic Grammatical Relations in English and German', *Linguistische Berichte*, 75, 1-25.

Hoijer, H. (ed.), (1946) 'Linguistic Structures of Native America', *Viking Fund Publications in Anthropology* 6, Viking Fund, New York.

—— (1964) 'Cultural Implications of some Navaho Linguistic Categories' in D. Hymes (ed.) *Language in Culture and Society*, New York, Harper and Row, pp. 142-53.

Hopper, P.U. and S.A. Thompson (1980) 'Transitivity in Grammar and Discourse', *Language* 56, 2, 251-300.

Jackendoff, R. (1972) *Semantic Interpretation in Generative Grammar*, MIT Press, Cambridge, Massachusetts.

Keenan, E.L. (1976) 'Towards a Universal Definition of "Subject of "' in C. Li (ed.) *Subject and Topic*, Academic Press, New York.

—— (1979) 'On Surface Form and Logical Form', *Studies in the Linguistic Sciences*, special issue Vol. 8, no. 2.

Larson, T.W. and W.M. Norman (1979) 'Correlates of Ergativity in Mayan Grammar' in F. Plank (ed.).

Li, C. and R. Lang (1979) 'The Syntactic Irrelevance of an Ergative Case in Enga and Other Papuan Languages' in F. Plank (ed.), cf. 16, pp. 307-24, Academic Press, New York.

Mardirussian, G. (1975) 'Noun Incorporation in Universal Grammar', *Chicago Linguistic Society XI*, 383-9, University of Chicago, Illinois.

Moravcsik, E. (1978) 'On the Distribution of Ergative and Accusative Patterns', *Lingua*, 45, 233-79.

Plank, F. (ed.), (1979) *Ergativity*, Academic Press, New York.

Rohdenburg, G. (1974) 'Sekundére Subjektivierungen im Englischen und Deutschen: Vergleichende Untersuchungen zur Verb- und Adjektivsyntax', *PAKS-Arbeitsbericht* 8. Cornelsen-Velhagen und Klasing, Bielefeld.

Shibatani, M. (ed.) (1976) *The Grammar of Causative Constructions. Syntax and Semantics*, Vol. 6. Academic Press, New York.

van Valin, R.D. (1980) 'On the Distribution of Passive and Antipassive Constructions in Universal Grammar', *Lingua*, 50, 303-27.

PART THREE:
RELATION-CHANGING RULES IN UNIVERSAL GRAMMAR

The articles in this section are all concerned with operations which effect a change in grammatical relations. Most of them focus on Passive. 'Some Universals of Passive in Relational Grammar' is perhaps the first paper to argue that Passive should be thought of as an *argument-eliminating*, or *demotion*, process, rather than as one which advances a Direct Object to Subject. This article was directly inspired by the then current work in Relational Grammar. The article 'Passive is Phrasal' is my first attempt to unite cross-language syntactic work on Passives with my semantic work. This approach is generalised in 'Parametric Variation' to the full range of relation-changing operations. The recent article with Alan Timberlake 'Predicate Formation Rules' both extends and refines the work in 'Parametric Variation', and introduces a much greater range of Passive structures — ones which can be naturally represented on our approach and which are, we argue, difficult to represent on other conceptions of Passive.

SOME UNIVERSALS OF PASSIVE IN
RELATIONAL GRAMMAR[1]

I shall present here several conceptions of the PASSIVE transformation and argue that for purposes of universal grammar one of
these is to be preferred over the others. I shall first distinguish
between relationally based PASSIVEs (rel-PASS) and structurally
based PASSIVEs (str-PASS) and argue for rel-PASS. Then I will distinguish two sub-types of rel-PASS and argue for one of those.

1. str-PASS versus rel-PASS

1.1

A rel-PASS is one defined in terms of the changes it induces in
the grammatical relations (GRs) which NPs bear to their verbs.
The GRs are 'subject of' (Su), 'direct object of' (DO), and 'indirect
object of' (IO). The specific conception of rel-PASS I shall argue
for stipulates: (i) the active Su ceases to bear any GR to its verb
and (ii) DO becomes the Su. This formulation is due to Perlmutter
and Postal (henceforth PP) (1974), though our claim is weaker
than theirs as they argue, roughly that conditions (i) and (ii)
(together with language specific 'side effects') constitute a *definition* of PASSIVE in the grammar of each language. But I am only
using (i) and (ii) as a universal schema, thereby allowing that in
some language PASSIVE might be defined differently, say in purely
structural terms, as long as the definition had the effect in that language of promoting the DO to Su and demoting the Su.

A str-PASS on the other hand is one defined primarily in terms
of changes induced in the dominance and linear ordering relations
of P-markers. Thus, the PASSIVE in Chomsky (1965) as well as
more recent proposals in Lakoff (1971), Hasegawa (1968) and
Langacker and Munro (1974) are all str-PASS.

1.2 The Primary Advantage of rel-PASS

It provides a basis for predicting the syntactic properties of passive
Ss in structurally distinct languages. Below we give three general

predictions and then several very specific predictions which follow from these (those discussed by Perlmutter and Postal, though perhaps somewhat differently than here, will be marked PP).

(A) The demoted Su either will not appear at all in the passive S, or else it will appear optionally in an obliqaue (Obl) case. Both options are natural ways to satisfy condition (i), that a demoted Su cease to bear any GR to the verb.

(B) Passive Ss are intransitive (PP). Reason: their main verbs lack a DO since it has become a Su by condition (ii).

(C) DOs promoted by PASSIVE acquire the coding properties of Su, i.e. they take on the characteristic position, case marking, and verb agreements of a basic Su (PP).

In support of (A) we note that many languages have PASSIVEs in which the demoted Su is obligatorily absent, e.g. Latvian (Lazdina 1966, 165) Machiguenga (Snell and Wise 1963, 125), Hungarian, classical Arabic, Maninka (Shopen and Bird 1974). Otherwise, a demoted Su is usually marked as a locative or instrumental.

As regards (B) we note that passive verbs will not be marked for object agreement even though their active counterparts are (Basque see (6), Gilbertese (3) and Fijian, Hungarian, Bella Coola). Other intransitivity properties are covered in (C).

To support (C) we have investigated PASSIVE in thirty odd languages and found that in the great majority the promoted DO did assume the coding properties of an intransitive Su. In a few cases, however, the full range of Su properties was not acquired by the promoted DO, and in a very few cases the promoted DO actually retained certain of its DO properties. These facts are summarised in the Appendix and discussed more thoroughly in Keenan (1974, 1975).

1.3 Specific Predictions

If the position of the DO in a language L is different from that of the intransitive Su then PASSIVE in L is a movement process. Reason: by (C) the DO will acquire the position of the Su, and by hypothesis it doesn't have it to begin with. Thus PASSIVE in languages whose basic word orders are S+Obl+(O)+V (e.g. Japanese, Turkish) S+V+(O), (e.g. Indonesian, Swahili) or V+(O)+Obl+S (e.g. Malagasy-1).

(1) Nahita azy tao   an-trano aho ⇒ Nohita-ko   tao   an-trano
                                                                    izy

    saw   him there in-house I   seen-by-me there in-house
                                                                    he

    'I saw him in the house'   'He was seen by me in the
                                                                    house'

The fact that rightward movement (rare) is correctly predicted for
a rare word order type is interesting confirmation of rel-PASS.

    If the transitive Su and the Obl NPs are not contiguous and if
the demoted Su can appear in the passive S, then PASSIVE moves
since the demoted Su must move to acquire the oblique position.
E.g. PASSIVE moves in languages whose basic word order is
V+S+(O)+Obl e.g. Welsh, Jacaltec (2) (from Craig 1974), Bella
Coola; S+V+O+Obl e.g. English, Tera, Shona; and
S+O+V+Obl (Bambara).

(2) Jacaltec x-ø$_j$-s$_i$-mak naj xuwan naj Pel   ⇒
        asp   hit cl Juan   cl Peter
        'Juan hit Peter'

        x-ø$_j$-mak-ot   naj Pel   y-u naj xuwan
        asp hit   pass cl Peter by cl Juan
        'Peter was hit by Juan'

    More interesting are cases where rel-PASS predicts that PASSIVE
will ot be a movement process. Thus, if the position of the DO is
the same as that of the intransitive Su then PASSIVE will not move
it. And if the transitive Su and the Obl NPs are contiguous, then
the Su need not move to become Oblique. One word order illus-
trating this is V+(O)+S+Obl.[2] Thus, an intransitive Su goes right
after the verb. So DO need not move under PASSIVE as it is already
immediately post verbal. Similarly, the transitive Su becomes
oblique and since it already follows the (derived) Su it need not
move to take an oblique position. Both Gilbertese (3) and Fijian
(Arms 1974,31) exemplify this word order, and as predicted,
nothing moves under PASSIVE in either language as (3) illustrates:

(3) E$_i$ kamatea$_j$ te naeta$_j$ te moa$_i$
        kill   the snake the chicken
    'The chicken killed the snake'

E$_j$ kamate<u>aki</u> te naeta$_j$ iroun te moa$_i$
   kill pass   the snake by the chicken
'The snake was killed by the chicken'

Again, the fact that rel-PASS makes a correct prediction about a rare word order type is strong support for rel-PASS. Note as well that the derived Su triggers subject agreement with the passive verb, the original object agreement being lost as predicted in B.

A final class of cases where rel-PASS predicts that PASSIVE will not move are languages in which Su and DO are contiguous in the active S and the demoted Su cannot appear in the passive S, as in classical Arabic (4).

(4)   qatala   ʔal ṣaya:<u>du</u>   ʔal-ʔasa<u>da</u>
     killed (act) the hunter-<u>nom</u> the lion-<u>acc</u>
     'the hunter killed the lion'

     qutila   ʔal-ʔasa<u>du</u>   (ʔ*min ṭaraf ʔal ṣayadu)
     killed (pass) the lion-<u>nom</u> (on part of the hunger)
     'the lion was killed'

The analogs above hold for case marking as well. Thus, e.g. if DO and intrans-Su are marked the same, then DO will not change case under PASSIVE. (5) from Gugu-Yalanji (Hershberger 1964) and (6) from Basque (Lafitte 1962) illustrate this case, as well as the final, not very surprising case of PASSIVE that is not (necessarily) a movement: namely the case of languages whose word order is sufficiently free that change in order will not signal change in GR.

(5)   Hank-angka minya-ø yaka-n ⇒ Hank-anda minya-ø
                                     yaka-ji-n
     Hank-erg   meat-nom cut-asp Hank-loc meat-nom
                                     cut-pass-asp
     'Hank cut the meat'   'the meat was cut by Hank'

(6)   Piarrese-k egin du   etxe<u>a</u>
     Peter-erg make have-he-it house-def ⇒
     'Peter built the house'

Piarrese-k egina   da   etxea
Peter-erg make (part) be-it house-def
'the house was built by Peter'

1.4

The primary disadvantage of a structurally based PASSIVE is that
there is no universally valid structural definition of PASSIVE. It
would be too space-consuming to illustrate the lack of universality
of the str-PASS mentioned in 1.1, but the following four problems
can prevent any given str-PASS from being universal.

(A) *Several languages have more than one structurally distinct
PASSIVE,*[3] e.g. Indonesian (Chung 1975), Dyirbal (Anderson
1974) and English (!). Thus, Lakoff (1971) argues that *be* and *get*
PASSIVES in English have different underlying sources and different transformational behaviour.

Note *I persuaded John to get/ *be himself fired, getting/ *being
yourself fired would be stupid,* etc.

(B) Any universal str-PASS must be able to identify those NPs
which PASSIVE affects (i.e. moves, in most languages) and must be
able to distinguish them from NPs not affected by PASSIVE. But
*there is no universally valid structural characterisation of just those
NPs affected by PASSIVE.* E.g. Su cannot even be structurally distinguished from DO universally (Keenan 1974, 1975).

Insufficiency of Linear Order: The existence of both verb final and
of verb initial[4] languages shows that both Su and DO may occur on
the same side of the verb, so position relative to the verb is not distinctive. Either Su or DO may be 'closest' to the verb. DO in SOV
languages, Su in VSO languages (Jacaltec−2, Bella Coola, Welsh,
classical Arabic−4, Maasai, Tongan). Further, while Su usually is
the leftmost major NP in a basic active S, with existence of VOS
order in Malagasy, Gilbertese, Fijian, and Toba Batak (Keenan
1972) shows that order of Su and DO is not universal.

Insufficiency of Dominance: While Su is usually the 'highest' NP
in the S, VSO languages show that it is not always higher than DO.

(7)   Na'e tamate'i 'e Tevita 'a Koliate
      killed   erg David acc Goliath
      'David killed Goliath'

Further, languages like Tagalog (Schachter and Otanes 1972), which are verb initial but have completely free word order of full NPs after the verb, also rule out relative dominance as a criterial distinction between Su and DO. And the case is even clearer in completely free word order ike Walbiri (Hale 1967).

Similarly, DO and IO, as well as DO and various Obl, are not structurally distinct. Relative order of DO and IO is generally freer than relative order of Su and DO. And very few languages present any evidence that any relative dominance difference exists between DO and IO (for arguments supporting this claim for English, see Johnson 1974).

(C) If the output of two structural operations is different, then the operations themselves are different. And in fact, the surface form of passive Ss presents certain systematic variation across languages. E.g.

(i) The derived verb is dominated by no other verb in surface. *Case* 1: the derived verb does not differ in form from the active one.

Tera (Newman 1970, 59)
(8) Ali xa ruɓa woy-a   ⇒   woy-a wa ruɓa
     Ali prf injure boy-the   boy-the prf injure
     'Ali injured the boy'   'the boy was injured'

Swahili (Givón 1972, 274)
(9) maji ya-meenea nchi   ⇒   nchi i-meenea maji
     water$_i$ it$_i$-covers land$_j$ land$_j$ it$_j$-cover water$_i$
     'water covers the land'   'the land is covered (by) water'

Case 2: the derived verb has a distinctive morphology (Bantu, Malayo-Polynesian, also Welsh, Japanese, Latin ...)

Welsh (Bowen and Jones 1960, 137)
(10) Dys<u>gir</u>   cymraeg gan yr athro   (to teach, active=
     teach-pass Welsh   by the teacher   *dysgu*
     'Welsh is taught by the teacher'

(ii) The derived verb is dominated by another verb in surface. *Case* 1: the higher verb is 'stative' or 'change of stative' (= 'be' in English, Luiseño etc. 'become' in German, Persian, and even 'go' in Hindi)

Hindi
(11) aurat   ne murgi mari ⇒   murgi   mari   gayee
      women erg chicken killed   chicken killed went
      'the woman killed the chicken' 'the chicken was killed'

> *Case* 2: the higher verb is a verb of reception or undergoing
> 'touch, receive' in Tai (Needleman 1973), 'undergo' (histori-
> cally) in Chinese, and even 'eat' in Sinhalese.

Tai
(12) Mary thúuk (John) kɔ́ɔt
      Mary touch (John) embrace
      'Mary was embraced (by John)'

Sinhalese[5]
(13) kikili laməjageŋ maeruŋ kæ:va
      chicken child-<u>inst</u> death eat
      'the chicken was killed by the child'

(D) It seems unlikely that the formally different PASSIVEs in
different languages share any formal properties that distinguish
them from other transformations. Referring back to the str-PASS
cited in 1.1 we find three major traits of PASSIVE: it involves reordering NPs (Chomsky 1965), Equi NP deletion (Hasegawa
1968), or some kind of Raising (Lakoff 1971, Langacker and
Munro 1974). But we have already seen that reordering is not
universal. And both Raising and Equi seem generally unmotivated
for languages which present no higher verb in the passive S, (see
(i) above). Further, many other syntactic processes besides
PASSIVE normally involve reordering, Equi or Raising, so these
cannot be taken as definitional of PASSIVE.

1.5 Motivation for a Universal Passive

Adopting a str-PASS appears to force us, then, to say that PASSIVE
is really a different transformation in different languages, and this
would mean that we would have no unified level of grammatical
description at which to state generalisations concerning PASSIVE.
Thus, if PASSIVE in all (or even most) languages must be restricted
from applying in certain universally specifiable environments, then
to state this regularity in the grammar of each language (which has
the restriction) is clearly to fail to describe what is general in

human languages – and that is the major goal of universal grammar.

What are these general regularities? We have already mentioned several in 1.2, and below we discuss four others of a rather different sort in that they do not, even informally, follow from the definition of PASSIVE as we have given it. Some of these generalisations are better established than others. All are in need of further clarification. Space precludes any attempt to justify them on universal grounds.

(A) PASSIVE is difficult[6] or impossible to apply if the reference of the promoted NP is not understood independently of that of the subject's.

Thus, in the a. sentences below, we do not understand what the object refers to independently of what the subject refers to, and as predicted, PASSIVE either doesn't apply, or else changes the meaning in an unusual way.

(14) a.   Joe smacked himself.
(15) a.   Joe$_i$ hit his$_i$ son.
(16) a.   Joe found a wife in Peoria.
(17) a.   Jean s'est lavé les mains. (lit: John washed to himself the
           hands=John washed his hands)
(14) b.   *He(-self) was smacked by Joe.
(15) b.   *?His$_i$ son was hit by Joe$_i$.
(16) b.   ?? A wife was found by Joe in Peoria.
(17) b.   **Les mains s'étaient lavées par Jean.

Cases (16) and (17) above are interesting because the DO is not overtly marked as being bound in reference to the Su, but we still understand that the person Joe found in (16) became *his* wife, and the hands Jean washed in (17) were *his* hands.

(B) If the DO is case marked in an unusual way for that language, then it may retain its case marking and not trigger verb agreement when 'promoted' to Su (Keenan 1974, 75).

E.g. in German and Latin DOs are usually marked accusative. But a few verbs e.g. *invidēre* 'to envy' in Latin, *helfen* 'to help' in German take dative DOs. And when PASSIVE applies, the promoted DO stays dative, the verb becomes 3sg., not agreeing with any NP; the transitive Su gets demoted as usual and the verb takes on the usual passive morphology.

Latin
(18) mihi   invide<u>tur</u>   (ab aliquo)
     me(dat) envy-pass 3sg (by someone)
     'I am envied (by someone)'

German
(19) Mir   wird   dadurch   nicht geholfen
     me(dat) become that-through not   helped
     'I am not helped by that'

(C) PASSIVE is harder to apply if the Su is not an agent and the DO is not a patient (See Trithart 1975).

Joe $\begin{cases} \text{recalls} \\ \text{misses} \end{cases}$ the old days.

?The old days are $\begin{cases} \text{recalled} \\ \text{missed} \end{cases}$ by Joe.

This car needs a new motor.

*A new motor is needed by this car.

Joe lost the race.
(natural: Joe=experiencer)

The race was lost by Joe.
(preferred: primary experiencer ≠ Joe. He caused the loss)

(D) Passive Ss are usually 'stative'. But the criteria of stativity are not fully agreed upon. E.g. if stative Ss do not have imperative forms, then passive Ss in Maori and Malagasy are not stative, since they do have imperatives.

Maori (Clark 1974)
(20) huti-a   te punga   o too taaua waka
     pull-pass art. anchor of our   canoe
     'pull up the anchor of our canoe'

Malagasy
(21) a. mamonóa azy   b. vonoy izy
        kill(act) him(acc)!   kill(pass) he(nom)
        'kill him'   'kill him'

If stative only means that the Su is not an agent then stativity follows from ref-PASS in any language in which the Su of the active S is agent (if an agent is present at all). If this is not the case, as in our analysis of Dyirbal (Keenan 1974, 1975) then the derived Su can express the agent, (Dixon 1972, 204).

2. Types of rel-PASS

2.1

We have been considering a rel-PASS to be any formulation containing both the Demotion Condition (DC): *Su ceases to bear any GR to the verb*, and the Promotion Condition (PC): *DO becomes Su*. But conceptions of rel-PASS may vary according to the primacy they accord one or the other of these conditions. Thus, in PP's formulation the PC is primary and the DC follows from it, taken together with certain general, and independently motivated, 'laws' of grammar; specifically the Relational Annihilation Law (RAL) 'an NP whose GR has been taken over by another ceases to bear any GR to its verb.' Since Raisings and Dummy Insertions also 'take over' GRs, it is clear that the RAL is more general than a mere constraint on PASSIVE. Now, since the RAL only applies to NPs whose GRs have been taken over, it follows that, in PP's formulation, the demotion of the Su depends on the logically prior promotion of the DO. Promoting the DO 'triggers' the demotion of the Su.

I should like to *propose* here an alternate formulation of rel-PASS in which the demotion of the Su is the primary, or independent condition, and the promotion of an NP follows from the universal, variable strength (Ross) condition:

Subject Presence Condition
For each language L there is a specific extent to which L requires that surface main clauses have independent NP subjects. This extent will be called the *subject number* of L. If L has a high subject number (and most do) then the gap created by the PASSIVE demotion of the Su will be filled by some NP. But if L has a relatively low subject number then passive Ss may lack surface subjects.

Determining the subject number of a language is of course problematic at the moment, but a first approximation would be to take it to be the percentage of basic S-types which are required to have subjects. Then languages like English, French, German, and Malagasy would have quite high subject numbers, as almost all basic S-types have surface subjects. On the other hand, languages like Turkish, Russian, and Latin will probably have lower subject numbers, since many basic S-types may lack overt subjects (e.g.

sentences whose English translations would express: (i) possession e.g. *I have a book*, (ii) location e.g. *a horse is behind the barn*, (iii) the weather e.g. *it is dark/raining*, (iv) agentless actions e.g. *the storm killed the chickens*).

Note: Our evidence here is impressionistic; we have not done a systematic study.

2.2 The Primary Evidence for Demotional-PASSIVE

is that in several languages PASSIVE can demote a Su without promoting anything else.

2.2.1 Thus Latin, Turkish, and Slavic all have 'canonical' PAS-SIVEs in which both the demotion and promotion conditions are met. But, in addition, they all also allow in various S-types that the Su be demoted without any attendant promotion of another NP.

Latin
(22) curri<u>tur</u>
     run-pass+3sg
     'there was running'

Turkish (Bailard 1975)
(23) a. Ahmet kadin-la   konuş-to
        Ahmet woman-with talk-past
        'Ahmet talked with the woman'
     b. Kadin-la   konuş-ul -du
        woman-with talk- pass-past
        'the woman was talked with'
     c. ben(im)-le konuş-ul- du- (*m)
        I   -with talk- pass-past-(1sg)
        'I was talked with'

N. Russian (Timberlake 1975)
(24) a. u   menja uže   vstato   bylo
        prep me(gen) already stand(part.neut.sg.)be(neut.3sg.)
        'I have already got up' (i.e. by me there has already
                                          been getting up)
     b. u menja bylo   telenka zarezano
        prep me(gen)be(3sg.neut)calf(acc) slaughtered(part.neut.sg.)
        'by me there was slaughtering a calf'

We should cite here as well the impersonal passives discussed in Langacker and Munro (1974).

Mojave
(25) inʸep   nʸ-   tapuy-č   -m
     me(acc) 1sg acc kill-'pass'-tense
     'I was killed'

2.2.2   In a few languages with high subject numbers, semantically vacuous NPs, 'dummies', are present as surface subjects of passive Ss, but no NP within the clause is promoted to Su.

Dutch (Kirsner 1975)
(26) a.   De jongens   flúiten
           the boys   whistle (3pl)
     b.   Er wordt   door de jongens gefloten
           Pro becomes by the   boys   whistled (part)
           'there is whistling by the boys'

French (Bailard 1975)
(27) Il en a   été   parlé.
     it of-it has been spoken
     'It was spoken about'

?English (Siegel 1973, example attributed to J. Ross)
(28) It was felt by many that John was incompetent.

2.2.3   In Japanese, sentences like (29) are problematic for any Promotional analysis of PASSIVE since there is no underlying source in which the derived subject of (29) has a grammatical relation to the verb.

(29) Taroo ga Hanako ni   nigerareru
     Taroo Su Hanako Agent run-away-pass
     'Taroo was run away on by Hanako'

The most plausible underlying source for (29) is one where *Taroo* is a topic and *Hanako*, the subject, as in (30). See Shimizu (1975) for more justification of this point.

(30) Taroo wa Hanako ga nigeru
     Taroo tpc Hanako Su run-away
     'Hanako runs away on Taroo'/'Speaking of Taroo, Hanako
                                  runs away on him'

Now, while (29) can perhaps be derived from (30), there exists an intermediate stage in which *Taroo* remains topic, and the subject, *Hanako*, is demoted and the verb becomes passive in morphology (and meaning) but the topic *Taroo* remains marked a topic.

(31) Taroo wa Hanako ni nigerareru
     Taroo tpc Hanako Agent runs-away-pass
     'Speaking of Taroo, he is run-away-on by Hanako'

Clearly the step from (30) to (31) indicates a spontaneous demotion of the Su independently of any promotion of anything else.

2.2.4 In some languages, e.g. Welsh, the promoted NP does not inherit all the coding properties of basic subjects (it takes on the position and case (in pronouns) but does not trigger verb agreement). We might expect on a promotional analysis of PASSIVE that the demoted Su would only lose those properties that the promoted DO took over. But, this is not the case. Rather the demoted Su ceases to trigger verb agreement and the verb reverts to a 3sg form.

Welsh (Bowen and Jones 1960, 137)
(32) a. Gwelir fi   b. Gwelir di, etc.
        see-pass I   see-pass you,
        'I am seen'   'You are seen' etc.

2.3

Final support for demotional-PASS is that it naturally allows that any NP functioning as a passive Su will satisfy the Subject Presence Condition. And it does appear that we get quite a variety, rather than the limited range predicted by a promotional analysis DO → Su. We note, without example: IO/BEN → Su (Japanese); IO → Su (Machiguenga); Topic → Su (Japanese); Agent → Su (Dyirbal); Loc → Su (Chicewa: see Trithart); Dummy → Su (German, Dutch, ?French, ?English); and perhaps even Possessor → Su (Japanese: see Shimizu).

3. Conclusion

We have argued two things: that a relationally based PASSIVE is to be preferred to a structurally based PASSIVE in universal grammar, and second, that a demotional PASSIVE has several advantages over a promotional PASSIVE. We have not, however, integrated the demotional concept of PASSIVE into a more comprehensive relationally based grammar. Thus, it remains merely a plausible, but not (yet) a convincing alternative to Perlmutter and Postal's conception. Further, the advantages of rel-PASS over str-PASS were only relative. Rel-PASS is more universal than str-PASS. However, rel-PASS can only make predictions about languages for which some reliable intuition of Su, DO, etc., is available. Schachter (1975) has argued with some persuasion, however, that these notions are not applicable to Philippine languages (Tagalog, Kapampangan, etc.) since the characteristic properties which usually define subjects are spread among several NPs in basic sentences (i.e. the NPs which undergo Equi, relativise, control reflexives etc. only very imperfectly overlap). If Schachter's arguments prove correct, then universal grammar will be in need of a still more general notion of PASSIVE.

Appendix

The left hand column represents possible combinations of coding properties of subjects. The right hand column, languages in which those properties are criterial and inherited by NPs promoted under PASSIVE. (We exclude from analysis the Philippine languages.)

Coding Properties	*Languages*
1. position, marking agreement	Luiseño, Buriat, Turkish, Romanian, Hindi, German, Hebrew, classical Arabic, Latvian
2. position and marking only	Japanese, Korean, Telugu, Malagasy, Sinhalese
3. position and agreements only	Bella Coola, Gilbertese, Jacaltec, Kinyarwanda, Fijian, Chicewa

4. marking and agreements only	Latin, Basque, Malecite-Passamaquoddy
5. only noun marking	Gugu-Yalanji, Dyirbal, Maori, Machiguenga
6. only position	Tai, Chinese, Tera, Maninka, Ainu, (full NP DOs)
7. only agreements	none

Notes

1. I would like to thank the Wenner-Gren Foundation for having supported the work on subject-final languages, grant 2944.

2. Other such orders are O+S+Obl+V, Obl+S+O+V, and V+Obl+S+O, but these orders are generally unattested in the world's languages.

3. Chung (1975) first discussed the problem of two passives in a given language (Indonesian) for Relational Grammar. The two passives in Japanese are discussed by Shimizu (1975) and those in Dyirbal by Anderson (1974), where it is shown that the passive that demotes the topic to dative does not feed the other major transformations in the language, whereas the one that demotes the topic to an instrumental does. In addition, Kimbundu (Givón, personal communication, see Chatelain 1888) and Swahili (Givón 1972) also present two PASSIVES, but we do not know whether their differences are ones of 'mere' surface form or rather indicative of deeper transformational behaviour.

4. Contrary to the opinion of some, VSO is a well attested, if minority, word order type across the world's languages. It is found in at least the following five major groups: Amerindian (e.g. Salish — Bella Coola, Mayan — Jacaltec), Celtic (Welsh), Semitic (classical Arabic), Nilo-Saharan (Maasai), and Malayo-Polynesian (Tongan). Note that for purposes of establishing that Su is not higher in the S than DO, those languages which are verb initial and relatively free word order, having some preference for VSO are also good support. They include e.g. Samoan and Maori.

5. The productivity of this construction is limited to those verbs which exhibit the required nominalisation, as in *mæruva* (killed) *mærung* (death). As e.g. 'see' had none, this type of construction cannot be used to translate 'I was seen', etc.

6. Note that when we say, 'It is more difficult to passivise statives than activity predicates', we mean that 'If a language can passivise statives, then, generally, it can passivise activity predicates.' It should be immediately apparent that this type of distributional regularity is one that we want to account for in universal grammar. But since a conditional regularity (If a language has P then it has Q) is not one which is present as a constraint on a rule in any given language some may feel it is different in status from an 'absolute' universal of the form 'All languages have P'. But in fact the conditional universal is the logically more general, for all absolute universals, all languages have P, can always be stated in conditional form, if a language has Q then it has P, where Q is taken as some predicate which trivially holds of all languages.

References

In addition to the works cited below, I would like to thank the following linguists for their help with the indicated languages: K. Bimson — Bambara; H. Hardy — Bella Coola; M. Mebarkia — Arabic; K. Radics — Hungarian; M. Shimizu — Japanese, and J. Yamada — Telugu.

Anderson S. (1974) 'Linguistic Institute Lectures'.
Arms D. (1974) *Transitivity in Standard Fijian*, Ph.D. dissertation, University of Michigan.
Bailard J. (1975) 'Promotional rules in French, Kinyarwanda and Turkish', unpublished paper, UCLA.
Bowen J. and T. Jones (1960) *Welsh*, Teach Yourself Books, English Universities Press, London.
Chatelain H. (1888) *Grammatica Elementar do Kimbundu*. Geneva, reprinted in Gregg.
Chomsky N. (1965) *Aspects of the Theory of Syntax*, MIT Press, Cambridge, Massachusetts.
Chung S. (1975) 'On the Subject of Two Passives in Indonesian', in C Li (ed.) *Subject and Topic*, Academic Press, New York.
Churchward C. (1953) *Tongan Grammar*, Oxford University Press, London.
Clark R. (1974) 'Transitivity and Case in Eastern Oceanic Languages', presented at the First International Conference on Comparative Austronesian Linguistics, Honolulu.
Craig C. (1974) *Jacaltec Syntax. A Study of Complete Sentences*, unpublished Ph.D. dissertation, Harvard University, Cambridge, Massachusetts.
Dixon R.M.W. (1972) *The Dyirbal Language of North Queensland*, Cambridge, Cambridge University Press.
Gildersleeve B.L. and G. Lodge (1913) *Latin Grammar* (3rd. ed.)
Givón T. (1972) Review of 'Some Problems of Transitivity in Swahili' by W.H. Whitely in *African Studies* 31, 5, 273-7.
Hale K. (1967) *Preliminary Remarks on Walbiri Grammar*, MIT Press, Cambridge, Massachusetts.
Hasegawa N. (1968) 'The Passive Construction in English', *Language* 44, 230-43.
Hershberger H. (1964) 'Notes on Gugu-Yalanji Verbs' and 'Gugu-Yalanji Noun Phrases' both in R. Pittman and H. Kerr (eds.) *Papers on the Australian Aborigines*, Australian Institute.
Johnson D. (1974) *Toward a Theory of Relationally Based Grammar*, University of Illinois.
Keenan E.L. (1972) 'Relative Clause Formation in Malagasy' in P.M. Peranteau, J.N. Levi, and G.C. Phares (eds.) *The Chicago Which Hunt*, Chicago Linguistic Society, Chicago, Illinois.
—— (1974) 'A Universal Definition of "Subject-of"' presented to Winter LSA.
—— (1975) 'Towards a Universal Definition of "Subject-of"', in C. Li (ed.) *Subject and Topic*, Academic Press, New York.
Kirsner R. (1975) 'On the Subjectless "Pseudo-Passive" in Standard Dutch and the Problem of Backgrounded Agents' in C. Li (ed.) *Subject and Topic*, Academic Press, New York.
Lafitte P. (1962) *Grammaire Basque*, Navarro-labourdin littéraire, Bayonne.
Lakoff R. (1971) 'Passive Resistance' *Chicago Linguistic Society*, VII, 149-63.
Langacker R. and P. Munro (1974) 'Passives and Their Meaning' *Language* 51, 4, 789-830.

Lazdina T.B. (1966) *Latvian*, Teach Yourself Books, English Universities Press, London.

Needleman R. (1973) *Tai Verbal Structures and Some Implications for Current Linguistic Theory*, Ph.D. dissertation UCLA.

Newman P. (1970) *A Grammar of Tera*, University of California, published in *Linguistics* 57.

Perlmutter D. and P.M. Postal (1974) 'Linguistic Institute Lectures', unpublished manuscript.

Schachter P. (1975) 'The Subject in Philippine Languages: Topic, Actor, Actor-Topic, or None of the Above?' in C. Li (ed.) *Subject and Topic*, Academic Press, New York.

—— and P. Otanes (1972) *Tagalog Reference Grammar*, University of California Press, Berkeley.

Shopen T. and C. Bird (1974) 'Maninka', Center for Applied Linguistics, unpublished.

Siegel D. (1973) 'Nonsources of Unpassives' in J. Kimball (ed.) *Syntax and Semantics* 2, Seminar Press Inc.

Snell B. and R. Wise (1963) 'Noncontingent Declarative Clauses in Machiguenga (Arawak)', *Studies in Peruvian Indian Languages* 1, 103-45, Summer Institute of Linguistics, University of Oklahoma, Norman, Oklahoma.

Timberlake A. (1975) 'Subject Properties in the North Russian Passive', in C. Li (ed.) *Subject and Topic*, Academic Press, New York.

8 PASSIVE IS PHRASAL (NOT SENTENTIAL OR LEXICAL)

1. Introduction

Following Keenan and Faltz (1979) and Keenan (1980) I shall argue here that Passive in English, and in fact quite generally in the language of the world, is a verb phrase derivational rule, not a sentence level one (transformation) and not a strictly lexical level one. More specifically I argue that Passive is best treated as a family of rules which derive n-place predicates from n + 1 place predicates, subject to certain conditions on semantic interpretation to be discussed below.

In Section 1.1 I briefly situate the treatment of Passive proposed here with respect to other treatments in the literature. In 1.2 I make explicit certain criteria which will be used to evaluate one syntactic analysis over another. In Section 2, I contrast sentential level derivational analyses of Passive, as a group, with an analysis which is at least limited to the derivation of verb phrases. In section 3, I contrast the phrasal analysis proposed here with the special case of strictly lexical passives. And in Section 4 I summarise some of the advantages and consequences of adopting the phrasal analysis of Passive proposed here.

1.1 Previous Treatments of Passive

Current treatments of Passive in the literature on generative grammar may be roughly grouped into three types: (1) sentential, (2) lexical, and (3) phrasal. Sentential treatments consider 'passives' to be sentences derived from another sentence (in the sense that they are derived from a structure having the category 'S'; that S need not be a fully formed surface form). Within this group we might distinguish 'one storey' analyses from 'two storey' ones. The two storey ones, exemplified in different ways by Awbery (1976), Hasegawa (1968), Lakoff (1971), and Langacker and Munro (1974), claim roughly that the sentential source for passives consists of one sentence embedded within another and the derivation of passives collapses these two Ss into a single surface clause. By contrast one-storey treatments derive passive sentences from a single sentence (clause). Such treatments have abounded in the generative literature from the earliest formulation (Chomsky 1957) to quite recent ones (Baker 1978, Perlmutter and Postal 1977).

Strictly lexical views are more recent in the generative literature (Friedin 1975, Bresnan 1978, Wasow, 1976) though we might note that traditional Latin/Greek based grammars treated Passive as a verbal not sentential category. (Here passives are lexical intransitive verbs derived from lexical transitive verbs.)[1]

Finally properly phrasal level treatments, in which passives are VPs derived from TVPs (transitive verb phrases) have been proposed in Thomason (1976), Dowty (1978), Bach (1979), and Keenan and Faltz (1978 and 1979). The treatment I propose here is a generalisation of that in Keenan and Faltz (1979), henceforth KF-79.

Note that the lexical and phrasal views are more similar to each other than either is to sentential views. The strictly lexical views can be treated in fact as a special case of the phrasal ones, the case where the only TVPs to undergo the passive derivation are lexical TVPs.

1.2 Adequacy Criteria for Syntactic Analysis

I accept here without discussion the standard adequacy criteria used in the literature — that we generate only structures judged as well formed by native speakers (the Soundness Criterion) and that we generate all of them (the Completeness Criterion). And I accept easily the principle that given two analyses of comparable descriptive adequacy according to the Soundness and Completeness Criteria we prefer one over the other if it is explanatorily more adequate in the sense that we can use the one to greater effect than the other to explain properties of natural language other than the judgements of grammaticality which justified the descriptive adequacy of the two analyses in the first place. The class of such other facts is of course an open class. But we all agree that we want to at least provide a basis for explaining that children learn to speak in a reasonable time period with only limited exposure to the language, exposure often contaminated with structures that are not fully well formed. And we all agree that we want to account in some way for how it is that competent speakers produce and comprehend sentences (and other structures) which they have not previously heard or produced.

So we naturally will prefer one grammar over another if it is drawn from a more restricted class of grammars; for then the child has fewer possibilities to choose from in deciding which of his genetically possible languages he is actually faced with, and thus we have a better basis for explaining how he learns quickly with limited exposure. And we shall in fact invoke precisely this reasoning in arguing for the phrasal analysis proposed here. Specifically, Passive on this view is largely a context-free phenomenon and so the class of passives the child has to learn to recognise is drawn from a more limited class of grammars than if passive were a sentence level transformational rule in the classical sense. Moreover our proposal does not require that language processors (children or other) recognise empty nodes or be able to invoke the process not fully specified in the literature, of coindexing phonologically empty nodes with full NPs and interpret them 'accordingly'. So in some sense then fewer demands are placed on interpreting passive surface forms (phonologically interpreted) than on many current views (cf. Chomsky and Lasnik 1977). (We are not however proposing that no 'traces' are necessary in general; only that we don't need them for passives, and a variety of similar 'relation changing' phenomena such as 'Raising', 'Equi', etc. Thus the presence of traces on this view is more limited and thus susceptible of a more restrained semantic interpretation — namely as bound variables in the logicians' sense.)

Accepting the goal of explaining (more exactly: providing the basis of an explanation) child acquisition and the comprehension/ production of novel utterances, I would like to make explicit two 'guidelines' for assessing the adequacy of a proposed analysis of any type of syntactic structure. The first, which I shall call the Minimal Domain Principle, and only discuss informally, is I feel accepted in the practice of working linguists though perhaps has not been explicitly acknowledged as a principle.

The idea behind the Minimal Domain Principle (MDP) is that in defining a particular derivational function, whether of a lexical, phrase structural, transformational, or morphophonemic sort, we take the domain of definition of the function to be the smallest class (level) of structures on which it can be defined giving adequate results. An example: consider the differences in form and meaning between (1a) and (1b):

(1)   a.   Every tall woman will object.
      b.   Every very tall woman will object.

We might (perversely, and rightly so, by current standards) attempt to derive these sentences by deriving (1a) in a 'standard' way and deriving (1b) from it by a sentence level transformation such as (2):

(2)   ... [$_{NP}$ (Det)-A-N-Y] ...   ⇒ 1-2-very-3-4-5

One might rule out such a rule on a variety of grounds, but I think the intuitively most convincing is that the differences in form and meaning between (1a) and (1b) are entirely given by the difference in form and meaning of the two NP subjects. If we treat this difference then at a level of NP syntax the rules we need anyway to combine NPs with VPs to yield sentences will generate both (1a) and (1b). So the presence of *very* in such cases is at most an NP level phenomenon not a sentence level one, and since, intuitively the class of NPs is a more restricted class than the class of Ss (if we generate all the Ss of English we have generated all the NPs, but the converse fails as some Ss, e.g. *Has John left*? do not naturally occur within NPs), the MDP tells us to prefer an NP level analysis over a sentence level one in such cases.

In fact of course we can go further. The same reasoning tells us that the differences in form and meaning between the two NPs is completely given by the differences in form and meaning between *tall* and *very tall*. If both are generated, as they would be on all views, as adjective phrases, then the independently needed syntax which combines APs with nouns and then puts determiners on generates the two NPs in question. So again by the MDP the distribution of *very* above is best handled at a level of AP syntax (if we generate all NPs we have generated all APs but the converse fails).

In a similar fashion I shall argue below that Passive, not only in English but in fact in languages in general, is a VP level phenomenon, not a sentence level one. This claim then argues against sentence level analyses of Passive, but is compatible with phrasal and lexical analyses.

Second, and avowedly more problematic for some, let us recall the learnability and comprehension facts we want to explain. When we comprehend a novel utterance we do not simply recognise it as well formed — we understand it. That is, we assign it a meaning. Similarly when we say that a child has learned a language we do not mean that he has merely learned to produce well formed sentences, etc. He has learned to use them meaningfully — to say things he intends as true, to say things he intends as false, to deny, to infer things from what others have said, to express desires he actually has, etc. Work in generative grammar has emphasised (the acquisition of) syntactic competence, perhaps at the expense of semantic competence. Clearly to explain our semantic competence (and its acquisition) we want a grammar which semantically interprets the syntactic structures of the language in a way that is learnable and in a way that allows us to explain (as always: 'provide the basis of an explanation for') how we assign an interpretation to a sentence which is novel to us. The following principle is the only one I know of which provides such an explanation (but this of course does not mean that others will not be discovered):

The Interpretive Principle (IP)
The semantic interpretation of an expression is a function of (determined by) the interpretation of the expression(s) it is derived from (up to some tolerable level of idiomaticity and systematic ambiguity).

(The IP is obviously very closely related to Compositionality, 'Frege's principle', etc. See Keenan 1979 and KF-1978 for much more discussion).

What this says in a nutshell is that if our grammar derives an expression A from an expression B then a competent speaker can determine the meaning of A if he knows the meaning of B. And given the IP (presented perhaps a little more explicitly, as per the references above) it is relatively easy to see how we assign interpretations to novel utterances, if we can recognise what they are derived from (which we should be able to if we're competent) and we know the interpretation of what they are derived from.

I'm not of course claiming that the IP is the only principle in terms of which we interpret sentences, but only that it is a basic one, one which enables us to account to a significant extent for our ability to interpret novel utterances. Other interpretative procedures surely exist. Idiom interpretation will not proceed as per the IP, and doubtless the interpretation of metaphors and various figurative usages (by no means trivial or marginal) will surely require additional principles.

In any event we shall argue for our analysis of Passive on the grounds that it satisfies IP to a greater extent than other analyses.

In particular since passives on our view are base-generated by context-free rules we will show that they can be interpreted as a function of the interpretations of their immediate constituents.

2. Phrasal versus Sentence Level Views of Passive

KF-79 report an investigation of passive structures in a large number of languages and present many properties of passives which they call *general* — that is, roughly, 90 % or more of the passive structures considered had those properties. I shall draw on these facts here to support a phrasal over a sentential view of Passive and refer the reader to KF-79 for examples and other supporting data. The first relevant fact is:

(3)   In *general*, if s is a passive sentence then (a) s differs from actives (non-passives) with respect to its VP and (b) s does not differ from actives in any other respect.

So up to ordinary limits of ambiguity, you can in general tell if a sentence is passive just by looking at its VP; moreover looking at anything else won't help. In particular the position and case marking of the subject does not differentiate passives from actives. For example passives are never formed (in distinction to yes-no questions) by inverting the Subject and the VP or the Subject and the Aux (if there is one). Nor are passives ever formed by placing a particle in an active, where the position of the particle with respect to the sentence as a whole, e.g. at the beginning of the sentence, at the end, between the subject and the VP, etc. Nor are passives ever formed by assigning an active sentence a distinctive intonation.

In short, to generate passives, not only in English but in languages quite generally, it is sufficient to derive VPs of a certain sort. Rules independently needed to combine VPs with NPs to form sentences will then generate passive sentences.

Thus by the Minimal Domain Principle Passive should be taken as a VP level derivational phenomenon, not a sentence level one.

Contrast Passive in this respect with the way yes-no questions are generally formed. Most treatments, correct to my mind, basically derive a yes-no question by modifying a declarative in some way — that is, yes-no question formation is a sentence level derivational rule. And this is correct since the syntactic distinctiveness of yes-no questions is not localised at a level of analysis smaller than the sentence. It is the whole sentence which carries the distinctive intonation; specifically interrogative particles are most commonly placed in a position defined with respect to the sentence as a whole, e.g. at the beginning, the end, etc. Even such uncommon ways of forming questions as inverting the subject and the VP (or the Aux) require that we mention two major constituents of the sentence, and the smallest unit of analysis which includes those items mentioned by the question-forming rule is the sentence itself.

Second, what holds of the syntax of passives and actives also holds of their semantic relations. Basically *there is no semantic relation which generally holds of active sentences and their passives.* But there are statable semantic relations between passive VPs and the TVPs they are derived from a phrasal view.

To support the first point consider first that by far the most widespread type of passive sentence is that exemplified by (4):

(4)   John was beaten.

The essential properties of (4) are that the passivised verb is a simple transitive verb denoting a physical activity and that it is agentless. (KF-79 list a half a dozen languages whose passives do not even permit the presence of agent phrases.)

Now to see that active and passive sentences, contrary to the early claims, are not 'cognitive paraphrases' in the sense of having the same truth conditions, it is sufficient to note that neither the (a) nor (b) sentences below entail the other, that is each could be true in a situation in which the other is false.

(5)   a.   Mary kissed no-one.
       b.   No-one was kissed.
(6)   a.   Mary interviewed few pupils' parents.
       b.   Few pupils' parents were interviewed.
(7)   a.   John ate many apples at the fair.
       b.   Many apples were eaten at the fair.
(8)   a.   Neither Fred nor Frank kissed Mary.
       b.   Mary was kissed.
(9)   a.   John kissed only Mary.
       b.   Only Mary was kissed.

(10) a. John rarely visits museums.
     b. Museums are rarely visited.

Of course for certain choices of NP an active sentence will entail its agentless passive. E.g. *Mary kissed John* entails *John was kissed.* None the less examples (5) to (10) clearly justify that if all we know of the sentence *s* is that it is a passive of a sentence *t* we can make no claim concerning whether *s* entails *t* or vice versa. For some choices of *s* and *t* certain entailments obtain and for many other choices they do not. In fact the only cases where actives regularly entail their agentless passives (we get to agented ones shortly) are ones in which the NPs in the sentence denote individual entities (as do e.g. proper nouns like *John*). Negative and quantified NPs, as well as conjunctions and disjunctions of NPs, do not in general denote individuals. Syntactically speaking most NPs are not of the individual-denoting sort.

We may conclude from the above that if agentless passive sentences are derived from actives then we cannot, in any natural way, give the semantic interpretation of the derived structures as a function of the interpretation of what it is derived from, and thus the IP fails on sentence level treatments of Passive.

But the IP holds for the phrasal derivational view we are proposing. On that view we derive a passive VP from a TVP (transitive verb phrase). Let us represent this derivation abstractly as follows: if tvp is a particular transitive verb phrase in a language then denote a passive of it by (Pass, tvp). So for English we shall here represent (ignoring tense and aspect) *was kissed,* the passive of the TVP *kiss,* by (Pass, *kiss*).

Now by the IP, we should be able to give the semantic interpretation of e.g. (Pass, *kiss*) as a function of that of *kiss.* And basically we can (though we shall ignore here a variety of subtle problems). Consider at least minimally what is involved. In a given state of affairs we may specify a VP (including passive ones) by stating which individuals they are true and false of. Once this is done we have determined whether the VP holds of what more complex NPs denote. That is, if I have determined for each individual whether *sing* (or *was kissed*) holds or fails of him, then we have determined the truth value of sentences like *everyone sings* (*was kissed*), *Neither John nor Fred sing* (*were kissed*), etc. So we may minimally think of (extensional) VPs semantically as functions from NP meanings into truth values, functions which are determined by the values they assign to individuals. (See KF-78 for a formal statement of how these functions are extended to the denotations of negative, quantified, and conjoined NPs.)

Similarly we can think, extensionally, of TVPs as functions which assign truth values to pairs of individuals, or equivalently, as functions which map each individual onto a VP meaning (a function which assigns truth values to single individuals). So if k is a function which interprets *kiss* in some state of affairs, and x and y are individuals in that state of affairs (possible world) then the truth value of (confusing levels) 'x kissed y' is represented by $(k(y)) (x)$, using standard function-argument notation.

And a decent first attempt at stating the relation between passive VPs and the TVPs they are derived from is given by (11), where tvp is some TVP, and x is an arbitrarily chosen individual:

(11) $(\text{Pass, tvp}) (x) = (\exists y) (\text{tvp}(x)) (y)$

For example, from (11) we have that (Pass, *kiss*) is that VP function which assigns to each individual x the truth value represented by 'for some y, y kissed x.'

Much more could be said here (and some more will) but even this primitive statement of the active-passive relation is sufficient to show that an active sentence will entail its agentless passive when the NPs used are the sort that denote individuals. If *John kissed Mary* is true then *Someone kissed Mary* is true and thus *Mary was kissed* is true by (11).

Consider now the syntactic and semantic properties of passives with agent phrases. Note first the following *general* fact from KF-79:

(12) In general agent phrases in passives take the case marking and pre- or post-position of some active oblique NP (usually a locative, instrumental, or sometimes a genitive) and generally agent phrases are positioned like the active obliques whose markings they take.

KF note some exceptions to (12) but still it appears that generally, i.e., for about 90% of the passive constructions with agent phrases, the claim holds. Recall as well that it is not uncommon that a language may have passives which don't allow agent phrases at all.

These two facts determine two more general deficiencies of the sentence level derivational views. Most such views (but not all, e.g. Awbery 1976 and Langacker and Munro 1974) derive the agent phrase in passives by moving and marking the subject of the active, not by independently generating it as an oblique NP. Yet, by (12), we have that syntactically it can be independently generated as an oblique NP and thus by the Minimal Domain Principle should be. Moreover, since several languages don't allow agent phrases we should in those cases have to obligatorily eliminate the agent phrase. In those languages it is not easy to see how children would learn such a rule since they have no direct evidence that an agent phrase could possibly be there in the first place. Finally, we note as well from KF-79 that, with the single exception of Achenese, agent phrases in passives are generally optional; that is, all languages having passives at all (except it appears, Achenese) present agentless passives. Thus most sentential views of Passive are more complicated than the one we propose as they require an additional rule of agent deletion which our approach, on which agent phrases are independently generated as oblique NPs, does not.

And finally, as regards the syntax of agent phrases, note that not uncommonly agent phrases can occur in structures which are clearly not passives. That is, quite apart from passives we shall need to generate agent phrases. So the sentence level derivation of agent phrases clearly duplicates what is needed anyway in the phrase structure (where basic oblique NPs are generated). To support the independent generation of agent phrases in English consider their presence on the (for lack of a better name) gerundive nominals in (13) and on the 'strong' or at least 'stronger' nominals in (14). In both cases we have chosen the verbs underlying the nominalisation as intransitive, and thus there is no motivation for saying that passive has anywhere applied to them.

(13) a. Cheating *by students* will be punished.
　　 b. Talking *by undergraduates* at High Table is forbidden.
(14) a. The move *by United* was unexpected.
　　 b. The march on Washington *by the farm workers* was a success.
　　 c. A wild pitch *by Tanner/* a left jab *by Ali*, ...

KF-79 give other non-passive environments across languages which take agent phrases.

One might have hoped that the sentential derivations of passives would handle the semantics of agent phrases however, since they are understood in basically the same way (in passives) as the subjects of the *TVP*s the passive VPs are derived from. But once again the IP is not satisfied. Agented passives are not always paraphrases of their actives nor do they bear a regular entailment relation to them. Similarly, for those approaches which have it, the agent phrase deletion rule is not paraphrastic. In the first case, the general problem of the logical equivalence of actives and agented passives is that for many choices of quantified NP we interpreted the subject of the passive as having wide scope over the agent phrase, whereas just the opposite scope assignment prevails in the active. That is, in general, subjects tend to have wide scope over elements of the VP, though the scope facts are often delicate and exhibit individual variation. None the less my feeling is that Chomsky's original assessment that (15b) is ambiguous in a way in which (15a) is not is clearly correct:

(15) a.   Everyone in this room speaks two languages.
     b.   Two languages are spoken by everyone in this room.

Some linguists have wanted to claim that in fact (15a) is ambiguous in the way (15b) is. While I think this is not to be the case, there are other examples which seem to me unimpeachable. Thus (16a) is not ambiguous and clearly fails to entail (16b), which shows that in general agented passives do not entail their corresponding actives:

(16) a.   No politician is admired by each student.
     b.   Each student admires no politician.

Similarly (17a) is unambiguous and clearly fails to entail (17b), which shows that actives do not always entail their agented passives:

(17) a.   No student kissed each politician.
     b.   Each politician was kissed by no student.

(18a) and (18b) is another case in which actives fail to entail their agented passives, and (19a/b) the corresponding case in which passives fail to entail actives.

(18) a.   Each student answered exactly half of the questions.
    b.   Exactly half of the questions were answered by each student.
(19) a.   Each question was answered by exactly half of the students.
    b.   Exactly half of the students answered each question.

A final example of a different but long familiar sort, taken again from Chomsky and never, to my knowledge rebutted:

(20) a.   Beavers build dams.
    b.   Dams are built by beavers.

Clearly (20a) can be true in a state of affairs in which men commonly build dams, but (20b) is not.

The phrasal analysis of agent phrases we suggest below can predict the syntactic (distributional) facts of agent phrases cited above and does give the correct predictions of entailment for the basic quantified and negative NPs (but we have no analysis of generics as in 20).

Syntactically we treat PPs, including the agentive by + NP as things which combine with n-place predicates (VPs are one-place predicates, TVPs are 2-place predicates, etc.) to form expressions of the same category. E.g., *sing*, and *sing in the garden* are both one-place predicates, *see* and *see from the porch* are both two-place predicates. Since PPs are not obligatory it follows immediately from this treatment that if a language has agented passives it also has agentless ones, which is generally correct. If a language has no agentive adposition then its passives (if it has any, and it may) will be obligatorily agentless, which as we have seen happens in some cases. Nor, perhaps surprisingly, is the semantics of agent phrases particularly difficult. (21) states the semantics for agent phrases applied to one place predicates. (vp is an arbitrary one-place predicate, x and y arbitrary individuals):

(21) $((by\ x)(vp))(y) = vp(x)$

E.g., *sing by x* assigns the same truth value to an individual *y* as *sing* itself does to *x*. This says unequivocally that the agent NP, *x*, is interpreted as the subject of the VP which the *by* phrase combines with. Semantically of course we cannot specify the (semantic) subject of *sing* by two differently referring NPs, so a 'sentence' like *John sang by Mary* (agentive reading on *by*) is nonsensical. So we would like to guarantee that once we have put an agent phrase on an n-place predicate we cannot in some other way put another NP into the sentence which also specifies the semantic subject of that n-place predicate. One such way is by nominalising the agentive VP derived with the *by*-phrase. So e.g., *the singing by the students* is both well formed and sensible, and clearly *the students* is interpreted as the semantic subject of *sing*, as our semantics says. Of course another way of guaranteeing that the subject of the n-place predicate will not be specified independently of the agent phrase is to passivise the n-place predicate. In English we cannot do this for one place predicates, but in many languages we can (Latin, cf. *curritur* = 'run + pass' meaning 'running is taking place/being done', Turkish, Shona, etc.).

The semantics for *by* + *x* which combine with TVPs is given below. (It is only a matter of notation to state a single definition covering agent phrases on n-place predicates in general, but the additional notation is not more enlightening than the examples given here.)

(22) $(((by\ x)\ (tvp))(y))(z) = ((tvp(y))(x)$

Sloppily, 'John kissed Mary by Susan' has the same truth value as 'Susan kissed Mary.' Again of course we cannot specify the semantic subject of the *TVP* 'kiss' twice. And passive, as well as nominalising, is one way of avoiding this. Note that our semantics for *by*-phrases plus the *independently given* semantics for Passive yield the correct semantic results (for the minimally simple cases considered):

$$
\begin{aligned}
(23)\ (Pass,\ ((by\ x)(kiss)))(y) &= (\exists z)((by\ x)(kiss))(y))(z) \\
&= (\exists z)((kiss(y))(x)) \\
&= (kiss(y))(x)
\end{aligned}
$$

That is, 'y was kissed by x' has the same truth value as 'x kissed y' (x and y understood to be individuals of course).

Overall then the phrasal generation of passives (in the simplest case) and the independent generation of agent phrases yields a large variety of generally (i.e., in roughly 90 % of the world's passives) correct syntactic and semantic predictions, ones which are either not made or more usually mismade by the sentential level approach.

And yet there are still further advantages of a phrasal approach of the sort outlined here. For one, we have a more natural way to state 'lexical' exceptions to Passive. It has always been embarrassing to a purely sentence level approach to attempt to restrict the Passive rule if the main verb of the sentence is drawn from a certain class, one which in English say might include *be, have, lack, resemble,* etc. It is not that it is impossible to do, but it is very hard to see the motivation for restricting the application of a rule in terms of something not mentioned by the rule. (We note that the classical, *Syntactic Structures,* view of passive did mention the category V, but that more recent views which move the direct object to subject by a move-NP rule, not specific to passives, do not.) Nor does there appear to be any hope of universally restricting the verbs which can undergo Passive. In KF-79 examples are given from Kinyarwanda which show that sentences like *This shirt has two buttons* have natural passives (*two buttons are had by this shirt*). Similarly *this book weighs two kilos* has a passive, *two kilos are weighed by this book.*

On the other hand, in our view lexical restrictions are more natural. Passive derives VPs from TVPs and to define Passive we must state just what TVPs are in the domain of definition of the rule. It is we submit more natural to restrict a rule in terms of items specifically mentioned in the rule than in terms of things not mentioned in the rule. There are after all infinitely many things not mentioned in any given rule. How would the child know to look for any particular choice among this infinitude?

Furthermore, the analogue of lexical constraints on the application of Passive exists on a semantic level as well. Thus the exact semantics of (Pass, tvp) will depend on the semantic properties of the tvp in question. For example, if the tvp is highly stative rather than being a simple physical activity one, then the truth value (Pass, tvp) assigns to an individual x is more accurately given by 'for most relevant individuals y, (tvp (x))(y).' Thus for *John was respected* to be true we require more than simply than *someone respected John* be true; we require that most relevant parties respected John, a point noted in Bach (1979).

Another case: TVPs which are not extensional on their objects, *seek, order,* etc. as opposed to ones like *kiss, hug,* etc. are also not extensional on their subjects when passivised. This shows up clearly in entailment differences like that below, where (24a) entails (24b) but (25a) does not entail (25b).

(24) a.   Mary was hugged in the garden.
     b. ⊨ Mary was in the garden.
(25) a.   Mary was sought in the garden.
     b. ⊭ Mary was in the garden.

See KF-78 for a treatment of such passives in which these entailment facts are represented.

Now treating Passive semantically as a way of forming VP functions from TVP ones it is natural to make the semantics of the derived function depend on the semantics of the one it is derived from, in the same kind of way that it is easy to make the value of a numerical function depend on properties the argument has. E.g. consider the function f from natural numbers to natural numbers such that $f(x) = x + 1$ if x is even and $f(x) = x + 2$ if x is odd.

But it is not natural to state these conditioning factors on the interpretation of Passive if Passive derives sentence meanings from sentence meanings. Extensionally speaking we cannot tell by looking at the truth value of a sentence whether the sentence is formed from an extensional or intensional TVP. So Passive at the very least would have to take sentence intensions (say functions from possible worlds = extensional interpretations into truth values) as arguments, and on anyone's account of intensional logic the semantics of intensional operators is much more complex than extensional ones. So this treatment again places a greater burden on the language learner and user than the generally extensional treatment given here. Worse, even if we are given a function from possible worlds to truth values there is still no way to tell whether a sentence expressing such a function is necessarily formed from an intensional TVP or an extensional one so it appears that invoking the complicated apparatus of intensional logic will not, at least in any obvious way, allow us to state the correct condition factors on the interpretation of passives.

And second, the phrasal view of passive presented here generalises easily in a way which permits the statement of certain universals of Passive. Thus Passive is not to be merely an operation which derives one-place predicates from two-place ones, but rather it derives n-place predicates from n+1 place ones, in such a way that, loosely, the last (or 'deepest') thing the n + 1 place predicate combines with is the subject of the n-place predicate; the subject argument of the n + 1 place predicate is eliminated, and the other arguments remain the same schematically.

$$(26) \quad P_n \quad \rightarrow \quad Pass \quad + \quad P_{n+1}$$
$$x_1, \ldots, x_n \qquad\qquad y, x_2, \ldots, x_n, x_1$$

The semantics of the derived P_n is given as the existential generalisation over the subject of the P_{n+1} as before. The rule basically defined by (26) is to be thought of as a rule of Core Grammar, stated using variables (parameters) such as n, for the number of arguments of the predicates (= the number of things it subcategorises, including its subject) and the x_1 and y, which range over possible arguments, e.g., full NPs, Ss (or perhaps $\bar{S}$s), etc. To state Passive in any particular language it suffices to state the values of the parameters realised by that language. Now we may associate each rule of Core Grammar with one or more Parameter Conditions which constrain the choice of values for the parameters in making up a grammar for any possible human language. In the case at hand for example we might require as a parameter condition that for each possible language L, the range of n in L includes 1 (if that range is not in fact empty). So if a language like Latin, Turkish, etc. can passivise intransitive verbs (so in that case n + 1 in the rule = 1 so n = 0) then we know that it can passivise transitive verbs; for the range of n is not empty so it contains 1 and thus we have passives of 1 + 1 = 2-place verbs. A much more detailed statement of the formalism needed to state Core Grammar along these lines is given in Keenan (1980). For now it is sufficient to say simply that the generalisation 'if a language can passivise intransitive verbs then it can passivise transitive verbs, but the converse fails' represents a basic statement about the nature of Passive in human language. It works best on TVPs and from there its domain of application may be extended. And this generalisation is naturally statable on a view of Passive in which it derives n-place predicates from n + 1 place ones, and it is not naturally statable on a view of Passive which does not mention n-place predicates, such as several of the sentence level derivational views.

3. Passive is Properly Phrasal not Merely Lexical

I shall present here a variety of cases in which we want to say that
what has been passivised is not merely a lexical TVP but a lexical
TVP together with other material, such as PPs.

The first type of argument takes the following form: we
establish first that semantically we want material other than simple
TVP meanings to be in the scope of passive. E.g. for certain types
of PPs we want the logical form of the passive of a tvp and pp to be
[*pass* (tvp + pp)] and not e.g. [(pass (tvp)) + pp]. Then by the IP,
which requires that the interpretation of a constituent generated by
phrase structure rules should be a function of the interpretation of
its immediate constituents, we can infer that syntactically the
immediate constituents of the passive VP should be the element
Pass on the one hand and the combination of the TVP + PP on the
other. We have in fact already considered one such case, that of
agentive PPs. We shall now look at this case in some detail justifying that what is passivised is the phrase *kiss by Mary* in *John was
kissed by Mary* and not simply *kiss*.

Suppose, contrary to what we want to show, that the VP *was
kissed by Mary* (ignoring tense/aspect as always) had the structure
shown in (27) in which only the lexical TVP *kiss* was passivised.

(27)   ((Pass, kiss), (by Mary))$_{VP}$

Then the interpretation of (27) according to the IP would have to
be given as a function of the interpretation of (Pass, *kiss*) = *was
kissed* on the one hand and of that of (*by Mary*) on the other. But
this can be shown to lead to incorrect semantic analysis, for by
parity of reasoning *was beaten by Mary* would be interpreted as the
function of the interpretations of *was beaten* and of *by Mary*. Now
imagine a state of affairs, clearly logically possible, in which just
the individuals who were kissed were beaten. That is, *was kissed*
and *was beaten* assign the same truth values to the same individuals (and hence the same truth values to denotations of quantified, negative, conjoined, etc. NPs) and thus are the same
(extensional) function from NP denotations to truth values. Call
that function F for the nonce. Now by the IP, the interpretation of
was kissed by Mary is determined by F and the interpretation of *by
Mary*. And the interpretation of *was beaten by Mary* is also
determined by F and the interpretation of *by Mary*, whence *was*

kissed by Mary and *was beaten by Mary* are extensionally the same function, that is, they must assign the same truth values to the same individuals whenever *was kissed* and *was beaten* do. And that is false.

We may easily construct a model in which the individuals who were kissed were just those who were beaten, but in which those who were kissed by Mary were not exactly those who were beaten by Mary. For example, imagine a state of affairs in which Mary kissed John and Susan beat John and nobody else either kissed or beat anybody else. Then *was kissed* and *was beaten* hold of the same individuals, namely just John, but *was beaten by Mary* holds of no-one while *was kissed by Mary* holds of John, so *was beaten by Mary* and *was kissed by Mary* do not hold of the same individuals even though *was beaten* and *was kissed* do.

Consequently if agent phrases are not part of the TVP which is passivised we cannot give the interpretation of simple passives like *was kissed by Mary* as a function of the interpretations of its immediate constitutents.

On the other hand, allowing Passive to operate on complex TVPs and treating PPs, including agent phrases, as things which combine with n-place predicates forming n-place predicates, as we are proposing, does yield correct results in these cases. Thus the general syntactic form for *John was kissed by Mary* and *John was beaten by Mary* is given in (28a) and (29a) respectively. The corresponding b-forms give the logical structure of the a-forms, and the b-forms, by our given rules for interpreting Passives and agent phrases, are logically equivalent to the c-forms.

(28) a. (John, (Pass, (kiss, (by Mary))))
     b. $(\exists z) ((((\text{ by Mary})(\text{kiss}))(\text{John}))(z))$
     c. (kiss(John))(Mary)
(29) a. (John, (Pass, (beat, (by Mary))))
     b. $(\exists z)((((\text{ by Mary})(\text{beat}))(\text{John}))(z))$
     c. (beat(John))(Mary)

And clearly (28c) and (29c) may have different truth values in an interpretation in which *was kissed* and *was beaten* assign the same truth values to the same individuals. And generally, it is quite possible for different TVPs to assign different truth values to at least one pair of individuals even though their passives assign the same truth values to the same individuals.

To summarise the argument type here: taking PPs in the syntactic scope of Passive allows us to interpret the passives of extensional TVPs directly as a function of their immediate constituents. Requiring that Passive be restricted in application to lexical TVPs, and thus not ones adjoined to a PP, does not.

Moreover agentive PPs, while logically special in one respect, are not special in this respect. That is, we argue below that many other types of PP will form a complex TVP from a simpler one, and that the simplest semantics in keeping with the IP is one in which the complex TVP undergoes Passive. We shall consider some of these PPs here (they do not have the logically constraining property of agentive ones that they pick out the semantic subject of the TVP) and then consider some objections on syntactic/semantic grounds to our analysis of complex TVPs.

Note first that agentive PPs are but an extreme example of what we might more loosely call subject oriented PPs, that is, ones which predicate something of the subject of the VP or TVP they combine with. Consider for example source locatives such as *from the attic* or *from London*, as they occur in (30a) and (31a) below. Note that the a-sentences entail the corresponding b-ones, and so clearly the source locative predicates a locative property of the subject of the VP.

(30)　a.　John fell/leapt/spoke/sang from the attic.
　　　　b.　John was in the attic.
(31)　a.　John came/ran/travelled from London.
　　　　b.　John was in (at) London.

The syntactic analysis of the VPs in the a-sentences is not problematic, so on the basis of these examples we are justified in positing a semantics for source-locative PPs which guarantees the entailment indicated in (32) below (which confuses levels of notation for ease of reading):

(32)　$[x, [_{VP} \text{ vp'd from } y]]$　⊨　x was in (at/on) y

(We hold the tense/aspect constant and ignore it.)

When source locatives combine with TVPs their subject orientation varies as a function of the semantic nature of the TVP. For those which are semantically causatives of verbs of motion the source locative now predicates of the surface direct object. Thus the a-sentences entail the b-sentences below but do not in general entail the c-sentences:

(33) a. John dragged/led/tugged/brought Bill from the attic.
    b. ⊨ Bill was in the attic.
    c. ⊭ John was in the attic.
(34) a. John took/lifted/removed/withdrew the clothes from the tub.
    b. ⊨ The clothes were in the tub.
    c. ⊭ John was in the tub.

On the other hand with other classes of TVPs the subject orientation of the source locative is preserved. This is so for example for 'action at a distance' TVPs. So (35a) entails (35c) but not (35b).

(35) a. John saw/attacked/signalled/roped Bill from the attic.
    b. ⊭ Bill was in the attic.
    c. ⊨ John was in the attic.

Now consider the passives of action at a distance TVPs with source locatives. (36a) does not entail (36b) but does entail (36c). Thus the source locative still predicates of the semantic subject of the TVP, not the derived subject of the passive VP.

(36) a. John was seen/watched/signalled/attacked/roped from the attic.
    b. ⊭ John was in the attic.
    c. ⊨ Someone who saw/watched/signalled, etc. John was in the attic.

Now suppose that the logical form of (36a) is given essentially by (37), in which only the lexical TVP is passivised and the source locative is adjoined to that passive VP.

(37) [John, ($_{VP}$ ($_{VP}$ Pass, see), from the attic)]

Then by the semantic constraints which guarantee that (33a) entails (33b) above, that is, that source locatives applied to VPs predicate of the subject of the VP, we should infer from (36a) that John was in the attic. Which is clearly incorrect. However, if what is passivised in (36a) is the complex TVP, *see from the attic* then the logical form of (36a) will be (38a) from which our semantics of Passive allows us only to infer (38b), and that correctly entails (38c) and not (38d).

(38) a. (John ($_{VP}$ Pass, ($_{TVP}$ see, from the attic)))
     b. for some x, (x, ($_{VP}$ ($_{TVP}$ see from the attic), John))
     c. ⊨ some x was in the attic.
     d. ⊭ John was in the attic.

So again taking TVP as a phrasal category allows us to interpret passives as a function of the interpretation of its immediate constituents whereas constraining Passive to apply only to lexical TVPs would force a more complicated semantics — harder to see how children would learn it, etc. — and would yield counter examples to the IP from simple, (non-idiom) sentences. The strictly lexical analysis of passives then would mitigate against the IP, leaving us with no way to explain the comprehension of novel utterances.

Nor is it just PPs of the source-locative sort which preserve subject orientation under passive. KF-79 give a large number of other types of such PPs. One fairly simple example concerns state-locatives, expressed by *at*, *in*, or *on*. When applied to simple VPs they predicate of the subject of that VP. So (39a) entails (39b).

(39) a. John spoke/fell/vomited/fainted at the meeting.
     b. John was at the meeting.

But state-locatives commonly predicate of the direct object (and sometimes also of the subject) of extensional TVPs. Thus (40a) entails (40b). Whether (40c) is entailed depends on the internal choice of extensional TVP — for some like *wash* the entailment obtains, for others like *see* it doesn't.

(40) a. John saw/found/killed/washed Bill at the meeting.
     b. ⊭ Bill was at the meeting.
     c. ⊨ ? John was at the meeting.

However the subject orientation of state-locatives is preserved when the TVP is drawn from the 'talk-about' class, ones which are generally non-extensional on their objects. So (41a) does not entail

(41b) but does entail (41c), contrary to the paradigm illustrated in (39) above.

(41) a. John criticised/cursed/mentioned Bill at the meeting.
     b. ⊭ Bill was at the meeting.
     c. ⊢ John was at the meeting.

And the passives of complex talk-about TVPs have an entailment paradigm like that of the action at a distance TVPs with respect to source locatives.

(42) a. Bill was criticised (cursed, mentioned) at the meeting.
     b. ⊭ Bill was at the meeting.
     c. ⊢ Someone who criticised (cursed, mentioned) Bill was at the meeting.

Again if Passive were merely lexical the VP of (42a) would consist of the PP *at the meeting* and the passive of *criticise*, which is of course a VP (e.g. *John was criticised*). So the semantics of state-locatives needed to account for the entailment in (39), that such locatives applied to VPs predicate of the subject of the VP, would yield the prediction that (42a) entails (42b) — which is incorrect. And again, if what is passivised in (42a) is the complex TVP *criticise at the meeting* then that passive only allows us to infer from (42a) that *someone ((criticised at the meeting) Bill)*, which will correctly entail (42c).

   In a similar way KF-79 give many other examples of complex TVPs formed from simpler ones plus a PP. Specifically they justify that the VPs in the a-sentences below should consist of Pass plus the complex TVP indicated in the b-sentences.

(43) a. The can was opened with a screwdriver.
     b. VP = [Pass, [$_{TVP}$(open)(with a screwdriver)]]
(44) a. Bill was caught/discovered/seen/surprised with Mary.
     b. VP = [Pass, [$_{TVP}$ catch, with Mary]]

TVP + PP is only one type of phrasally complex TVP which may be passivised however. KF-79 present several other types. Before considering them however let us countenance one quite reasonable objection to our analysis of Passive so far. We are claiming that the combination of a TVP + a PP undergoes Passive but in fact only the embedded TVP carries any passive markings. Couldn't we, by the Minimal Domain Principle, argue that only that TVP is in the domain of Passive. Moreover, aren't we forcing the morphology assignment function which yields past participle forms to apply to full phrases and not just lexical items?

The answer to the second question is clearly yes. And quite independent of passive morphology assignment we want morphology assignment rules in general to apply to phrases. One obvious case is that of Case Marking. Clearly it is entire NPs which are nominative, ergative, accusative, etc. Yet often enough it is only the head N which actually carries morphological indications of case. But also often enough other elements of the entire NP carry such markings, such as the adjectives and determiners (Latin, Russian, etc.).

A second case of phrasal constituents being in the domain of a morphological function is illustrated by so called verb agreement — which is clearly at least verb phrase agreement. For example, VPs which consist of a copular verb + adjective phrase commonly mark agreement both on the copular verb and on the predicate adjective, as illustrated below from French:

(45) Marie et Françoise sont heureuses.
       fsg   fsg   3pl   fpl
       Marie and Françoise are happy.

Analogous claims hold for VPs consisting of a copular verb plus predicate nominals. E.g. *John is a soldier* but *John and Bill are soldiers.*

Yet another case: if a VP is a conjunction of two VPs, normally both conjuncts carry agreement features, as illustrated in (46) below from modern Hebrew.

(46) Ruti v- Miriam shot-ot kafe   v- medabr-ot
       fsg   fsg   fpl   fpl
       Ruth and-Mary drink coffee and talk
       'Ruth and Mary are drinking coffee and talking'

Notice further that there are certain rather general patterns in morphology assignment regardless of the particular type of assignment, e.g. case marking, verb agreement, etc. One regularity is that if a conjoined structure is to be marked, normally both conjuncts carry such marking. (This constraint is referred to as the Morphological Coordinate Structure Constraint in Keenan, 1980.) There is to be sure the odd exception, but marking both conjuncts is the overwhelming norm. A second regularity is that commonly enough though clearly not always, morphological marking of a functionally complex structure tends to attract to the head of the structure. So e.g. it is reasonably common to find cases where case marking affects only the head N of a Det-A-N structure. We don't however find cases where only the adjective carries the case marking morphology.

And of particular interest to us here is that commonly if we are to mark an expression of category X which consists itself of an X + a PP, normally only the head X and not the PP carries the marking. So if *sing in the shower* is to be marked plural only the head *sing* is so marked, not the PP *in the shower*. And if *the man in the shower* is to be marked accusative, say, then normally *in the shower* will not itself carry any specifically accusative marking.

So the fact that the assignment of passive morphology to the TVP + PP does not affect the PP is what one would expect of morphology assignment rules in general, and thus our treatment of Passive is quite unexceptional in this respect.

Furthermore there are other types of complex TVPs in which passive morphology is reflected more than once internal to the TVP and thus the Minimal Domain Principle will require application of Passive to the entire TVP, not just lexical TVPs.

Probably the most obvious case here concerns the passives of conjoined TVPs. Following KF-78 here we assume that natural language grammars have a generalised coordinate structure rule of the form $X \rightarrow (X, \{^{and}_{or}\}, X)$, for X almost any category, including at least S, VP, TVP, DTVP (ditransitive verb phrase), NP, AP, PP, and ADVP (adverb phrase). KF-78 give a general and straightforward semantics for interpreting such conjunctions directly generated. Conversely, the more traditional assumption of conjunction reduction rules has never rigorously been formulated in such a way that a natural semantics can be assigned. No-one to my knowledge can successfully relate (47ab) to their presumed sources on a conjunction reduction analysis.

(47) a. John either hugged or kissed every student in his class.
    b. Some student robbed and beat some professor.

Rather obviously (47a) is not logically equivalent to e.g. *John hugged every student in his class or kissed every student in his class.* However the semantic analysis of coordination and quantified NPs in KF-78 yields the correct results here, and does do with a much simpler grammar than one which posits length decreasing rules such as conjunction reduction: the rules in KF-78 being all context-free as regards conjunction. Accepting this motivation for generating complex TVPs by conjoining simpler ones, the syntactic form of (48a) below would be roughly given by (48b). And this shows that the passive morphology, specifically the past participle morphology, is present on each conjunct of the TVP passivised, which is of course in conformity with what we know about morphology assignment in general on coordinate structures.

(48) a.   Mary was hugged or kissed by John.
     b.   (Mary, [$_{VP}$Pass [$_{TVP}$ [$_{TVP}$ hug or kiss] [$_{PP}$ by John]]])

There is moreover a second, less well attested, type of case where passive morphology is present on two different parts of complex TVPs. This case concerns the passives of TVPs modified by certain sorts of 'higher' verbs, notably aspectual type verbs like *begin* and desiderative verbs like *want.* Thus traditional grammars of Turkish (Lewis 1967) point out that sentences like (49a) below passivise to (49b) in which both the TVP and the aspectual or desiderative verb show passive morphology.

(49) a.   Ahmet kitab-i   oku-maya   başladi
          Ahmet book-acc read-inf+dat begin+past
          'Ahmet began to read the book'
     b.   Kitap (Ahmet tarafından) oku- n-   maya   başla-n-
                                                                  di
          book   Ahmet by   read-pass- inf+dat begin-pass-
                                                                  past
          'The book was begun to be read'

More recent studies such as Balpinar (1979), from which the above example is taken, and Georges and Kornfilt (1977) support the claim that Passive has not applied independently on the two verbs. That is, (49b) exemplifies only one passive.

Similarly Keenan (1976) argues for a similar analysis of Malagasy passives, illustrated in (50).

(50) a.   Te- h- am- ono ny omby Rakoto
          want-fut act- kill the cow   Rakoto
          'Rakoto wants to kill the cow'

     b.   Tian-dRakoto   vonoina ny omby
          wanted-by-Rakoto be+killed the cow
          'The cow was wanted to be killed by Rakoto'

(In the last example we note that both *tia* 'want' (contracted from *te-*) and *mamono* 'to kill' appear in their normal independently attested passive forms; moreover (50b) does not indicate desire on the part of the cow but only on Rakoto's part. Further, Rakoto clearly wants that he do the killing, not simply that the cow be killed.)

The grammar of passives we are developing lends itself nicely to a description of these facts. We simply allow that certain verbs, (in certain languages) such as *begin* and *want*, combine directly with TVPs to form complex TVPs. Then in the definition of the function which assigns passive morphology to TVPs we state that $f_{pass}(begin\text{-}read) = f_{pass}(begin) + f_{pass}(read)$.

We have so far considered two principle types of phrasally complex TVPs which should be under the scope of Passive: TVP + PP, and TVP+c+TVP. In addition, some languages such as Turkish and Malagasy appear to offer complex TVPs of the form V_x + TVP, where the V_xs are drawn from aspectual and desiderative verbs, and perhaps others.

There are however several other types of complex TVPs in English. We note our analysis of the three types of cases illustrated in (51) to (53). The first type illustrates passives of 'raised' structures, the second passives of 'equi' structures, and the third passives of 'manner-causatives', not to my knowledge well studied in the generative literature.

(51) a.   John was believed/thought/said/held/known/ rumoured to be an imposter.

     b.   VP = [Pass, [$_{TVP}$ believe to be an imposter]]

(52) a.   John was advised/encouraged/made/persuaded/forced to sign the petition.

     b.   VP = [Pass, [$_{TVP}$ advise to sign the petition]]

(53) a.   Mary was talked/inveigled/cajoled/frightened/ embarrassed into signing the petition.

     b.   VP = [Pass, [$_{TVP}$ talk into signing the petition]]

To see the plausability of analysing the TVPs as complex in the way indicated consider the lexicalist alternative: The VPs above would consist of an infinitival phrase or an *into* complement together with the passive of the 'main' verb, *believe, advise,* or *talk.* If the passive forms of these verbs independently constitute VPs, as is at least the general case of passives we have seen so far, then a variety of unintuitive results ensue. For one thing several of these verbs don't seem to form a passive VP since e.g. *John was said/rumoured, Mary was talked/inveigled,* etc. do not appear to be well formed sentences. Doubtless the syntactic problems could be handled, at the expense of course of complicating the grammar, but more important, the semantic problems remain. Namely, we have no independent motivation for assigning expressions like *was said* or *was talked* a meaning at all. So in particular we will not assign a meaning to the entire VP in the passive sentences above as a function of the meanings of their parts.

And more generally, those 'main' verbs above which do naturally passivise in isolation often have different meanings than the one they would have to be assigned as they occur in (51)-(53) on the lexicalist analysis. For example, *John was known/held* is well formed but we do not assign *was known* or *was held* that meaning in (51a). For example (51a) does not entail *John was believed/John was known/John was held,* etc. At best in this approach we would have to say that the interpretation of *was known* etc. varies with the context in which it occurs. While this doesn't seem outlandish it does make assigning a meaning to such expressions a more complicated matter than in our approach in which the passives of *know, advise,* and *talk* do not occur at all in the sentences cited. Rather what is passivised is the complex TVP; the appearance of passive morphology on the 'head' verb is simply a matter of morphology assignment, one for which we have ample motivation from other types of morphology assignment functions (case marking, verb agreement, etc.).

Consequently in our approach it is easier to see how children learn the meanings of sentences like (51)-(53) than it is in the strict lexicalist approach to Passive.

We might note finally that sentences like (54) and (55) are subject to the same analysis as we have given for (51)-(53).

(54) John was considered/called a thief.

(55) John was regarded/known/elected/remembered as a
      Democrat.

So e.g. (54) does not entail *John was considered*. Concerning (55),
John was regarded seems uninterpretable, just as *Mary was talked*
is in (53), etc. Of course if we *consider a thief, regard as a
Democrat* as complex TVPs then these problems disappear; *was
regarded* for example will not be a constituent of (55) and we shall
not be obliged to assign it a meaning or worry about how to not
generate *John was regarded,* etc.

4. Conclusions and Consequences of the Proposed Analysis

Our purpose here has been to establish that, in the general case
across languages, Passive is best represented as a phrase-structural
way of deriving n-place predicates from n+1 place ones. This conception of Passive is assumed embedded in a conception of Core
Grammar in which rules are stated generally using variables
ranging over grammatical categories (and a few other things, such
as the number of elements in the subcategorisation of a predicate,
adjective, etc.), and rules for particular languages are drawn from
those in Core Grammar by specifying values for the variables in
accordance with stipulated Parameter Conditions. An explicit and
reasonably extensive version of this conception of Core Grammar
is given in Keenan (1980), to which we refer the reader.
   It will be worth emphasising here however one consequence of
our conception of Passive, which has rather far reaching implications for the design of Core Grammar, and which is worked out
in considerable detail in Keenan (1980). Namely, since Passive is a
phrase structural operation it cannot 'be fed' (adapting a line of
argument in Wasow 1976) by (sentence level) transformations.
Thus all the operations which were originally considered to be
transformational in this sense and which fed Passive in a significant
way must also be construed within the phrase structure part of the
grammar. This has in fact been done in Keenan (1980) for Conjunction Reduction, Neg Lowering, all the Raisings, all the Equis,
and all the Sentential Extrapositions. (In the latter case we base
generate both *That Fred left was clear* and *It was clear that Fred
left*. This we do so that the *it* in the latter sentence can 'Raise' and
then be passivised to subject: *John believed it to be clear that Fred*

left; *It was believed to be clear that Fred left.*) We have also treated
Dative Shift in Keenan (1980) but we have not treated the *there*-
insertion cases (*John believed there to be mice in the barn, There
were believed to be mice in the barn*). So although the *there*-
insertion cases remain, the prognosis that all relation changing
rules which feed Passive are naturally represented, both syntactically and semantically, in the Base seems excellent. And this
achieves a very considerable simplification of the grammar as a
whole. Many length decreasing transformations — these are the
culprits responsible for the excessive generating capacity of current
formulations of generative grammar — are eliminated, e.g. Conjunction Reduction. And this conception of grammar claims that
many of the productive processes in language — namely the basic
relation changing operations — can be represented in a strictly
context free way. Even more important to our mind, this conception of grammar shows that the structures generated by these
relation changing processes can be directly interpreted as a
function of the interpretation of their immediate constituents, and
thus our grammar satisfies very strong conditions on learnability
and provides a clear basis for explaining the comprehension of
novel utterances.

On the other hand, we have not been concerned here to choose
among the several current proposals for representing Passive in a
phrasal way. These are discussed in KF-79. Suffice it to say here
that these proposals are highly similar as regards the generation of
Raising and Equi structures to which Passive applies. They differ
rather more in two respects. First, the treatment of PPs. The
proposal in KF-78 is perhaps the only one to explicitly allow PPs
to combine with n-place predicates to form n-place predicates,
rather than merely with 1-place predicates; in particular it is the
only proposal which gives an explicit semantics accounting for at
least some (but not all) the basic entailments involving such PPs.
Moreover the extension of the class of PPs to include agent
phrases is perhaps unique to our proposal. Most other treatments
(Thomason 1976; Bach 1979; Gazdar 1979; and Dowty 1978) in
one way or another basically claim that there are two passive
operations in English, one which is accompanied by agent phrases
and one which is not. This claim of course gives the wrong distributional prediction concerning agented and agentless passives.
Namely, without additional, and so far unmotivated, constraints on
how two independent transformations can be distributed across

languages, this approach allows that a language could have only agented passives with the same ease with which it could have only agentless passives. But as we have seen this is incorrect. Many languages (Latvian, Classical Arabic, Maninka, etc.) present only agentless passives, while there is only one case, Achenese (Lawler 1977) cited as presenting only agented passives.

Still these differences are rather minor. Our analysis of PPs can easily be adopted in these other approaches, and overall we must note that the independently arrived at phrasal treatments show far more similarities than divergences, which encourages me to think that the phrasal approach is basically on the right track.

And secondly, the phrasal approaches differ among themselves as regards the specific mechanism for deriving VPs from TVPs. (Ours is in fact the only approach which states Passive with sufficient generality to capture passives in intransitives as well as in verbs of higher degrees of transitivity.) In some approaches the passive VP is directly derived from the TVP, as in KF-78/79. In others, (Thomason 1976) and (Gazdar 1979) adjective phrases are derived from TVPs and the passive VPs are formed by an independent rule which adjoins copular verbs like *be* with adjective phrases. In still other cases (Bach 1979) a distinct category *passive participle* (not semantically distinguished from adjective phrases, only syntactically distinguished) is derived from TVPs, and then *be* + passive participle yields VPs.

All of these analyses receive at least some support from English as well as from many other languages. KF-79 present a summary of the observed possible types of internal structure presented by passives of simple (lexical) TVPs. We have chosen not to take a position on the internal structure of *be* + *kissed* in English since all of the proposals are compatible with the phrasal analysis we have proposed here and thus do not argue against a phrasal analysis as opposed to either sentential or lexical analyses.

Note

1. This sentence was omitted in the original of this paper.

References

Awbery, G. (1976) *The Syntax of Welsh: A Transformational Study of the Passive,* Cambridge, Cambridge University Press.

Bach, E. (1979) 'In Defense of Passive', *Linguistics and Philosophy* 3, 297-342.

Baker, L. (1978) *Introduction to Generative Transformational Syntax,* Prentice-Hall, Englewood Cliffs, New Jersey.

Balpinar, Z. (1979) 'Some Aspects of Turkish Passivisation', manuscript, LSA Institute, Salzburg, Austria.

Bresnan, J. (1978) 'A Realistic Transformational Grammar' in M. Halle, J. Bresnan, and G.A. Miller (eds.) *Linguistic Theory and Psychological Reality,* MIT Press, Cambridge, Massachusetts.

Chomsky, N. (1957) *Syntactic Structures,* Mouton, The Hague.

—— and H. Lasnik. (1977). 'Filters and Control', *Linguistic Inquiry* 8, 3, 325-505.

Dowty, D. (1978) 'Governed Transformations as Lexical Rules in Montague Grammar', *Linguistic Inquiry* 9, 3, 393-427.

Friedin, R. (1975) 'The Analysis of Passives' in *Language* 51, 384-405.

Gazdar, G. (1979) 'Constituent Structures', manuscript, School of Social Sciences, University of Sussex, Brighton, England.

Georges, L. and J. Kornfilt (1977) 'Infinitival Double Passives in Turkish', *NELS* VII.

Hasegawa, N. (1968) 'The Passive Construction in English', *Language* 44, 230-43.

Keenan, E.L. (1976) 'Remarkable Subjects in Malagasy', in C. Li (ed.) *Subject and Topic,* Academic Press, New York.

—— (1979) 'On Surface Form and Logical Form', *Studies in the Linguistic Sciences,* special issue, 8, 2.

—— (1980) 'A conception of Core Grammar', manuscript presented at the Stanford Workshop on Non-transformational Grammars.

—— and L. Faltz (1978) *Logical Types for Natural Language,* UCLA Occasional Papers in Linguistics, No. 3, Department of Linguistics, UCLA.

—— (1979) 'Passive in Universal Grammar', presented to the Sloan Foundation Workshop on the Lexicon.

Lakoff, R. (1971) 'Passive Resistance', *Chicago Linguistic Society* VII, 149-63.

Langacker, R. and P. Munro (1974) 'Passives and their Meaning', *Language* 51, 4, 789-830.

Lawler, J. (1977) 'A Agrees with B in Achenese: a Problem for Relational Grammar' in P. Cole and J. Sadock (eds.) *Syntax and Semantics 8: Grammatical Relations,* Academic Press, New York.

Lewis, G. L. (1967) *Turkish Grammar,* Clarendon Press, Oxford.

Perlmutter, D. and P. Postal (1977) 'Toward a Universal Characterisation of Passivisation', *BLS* III, 394-417.

Thomason, R. (1976) 'Some Extensions of Montague Grammar', in B. Partee (ed.) *Montague Grammar,* Academic Press, New York.

Wasow, T. (1976) 'Transformations and the Lexicon' in P. Culicover, T. Wasow, and A. Akmajian (eds.) *Formal Syntax,* Academic Press, New York.

9 PARAMETRIC VARIATION IN UNIVERSAL GRAMMAR[1]

1. Goals of this Paper

> The grammar of a particular language can be regarded as simply a specification of values of parameters of Universal Grammar.
> Chomsky, *Lectures on Government and Binding.*

We share a conception of Universal Grammar (UG) of which the grammars of particular languages are special cases: the categories, rules, and constraints on rules of any particular language must be chosen from those specified to exist by UG.

The principle goal of this paper is to present a formal conception of UG in which it is made explicit just how we choose particular categories, rules, and constraints from those provided by UG to form the grammars of particular languages. A general consequence of our proposal is that typological universals logically follow from a correct statement of UG. (By typological universals we understand statements describing the distribution of syntactic properties across languages, e.g. 'If a language has a certain property P then it also has Q, but the converse fails.' Not all such universals of course need be given in this conditional format.) Thus I see the proposals put forward here as providing a formal framework which unites the current research trends in typology on the one hand and generative grammar on the other.

In Sections 3 and 4 I illustrate the conception of UG proposed by a detailed study of Passive in UG. The study is intended as a substantive contribution to our understanding of passive constructions in the world's languages, and argues that Passive is best represented by a context-free phrase structure rule whose outputs are semantically interpreted as a function of the interpretations of their immediate constituents. The rule involves no NP movement or traces and is not limited to lexical passives. In Section 5 the results of this study are shown to carry over to relation changing rules in general, e.g. 'Raising', 'Conjunction Reduction', 'Extraposition', 'Tough Movement', etc. In Section 6 summary solutions are provided to certain questions raised by the preceding analysis. In particular I give one proposal for incorporating into the universal Base rules involving unbounded 'movement' whose outputs are interpreted by variable binding operators. The general conclusion then is that a very significant portion of the productive processes in a language may be enlighteningly represented both syntactically and semantically in the Base.

2. Overview of the Proposal

In the spirit of the quote from Chomsky above, the rules (R) and the constraints (C) of UG will be stated using parameters (= variables) ranging over various linguistic entities. Thus the Rs and Cs of UG actually define sets of rules and constraints, one for each choice of values for the parameters. Grammars of particular languages vary according to the choices they make from these sets. To define the class of *possible human languages* (phl's) we must state which choices of rules (constraints) from a given set R (C) are sufficient to constitute the R-rules (C-constraints) of a phl.

We propose then that each R and C of UG is accompanied by one or more *parameter conditions* (PC's) stipulating conditions on the choices from these sets that the grammars of phl's must satisfy. Then the class of phl's is *defined* to be the class of languages whose grammars draw their rules and constraints from those specified in UG in such a way as to satisfy the PC's.

2.1 An Illustrative Example

Let us illustrate the form and functioning of PC's with the familiar example of Subjacency. We are not concerned with the empirical accuracy of our statement of Subjacency, but only desire to illustrate how parameter conditions are used to define the class of phls, and with how they determine typological universals.

Informally, we want to impose a constraint on syntactic rules to the effect that no rule can mention two nodes if one is dominated by more than one *bounding node* which does not dominate the other. *Bounding node* (BN) is a parameter in the constraint, and languages vary somewhat with regard to which nodes they choose as bounding. Plausibly for example PP is bounding in German but not in English; perhaps both S and S̄ are bounding in English but not both are bounding in Italian, etc. In effect then different languages have somewhat different Subjacency constraints, and the statement of Subjacency in UG must specify just the correct class of Subjacency constraints which phl's may have. To do this it must specify the set of *possible bounding nodes* (BN_{UG}) — those nodes which are bounding in at least one phl. And then it must specify for an arbitrary phl L just what conditions the *bounding nodes in L* (BN_L) must satisfy.

Let us assume, for sake of illustration, that BN_{UG} has been empirically determined to be {NP, S, Š, PP}. Then Subjacency in UG might be given as in (1) below. The PCs proposed are given *en bloc* for purposes of reference and discussion. In fact PC(v) will be rejected as not a possible PC, and PC(iii) entails PC(ii).

(1)   *Subjacency$_{UG}$*
    a.   For each BN $\subseteq BN_{UG}$.
       'No rule mentions nodes x and y in a structure if more than one node whose label is in BN dominates x but not y.'
    b.   *Parameter Conditions*
       For all languages L,
       (i) $BN_L \subseteq BN_{UG}$
       (ii) $BN_L \neq \varnothing$
       (iii) $BN_L \cap \{S, Š\} \neq \varnothing$
       (iv) if PP $\in BN_L$ then NP $\in BN_L$
       (v)   if L is verb final then PP $\in BN_L$

Note first that in (1a) BN is a variable ranging over subsets of BN_{UG} and that (1a) defines 16 subjacency constraints, one for each value of BN.

PC(i) appears trivial. It merely says that the bounding nodes in any phl L are a subset of the possible bounding nodes. We shall henceforth assume by convention that where P is a parameter in a R or C of UG, P_L, the values of P in an arbitrary phl L, are a subset of the range of P as given in the R or C. So PC(i) need not be explicitly stated. Its content however is not logically trivial. It says explicitly that any language whose bounding nodes are not a subset of BN_{UG} is not a human language; it entails that Determiner is not bounding in any human language, etc. Moreover, if PC(i) were the only PC on Subjacency it would logically follow that there are *exactly* 16 types of language with respect to Subjacency, one for each of the possible values of BN, since the set of phl's is *defined* to be the set of all languages whose rules and conditions are drawn from those of UG in such a way as to satisfy the PC's, and there are 16 different ways of satisfying PC(i), one for each possible value of BN. Thus all the languages which differed from English solely with regard to choice of bounding node would be phl's.

PC(ii) says that for all phl's L the set of bounding nodes of L is not empty. Accepting PC(ii), there are only 15 types of phl's with respect to Subjacency, and all phl's present some non-trivial form of it.

PC(iii) says that for all phl's at least one of S or S̃ is bounding. It entails PC(ii) and rules out three other cases; those in which only NP is bounding, only PP is bounding, and only NP and PP are bounding. Accepting PC(iii) then there are only twelve types of languages with respect to Subjacency.

PC(iv) is somewhat more interesting. It rules out of the set of phl's those in which PP is bounding but NP is not. This includes three cases not covered by PC(ii), thereby reducing the number of language types in question to nine. (The case where only PP is bounding is ruled out by both PC(iii) and PC(iv).)

Note that independent of our framework PC(iv) might have been stated as a typological universal: 'If PP is bounding in L then so is NP but not conversely.' But this universal (if true) is entailed by Subjacency$_{UG}$ as stated. In fact our PCs entail a much stronger claim, as the typological universal does not rule out languages with no bounding nodes, or ones where only NP is bounding, or ones where only PP is bounding, but Subjacency$_{UG}$ clearly does. Clearly then typological universals are entailed by a correct formulation of UG.

PC(v) seems of a different character from the others. It says that if a language places the verb rightmost in simplex declarative sentences then PP is binding in that language. Thus PC(v) mentions a property of L not mentioned in the constraint (1a) it is a PC of. There will of course be infinitely many linguistic properties not mentioned in any given R or C of UG. Allowing PCs to refer to such properties would appear to require that an adequate formulation of an R or C in UG necessitated checking infinitely many possible PCs, something we cannot in principle do, and would thus leave the notion of a PC in some sense undefined. We would simply not know from what class of possible conditions we could choose PCs. Why not have PCs like: PP is bounding in L if L has an odd number of tones, or if L is spoken in the Southern hemisphere, or if Fermat's Last Theorem is true, etc.? In order then for the notion parameter condition to be well defined we shall impose the following metalinguistic condition on possible PCs:

(2)   Parameter conditions on an R or C of UG are expressible as boolean (set theoretical) functions of the range of the parameters in the R or C.

Thus we rule out PC(v) by (2).

2.2 A Surprising Result

The conception of UG we have so far presented implies the following:

(3)   *The Principle of Language Interdependence* (PLI)
      The correctness of a grammar for one language cannot be evaluated independently of those of other languages.

   To see why PLI holds consider that the correctness of the statement of a R or C in UG depends crucially on data from a fair sample of the phl's. It is obvious that the correctness of PCs so depends, since they directly make predictions concerning the distribution of syntactic properties across phl's. For example, both PC(iii) and PC(iv) are falsified if we find one human language in which only PP is bounding. Moreover we can argue in favour of one proposal over another in UG on the grounds that the one permits the statement of PCs which give an empirically more adequate prediction concerning the distribution of syntactic properties of the structures in question. This may be the case, given (2), if the two proposals do not contain exactly the same parameters. For example, in our discussion of Passive$_{UG}$ in the next section we argue that Passive$_{UG}$ must contain a parameter ranging over the degree (= number of arguments) of the predicates passivised (or, for the nonce, the degree of the main predicates in the sentences passivised). Thus proposals which have such a parameter are preferable to those which don't as they permit the statement of PCs which more adequately represent the properties of passives across the world's languages.
   Given then that the form of Rs and Cs in UG depends on data from many languages it follows immediately that the form of rules and constraints in a given language depends on those of other

languages since the rules and conditions of the given language must be instances of those in UG.

3. Passive in UG

3.1 Phrasal Passive: an Informal Statement

Let us think informally on n-place predicates (P_ns) as expressions which combine, in whatever ways languages allow, with n argument expressions of whatever categories to form a sentence. For example, ignoring both here and later tense and aspect marking, *slept* and *is probable* are one-place predicates (P_1s) in English, *kissed* and *believes* are P_2s, etc. P_0s then are sentences (they combine with zero arguments to form a sentence), and we shall use the symbols P_0 and S interchangeably. Note that P_ns in general may be syntactically complex rather than single lexical items. Indeed P_0s are almost always complex, and in general the greater the value of n the fewer the means languages dispose of to form complex P_ns. Thus there are more ways of forming complex P_0s than P_1s, though P_1 is respectably rich syntactically, including expressions such as *is probable, fell down, wants to leave, sang and danced*, etc. in English. P_2s are less rich than P_1s, though probably most would agree that *write down*, and *hugged and kissed* are complex P_2s.

Using this notation I want to say that Passive$_{UG}$ is best represented as a particular way of deriving n-place predicates from n+1-place ones. Thus we shall treat e.g. *was kissed* as a passive P_1 derived from the P_2 *kiss*. So English passives are but a special case of deriving P_ns from P_{n+1}s where n = 1. Many languages of course also allow P_0s to be derived from P_1s via Passive$_{UG}$. Some examples (from Keenan 1980a) are: Latin, Turkish, Shona (Bantu), Dutch, German, commonly in Uto-Aztecan, etc. Thus in Latin, in the same way as the P_1 *amatur* 'is loved' is derived from the P_2 *amat* 'loves' so the P_0 *curritur* 'running is being done' is derived from the P_1 *currit* 'runs'. Similarly many languages, e.g. Japanese, Tagalog, Malagasy directly allow P_3s such as *give* to be passivised, forming P_2s such as *was given*. Note however that the existence of passives formed from P_1s or P_3s in a language is not independent of ones formed on P_2s. The following for example is a typological universal: 'If a language can passivise P_1s (to form P_0s) then it can passivise P_2s to form P_1s.' So one motivation for treating Passive$_{UG}$ as a predicate level rule is that we want the degree (number of arguments) of the predicates to be a parameter in the rule so that such typological universals may be captured in the parameter conditions on the rule. A preliminary formulation of Passive in UG sufficient to capture such universals is given by the context-free expansion rule below:

(4) *Passive$_{UG}$* (First Approximation)
   a. *Rule:* $P_n \rightarrow \{Pass, P_{n+1}\}$ all $n \geqslant 0$
   b. *Parameter Conditions*
   (i) if $n_L \neq \varnothing$ then $1 \in n_L$

3.2 Discussion

(4a) defines an infinite set of rules, one for each value of n. Thus $P_0 \rightarrow \{Pass, P_1\}$ is one such rule, $P_1 \rightarrow \{Pass, P_2\}$ is another. And the PC states that if the range of n in L is not empty, i.e. L has some rule of the form $P_k \rightarrow \{Pass, P_{k+1}\}$, then 1 is in that range, that is, $P_1 \rightarrow \{Pass, P_2\}$ is a rule of L. The typological universals cited above obviously follow from Passive$_{UG}$ as stated. For if L can passivise P_1s then it forms P_0s via Passive, so $0 \in n_L$, so $n_L \neq \varnothing$, whence by PC(i) $1 \in n_L$, so $P_1 \rightarrow \{Pass, P_2\}$ is a rule of L, i.e. L passivises P_2s. PC(i) of course does not claim that n_1 is not empty for all phl's L. And this is correct. Many languages, e.g. Enga (New Guinea), Tamang (Sino-Tibetan), and Isthmus Zapotec (Oto-Manguean), see Keenan (1980a) for supporting data, have no passives. And since PC(i) is satisfied by languages with no passives, it follows from the definition of phl that there exist phl's with no passives.

Let us consider briefly the form of the rule itself. It is a (context-free) expansion rule, and thus part of the universal Base rules (Base$_{UG}$). The righthand side of the rule consists of two unordered (hence the use of set brackets) symbols, a category symbol P_{n+1} and a constant of UG, *Pass*. Formally such constants are non-lexical elements which do not appear on the left of any expansion rule in Base$_{UG}$. Their expression in surface will be handled by morphophonemic rules of UG, constrained to be expressed by *broad morphological functions*, ones whose output differs from the input by at most *strict morphological modification* (affixing, internal vowel change, reduplication, tone change) and the presence of 'grammatical constants' — items drawn from small closed classes such as plural morphemes, auxiliary verbs, coordinate conjunctions, etc. Thus we are claiming that Passive$_{UG}$ is best represented by processes in which P_ns are derived from P_{n+1}s in broad morphological ways.

Let us stress an obvious property of the rule: regardless of how the basic expansion rules of Base$_{UG}$ are formulated, a P_{n+1} will combine with n+1 argument expressions to form a sentence. But the passive of a P_{n+1} only combines with n argument expressions to form a sentence. In this sense then Passive 'absorbs an argument' (rather than just the case of an argument expression, as in e.g. Chomsky 1981). For example, making some inessential assumptions regarding Base rules other than Passive$_{UG}$, we might represent the Base structure underlying *Mary was kissed* by the following *unordered* tree:

(5)

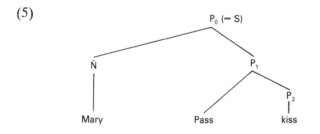

Similarly passives on P_1s may be represented as:

(6)

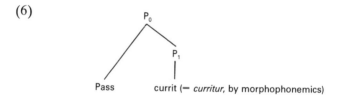

Thus at no stage in the derivation is *kiss* constructed with two argument expressions. And in particular no 'trace' of the 'object' argument expression is present in surface.

Note that to say that the tree in (5) is unordered is to say that no linear-order relation is defined among the constituents, in particular among the terminal elements. Thus the tree structures expressed linearly and schematically by [Mary, [Pass, kiss]], [[Pass, kiss], Mary], and [[kiss, Pass], Mary] represent the same unordered tree. Both the trees and rules used in this paper do not represent linear order, as that syntactic property is universally irrelevant to the phenomena such as Passive which we are discussing.

Passive$_{UG}$ as formulated so far seems obviously inadequate in certain respects. It does not tell us for example that the argument of the P_{n+1} which is absorbed is the subject argument and that the subject argument of the derived P_n is in any sense the same as some non-subject argument of the P_{n+1}. And more generally it does not tell us (yet) how the interpretation of the derived predicate is dependent on that from which it is derived. So we cannot yet distinguish Passives from other 'detransitivising' processes, such as (in one language or another) Reflexive, Reciprocal, Antipassive, Unspecified Object Deletion, etc. Nonetheless even this incomplete formulation can be profitably distinguished from several other analyses of Passive in the literature.

3.3 Phrasal versus Sentential Views of Passive

By sentential (i.e. transformational) views of Passive we understand ones which derive sentences (Phrase markers dominated by S, or perhaps Š) from sentences. So on this view passives are types of sentences, not as on our view, types of n-place predicates. Such views are instantiated in various ways in Chomsky (1957), Hasegawa (1968), R. Lakoff (1971), Langacker and Munro (1974), Awbery (1976), and Perlmutter and Postal (1977). Of these proposals, only the latter, the Relational Grammar view, is intended as universal.

There are several reasons why predicate level views of Passive are preferable to S-level views quite generally. First, and perhaps most impressive when passives in a wide range of languages are considered, is that passive 'sentences' (in our view ones which have a main predicate which is passive) are universally distinct from active sentences not with respect to properties of sentences but only with respect to properties of their P_ns. To be more specific: if Passive were universally a sentence level derivational process we would expect that the syntactically distinctive properties of passives would be ones of necessity defined on sentences as a whole. Consider for example the clear case of yes-no Questions (Qs), which on all views are formed by sentence level derivational processes: from (a structure underlying) a declarative S an interrogative S is derived. There are only two common (not exclusive) ways of deriving such interrogative Ss: either a characteristic intonation contour is assigned to the declarative S or a particle is inserted into the declarative S, where the position of the particle is defined with respect to the sentence as a whole, e.g. most commonly at the *beginning of* the S or at the *end of* the S, less commonly between the subject and the predicate. Obviously then Contour Assignment and Q-Particle Placement must crucially mention the category S as the intonation contour is straightforwardly a property of the entire S and the position of the particle must be given as the beginning (end, etc.) of the S. Even such uncommon ways of forming Qs as by Subject–Verb (or Aux) inversion are S-level processes, since the smallest syntactic unit which contains all the items mentioned by the rule is the S.

But passives are never formed in such ways. No language forms passives by modifying the intonation contour of an active, or by inserting an S-level particle into the active, or by inverting the subject and the verb.

Note that in our proposal these facts are *predicted* for the most widespread type of passives (P_1s derived from P_2s) since the rule only mentions P_1s and P_2s and cannot thus determine any sentence level properties.

Conversely, if Passive$_{UG}$ is a predicate level rule we do expect that the distinctive form of passives will be localised within the derived P_n, and this is correct. Thus (see Keenan 1980a for detailed examples) a passive P_n in a language consists of a morphological modification of a P_{n+1} (limited in fact to affixing, internal vowel change, and occasionally zero; reduplication and tone change are to my knowledge never used to form passives) and, in some cases, an auxiliary verb selected by Passive. Thus to form a passive 'sentence' in English it is sufficient to generate a passive P_1, e.g. *be kissed* (ignoring as always tense). The rules we need independently to combine P_1s with Ns to form sentences can then form *Mary was kissed* in the same way as they form *Mary sang*.

A second general reason for taking passives as types of predicates, not types of sentences is that as predicates they share many properties with items which are unequivocally predicates, namely lexical verbs. Let us mention briefly two such properties.

First, as already noted above, they select their auxiliary. Thus, independent of Passive, we know that the choice of auxiliary verb in say compound past tenses in many European languages depends on the choice of main verb. Thus in German and French some verbs (in fact most lexical verbs) form their compound past tenses with *have*, but some, typically including verbs of motion, form them with *be.* So the choice of Aux depends on the choice of main verb. And so in passives. Thus in French all passive verbs choose *be* as the Aux; in German they choose *be* for 'stative' passives (*Das Haus ist verkauft* 'The house is sold' (You're too late to buy it)) and *becomes* for 'dynamic' passives (*Das Haus wird verkauft* literally: 'The house becomes sold' (so you still have a chance to buy it)).

Note here then that we are committed to the passive auxiliary as being part of the P_1 at some level of analysis even if it may occur separated from it in surface. This is consistent with current EST work in which the basic S expansion rule would be S → NP + (INFL) + VP. The 'category' INFL may include tense marking and perhaps modals, but will not include the use of *have* and *be* in compound past tenses or progressive verb forms. Thus e.g. in environments where we generate Ss with no INFL, as in 'Raising' contexts, we fail to get tense and modals but we do get *have* and *be: John believes Fred to have been cheating* but **John believes Fred to will cheat,* etc.

Second, other processes in a language which are sensitive to subtypes of lexical predicates are also sensitive as to whether the predicate is passive or not. Verb (phrase) agreement is one such case. Thus in many languages the actual agreement affixes vary according to subclasses of verb — the so called conjugations in Romance for example. Similarly the agreement paradigms may vary according as the verb is passive or not. Compare for example the following present indicative paradigms for active and passive predicates in Latin:

	active			*passive*	
amo	amamus		amor	amamur
amas	amatis		amaris	amamini
amat	amant		amatur	amantur

Clearly for example the 2pl endings are completely different, *-tis* and *-mini.* Keenan (1980a) supports as well that active and passive agreement paradigms differ in one way or another in Welsh, Kapampangan, and Maasai. Note that if Passive were a sentence type then the agreement rules would have to mention not only what agreed and what it agreed with but also some independent parameter of the sentence to know whether the sentence was passive or not.

A third general reason for taking Passive as a predicate level rule rather than a sentential level one concerns the statement of 'lexical' exceptions to Passive in particular languages. In general exceptions to rules are constraints on the domain of definition of the rule over and above what is specified in the rule itself.

The BPC below is a highly motivated and generally adhered to principle which conditions on particular rules should satisfy:

(7)   *The Basic Parameter Constraint* (BPC)
       Constraints on a syntactic rule may only mention parameters actually used in the rule.

The motivation for the BPC is substantive: there are infinitely many things not mentioned in any given rule. The BPC limits to a finite number the number of ways that a rule can be constrained. Thus adopting the BPC makes it easier to understand how someone could learn a given rule in a limited amount of time with imperfect exposure to instances, etc.

Accepting the BPC consider the Passive rule(s) of English. Somehow we must state that certain P_2s, e.g. *have, be, become, lack*, etc. do not productively passivise. These 'exceptions' to Passive constitute a constraint on the Passive rule. However *we* state the constraint it satisfies the BPC since English Passive must be an instance of Passive$_{UG}$ and P_n is a parameter in that rule. But if Passive$_{UG}$ did not mention predicates as a parameter, as the Relational Grammar view does not (Passive merely changes the relations which certain NPs bear to their *clause*), then no such constraint can be stated satisfying the BPC. Note further that we cannot appeal to some universal exceptions to Passive stated at the level of UG. Thus we find in languages like Kinyarwanda (Kimenyi 1980) and Malagasy (Keenan 1980a), languages in which passives bear a high functional load serving for example to present certain Ñs in positions from which they can be extracted, that possessive *have* does passivise. E.g. in Kinyarwanda we can say things like *Two buttons are had by this shirt.*

Finally, a fourth general reason for taking Passive$_{UG}$ as a predicate level rule is that syntactic properties of passives across languages may be correctly characterised as long as the number of arguments of the predicates is a parameter in the rule. PC(i) above is one such constraint. None of the sentence level rules presented above however include any such parameter. In fact none of the above approaches to Passive naturally suggests that languages will present passives of P_1s (though Perlmutter, has discussed them in a Relational Grammar framework). Our view however does correctly predict their existence and moreover predicts that P_2s are universally the most passivisable of the P_ns. Thus we predict that there exist languages with passives on P_2s but not on P_1s.

3.4 Agent Phrases

Agent phrases, such as *by Mary* in (8), are not represented in our formulation of $Pass_{UG}$ at all.

(8)   John was kissed by Mary.

We are then assuming that agent phrases are generated independently of the Passive rules of UG. There is in fact ample support from UG for this assumption. Note first that when we claim *by Mary* is an agent phrase in (8) we intend something in part semantic and in part syntactic. Semantically we intend that Mary satisfies the thematic role requirements and selectional restrictions of the P_2 *kiss*. Syntactically *(by) Mary* is presented differently from the argument expressions of P_1s in general. In fact, *by Mary* is presented like ordinary oblique noun phrases in active sentences in English. Moreover this property of agent phrases is not peculiar to English: quite generally across languages (see Keenan 1980a for supporting data) agent phrases are constructed with an adposition which exists independently in the language and which marks locative, instrumental/means, or possessive NPs in active sentences. E.g. *by* in English marks locatives, as in *John sat down by the window*; similarly *von* and *de* function both as locatives and possessive markers in German and French respectively. We refer the reader to Keenan (1980a) for more extensive documentation of this point.

Thus our principal motivation for generating agent phrases independently of Passive is that expressions which function as agent phrases occur in non-passive structures. Of course since part of what is intended by *agent phrase* is semantic we must show that such phrases occur in non-passive structures with the appropriate semantics. English amply illustrates such cases. Consider for example the nominalisations in the following sentences:

(9)   a.   The University forbids *talking by students during exams.*
      b.   *Cheating by students* will be punished by expulsion.

c.   *The march on Washington by the Farm Workers* was successful.
d.   *The strike by the UA W* was unsuccessful.

Clearly for example *students* in (9a, b) functions as the 'semantic subject' of the underlying P_1s *talk* and *cheat*. As P_1s do not passivise in English we must clearly generate these agent phrases independently of the passive rules of English. Thus the rules we need to both generate and interpret agent phrases must be stated independently of Passive and thus will apply to agent phrases in passives as a special case; so there is no need to include agent phrases specifically in the statement of Passive$_{UG}$ itself. Again we refer the reader to Keenan (1980a) for types of structures other than Passives in which agent phrases occur.

A final reason for not including agent phrases in the statement of Passive$_{UG}$ is that in several languages cited in Keenan (1980a), e.g. Latvian, Classical Arabic, Sonrai, etc. only agentless passives occur. Were Passive$_{UG}$ to require the presence of agent phrases, as it does on many sentential level views, then the grammars of these languages would require a totally opaque rule — one that it is hard to see how children could learn, etc. Moreover, in essentially all languages (Achenese is cited in Keenan (1980a) as an exception), agent phrases are at most optional. That is, we have the typological universal that if a language presents agented passives then it presents agentless ones, but the converse fails. This universal is predicted if we take agent phrases as independently generated oblique NPs, as they are independently optional.

4. Enriching Passive$_{UG}$

Our statement of Pass$_{UG}$ is, on intuitive grounds, woefully incomplete. We have for example said nothing concerning how a passive P_1 is interpreted relative to the P_2 it is derived from, though clearly the meaning of *was kissed* is not independent of that of *kiss*. We have not even indicated that the category of the argument of a passive P_1 must be the same as that of one of the arguments of the P_2 it is derived from. And there are clear typological regularities here. For example, if a language can derive passive P_1s taking $\bar{S}$ arguments, as in *that arithmetic is incomplete was proven years ago*, then it can derive passive P_1s taking ordinary NPs as arguments, e.g. *Mary was kissed.* For these reasons and many others then we are motivated to subcategorise predicates not only for the number of arguments they require, as we have already done, but also for the categories of their arguments. Thus we want to say that while *is sleeping* and *is probable* are both one-place predicates, they differ in that *is probable* takes an $\bar{S}$ argument while *is sleeping* takes an ordinary NP argument, henceforth denoted $\bar{N}$. This syntactic difference of course is directly reflected in their semantics. Semantically *is probable* predicates something of $\bar{S}$ denotations, while *is sleeping* predicates something of ordinary individuals like John and Mary. We may express this difference, without loss of generality, by semantically interpreting *is probable* as a function from $\bar{S}$ denotations into sentence (S) denotations and by interpreting *is sleeping* as a function from $\bar{N}$ denotations into S denotations. So the two P_1s are semantically distinct in that they are interpreted by functions with different domains, but they are semantically similar in that they are interpreted by functions with the same range.

Thus the subcategorisation notation we introduce for n-place predicates will be both syntactically and semantically significant: syntactically it will give the number and category of the argument of the predicate; semantically it will specify the domain and the range of the functions which may interpret the predicates. Somewhat more formally, we shall assume that UG associates with each category C a set T_C of possible denotations (relative to a model) for expressions having the category C. The set T_C will be called *the type for* C (relative to a model) and its precise nature will not concern us here. We may now give the subcategorisation notation as follows:

(10) *A Formation Rule for Category Symbols in UG*

    a.   Where W and $X_1, X_2, \ldots, X_n$ are category symbols in UG, the complex symbol $\underset{< X_1, X_2, \ldots, X_n >}{W}$ is the category symbol for expressions which combine with n argument expressions of categories $X_1, X_2, \ldots, X_n$ to form an expression of category W. The sequence $< X_1, X_2, \ldots, X_n >$ will be called the *subcategorisation* of the complex symbol and X_i will be called the *i^{th} argument* of the symbol.

    b.   The type for the complex category will be some set of

functions mapping n-tuples $< X_1, X_2, \ldots, X_n >$ into T_W, where each X_i is an element of T_{X_i}.

Using this notation we might assign the category $\frac{S}{\bar{N}}$ to *is sleeping* in English and the category $\frac{S}{\bar{S}}$ to *is probable*. Formally this means that English might have a rule expanding $\frac{S}{\bar{N}}$ to *is sleeping*, etc. Similarly we *might* assign *believe* as it occurs in *John believes that Fred is a thief*) the category $\frac{S}{\bar{N}\bar{S}}$ and we *might* assign *surprise* (as it occurs in *That Fred is a thief surprises John*) the category $\frac{S}{\bar{S}\bar{N}}$. We insist here on the *might* since our subcategorisation notation says nothing concerning how expressions combine with predicate symbols to form sentences. It only gives the number and category of these expressions. Just how predicates enter into combinations with other expressions to form sentences will depend on other rules, the primary constituent building rules, of the Base$_{UG}$. Any way of designing these rules so that predicates combine with the right number of expressions in the right categories is compatible with our notation. And since Passive$_{UG}$ only derives predicates from predicates we can by and large avoid having to commit ourselves here to any particular choice of base rules (see Bach 1975, for an enlightening discussion of the possibilities here).

On the other hand it is important that the elements of a subcategorisation $< X_1, X_2, \ldots, X_n >$ are ordered. If they weren't, then, since $\{\bar{N}\}$ and $\{\bar{N},\bar{N}\}$ are the same set (they have the same members) we would fail to indicate for example that *sleep* and *kiss* have different categories. Moreover, expressions whose categories differ solely in terms of the order of items in the subcategorisaton will be semantically interpreted in different ways. Accepting for example the category assignments given above to *believe* and *surprise* we will have that the former is interpreted by some function whose domain is $T_{\bar{N}} \times T_{\bar{S}}$, while the latter is interpreted by a function whose domain is $T_{\bar{S}} \times T_{\bar{N}}$. So these two P$_2$s are represented as semantically distinct as they are interpreted by functions with different domains. The first argument of the believe-function is an $\bar{N}$ denotation, while that of the surprise-function is an $\bar{S}$ denotation. Similarly their second arguments differ. Note that the order of elements in a subcategorisation corresponds to the order of arguments of the functions which interpret predicates having that subcategorisaton. This is an *arbitrary* convention. We could have given the order or argument of the semantic functions as just the opposite of the order given in the subcategorisation. But some fixed association of semantic with syntactic arguments must be given. And fixing it in the way we have (or in its mirror image) is sufficient to semantically distinguish *believe* from *surprise* without regard for how these expressions combine with others to form sentences.

Note also that the notation we have used for complex category symbols is apparently more general than needed for Passive$_{UG}$ since W can be any category, not necessarily S. This notation will be useful for other sorts of 'predicatives'. For example, taking $\bar{A}$ as the category of adjective phrases, $\frac{\bar{A}}{\bar{N}}$ would be the category for expressions which combine with $\bar{N}$s to form $\bar{A}$s. Arguably for example expressions such as *fond (of), jealous (of)*, etc. in English are in that category, as they combine with full noun phrases to form adjective phrases such as *fond of children, jealous of Mary*, etc. Similarly taking N as the category name for common nouns such as *man, woman*, etc., $\frac{N}{\bar{N}}$ would be the category of expressions such as *father (of), friend (of)*, etc. as they combine with full noun phrases to form complex Ns, e.g. *friend of the President*, etc. (We treat the *of* in such expressions as part of the case marking, see below, imposed by the 'predicative' on its arguments.)

Note finally that the symbols P_1, P_2, etc. now do not appear as category symbols in UG. Technically we may use the complex symbol $\frac{S}{X}$ as a variable ranging over the categories of UG. In cases where we are not interested in specifically mentioning the sub-categorisation of an n-place predicate we shall still informally refer to them as P_ns.

Using the new notation let us now give a more adequate statement of Passive$_{UG}$. We shall include now the interpretative rule for passives as well as the syntactic rule proper.

(11) *Passive$_{UG}$* (Second Approximation)
 a. *Syntax*

$$\frac{S}{< X_1, X_2, \ldots, X_n >} \rightarrow \left\{ \text{Pass,} \quad \frac{S}{<Y, X_2, \ldots, X_n, X_1 >} \right\}$$

 b. *Semantics*

Where e of category $\frac{S}{< Y, X_2, \ldots, X_n, X_1 >}$ is interpreted by a function f_e, interpret (Pass, e) by that function which maps n-tuples of individuals $<x_1, x_2, \ldots, x_n >$ onto $(V\ y)\ (f_e\ (y, x_2, \ldots, x_n\ x_1))$, where y is an individual in T_Y and each x_i is in T_{X_i}

c. *Parameter Conditions*

(i) if the range of $\genfrac{}{}{0pt}{}{S}{S}\langle Y, X_2, \ldots, X_n, X_1 \rangle$ is not empty
in L then $\genfrac{}{}{0pt}{}{S}{\langle \check{N}\,\check{N} \rangle}$ is in that range.

4.1 Discussion

Let us consider first the syntactic part of (11). It defines an infinite set of rules, one for each n+1-ary sequence of categories $\langle Y, X_2, \ldots, X_n, X_1 \rangle$. Some of these rules are given below:

(12) a. $\genfrac{}{}{0pt}{}{S}{\check{N}} \rightarrow \left\{ \genfrac{}{}{0pt}{}{\text{Pass,}}{} \genfrac{}{}{0pt}{}{S}{\langle \check{N}\,\check{N} \rangle} \right\}$

  b. $\genfrac{}{}{0pt}{}{S}{\check{S}} \rightarrow \left\{ \genfrac{}{}{0pt}{}{\text{Pass,}}{} \genfrac{}{}{0pt}{}{S}{\langle \check{N}\,\check{S} \rangle} \right\}$

  c. $S \rightarrow \left\{ \genfrac{}{}{0pt}{}{\text{Pass,}}{} \genfrac{}{}{0pt}{}{S}{\langle \check{N} \rangle} \right\}$

  d. $\genfrac{}{}{0pt}{}{S}{\check{N}\,\check{N}} \rightarrow \left\{ \genfrac{}{}{0pt}{}{\text{Pass,}}{} \genfrac{}{}{0pt}{}{S}{\langle \check{N}\,\check{N}\,\check{N} \rangle} \right\}$

The parameter condition on (11) tells us that if a language has any passives at all it has ones in which P_2s subcategorised for $\check{N}$ first argument and $\check{N}$ second argument are passivised. Thus the new PC entails the old one. In addition it entails the typological universal mentioned earlier that if a language forms passive P_1s taking $\check{S}$ arguments then it forms passive P_1s taking $\check{N}$ arguments. Thus the new formulation gives a descriptively more adequate characterisation of the syntactic properties of passive constructions across languages and is to be preferred to the old formulation.

By far however the greater advantage of the new formulation concerns the possibility of correctly interpreting passive structures as a function of what they are derived from. While the issues in detail here are complex, consider that for basic first order P_ns the interpretative rules we have given are (grossly) correct. Thus as a special case our rules state that a P_1 like *was kissed* holds of an *individual* Mary just in case for some individual y, *kissed* holds of the pair $\langle$ y, Mary $\rangle$ — which is just to say that *y kissed Mary* is true. Similarly *curritur* 'running is being done' holds (= is true) if for some individual y, *currit* 'is running' holds of y. These results are essentially correct and in striking contrast to the standard classical 'paraphrastic' approach to Passive.

Thus on our approach we have given the interpretation of a derived P_n by stating what individuals it holds of in terms of those which the P_{n+1} it is derived from holds of. Note crucially that a (first order) P_n combines with many expressions which do not in general denote individuals. E.g. while *John* and *the president* may denote individuals (see Keenan and Faltz 1978 for a formal definition of individual in semantic terms) expressions like *every student, John and Mary, no student, neither John nor Mary*, etc. do not in general denote individuals. Nonetheless the values of first order predicates on these more complex denotations is determined by their values on individuals. Thus if we have stated of each individual whether he is sleeping or not, we have determined the truth value of *everyone is sleeping, neither John nor Mary are sleeping*, etc. Thus our general semantics for applying P_1 denotations to $\bar{N}$ denotations guarantees that e.g. *everyone is sleeping* is true iff for every individual x, x *is sleeping* is true. Similarly, since *is being kissed* is a P_1, our general semantics for P_1s guarantees that (13a) below has the same truth value as (13b).

(13) a.   Everyone is being kissed.
     b.   For every individual x, x is being kissed.

And our semantics for Passive states that a P_1 like *is being kissed* holds of an individual x iff for some individual y, *is kissing* holds of $< y, x >$. Thus (13b) above is semantically identical to (13c):

(13) c.   For every individual x, there is an individual y such that
          is kissing (y, x) holds.

Notice that (13a) does not even entail (13d):

(13) d.   For some individual y, y is kissing everyone.

Moreover it is quite general that agentless passives do not entail the 'corresponding' existential generalisation of the active. Thus the a-sentences below do not entail the corresponding b-sentences:

(14) a.   Both John and Bill were kissed.
     b.   For some individual y, y kissed both John and Bill.
(15) a.   More than three students were kissed.

      b.   For some individual y, y kissed more than three
           students.
(16) a.   Exactly three students were kissed.
      b.   Some individual y kissed exactly three students.

Note of course that passives do entail the existential generalisation of the actives when the NPs used denote individuals. E.g. *Mary was kissed* does entail *some individual y kissed Mary.* And this entailment is predicted on our analysis.

    Similarly note that quite generally active sentences do not entail their corresponding agentless passives. E.g.

(17) a.   John kissed no-one.
      b.   No-one was kissed.
(18) a.   John kissed few pupils' parents.
      b.   Few pupils' parents were kissed.
(19) a.   John kissed at most three students.
      b.   At most three students were kissed.
(20) a.   No student kissed Mary.
      b.   Mary was kissed.
(21) a.   Neither John nor Fred kissed Mary.
      b.   Mary was kissed.

The entailments only obtain in general when the NPs in question are of the individual denoting sort. Thus *John kissed Mary* does entail *Mary was kissed.* And again this entailment is predicted on our analysis.

    We may infer from these examples then that there is no regular entailment relation between actives and agentless passives other than that predicted by the relation between active and passive predicates we have given. Whether entailments between sentences whose NPs are not of the individual denoting sort obtain or not is determined as a function of the semantics for complex NPs plus that of the active-passive relation between the predicates. It thus appears then that the only semantic relation between actives and passives is that which is statable between active and passive predicates. And this constitutes strong motivation for taking Passive$_{UG}$ as a derivational relation between predicates, for it is only on that level that we can give the semantics of derived structures as a function of that from which they are derived.

    Nor does this conclusion depend on taking only agentless

passives. For example, (22a) clearly does not entail (22b).

(22) a.   At most three politicians kissed every baby.
     b.   Every baby was kissed by at most three politicians.

Imagine a situation in which there are four politicians and two babies, each politician kisses baby$_1$ and none kisses baby$_2$. Then (22a) is true since in fact no politician kissed every baby. But (22b) is false since baby$_1$ was kissed by more than three politicians. Thus (22a) does not entail (22b). An analogous lack of entailment obtains if *at most three politicians* is replaced by other 'non-increasing' NPs, e.g. *no politician, neither John nor Fred, fewer than ten politicians, exactly three politicians*, etc. Thus it is not in general the case that actives entail their corresponding passives, though the entailments do obtain, as we predict, when the NPs denote individuals. E.g. *John kissed Mary* does entail *Mary was kissed by John.*

It is equally easy to see that agented passives do not in general entail the corresponding actives. Thus (23a) fails to entail (23b).

(23) a.   At most three babies were kissed by every politician.
     b.   Every politician kissed at most three babies.

Imagine a situation in which there are four babies and two politicians, one politician kisses each baby and the other kisses none. Then (23a) is true since in fact no baby was kissed by every politician, but (23b) is false since one politician kissed more than three babies.

In general then the only semantic relation between actives and passives is the one predicated from the relation we have given between active and passive predicates. Whether the sentences formed from such predicates entail each other varies with the semantics of the NPs in the sentence; the entailments are predicted given our semantics for passives plus that of the complex NPs in question. We refer the reader to Keenan and Faltz (1978) for a detailed statement of this semantics and the correct results for basic first order P_ns in natural language. We note here without argument that the claims made here concerning individuals with respect to Ň denotatons in general extend directly (surprisingly) to individuals in Š denotations. The semantics must be extended however for nonfirst order predicates, e.g. ones which predicate of sets of individuals or yet more complex structures. That is, *the students were outnumbered* does not, obviously, mean *For each student x, some individual y outnumbered him.*

Note however that the fact that the semantics of Passive must be made contingent on the semantic type of the P_ns in question is something which supports our view of passive. That is, we expect to condition the interpretation of passive P_ns in terms of the semantics of the P_{n+1} they are derived from in the same way that Passive may apply differentially to syntactically distinct P_{n+1}s.

4.2 The Semantics of Agent Phrases

The classical paraphrastic sentence level derivation of passives, however misguided in general as regards its semantic claims, did have the advantage that it predicted the paraphrase relation between actives and passives when the NPs in question were simple, i.e. individual denoting (and the predicates were otherwise simple). On our approach we independently generate agent phrases as PPs or oblique case NPs and one might (for a fleeting moment) doubt the feasability of correctly characterising this paraphrase relation on our approach. Surprisingly however, it turns out to be quite easy to assign agent phrases a semantics in which the paraphrase does hold when the agent NP is of course an individual denoting one.

Thus let us assume that in general PPs have categories of the form $\frac{X}{X}$, for various choices of category X. That is, in general they combine with Xs to form Xs. For example, *sing* and *sing in the garden* are both P_1s, *vase* and *vase on the table* are both common nouns, etc. Using BY as the agentive adposition of UG we may then give a general semantics for agent phrases when applied to P_ns as follows:

(24) If f is a P_n interpretation then for all individuals x, (BY x) (f) is that P_n interpretation which maps an n-tuple $< y_1, y_2, \ldots, y_n >$ of individuals onto the same S denotation as f maps $< x, y_2, \ldots, y_n >$.

For example, using English predicates themselves to represent their semantic interpretations for simplicity of representation, we have from (24) that (BY x) (*run*) is that P_1 which holds of an individual y iff *run* holds of x. And (BY x) (*kiss*) is that P_2 interpretation which holds of a pair (y_1, y_2) iff *kiss* holds of (x, y_2). This says directly that agent nominal x is functioning as the first argument of the interpretation of the P_2 *kiss*. And as that argument is in general the one denoted by 'subject' phrases of *kiss* we have said that agent nominals are functioning as the semantic subjects of the P_ns the agent phrase combines with.

To see that this semantics yields the correct results in simple cases consider that the S denotation of (25a) below is represented in our semantics by (25b).

(25) a. Mary was kissed by John.
     b. [Pass, ((by John) (kiss))] (Mary)

The active *John kissed Mary* is represented of course by *kiss* (*John, Mary*). Now the P_1 in (25b) is a passive, so our semantics for Passive tells us that (25b) is interpreted identically to (25c):

(25) c. $(\exists y) [((by John) (kiss)) (y, Mary)]$

And our semantics for agent phrases tells us that the inner S in (25c) is equivalent to *kiss* (*John, Mary*), whence (25c) is equivalent to (25d).

(25) d. $(\exists y) [kiss (John, Mary)]$

And by vacuous quantification, (25d) is equivalent to *kiss* (*John, Mary*), the desired result.

Notice then that we have successfully treated agent phrases as PPs and provided them with a semantics which yields the correct predictions of semantic relatedness for passive sentences in which they occur independently generated. We should note however that the treatment does have some consequences which some may find objectionable. In particular it treats ((*by John*) (*kiss*)) as a syntactically complex P_2 and it allows such to be passivised, whence the morphology assignment rules we associate with Passive$_{UG}$ will have to be allowed to apply to expressions other than lexically simple ones. The latter point is in fact not problematic and will be discussed later. As regards the former point, we refer the reader to Keenan (1980) for a detailed semantic justification for taking agent phrases directly as P_2 modifiers, though we shall note a few additional points in support of that analysis here.

First, note that agent phrases are but a logically special case of 'subject' oriented P_n modifiers. Other PPs and certain types of adverbials may also profitably be regarded as P_n modifiers where n may take the value 2. For one example consider source locatives such as *from the roof*. When they apply to simple P_1s they predicate a locative property of its 'subject'. E.g. *John sang/spoke/ fell/leapt from the roof* entails that John was on the roof. The inter- pretation of source locatives in sentences formed from P_2s is complex, depending on the semantic nature of the P_2. For certain 'action at a distance' P_2s such as *see, observe, watch* the source locative unambiguously predicates of the 'subject'. Thus (26a) entails (26b).

(26) a.   John watched Mary from the roof.
     b.   John was on the roof.

On the other hand for many 'causative verbs of motion' (perhaps best analysed as ditransitive verbs, P_3s) the source locative is most naturally understood to predicate of the 'object' argument. Thus *John dragged/brought/led Mary from the roof* entails that Mary was on the roof. And for many other P_2s the source locative seems inherently ambiguous according as it predicates of the 'subject' or the 'object'. Thus *John grabbed/shot/called/summoned Mary from the roof* seems ambiguous according as John or Mary was on the roof. Note that on the reading in which Mary is on the roof we interpret the P_2 in some sense as a verb of motion like *drag*, as the sentences imply that Mary moved from the roof (in the case of *grabbed* and *shot*) or was at least requested to move from the roof (in the case of *called, summoned*, etc.).

    This variation in the interpretation of source locatives is itself evidence for taking them as P_2 modifiers since if they are inter- preted as functions on P_2 denotations we can condition their inter- pretation according to the semantic nature of the P_2 in question. Moreover, consider the passives of the action-at-a-distance P_2s, where the source locative is subject oriented. Note that (27a) unambiguously entails (27b) and does not entail (27c).

(27) a.   Mary was watched from the roof.
     b.   Someone who watched Mary was on the roof.
     c.   Mary was on the roof.

These facts are predicted if *from the roof* is taken as a P_2 modifier and thus the logical form of (27a) is essentially as in (28) below:

(28) [Pass (from the roof (watch))] (Mary)

Our semantics for Passive says that (28) is true iff for some individual y, *watch from the roof* holds of the pair $<$ y, Mary $>$ and the independently needed semantics for source locatives applied to action-at-a-glance P_2s guarantees that the source locative predicates the location of the 'subject' argument y.

On the other hand, if *from the roof* could only be a P_1 modifier the logical form of (27a) would have to be that in (29) below:

(29) [from the roof (Pass (watch))] (Mary)

Now (*Pass, watch*) is a P_1 and when applied to P_1s source locatives unambiguously predicate of the subject argument, Mary in this case. Thus (27a) would entail that Mary was on the roof, which is incorrect.

More direct evidence for directly modifying P_2s to form P_2s comes from the behaviour of adverbs of intent, such as *reluctantly, willingly, eagerly*, etc. And our analysis here enables us to represent an ambiguity noticed much earlier in the literature but never to our knowledge satisfactorily explained. Consider first that these adverbs for example unambiguously predicate of the subject argument of a P_n regardless of whether the P_n is a P_1 or a P_2. Thus the a- and b-sentences below are roughly logically equivalent:

(30) a.   John sang reluctantly/eagerly.
　　　b.   John sang and John was reluctant/eager to sing.
(31) a.   John kissed Mary reluctantly/eagerly.
　　　b.   John kissed Mary and John was reluctant/eager to kiss Mary.

Note in particular that (31a) does not have a reading on which Mary was the reluctant/eager partner. So (31a) is not ambiguous in this respect. But the passives are ambiguous in this respect. Thus *Mary was kissed reluctantly/eagerly* may mean either that Mary was reluctant/eager or that the one who kissed her was. This ambiguity is predicted on our analysis which assumes that these adverbs may be both P_1 and P_2 modifiers. The reading on which Mary is reluctant/eager is given by:

(32) [reluctant (Pass (kiss))] (Mary)

Here *reluctant* modifies the P_1 *was kissed* and thus pertains to the subject argument Mary. The second reading is represented by

(33) [Pass (reluctant (kiss))] (Mary)

Here our semantics for Passive says that (33) is true iff for some individual y, (*reluctant kiss*) holds of the pair $<$ y, Mary $>$ and the subject orientation of *reluctant* guarantees that that holds just in case y kissed Mary and y was reluctant to kiss Mary.

Note further that more direct syntactic evidence for such structures being complex P_2s is given by the fact that they co-ordinate with items which are clearly P_2s as in *John sought and eagerly accepted the nomination.* Such immediate syntactic evidence for the P_2 status of *kiss by John* (or the P_1 status of *run by John*) seems lacking however. The basic reason seems to be a constraint on languages prohibiting double specification of the semantic subject of a given P_n. Thus once we have generated a P_n with an agent phrase the only way the structure can surface is if some other operation applies which eliminates the subject argument of the P_n. Passive is one such operation; the *-ing* nominals cited earlier are another. That is, once a P_1 such as *talk by students* is nominalised yielding *talking by students* the resultant structure no longer is a predicate at all and cannot take further arguments.

To summarise briefly this section: our principal reason for taking various PPs and adverbs as P_2 modifiers (as well as P_1 modifiers) is that if we do we can interpret (correctly) a variety of structures as a function of their form. Moreover we can represent certain ambiguities heretofore mysterious and we can represent some surprising predication properties of PPs, to wit that *from the roof* in *Mary was watched from the roof* predicates of something not overtly represented in the sentence at all. And finally, for some of the P_n modifiers discussed we have evidence independent of the passives that they have the category of P_2s.

4.3 Passives on Syntactically Complex P_ns

Taking passives of P_2s such as *reluctantly kiss, kiss by John*, etc. as discussed above is one type of example of passives of complex[2] P_2s. The arguments in support of analysing such expressions as P_2s were mostly though not entirely semantic in nature. Here we present two types of case more directly syntactic in nature. The first concerns passives of complex P_1s in languages such as Latin which permit them.

Passives such as *curritur* 'running is being done', *pugnatur* 'fighting is being done', etc. clearly are P_0s in Latin and have, obviously enough, no overt subject. They may of course take agent phrases e.g. *curritur ab aliquo* 'running is being done by someone' constructed in the same way as agent phrases in passives of P_2s. And for reasons similar to those given above for English we want the agent phrases to be part of the P passivised, not simply a modifier of a derived P_0.

Recall now that a variety of P_2s in Latin take their second argument in the dative, rather than the more usual accusative case. Some examples are *invidere* 'to envy', *parere* 'to obey', *servire* 'to serve', etc. Now consider a typical active/passive pair as in (34):

(34) a.   Marcus mihi invidet
          Marcus to + me envies
          'Marcus envies me'
   b.   mihi   invidetur
          to + me envy + 3sg + pass
          'I am envied' (literally to me (it) is envied)

There is no reason to consider that *mihi* 'to me' in (34b) has changed its grammatical relation to the verb compared to the one it has in (34a). It is still dative in case and does not trigger verb agreement. Thus (34b) is overtly subjectless in the same way as *curritur* is. In our approach we may generate such passives by taking *mihi invidet* 'envies to me' as a complex P_1 and passivising it to a P_0 just as was done for *currit → curritur*:

(35)

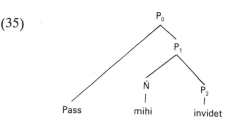

Additional, and rather striking support for allowing Passive to apply to both P_1s and P_2s comes from the fact that P_2s such as *invidere* can, at least in poetical usage, be directly passivised to yield P_1s taking a nominative subject argument. Thus from Horace (cited in Allen and Greenough, 1903, p. 232) we have:

(36) cur invideor
      why envy + pass + 1sg
      'Why am I envied?'

A rough constituent tree for (36) would be:

(37)

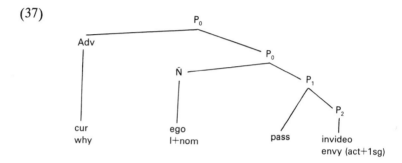

The independent first person pronoun *ego* of course regularly drops yielding the form in (36) once passive morphology and agreement forms are added to the verb in (37).

Note that the two passives cited above are particularly difficult to represent on a strictly lexicalist view of Passive in which only lexical P_ns can be passivised. We would need somehow to say that *the* passive of *invidere* is a P_1 which takes its argument only in the nominative for all persons and numbers except the third singular. That one allows its argument to be either nominative or dative, and thus is in effect two verbs. We should perhaps stress as well that dative object verbs in Latin are not a mere handful of lexically idiosyncratic P_2s. Allen and Greenough (1903) give an avowedly incomplete list of 23, a list which does not include for example such basic dative object taking verbs as *respondere* 'to reply, answer'. Thus in the active we have *Caesari respondet* '(he) replies to Caesar' and in the passive *Caesari respondetur* 'to Caesar (it) is replied'.

Similar examples of 'dual' passives can be found in North Russian, which in addition to canonical passives (P_1s derived from

P_2s) also presents passive P_0s derived from P_1s. Thus consider (38), cited from Timberlake (1976):

(38) u mena bylo   telenka   zarezano
      at me   was (3sg, neut) calf (fem, acc) slaughtered (3sg, neut)
      'By me there was slaughtering a calf'

The construction is clearly superficially subjectless, the predicate being third person neuter in form and thus not agreeing either with *mena* 'me' which is first person or with *talenka* 'calf' which is feminine. As P_2s like 'slaughter' regularly form passive P_1s (which would take 'calf' above as a nominative argument, though this particular example is not given in Timberlake 1976), we have another case where we may either passivise a P_2 directly forming a P_1, or we may passivise the result of combining the P_2 with an $\bar{N}$ (the result being a P_1) yielding a P_0.

A different sort of argument for applying Passive to complex P_ns is given by cases where the distinctive passive morphology shows up in more than one part of the P_n, in such a way that the two pieces of the passive morphology cannot be independently generated. To illustrate such cases we must find complex P_ns formed from two or more predicates, as passive morphology is limited to predicates. Two such cases may be found in the literature.

The first case unspectacularly concerns passives of coordinate P_2s. Thus (see Section 5) we shall form complex P_2s such as *hug and kiss, hug or kiss,* etc. and these may be passivised yielding passive morphology on both conjuncts. Thus we shall analyse *Mary was robbed and beaten by some irate student* as containing the passive of the complex P_2 *rob and beat by some irate student,* where *rob and beat* is itself a complex P_2. Evidence for taking coordinations in all categories as base-generated is both syntactic and semantic. Syntactically we generate a very large range of coordinate structures without the never well defined and most cumbersome apparatus of conjunction reduction and the across the board constraints (see Gazdar 1981, for an enlightening discussion). Semantically (for first order P_ns) we obtain a more correct semantic interpretation than on 'reduction' approaches. E.g. note that (39a) and (39b) are not paraphrases:

(39) a. Some students both hugged and kissed Mary.
     b. Some student hugged Mary and some student kissed
         Mary.

But correct predictions of semantic relatedness are in general
obtained by base-generating conjunctions and disjunctions of P_ns
(see Keenan and Faltz 1978 and to appear, for an extended
discussion of these rules).

Once *hug and kiss*, etc. is admitted as a complex P_2 it is trivial to
observe that passive morphology appears in both conjuncts in
Mary was hugged and kissed. Note by the way that *Mary was
robbed and beaten by some irate student* is not a paraphrase of
*Mary was robbed by some irate student and (was) beaten by some
irate student*, so semantically we want the agent phrase to be outside the scope of the co-ordinate conjunction.

A second, more interesting though more problematic, case of
complex P_ns formed from more than one P_n concerns predicates
formed from verbs of aspectual meaning (*begin, finish*, etc.), verbs
of desire (*want*), and verbs of intent (*intend, plan*, etc.). It is
arguably the case in several languages, e.g. Turkish (Georges and
Kornfilt 1977), Malagasy (Keenan 1976) and Hebrew that such
verbs combine with P_2s to form complex P_2s. Consider for example
the following active and passive pair from Turkish (Lewis 1967):

(40) a. bu iş-i   yap-may-a   başliyor-lar
         this job-acc do-   dat   begin -3pl
         'They are beginning to do this job'
     b. bu iş   yap-il- may-a başla-n- iyor
         this job(nom) do- pass-   dat begin-pass-pres
         'This job is being begun to be done'

(The passive affix *-il* and *-n* are conditioned variants, *-n* being the
form used after vowels and *l*). The important point to note in
(40b) is that both the main verb *begin* and the nominalised verb *do*
show passive morphology. Georges and Kornfilt (1977) show that
the two verbs cannot be assigned passive morphology independently. That is, Passive has applied only once in (40b). We can
naturally represent this if we take *begin to do* in (40b) as a complex
P_2. Then we need merely design the assignment of passive morphology assignment rules of Turkish in such a way that the passive
of a P_2 consisting of predicates like *begin, want, intend*, etc. plus an

infinitive (verbal noun) of a P_2 assigns passive morphology to both constituents.

Comparable examples are given for Malagasy in Keenan (1976). Similarly note the Hebrew active/passive pair below:

(41) a. (hem) igmeru   la'asof et ha- tvu'a ba-   stav
     they finish   gather acc the-harvest in+the- fall
        (act, fut, 3pl) (inf, act)
     'They will finish gathering the harvest in the fall'

    b. ha- tvu'a   tigamer   lehe'sef ba-   stav
     the-harvest finish   gather in+the- fall
      (fem)   (pass, fut, 3sg, fem) (inf, pass)
     'The harvest will be finished to be gathered in the fall'

We note that if the passive *tigamer* 'finish' is replaced by the appropriate form of the active, *tigmor*, in (41b) the result is ungrammatical. Similarly if the passive infinite *lehe'sef* 'to be gathered' is replaced by the active infinite *la'asof* the result is ungrammatical. Thus we cannot independently generate the two passive forms in (41b). But as in the Turkish example, if *finish to gather* is treated as a complex P_2 then Passive applies only once in the derivation of (41b) and the correct result is obtained merely by designing the passive morphology rule so as to assign passive morphology to each of the predicates in the complex P_2.

In fact it is possible that the English passives in (42) should be analysed as passives of such complex P_2s. But the case is less clear than the Turkish, Malagasy, and Hebrew cases above, since the paradigms illustrated in English are much less productive, examples are of more doubtful grammaticality and the claim that the two passive forms cannot be independently generated is less convincing.

(42) a.   The room *was finished being decorated* at six.
    b.   Algebra *was begun to be studied* in the Middle Ages.

4.4 Extending Passive$_{UG}$: Thermatic Roles and Case Marking

Recall that we justified enriching our original formulation of Passive$_{UG}$ in (4) by the addition of the subcategorisation notation used in (11) on the grounds that the inclusion of the additional parameters in the rule permitted a more adequate statement of parameter conditions on the rule, that is, a more accurate representation of the properties of passives in the world's languages. Specifically the new formulation allows us to distinguish among types of P_2s and say that Passive applies most productively to those whose subcategorisation is $< \check{N},\check{N} >$. In the same vein we would now like to discriminate among such P_2s according as to the thematic (θ) roles which the arguments bear to the predicate. Specifically we would like to be able to guarantee that P_2s whose two $\check{N}$ arguments bear respectively the Agent and Patient roles to the predicate are the most passivisable of P_2s. And this will require that we have parameters in the passive rule ranging over thematic roles.

Let us assume then that we have among the Constants of UG a set of θ-role markers including Agt (agent), Pat (patient), Exp (experiencer), etc. And let us enrich our notation for category names in UG to include expressions of the form (43):

$$(43) \qquad \begin{array}{c} W \\ < X_1, X_2, \ldots, X_n > \\ < \theta_1, \theta_2, \ldots, \theta_n > \end{array}$$

Expressions having such a category will as before be ones which combine with n argument expressions of categories X_1, X_2, ..., X_n to form an expression of category W. They will be interpreted as before by functions mapping n-tuples $< x_1, x_2, \ldots, x_n >$ into T_W, where now each x_i is not only an element of T_{x_i} but in addition is required to bear the θ-role θ_i to the predicate. We assume that the θ-roles are given a universal semantic definition. We may now more adequately represent Passive$_{UG}$ as follows:

(44) *Passive$_{UG}$* (Third Approximation)
    a. *Syntax*

$$\begin{array}{c} S \\ < X_1, X_2, \ldots, X_n > \\ < \theta_1, \theta_2, \ldots, \theta_n > \end{array} \rightarrow \left\{ \begin{array}{cc} \text{Pass,} & S \\ & < Y, \ X_2, \ldots, X_n, X_1 > \\ & < \theta_{n+1}, \theta_2, \ldots, \theta_n, \theta_1 > \end{array} \right\}$$

    b. *Semantics*
       identical to that given in (11)
    c. *Parameter Conditions*
       (i) if the range of the complex symbol to the right of the arrow above is not empty in L then $\begin{array}{c} S \\ \check{N} \quad \check{N} \\ \text{Agt} \quad \text{Pat} \end{array}$ is in it.

(ii) if $\frac{S}{N}$ is in the range of the complex symbol on the

right of the arrow then $\frac{S}{\underset{Agt}{N}}$ is in it.

Note that Passive$_{UG}$ as stated above preserves θ-roles of its arguments (in distinction e.g. to its approximate inverse, Causative). Moreover PC(i) clearly entails the parameter condition on the earlier formulation of Passive$_{UG}$ and in addition now says that P_2s taking agent and patient arguments are among the most passivisable of P_2s. PC(ii) states that if L allows passives on any P_1s then it must allow them on P_1s taking agent arguments. If we define (questionable but not unreasonable) a predicate to be *stative* if the θ-role of its first argument is not agent then the PCs on (44) jointly say that non-stative P_ns (for n = 1 or n = 2) are the most passivisable of P_ns. The observation could be generalised to P_ns for any n.

Consider finally the interaction of case marking and Passive. In the same way that predicates taking the same number and categories of arguments may vary according to the θ-role of those arguments (e.g. *kiss* and *need* in English) so also they may vary with respect to the case they impose on the corresponding argument expressions. For example *amare* 'to love' takes its first argument in the nominative and its second in the accusative, while *invidere* 'to envy' takes its first in the nominative but its second in the dative. And clearly in Latin accusative-taking P_2s passivise more readily than dative-taking ones. We would like to capture this regularity in the PCs for Passive$_{UG}$ and thus want that rule to contain parameters ranging over case markers. Since in any given language with a significant case-marking system there is serious redundancy between θ-role marking and case marking it might be thought that including parameters in Passive$_{UG}$ for both θ-roles and case marking is unnecessary. Perhaps this is so, but we think it unlikely. For example in Latin there are several pairs of P_2s with approximately the same meaning but which differ according as the second argument case marker is *accusative* or *dative*. For example *placere* 'to please' takes its second argument in the dative, but both *delectare* and *iuvare* 'to delight' take their second argument in the accusative. The three verbs are close enough in meaning that it is unlikely that their second arguments bear different thematic roles. Let us then enrich our category notation once more to include subcategorisation for case marking of arguments as well as θ-role. Then Passive$_{UG}$ may be stated as follows:

(45) *Passive$_{UG}$*
    a. *Syntax*

$$
\begin{array}{c} S \\ < X_1, X_2, \ldots, X_n > \\ < \theta_1, \theta_2, \ldots, \theta_n > \\ < c_1, c_2, \ldots, c_n > \end{array} \rightarrow \left\{ \begin{array}{cc} \text{Pass,} & S \\ & < Y, X_2, \ldots, X_n, X_1 > \\ & < \theta_{n+1}, \theta_2, \ldots, \theta_n, \theta_1 > \\ & < c_{n+1}, c_2, \ldots, c_n, c_1 > \end{array} \right\}
$$

    b. *Semantics*
       as before
    c. *Parameter Conditions*
       (i) if the range of the complex symbol on the right above

is not empty in L then $\underset{\underset{c_1}{\underset{\text{Agt}}{N}}}{S} \underset{\underset{c_2}{\underset{\text{Pat}}{\tilde{N}}}}{}$ is in it, where $< c_1, c_2 >$

$= < \text{nom, acc} >$ or $< c_1, c_2 > = < \text{erg, abs} >$.

       (ii) if S is in the range of the complex predicate on the

right of the arrow in L then $\underset{\underset{c'}{\underset{\text{Agt}}{\tilde{N}}}}{S}$ is in it, where c' is nom

or c' is erg.

This completes the statement of Passive$_{UG}$ to the extent that we shall develop it here. We refer the reader to Keenan (1980a) for further typological properties of passives which would justify enriching Passive$_{UG}$ to include further parameters. In particular, we may note that many languages with passives present more than one distinct type of passive. For example in Latin alongside *amor* 'I am loved' we have *amatus sum* 'I have been loved', this latter being interpreted in a strictly perfective way in distinction to the former which is not strictly perfective. Similarly both Russian and Tzeltal (Mayan) present two passives, one of which is strictly perfective, the other of which is not (being strictly imperfective in Russian). One way to represent these facts in our framework would be to subcategorise *Pass* in UG as ± perfective. But we shall not pursue that approach here.

4.5 Conclusion

We have given a variety of syntactic and semantic reasons why Passive in UG is best treated as a parametrised phrase structure rule deriving predicates from predicates. We note here two somewhat more general advantages of this approach. First, we have provided a uniform treatment, both syntactically and semantically, for passives on predicates of different number and categories of arguments. It is thus expected on this approach that we will find passives on P_1s as well as on P_2s.

Second, and farther reaching, by treating Passive$_{UG}$ as a phrase structure rule rather than a transformational (= sentence-level derivational) rule we have relegated a piece of the syntax and semantics of natural languages to a simpler component. Thus for example on our view as opposed to the transformational one, children have fewer options to choose from in deciding which of the possible passive rules are the rules of their language. Thus we provide a better basis for explaining how children learn languages quickly with limited exposure to imperfect data, etc.

Of course Passive$_{UG}$ is but one family of rules, so our simplification is not perhaps massive. However in the next section we show that other rules which affect the argument structure of predicates — rules such as Raising (to Subject and to Object), Conjunction Reduction, Extraposition, Tough Movement, etc. can also be treated as phrase structure rules within Base$_{UG}$. In fact, as we show below, our treatment of Passive$_{UG}$ actually forces us to treat these other argument affect operations in the Base$_{UG}$. The more general conclusion of the next section then is that a very significant part of the syntax and semantics of a natural language may be treated within a class of simple grammars, the context free phrase structure ones.

5. Relation-Changing Rules and the Universal Base

The domain of definition of syntactic transformations is recursively given beginning with the structures generated by the Base. Hence, as Wasow (1977) observes in a slightly different context, there is no sense in which transformations can 'feed' Passive$_{UG}$ as formulated by us. Hence, roughly, the outputs of many relation changing rules on the classical view of transformational grammar must be base-generated in order to yield structures to which Passive$_{\text{UG}}$ can apply.

The two primary rules which fed Passive on that view were Dative (DAT) and Raising to Object (R-to-O). Thus DAT derived *John gave Mary the book* from *John gave the book to Mary*, and the resultant structure could be analysed by Passive to yield *Mary was given the book.* R-to-O derived structures like *John believed Fred to be a linguist* from ones like *John believed that Fred was a linguist*, which could in turn be passivised to yield *Fred was believed to be a linguist.* Of these two rules DAT is relatively easy to handle in the Base. It is sufficient to define a rule analogous in some respects to Passive$_{\text{UG}}$ which derives P$_3$s from P$_3$s by interchanging the second and third arguments, preserving θ-roles and making appropriate changes in case marking. See Dowty (1978) for one such approach.

The more serious case concerns that of R-to-O, for any rule which created derived subjects, intuitively speaking, fed R-to-O and thus directly fed Passive. Hence in our view all rules which created derived subjects must have their 'outputs' base-generated. The principal cases here are *Conjunction Reduction (Conj), Neg Lowering (Neg), Raising to Subject (R-to-S), Extraposition (Extra)* (or *Intraposition*), *There Insertion (There)*, and *Tough Movement (Tough)*. *Conj* created structures like those in (46b) from ones like (46a). Embedding (46b) and applying R-to-O and then Passive yielded structures like (46c).

(46) a.   John is honest and John works hard.
    b.   John is honest and works hard.
    c.   John is believed to be honest and to work hard.

Similarly the other classical transformations mentioned above derive the b-sentences below from the a-sentences, and embedding the result allows R-to-O to apply which feeds Passive yielding the indicated c-sentences.

(47) a.   That John will win is certain. $\Rightarrow$ (R-to-S)
    b.   John is certain to win.
    c.   John was believed to be certain to win.
(48) a.   Neg [many arrows hit the target] $\Rightarrow$ (Neg)

   b.   [not many arrows] hit the target
   c.   Not many arrows were believed to have hit the target.
(49) a.   That Fred will win is certain. ⇒ (Extra)
   b.   It is certain that Fred will win.
   c.   It is believed to be certain that Fred will win.
(50) a.   A cat is on the mat. ⇒ (There)
   b.   There is a cat on the mat.
   c.   There is believed to be a cat on the mat.
(51) a.   To read these books is easy. ⇒ (Tough)
   b.   These books are easy to read.
   c.   These books are believed to be easy to read.

Our problem now is to formulate R-to-O and the other rules mentioned above as phrase structure rules so that the passives in the c-sentences above can be generated by the Passive rule we have already motivated. To illustrate the derivations determined by such rules we shall have to give first some formulation of the basic constituent-building rules of UG.

5.1   Basic Constituent-Building Rules of UG

Among the primitives of UG we assume defined a set PH of possible *phonological systems*, and for each $p \in$ PH the sets W_p of *possible phonological words over* p. Specifically as part of the universal Base we assume that UG will define a set CON of constants. This set will include various distinguished subsets, in particular a set of *boolean operators* including AND, OR, and NEG; a set of *valency-affecting operators* including *Pass, Cause, Dat*, etc.; a set TR of *thematic role markers* including *Agt, Pat, Exp*, etc.; a set CM of *case markers* including *nom, acc, erg, gen, dat, abs*, etc.; and a set SCF of *inherent subcategorisation features* including *plural, mass, indicative*, etc.

Base$_{UG}$ defines the set CAT of *possible grammatical categories* recursively as follows:

(52) (i)   N $\in$ CAT and S $\in$ CAT
     (ii) if C $\in$ CAT and K $\subseteq$ SCF then C$_K$ $\in$ CAT
     (iii) if C $\in$ CAT then Č $\in$ CAT
     (iv) if C $\in$ CAT then C $\in$ CAT, where X ranges over
                     X
                     θ
                     c

CAT^n (the set of n-ary sequences over CAT), θ ranges over TR^n and c ranges over CM^n, all $n \geqslant 1$.

As before N is the category of common noun phrases and Ñ that of full noun phrases (the exact bar level difference will not be important in what follows). S of course is the category sentence. By clause (iv) of the definition it combines with n-tuples of category names, θ-role markers and case markers to form predicatives of degree n. Thus intuitively S is as before the category of zero place predicates, and definition (52) says that 'nominals' and 'predicatives' are the basic categories of natural language, other categories being formed from them in any of three ways.

In stating rules using the category names so defined we shall often omit case and θ-role markers when not relevant. We shall use COMP as an abbreviation of $\frac{S}{S}$, and assume that *that* in English is of this category. Similarly we shall use INF to abbreviate $\frac{\check{X}}{X}$ where X is any P$_n$ category, $n \geqslant 1$, and we shall assume that *to* in English has this category. So *to* combines with P$_n$s to form P̌$_n$s, for all $n \geqslant 1$. Note that our category notation is ambiguous. E.g. $\frac{S}{\check{N}}$ might be bar over $\frac{S}{\check{N}}$, viz. the infinitive of P$_1$s taking Ñ arguments, or it might be Š over Ñ. In the former case we shall use a long bar over S. We may easily disambiguate our notation with the use of parentheses but few enough cases occur that it is not worth the trouble.

We may now state the primary constituent building rule of UG as follows:

R. 1   *PCB* (or the Primary Constituent Building Rules of UG)
For all $W \in$ CAT, all $n \geqslant 0$ and $m \geqslant 1$,

$$\begin{matrix} W \\ X \\ \theta \\ c \end{matrix} \rightarrow \left\{ \begin{matrix} Y, & W \\ & X, Y \\ & \theta, \delta \\ & c, d \end{matrix} \right\} \text{ is a rule of UG,}$$

where X, θ, c are any elements of CAT^n, TR^n, and CM^n respectively and Y, δ, d are any elements of CAT^m, TR^m, and CM^m, respectively.

Parameter Conditions
(i) For all languages L, $\begin{matrix} S \\ \check{N} \\ Agt \\ c \end{matrix}$ is in the range of the complex

symbol on the right of the rule for some c ∈ CM.

The following are three of the rules defined by PCB:

(53) a. $S \rightarrow \left\{ \bar{N}, \begin{array}{c} S \\ \bar{N} \end{array} \right\}$

                Agt

                nom

  b. $\begin{array}{c} S \\ \bar{N} \end{array} \rightarrow \left\{ \bar{N}, \begin{array}{c} S \\ \bar{N}\ \bar{N} \end{array} \right\}$

        Agt   Agt Pat

        nom   nom acc

(54) $S \rightarrow \left\{ <\bar{N}, \bar{N}>, \begin{array}{c} S \\ \bar{N}\ \bar{N} \end{array} \right\}$

                         Agt Pat

                         nom acc

As before the use of curly brackets indicates an unordered set, whereas angled brackets indicate sequences.

The parameter condition says simply that in all languages sentences may be formed which consist of an $\bar{N}$ and a P_1 taking $\bar{N}$ arguments marked for some case and interpreted as agents. Rather obviously much more should be said by way of parameter conditions. For example the choice between (53a, b) and (54) will in part determine whether the language is a 'flat' one or not. These issues run deep, but they are of only secondary concern in defining relation-changing rules, as these are in general rules which derive predicates from predicates. We may then continue avoiding any particular commitment as to how argument expressions in a language are matched for interpretative purposes with elements of a subcategorisation. Languages obviously vary considerably with regard to the case marking, linear order, and constituent structures they assign to simple sentences, and the regularities here must be accounted for by parameter conditions both on PCB as well as the linear order assignment rules if these are done independently of PCB (as we believe they should be, as linear order cannot in general be determined on the basis of mere category membership of constituents, it depends in part on relative length of the lexical items having these categories in particular cases).

R. 2   *The Lexical Rules of UG*

$W \rightarrow w$, all $W \in CAT$, all $w \in \cup \{\cup W_p : p \in PH\}$

Parameter Conditions

(i) the range of w in L is a subset of some W_p, for some p $\in PH$

The PC here merely states that the words in a given language are all drawn from a same possible phonological system. Obviously again much more could be said. All languages have one-syllable words, etc. Note however that as given the lexical items in a given language are all values of parameters of the lexical insertion rules of UG — consistent with an early remark of Chomsky's.

5.2 Raising in UG

Our goal here is to base-generate sentences like (55) below:

(55) John is believed to be a genius.

Plausibly enough (55) consists of an $\bar{N}$ *John* and a P_1 taking $\bar{N}$ arguments and is generated from these two elements by PCB. The P_1 arguably is passive, and is thus the passive of a P_2. We shall take the P_2 in question to be *believe to be a genius*. It is thus a complex P_2 consisting of *believe*, of category $_{\bar{N}\bar{S}}^{S}$ and the infinitive of a P_1 taking $\bar{N}$ arguments, *to be a genius*. Thus we want a base rule which combines $_{\bar{N}\bar{S}}^{S}$ with $_{\bar{N}}^{\check{S}}$ to yield $_{\bar{N}\bar{N}}^{S}$. Generalising, we want a rule of UG which combines n-place predicates whose last argument is $\check{S}$ with infinitives of P_1s taking X as argument to yield an n-place pedicate like the original, except that the last argument is X rather than $\check{S}$. The syntactic part of $Raise_{UG}$ is then formulated as follows:

R.4   *$Raise_{UG}$*

a. *Syntax*

$$\overset{S}{X_1, X_2, \ldots, X_n} \rightarrow \left\{ \overset{S}{X_1, X_2, \ldots, X_{n-1}, \check{S}, \overset{\bar{S}}{X_n}} \right\},$$

all $n \geqslant 1$

(We have for the moment ignored case and θ-role marking in the statement of the rule.) Let us consider some of the rules in R. 4, beginning with the simplest case where $n = 1$. Two such rules are given opposite:

(56) a. $\begin{matrix} S \\ \tilde{N} \end{matrix} \rightarrow \left\{ \begin{matrix} S, \bar{S} \\ \bar{S} \ \tilde{N} \end{matrix} \right\}$

b. $\begin{matrix} S \\ \tilde{S} \end{matrix} \rightarrow \left\{ \begin{matrix} S, \bar{S} \\ \tilde{S} \ \tilde{S} \end{matrix} \right\}$

For completeness we might note the Inherent Subcategorisation rules of UG below, though we shall not use these rules in what follows.

R. 3   *The Inherent Subcategorisation Rules of UG*

$$C \rightarrow C_f, \text{ all } C \in \text{CAT, all } f \subseteq \text{SCF}$$

For example, taking *proper* as an element of SCF we have that $\bar{N} \rightarrow \bar{N}_{proper}$ is a subcategorisation rule of UG.

The reader may verify that using PCB and the lexical rules above and making some obvious assumptions about which of these rules English chooses, the sentence *John is a linguist* can be generated in the way indicated in the following unordered tree:

(57)

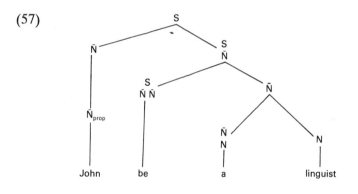

Similarly *Fred believes that John is a linguist* is generated as follows:

(58)

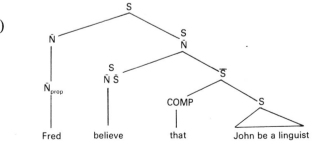

Let us turn now to the relation-changing rules of UG. Passive$_{UG}$ of course has already been given. So let us consider the crucial case of Raising.

Note that these are just the *Raising to Subject* rules of UG! To see this let us assume, standardly, that English expressions like *seem, appear, be certain,* etc. are P_1s taking $\bar{S}$ arguments, that is, they have the category $\frac{S}{\bar{S}}$. Then PCB generates the structures in (59). Note that for ease of reading we have marked verb agreement where it should be marked, that is, in finite verbs but not in infinitives. We shall continue this practice in later examples.

(59) a.

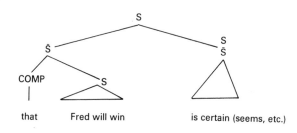

b.

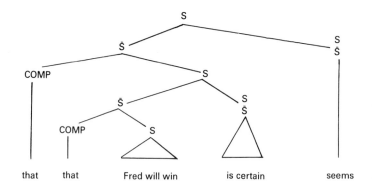

Consider now that the rule in (56a) generates *Fred is certain to win,* classically the result of applying raising to Subject to (59a).

(60)

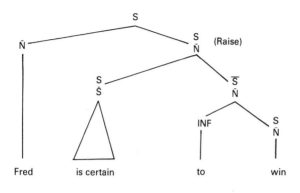

Similarly the classical result of Raising the embedded sentential subject from (59b) is base-generated by (56b) as follows:

(61)

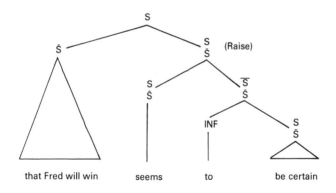

Thus just as Passive$_{UG}$ may create P$_1$s taking either Ñ or S̃ arguments, so Raising may create such P$_1$s. Note further that Raising to Subject iterates in an intuitive sense:

(62)

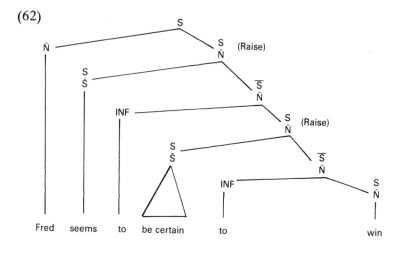

Fred   seems   to   be certain   to   win

Consider now the Raising to Object rules in R. 4. The basic case is:

$$(63) \qquad \underset{\check{N}\ \bar{N}}{S} \rightarrow \left\{ \underset{\bar{N}\ \check{S}}{S}, \overline{\underset{\bar{N}}{S}} \right\}$$

This rule (plus the lexical rules of English of course) clearly generates *believe to be a genius* as a P_2 taking two Ñ arguments since *believe* has the category $\underset{\check{N}}{\overset{S}{}}_{\check{S}}$ and *to be a genius* is an infinitive of a P_1 taking an Ñ argument. Thus *believe to be a genius* passivises by Passive$_{UG}$ yielding (64) as was our goal:

(64)

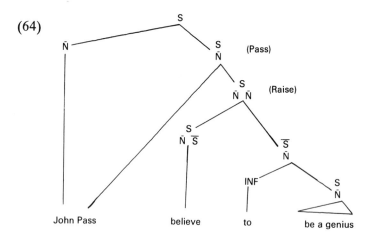

John Pass   believe   to   be a genius

Note that the Raising to Subject rules given above 'feed' Raising to Object, (63), which in turns feeds Passive, as in (65):

(65)

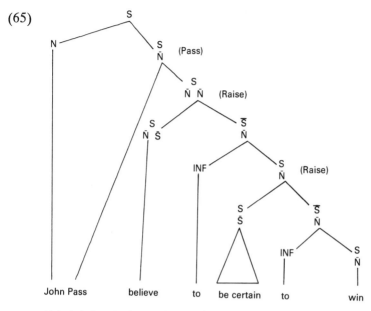

'John is believed to be certain to win.'

Similarly in these rules Passive itself feeds Raising, as in (66):

(66)

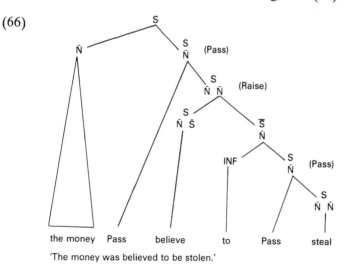

'The money was believed to be stolen.'

Example (66) shows that whatever merit the classical 'sandwich' arguments may have had they certainly did not show that repeated application of Passive, Raising, etc. in a derivation justified the existence of transformations. The reader may test his knowledge of the rules so far proposed by giving trees for:

(67) a.   That Fred left is believed to be certain.
  b.   John is expected to be certain to be believed to be kidnapped.

We may note that, as on the classical approach, (67a) has two derivations in this system. In each case the first rule to apply is the PCB rule $S \rightarrow \left\{ \bar{S}, \frac{S}{S} \right\}$. Then either R-to-S applies and then Passive applies to the $\frac{S}{S}$ created by that rule, or else Passive applies first and then R-to-O applies to the $\underset{N}{S}\bar{S}$ created by that rule. Similarly (67b) has multiple derivations. Perhaps the easiest to work out is the one where the PCB rule $S \rightarrow \left\{ \bar{N}, \frac{S}{N} \right\}$ applies first and then, ignoring applications of PCB, Passive, Raising, Raising, Passive, Raising, and Passive apply in that order. We note that when the semantics for Raising is given the multiple structures for these sentences can be shown to be logically equivalent.

As a final illustration of the generality of the Raising and Passive rules we have proposed let us illustrate a plausible case where a $\bar{P}_1$ has been raised to object and then passivised to subject. We shall assume that 'Tough' predicates like *be difficult, easy*, etc. are P_1s taking $\bar{P}_1$s as arguments. Then PCB and the lexical rules base generate:

(68)

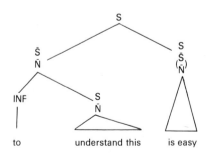

Then (69) illustrates Passives and R-to-O where the affected argument is a $\bar{P}_1$. To simplify the tree we use $\bar{P}_1$ instead of $(\bar{\bar{S}}_N)$.

(69)

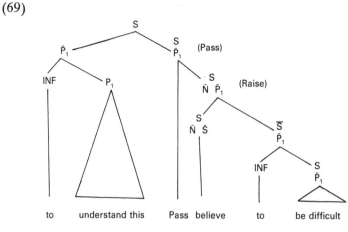

'To understand this is believed to be difficult.'

To complete our statement of Raising$_{UG}$ we must first include the variables in the rule ranging over case and θ-role markers, and then give the interpretation of the n-place predicate generated by the rule as a function of the interpretations of what it is generated from. Neither is problematic. As regards the former, add the sequences of variables $\theta_1, \theta_2, \ldots, \theta_n$ and $c_1, c_2, \ldots, c_n$ under $X_1, X_2, \ldots, X_n$ on the left of the rule. Use the same variables in both cases for the X_i on the right, for $i < n$. Otherwise, for $\check{S}$ and X_n on the right of the rule use new variables in all cases. The relations between the derived case and θ-role markers on the left and those on the right will be constrained by parameter conditions. Most usually for example the case of X_n on the left is the unmarked case for n^{th} arguments. In a few cases (Icelandic, see Andrews, 1979) it may be the same as that for X_n on the right.

As regards the semantics of Raising$_{UG}$ we want to say e.g. that the derived P_2 *believe to be a genius* maps the denotation of *every student* onto that P_1 denotation which holds of an individual x iff *believe [be a genius (every student)]* holds of x. Referring the reader to Keenan and Faltz (1978 and to appear) for details, we can give a generalised semantics for Raising$_{UG}$ which guarantees this relation as follows:

R.4   *Raising$_{UG}$*
  b.   *Semantics*
      Where e of category $<X_1, X_2, \ldots, X_{n-1}, \bar{S}>$ is
      interpreted by f_e and b of category S is interpreted
      by f_b, interpret (e,b̄), generated by Raising$_{UG}$,
      by that function which maps n-tuples $<x_1,$
      $x_2, \ldots, x_{n-1}, Q>$ onto $(f_e \ (f_b \ (Q)) \ (x_1, \ldots, x_{n-1})$, where
      each x_i is an individual in T_{X_i} and Q is any element of
      T_{X_n}.

We note without argument that this guarantees the paraphrase
relation between raised and unraised structures which motivated
the classical treatment of Raising. It says in effect that *John
believes every student to be a genius* is logically equivalent to the
claim that John believes that *be a genius* holds of the denotation of
every student.

5.3   *Flatten: A Problem of Derived Constituent Structure*

In the case of Raising to Object (but not Raising to Subject), R.4
yields an apparently unintuitive constituent structure for *John
believes Fred to be a genius,* namely:

(70)

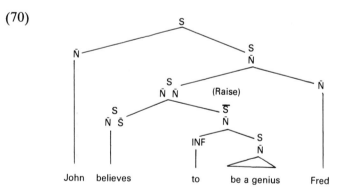

Although linear order is not determined by our rules, it is clear
that the natural English *John believes Fred to be a genius* cannot be
assigned the constituent structure given in (70) since *Fred* separ-
ates the two parts of the complex P_2 *believes to be a genius.* Consequently in our approach English will need some sort of flattening
rule whose effect is illustrated in (71):

(71)

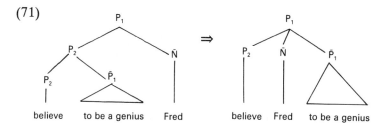

It is then reasonable to query first, whether there is any independent evidence for the existence of such a flattening rule, and second, whether there is motivation for taking *believe to be a genius* as a complex P_2 in addition to that already provided — namely that we correctly generate and interpret a class of complex passives.

We consider there to be a lot of evidence for flattening rules of the sort illustrated above. Roughly the process is one in which the argument expression of a complex 'headed' P_n is attracted to the 'head' (or equivalently the 'body' of the complex P_n is extraposed around the argument). Formally let us define:

(72) Let W be a P_n whose immediate constituents are X_1, X_2, ..., X_k for some $k \geqslant 2$. Then W is said to be *headed* iff exactly one of the X_i is a P_m for some $m \geqslant n$, and that X_i is said to be the *head* of W, the remainder of W being called the *body*.

For example, the expressions in (73) are headed P_0s, those in (74) are headed P_1s, the heads being italicised in all cases:

(73) a. John *sang.*
     b. John *began to sing.*
     c. John *kissed Mary.*
(74) a. *is certain* to win.
     b. *fall* on the desk.
     c. *die* young.
     d. *kiss* Mary.
     e. *want* to leave.
     f. *wake up* screaming.
     g. *fall* down.

Let us now give a formulation of Flatten$_{UG}$ which is sufficiently general for our purposes:

(75) *Flatten*$_{UG}$ (A stylistic rule)
    ... $[_X[_{P_n} \text{Head} + \text{Body}] + \text{Arg}]$ ... $\Rightarrow$ $[_X \text{Head} + \text{Arg} + \text{Body}]$

Parameter Conditions
For all L, the applicability of the rule varies directly according as the argument is:
(1) invisible (e.g. a trace)
(2) a proform
(3) small compared to the body
(4) large compared to the body

Roughly then the acceptability of breaking up the head and body of a complex P_n is proportional to the size of the element breaking it up. Moreover let us accept that the acceptability ordering of the inputs to a stylistic rule is the inverse of that of the outputs. Notice that this is just the natural generalisation of the two-valued obligatory/optional distinction. Then it will follow that the easiest arguments to 'strand' i.e. not attract to the head will be long ones; the next easiest will be small ones which are not proforms, etc.

Consider now the independent motivation for Flatten$_{UG}$. Note that basically all approaches to generative grammar would agree that the structures represented in (74) are headed P_1s (though they might not find this a useful definition to make). In English the P_0s formed by such P_1s do not in surface meet the structural definition of Flatten$_{UG}$ since the subject argument does not occur to the right of the body. However in languages in which 'subjects' normally follow P_1s Flatten can apply. The clearest cases here of course are VOS languages, e.g. Otomi, Ineseño Chusmash, Tzeltal, Toba Batak, Malagasy, etc. (see Keenan 1978 for supporting data). In these languages then the expected order of *John began to sing* will be *began to sing John*. Thus the argument of the P_1 *began to sing* is separated from the head *began* by *to sing*. And we find in many such cases (Keenan 1978 cites Batak, Tzeltal, and Malagasy) that the argument may (but need not) attract. (76) from Toba Batak is illustrative:

(76) a. nunga   mulai   manussi abit   si   Rotua
         already begin   wash   clothes art   Rotua
         'Rotua has already begun to wash clothes'
     b. nunga   mulai   si   Rotua manussi abit
         already begin   art   Rotua wash   clothes
         'Rotua has already begun to wash clothes'

Clearly (76b) will be derived from (76a) by Flatten$_{UG}$, giving thus independent motivation for that rule.

Consider now that in syntactic and semantic analogy to (76) above, we consider the structures in (77) below to be headed P$_2$s.

(77) a. *believe* to be a genius
   b. *find* on the desk
   c. *find* unacceptable
   d. *give* the book
   e. *persuade* to leave
   f. *catch* stealing hubcaps
   g. *write* down

Note that again most approaches would agree that *write down* and similar verb + particle constructions are headed P$_2$s. And note that the acceptability ordering in (78) is consistent with that given for Flatten$_{UG}$ thus constituting additional support for that rule in English:

(78) a. the names that$_t$ John wrote t down
   b. John wrote them down
   c. John wrote the names down
   d. ?John wrote the names of all the candidates from the third precinct down
   e. ?*John wrote whatever Fred put on the blackboard down

And accepting as P$_2$s the other expressions in (77) it is not hard to construct paradigms like (78) supporting the correctness of the predictions made. In particular pronominal and small N̄ 'objects' of *believe to be a genius* must attract to the head; on the other hand large 'objects' need not, as illustrated in (79):

(79) a. John believes to be a genius the undergraduate student who he nominated for the Linguist of the Year award.
   b. I believe to be false the rumour that Fred stole the money and fled to South America.

We thus have some direct evidence that English expressions of the form *believe to be false/a genius* should be analysed as complex P$_2$s. Let us consider now further, more direct, evidence.

There is in the first instance what we might call the obvious evidence — namely that which was cited in support of the classical R-to-O analysis. For notice (see 70) that the 'raised' NP in our analysis is the 'object' argument of a P_2. E.g. *Fred* is the object of *believe to be a genius* in (70) and thus is expected to be affected by object sensitive rules such as Reflexivisation, Accusative Case Marking, Object Proforms, and Object Clitics. Similarly it is expected that expressions like *believe to be clever* will occur in syntactic contexts diagnostic for P_2s in general. The domain of Passive in English is one such context; so also are co-ordinate structures. E.g.

(80) No teacher both admires and believes to be clever every student that he advises.

Similarly in the simplest cases of Tough Movement the expression following the 'Tough' predicate is an infinitive of a P_2, and we find sentences such as (81) in English:

(81) John is difficult to believe to be a genius.

Let us consider now two pieces of slightly less obvious evidence. First, it is an embarrassment to both the classical approach to Raising as well as to current EST approaches that passives on raised structures are often grammatical where the supposed output of Raising is not. E.g.

(82) a.   *John said/claimed/alleged Fred to be a thief.
      b.   Fred was said/claimed/alleged to be a thief.

Thus in one way or another classical and current approaches must countenance deriving structures from intermediate forms which cannot surface. In our view however (82b) is not derived in any sense from structures like those in (82a); the forms in (82b) are independently generated. Thus we do not need to posit underlying structures which are ungrammatical in the derivation of (82b). We need only to treat expressions like *say to be a thief* as P_2s, which the existence of (82a) motivates, and restrict the occurrence of such P_2s. For example we might posit a filter which would star P_1s of the form in (70) when the lowest P_2 was a verb of saying like *say, claim*, etc. Note that such a filter correctly predicts the grammaticality assignment in (83):

(83) a.   John was said to be a thief.
  b.   ?*Who$_t$ did Fred say t to be a thief.
  c.   *Fred said John to be a thief.

(83) points up a yet deeper advantage of our treatment of Raising$_{UG}$ and Passive$_{UG}$. Namely, current work in EST derives both (83a) and (83b) from structures of the form (83c), in both cases by moving an Ñ and leaving a trace behind. However for various semantic reasons the traces left by the movement in Passive and Raising to Subject is treated like an ordinary Ñ whereas that left by wh-movement is treated like a bound variable. So EST must posit distinct types of traces. Yet it is not easy to see how learners of the language distinguish among completely invisible elements. In any event, we do not need to make such a distinction. In the derivation of (83a) in our view *John* never occupied the subject position of *to be a thief* and was never moved, whence there is no trace in that position in (83a). Similarly in the Raising to Subject cases, (59), no Ñ was moved, whence no traces are left. Thus we have eliminated the basic cases in which moved Ñs leave traces not interpreted as bound variables, and thus our approach yields a more uniform interpretation of traces than current EST approaches.

Let us consider now, more briefly, the other relation-changing rules illustrated earlier.

5.4 Conjunction Reduction

Ignoring case and θ-role marking a first approximation to Conj$_{UG}$ is given by:

R.5   *Conjuction$_{UG}$* (First Approximation)
  a.   *Syntax*
      $W \rightarrow \{<W,W>,k\}$ all $W \in$ CAT, all $k \in \{$AND, OR$\}$
  b.   *Semantics*
      For all e, e' of category W, interpret $\{<e,e'>$, AND$\}$ as $f_e \wedge f_{e'}$ and interpret $\{<e,e'>$, OR$\}$ as $f_e \vee f_{e'}$ where f_e is the interpretation of e and $f_{e'}$ that of e', and $\wedge$ and $\vee$ refer to the boolean operations of meet and join respectively in the type for W.

Conj$_{UG}$ will of course be subject to many parameter conditions: e.g. if we can form co-ordinations with OR in L we can form them with AND, if you can conjoin P_{n+1}s you can in general conjoin P_ns, etc. Moreover the above rule can easily be generalised to allow arbitrarily many conjuncts, not just two as given in R.5. Even so the rule is inadequate in certain respects (see below) but is sufficiently general to generate the passives mentioned earlier:

(84)

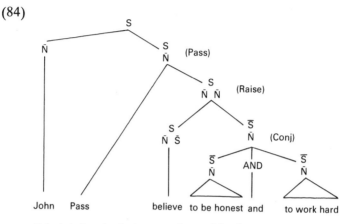

'John is believed to be honest and to work hard'

As regards the inadequacy of R.5 note that it only allows conjunctions of n-place predicates which take their arguments with the same θ-roles and in the same case, otherwise the category symbols are distinct. And while languages sometimes seem to approach such stringent restrictions on coordinate structures they clearly do not always do so. For example the first argument of *need* in English is clearly not Agent; let us call it Experiencer. And we may form *John needed and hired a new secretary. Hire* does of course take its first argument as Agent. Now what θ-role should *John* be required to satisfy in the interpretation of the above sentence? Clearly his role is not identical to Agent or to Experiencer, but equally clearly it is determined as a function of them. Let us, anticipating slightly, call that function $\wedge$. Intuitively an individual will bear the θ-role $(\delta \wedge \gamma)$ to an action just in case he bears δ and he bears γ. So intuitively the function $\wedge$ should be commutative $(x \wedge y) = (y \wedge x)$, and satisfy the idempotent laws, $(x \wedge x) = x$. Thus if we conjoin two predicates both of which take their first argument in say the Agent role then the derived role of the first argument expression will be (Agt $\wedge$ Agt), which by the constraint on $\wedge$ is the same as Agt, intuitively correct. That is, John is an agent in *John hugged Mary and kissed Ruth.* Similarly the θ-role assigned to the ith argument of a disjunction, of P_ns will be denoted as the value of the join function, v, of the ith θ-roles of the ith arguments of the disjuncts. Intuitively an individual will bear the θ-role $(\delta \vee \gamma)$ to an action if either he bears δ or he bears γ.

In general then a co-ordinate P_n does not preserve θ-roles but creates new θ-roles for its arguments. Case marking however seems to behave differently. Often languages do not permit conjunctions of predicates taking their i^{th} arguments in different cases. Where they do the case of the ith argument of the conjunction is probably most commonly either the case of one of the conjuncts (possibly there are some universal hierarchies here) or else the case of the closest conjunct in linear order in surface. But I am unsure enough of the facts not to want to hazard any serious parameter conditions here. Thus we shall settle for the moment for the following formulation of Conjunction$_{UG}$.

R.5 *Conjunction$_{UG}$*
   a. *Syntax*

For all $n \geqslant 0$, all $W \in CAT$, all $k \in \{AND, OR\}$,

$$
\begin{array}{ccc}
W & & \{<W, W>, k\} \\
X & \longrightarrow & X \ \ X \\
\theta & & \delta \ \ \gamma \\
c & & d \ \ g
\end{array}
$$

where $\delta, \gamma \in TR^n$ and $c, d, g \in CM^n$ and $\theta_i = \delta_i \wedge \gamma_i$ if k = AND, and $\theta_i = \delta_i \vee \gamma_i$ if k = OR, and $c_i = d_i$ if $d_i = g_i$.

θ_i above is of course the ith element in the sequence θ; analogously for δ_i, c_i, etc.

5.5 Negation

R.6 *Neg$_{UG}$*
   a. *Syntax*

$$
\begin{array}{ccc}
W & \{Neg, W\} & \text{all } W \in CAT, \text{ all } X \in CAT^n, \text{ all } \theta \in TR^n \\
X & X & \text{and all } c, d \in CM^n \\
\theta & \longrightarrow \ \ \theta & \\
c & d &
\end{array}
$$

   b. *Semantics*

Interpret $\{Neg, e\}$ as the boolean complement in T_W of the interpretation of e.

The rule says that negation preserves θ-role, so e.g. John has the same θ-role in *John didn't sing* as he does in *John sang.* But it does not preserve case. For example, in Slavic various P_ns impose nominative or accusative case on certain arguments in the affirmative, but when negated force or allow a genitive case. (85) shows that the Passives we want are generable with this rule:

(85)

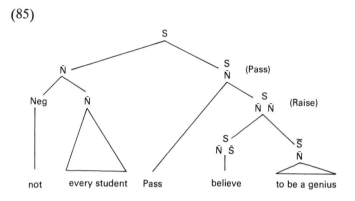

'Not every student was believed to be a genius.'

5.6   *Extra (Intra)-position and There Insertion*

For many reasons in addition to our treatment of Passive$_{UG}$ we want to say that the expressions *it* and *there* in (86) below are argument expressions, the remainder of the sentence being a P_1 in each case. Moreover *it* and *there* are semantically similar in that neither makes an independent contribution to the meaning of the sentence, the interpretation of *it* in (86a) being given by the Š *that Fred left* and that of *there* by *unicorns.* In this sense

(86) a.   It is certain that Fred left.
      b.   There exist unicorns in Israel.

we may say that such elements are *dumb* and, adopting the terminology of Relational Grammar, refer to them as *dummies.* We shall represent their status in UG as follows: for each category C, we shall add to the Constants (CON) of UG a symbol D_C, called *the dummy for C.* Semantically each such D_C will be interpreted freely in the type for C. (We might also choose a fixed element of that type, but the interpretation of a D_C will play no role in the interpretation of sentences in which they occur, rather like that of bound variables in logic.) The basic rule we need to introduce such symbols into sentences is given by:

R.6[1] *Dummy$_{UG}$*
    a. *Syntax*

$$\begin{matrix} S \\ D_C \end{matrix} \rightarrow \left\{ \begin{matrix} S, C \\ C \end{matrix} \right\}$$

    b. **Semantics**

Given e of category S interpreted by f_e and e′ of category C

C interpreted by $f_{e'}$, interpret {e,e′} by any function f from T_C into T_S such that $f(f_{D_C}) = f_e(f_{e'})$.

Let us consider first the syntactic part of R.6. To complete the statement we may assign the same θ-role and case marker variables to the P_1s on both the left and right of the arrow. We shall assume that English has lexical rules for dummies as follows:

(87) a. $D_{\bar{N}} \rightarrow$ there
        b. $D_{\bar{X}} \rightarrow$ it, for all P_n categories X.

Then the basic sentences in English containing such dummies are generated as follows:

(88)

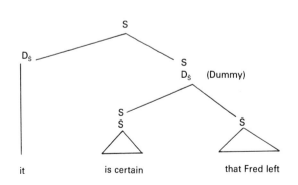

(89)

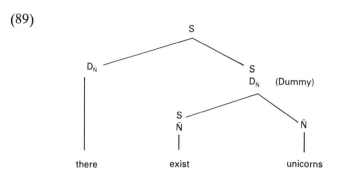

(90)

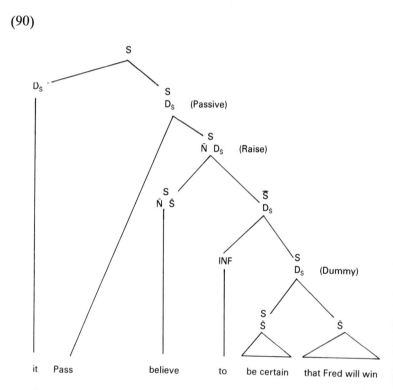

'It is believed to be certain that Fred will win.'

Note that in (89) we could have expanded the lower $\frac{S}{N}$ to an $\frac{S}{N}$ and a modifier such as *in Israel*. This would generate *There exist in Israel unicorns* in which *exist in Israel* is a headed P_1. Thus Flatten could apply yielding *There exist unicorns in Israel*. As usual of course if the argument expression is long it may remain outside the P_1: *There exist in Israel unicorns of a great variety of types.*

Consider now the semantics of R.6. To take an example, it says that the P_1 *is certain that Fred left* maps the denotation (whatever it is) of *it* onto the same S denotation as *is certain* maps *that Fred left* onto. Similarly the interpretation of *exist unicorns* maps the denotation of *there* onto the same S denotation of that of *exist* maps that of *unicorns*. Thus the classical paraphrase relation between sentences and their extraposed versions is captured in our semantics. Notice finally of course that we can now generate the passives we want.

(91)

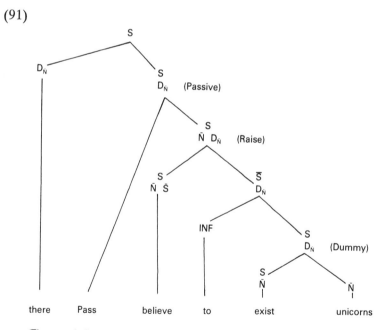

'There are believed to exist unicorns.'

It is worth noting perhaps that (91) has, as in the classical approach, two derivations in our system. In the second, illustrated in (92), we have first passivised *believe* yielding *That Fred will win is certain* as the derived 'subject'. Then we raise the subject of that sentence to subject, and then extrapose:

(92)

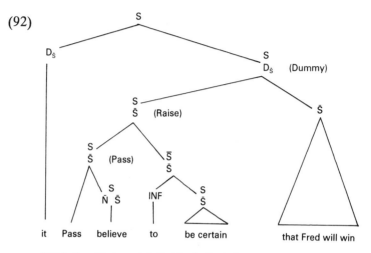

'It is believed to be certain that Fred will win.'

The reader may verify that (91) and (92) are assigned the same interpretation on our semantics.

Note that Dummy$_{UG}$ as formulated only allows dummies in 'subject' position. We may however easily generalise away from that restriction, though motivation for same is not massive:

R.6   *Dummy$_{UG}$*
   a.   *Syntax*

$$\langle X_1, X_2, \ldots, X_n, D_c \rangle \overset{S}{\rightarrow} \{\langle X_1, X_2, \ldots, X_n, C \rangle, C\}$$

   b.   *Semantics*
      the natural generalisation of that given in R.6[1] before.
   c.   *Parameter Conditions*
      (i) if $m > 0$ is in the range of n in L then $m = 0$ is in that range.

PC(i) just says that if you can have dummies in non-subject position then you can have them as subjects. Some motivation in English for allowing dummy 'objects' is given by sentences like *John'll guarantee it that Fred will be there on time.* The relevant derivation is illustrated in (93) opposite:

(93)

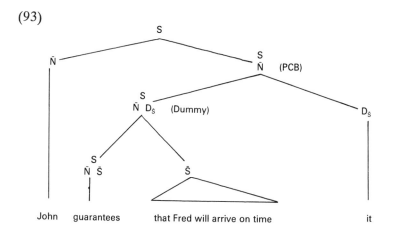

Of course the node expanded by the Dummy rule dominates a headed P_2, so Flatten applies moving *it* into the complex P_2 yielding *John guarantees it that Fred will arrive on time*.

Note further that taking 'Tough' predicates like *is tough* as P_1s with $\bar{P}_1$ arguments, and noting that rule (87b) takes *it* as a dummy for P_1s (as well as P_0s), our rules generate (94):

(94)

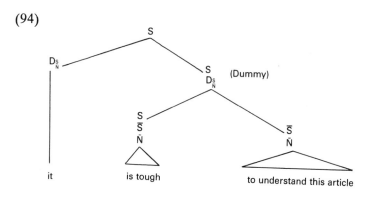

5.7 Tough Movement

Of the relation-changing rules considered, *Tough* is perhaps the least well understood, both syntactically and semantically; moreover it is not well attested across languages. So we have only a poor idea what its universal formulation might look like. Here we shall attempt only a primitive first approximation to the rule, pointing out certain problems which will remain open. Our goal then is to provide a rule which will generate structures such as:

(95) a.   Rabbits are easy to catch.
     b.   That Fred stole the money is difficult to believe.

The category of *be easy* in (95a) has already been given; *to catch* is obviously a P_2 infinitive. And *be easy to catch* is straightforwardly a P_1 whose argument is the same as the second argument of *catch* and which appears to be understood as a Patient in both cases. Note that (95a) is similar to Passive: something (*be easy*) has combined with a $\check{P}_2$ to form a P_1 whose argument is the same as that of the P_2. Passive differs only in that the combining item is a constant, *Pass*, and it combines with a P_2 not a $\check{P}_2$. The two structures are also semantically similar in that the derived P_1 is semantically determined by its values on individuals. Thus in the same way that the passive *was kissed* holds of the denotation of *every student* iff for every individual x with the student property, *was kissed* holds of x, so *is easy to read* holds of every book iff for each individual x with the book property, *is easy to read* holds of x. And that is so, if and only if *is easy* holds of the denotation of *to read x*. Thus *every book is easy to read* is not a paraphrase of *to read every book is easy*.

R.7   *Tough$_{UG}$*
    a.   *Syntax*

$$S \rightarrow X \quad \left\{ \begin{matrix} S \\ \binom{\bar{S}}{Y} \end{matrix} \quad , \quad \begin{matrix} \bar{S} \\ Y,X \end{matrix} \right\}$$

    b.   *Semantics*

Where e of category $\binom{\overset{S}{\bar{S}}}{Y}$ is interpreted by f_e and e′ of

category $\overset{S}{Y,X}$ is interpreted by $f_{e'}$, interpret (e,e′) by that function f which sends each individual $x \in T_X$ to f_e $(f_{e'}(x))$.

Then (95a) is generated as follows:

(96)

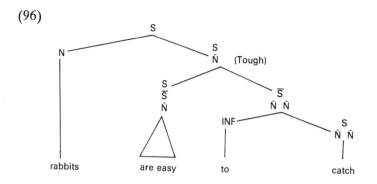

(95b) is generated analogously, replacing the relevant occurrences of Ñ above by S̃. And the passives we want to generate are now represented as follows:

(97)

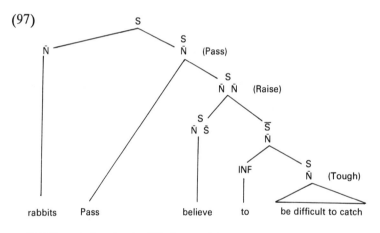

'Rabbits are believed to be difficult to catch.'

(The expansion of the node marked *Tough* is the same as in (96)).

Adding case and θ-role markers to Tough$_{UG}$ may be done as follows: both occurrences of Y are subtended by the same case and θ-role variables; both occurrences of X take the same θ-role variable but different case variables; and the complex symbol $\frac{\text{S}}{\text{S}}$ itself takes new case and θ-role variables.
Y

We note that we have not explicitly given the relation between sentences like *For John to read this book is tough* and *This book is tough for John to read,* though it would appear plausible to treat *for John* as an 'oblique subject' as was done for agent phrases earlier. We mention the unbounded nature of Tough below.

6. Conclusion and Some Open Problems

We have shown above that the major relation-changing rules can be plausibly represented directly in Base$_{UG}$, their feeding relation to Passive$_{UG}$ can be adequately accounted for, and the classical paraphrase relations represented by these rules, to the extent that they existed, are directly expressed by the semantic interpretations associated with these rules. On the other hand these rules were not given the more thorough treatment that Passive was in terms of their universal properties and the associated parameter conditions they determine. Moreover incorporating these rules as well as Passive in Base$_{UG}$ raises many other questions which this approach must answer if it is to prove successful. Below we mention a few, indicating lines of solution in most cases.

6.1 Passive Morphology Assignment

Since complex P$_2$s can be passivised in English we must state how the 'passive participle' morphology is assigned recursively as a function of how the P$_2$s are formed. For the cases considered so far from English this may be done as follows:

(98) {Pass,e} ⇒ be + EN(e), where
    (1) EN(e) = the past participle of e if e is lexical and
    (2) EN(e) = [EN(e$_1$) + c + EN(e$_2$)] if e = (e$_1$,c,e$_2$) for
           c∈{and,or}, and
    (3) EN(e) = [EN(e$_1$),y] if e = {e$_1$,y} where e$_1$ is a P$_2$ and y is
           any other constituent, e.g. *to be a genius, on
           the desk, down,* etc.)

A slightly more refined statement would be necessary for the cases of complex passives in Turkish and Latin cited earlier, but their statement is not in principle different from the above. We might note moreover that EN above is a strict morphological function, its outputs differ from its inputs in strictly morphological ways. Moreover (98) should be subject to the parameter condition that the strict morphological function may not be one which merely effects tone change or reduplication, since languages do not form passives in these ways. Finally, clause (2) of the definition of EN is clearly factorable as a general constraint on strict morphological functions:

(99)   *The Morphological Co-ordinate Structure Constraint*
       If f is a strict morphological function then $f(e_1,c,e_2) = [f(e_1),c,f(e_2)]$.

There will be some neutralisation phenomena which counter-exemplify (99), but the principle seems general enough that exceptions should somehow be handles as marked cases.

6.2 Should Passive iterate?

Since our rules generate (*Pass, kiss*) as a P_1 they will also generate (*Pass, (Pass, kiss)*) as a P_0, one that is true iff for some individual y there is an individual x such that x kissed y. English of course blocks such derivations by its general prohibition against passivising P_1s, but Latin and other languages will not. Do we want to universally prohibit such double passives? We shall leave the question open, as there do appear to be some cases where we may want such passives, though the evidence is not yet perhaps strong enough or widely attested enough to be thoroughly convincing. In the first instance we note without example that just such double passives are cited by Noonan (1978) for Irish (see Keenan 1980a for examples). We note that the passive of the already passive P_1 is effected by a different morphology, called impersonal, than that by which the personal passive of the P_2 is effected.

A second possible case concerns passives of certain P_3s in English. Let us assume, reasonably on our approach, that *forbid* and similar verbs have the category indicated in (100):

(100)

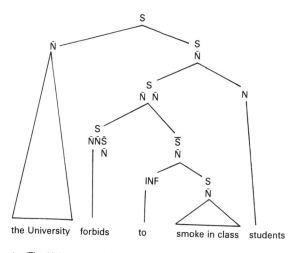

the University   forbids   to   smoke in class   students

(= 'The University forbids students to smoke in class' by Flatten)

Then the straightforward P₂ passive in English is given by:

(101)

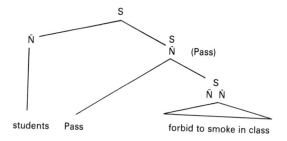

students   Pass   forbid to smoke in class

'Students are forbidden to smoke in class'

(The node $_\bar{N}^S\bar{N}$ is expanded above identically to that in (100) above.)

Then the double P₂-P₃ passive may be generated as follows:

(102)

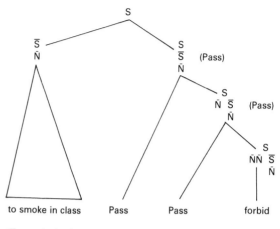

'To smoke in class is forbidden'

If such derivations are allowed in English the passive morphology rule, (98), would have to be enriched to include the clause EN (Pass, e) = EN(e). And generally it seems to us that the basic problem in iterating rules like Passive and Causative, both of which make semantic sense when iterated, lies in the morphological nature of these rules. Roughly, it is hard to passivise twice in English because you can't form the past participle of a past participle, though neutralisation phenomena like that in (102) above may provide a way out.

6.3 'Construing' Complex P_2s

How are we on this approach to account for the oddity of expressions as *I believe Fred to admire herself/each other?* For cases such as these the problem can be treated in purely semantic terms. The P_1 in the above sentence is interpreted identically to *believe (Fred admires herself/each other)*, so if the interpretation of the latter is odd, then so is that of the former, since they are the same. On the other hand, there will be cases of purely syntactic/morphological dependency between 'bodies' of complex P_2s and the argument of the entire P_2. For example, suppose English had gender agreement in predicate adjectives. Then the surface form of [*(believe to be clever), Mary*] would have to mark *clever* as feminine. But this just says that the rules which assign agreement morphology must be recursively defined on complex P_ns in the same sort of way that Passive morphology assignment is. The principle then is unproblematic and moreover independently motivated. For example in languages in which lexical P_2s object-agree we must assign 3pl morphology to each of the lexical P_2s in *John hugged and kissed both Mary and Ruth.*

6.4 Unbounded Rules Feed Passive

Tough in English is somewhat unbounded, as illustrated by sentences like (103):

(103) This book is difficult to believe that Fred stole.

To generate (103) by our rule of *Tough* we are motivated to assign *believe that Fred stole* the category P_2. Then passives such as *This book is believed to be difficult to believe that Fred stole* are routinely generated by the Raising and Passive rules already proposed.

There are several ways we may generate such complex P_2s. Perhaps the easiest formally speaking is to in effect mimic the (context-free) rules used to generate variable binding operators in formal languages. This we may do as follows:

First, for each integer i and each category C, add i_C to CON. Intuitively i_C is to be the ith index (variable, trace) of category C. We then add the following lexical rules to UG[3]:

(104) $C \rightarrow i_C$, all $C \in$ CAT, all integers i
   Interpret i_C freely in the individuals of T_C.

Now we must add operators which bind the variables (or indices) so added. This we may do as follows:

For each integer i and each category C, add $<C,i>$, abbreviated C_i, to CON. The rules which introduce them are as follows:

R.8 *Binding$_{UG}$*
   a.   *Syntax*
$$\overset{W}{<X_1,X_2, \ldots, X_n, Y>} \rightarrow \{Y_i, \overset{W}{<X_1,X_2, \ldots, X_n>}\}$$
   b.   *Semantics*

   Where f is an interpretation mapping e in $\overset{W}{X_1, X_2, \ldots, X_n}$

onto $f_{e'}$ interpret $\{Y_i, e\}$ by that function f which maps
each individual $y \in T_Y$ onto $f_{e'}$ where f′ differs from f in
that f′ $(i_Y) = y$.

We note that Binding$_{UG}$ may be generalised to include more than
one sort of binding operator, but the generalisations need not concern us here. Sentence (105) illustrates the use of Binding:

(105)

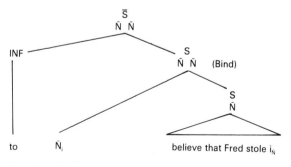

'Some woman every man kissed.'

And we may now generate *to believe that Fred stole* as a P_2 infinitive as follows:

(106)

'to believe that Fred stole'

Another way of incorporating variable binding rules into a context-free system is given in Gazdar (1981) and shown to possess certain linguistic advantages. We refer the reader to that work, only noting here that since Gazdar's rules are context free our rules can be directly given in his notation.

Notes

1. The research for this paper was supported by NSF grant BNS 79-14141. An early version of the work was presented during a linguistic symposium at the Universities of Trier (West Germany) and Hasselt (Belgium), spring 1980.

2. We should note that we are not alone in countenancing the existence of syntactically complex P_2s. Early work in generative grammar, such as Chomsky (1955) used such categories, as has later work such as Bach (1979).

3. If one objects to having an infinite number of elements in CON or an infinite number of lexical rules, we may easily replace these by a finite number of rules as follows: define the infinite number of indices of category C by: $Index_C \rightarrow I_C$ and $Index_C \rightarrow I\ Index_C$. Then add to UG: $C \rightarrow Index_C$.

References

Allen and Greenough (1903) *New Latin Grammar*. J.B. Greenough *et al.* (eds.), *College Classical Series* (1981) Caratzas Brothers, New Rochelle, New York.

Andrews, A.D. (1979) 'A Lexically Based Analysis of Case-Marking and the Complement System in Icelandic', paper presented at the Brown Workshop on Syntactic Theory, Brown University.

Awbery, G. (1976) *The Syntax of Welsh: A Transformational Study of the Passive.* Cambridge University Press, Cambridge.

Bach, E. (1975) 'Order in Base Structure' in C. Li (ed.) *Word Order and Word Order Change*, University of Texas Press, Austin.

—— (1979) 'In Defense of Passive', *Linguistics and Philosophy* 3, 297-342.

Chomsky, N. (1955) *The Logical Structure of Linguistic Theory* published in Plenum, New York 1975.

—— (1957) *Syntactic Structures*, Mouton, The Hague.

—— (1981) *Lectures on Government and Binding*, Foris, Dordrecht.

Dowty, D. (1978) 'Governed Transformations as Lexical Rules in Montague Grammar', *Linguistic Inquiry* 9, 3, 393-427.

Gazdar, G. (1981) 'Unbounded Dependencies and Co-ordinate Structures', *Linguistic Inquiry* 12, 155-85.

Georges, L. and J. Kornfilt (1977) 'Infinitival Double Passives in Turkish', *NELS* VII.

Hasegawa, N. (1968) 'The Passive Construction in English', *Language* 44, 230-43.

Keenan, E.L. (1976) 'Remarkable Subjects in Malagasy' in C. Li (ed.), *Subject and Topic*, Academic Press, New York.

—— (1978) 'The Syntax of Subject-Final Languages' in W. Lehmann (ed.) *Syntactic Typology*, University of Texas Press, Austin.

—— (1980) 'Passive is Phrasal (not Sentential or Lexical)' in T. Hoekstra *et al.* (eds.) *Lexical Grammar*, Foris, Dordrecht, pp. 181-215.

—— (1980a) 'Passive in the World's Languages', to appear in T. Shopen *et al* (eds.), *A Field Guide to Syntactic Typology* (tentative title).

—— and L. Faltz (1978) *Logical Types for Natural Language,* UCLA Occasional Papers in Linguistics, No. 3, Department of Linguistics, UCLA.

—— (to appear) *Logical Types for Natural Language.* Reidel, Dordrecht

Kimenyi, A. (1980) *A Relational Grammar of Kinyarwanda* in University of California Publications in Linguistics, vol. 91 University of California Press.

Lakoff, R. (1971) 'Passive Resistance', *Chicago Linguistic Society* VII, 149-63.

Langacker, R. and P. Munro (1974) 'Passives and Their Meaning', *Language* 51, 789-830.

Lewis, G.L. (1967) *Turkish Grammar*, Clarendon Press, Oxford.

Noonan, M. (1978) 'Impersonal Constructions: Evidence from Irish', manuscript, Department of Linguistics, SUNY Buffalo, New York.

Perlmutter, D. (1978) 'Impersonal Passives and the Unaccusative Hypothesis', *BLS* IV.

—— and P. Postal (1977) 'Towards a Universal Characterisation of Passive', *BLS* III, 394-417.

Timberlake, A. (1976) 'Subject Properties in the North Russian Passive' in C. Li (ed.) *Subject and Topic*, Academic Press, New York.

Wasow, T. (1977) 'Transformations and the Lexicon' in P. Culicover, T. Wasow, and A. Akmajian (eds.) *Formal Syntax*, Academic Press, New York.

10 PREDICATE FORMATION RULES IN UNIVERSAL GRAMMAR

(Written with Alan Timberlake)

Introduction

We present a conception of Predicate Formation Rule (PFR) which we believe provides a general and reasonably elegant account of a variety of syntactic phenomena that are largely under-represented in other approaches (RG, GPSG, LFG, and GB).

Central to the notion of a PFR is the notion of an n-place predicate (Pn). We identify P0 with S(entence), and for $n > 0$, a Pn is a function mapping an expression of an appropriate argument category to a Pn-1. Thus in (1) we think of *tell* as a (syntactically simple) P3 which maps *Bill* of category NP to the (syntactically complex) P2 *tell Bill*, which maps *that Fred left* of the category P0 to the (syntactically complex) P1 *tell Bill that Fred left*, which in turn maps the NP *John* to the P0 illustrated.

(1)

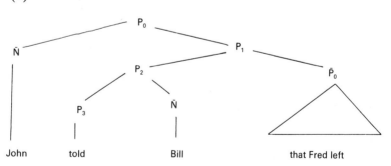

For a given $n > 0$, Pn's may differ among themselves with respect to the categories of their argument expressions and the cases and theta roles they assign them. Thus a given Pn will have a category of the form in (2), where the Ai, ci, and θi range over the (universally defined) sets of possible argument categories, case markings, and theta roles respectively.

(2)   S
         A1 A2 ....An-1 An
         c1 c2 ....cn-1 cn
         θ1 θ2 ....θn-1 θn

We allow as possible argument categories not only $\bar{N}$ (= NP) and $\bar{P}\bar{0}$ but also nominalised Pn's, noted $\bar{P}\bar{n}$. Specifically, P1 infinitives such as *to sleep, to sleep and to dream, to sleep soundly* are $\bar{P}\bar{1}$s and P2 infinitives such as *to hug, to hug and to kiss, to kiss loudly* are $\bar{P}\bar{2}$s.

Predicate Formation Rules are ways of deriving Pn's. We distinguish four such ways here:

(3)   a.   *Basic rules*: Pn+1(A) = Pn
      b.   *Modifier rules*: MOD(Pn) = Pn
      c.   *Boolean rules*: AND(Pn,Pn, ...,Pn) = Pn
      d.   *Valency Affecting rules*: F(Pm) = Pn

In (3a) we intend that an expression of a Pn+1 category maps an expression of category An+1 to a Pn of the appropriate category. Specifically, an expression of the category given in (2) will map an expression of category An to a Pn-1 whose category is like that in (2) less the last column.

Regarding (3b), MODifiers map Pn's to Pn's preserving (in general) subcategorisation. We treat as MODs adverbs, gerunds, PPs and optional oblique NPs, including agent phrases. Thus *in the park* will map the P1 *sleep* to a P1, and the P2 *find* to a P2.

The major concern of this paper is (3d), Valency Affecting rules (VARs). They directly derive Pn's from Pm's and may be classed as valency increasing, decreasing, or preserving according as n is greater than, less than, or equal to m. For example, Causatives are formed by Valency Increasing rules (VIRs) and Passives by Valency Decreasing rules (VDRs). Below we give some examples of VARs. We note that, despite certain appearances, our notation is essentially a categorial one and thus builds on earlier treatments in Bach (1980), Dowty (1978), Keenan (1980), and Thomason (1976).

Valency Affecting Rules

A simple illustration of VIRs is given by Latin, where a Pn may be prefixed by any of several locative 'prepositions' to form a Pn+1, the case and theta role assigned to the new argument category being determined by the 'preposition'. Thus from P1s such as *ire* 'to go' we may form ad(*ire*) = *adire* 'to go towards', ex(*ire*) = *exire* 'to go from', and from P2s such as *ferre* 'to carry, bear' we may form ad(*ferre*) = *affere* 'to carry to', ex(*ferre*) = *efferre*, in(*ferre*) = *inferre* 'to carry into', etc.

More productive use of VIRs is given by Bantu languages. Thus Kinyarwanda (Kimenyi 1978) may derive Pn+1s from Pn's by affixing IR (in various shapes), the new argument category being assigned the unmarked (= accusative) case and a Benefactive/Recipient theta role. The rule is given in (4):

(4)   IR(S   ) =   S
         $A_1...A_n$ $A_1...A_n A_{n+1}$
         $c_1 ...c_n$ $c_1 ...c_n$ acc
         $\theta_1 ...\theta_n$ $\theta_1 ...\theta_n$ ben

For example, from the P1 -*byin*- 'dance' we may derive the P2 IR(-*byin*-) = *byin-i*- 'dance-for'. (5a, b) illustrate the use of these two predicates.

(5)   a.   Maria   y- a- byin- ye
            Mary she-pst-dance-asp
            'Mary danced'
      b.   Maria   y- a- byin i- ye   umugabo
            Mary she-pst-dance-IR-asp man
            'Mary danced for the man'

Equally from the P2 -*oher*- 'send' we may derive the P3 IR (-*oher*-) 'send to/for', and from the P3 -*he*- 'give' we derive IR (-*he*-) = -*he-er*-, as in (6a, b) below:

(6)   a.   Umugore $[_{P_1}[_{P_2}[_{P_3}$ a- ra- he- a] imbwa] ibiryo]
            woman   she-pres-give-asp dog   food
            'The woman gave the dog the food'
      b.   Umugore $[_{P_1}[_{P_2}[_{P_3}[_{P_4}$ a- r- he- er-a]   umugabo]
                                                              imbwa]ibiryo]
            woman   she-pres-give-IR-asp man dog   food
            'The woman gives+on+behalf+of the man the dog the
                                                              food'

Note that there is no sense in which the b-sentences above are derived from the a-sentences. The only derivational relation that exists is between their respective predicates. In fact, in Kinyarwanda, as in many other Bantu languages, it is not possible to present benefactive NPs as obliques governed by a preposition. It is thus prima facie implausible to derive the b-sentences by a BEN→DO advancement rule (a point made by Hodges 1977 for Kimeru and by Gary 1977 for Mashi). The simplest account is clearly that given by the IR rule in (4). Moreover, PFRs like (4) are very much part of the 'core' syntax of Bantu languages. Thus Kinyarwanda possesses rules like (4) which introduce instrumental, manner, and various types of locative arguments. More than one such rule may apply in deriving e.g. a P3 from a P1. See Kimenyi (1978) for a thorough discussion.

Lastly we consider Valency Decreasing rules (VDRs) such as Passive, Middle, Antipassive, Reflexive, etc. It is specifically with Passive that we will be concerned in this paper:

(7) PASSIVE$_{UG}$
    a. syntax: $\text{PASS}(\quad S\quad)\quad=\quad S$
                              $A1 \ldots An{+}1 \quad An{+}1 \; A2 \ldots An$
                              $c1 \ldots cn{+}1 \quad d \quad\;\; c2 \ldots cn$
                              $\theta1 \ldots \theta n{+}1 \quad \theta n{+}1 \; \theta2 \ldots \theta n$
    b. semantics: $[\text{pass}(P_{n+1})](x_n) \ldots (x_1){=}$
                    $(\exists y)[p_{n+1}(x_1)(x_n) \ldots (x_2)(y)]$
    c. parameter conditions: if Pn's with property X ϵ
                                Domain(PASS_L), then Pm's with
                                property Y ϵ Domain (PASS_L)

Regarding (7a), Passive derives Pn's from Pn+1s in such a way that the subject category and theta role of the derived Pn is the same as that of the rightmost category of the Pn+1 it is derived from. Its case may however be different (subject to parameter conditions). The subject argument and theta role of the Pn+1 are lost entirely. For the other argument categories the association between case and theta role is preserved.

(7b) states how the derived Pn is interpreted relative to the Pn+1 it was derived from.

(7c) gives the form of conditions on the choice of passive rules in an arbitrary possible language. Our intent here is to suggest that any choice of rules conforming to (7a,b) which satisfies the parameter conditions (PCs) is a possible set of passive rules for a language. Examples of PCs will be given later.

We note further that since Pn+1s which undergo Passive may be syntactically complex, we must state how passive morphology is assigned to complex Pn+1s as a function of how they are built up. We sketch this in (8), where *pass* is the Passive Morphology Assignment function.

(8) a. $\text{pass}(p_{n+1}, \text{AND}, p_{n+1}) = (\text{pass}(p_{n+1}), \text{AND}, \text{pass}(p_{n+1}))$
     b. $\text{pass}(p_{n+1}, \text{mod}) = (\text{pass}(p_{n+1}), \text{mod})$
     c. $\text{pass}(p_{n+2}, \text{arg}) = (\text{pass}(p_{n+2}), \text{arg})$

Thus, in the unmarked case, passive morphology distributes across co-ordinate predicates and skips modifiers and arguments. The value of *pass* at a lexical predicate is provided by the proper morphological analysis of the language in question.

Finally we note that agent phrases are generated independently of Passive as oblique NPs (modifiers). (They are normally constructed with an adposition which occurs in non-passives, and even when interpreted as 'agents' they are not limited to passives, as in *The University forbids talking by students during exams*.) Semantically agent phrases are interpreted as per (9):

(9) $(\text{BY } y)(p_n)(x_n) \cdots (x_1) = p_n(x_n) \cdots (x_2)(y)$

This semantics, together with (7b), is sufficient to guarantee that *John was kissed by Mary* is logically equivalent to *Mary kissed John*. See Keenan (1980) for details.

To illustrate our conception of Passive, consider that in Latin *Marcus amatur* 'Marcus is loved' has the structure in (10).

(10)

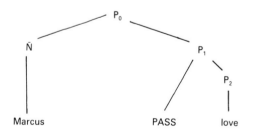

Note here that the P2 'love' has never taken an object argument in the derivation of 'Marcus is loved'.

Advantages of this approach

We show below that a PFR approach to Passive enables us to represent in a natural way many attested constructions which are not naturally representable on other approaches. The greater expressive power of our approach is largely due to the fact that the P_{n+1}s which undergo Passive may be syntactically complex.

Case 1: PASS(P1) = P0

The most widespread Passives are those illustrated in (11):

(11) PASS(S) = S [English, Latin, Lithuanian]
         N̄ N̄   N̄
         c1 c2   c
         agt pat   pat

Equally passives of the sort in (12) are well attested:

(12) PASS(S) = S [Latin, Lithuanian]
        N̄
        c
       agt

A typical example (Virgil) is: (*Sic*) *itur ad astra* '(Thus) is gone to the stars'. (13) gives the structure of this example.

(13)

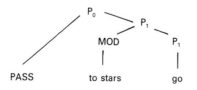

Note that the P1 passivised is syntactically complex, containing the goal locative modifier 'to the stars' in the same way as in 'Marcus went to the stars'. If we analysed (13) in such a way that 'to the stars' combined with P0s outside the scope of PASS, then it would freely combine with any predicate, thus incorrectly enabling us to generate *Marcus stayed to the stars*.

Less widely appreciated are Passives of the form:

(14) PASS(S) = S [Lithuanian]
$\quad\quad\quad$ Ñ
$\quad\quad\quad$ c
$\quad\quad\quad$ pat

In fact, Lithuanian (Timberlake, 1982) allows Passives of virtually all types of P1s: life cycle (15a), inchoative (15b), phenomenological (15c), existential (15d), copular (15e), and P1s derived from Subject-to-Subject Raising (15f).

(15) a. Kur   mūsų gimta   , kur   augta?
$\quad\quad\quad$ where by+us bear(nt.sg.PASS) where grow
$\quad\quad\quad\quad\quad\quad\quad\quad\quad\quad\quad\quad\quad\quad\quad\quad\quad\quad$ (nt.sg.PASS)
$\quad\quad\quad$ 'Where by us was getting born, where getting grown up?'

$\quad\quad$ b. Ko   čia   degta   /plysta?
$\quad\quad\quad$ what here burn (nt.sg.PASS)/ burst
$\quad\quad\quad$ 'By what was (it) burned/burst here?'

$\quad\quad$ c. Naktį gerokai palyta
$\quad\quad\quad$ night goodly   rain (nt.sg.PASS)
$\quad\quad\quad$ 'Last night (it) got rained a goodly amount'

$\quad\quad$ d. Ar būta   tenai   langinių?
$\quad\quad\quad$ and be (nt.sg.PASS) there   windows (gen.m.pl.)
$\quad\quad\quad$ 'And had there really been any existing going on by win-
$\quad\quad\quad\quad\quad\quad\quad\quad\quad\quad\quad\quad\quad\quad\quad\quad\quad\quad$ dows there?'

$\quad\quad$ e. Jo   būta   didelio
$\quad\quad\quad$ gen.m.sg.3 be(nt.sg.nom.PASS) tall (gen.m.sg)
$\quad\quad\quad$ 'By him there had been being tall'

$\quad\quad$ f. Jo   pasirodyta   esant didvyrio
$\quad\quad\quad$ gen.m.sg.3 seem (nt.sg.nom.PASS) being hero
$\quad\quad\quad$ 'By him (it) was seemed to be a hero'

As with passives of P2s in Lithuanian, the lexical predicate appears in participial form (in fact, in either of two aspectually differentiated forms), and the agent is optionally expressed in the genitive. But unlike passives of P2s, the passive predicates in (15) appear in the non-agreeing nominative neuter singular, in honour of the absence of any subject.

Comparable examples of (14) can be found in Turkish (Özkaragöz, 1982) and N. Russian (Kuz'mina and Nemčenko, 1971). We note that such passives violate explicit predictions of RG (Perlmutter and Postal, 1983) and are not generable on current versions of GB.

Case 2: PASS(PASS(P2)) = P0

Since P2s passivise to P1s, and P1s passivise to P0s, our approach, unless constrained, admits the existence of iterated Passive by the equation above. And in fact, Özkaragöz (1982) cites numerous examples for Turkish:

(16) Harp-te vur- ul- un- ur
      war-in shoot-PASS-PASS-aor
      'In war one is shot (by one)'

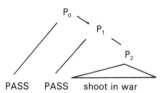

PASS   PASS   shoot in war

Lithuanian likewise allows iterated Passives, with both agent phrases expressed:

(17) Lapelio   būta   vėjo nupūsto
      leaf(gen.m.sg) be(nom.nt.sg.PASS) wind blow(gen.m.sg.
                                              PASS)
      'By the leaf there was getting blown down by the wind'

The semantics in (7b) applies straightforwardly to iterated Passives: PASS(PASS(shoot)) is true iff $(\exists y)[\text{PASS(shoot)}](y)$ iff $(\exists y)[(\exists x)(\text{shoot}(y)(x)]$. That is, PASS(PASS(shoot)] is true iff someone shoots someone. Although there remains much to be said about the pragmatics of iterated passives, we may note that in Lithuanian, at least, it involves the notion of evidentiality, broadly construed.

Cases 1 and 2 combine, to the best of our knowledge, to yield the following PC: if L has iterated passives, Case 2, then L has passives of unaccusatives, (14), which in turn entails that L has passives of unergatives, (12), and that entails that L has 'canonical' passives, (11).

Case 3: PASS(P1) = P0, where P1 = P2(A)

Here we consider Passives of P1s which themselves consist of a P2 and an argument expression. Observe first from Latin:

(18) a. [$_{P0}$ Marcus [$_{P1}$ mihi [$_{P2}$ invidet]]]
        nom   dat   envy(3.sg)
     'Marcus envies (to) me'
  b. [$_{P0}$ mihi invidetur] = 'to me is envied'
        dat   envy(3.sg.PASS)
  c. [$_{P0}$ (ego) invideor]
        nom envy(1.sg.PASS)
     'I am envied'

(18b) is the straightforward passive of the P1 in (18a), the verb being 3sg since it has no subject to agree with. *Mihi* is dative for the same reason as in (18a); it has combined with the P2 'envy', which assigns its argument dative in forming the P1 'envies me'. Of more interest here is the more literary (18c), used e.g. by Horace *Cur invideor?* 'Why am I envied?'. Here we passivise the P2 'envy' to form the P1 'be envied', which, like other P1s in Latin, puts its argument in the nominative and agrees with it. Thus our approach, in distinction to others, naturally generates both passives (18b,c). More generally, most approaches to generative grammar are simply not equipped to generate what in their view would be two passives 'off the same source'. In what follows we shall see several other examples of 'dual passives'.

A particularly troublesome case in this regard is illustrated by Polish (19a,b), in which the dual passives are formed from P2s which take their argument in the accusative. (Latin by and large does not permit dual passives in such cases.)

(19) a. [$_{P0}$ Lipa   [$_{P1}$ PASS   [$_{P2}$ ścięta   ]]]
        linden(nom.fem.sg.)   cut(nom.fem.sg.
       'The linden was cut down'   Pass)
  b. [$_{P0}$ PASS [$_{P1}$ [$_{P2}$ Ścięto   ] lipę   ]]
                    cut(nt.nom.sg.   linden(fem.acc.
                       PASS)   sg.)

In (19a) we see the passive of the P2 'cut down', which is a P1, taking its argument in the nominative and agreeing with it in gender, number, and case. In (19b) we see the P0 formed as the Passive of the complex P1 'cut down the linden'. 'Linden', as it has combined with the P2 'cut down' to form a P1 (just as it would in an active), occurs postverbally in the accusative and does not trigger verb agreement. The verb itself is in the non-agreement form: neuter, nominative, singular. Similar dual passives are cited for Hindi (20) (see Sinha, 1978) and N. Russian (Kuz'mina and Nemčenko, 1971) in (21).

(20) a. Siksək ne lərki ko klas se   nikal diya   [active]
          teacher erg girl DO class from drive out
          'The teacher drove the girl out of the class'
     b. Lərki-Ø klas se   nikal di gəyi   [PASS(P2)=P1]
          girl-abs class from drive out PASS
          'The girl was driven out from the class'
     c. Lərki ko klas se   nikal diya gəya   [PASS(P1)=P0]
          girl DO class from drive out PASS
          '(It) was driven out the girl from the class'

(21) a. Ja   zarezal   talenka   [active]
          l.nom. slaughter calf(acc.sg.)
          'I slaughtered a calf'
     b. (U menja) telenok   zarezan   [PASS(P2)=P1]
          by me   calf(m.nom.sg.) slaughter(PASS.m.nom.sg.)
          '(By me) a calf was slaughtered'
     c. (U menja) zarezano   telenka   [PASS(P1)=P0]
                    nt.nom.sg.PASS acc.sg.
          '(By me) there occurred slaughtering a calf'

Lest one be tempted to suggest that passives of complex P1s with accusatives are not 'real' passives, we may note that in N. Russian, for example, the passive participle is morphologically the same for passives of P2s and complex P1s, and the behaviour of agent phrases is likewise identical (see Timberlake 1976). We note that these passives are a direct counterexample to Burzio's generalisation within GB theory.

We may note as well the following parameter condition: if P1s formed from accusative-taking P2s are in the domain of PASS$_L$, then this guarantees that lexical unergative P1s are in Domain(PASS$_L$).

Case 4: PASS(Pn) = Pn-1, for n ≥ 3.

Just as we obtained multiple passives above according as we passivised a P2 or a complex P1, so in general we obtain multiple passives according as we passivise a Pn+1 or a complex Pn. A simple case is illustrated below from Kinyarwanda. Note first the active P0 in (22).

(22) [$_{P0}$ Umugabo [$_{P1}$ [$_{P2}$ [$_{P3}$ yahaa-ye] umugore] igitabo]]
      man   gave-asp woman   book
    'The man gave the woman the book'

The structure we assign to (22) is justified by the fact that 'give' selects two unmarked NPs as non-subject arguments. Recall that Recipient or Benefactive NPs in Kinyarwanda may not be constructed with a preposition.

Now passivising on the P3 'gave' gives by PASS$_{UG}$ (7) a P2 theta marking its subject argument as Recipient, as per (23):

(23) [$_{P0}$ Umugore [$_{P1}$ [$_{P2}$ PASS[$_{P3}$ -haa-ye] igitabo]]]

    = Umugore ya -haa -w   -ye igitabo
      woman   she-give-PASS -asp book
      'The woman was given the book'

Similarly, passivising the complex P2 'gave the woman' yields the P1 instantiated in (24).

(24) [$_{P0}$ Igitabo [$_{P1}$ PASS [$_{P2}$ -haa-ye umugore]]]

    = Igitabo   cy-ahaa-w-   ye   umugore
      book   it-gave-PASS-asp woman
      'The book was given (to) the woman'

Moreover, these examples are but the tip of an iceberg. Recall the magnificent P4 in (6b), repeated below as (25).

(25) [P0 Umugore[P1[P2[P3[P4 a- ra- he- er- a]
umugabo] imbwa]ibiryo]]

    woman   she-pres-give-IR-asp man   dog
food

'The woman gives on behalf of the man (to) the dog the food'

Now passivising on the P4 'give-for' yields a P3 taking a Benefactive subject, as in (26a). And passivising on the P3 'give-for the man' yields the P2 in (26b) taking a Recipient subject, and passivising on the P2 'give-for the man (to) the dog' yields the P1 in (26c) taking a Patient subject.

(26) a. Umugabo a- ra- he- er- w-   a imbwa ibiryo
      man   he-pres-give-IR-PASS-asp dog   food
      'The man has food given to the dog on his behalf'

  b. Imbwa i- ra- he- er- w-   a umugabo ibiryo
      dog   it-pres-give-IR-PASS-asp man   food
      'The dog is given food on behalf of the man'

  c. Ibiryo bi-ra- he- er- w-   a umugabo imbwa
      food   it-pres-give-IR-PASS-asp man   dog
      'The food is given (to) the dog on behalf of the man'

Let us stress here that all these delightful passives are but special cases of PASS$_{UG}$ as defined in (7). We turn now to some rather more complicated examples.

Case 5: PASS(Pn+1) = Pn, where An+1 $\neq$ NP.

Passives such as those in (27) are straightforwardly generated from P2s which take P̄0 second arguments:

(27) a. That the Earth is flat is widely believed.
  b. That arithmetic is incomplete was proved by Gödel.

More interesting cases here are given by subject control predicates (e.g. *begin, want, intend*) which we treat (in the first instance) as P2s taking P1 infinitives (P̄1s) as argument and yielding P1s whose subject category is the same as that of the P1 infinitive. Thus we may analyse (28a) (Kinyarwanda) as having the gross structure given in (28b).

(28) a.   Abaana ba- taangi-ye gu-soma igitabo
           children they-start- asp to-read books
           'The children are starting to read books'
     b. $[_{P0}$ children $[_{P1}$ $[_{P2}$ start] $[_{\bar{P}\bar{1}}$ to read books]]]

And the passive of the P2 'start' is a P1 which takes a P1 infinitive
as a subject argument, as illustrated in (the well-formed) (29).

(29) a.   Gu-soma igitabo bi-taangi-w-   e   (na-aabaana)
           to-read   books it-start- PASS-asp (by-children)
           'Reading books is begun (by the children)'
     b. $[_{P0}$ $[_{\bar{P}\bar{1}}$ to read books] $[_{P1}$ PASS P2]]

Of interest here is that our semantics for agent phrases allows us
to represent the control of *to read* by the agent *children* in the passive just as in the active (assuming the nominalising operation itself
is transparent to control). Replacing *children* by *John* for simplicity and mixing levels, our semantics tells us:

(30) [pass((BY John)(start))]($\bar{P}_1$)=($\exists$y)(((BY John)(start))($\bar{P}_1$)(y)
                                    =($\exists$y)((start)($\bar{P}_1$))(John)
                                    =((start)($\bar{P}_1$))(John)

Thus 'to read books was started by John' has the same truth conditions as 'John started to read books' (always assuming that the
nominalisation of 'read books' is transparent).

The analysis in (28) and (29) generalises along two dimensions
of interest here. First we consider object control predicates such as
allow, order, and *forbid.* We may treat them as P3s taking an NP
argument to yield P2s of the same category as *start.* Thus (31)
would have the gross structure as indicated:

(31) $[_{P0}$Umugabo $[_{P1}[_{P2}[_{P3}$y- akuundi-ye]abaana]gu-soma
                                                              igitabo]]
     man   he-allow- asp children   to-read
                                                       books
     'The man allowed the children to read books'

(We note that 'allow' above is itself the IR form of the P2 'like').

Now, since we already know that Kinyarwanda can passivise P3s
as well as P2s taking infinitival arguments, we correctly predict the

existence of two passives from the predicates in (31). (32a) illustrates the case where we have passivised the P3 *allow* making the Benefactee the subject, and (32b) the case where we have passivised the complex P2 *allow the children* creating a P1 infinitive taking predicate.

(32) a. Abaana y- akuunki-w-   e gu-soma igitabo
children they-allow-   PASS-asp to-read books
'The children were allowed to read books'

b. Gu-soma igitabo bi-akuunki-w-   e abaana
to-read   books it-allow-   PASS-asp children
'To read books was allowed the children'

As before, other approaches will fail to get both these passives.

The second direction of generalisation concerns the proper categorisation for subject control predicates (*begin, intend,* etc.). We treated them above as functions deriving P1s from P1 infinitives preserving subcategorisation. But just as we treat MODifiers as functions mapping Pn's to Pn's, all n, so here the natural analysis treats *begin, intend,* etc. as functions taking Pn infinitives, Pn's, to Pn's, preserving subcategorisation. Thus UG in principle allows two analyses for *John intended to buy a watch.* On the first *intend* combines with the P1 infinitive *to buy a watch* to form the P_1 *intend to buy a watch.* On the second, it combines with the P_2 infinitive *to buy* forming the P2 *intend to buy* whose (object) argument is of the same category and theta role as that of *buy.* (33) illustrates this structure from Lithuanian.

(33) Jonas numatytė pirkti laikrodį iš   honoraro
John intend   buy   watch   from salary
'John intended to buy a watch from (his) salary'

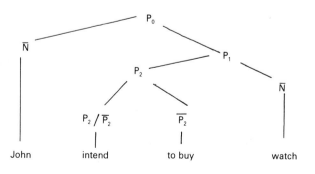

Now, since *intend to buy* in (33) is a P2 taking *watch* as argument, we may hope to passivise deriving a complex P1. (34) shows that our hope was not in vain:

(34) Laikrodis   numatytas   pirkti iš   honoraro
     watch(nom.m.sg.) intend(nom.m.sg.pass) buy from salary
     'A watch was intended to be bought from (his) salary'

Similar passives are noted for Malagasy in Keenan (1975) and for Turkish in descriptive grammars (Lewis, 1967) as well as in more recent generative treatments (Georges and Kornfilt, 1977):

(35) a. Ahmet kitab-i   oku-maya başla-di
         Ahmet book-DO   read-inf   begin-pst
         'Ahmet began   to   read   the   book'
     b. Kitap (Ahmet tarafindan) oku- n-   maya başla-n- di
         book   Ahmet by   read-PASS-inf begin-PASS
                                                                    -pst
         'The book was begun to be read (by Ahmet)'

We note that passive morphology applies to both the 'matrix' and the infinitival predicates in Malagasy and Turkish but only to the matrix predicate in Lithuanian. Keenan (1975) and Georges and Kornfilt (1977) argue for Malagasy and Turkish respectively that the double passive morphology cannot be due to the independent application of Passive. (We treat it as a language-particular fact concerning the passive morphology assignment rule.) But if Passive hasn't applied twice, current views other than ours provide no way to get two passive morphologies.

We turn now to our last case, which concerns scope ambiguities between Modifier functions and the Passive function.

Case 6: Pass(MOD(Pn)) = MOD(PASS(Pn+1))

We have been treating MODs as maps from Pn's to n's preserving subcategorisation, where n may take on both 1 and 2 as values. (Here we have only used this for the special case of agent phrases, but see Keenan (1980) for justification from other types of PP modifiers.) This means that in principle we allow two structures for (36), given in (37a,b).

(36) John arrested Mary willingly

(37) a. [willingly(arrest(Mary))](John)
    b. [willingly(arrest)](Mary)(John)

In fact (36) is not ambiguous; 'subject-oriented' adverbials like *willingly* determine a property, call it AW 'act willingly' for the nonce, which holds for the subject argument regardless of the valency of the Pn they combine with. A sufficient approximation to the semantics of *willingly* is given below:

$$(38) \quad [W(p_n)](x_n) \ldots (x_1) = p_n(x_n) \ldots (x_1) \wedge AW(x_1)$$

In fact (38) guarantees the logical equivalence of (37a,b) since each is true iff John arrested Mary and John acted willingly. The Passive in (39), however, also has two structures, (40a,b), which differ accordingly as *willingly* is inside or outside the scope of PASS. And these structures are not logically equivalent. In (40a) it is Mary who acted willingly, whereas in (40b) it is the agent of *arrest* who so acted.

(39) Mary was arrested willingly

(40) a. [willingly(PASS(arrest))](Mary)
        = (PASS(arrest))(Mary) $\wedge$ AW(Mary)   [by (38)]
    b. [PASS(willingly(arrest))](Mary)
        = ($\exists y$)[willingly(arrest)](Mary)(y)   [by (7b)]
        = ($\exists y$)[(arrest)(Mary)(y) $\wedge$ AW(y)]   [by (38)]

Our approach, then, correctly predicts the unambiguity of an active (36) and the ambiguity of the Passive (39). This is in principle impossible for analyses which 'reduce' the semantics of Passives to that of the corresponding actives.

We note further that comparably treated ambiguities of the same sort are more productive in Rusian, where sentences like *Priexav na front, vojska byli vstrečeny generalom* 'Having arrived at the front, the troops were greeted by the general' allow either the passive subject or the passive agent to be interpreted as the subject of the adverbial participle 'having arrived' (see Rappaport, 1984).

Finally, consider 'argument-oriented' MODifiers such as *in shorts, naked*, etc. (41) gives a sufficient (for our purposes here) semantics for such MODs. (41) states that they map Pn denotations to Pn denotations in such a way as to predicate of the argument of the Pn they derive.

(41) $[\text{naked}(p_n)](x_n \ldots (x_1) = p_n(x_n) \ldots (x_1) \wedge (\text{naked})(x_n)$

Given (41), a sentence such as *We baptised Bill naked* is correctly predicted to be semantically ambiguous. Combining the MOD *naked* with the complex P1 *baptise Bill* we have the reading on which we are naked. Combining it with the simplex P2 *baptise* we get the reading on which Bill is naked.

But next observe that while we have two structures for the Passive *Bill was baptised naked,* they are logically equivalent:

(42) a. $[\text{naked}(\text{PASS}(\text{baptise}))](\text{Bill})$
   $= (\text{PASS}(\text{baptise})(\text{Bill}) \wedge (\text{naked})(\text{Bill})$ [by (41)]
   $= (\exists y)(\text{baptise})(\text{Bill})(y) \wedge (\text{naked})(\text{Bill})$ [by (7b)]
   b. $[(\text{PASS})(\text{naked}(\text{baptise}))](\text{Bill})$
   $= (\exists y)[(\text{naked}(\text{baptise}))(\text{Bill})](y)$ [by (7b)]
   $= (\exists y)[\text{baptise}(\text{Bill})](y) \wedge (\text{naked})(\text{Bill})$ [by (41)]
   $= (\exists y)(\text{baptise}(\text{Bill}))(y) \wedge (\text{naked})(\text{Bill})$

Thus both (42a,b) entail that it was Bill who was naked, not the agent of *baptise.* So here we correctly predict the ambiguity in the active but not in the passive. And again approaches which reduce the interpretation of Passives to the corresponding active will wrongly predict an ambiguity in the Passive.

Conclusion

We have been able here to present only a small part of the potential of predicate formation rules and the notion of n-place predicate on which they are based. We have concentrated on Passive, and even here have not been able to discuss the many other PFRs which interact in substantive ways with Passive: Raising-to-Object, Tough Movement, Extraposition, Causatives, and Small Clause Structures. Even so, we have been able to characterise a range of structures not naturally representable on other approaches.

We should like to conclude with one methodological obser-vation: as we pursue our work on PFRs it becomes increasingly clear that the structures instantiated in any given language are but a small portion of those which must be made available at a level of UG. In line with our statement of Passive at UG given above, we conceive here of UG as specifying, directly or indirectly, the entire set of structures from which we may draw in constructing a particular language. The choice from among these structures will be subject to parameter conditions, of which we have tentatively suggested a few of an implicational nature.

As the characterisation of possible structures at UG must generalise over the various language-particular instantiations, it is reasonable to believe that an explicit characterisation of UG will be conceptually simple and elegant, as we would like to think that our statement of Passive at UG is. By contrast, the complete specification of any particular language, or even of the Valency Affecting rules of that language, may exhibit unsystematic and even random shortfalls from what is universally possible. We are left, then, in the possibly unsurprising position that it will be easier to define the class of possible human languages than it will be to define any particular member of that class.

References

Bach, E. (1980) 'In Defense of Passive', *Linguistics and Philosophy* 3, 297-342.

Dowty, D. (1978) 'Governed Transformations in Montague Grammar', *Linguistic Inquiry* 9, 3, 393-426.

Gary, J.O. (1977) 'Implications for Universal Grammar of Object-creating Rules in Luyia and Mashi', *Studies in African Linguistics*, Supplement 7, 85-97.

Georges, L. and J. Kornfilt (1977) 'Infinitival Double Passives in Turkish', *NELS* VII.

Hodges, K.S. (1977) 'Causatives, Transitivity and Objecthood in Kimeru', *Studies in African Linguistics*, Supplement 7, 113-27.

Keenan, E.L. (1975) 'Remarkable Subjects in Malagasy', in C. Li (ed.) *Subject and Topic*, Academic Press, New York, pp. 247-303.

—— (1980) 'Passive is Phrasal (not Sentential or Lexical)' in T. Hoekstra, H. van der Hulst, and M. Moortgat (eds.) *Lexical grammar*, Foris, Dordrecht, pp. 181-215.

—— (1982) 'Parametric Variation in Universal Grammar', in R. Dirven and G. Radden (eds.) *Issues in the Theory of Universal Grammar*, Gunter Narr, Tübingen.

Kimenyi, A. (1978) *A Relational Grammar of Kinyarwanda* University of California, Berkeley, California.

Kuz'mina, I.B. and E.V. Nemčenko (1971) *Sintaksis pričastnyx form v russkix govorax*, Nauka, Moscow.

Lewis, G.L. (1967) *Turkish Grammar*, Clarendon Press, Oxford.

Özkaragöz, I. (1982) 'Monoclausal Double Passives in Turkish', unpublished manuscript, Department of Linguistics, UCSD.

Perlmuter, D.M. and P.M. Postal (1983) 'The 1-advancement Exclusiveness Law', in D.M. Perlmutter and C.G. Rosen (eds.), *Studies in Relational Gramar*, 2, University of Chicago, Chicago and London.

Rappaport, G. (1984) *Grammatical Function and Syntactic Structure: The Adverbial Participles of Russian*, Slavica, Columbus, Ohio.

Sinha, A.K. (1978) 'Another Look at the Universal Characterisation of the Passive Voice', *Chicago Linguistic Society* 14, 445-57.

Thomason, R. (1976) 'Some Extensions of Montague Grammar' in B. Partee (ed.) *Montague Grammar*, Academic Press, New York.

Timberlake, A. (1976) 'Subject Properties in the North Russian Passive' in C. Li (ed.) *Subject and Topic*, Academic Press, New York, pp. 545-70.

—— (1982) 'The Impersonal Passive in Lithuanian', *BLS* 8, 508-24.

PART FOUR:
EXPLANATION IN UNIVERSAL GRAMMAR

The articles in this section all attempt to relate observable syntactic phenomena, specifically patterns of cross-language variation, to semantic phenomena. To the extent that either of these domains may be thought of as independent of the other, the principles relating them may be considered 'explanatory'. For example, in 'The Logical Status of Deep Structures' I attempt to explain the fact that languages which regularly present resumptive pronouns in relativised positions characteristically present a wider range of relative clauses than languages which do not present such pronouns. The basic idea here is that pronoun-retaining languages present overtly (in surface) more of what we need to know to understand what the relative clause refers to. In 'The Functional Principle' I attempt to relate permissible and impermissible patterns of co-reference to the function-argument structure of the relevant expressions. In 'On Surface Form and Logical Form' both word-order patterns and agreement patterns are characterised in terms of semantic function-argument structure . In 'The Logical Diversity of Natural Languages', while several regularities between syntactic and semantic structure are offered, the principal point made is that languages differ significantly with respect to their logical expressive power.

11 THE LOGICAL STATUS OF DEEP STRUCTURES: LOGICAL CONSTRAINTS ON SYNTACTIC PROCESSES[1]

In Section 1 we propose a certain property that the logical form of restrictive relative clauses should have in order to correctly determine the logical properties of such relative clauses. In Section 2 we present syntactic evidence from universal grammar that the deep structure of relative clauses has the property proposed in Section 1, and that languages differ with respect to how much of the logical structure of relative clauses is presented in surface. In Section 3 we present some language universal generalisations relating logical structure and surface structure. Specifically we argue that the more a syntactic process, such as relative clause formation, preserves logical structure, the greater the variety of contexts in which it applies and the more 'difficult' the positions it applies to. In this respect then some languages are argued to be logically more expressive than others.

1.

Sentences (1) and (2) are logically distinct in that they are not necessarily true in exactly the same circumstances.

(1) Every student was surprised that he passed the exam.
(2) Every student was surprised that every student passed the exam.

Imagine for example the following plausible situation: each student takes and passes the exam; each student is confident of passing, but knows that it is usual for a fixed percentage of the people taking any exam to be failed. In such a situation (1) might easily be false but (2) true.

Similarly, the restrictive clauses (3) and (4) are logically distinct in that they specify different sets.

(3) every student who was surprised that he passed the exam
(4) every student who was surprised that every student passed the exam

337

(3) specifies a set of students about whom (1) is true, whereas (4) specifies a set about whom (2) is true, and the truth conditions of (1) and (2) are different. Thus the *difference* in logical form of (3) and (4) is essentially the same as that between (1) and (2). Note that it is the fact that (3) and (4) specify different sets which accounts for the difference in truth conditions of (5) and (6).

(5)   Every student who was surprised that he passed the exam was tired.
(6)   Every student who was surprised that every student passed the exam was tired.

Notice that the choice of determiner used in the quantified noun phrase 'every student' is immaterial in establishing the logical differences cited above. Thus if 'every student' is everywhere replaced in (1) and (2) by 'some student who was drunk', 'many students' or even 'the student who studied the least', the resulting pairs of sentences are still true under somewhat different conditions and thus logically distinct.

In the formal languages whose logical properties are represented in standard predicate logic, the sort of meaning difference we have been discussing exists and is represented by the use of quantifiers. Thus, in the language of elementary arithmetic, the logical form of the a. sentences below is represented by their corresponding b. sentences.

(7)   a.   Every number is either even or not even.
       b.   (every x) (x is even or x is not even)
(8)   a.   Every number is even or every number is not even.
       b.   ((every x) (x is even) or (every y) (y is not even))

Of course in a normal mathematical language the objects we use the language to talk about are agreed upon ahead of time and so need not be specified in the formal sentences. That is, in (7b) for example, it is understood that we are talking about numbers. But in ordinary language we may talk about many different sorts of things, so it is usually necessary to specify this information in the sentence. Thus our logical representation of (7a) would be (7c):

(7)   c.   (every number, x) (x is even or x is not even)

It is a trivial matter to modify the syntax of standard logic to accommodate sentences of the form (7c) rather than (7b). And it is basically this modification which we adopt to represent the logical form of (1) and (2), given as (9) and (10) below:

(9)   (every student, x) (x was surprised (x passed the exam))
(10) (every student, x) (x was surprised ((every student, y) (y passed the exam)))

In Keenan (1972a) we have rigorously specified the logical form of sentences such as (1) and (2) and defined the notion 'true in an arbitrary state of affairs (model)' in such a way that the difference in truth condition of (1) and (2) is represented, as is consequently the difference in the sets specified by (3) and (4).

Syntactically (9) consists of two parts: a quantified noun phrase and the sentence quantified into. The quantified noun phrase consists of a determiner, 'every', a common noun which represents the domain of things talked about, and a variable or pronominal index, 'x'. The sentence quantified into, considered in isolation, is one in which the pronominal index x occurs free and marks the positions quantified into by the quantified noun phrase. In the logical forms we have proposed, sentences such as (9) are recursively nominalised, forming complex quantified noun phrases — those which represent the logical form of restrictive relative clauses — and can be used to quantify into further sentences, as illustrated in (5). (And these sentences can further be nominalised, etc.) When a complex sentence like (9) is nominalised and used to quantify into other sentences it must carry a variable or pronominal index as in the case of simple quantified noun phrases. Thus the logical structure we propose for (3) would be essentially (11):

(11) ((every student, x) (x was surprised (x passed the exam)), y)

The pronominal index y above is used only as the reference point for some sentence that (11) might be used to quantify into. It plays no role in determining the set of objects specified by (11). Noting this then, we can say that the essential logical form of relative clauses consists of two parts: a *head noun phrase* which carries a pronominal index, and a *subordinate sentence* in which the pronominal index occurs and identifies the positions relativised into by the head noun phrase. The set specified by a restrictive relative clause then will consist of just those objects specified by the head noun phrase which the subordinate sentence is true of.

This proposal does not differ greatly from many current in generative grammar, except that it requires that the subordinate sentence should not contain a repetition of the head noun phrase but only of its pronominal index (repetition of the full noun phrase would lose the distinction between (3) and (4)).

2.

Any language which has relative clauses must provide some strategy to identify the role that the head noun phrase plays in the subordinate sentence, or else the relative clauses would be intolerably ambiguous — and we would not be able to distinguish the referents of 'the girl that John loves' and 'the girl that loves John'. We stress that identifying the position relativised into by the head noun is logically important, for only if the position is known can we clearly determine the sentence which must be true of the objects specified by the head noun, and thus understand the reference of the entire relative clause.

Logically we have solved this problem marking the positions relativised into with pronouns that match the index on the head noun phrase. It does not appear however that natural languages avail themselves of exactly this solution. Some languages, e.g. Czech,[2] Hadza,[3] do present sentences containing full noun phrases together with co-referential pronouns with which they form a constituent. But we know of no language which regularly retains these indexical pronouns in noun phrases which occur as head noun phrases of relative clauses.

Co-reference in natural language is not generally indicated by matching pronouns with pronominal indices of nouns. But co-reference is normally indicated by matching pronouns with the noun class and subclass of noun phrases. Such referencing power varies considerably across languages. Some, e.g. Malagasy, possess essentially only one third person subject pronoun. Others, such as English, possess a few, *he, she, it, they*. And some Bantu languages may possess upwards of 10 to 15, as weak pronouns may agree in noun class and number with the head noun. Luganda for example has 16 distinct weak subject-pro-forms.

One quite general solution to the strategy problem for relative clauses then is illustrated by languages which retain a personal pronoun in the position of the subordinate sentence relativised into. Our current research indicates that languages in which pronoun retention is a major strategy (used in relativisation in major noun phrase positions in simplex sentences) fall naturally into two groups: a *strong* group which includes modern Hebrew, modern Arabic, Welsh, Persian[4] and to some extent Batak,[5] and a *weak* group which includes Roumanian, Luganda, Swahili and Yoruba.

The strong group typically does not distinguish both a strong and weak form of the personal pronoun for given grammatical cases, (although there may be emphatic forms of the personal pronoun). Typically the relative clause complementiser (hereafter *Rel*) is a generalised subordination marker which may introduce other sorts of subordinate sentence and which is often not marked for case.[6]

Usually in these languages it is difficult or impossible to retain subject pronouns in relative clauses;[7] direct object pronouns are somewhat easier (e.g. not usually retained in Welsh, optionally retained in Hebrew, normally retained in Arabic — Colloquial Egyptian); and oblique case pronouns are usually obligatorily retained.

Hebrew is a representative example of this group. In the relative clause (12), the subordinate marker *še* is invariable in form — not marked for gender, number, or case. It also serves to introduce sentence complements as in (13).

(12) Dan makir- et   ha- iš   še- ha- iša   hikta oto
      Dan knows DO the man that the woman hit   him
(13) Miriam amra še- ha- iš   hika et   ha- iša
      Miriam said that the man hit   DO the woman

The direct object pronoun *oto* agrees in gender and number with the head noun *ha-iš*. It may be optionally omitted from (12). And most important, the subordinate clause following *še-* in (12) has the surface structure of a sentence. If a man had already been identified one might say (14) as a complete sentence:

(14) Ha-iša hikta oto (The woman hit him)

Clearly then Hebrew preserves in surface the sentential status of the subordinate part of the relative clause. On the other hand English and many European languages do not preserve the sentential status of the subordinate clause in surface. That part of the relative clause following the optional 'that' in (15) is not a surface structure sentence in English.

(15) the girl (that) John kissed

As the subordinate clause is a sentence in logical structure, we are justified in saying that the strong pronoun retaining languages preserve in surface more of the logical structure of relative clauses than do languages like English.

The weak pronoun retaining languages usually distinguish strong and weak forms of the personal pronoun (and may have yet another form for emphatic pronouns). It is generally the weak form that is retained in the subordinate position of relative clauses. Typically the weak form is affixed to the verb. Frequently it also occurs in simple sentences when the full noun phrase it refers to is present. The full noun phrase may be the stressed form of the pronoun. Typically weak pronouns only occur in subject, direct object, and indirect object positions and usually not in all of these (e.g. Yoruba has only weak subject pronouns, Luganda weak subject and object pronouns, and Roumanian weak object and indirect object pronouns but no weak subject pronouns). Frequently *Rel* does mark the grammatical case the head noun would have in the subordinate sentence. (Luganda marks subject and object cases, Roumanian marks subject, object, indirect object, and genitive. But Yoruba does not mark case, having an invariable *Rel*). (16), (17), and (18), from Yoruba, Luganda, and Roumanian respectively illustrate the diversity of relative clause formation in the weak group.

(16) omodé t'ó (= tí + ó) rí   okùnrin nye
      child   that he saw man   the
      (the) child who saw the man
(17) omukazi e- ye- basse
      woman   she Rel sleep
      (the) woman who is sleeping
(18) barbatul pe care femeia   l- a lovit
      the man whom   the woman him hit

The weak pronoun retaining languages also appear more structure preserving than e.g. English, for the subordinate clause following the *Rel*-marker in (16)-(18) above has the surface structure of a sentence. But these languages seem somewhat less structure preserving overall than the strong group. In the first place weak pronouns occur in relatively few positions — subject, object, indirect object — which include the easiest positions to relativise into regardless of the syntactic strategy used in relativisation (the notion of 'easiest' will be explicated shortly). The typically enclitic nature of the pronouns further restricts their freedom of occurrence in that, for example, they cannot be conjoined to form a noun phrase of the form 'he and she' — only the strong forms could be used here. In the second place, the fact that the *Rel*-marker is marked for case indicates that presence of the weak pronoun is not sufficient to mark the function of the head noun in the subordinate clause. Thus in Roumanian and Luganda the *Rel*-marker codes as many or more grammatical cases than can be represented by weak pronouns. Notice too that within Bantu languages the *Rel*-marker frequently occurs within rather than preceding the subordinate sentence. Thus when non-subjects are relativised on in Luganda the *Rel*-marker usually follows the subject of the subordinate sentence, as in (19) where *gwe* is the object *Rel*-marker agreeing in number and noun class with the head noun *omuggo*.

(19) Fred yalaba omuggo John gwe yakubisa embwa
     Fred saw   stick   John that hit-with dog
     (Fred saw the stick that John hit the dog with)

We conclude this section with two remarks: (a) the existence of many languages, from diverse language families, which present pronouns in the subordinate sentence referring to the head noun phrase constitutes evidence in favour of using the logical structures proposed in Section 1 as the underlying syntactic sources of relative clauses. What differs primarily across languages in this approach then is the specification of the environments in which deletion of the subordinate pronoun is optional and obligatory — and this sort of variation is already known to be natural across languages. (b) The pronoun retaining languages present in surface more of the logical structure of relative clauses than languages which do not retain the subordinate pronoun.

3.

Since the communicating function of natural language depends in part on how clearly semantic information is coded in the syntactic structures of the language we might expect that a syntactic strategy that preserved more logical structure than some other would, in some sense, be the more successful. The following principle is one way of making this intuition explicit.

Conservation of Logical Structure (CLS)

The more a syntactic process preserves logical structure the greater the range of such structures expressible in surface.

We present two major pieces of evidence in support of CLS:

1. *Pronoun retaining languages permit relative clause formation in a greater variety of contexts than non-pronoun retaining ones.*

In the strong pronoun retaining languages it is not unusual to find that relativisation is possible into sentence complements of nouns, as in Hebrew (20), into single members of conjoined noun phrases, as in Arabic (21), and even into relative clauses themselves, as in the Welsh (22).

(20) Ani roa et   ha- iš   še- Sally ma'amina la- šmo'a še-
                                                      Miriam hikta oto
     I   see DO the man that Sally believes   the rumour that
                                                      Mary   hit   him.
(21) Ra'ayt alrajul   allathi hua wa ibnahu thahabu ille N.Y.
     (I) saw the man that   he and son his went   to New York
(22) Dymar'r het y gwn y dyn a'- i gadewodd ar y ford
     Here-is the hat that I-know the man who it left on the table
     (Here is the hat that I know the man who left (it) on the
     table)

Table 11.1 compares relativisation possibilities of the five strong pronoun retaining languages with two non-pronoun retaining ones, English and Malagasy. The key to the headings is: *co-S*: one member of co-ordinate sentences. *co-NP*: one member of co-ordinate noun phrases. *S-cmp-NP*: sentence complement of noun phrase, as in 'the rumour that *Mary left John*'. *Emb-Q*:

embedded question, as in 'I don't know *who hit John*'. *Rel-Cl*: relative clause. *O-Prep*: object of a preposition. *Conj*: occurring in different grammatical cases in each of two conjuncted sentences, as in '*The boy* came early and Mary loves *the boy*'. *Poss-NP*: possessor noun phrase as in '*John's* car'.

Table 11.1: Relativisation is Possible into:

	co-S	co-NP	S-cmp-NP	Emb-Q	Rel-Cl	O-Prep	Conj	Poss-NP
Hebrew	no	yes	yes	yes	yes	yes	yes	yes
Arabic	no	yes	no	yes	yes	yes	yes	yes
Welsh	no	no	yes	yes	yes	yes	—	yes
Persian	no	yes	yes	yes	yes	yes	—	yes
Batak	no	yes	no	no	no	yes	yes	yes
English	no	no	no	no?	no	yes	yes	yes
Malagasy	no	no	no	no	no	no	no	no

The questioned entry under English embedded questions is due to the fact that typically they are ungrammatical when formed in the usual way, but are frequently accepted if a pronoun is retained in the position relativised into. Compare:

(23) *This is the road which I don't know where goes
(24) This is the road which I don't know where it goes

Although our table has a few blanks, it overwhelmingly supports the claim that pronoun retention extends the domain of relativisation. Whenever it indicates that relativisation by pronoun deletion is possible in English or Malagasy it is also possible (ignoring the few blanks) in *all* the pronoun retaining languages. But the converse fails badly.

The somewhat poor showing of Batak in this respect is explained as follows: the principal relativisation strategy in Batak is a pronoun deleting strategy. But as with many W. Malayo-Polynesian languages[8] only subjects may be relativised with this strategy. As Batak has but two voices, active and passive, this means that from the point of view of underlying structures only subjects and objects can be relativised. So a morphologically more complex strategy is used for many constituents that cannot be made a subject — and this strategy permits retention of non-subject pronouns.

Note also the difference between English and Malagasy. Of the pronoun deleting languages English is one of the most liberal we have looked at from the point of view of relativisation. The use of a relative pronoun which carries case markers and full prepositions appears responsible for this. Thus in 'the table on which Fred put the money' the phrase 'on which' codes quite explicitly the role that 'table' plays in the subordinate clause. In Malagasy the coding is much less explicit, since the *Rel*-marker is invariable in form. As with Batak basically only subjects can be relativised. Malagasy however has three voices, an active, a passive, and a catch-all voice that will make almost any major constituent of an active sentence the subject. But in making it the subject no preposition is retained marking the underlying function of the NP. Consequently the semantic role of the head noun of a relative clause whose subordinate verb is in the third voice may play any function in that clause except that of underlying subject or object. It is impossible to distinguish in surface for example between 'the table under which Fred put the money' and 'the table on top of which Fred put the money'. The best we can do is *ny latabatra izay nametrehan'i Fred ny vola* 'the table where Fred put the money'.

Since English can discriminate very many particular functions that head nouns play in subordinate clauses, whereas Malagasy can only discriminate three explicitly, it is not unreasonable to think that English explicitly preserves more of the logical structure of relative clauses than Malagasy, given that they both preserve less than the strong pronoun retaining languages which in addition to preserving the function of head noun also preserve the sentential status of the subordinate clause. That English can form more relative clauses than Malagasy then conforms to CLS, but we do not pursue further here the differential relativising power of languages with invariable *Rel*-markers and those with case marked ones.

A final remark on Table 11.1: note that none of the strong pronoun retaining languages admits that relative clauses may naturally be formed into only one member of a co-ordinate sentence. Similarly relativising twice into the same relative clause e.g. 'This is the book which I saw the girl that you know the man who gave it to her' was not generally accepted, although it could be puzzled out. Consequently retaining subordinate pronouns in relative clauses does not give us unrestricted relativising power, it merely enlarges the class of relative clauses by comparison with non-pronoun retaining languages, but both sets of languages share some impressive common restrictions on relative clause formation.

Table 11.2 compares three weak pronoun retaining languages with English and Malagasy.

Table 11.2: Relativisation is Possible into:

	co-S	co-NP	S-cmp-NP	Emb-Q	Rel-Cl	O-Prep	Conj	Poss-NP
Roumanian	no	no	no	yes	no	yes	yes	yes
Luganda	no	no	no	yes	yes	no?	yes	yes
Yoruba	no	yes	no	no	no	yes	*	yes
English	no	no	no	no?	no	yes	yes	yes
Malagasy	no	no	no	no	no	no	no	no

The * in the Yoruba row indicates that while relativisation was not judged natural in conjoined sentences the difficulty seemed to pertain more to the difficulty in conjoining sentences rather than the difficulty in relativisation. Conjoining sentences in Yoruba by overt co-ordinate conjunction was not judged natural. Noun phrases could be overtly conjoined, but sentences were merely said one after the other. The problem of relativising into conjuncts then does not arise in a natural way.

The questioned *no* in the Luganda row is of more interest. One cannot relativise on the object of a preposition, either stranding the preposition or attaching it to the *Rel*-marker. Basically the Lugandan relativisation strategy works on subjects and objects (including many things one might want to call indirect objects), providing distinct series of subject and object *Rel*-markers which agree in number and noun class with the head noun. Rather than permitting relativisation on oblique case constituents such as instrumentals however, Luganda provides a way of systematically modifying the simple active verb to form a 'prepositional' verb whose direct object would be the oblique case constituent of the simple verb. It then can form relative clauses on these constituents as direct objects. (25) and (26) illustrate this formation. No relative clause can be formed on *olutti* 'stick' from (25) but only from (26) as illustrated in (27).

(25) John ya-sima   lumonde n'olutti
     John he dug up a potato   with a stick
(26) John lumonde ya-mu-simisa   lutti
     John a potato   he it dug up-with a stick

(27) Fred yalabu olutti John lwe- ya-sim*isa* lumonde
      Fred saw   (the) stick that John dug up-*with* a potato

So inability to form relative clauses directly on oblique case constituents in Luganda does not result in a loss of expressibility. It
suffices to convert the verb to a 'prepositional' form making the
oblique case NP a direct object, whence it can be relativised. Note
the similarity of this strategy to the use of the voice system in
Malagasy and other W. Malayo-Polynesian languages (including
Kalagan,[9] Batak, and Ivatan[10]).

The information in Table 11.2 basically supports CLS but the
evidence is not nearly so striking as that presented in Table 11.1.
Relativisation in Yoruba in fact seems slightly more constrained
than in Malagasy. This is not surprising since Yoruba retains only
subject pronouns in the subordinate clause and its *Rel*-marker,
being invariable, does not code the function of the head noun in the
subordinate clause.

Roumanian and Luganda do have a slight edge over English
and Malagasy with respect to freedom of relativisation, but both
are clearly more restricted than the strong pronoun retaining languages. This confirms our intuition that weak pronoun retention is
less preserving of logical structure than strong pronoun retention.

2.   *Across languages, the use of pronoun retaining strategies for
      given noun phrase positions is proportional to the
      inaccessibility of the noun phrase as determined by its
      position in the (independently motivated) Noun Phrase
      Accessibility Hierarchy.*

In the course of our comparative work on relativisation in different languages it has become quite apparent that the relativisability of certain positions is not independent of others. These
dependencies are largely independent of the syntactic strategy a
given language may use in relativisation. Furthermore the same
dependencies appear to hold for a variety of syntactic processes
whose effect is to make a noun phrase occurring in a sentence the
head of that sentence such that the sentence becomes, in some
sense subordinate to the noun phrase that was originally an
undistinguished part of it. Such processes in English include *Rel-
Cl, Quest* (e.g. Which girl did John kiss?), *Emb-Quest* (e.g. Fred
knows *which girl John kissed*), *Cleft* (e.g. It was Mary who John

kissed), *Strong-Top* (e.g. As for Mary, no-one likes her anymore), *Exist* (e.g. There was a young girl who John thought could play the part), and *What-Cl* (e.g. *Whoever Mary looks at* will turn to stone).

Basically we are claiming that whenever the difficulty in applying one of these processes to some noun phrase x is greater than or equal to the difficulty in applying the process to y, then the difficulty in applying any other one of the processes to x will be greater than or equal to applying that process to y. In other words, some NP positions are inherently less easy than others to make dominant with respect to the entire sentence they occur in.

Our formulation allows that the absolute ease of applying two different processes to the same NP might be very different. In Malagasy for example it is possible to apply *Quest* and *Cleft* to objects of true prepositions — positions which are not relativisable. And in English there are cases where *Rel-Cl* operates on an NP occurring in different cases across conjunctions but where *Quest* doesn't — presumably because the structure preserving property of repetition of the relative pronoun is not part of the syntactic strategy of *Quest.*

(28) The man who Mary kissed and who called the police
(29) *Which man did Mary kiss and called the police?

A full statement of the Accessibility Hierarchy would go well beyond our data and the bounds of this paper. Still, we give two principles of the hierarchy in order to justify our claim in 2. above. We use ⩾ to mean 'greater than or equal to in accessibility'.

(A) major NP ⩾ minor NP
     (A major NP of a sentence S is an NP which functions as a major constituent of the main verb of S, such as 'subject', 'direct object', etc.)
(B) For major NP, we have that Subj NP ⩾ Dir-Obj NP ⩾ Ind-Obj NP ⩾ other oblique case NP ⩾ object of comparison

Specifically then (A) predicts that it will generally be harder to relativise on minor NP than on major NP. (Note that the comparison in Tables 11.1 and 11.2 is almost entirely on minor NP.) (B) claims that whenever a language permits one to relativise on objects of comparative constructions then you can also do so on objects of true prepositions. And if these work, then direct objects and then indirect objects can be relativised. Finally, the easiest of all to relativise on are subject NP. The converse of these statements in general fail.

The evidence in support of the hierarchy is of two sorts. The first is direct. Informants simply judge that questions, relative clauses, etc. formed on NP far down the hierarchy are less well formed than those formed on NP highly placed on the hierarchy. The second is indirect. Namely, the principle of accessibility allows us to explain the existence of certain syntactic phenomena across languages, thereby increasing the generality of our linguistic descriptions.

We saw earlier that Malagasy and several other W. M-P languages permit *Rel-Cl* to work only on subjects. We can now point out that the function of the multiplicity of verb voices in these languages (e.g. three in Malagasy, four in Kalagan)[11] is to move noun phrases from inaccessible positions to accessible ones. Nor is it any accident that if only one position is to be accessible it is the subject position. It is easy for a non-speaker of these languages, even one who has read carefully their grammars, to get the impression that the principal function of the large number of voices is simply to allow people to say basically the same thing in different ways and with a slightly different emphasis, just as actives and passives in English differ in emphasis but presumably have the same propositional content. But this analysis completely overlooks the major function of the voice: to make noun phrase accessible for questioning, relativising, etc.

Similarly, the function of the various prepositional forms of verbs in Luganda (an plausibly many other Bantu languages)[12] is to move oblique case NP into an accessible position — the direct object position. And as with the M-P languages referred to above, it is natural to wonder why a language would provide a systematic way of saying 'hit-with', 'planting-with' given that we already can say 'hit', 'plant', etc. The Accessibility Hierarchy provides the basis of the answer. It also enables us to see that two apparently rather unrelated phenomena — the verb voices in W. M-P and the prepositional verbs in Bantu — function in very similar ways: namely, to make inaccessible NP accessible.

Returning now to the second generalisation in support of CLS we note that across languages the likelihood of using a pronoun retaining strategy in *Rel-Cl* increases as we move down the

Accessibility Hierarchy. For the languages we have considered in which pronoun retention is a major relativisation strategy the evidence in favour of this generalisation is striking. In Batak for example, the primary strategy is a deletion one, but it only works on underlying subjects and objects — those NP which can be made subject in surface. The second strategy, a pronoun retaining one, allows relativisation into sentence complements of verbs as well as in the positions indicated in Table 11.1. Thus we have:

(30) Ndang huberang boru-boru i, ima na dirippu s si Bissar na
     Not seen-by-me woman the that thought by Bissar that
     manussi abit {ibana}
                 {*Ø}
     was-washing clothes she

The *Rel*-marker *ima na* is different in this strategy than in the deletion one in which it is merely *na*. A similar phenomenon occurs in Welsh. In the pronoun deleting strategy, which works principally on just subjects and objects, the subordinate clause is, in affirmative sentences, introduced by *a*, referred to in grammars[13] as a relative pronoun. In the pronoun retaining strategy, which allows relativisation to occur in the various difficult position in Table 11.1, the subordinate sentence is introduced by a 'relative particle' *y*.

Even Hebrew and Arabic, which cannot be said to have morphologically distinct strategies, still support our generalisation. Thus in Hebrew subject pronouns of full verbs are not usually retained in relativisation, but if the subject position is low on the hierarchy the pronoun may be retained, sometimes obligatorily. Thus:

(31) Ani roa et ha- iš še- {hu} -ovno halxo le New York
                           {*Ø}
     I see the man that he and his son went to New York

Similarly it is preferred to retain direct object pronouns in difficult positions even though retention is optional when relativising on direct objects of simplex sentences. Clearly these apparent anomalies in the retention of pronouns in Hebrew are simply further instances of a broader generalisation, given the Accessibility Hierarchy.

The evidence from Arabic (Colloquial Egyptian) is even more striking. In the respects that concern us there are basically two types of personal pronoun: independent pronouns which function as subjects, and dependent pronouns which normally occur either suffixed to verbs or prepositions, functioning as objects of these, or else suffixed to nouns and functioning as genitives. It is only the dependent pronouns — the ones representing the less accessible positions — that are normally retained in relativisation. However if we attempt to relativise into certain inaccessible subject positions we find that dependent pronouns are occasionally used as subjects!

(32) ra'ayt alrajul allathi Mona farihat   an- {hu}-daraba
                                                   {*Ø}
                                                         Ahmed
      (I) saw the man that   Mona was pleased that he hit
                                                         Ahmed

In other cases of inaccessible positions it sometimes happens that the independent form of the pronoun is retained even though it functions more as an accusative rather than a nominative.

(33) ra'ayt alrajul   allathi {hua}wa ibnahu thahabu ille New
                               {*Ø}
                                                           York
      (I) saw the man that   he and son-his went   to New
                                                           York
(34) ra'ayt alrajul   allathi Mona ta'rafu-hu {hua}wa zawgati-hi
                                               {*Ø}
      (I) saw the man that   Mona knows him he and wife   his

Again CLS and the Accessibility principle provide a basic explanation for these apparent anomalies: given that the position relativised into is inherently rather inaccessible we must present in surface the logical structure of the sentence relativised into in order that the logical structure of the entire relative clause be clear. Extending the usages of so-called subject and object pronouns is simply the natural way in Arabic of preserving logical structure in surface.

Further evidence in support of our generalisaton comes from languages in which pronoun retention is not a major relativisation strategy. It happens frequently that such languages do admit of pronoun retention in certain relatively inaccessible positions, specifically possessor-NP and NP occurring in different cases across conjunctions. We have documented examples of genitive pronouns retained in relative clauses in Norwegian, Icelandic, Turkish, and Malay.

(35) (Malay): lelaki yang Ali telah menchuri ayam- nya
             man that Ali perf stole   chicken-his

Even in English certain speakers show a preference for 'Here comes the man that I can never remember his name' rather than '... whose name I can never remember'.

Similarly in Ancient Greek (Goodwin 1894, 222), Latin (Gildersleeve 1895, 407) and Serbo-Croat, (36), examples[14] can be found in which a pronoun is retained in second conjuncts when the NP position is of a different grammatical case than in the first conjunct.

(36) zemla o   kajoj znamo vrlo malo a   smatramo je
                                                 yaznom
     land   about which we-know very little and we-consider it
                                                 important

Another anomaly explainable in term of CLS and the Accessibility principle is that in all languages we have considered it is difficult, and usually impossible (see Table 11.1), to directly relativise into a sentence complement of a lexical NP, e.g. 'the country' in (37).

(37) John believes the prediction that the country will fall.

But many of these languages (e.g. English, French, Roumanian, Arabic) do present a relative clause which is semantically equivalent to the one we would expect to get by relativising directly into the complement sentence. Thus (38a) is ill formed in English but has the same meaning essentially as the well formed (38b).

(38) a. *the country that John believes the prediction that will
          fall

b.   the country about which John believes prediction that it will fall

(38b) clearly appears to be formed by relativising into a position directly governed by the main verb of the sentence rather than of the complement sentence. Thus the relativisation has taken place on a more accessible NP in (38b) than (38a), which given our principles is not surprising. But what is most interesting here is that in general the apparent underlying source for the acceptable relative clause is less acceptable than the direct underlying source for the unacceptable relative clause. Thus (39) below is less acceptable in English than (37).

(39) ?John believes about the country the prediction that it will fall

It would appear then that relative clause formation does not, in this case, preserve the relative acceptability ordering of sentences — a surprising fact since it usually does. And again CLS together with the Accessibility principle explain the greater acceptability of (38b) than (38a). Accepting that (37) and (39) have essentially equivalent logical structures (something that may not be true for all sentence pairs differing in this way) it is easy to see that the surface structure of the acceptable relative clause (38b) preserves the structure of (37) intact following the *Rel*-marker 'about which'. Its greater acceptability then is due to its logical transparency.

A final piece of evidence supporting our major generalisation is that even in languages where pronoun retention is not a norm, a relative clause formed on an inaccessible position is typically more understanding, logically speaking, than the corresponding one without the subordinate pronoun. Compare:

(40) This is the girl which the fact that John kissed {*her} sur-
                                                      {**Ø}
      prised everybody
(41) This is the girl that {*she} and her brother were expelled
                            {**Ø}
      yesterday

In conclusion: we have argued that the logical structure of relative clauses should consist of head noun phrase and a sentence which contains a pronominal reference to the head noun phrase. We have shown that many languages present such pronouns in surface and that these languages permit relative clause formation to apply in a greater variety of contexts, including the less accessible ones, than languages in which these pronouns are not retained. Our principle of Accessibility and of the Conservation of Logical Structure provide an explanation for these, and other, syntactic facts.

A closing note on method: some linguists might object to our proposals on the grounds that the difficult relative clauses that we have judged acceptable in pronoun retaining languages are often cumbersome and not frequently used. Certainly in some cases such as relativising into relative clauses, this is so. But as an objection to our work we feel it is not well taken since the purpose of our work has not been merely to enumerate certain sometimes clumsy structures that grammars of particular languages should generate, but rather to compare different relative clause strategies. To this end we have performed grammatical 'experiments' in submitting different strategies to the same stress conditions (by trying to force them to operate on relatively inaccessible NP) and attempted to make generalisations concerning the nature of the strategies as a function, in part, of how they behave under similar stress conditions. Essentially we are claiming that pronoun retaining strategies hold up better under stress than pronoun deleting ones — and the principles of CLS and Accessibility are our attempt to explain this behaviour.

Discussion

T. Vennemann: The ungrammatical translations of sentences taken from languages in which the relativised noun is retained in the relative clause as a pronoun all become grammatical (though not very felicitous) English sentences when we replace *that* by *such that*, e.g. *Here is the hat such that I know the man who left it on the table.* Perhaps the difference between languages with relative pronouns ('*who*-languages') and languages with a non-pronominal relative marker ('*such-that*-languages') could serve as a basis for a typology. It seems to me from the very little experience I have with relative clause formation in different languages that pronoun retention is more likely to occur in *such-that*-languages than in *who*-languages, the reason being, of course, that in the latter the relative pronoun is itself a 'retained pronoun'. I would expect that consistent (or 'pure') *such-that*-languages have retained pronouns, while consistent (or 'pure') *who*-languages do not have (additional) retained pronouns. As a language changes type, inconsistent pronoun retention behaviour may occur. I believe that the occurrence of pronoun retention in certain dialects of English heralds the change of this language from a *who*-language to a *such-that*-language (with *that* as a relative clause marker meaning 'such that').

E. Keenan: I basically agree with Mr. Vennemann's main point: namely, that pronoun retention is more likely in languages whose relative marker (RM) is non-pronominal than in languages in which the RM is pronominal. All the pronoun retaining strategies I cited were cases where the RM was non-pronominal. Notice however that even in those cases, not all pronouns are retained. In particular when the relative clause is formed on a subject position the pronoun is not normally retained. Furthermore it often happens that languages with non-pronominal RM do not normally retain a personal pronoun at all. This is the case for example in Malagasy (RM = *izay*), Tagalog (RM = *na/ng*), Javanese (RM = *seng*), and the Malayo-Polynesian languages generally. It is also the case in Scandinavian languages e.g. Swedish (RM = *som*). In fact, even in English the RM *that* is not pronominal, yet personal pronouns are not normally retained in relative clauses formed with *that*.

In addition there are languages whose RM is pronominal but which retain certain pronouns. Examples are not hard to find in Romance, e.g. certain dialects of Spanish, Italian, and quite generally in Roumanian, as in (1):

(1)   Femeia   careia   John i-   a dat cartea   doarme
      the woman to whom John to her gave the book is sleeping
      (The woman that John gave the book to is sleeping)

However, as indicated in the body of my paper, these languages distinguish a stressed and unstressed form of the personal pronoun, and it is only the unstressed one that is retainable in relative clauses. Excluding retention of unstressed pronouns then (whose presence is probably dependent on factors irrelevent to relative clause formation since they may sometimes occur in otherwise simplex sentences in the presence of full, co-referential, NP) it does appear unusual for personal pronouns to be retained in languages with pronominal RM.

We should note however that the pronominal status of the RM is not always easy to determine. Thus in many Bantu languages the RM are not obviously related morphologically to personal pronouns, but they do agree with their head NP in noun class and number, and they do distinguish subject heads from object heads (there being a different series of RM for relative clauses formed on subjects and those formed on objects). Further, in some of these languages, notably Shona, personal pronouns are retainable in relative clauses formed on oblique case NPs, as indicated in (2):

(2)   Ndirikuona jira   rakagukidwa   (na-ro) michero na
                                                              John
        I-see   cloth (that) covered-with-by (with-it) fruit   by
                                                              John
      (I see the cloth that John covered the fruit with)

So while I agree with Mr. Vennemann's main point, it must be noted that the typology determined by the different relativisation strategies is not 'clean' — languages can, to some extent, be more or less pronoun retaining.

Secondly, I would take issue with Mr. Vennemann on a minor point: namely, that the non-pronominal RM strategies discussed can be assimilated to *such-that* constructions in English. It seems to me that *the hat such that I know the man who left it on the table* is simply a reduced form (using the quite common deletion of *WH + is* in English) of *the hat which is such that I know the man who left it on the table.* This relative clause is quite possible because it is formed on the subject position of the predicate *is such.* The pronoun *it* must be retained because what follows the sentence complementiser *that* must be a sentence. Note in this regard that if *such-that* were regarded as a RM it would appear anomalous relative to other non-pronominal RM since it would require the retention of subject pronouns, as in *the hat that it fell on the floor* and not *the hat such that fell on the floor.*

And lastly, I am inclined to disagree with Mr. Vennemann's suggestion that the retention of pronouns in certain dialects of

English is indicative of an evolutionary trend in English. Rather the trend seems to be in the other direction, since, as the example below shows, pronoun retention was the norm in certain positions in Old and Middle English:

(3)   (cited from Bever and Langendonen 'A Dynamic Model of the Evolution of Language', *Linguistic Inquiry* II, 433-63)
        a jantyllwoman that semeth *she* hath grete nede of you

Hagège: Je ne suis pas insensible à la séduction de ce grand principe de division des langues en un groupe où le pronom est supprimé et un groupe où il est conservé, encore que l'intérêt typologique de ce critère ait été aperçu, dans les travaux sur la 'proposition relative', depuis assez longtemps. Mais je ne suis pas aussi persuadé que vous de la suppression du pronom dans les langues comme l'anglais ou le français. Dans ces langues, le pronom est tout simplement condensé dans le relatif, comme cela s'aperçoit bien dans les langues à déclinaison, par exemple le russe, qui dit *čelovek kotorogo ia uvidel*, ou l'allemand, qui a *der Mann, den ich gesehen habe*. De plus, dans les langues où le pronom est 'supprimé', il ne l'est pas par tout le monde, et en particulier, les enfants au stade de l'apprentissage, et beaucoup de personnes qui ont peu fréquenté l'école disent, en français, '*l'homme que je l'ai vu*'. C'est qu'on est devant deux procédés qu'adoptent les langues pour résoudre le problème de la subordination: la parataxe ou l'hypotaxe; je vous accorde bien volontiers que la parataxe de l'hébreu, de l'arabe ou du batak est un procédé plus transparent et plus simple que l'hypotaxe, mais il me paraît nécessaire de préciser qu'au sein d'une même langue, elles peuvent parfaitement co-exister, ce qui conduit à assouplir la grille typologique ici proposée; d'autre part et surtout, il existe un troisième procédé qui me paraît devoir être mentionné, c'est celui du chinois, qui se sert ici du joncteur employé dans le syntagme nominal, et qui n'a donc pas de proposition relative, puisque la structure, par exemple, de *pengyou* et de *zuotan lai de pengyou* ('mon ami' et 'l'ami qui est venu hier') est exactement la même.

E. Keenan: J'accepte bien volontiers que le pronom relatif des langues européennes incorpore en quelque sorte le pronom personnel. Et si ce que je faisais dans mon exposé c'était de pro-poser une typologie, alors j'aurais certainement à tenir compte de ce que le pronom personnel ne soit pas entièrement supprimé dans ces langues-là. Mais le but de mon exposé n'était pas de présenter de typologie, c'était plutôt de présenter d'abord certains faits linguistiques et ensuite de proposer une explication de ces faits.

Le fait principal que j'ai presenté c'est ceci: les langues qui retiennent les *pronoms personnels* dans les positions relativisées présentent un plus grand nombre de subordonnées relatives que les langues qui ne présentent pas de pronoms personnels dans ces positions.

Et l'explication que j'ai proposée c'est ceci: retenir le pronom personnel c'est en effet conserver en surface la structure logique de la subordonnée. Et la raison de cela, c'est qu'en structure logique la subordonnée est représentée par une phrase logique (celle qui est vraie du référent de la construction nominale tout entière). Et justement, les langues qui retiennent les pronoms personnels présentent la subordonnée relative en surface comme une phrase entière. Par contre, les langues qui suppriment le pronom personnel, ou qui le déguisent comme pronom relatif, détruisent un peu la structure logique de la subordonnée relative car la phrase logique n'est pas présentée comme phrase grammaticale en surface. C'est-à-dire, dans *la femme que j'ai vue* la subordonnée *que j'ai vue* n'est pas une phrase en surface.

Ceci étant établi il ne reste qu'à remarquer que la stratégie qui est la plus explicite logiquement est, naturellement, la stratégie qui fonctionne dans le plus grand nombre de contextes linguistiques.

Notes

1. This paper was written while the author was a fellow of King's College, Cambridge. Research on the material from the Malayo-Polynesian languages was supported in part by the Wenner-Gren Foundation for Anthropological Research, and in part by a National Science Foundation Post-doctoral Fellowship.
2. See Vanek, A. (1960).
3. I am indebted to Dr. James Woodburn for the Hadza data.
4. I am indebted to John Paine for both the Welsh and Persian data mentioned here and later.
5. Batak has two major relative clause strategies. They are discussed below, and in detail in Keenan (1972b).
6. In spoken Egyptian Arabic it is common to use an invariable *Rel*-marker *ille*. But in written, newspaper, Arabic the *Rel*-marker agrees with the head noun in gender — masculine and feminine — and in number — singular, dual, and plural. In the dual forms a distinction is made between nominative and non-nominative case marking (in agreement with the role of the head in the matrix clause).

7. A possible exception is Iai, a Melanesian language presented in Tryon (1968) in which apparently a third person subject pronoun is retained both in relative clauses and in simplex sentences co-occurring with a co-referential NP. No distinction appears to be made between strong and weak forms of the pronoun. Too few examples of the appropriate sort of relative clause are given for us to be able to consider this strategy in Iai.

8. See Keenan (1972b), for a detailed discussion of this strategy.

9. See Collins (1971).

10. See Reid (1966).

11. See Collins (1971).

12. See for example Perrott (1957).

13. See Bowen and Rhys Jones (1960).

14. I am indebted to Bernard Comrie, personal communication, for these examples. The Serbo-Croat example is due originally to Wayles Brown.

References

Bowen, J. and T.J. Rhys Jones (1960) *Welsh*, Teach Yourself Books, English Universities Press, London.

Collins, G. (1971) *Two Views of Kalagan Grammar*, Ph.D. dissertation, Department of Linguistics, Indiana University, Bloomington, Indiana.

Gildersleeve, B. (1895) *Latin Grammar*, 3rd edn. Macmillan, London.

Goodwin, G. (1894) *Greek Grammar*, Macmillan, London.

Keenan, E.L. (1972a) 'Semantically Based Grammar' *Linguistic Inquiry* 3, 4, 413-61.

—— (1972b) 'Relative Clause Formation in Malagasy (and some related and some not so related) Languages' in P.M. Peranteau, J.N. Levi, and G.C. Phares (eds.) *The Chicago Which Hunt*, pp. 169-90, Chicago Linguistic Society, Chicago, Illinois (1972).

Perrott, D.V. (1957) *Swahili*, Teach Yourself Books, English Universities Press, London.

Reid, L.A. *An Ivatan Syntax*, Oceanic Linguistics Special Publication No. 2, 1966, Pacific and Asiatic Linguistics Institute, University of Hawaii.

Tryon, D.T. (1968) 'Iai Grammar', *Pacific Linguistics* 8 (Series B) the Australian National University, Canberra.

Vanek, A. (1960) 'Pronominalisation Revisited', *Papers in Linguistics* 1, 3.

12 THE FUNCTIONAL PRINCIPLE: GENERALISING THE NOTION OF 'SUBJECT'

We argue that subjects of simplex sentences, *heads* of restrictive relative clauses, and *possessor phrases* of possessive constructions are logically similar in one basic respect. This similarity together with the Functional Principle below allows us to explain several generalisations which hold of these constructions across languages.[1]

1. Preliminary Terminology and the Functional Principle

A function f from a set A to a set B is an operation which associates with each element x of A a unique element $f(x)$ of B. Expressions of the form $f(x)$ are called *functional expressions* (FEs). They come in two parts: first, the functional symbol, e.g. 'f' which denotes a function and which, as I'm using the term, may be complex — not just a single symbol; and second, the *argument expression* e.g. 'x', which denotes an *argument* of the function, i.e. an object the function applies to. A FE $f(x)$ itself denotes the thing that the function f associates with the argument x. For example, in arithmetic 5^2 is a FE. The numeral '5' is the argument expression and denotes the number 5. The superscript ^{2} is the function symbol and denotes the squaring function. '5^2' itself denotes the number 25, since that is the number the squaring function associates with 5.

I shall refer to the process of understanding the reference of a FE as *evaluating the FE*. We don't know exactly what this involves psychologically, but it at least requires that we mentally identify the argument of the FE as well as the functions which apply to it. These identifications are subject to the two conditions below, which we call collectively

The Functional Principle (FP)
(i) The reference of the argument expression must be determinable *independently* of the meaning or reference of the function symbol.

(ii) Functions which apply to the argument however may vary with the choice of argument (and so need not be independent of it).

FP(i) merely says that e.g. to evaluate 5^2 we must be able to determine the referent of '5' regardless of whether we are going to square it, cube it, or whatever. FP(ii) is designed for complex functions. E.g. consider the function h which raises any number n to the power n-1. To evaluate h(3) we must apply the squaring function to 3. To evaluate h(4) we must apply the cubing function to 4, etc. Clearly the function we apply varies with the choice of argument of h.

2. Three Examples of Functional Expressions in Natural Language (NL)

We shall only consider in this paper FEs whose arguments are referential, that is, nominal in nature, (rather than e.g. verbal or sentential).

(i) *simplex (declarative) sentences.* The subject (phrase) is the argument expression and the predicate phrase denotes the function. It associates with the referents of the subject a sentence-meaning (say a truth value in a state of affairs). So to evaluate the truth of a simple sentence we must mentally identify the referent of the subject and then determine whether the predicate holds of it or not.

(ii) *restrictive relative clauses (RRCs)*. The head[2] NP is the argument expression and the restricting clause denotes the function. It applies to the set of objects denoted by the head to yield a subset of that set consisting of those members that the restricting clause is true of. So, to evaluate *men who Mary likes* we must mentally consider the set of men and then restrict that set to those members of which the sentence *Mary likes him* is true. Note: we only consider in this paper RRCs whose restricting clauses are simplex.

(iii) *possessive constructions* (specifically inalienable ones and 'abstract' ones, like *the inside of the bottle, the rest of the cake, the temperature of the air*, etc. Here the possessor (genitive) NP is the argument expression and the head NP represents the function (just the opposite function-argument relation exhibited by RRCs). To evaluate e.g. *the inside of the bottle* we must identify the referent of *the bottle* and then determine its inside. We do not in any sense first conceive of the set of all 'insides' and then pick the one which the bottle in question just happens to have.[3]

3. Some Generalisations Concerning Functional Expressions

3.1 NPs in Function Symbols Cannot Control the Pronominalisation of their Argument Expressions

If they could, then the reference of the argument expression would not be given independently of that of the function symbol. So Section 3.1 follows directly from FP(i). On the other hand, *argument NPs can usually control pronominalisation into function symbols.* This follows (loosely) from FP(ii), which states that the meaning of functions can depend on their arguments, though it doesn't state that the dependency can be exactly of the sort coded by pronominalisation in English.

Below we substantiate these claims for the three types of FEs we consider. Note that Section 3.1 holds regardless of the linear order of the function symbol and its argument. (An asterisk by a phrase means that it cannot be understood to have the cross reference stipulated by the matching indices.)

3.1.1 NPs in predicates cannot pronominalise their subjects — though they may precede them.

John$_i$ hit him self$_i$ *He$_i$/he-self$_i$ hit John$_i$
The men$_i$ insulted each other$_i$ *Each other$_i$ insulted the men$_i$

Malagasy
Namono tena$_i$ Rabe$_i$; *Namono an-dRabe$_i$ izy$_i$/ny tena-ny$_i$
killed   self Rabe   killed   Rabe he /the self-his
'Rabe killed himself'

Tzeltal (Penny Brown, personal communication)
la   s-mah s$_i$ -ba Ziak$_i$; *la ṡ-mah Ziak$_i$ s$_i$ -ba
past strike his-self Ziak   past strike Ziak his-self
'Ziak struck himself'

3.1.2 Heads of possessive constructions cannot pronominalise possessor NPs (though they dominate them, often precede them, and may command them).

*the inside$_i$ of $\left\{ \begin{array}{l} \text{it}_i \\ \text{itself}_i \end{array} \right\}$ *Malagasy*
*ny fahalehiben$_i'$-ny$_i$
the size$_i$ (of)-it$_i$

*his$_i$ lawyer$_i$
*a friend$_i$ of his$_i$ *ny naman$_i'$-   ny
the friend$_i$ (of)-his$_i$

John'$_i$s picture/analysis of himself$_i$
*his$_i$ picture/analysis of John$_i$

3.1.3 Heads of RRCs cannot be pronominalised by an NP in the restricting clause (though they often occur in the right of such clauses and can control pronominalisation into the restricting clause).

Hebrew
ha- ish$_i$ she- Miriam hikta oto$_i$;   *hu$_i$ she- Miriam hikta
the man$_i$ that Miriam hit   him$_i$ he$_i$ that Miriam hit
                                                    et   ha- ish$_i$
                                                    ACC the man$_i$

Japanese
Sono otoko$_i$-ga   Taro$_j$-o   tataita ; Taro$_j$-o tataita otoko$_i$
That man$_i$ SUBJ Taro$_j$ ACC hit   Taro$_j$ hit   man$_i$
'That man hit Taro'   'The man who hit Taro'

zibun$_i$-o tataita otoko$_i$;   *Taro$_i$-o tataita $\left\{ \begin{array}{l} \text{kare}_i\text{-} \\ \text{zibun}_i\text{-} \end{array} \right\}$
self$_i$ hit   man$_i$
'the man who hit himself'

                                              Taro$_i$ hit $\left\{ \begin{array}{l} \text{he}_i \\ \text{he}_i\text{-self} \end{array} \right\}$

*sono otoko$_i$-ga Taro-o tataita $\left\{ \begin{array}{l} \text{kare}_i\text{-} \\ \text{zibun}_i\text{-} \end{array} \right\}$

that   man$_i$ Taro   hit $\left\{ \begin{array}{l} \text{he}_i \\ \text{he}_i\text{-self} \end{array} \right\}$

'the man who hit Taro'

Note incidentally that in Japanese it is possible for the head of a RRC to be a controlled pronoun (Kuno 1973, 235); what is impossible is that the controller be within the restrictive clause.

Taro_i wa   kanemochi ka?   ;   Tokyo de hataraku kare_i wa
Taro_i TPC wealthy   QUEST   Tokyo in works   he_i   TPC
'Is Taro_i wealthy?'

totemo kanemochi da
very   wealthy   is
'(Yes) he_i who works in Tokyo
is very wealthy'

3.2 Quantified NPs in Argument Position can Generally have Wider Logical Scope than NPs in the Function Symbol

In fact, to say that A has wider scope than B is basically to say that a referent of B can be chosen in function of that for A but not vice versa — A's referent must be chosen independently. A standard example will make this clear.

3.2.1 Subjects can have wider scope than objects.
In a sentence like (1)

(1)   Every girl kissed some boy.

to say that *every girl* has wider scope than *some boy* is to say that (1) is true just in case no matter what girl we identify we can choose a boy (possibly different for different choices of girl) who she kissed. But this is just to say that the choice of subject referent is independent of anything else in the sentence while that of object referent can depend on that of the subject. This dependence is made explicit in (2b) which is logically equivalent to (2a), the standard logical representation of (1) on which *every girl* has wider scope.

(2)   a. $(\forall x)(\exists y)\, K(x,y)$ i.e. for each girl x there is a boy y such that x kissed y

      b. $(\exists f)\,(\forall x)\, K(x,f(x))$ i.e. there is a function f (from girls to boys) such that for every girl x, x kissed $f(x)$.

Note that if we want to force the reading of (1) on which *some boy* has wider scope Section 3.2 predicts that it should be sufficient to present that constituent as a subject. And since that is what PASSIVE does, Section 3.2 correctly predicts that PASSIVE changes the relative scope preferences in sentences like (1).

Note as well that the predictions made by Section 3.2 also seem independent of the linear order of subject and object NPs, as (3) supports, although the data are more problematic since, as Ioup (1973) has shown, many factors, most notably the lexical identity of the determiners, are needed to account for our judgements of relative scope.

(3)   *Malagasy*
       mamaky boky ny mpianatra rehetra
       read   book the student   all
       'All the students are reading a book' (possibly different in
                                                  each case)

3.2.2 Heads of RRCs can have wider scope than NPs in the restricting clause.   Thus *every girl who kissed some boy* most naturally specifies the set of girls such that for each one there is some boy she kissed. And *some boy who every girl kissed* specifies a single boy such that each girl kissed him. And again, the FP predicts that one way to force *some boy* to have wider scope in (1) would be to reorganise (1) so that *some boy* was the head of a restrictive relative clause. And indeed sentences like *There was some boy who every girl kissed* are often used for just this effect.

3.2.3 Universal NPs in possessor position can have wider scope than NPs in their heads.   Thus *a representative of every country attended the meeting* means (preferably) that every country was such that one of its representatives attended, and not that one individual who represented all the countries attended. So the referent of *representative* depends on that of *country*. The same is true in *every country's president attended*, which may require that each country have only one president, but still allows that as many presidents attended as there were countries. Similarly *the temperature of everyone in the ward was high* means that each person there had a high temperature, but not that they all had the same temperature.

4.

The examples of pronominalisation and relative scope that we have discussed are both cases where the meaning we assign to a function symbol depends on that we assign to the argument expression. Assuming that, other things being equal, *logically similar constructions are expressed in syntactically similar ways*, we might expect that the morphological shape of a function symbol could depend on the argument expression. And, in fact,

4.1 Function Symbols May Present a Morpheme Whose Form is Determined by the Noun Class of the Argument Expression

4.1.1 Predicates may 'agree' with subjects. A commonplace, though in many languages e.g. Swedish, Thai, Japanese it doesn't occur at all, and in many others e.g. Basque, Georgian, Chinook verbs agree with objects of various sorts as well.[4]

4.1.2 Heads of possessive constructions may 'agree' with possessor NPs. Less common than predicates agreeing with subjects, but still quite general, occurring e.g. in Turkish (Underhill 1972), Eskimo (Allen 1964), Arosi (Capell 1971), Fijian (Milner 1956), Dharawal (Wurm 1972), Quechua (Snow 1973), Zurich German (Henk van Riemsdijk, personal communication), Yurok (Robins 1958) and, restricted to pronouns, Welsh (Bowen and Jones 1960).

Turkish (Underhill 1972)		*Zurich German*	
Ahmed-in	shapka-sɨ	əm buəb zini muətər	
Ahmed-GEN hat	3SG	the boy his mother	
'Ahmed's hat'		'The boy's mother'	

Note in passing that in all the languages mentioned where heads agree with possessors the verb also normally agrees with its subject. We suggest then the following implicative universal: *If heads of possessive constructions agree with their possessors in a given language then verbs agree with subjects in that language.* This putative universal is not arbitrary. In many languages the subject agreement affixes on the verb *are* the bound forms of the possessive pronoun. This is the case in many Amerind languages e.g. Quechua (Snow 1973), Tojolabal (Furbee 1973), and Yurok (Robins 1958), as well as in Turkish (historically speaking, see Lewis 1967) and certain Caucasian languages e.g. Abaza (Allen 1964).

Abaza: d- l- pa- b   ;   d- l- sh' - d
        he-her-son-is   him-she-kill-ed

Possibly, but this is *only* a suggestion, in many NLs the verbs derive historically from possessive constructions plus a copula i.e. *John left* is *John's leaving is,* and the verbs retain the possessive agreement affixes even where they have later been lost on independent possessive constructions.

4.1.3 Restricting clauses of relatives 'agree' with heads.   That is, they present a morpheme coding noun class features of the head. These may appear as relative pronouns, but surface as personal pronouns in the position relativised in many NLs (e.g. Welsh, spoken Czech, Arabic, Gilbertese, Urhobo) and are presented simply as preverbal clitics in Bantu languages.

Hebrew   *Luganda*
ha- ish she- Miriam hikta oto   omusajja omukazi gwe -yakuba
the man that Miriam hit   him   man   woman   whom-hit
                                  'the man that the woman hit'

4.2 When Sentences are Nominalised the Subject May Become a Possessor NP

The possessor marks the independently referring part of FEs which are NPs. So if we convert a sentence to a NP and want to preserve the independent referring status of the subject it is natural to mark it in a way appropriate to NPs. Action nominalisations in English are characteristic: *John left* ⇒ *John's leaving (annoyed us).* Similar examples can be found in Turkish (Comrie 1974), Tagalog (Schachter and Otanes 1972), Quechua, Arosi (Capell 1971), Malagasy, Finnish, Mojave (Munro 1973), and Polish (Comrie 1974). Not all languages make such a change of course. E.g. action nominalisations in Tamil (Comrie 1974) retain the subject in the nominative and just mark the VP as being nominalised.

5.

We have largely restricted ourselves thus far to FEs in NL which are relatively simple. This is because the function-argument relations in complex structures are not trivial extensions of those in simple structures. For each type of complex structure the function-argument relations and hence the applicability of the FE must be determined independently. Below we shall illustrate this point by analysing in some detail the function-argument relations present in RRCs, the most complex of the FEs we consider. Several universal properties of RRCs will be explained in terms of the FE.

The head of a RRC, as we have argued, is the argument expression, and the restricting clause the function symbol. But the restricting clause is basically sentential in nature, and has its own function-argument structure, its subject being its argument, its predicate its function symbol. Further, since the restricting clause talks about the referents of the head NP, the head has a grammatical role (subject, object, etc.) in the restricting clause. E.g. in *men who like Mary* the head NP *men* is felt to be the subject of the restricting verb *like*, whereas in *men who Mary likes* it is object. Hence,

5.1   If the Head of a RRC Does Not Function as the Subject of the Restricting Clause then that Subject Must Refer Independently of the Head

This follows from the FP, given that the subject in question is the subject of a sentence in which the head NP functions as a non-subject. In particular note that if the subject is a pronoun it cannot be understood to be co-referential with the head.

*the man$_i$ that $\left\{ \begin{array}{l} \text{he}_i \\ \text{the man}_i \end{array} \right\}$ hit

Japanese
*kare$_i$-ga tataita otoko$_i$- ...
he$_i$ hit   man$_i$
'the man$_i$ that he$_i$ hit'

Basque (thanks to G. Brettschneider)
bere$_i$ burua jo zuan gizona$_i$
his$_i$ head hit had man$_i$.
'The man who hit himself'

*berak$_i$ jo zuan gizona$_i$
he$_i$ hit had man$_i$
'The man$_i$ that he$_i$ hit'

(Note that the Crossover Principle (Postal 1971) cannot explain either the Japanese or Basque data above. Japanese is an SOV language whose RRCs present the head on the right. So heads which function as objects of the restricting verb, as above, will not have crossed over the subject. And in Basque, equally an SOV language, the Crossover Principle is simply inapplicable since in the first relative clause above the head is subject of the restricting verb and so has crossed over the object. Yet in the Basque version of *the man that he hit* the facts of co-reference are the same as in English and Japanese.)

5.2 If the Head NP of a RRC Does Function as the Subject of the Restricting Clause then no Personal Pronoun will be Present in the Subject Position of the Restricting Clause

This prediction is surprisingly substantive, since a great many languages, as we have indicated, characteristically present personal pronouns in the position relativised. (See Keenan and Comrie 1972 and 1977 for a discussion of this in 20-odd languages.) Yet the one major position in which personal pronouns are not present is the subject position[5] of the main verb of the restricting clause.

> *Hebrew*: ha- isha$_i$ she- *hi$_i$ hikta et   ha- ish
>   the woman$_i$ that *she$_i$ hit   ACC the man
>   'The woman who hit the man'

This is explained by the FP since if such a pronoun were present it would be interpreted as being not necessarily co-referential with the head NP — just the opposite of the intended meaning.

5.3

No language has reflexive relative pronouns (where 'reflexive' here means co-referential with another NP in the same clause). That is, no language can say anything like *the man$_i$ whoself$_i$ {he$_i$/the man$_i$} saw*. This is basically because a relative pronoun, reflexive or otherwise, must co-refer to the head, and thus a reflexive relative pronoun would stipulate that the head NP was necessarily co-referential with a NP in the restricting clause other than the NP relativised — which cannot be since the head must be an independently referring expression. In fact, the following universal makes the case against reflexive relative pronouns even stronger: *Subjects universally control reflexivisation.* That is, in general a reflexive pronoun in a sentence can be understood to co-refer to the subject of that sentence. And in many languages e.g. German, Malagasy, Japanese, and (largely) Hindi (McGregor 1972) must be understood to refer to the subject. So a reflexive relative pronoun would in general mean that the head NP co-referred with the subject of the restricting clause. But both heads and subjects of restricting clauses (pronominal or otherwise) must be understood to refer independently of anything else in the RRC, including each other, and so cannot be stipulated as being co-referential.

5.4 Subjects are Universally the Easiest NP Positions to Relativise

Thus within languages it appears (Smith 1974) that children acquire the ability to understand RRCs whose heads function as the subject of the restricting clause before they acquire ones whose heads function as objects. And across languages we find that if a language has RRCs at all it has ones whose heads function as subjects of the restricting clause. And some languages, e.g. Malagasy, and Tagalog, have only such RRCs. The explanation of these facts is this: evaluating RRCs whose heads function as subjects of the restricting clause is psychologically simpler than evaluating ones whose heads function as non-subjects. For to evaluate a RRC we must in general determine the reference of two independently referring expressions: the head NP and the subject of the restricting clause. But in the special case where the head functions as the subject there is only one independent reference to make.

To put the same point differently, relativising on objects forces them to be independently referring expressions — a property they do not generally have. So object relativisation distorts our usual way of understanding sentential functional expressions. But relativising on subjects introduces no such distortion since subjects are already independently referring expressions.

6. Conclusions, Caveats, and Counterexamples

6.1 The Functional Principle and Primacy Relations

We want to stress here that we are *not* claiming that the FP alone can be used to determine all and only the correct predictions of cross reference and relative scope of NPs in surface. Such a determination is a complex function of several variables, of which the FP is one. But linear order and command are also needed. This need can be seen by considering cross reference in sentences with complex subjects. The data of relative acceptability in (4)-(6) justify the independent need for linear order as a primacy relation and possibly command as well. They further support a weakening of the FP along the following lines: *namely, to the extent that the identification of the reference of the argument expression depends on that of the function symbol the FE is unacceptable.* Thus the earlier cases we considered, and (4), indicate total dependence and hence total unacceptability. But (5) indicates only partial dependence. The sentence is still out in English, though possible in subordinate constructions and clearly not as bad as (4). Further its rendition in Malagasy, a subject final language, is perfectly acceptable — presumably due to the influence of *linear order.* And finally (6) is somewhat more acceptable yet (more frequently judged acceptable by linguists than non-linguists), indicating the need perhaps for *command* in this context as well.

Malagasy

(4)   **Heself$_i$ loves John$_i$ **Tia an-dRakoto$_i$ izy$_i$/ny tena-ny$_i$

(5)   *His$_i$ father looked at John$_i$ Nijery an-dRabe$_i$ ny rəi-ny$_i$

If his$_i$ father looks at John$_i$ again he'll scream

(6)   ??The man who loves her$_i$ didn't see Mary$_i$ Tsy nahita an'i Maria$_i$ ny lehilahy tia azy$_i$

6.2 The Relative Importance of the FP and other Primacy Relations is not Universal

Thus in certain Austronesian languages e.g. Maori, Samoan, and Tagalog many of the functions we usually associate with 'subject' are in fact shared by two or more NPs — 'subjects' and 'passive agents'. Our data indicate to us that in such languages primacy relations like linear order are more important than *subject of* in determining e.g. reflexivisation in simplex sentences. It is in general very difficult or impossible to get *any* backward pronominalisation in these languages, even though 'subjects' may sometimes follow objects. We are currently applying a checklist of 25 subject diagnostics to various languages to determine how concentrated or diffuse their 'subjects' are.

Notes

1. I wish to thank the Wenner-Grenn Foundation for Anthropological Research for having supported the research on subject-final languages reported herein.

2. By 'head NP' we mean whatever NP in surface specifies the domain of objects that the restricting function applies to. Thus the apparently headless relative clauses of Diegueño (Gorbet), Bambara (Bird 1966), and Hindi (Keenan and Comrie 1977) merely present in our sense the head NP inside the restricting clause. In many of these cases e.g. Bambara, Hindi, it is identifiable by its morphological marking, not by its position.

3. But this pattern of evaluation does seem more characteristic of alienable possession. *John's car* may well be evaluated in the same way as *the car which John possesses.* Many of the generalisations we make about possessive constructions hold regardless of which way we consider alienables. Note that as a reduced RRC, the possessor NP would represent the subject of the restricting clause, so its reference would be, correctly, predicted to be independent of that of the head.

4. Occasionally, in ergative languages, we find verbs agreeing with objects but not with subjects. This is so in Avar (Keenan and Comrie 1977), Mabuiag (Klokeid 1972) and Hindi in certain cases in the perfective (McGregor 1972).

5. Hausa (Schachter 1973), Yoruba, and Urhobo (a Kwa language related to Yoruba) would appear to be counterexamples of this claim. However, in Keenan and Comrie (1977) we argue that the subject pronoun present in the restricting clause is simply a verb agreement which co-occurs with full NP subjects in simplex sentences, and so does not count for our purposes as an independently determinable subject. That is obvious in Hausa but considerably more subtle in Yoruba. The Urhobo data bear some morphological similarities to that from Yoruba, but we do not know if arguments similar to those used for Yoruba will obtain.

References

Allen, W.S. (1964) 'Transitivity and Possession', *Language* 40, pp. 337-43, reprinted in F. Householder (ed.) *Syntactic Theory: 1 Structuralist*, Penguin Modern Linguistics Readings, 1972.

Bird, C. (1966) 'Relative Clauses in Bambara', *Journal of West African Languages* 5, 35-47.

Bowen, J.T. and T.J. Rhys Jones (1960) *Welsh*, Teach Yourself Books, English Universities Press, London.

Capell, A. (1971) 'Arosi Grammar', *Pacific Linguistics* 20 (Series B) The Australian National University, Canberra.

Comrie, B.C. (1974) 'Syntax of Action Nominals: A Cross Language Study', paper read at the Cambridge Universal Grammar Seminar.

Furbee, N.L. (1973) 'Subordinate Clauses in Tojolabal-Maya', in *You Take the High Node and I'll Take the Low Node*, Chicago Linguistic Society.

Gorbet, L. 'How to Tell a Head when You see One: Disambiguation in Diegueño Relative Clauses', unpublished paper.

Ioup, G. (1973) 'Some Universals of Quantifier Scope', paper presented at the Second Conference on New Ways of Analyzing Variation, Georgetown University, Washington, D.C.

Keenan, E.L. and B. Comrie (1972) 'Noun Phrase Accessibility and Universal Grammar', paper presented to the Winter Meetings of the Linguistic Society of America.

—— (1977) 'Noun Phrase Accessibility and Universal Grammar', *Linguistic Inquiry* 8, 1.

Klokeid, T.J. (1972) 'Relative Clauses in Mabuiag', unpublished paper, MIT, Cambridge, Massachusetts.

Kuno, S. (1973) *The Structure of the Japanese Language*, MIT Press, Cambridge, Massachusetts.

Lewis, G.L. (1967) *Turkish Grammar*, Clarendon Press, Oxford.

McGregor, R.S. (1972) *Outline of Hindi Grammar*, Clarendon Press, Oxford.

Milner, G. (1956) *Fijian Grammar*, Government Press of Fiji, Fiji.

Munro, P. (1973) 'Nominalisation and Plurality in Mojave' in *You Take the High Node and I'll Take the Low Node*, Chicago Linguistic Society.

Postal, P. (1971) *Crossover Phenomena*, Holt, Rinehart and Winston, New York.

Robins, R.H. (1958) *The Yurok Language*, University of California Press, Berkeley.

Schachter, P. (1973) Focus and Relativisation, *Language* 49, 19-46.

—— and Otanes (1972) *Tagalog Reference Grammar*, University of California Press, Berkeley.

Snow, C.T. (1973) 'Equi-NP Deletion and Reflexivisation in Quechua: Evidence for the Syntactic Structure of Complements', paper read at the Linguistic Society of America Winter Meeting.

Underhill, R. (1972) 'Turkish Participles', *Linguistic Inquiry*, 3, 1.

Wurm, S.A. (1972) *Languages of Australia and Tasmania*, Mouton, The Hague.

13 ON SURFACE FORM AND LOGICAL FORM

The body of this chapter, Sections 2, 3 and 4 presents two quite general correlations between the surface forms (SFs) of natural languages and their logical forms (LFs). Section 1 discusses briefly the nature of SFs and LFs, and Section 5 assesses the significance for linguistic theory of establishing relations between SFs and LFs.

1 The Nature of SFs and LFs

I will assume a SF (= a surface structure) can be represented by a labelled tree (phrase marker) of the sort usual in generative grammar. Subtrees of a tree represent constituents of the SF and are themselves SFs (since they are also labelled trees). The labels on the nodes of a tree represent the grammatical categories and subcategories of expressions of the language.

It is worth emphasising that the SFs of a language are defined by a complex set of rules which may be empirically validated (judged *descriptively* adequate) according to (i) the phonologically interpreted SFs they define are judged grammatical (the soundness criterion) and (ii) according as all the forms speakers judge grammatical are in fact defined (generated) by the rules (the completeness criterion). In addition a set of rules may be judged *explanatorily* adequate according as it is useful in explaining other facts about the language, such as that children learn languages quickly on the basis of limited exposure.

Consequently there can be no simple direct argument concerning the correctness of a particular assignment of SF to a particular expression of a language. We can only assess the descriptive and explanatory adequacy of the entire set of rules, and it is this set which determines assignments of SFs in particular cases. Further, as we modify the rules to make them descriptively more adequate our assignments of SF will change (as the history of generative grammar amply demonstrates).

The nonobvious nature of structure assignment is something

linguistic theories share with all scientific theories. There is for example nothing obvious, or given, or natural, about the atomic structure which physical theories assign to oxygen. Our representations here are part of a theory which assigns structures to many compounds and elements and whose correctness is determined by its predictions of the chemical and subatomic properties of these elements and compounds. Further, our assignment of structure in particular cases has undergone massive changes over time as our understanding of the chemical and subatomic properties has grown.

What holds of SFs and atomic forms also holds of LFs. Thus given a set of expressions of a language (e.g. English, elementary arithmetic, etc.) a logical theory defines a set of LFs (logical structures) whose descriptive adequacy is determined by the correct predictions they make concerning the logical properties of the expressions of the language. For example it is a logical property of (1) that is entails (logically implies) (3), whereas (2) does not have this property.

(1)   Both John and Mary can swim.
(2)   Either John or Mary can swim.
(3)   Mary can swim.

(To say that a sentence A entails a sentence B is just to say, informally, that in any state of affairs in which A is true, B is true. That is, whenever the world is the way A says it is, it is also the way B says it is.)

Furthermore, logical theories for a natural language can also be assessed as more or less explanatorily adequate according as the set of LFs the theory defines is useful in the explanation of other properties of the language. For example, in *Logical types for natural language* (Keenan and Faltz 1978, henceforth *Logical types*) it is argued on several different grounds that the LFs that theory provides are explanatorily more adequate (in addition to being descriptively more adequate) than those provided in 'The proper treatment of quantification in ordinary English' (Montague 1973). We argue for example that our LFs make fewer demands on the logical competence of speakers (and hence learners) of the language.

As with SFs then there is nothing obvious or given about the assignment of LF to a particular expression of a language. The assignment depends on the descriptive and explanatory adequacy of the logical theory which defines the set of LFs. And as with SFs, as we modify our logical theories for a natural language in the direction of increasing descriptive adequacy, the assignment of LFs to expressions of the language will change. For example, a purely sentential logic for English is not rich enough to show that the (a) sentences below entail the corresponding (b) sentences:

(4) a. All men are mortal and Socrates is a man.
     b. Socrates is mortal.
(5) a. All horses are animals.
     b. All heads of horses are heads of animals.

First order logics, which distinguish a predicate argument structure in simple formulas and which allow quantification over arguments, can represent the entailment relations given above. And recent work in natural logic, such as Montague Grammar generally (cf. Partee 1976) and *Logical types* distinguishes more structure than the classically-given first order predicate calculus (CL) and is descriptively more adequate for English than is CL. (Richness of logical structure does not necessarily correlate with being a higher than first order logic. See Section 5 for discussion.)

In addition to the theoretical and methodological properties which scientific theories in general share, syntactic theories and logical theories have some additional properties in common. Namely the structures which both define are representable by labelled trees. That is, they are linguistic objects, having a constituent structure, etc. It thus makes sense to ask to what extent the SF a syntactic theory assigns to an English expression corresponds or 'looks like' the LFs assigned to that expression by a logical theory. Is there for example a one-to-one correspondence between the constituents of the SF and those of its LFs? Do constituents of different grammatical categories correspond to logical constituents of different logical categories? And so on.

Answers to these questions depend of course on the exact nature of the SFs and the LFs the two theories define. Consider for example the English SF in (6).

(6)

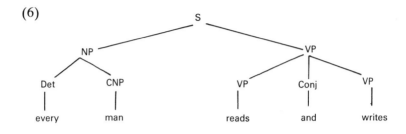

The example is for illustrative purposes and does not for example represent the nonsegmented Auxiliary or the verb agreements. Further we do not insist on the label CNP, *common noun phrase*, but we do insist that *every man* and *man* in (6) be assigned different category labels, a distinction recognised both by traditional grammar and X-bar notation. We shall henceforth for clarity refer to expressions like *student, fat student,* etc., as CNPs and expressions like *every student, a student, John, he,* etc. as DNPs, determined noun phrases.

A plausible LF for (6) in CL would be:

(7)

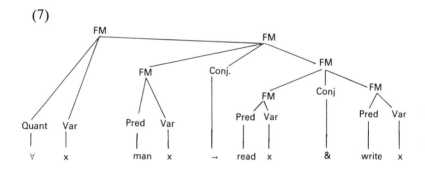

Clearly the correspondence between (7) and (6) is none too good. (7) for example contains five properly embedded formulas (FMs), the category which corresponds to Sentence, whereas (6) has no properly embedded sentences. Further the category distinction in English between CNP and VP is lost in CL, both being represented as one-place Predicate symbols.

By contrast the LF for (6) given in *Logical types* is:

(8)

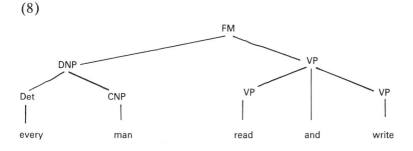

Obviously the correspondence between constituent structures is close to one-to-one here, and all the category distinctions in English are preserved in the LF. *Logical types* does not represent Auxiliaries or verb agreements however and further the trees are unoriented. That is, left-to-right order is not represented in (8). (8) is in fact a set of two expressions, the DNP *every man* and the VP *read and write*. The DNP is itself a set of two expressions whose members are *every* and *man,* and the VP is a set of three expressions: *read, and,* and *write.*

On the other hand, (9) would be, if I am not mistaken, a LF assigned to (6) in Montague Grammar. (I have used where possible 'standard' names for categories rather than those actually used in MG.)

(9)

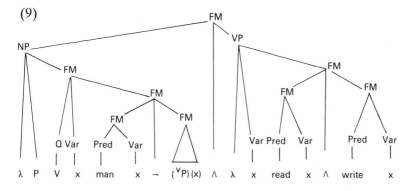

Clearly the correspondence here is less good than in CL. Not only do we lose the distinction between CNP and verb but (9) presents seven properly embedded formulas.

Given a set of SFs and a set of LFs for a natural language we may now say that a property P defined on the SFs *corresponds* to a property P′ defined on the LFs just in case a SF has P iff some (all) of its LFs have P′. And in general SFs will correspond to LFs to the extent that their properties correspond. Further, this notion of correspondence can be naturally generalised in several ways. We may replace P and P′ by n-place relations R and R′ and we may allow the arguments of R and R′ to be not simply SFs and LFs themselves but sets of SFs and LFs.

To support our claim that in general there is a significant correspondence between the SFs for a natural language and their LFs we shall consider here two relations defined in SFs, the *agreement* relation and the *left-to-right order* relation, and argue that in a large class of syntactically specifiable contexts these relations do correspond to relations defined in LFs.

2 The Agreement Relation

We observe across a wide range of languages that certain constituents of SFs 'agree' with certain others. For example in a SF for a sentence consisting of a VP and a DNP (regardless of their relative order) the VP may agree with the DNP. That is, a given expression of the VP will vary in form according as expressions for the DNP are drawn from different gender classes and have different numbers. In the same sense we find that transitive verbs (TVs) and in fact transitive verb phrases (TVPs) sometimes agree with their DNP objects (the DNP they combine with in whatever way to form a VP), though this agreement is less common than VP agreement with subjects. Another common case is that of adjective, and more generally adjective phrase (AP) agreement with their CNP 'heads'.

But we don't expect that just any constituent of a SF may agree with any other. It is then an interesting problem in Universal Grammar to specify the pairs of SFs < A,B > such that A may agree with B in a syntactic structure E. (By 'may agree' I mean that there are possible human languages in which they do agree.)

To define the problem somewhat more precisely, let us consider here a *syntactic structure* (and so in particular a SF) to be a labelled tree of the usual sort *less* the terminal symbols, that is, less the actual expressions of the language. We may then say of two expressions in a language that they have, or *express*, a same SF. Arguably for example both *some tall man* and *every woman* express (10a), though only *some tall man* expresses (10b).

(10) a.   b.

We may now define:

(11) Given A and B distinct constituents of a syntactic structure E
in a language L, A agrees with B iff the form of expressions
of A varies with the choice of expressions of B.

(To say that A and B are *distinct* is to say that neither is a sub-
constituent of the other.) And our problem may now be stated
thus:

(12) For which choices of E, A, and B as above is it the case that
there exist languages in which A agrees with B?

A reasonable starting point is the common cases of agreement
cited above: VPs may agree with their DNP subjects; TVPs with
their DNP objects; and APs with their CNP heads. Do these cases
have anything in common? I think so. Namely, there is a sense in
which how we semantically interpret the item which agrees varies
with how we interpret the item it agrees with. This claim is not
obvious and will be justified below. Specifically, let us consider the
Meaning-Form Dependency Principle as a first attempt to characterise the class of possible agreement phenomena.

The Meaning-Form Dependency Principle (MFDP)

Given A and B distinct constituents of a syntactic structure E,
A may agree with B iff the semantic interpretation of
expressions of A varies with the semantic interpretation of
expressions of B in the interpretation of E.

Loosely, the form of As varies with that of Bs just in case the interpretation of As varies with that of Bs. Which is to say that a surface relation holds of A,B pairs just in case a certain semantic relation holds between their interpretations. And this is just the kind of correspondence we are looking for, although the MFDP does not specifically mention a relation defined in LFs to which the agreement relation in SFs corresponds. We will state such a relation shortly, but as it is the MFDP which gives the intuition behind the principle, let us first see what justification there is for it.

Consider first the case of Adjective Phrases. If the principle is correct it should be the case that how we interpret modifying adjectives varies with the interpretation of the CNP they modify. And this is in fact the case. Consider for example an ordinary adjective like *flat*. In expressions like *a flat road, a flat table*, etc. *flat* means something like 'without bumps or depressions'. And this in general seems to be the interpretation of *flat* when the CNP it modifies refers to a class of objects with extended surfaces. But if the CNP refers to a normally tasty liquid, as in *flat beer/ champagne* then *flat* means something like 'lacking its normal taste, having lost its "zip"'. And if the CNP refers to a class of objects which, in their usable state, are inflated with a gas of some sort, as in *a flat tyre/balloon* then *flat* means something like 'deflated'. And if the CNP refers to singing or voice quality, as in *a flat voice, flat sopranos*, then *flat* means something like 'too low in pitch'. In short, our interpretation of *flat* is adjusted to, or varies with, the kind of thing we are predicating it of.

And this is commonly the case for common adjectives. Thus *strong* tables or fortresses are ones which can *withstand* much force, whereas strong wrestlers or weightlifters are ones that can *exert* much force; and strong tea or tobacco are substances which *produce a marked effect* on those who ingest them. Similarly *solid* buildings or tables are basically strong ones; but solid bars or cubes are ones which are not hollow, solid gold or silver are substances of a high degree of chemical purity, and solid lines or rows of buildings are ones without a break.

We may infer then that how we interpret modifying adjectives, and thus APs in general, varies according to the meaning of the CNP they modify.

Analogous claims hold for basic transitive verbs. Consider for example *cut*. If its object is (roughly) an animal or a largish body part of an animal, *cut* means something like 'to make an incision in the surface of'. Note that the integrity of the object cut is understood to be preserved. A finger which has been cut is still a finger, and can be cut again. Thus *cut* when applied to animals or body parts does not imply cutting all the way through. Nor does it imply intentionality or a purpose on the part of the agent. I may cut John either accidentally or on purpose, and in each case the adverbial phrases *accidentally, on purpose* adds information not present in the meaning of *cut* itself. On the other hand, if the object of *cut* is a prepared foodstuff, as in *to cut a cake, the roast, cut* is now interpreted as something like 'to divide into portions for the purpose of serving'. So the action *cut* specifies in these cases is an intentional or purposive one. Further, the integrity of the object cut is seriously affected and normally destroyed as we do now cut all the way through. On the other hand, if the object of *cut* refers to the kind of object consisting of many uniformly elongated objects, as in *to cut the lawn, your hair, one's fingernails, cut* is interpreted to mean something like 'trim'. In distinction to the first sense of *cut* above (cut a person), we do cut all the way through in that the parts of the whole are cut off. And in distinction to the second sense above (cut the cake) we do preserve the integrity of the whole. Once we have cut the lawn there is still a lawn there. And further, some notion of purpose is implied. We cut the lawn or our hair to make them more regular, pretty, or something like that.

Further, if the object of *cut* is a concrete mass noun, as in *to cut alcohol* or *cut heroin, cut* means something like 'diminish the potency of by admixing a physically comparable substance'. Thus we may cut whisky with water, marijuana with tea, etc. No notion of making an incision is present in any sense in this interpretation of *cut*. And if the object of *cut* is an abstract one of certain sorts, as in *to cut working hours/production quotas/prices, cut* means something like 'to decrease the value of along a numerically continuous dimension' (the dimension in question of course is one appropriate to the nature of the object cut). And matters are still more varied. Thus *to cut a class* or *a meeting* means to not attend when supposed to; *to cut a path* (through a field) or *a tunnel* (through a mountain) means to create a path or a tunnel by cutting something else and removing it; *to cut a film* or *a dissertation proposal* means to eliminate parts of it (destroying integrity) and put the result back together again (restoring integrity) yielding a shorter and presumably better work (notion of purpose involved).

In short then, the action we interpret *cut* as specifying is one appropriate to the object affected. And what holds of *cut* here holds as well of other common transitive verbs. To *drive cars* or *buses* is a different action from driving *cattle* or *sheep*; and both actions are different from driving *a motor* or *a generator*. *To drill* means something different in *to drill recruits* than in *to drill metal,* etc. Thus transitive verbs, and so transitive verb phrases in general, vary in their interpretation with the interpretation of the object affected.

Finally, intransitive verbs, and so VPs in general, behave similarly. Thus to say of an animal that it *is running* is to say both that the animal is moving its parts (internal movement) and that it is changing location however momentarily relative to other things (external movement). But to say that a watch or a car motor is running is at best only to make a claim concerning internal movement; no external movement is implied. If you are running with your watch it does not follow that your watch is running. And to say that your nose or the tap is running implies neither internal nor external movement on the part of the nose or the tap. Rather it implies that liquid, of a sort appropriate to the referent of the subject phrase, is moving out of that referent. And to say of a play or an exhibition that it is still running is to say that it is still available for public enjoyment, with no implication of physical movement at all. In short, how we interpret *run* in a context 'DNP is still running' depends on what sort of object the DNP refers to.

Note that the dependency here is clearly semantic. If we say *it is still running* how we interpret the verb depends on what *it* refers to. And if I ask you to *cut them* the action I'm asking you to perform is different according as *them* refers to production quotas or salamis. And the interpretation of flat in *a flat one* or *flat ones* depends on the class of item referred to by *one* or *ones*.

It does appear then that the MFDP holds for the common cases of agreement considered. But many questions concerning this dependency still need to be answered. At what level of linguistic description should this meaning dependency be represented? Semantic? Pragmatic? (We have remained non-committal on this point.) Does the same sort of form-meaning dependency obtain for other cases of agreement phenomena? And is there any correlation between what varies in meaning with what, and the logical structures assigned to agreement pairs?

Let us consider the last question first. Within Classical Logic there seems no complete description of the agreement pairs (VP and NP, TVP and NP, AP and CNP). Simple VPs correspond to one-place predicate symbols, and a limited class of DNPs, such as proper nouns, corresponds approximately to individual constants (0-place function symbols), so we may consider that simple cases of [$_S$DNP, VP] structures correspond to atomic formulas, in which, semantically, the VP is interpreted as a function taking the DNP interpretation as an argument. But the correspondence breaks down when more complex DNPs in English are considered. Thus *every man is running* does not correspond to a formula with a function-argument structure even grossly isomorphic to that of *John is running*. The two cases may be compared as follows:

(13) a. John is running.
     b. $R(j)$
(14) a. Every man is running.
     b. $(\forall x)(M(x) \rightarrow R(x))$

In fact, nothing in (14) corresponds to (interprets) the English DNP *every man* at all.

Transitive verbs correspond somewhat to two-place predicate symbols in CL, but a VP in English consisting of a transitive verb plus object does not correspond to any logical category in CL. On the other hand, it is easy to reformulate CL without changing the entailments of any of the formulas in such a way that transitive verbs do correspond to something which combines with a simple DNP to form a VP. A classical two-place predicate is semantically interpreted as a function U^2, the set of ordered pairs in U, the universe of discourse (i.e. the entities which exist in that state of affairs) into the set of truth values, represented as 0 (false) and 1 (true). Given such a function f, there is a unique other function g which maps members of U onto VP meanings, that is functions from U into $\{0,1\}$ such that for all x,y in U, $(g(x))(y) = f(y,x)$. So CL could be trivially reformulated so that, for a very simple class of DNPs, transitive verbs in English would correspond to functions taking DNP meanings as arguments, and thus, for this limited class of DNPs, there would be a similarity between VP and TVP representations in CL. Namely, both would be functions taking DNP meanings as arrangements.

But when the AP,CNP pairs are considered CL has nothing to offer us. Expressions like *flat road* are not directly assigned any logical category. Nor is there anything in CL equivalent to a modifying adjective. The best translation in CL of (15) below would be (16).

(15) Every happy man is laughing.
(16) $(\forall x)$ $(man(x)$ & $happy(x) \longrightarrow laugh(x))$

So the correspondents of 'happy' and 'man' do not form a logical constituent, and are in fact of the same logical category (one-place predicate), and that category is the same as that for simple VPs (*laugh*).

Montague Grammar might appear to offer a more promising set of logical structures since at least the formal English (which is 'translated' into the formulas of an intensional logic and only then interpreted) does have categories of AP and CNP. However, even ignoring the fact that the distinction between CNP and VP does not survive the translation into the set of logical structures, I can still find no basis for a similarity between the three agreement pairs we have considered. It is the case that APs and CNPs form logical constituents, and the APs are interpreted as functions taking CNP meanings as arguments. And it is also the case that TVPs and DNPs form a constituent in the logic and TVPs are interpreted as functions taking DNP meanings as arguments. So for these cases we can say that that English item which shows agreement is in each case interpreted as a function taking an argument the (interpretation of the) item it agrees with. But the similarity breaks down when the NP,VP pairs are considered. For here, while such pairs are a logical constituent (formulas), it is not the case that the agreeing item, the VP, is interpreted as a function taking as argument the item it agrees with. Rather the DNP is interpreted as a function taking the VP meanings as arguments.

On the other hand, in *Logical types* there is a uniform function-argument assignment. VPs are interpreted as functions of their DNP Subjects, TVPs as functions of their DNP objects, and APs as functions on their CNP arguments. Further, the function-argument assignment holds regardless of whether the NPs in question are simple ones like proper nouns, or complex ones like *every flat road*. Thus the LF assigned in that theory to *every handsome man loves a beautiful woman* is:

(17)

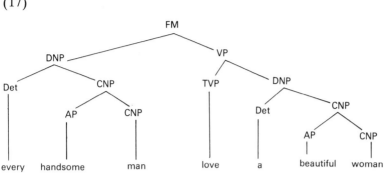

We should stress here that (17) is itself a LF in *Logical types*; that is, it is directly interpreted, not mapped onto a formula in some intensional logic, that is a different structure, and then interpreted.

Assuming the LFs defined in *Logical types* we may directly characterise the correspondence between agreement pairs and LFs by:

The Functional Dependency Principle (FDP)

Given A and B distinct constituents of a SF, E, A may agree with B iff in the LF of expressions of E, the LFs of expressions of A are interpreted as *functions* taking the interpretations of expressions of B as arguments.

In such cases we shall refer to expressions of A as *functional expressions* and expressions of B as *argument expressions.*

Further, as *Logical types* defines a rather large number of function-argument structures involving DNPs and CNPs, we have at hand a ready set of predictions concerning possible agreement phenomena involving these categories. Let us note the following assignments given in *Logical types*:

(18) Functions taking DNP arguments:
    a. VPs
    b, TVPs
    c. Possessive Phrases (e.g. *the father of, 's father*)
(19) Functions taking CNP arguments:
    a. APs
    b. Relative Clauses

c.   Articles (*the, a*)
d.   Quantifiers (*every, no*)
e.   Numerals (*one, two,* etc.)

Considering the second category first, the FDP predicts the existence of languages in which APs agree with CNPs, which we have already seen to be correct. Second, it predicts agreement between Relative Clauses and their CNP heads. This is also correct, for recall the definition of agreement: A agrees with B iff the form of expressions of A varies with the choice of expressions of B. Now a great many languages form Relatives by presenting in the position relativised a personal pronoun agreeing in noun class with the CNP head of the Relative, as illustrated below from Hebrew:

(20) a.   *ha- ish* [*she- natati* <u>*lo*</u>   *et   ha- sefer*]
                        RC
          the-man that-I+gave to-him DO the-book
          'the man that I gave the book to'
     b.   *ha- isha* [*she- natati* <u>*la*</u>   *et   ha- sefer*]
                         RC
          the-woman that I+gave to-her DO the book

Clearly the forms of the Relative Clauses vary (one contains *lo* where the other has *la*) according to the gender class of the head CNP. Similarly languages which use special forms of pronouns in Relatives, so-called relative pronouns, often present cases where the relative pronoun agrees in gender and number with the head CNP, as thus the form of the entire RC varies with certain choices of expressions for the CNP. So the prediction is verified. Note however, that the FDP does not predict in this case which part of the Relative Clause will vary in form but only that the Relative Clause as a whole will vary.

Third, the FDP predicts that articles may agree with the CNPs they are functions on, and such cases (e.g. Romance) are well known, though perhaps less widespread than the accessibility of confirming cases would indicate.

Fourth, the FDP predicts that quantifier words like *every* and *no* will agree with the CNPs they combine with, and again confirming instances are easy to come by:

(21) a. *tous les hommes*   b. *toutes les femmes*
    all   the men   all   the women

And finally, the FDP predicts that Numerals may agree with their CNPs. Again this is correct; though it is very common that the internal structure of numerical DNPs is complex and nonuniform from one number to another. Nonetheless Russian provides a confirming instance. The numeral 'one' has four forms, one plural form (*odnix*, used before inherently plural CNPs of the sort *pants*, *scissors*, etc.) and three singular forms, one for each of the three genders of CNPs. The amount of agreement decreases rapidly as we consider the higher numbers, but still 'two' in the singular makes at least two gender distinctions.

Recalling now that the motivation for the function-argument assignment given in *Logical types* (or any logic) is semantic — that is, given that function-argument assignment we get many right and few wrong predictions of entailments, the fact that all the predictions in (19) are correct is rather striking confirmation of the FDP.

Consider now (18). The FDP predicts, correctly as we have already seen, that VPs may agree with their Subjects, and TVPs with their Objects. Further, within the logic, heads of possessive constructions are assigned a logical category and are semantically interpreted as functions on the Possessor NP. E.g. *John's father* and *the father of John* would be assigned the following LFs:

(22) a.   b.

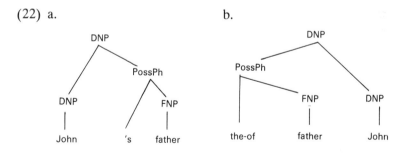

(FNP abbreviates Function Noun Phrase, a primitive category in the system.)

And the FDP predicts, correctly that heads of possessive constructions, Possessive Phrases in *Logical types*, may agree with their possessors. This in fact is massively common in Amerindian languages, and is evidenced in many others as well, e.g. Turkish, Arosi (Melanesian), Daga (New Guinea), and Hebrew. (23) from Hebrew is illustrative:

(23) a. *beit-o   shel Dan*   b. *beit-a   shel Miriam*
         house-his of Dan   house-her of Mary
         'Dan's house'   'Mary's house'

It is perhaps fair to mention here that while the form of possessive agreement cited above is very widespread — my impression is that it is as widespread as is adjective agreement with CNPs and TVP agreement with their NP Objects — there are some limited cases in which the agreement goes the other way. One obvious case is the pronominal possessives in Romance. Thus we have *son frère* 'his/her brother' and *sa soeur* 'his/her sister'. The possessives here behave in fact like adjectives as regards agreement and are traditionally called possessive adjectives. The paradigm however is limited to the pronominal possessive forms. The productive possessive construction shows no such agreement, e.g. *le frère de Jean* 'the brother of John' and *le frère de Marie* 'the brother of Mary'. A somewhat larger class of 'wrong' agreements can be found in certain Slavic languages where a DNP with a possessor reading may, in certain cases, be constructed with an adjectival ending and thus agree with the head CNP as an adjective would. Comrie and Thompson (1978) cite the following from Czech:

(24) a. *vědcova kniha*   b. ?*kniha vědce*
         scientist-f.sg. book   book scientist-gen
         'the scientist's book'"   'the scientist's book'

Note that (24a) clearly has a possessive meaning, not something like 'a scientific book' (which would be *vědecká kniha*). And contra the FDP the logical possessor shows agreement with the CNP head. Again however the productivity of this paradigm is limited, in fact listable (though the list would be much longer than for the Romance cases cited above). Thus only definite, singular, unmodified possessors can be construed as adjectival. To say *the old scientist's book, the (many) scientists' books,* or *a scientist's book* we could only use the 'proper' possessive construction illustrated in (24b). Bob Rothstein (personal communication) points out however that at least certain proper noun possessives, as

Newton's theories, may also be constructed with the possessor as an adjective.

It would seem then that to maintain the FDP as stated we should weaken it to allow for listable exceptions. And this is not unreasonable. If we establish a correlation between the most productively generated SFs and their LFs we have surely established a correlation between SF and LF in general. Exceptions to the general pattern will have to be learned as special cases. Indeed for other types of correlation between SF and LF, such as some version of the Fregean Principle (meaning of the whole is a function of the meaning of the parts) various types of fixed expressions — proverbs, idioms, etc. — will clearly be listable exceptions.

Finally, FDP predicts that prepositions may agree with the NPs they govern, although the LFs in *Logical types* are less clear here, as Prepositions have multiple categories.[1] Thus in addition to combining with DNPs to form various classes of modifiers they may also combine directly with VPs and TVPs to extend the class of DNP arguments they take. Thus in *Logical types* (*sleep, in*) is a derived TVP requiring a DNP object to make a VP again (so [(*sleep, in*), (*the bed*)] is a derived VP). Further, cases of Preposition agreement with DNPs are harder to find across languages, but some cases do exist. (25) from Arosi (Melanesian; see Capell 1971 for supporting details) is one example:

(25)   'ini- a mada
      with-it club
      'with a club (he hit me)'

Worth noting here is that not all prepositions show agreement with the NP they govern, and those that do, show an agreement paradigm similar (perhaps identical) with that that transitive verbs show with their Objects. However, given the similarity in function-argument structure between transitive verbs and their Objects and prepositions and their Objects, it is perhaps not surprising that transitive verbs can historically become reduced to function as dependent forms, i.e. Prepositions. Note as well that another very common source for prepositions is possessive constructions. Thus for example *behind it* will in many languages be something like *at its back*. If the language were such as to have agreement between possessive heads and Possessors we could expect that prepositions so derived historically might show such agreement as well. Something like this may be the explanation for the postposition agreement in Daga (New Guinea; see Murane 1974 for details). In any event there are several clear cases of postpositions agreeing with their DNP Objects, and the agreement suffixes are the same as the intimate possessive agreements with possessors:

(26) *ge orup ame ena- m   ak*
      you fellow that with-their go+2sg+imp
      '(You) Go with those fellows'

Thus for all the function-argument structures in *Logical types* which concern either DNPs or CNPs, the Functional Dependency Principle correctly predicts the possibility of agreement. And as these nine cases represent a reasonably large sample of the possible agreement phenomena known to me, I feel that even if the FDP were restricted to hold for just these cases it would still represent a very significant correlation between SF and LF and thus support the general claim that there exist correspondences between SF and LF. On the other hand, a large number of questions concerning the FDP remain. In Section 2 we raise some of these questions.

3 Refining the FDP

We have replaced the original intuition expressed in the Meaning-Form Dependency Principle by one, the FDP, stated in formal logical terms. It is reasonable to ask how well the original intuition behind the MDFP carries over to the larger range of cases. The results here are mixed and interesting, and suggest some additional correlations between SF and LF.

Consider first the Possessive Phrases. Do the heads of such constructions vary in their interpretation with the reference of the Possessor in anything like the same way in which say *flat* varies with the interpretation of the CNP it modifies or *cut* varies with the semantic nature of its Object? Here there does seem to be some variation, though it is not clear that it is of exactly the same sort as the very idiosyncratic variation exhibited by *flat, cut,* and *run*. Thus consider a PossPh like *the middle of.* If its argument, the Possessor, denotes an activity, such as the performance of a play or a radio program, then *the middle of* picks out that part of the performance which occurs at a moment, or period, of time midway between the beginning and the end of the activity. Analogous claims hold for arguments that denote specified periods of time, such as *day, night,* etc. But if the argument refers to a concrete physical object *the middle of* has different senses. Thus the middle of the Earth is a physical point, or region, more or less equidistant from all the points on the surface of the Earth. So *the middle of* may have a temporal or physical interpretation according to the nature of the Possessor — a fact which is well known. But this variation is not wholly similar to that evidence for *flat, cut,* etc. That is, the same variation shows up for a few other such expressions, e.g. *the end of, the length of,* whereas I don't expect (but haven't in fact checked) that any other adjective besides *flat* would have exactly the four senses attributed to it earlier. On the other hand, *the middle of* does show further different senses which do seem more idiosyncratic when applied to different sorts of physical objects. Thus if the Possessor refers to something conceived of in two dimensions, *the middle of* may pick out a *point* at the geometrical centre, as in *the middle of the stage* or *the middle of a sheet of paper.* But if the two dimensional object is notably elongated, *the middle of* picks out a *line* more or less equidistant from the edges, as in *the middle of the road.* Further, if the object is conceived of in three dimensions, then differences in the interpretation of *the middle of* show up according as the object is solid or one habitually entered by human beings. Thus *the middle of the Earth (the Sun) consists of molten iron (Helium atoms)* means that the space at the geometrical centre is filled with molten iron, etc. But *John is sitting in the middle of the room* does not suggest that John is suspended in midair. Rather the middle of the room defines a region of space with reference to the centre of the (two dimensional) floor.

In addition, many overtly possessive constructions lend themselves easily to 'metaphorical' interpretations of the head (or PossPh). Thus one might argue that *the head of* in *the head of the animal* is interpreted literally, and picks out a certain body part of the animal. But *the head of the table* or *the head of the department* forces *the head of* to be understood in a nonliteral (metaphorical) way. This sort of metaphor is what Reinhart (1976) calls nonpoetic metaphor and is characterised, in our terms, by a reinterpretation of the function expression given a 'nonordinary' argument expression (the Possessor). But whether we take one sense as basic and the others as metaphorical or not, it is still the case that it is the function expression which is subject to various interpretations depending on the (literal) meaning of the argument expression.

In addition we might note that nominalisations of various other sorts of functional expressions (adjectives, VPs, etc.) commonly take the form of possessive constructions, and some, but not all, of the sense variation in the original may be preserved under the nominalisation. Thus *the strength of* has a similar range of senses to *strong* (person, fortress, tobacco, etc.). On the other hand, *the solidity of* loses some of its senses. Thus while *the solidity of the chair* presumably does refer to its capacity for withstanding force, *the solidity of the bar* or *the cube* is unclear in meaning, referring most likely in my opinion not to its quality of being not hollow but to its capacity of withstanding force. And the solidity of the gold or silver cannot be used to refer to its chemical purity but must refer to its capacity to withstand force, if indeed it refers to anything at all. Nor can *the solidity of a line* or *a row of buildings* naturally refer to their quality of being 'perceptually unbroken'. Note also that *solid* loses its chemical purity sense when used predicatively. *This gold is solid* does not mean it is chemically pure. These observations suggest:

The Functional Depth Principles

    (i)   The meaning range of functional expressions decreases in proportion to its internal function-argument complexity, and

    (ii) for f a functional expression and e an argument expression, the meaning range of f(e) is less than or equal to that of e.

Thus (i) says basically that more derived items exhibit less meaning variation than less derived items of the same category. And (ii) says that a derived item exhibits less (or at least not more) meaning variation than the item it was derived from.

Thus (ii) would predict for example that *run slowly* should have a narrower (or at least not greater) meaning range than *run*, given that *slowly* is interpreted as a function of the interpretation of *run*. And this appears to be correct. While we can understand *John/the motor/the tap is running slowly* using *run* in the same sense as if *slowly* were absent, we cannot say *My Fair Lady* or *the Braque exhibition is running slowly*, so *run* has lost one of its senses.

    (i) would predict that VPs consisting of a TVP plus object

would exhibit less meaning variation than simple lexical intransitive verbs. And this also seems correct. It is not easy to find TVP
+ DNP combinations in English which exhibit the gradient,
idiosyncratic variation exhibited by *run,* though some variation still
does exist. Thus *to cross the river here* is interpreted as an activity if
the subject is animate (e.g. *the soldiers*), but it is interpreted as
denoting a state or a locative relation with various choices of
inanimate subject, e.g. *the bridge, the telephone lines,* etc. The
Depth Principle also suggests that a predicate adjective may have
fewer senses than its modifying use since, e.g., *be solid* is functionally more complex than *solid.* And at least for *solid* this appears to
be correct.

The Depth Principle very likely has something right about it
then, though much more work investigating particular cases would
be needed to place it on firm ground. Furthermore there are other
restrictions on the meaning range of functional expressions besides
those covered in the Depth Principle. Thus some lexical adjectives
(intransitive verbs, etc.) simply exhibit much less meaning variation
than do others. Thus the *Random House College Dictionary*
(1973) lists only one sense for *eleemosynary,* two for *perspicacious*
(one archaic), and three for *melancholy,* whereas it gives 23 for
flat, 23 for *strong,* and 26 for *solid.*

A kind of limit case here may be *logical constants,* items like
every and *not* whose interpretations do not vary from state of
affairs to state of affairs. And as *Articles, Quantifiers,* and
Numerals are logical constants in this sense we would perhaps not
expect them to exhibit meaning variation. And that appears correct.
We shall not here present and substantiate a principle which would
predict that, however. Prepositions, few in number in any language
compared to for example CNPs and VPs, seem to lie somewhere
between ordinary 'content' items and logical constants. And it is
unclear to me whether we want to say that *with* in *to fill the tub
with Harry/with water/with joy* exhibits meaning variation or is
simply mutiply ambiguous.

So more research is needed here. But it does seem to me likely
that some version of the MFDP, suitably restricted to allow for
inherent restrictions on the meaning ranges of specific items, can
be made to work.

It is reasonable to query whether functional expressions taking
items other than DNPs and CNPs as arguments also show agree-

ment. If not, the FDP should be restricted to only cover nominal agreement. But our linguistic knowledge is limited here, so we shall not at the moment impose such a restriction. Further, we can find cases where adverbs and PPs inflect for categories that the VPs (and TVPs) they are functions of also inflect for. In Malagasy for example locative complements of verbs are marked for tense, and their marking must be the same as that of the verb:

(27)

$$n\text{- }andeha \begin{Bmatrix} t\text{-} \\ {}^*\!\varnothing\text{-} \\ {}^*\!ho\text{-} \end{Bmatrix} any \quad Antsirabe \; Rabe$$

$$\text{past-go} \begin{Bmatrix} \text{past} \\ \text{pres} \\ \text{fut} \end{Bmatrix} \text{there Antsirabe Rabe}$$

'Rabe went to Antsirabe'

And in Avar (NE Caucasian; see Anderson 1977) certain adverbial constructions agree with the subject, as do the verbs:

(28) a. *emen roq-'o-ve v-us:ana*
         father home- m. m.-returned
         'Father returned home'
     b. *ebel   roq'o-je j-us:anax*
         mother home- f.   f.-returned
         'Mother returned home'

But in the Avar case it is 'surely' more natural to consider that it is the entire VP *returned home* which is agreeing in gender with the subject. The apparent agreement between the VP and adverb is an artefact of how VP agreement is internally realised and not a case of the form of the adverb varying with the choice of verb, as would be required by the FDP.

The Malagasy case is perhaps less easily explained away. Given sentences like *John works and has always worked very hard*, where plausibly VPs with different tense marking occur within the scope of the adverb, it is reasonable to think that tense marking is a property of verbs, and so the adverbs or PPs which must have the same tense marking may well be instances of agreement as per the FDP. But it is also not implausible to think that tense marking is a property of the whole VP or even the entire sentence, in which case apparent agreement in tense internal to the VP would be a result of spreading of the marking on the VP as a whole and not a case of the form of the PP varying with the choice of verb.

A clear case of feature spreading rather than agreement is given by case marking of modifying adjectives. While it would be tempting to consider, with traditional grammar, that modifying adjectives agree in case with their CNP heads, it seems clear (see pp. 400 ff.) that case marking is a process which takes the entire DNP in its domain and that in certain languages the case marking on the DNP spreads into adjectives and determiners. So agreement in case, as opposed to agreement in gender class, is not a case of the form of one expression varying with the choice of another as the FDP requires.

The cases of feature spreading above neither support nor refute the FDP, but they do in certain cases support the *phrasal* as opposed to the merely lexical nature of agreement phenomena. Thus the FDP claims that VPs in general, not just lexical VPs (intransitive verbs) may agree with their DNP subjects. The claim is not falsified if only lexical VPs show agreement since variation in form of part of the VP is variation in form of the whole VP, but the FDP still does suggest that other parts of the VP may vary in form since it does not restrict agreement to lexical VPs.

Thus the examples of verb and adverb agreement with subjects cited for Avar above clearly illustrate full VP agreement as opposed to merely lexical VP agreement. (29) and (30) from English also illustrate full VP agreement.

(29) a. He *is* behaving *him*self.
     b. She *is* behaving *her*self.
     c. They *are* behaving *them*selv*es.*
(30) a. He *has* lost *his* way.
     b. She *has* lost *her* way.
     c. They *have* lost *their* way.

Note that the VP agreement is still evidenced in cases where the lexical verb itself does not agree, as in (31):

(31) a. They should/might/must/won't/behave *them*selv*es*
         (*himself/*oneself)
     b. She may/must/should/have lost *her* way (*his way/
         *their way)
     c. She tried/promised (Bill)/wanted/to lose *her* way

Similarly both copular verbs and predicate adjectives and predicate nominals show agreement with Subjects in many languages.

(32) a. John *is a* doctor.
  b. John and Mary *are* doctors.
(33) a. Marie *est* intelligent*e*.
  b. Marie et Francoise *sont* intelligent*es*.
  c. Jean et Marie *sont* intelligent*s*.

(33b,c) show as well that what the form of the VP varies as a function of is the entire DNP Subject and not just the 'head'. To know whether *intelligent* is feminine plural, (33b), or masculine plural, (33c), we must in principle check the gender of each conjunct of the Subject. The point is perhaps even more obvious in languages in which full verbs agree in gender, as the Hebrew examples below illustrate:

(34) a. *Miriam v-Ruti medabro̱t*
    Mary and Ruth are speaking (f.pl.)
  b. *Miriam v-Dan medabri̱m*
    Mary and Dan are speaking (m.pl.)

Overall then the fundamentally phrasal (rather than merely lexical) nature of the agreement phenomena that the FDP predicts seems to us basically correct. On the other hand, whether the FDP makes correct predictions concerning function argument structures not involving DNPs and CNPs must await further logical and linguistic research.

But what about further function-argument structures which do involve DNPs and CNPs? A few plausible cases do come to mind. Thus we strongly expect that ditransitive verbs like *give* and *hand* will be treated semantically as functions taking, at some level of analysis, their Indirect Objects (IOs) as arguments. Assuming that, the FDP would predict the possibility of ditransitive verb phrase agreement with IOs, and this is in fact correct. E.g., Spanish, Basque, and Daga (New Guinea) all evidence such agreement.

What about the logical functions represented by *and, or,* and *not*? In *Logical types* these operators do directly form derived DNPs, but they are treated as operators of a different sort from those already considered. The main difference is that they also combine directly with Formulas, VPs, TVPs, and APs to form derived members of those categories. Further, *and* and *or* are two-place functions rather than the one-place ones considered so far. Linguistically, relative to the category they combine with, a certain minimal variation is known. That is, many languages, for example, use different morphemes for *and* according as the category of items conjoined is different. The examples below from Malagasy are illustrative, and Payne (1978) provides large numbers of other examples.

(35) a. *mininam-bary Rabe ary (*sy) misotro taoka Rasoa*
     eat-   rice Rabe and   drink booze Rasoa
     'Rabe is eating rice and Rasoa is drinking booze'

   b. *mihinam-bary sy   (*ary) misotro taoka Rabe*
     eat-   rice and   drink booze Rabe
     'Rabe is eating rice and drinking booze'

   c. *mihinam-bary Rabe sy (*ary) Rasoa*
     eat-   rice Rabe and   Rasoa
     'Rabe and Rasoa are eating rice'

On the other hand, I know of no language in which the form of *and* varies with the choice of conjuncts within a category. Thus, as far as I know, if a language has an overt conjunction for DNPs at all then it uses the same form for *John and Bill* as it does for *Mary and Susan.*

We have considered a rather large number of function-argument structures and at least those which involve DNPs and CNPs are commonly enough expressed in SF by items which satisfy the agreement predictions of the FDP. But are there cases of agreement in SF which are not expressed by function-argument structures of the right sort? There would appear to be at least one: That of pronominal agreement with full DNP 'antecedents'. As 'bound pronouns' can occur in constituents in which their antecedents do not occur, the pronoun will not in general be represented as a function taking the interpretation of the full DNP as an argument. This at least is not the case for pronominal representation in *Logical types,* nor is it the case in any of the commonly used versions of LFs for natural languages or formal languages. Rather pronominal co-reference is represented by the use of Variable Binding Operators (VBOs), illustrated in (36) from Classical Logic and (37) from *Logical types.*

(36) a.　Every student laughed and cried.
　　 b.　$(\forall x)\ (student(x) \rightarrow laughed(x)\ and\ cried(x))$
(37) a.　Every man loves his mother.
　　 b.　$((every, man), (\lambda x(x, (love, (x's\ mother)))))$

The use of such VBOs seems 'unnatural' in the sense that they do not seem to correspond to anything in SF. Indeed we count it as an advantage of *Logical types* that very many SFs using quantified NPs which bind the reference of more than one position can be represented without the use of VBOs. For example, (36a) would be represented in *Logical types* by:

(38)　$((every, student)(laughed, and, cried))$

However in the LF for (37a) there is no way to bind *his* without using the lambda operator. And it is clearly not the case that what corresponds to *his*, namely the bound occurrence of x, is interpreted as a function taking the interpretation of (*every,man*) as an argument. Similarly the position relativised into in the representations for Relative Clauses in *Logical types* is represented by a bound variable.

The best tentative conclusion I can reach concerning these phenomena is that the kind of agreement we see between pronouns and full NP antecedents is different in kind from that that we have considered so far, and a logical characterisation of it should proceed along lines different from those in the FDP. I would propose then that the FDP be restricted so as to require that the distinct constituents A and B of E are further required to be of distinct categories (not merely subcategories of one and the same larger category). Since pronouns and full NPs are all DNPs, the FDP would then make no prediction about their agreement possibilities. An additional principle would be required then to characterise pronominal agreement. The principle is in fact easy to state, though we shall not be concerned with its details or justification here. But roughly, if A and B are of the same major category, then A is represented in LF by a bound variable and B is what binds it (i.e., in *Logical Types*, B is the argument of the structure created by that VBO).

A final potential restriction on the FDP concerns case marking of DNPs. In many languages a DNP Subject may have one case marker, the absolute, if the main verb of the VP is intransitive, and another marker, the ergative, if the main verb is transitive. So the form of the DNP would vary with that of the VP, in violation of the FDP. Similarly in many languages Experience 'Subjects' will be marked like IOs (that is, dative) whereas Subjects of activity VPs will be nominative (or unmarked).

Appearances then might suggest that the FDP should be restricted so as to cover just the traditional *agreement* cases and not, as Emmon Bach points out to me, traditional cases of *government*. To impose such a restriction we might for example stipulate that the variation in form mentioned in the FDP be restricted to variation with respect to inherent nominal properties such as number and gender. Even so restricted, the principle would correctly account for a large number of specific correspondences between SF and LF and so still support the general conclusion that there exist correspondences between SF and LF.

I doubt however that such a restriction need be imposed. Even a brief look at case marking properties of languages shows, as I shall briefly argue below, that case marking is a sentence-level phenomenon. That is, case marking, despite the fact that it sometimes (see below) shows up morphologically bound to DNPs, is a property of sentences or more exactly a relation between a DNP and the entire sentence in which it occurs, and not a property of DNPs given as a function of the verb in the clause in which they occur.

To support this claim, I shall summarise a very large number of cases in which DNP case marking is independent of the choice of the verb. Thus for a given choice of verb a given DNP may have any of several case markers (CMs), and the conditioning factors appear to be almost any conceivable property of the sentence containing the DNP. (The latter claim is surely too strong, but a quick look at case marking systems reveals an astounding variety of such conditioning factors.)

First, it is obvious that locative cases are not predictable from the verb generally. Thus in the same way that in English we may say *John fell on the sidewalk/near the station/in the bathroom*, etc., so in case marking languages in the narrow sense, such as Finnish, a given verb like *fall* may take DNP complements in any of various locative cases. We may then dismiss locative cases, and indeed all the semantically rich oblique cases (e.g. instrumentals) from consideration and concentrate on case marking affecting Subjects and Direct Objects.

But even here there are a massive number of cases where the CM on a DNP may vary with the verb held constant.

First, consider the very widespread use of 'definite DO marking'. Many languages, such as Hebrew, Turkish, Persian, Spanish, Malagasy, etc., present DOs of the same verb in different cases according as the DO is ± definite and/or ± animate, the exact conditioning factors varying from language to language. (39) from Hebrew is illustrative:

(39) a.   *ani ohev yeladim*
        I   like   child-pl
        'I like children' (no CM on the DO)
   b.   *ani ohev et   ha- yeladim ha- ele*
        I   like   DO def-child-pl def-those
        'I like those children'

A second, very widespread phenomenon among case marking languages concerns differential marking according as the DNP is understood to be partitively or wholly affected. Thus the differences discussed in Anderson (1971) as between *chew the meat/ chew on the meat, shoot Bill/shoot at Bill*, etc., show up in the case marking in many languages. The case of Finnish is well known. DOs of many affirmative transitive verbs may be partitive in case if they are only partially affected by the action (and so the action may be understood as incomplete). If they are wholly affected, the CM may be either 'accusative' or nominative depending on other factors to be discussed shortly (see Timberlake (1975 and 1977) for detailed discussion). Edith Moravcsik (1978) points out furthermore that this distinction exists in a great many languages and includes Subjects of intransitive verbs as well. She cites, for example, (40) from Russian:

(40) a.   *kash-a   ostalas'   na stole*
        kasha-nom remained   on table
        'Kasha remained on the table'
   b.   *kash- i   eshcë ostalos'*
        kasha-gen still   remained
        'Some kasha was still left'

Similarly many of Fillmore's pairs show up in the case marking of heavily case marking languages. (41) from Hungarian is also taken from Moravcsik (1978):

(41) a. *János beültette   a   kertet   fákkal*
        John planted (def) the garden (acc) trees+with
        'John planted the garden with trees'
   b. *János fákat ültetett   a   kertbe*
        John trees planted (indef) the garden+into
        'John planted trees in the garden'

(Note that as per the FDP, the verb in (41a) agrees with the definiteness of the DO, but does not agree with indefinite DOs as in (41b).)

Third, note that in some ergative languages intransitive subjects may sometimes take either the absolutive case or the ergative case, with a difference in meaning: the ergative indicating Subject intention or responsibility, the absolutive indicating accidental action. E. Pomo (Uto-Aztecan; Moravcsik 1978) and Bats (Caucasian; Comrie 1973) are examples. (42) below is from Bats:

(42) a. *so   wože*
        I-abs fell
        'I fell (not implied that it was my fault)'
   b. *as   wože*
        I-erg fell
        'I fell (it was my fault)'

Further, even a bare animacy distinction may occasionally trigger different CMs on transitive Subjects. (43) from Gugu-Yalanji (Australia) is cited from Gary and Keenan (1977).

(43) a. *dingkar-angka   kaya kunin*
        man-   erg+anim dog hit
        'The man hit the dog'
   b. *kalka-bu   kaya kunin*
        spear-erg+inanim dog hit
            (= instr)
        'The spear hit the dog'

The above cases are all ones in which semantic properties of the marked DNP are reflected in the CM but are not predictable from the verb itself. Some of these properties, such as definiteness, may also have a syntactic characterisation, in which case it is not easy to decide whether the conditioning factor is semantic or syntactic. But other cases are more clearly syntactic. Thus, as is well known, many languages may case mark full DNPs and pronouns differently. Thus English does not mark full DNPs but does mark pronouns. And Dyirbal (Dixon 1972) and many other Australian languages may case mark full DNPs on an ergative-absolutive basis but pronouns on a nominative-accusative basis.

Furthermore, if a language distinguishes noun classes and also case marks, the form of the case marking may vary with the noun class. E.g., Russian and Latin case marking varies according as the nominal marked is masculine or feminine, singular or plural, etc.

The above collection of facts shows that case marking is sensitive to a large number of syntactic and semantic properties of the DNP affected by the marking, where these properties are not predictable from the verb. Further case marking will also be sensitive to whether the DNP in question forms a logical constituent with a VP or a TVP, and will need to have information regarding the semantic and/or syntactic subclass of the verb. Yet even with all this information the CM is not completely predictable. It still might, for example, mark the DNP as partitive or not, as in the Russian cases above, or it might mark it as ergative or absolutive, as in the Bats cases above. In either case the CM itself brings in new information (partial affectedness, purposive activity, etc.). All this rather suggests the, in fact quite intuitive, view that case marking is both syntactically and logically a relation between a DNP and a VP or TVP. And if case marking is treated as a two-place function taking DNPs and verbs of various sorts as arguments then the FDP simply has no prediction to make, except the correct one that the form of the CM may vary with the nature of the arguments (stative vs activity VP, definite vs indefinite DNP, etc.).

Even this rather appealing picture however is very badly oversimplified. Evidence from very many languages shows that case marking must have much information available concerning the structure of the entire sentence in which the marked DNP occurs.

Thus, for example, several different cases are available where the CM of a given DNP varies with properties of *other* DNPs in the clause. Recall the Finnish cases mentioned above. The Object of many affirmative transitive verbs if not semantically partitive, and so marked by the partitive case, may still be either nominative or 'accusative'. The conditioning factor here is whether the transitive verb presents an overt subject or not. Thus, using the traditional case labels, we note the following examples from Comrie (1978) (see Timberlake 1975 for a thorough discussion):

(44) a.   *Maija-Ø   söi kala-n*
      Maija-nom ate fish-acc
      'Maija ate the fish'
   b.   *Syö   kala-Ø !*
      eat-imp fish-nom
      'Eat the fish!'

Similarly objects of impersonally used (i.e. subjectless) transitive verbs also take nominative objects. On the other hand, if the subject of the (affirmative) transitive verb is present, the nonpartitive object is 'accusative' ('antiergative' in Comrie's terminology, but in any event different from the nominative). So case marking of one DNP then is contingent on the presence or absence of another.

A different type of dependency between DNPs is illustrated in Dalabon (Australia; Silverstein 1976, cited in Comrie 1978). Here case marking is contingent on the 'chain of being' relations between the transitive subject and the object. Thus if the subject is animate (as in (45)) and the object inanimate the subject is not case marked. But if both are animate the subject takes an ergative marker:

(45) *Buluŋan-Ø   ga'manbuniŋ*
    my-father   he-made-it
    'My father   made it'
(46) *Buluŋan- yi wuduwud ga'nan*
    my-father- erg baby   he-looks+at-him
    'My father is looking at the baby'

A third related type of example is given by case marking in ergative languages when a 'normally' transitive verb is used 'absolutively' as *He wrote and wrote* as opposed to *He wrote the letter*. Some ergative languages cited in Comrie (1973) use an absolutive ending for the absolutive use, and others, like Hindi, use the ergative. In the former case then, case marking of the subject is not predictable from the identity of the verb.

It appears then that the domain of case marking must not only include the DNP and the VP or TVP but also other DNPs in the clause. And yet we have only begun to touch upon the other properties of the sentence to which case marking must be made sensitive. Thus in many languages (Hindi, Georgian) case marking is sensitive to Aspect. Subjects of perfective sentences are marked in one way, subjects of imperfectives another. And since the same verb can occur in many different aspects this property of case marking is not predictable from the verb.

Further, it is quite common that case marking of DNPs is different according as the sentence they are in is negative or not. Thus, as is well known, DOs in Russian and Czech may be genitive if the sentence they occur in is negative. This is also true for Finnish and Lithuanian, as Moravcsik (1978) points out, and further the same holds for certain intransitive subjects. Compare (47a,b) from Moravcsik:

(47) a. *proexal avtomobil'*   (Russian)
         went-by car (nom)
         'A car went by'
     b. *ne proexalo aytomobilja*
         neg went-by car (gen)
         'Not a car went by'

Analogous claims again hold for Finnish and Lithuanian. Worse, in Kawaiisu (S. Numic, Uto-Aztecan; see Munro 1976 for details) Subjects of negative sentences are marked (overtly) like DOs, whereas in nonnegative sentences they are not overtly case marked. In fact, Subjects of embedded clauses generally take object marking. So it may be the case that case marking is not independent of whether the sentence the DNP occurs in is a main clause or an embedded clause. In Wappo (Li and Thompson 1975, cited in Gary and Keenan 1977) the overt case marking of Subjects is simply lost in finite subordinate clauses:

(48) a. *ce kew-i   ew toh- ta?*
         that man-Subj fish catch-past
         'That man caught a fish'
     b. *Ah ce   kew-Ø ew toh- ta? hatiskhi?*
         I   that man fish catch-past know
         'I know that that man caught a fish'

It appears then that case marking is fully clausal in nature. And on reflection this is not surprising. In very many languages pre- or postpositions not only mark DNPs, they also mark various types of subordinate clauses. Thus subordinate clauses like *on arriving at the station, John went straight to the ticket counter; The meeting began upon John's arrival*, etc., may well be translated in heavily case marking languages by ordinary morphologically bound case markers. Recall in this connection the widespread use of the 'absolutive' constructin in the IE languages. (49) from Ancient Greek is illustrative (diacritics omitted):

(49) *elthont-a   eis ten polin, ho didaskal-os   edeixe*
                                        ton paid-a to sokrat-e
     coming-acc into the city, the teacher- nom showed
                                        the child-acc the Socrates-dat
     'Coming into the city, the teacher showed the child to
     Socrates'

The nonfinite verb on the (subjectless) subordinate clause is case marked accusative, which indicates that the understood Subject of *coming* is co-referential with the DNP marked accusative in the main clause, namely the child. Had *coming* been marked nominative, it would have been the nominative DNP, *the teacher*, who was coming; and had it been marked dative it would have been *Socrates*. And had it been in the 'absolutive' form, the genitive case (ablative in Latin, dative in Gothic, locative in Sanscrit), the understood Subject of *coming* would have had to be different from any of the major participants in the main clause and thus already understood from the prior discourse.

The general point here is that case marking commonly has a variety of clausal and cross clausal functions. The domain of case marking then, even restricted to DNP marking, is properly the entire sentence in which the DNP occurs.

Note finally, that if case marking is a sentence level property we might expect reflexes of it to show up elsewhere than on the DNPs. And this in fact is correct, at least where case marking is understood broadly enough to cover markings on indirect objects and obliques. Recall the Latin paradigms in which 'prepositions' may show up either on the DNP, or on the verb, or both. Thus from a verb like *ferre* 'to carry' we may form derived verbs such as *inferre* 'to carry into', *transferre* 'to carry across', *ex+ferre* 'to carry from', *ad+ferre* 'to carry to', etc. The DNP 'Object' of such verbs may or may not also carry the preposition. Thus Caesar may carry the war into Italy, he may 'incarry' the war into Italy, or he may 'incarry' the war Italy. Similar double markings occur in Hungarian and to a lesser extent Modern Russian. (50) from Hungarian is illustrative.

(50) *Janos <u>ra</u>- Ø- te- tt- e   a   kalap-ot az asztal-<u>ra</u>*
      John <u>on</u>-it-put-past- 3sg3sg the hat- acc the table-<u>on</u>
      'John put the hat on the table'

Further, it is in fact quite common to find that that element which marks the relation a DNP bears to the action expressed by the verb may be marked exclusively in the verb. Such cases arise commonly in Caucasian languages, Penutian languages (Chinook, Totonac), Ancient Greek (see Keenan 1976 for examples), Arawakan languages (e.g. Machiguenga; see Gary and Keenan 1977 for examples) and Bantu languages. (51) from Kinyarwanda (see Kimenyi 1976 for a thorough discussion) is illustrative:

(51) *Yohani y- a- andik-iish-ije-ho ameza ikaramu*
      John   he-past-write-inst-asp-loc table   pen
      'John wrote on the table with the pen'

We may conclude then that syntactically speaking case marking is a function taking the entire sentence as its domain and thus the only prediction made by the FDP is the correct one, namely that the form of case markers may vary with the properties of the sentence it applies to.

4 The Left-Right Order Relation

The function-argument structures concerning CNPs and DNPs distinguished in *Logical types* turn out to support, quite unexpectedly, another correlation between SF and LF: namely, the characteristic left-to-right order of the constituents which express these structures. Thus:

The Serialisation Principle (SP)

    Different functional expressions taking the same class of argument expressions tend to serialise on the same side of their argument expressions.

The Dissimilation Principle (DP)[2]

Functional expressions taking DNPs as arguments and functional expressions taking CNPs as arguments tend to serialise on the opposite side of their argument expressions.

The SP predicts that VPs, TVPs, PossPhs, and Adpositions (= Prepositions in English) will all occur on the same side of their DNP arguments. Similarly, APs, Relative Clauses, Articles, Determiners, and Quantifiers will tend to occur on the same side of their CNP arguments. And the DP says that these two sides are different. Thus there should only be two characteristic word order types with respect to functional expressions of DNPs and CNPs: either Function + DNP and CNP + Function or DNP + Function and Function + CNP. Although these predictions are too strong in one respect and so will be weakened slightly below they do make a very substantial number of correct predictions as we shall show and thus do constitute evidence in support of a general correlation between SF and LF.

Thus consider the characteristic word order patterns in Verb Final (SOV) languages, easily the most widespread word order type across different geographical areas and genetic groupings. The relevant word order correlations are:

(52) a. Subject + VP (e.g. John sings; John Mary kissed)
Object + TVP
DNP + Postposition (e.g. the garden-in)
DNP + PossPh (e.g. John's father)
b. Adjective + CNP (e.g. tall man)
Relative Clause + CNP (e.g. the apple eating man)
Article + CNP (the man; this man)
Quantifier + CNP (every man)
Numeral + CNP (two man)

Clearly all the functions of DNPs occur on the same side of the DNP, the right, and all the functions of CNPs occur to the same side, the left. So the SP is fully supported. And these two sides are different, so that the DP is fully supported, at least as far as our current knowledge of the word order correlates goes. Specifically, we know more about some of the word order patterns than we do about others. In particular, as indicated earlier, the internal construction of numeral expressions is complex, nonuniform, and not well known across languages. Further, in all cases here, and below, it should be recognised that we need large-scale studies of the word order correlates to make our claims more accurate, and the few such studies we have (see e.g. Hawkins 1979a and 1979b) will surely show that the internal analysis of word order patterning is more complex than indicated above. None the less, relative to the current state of our ignorance, the above mentioned correlates are (with the serious hedge regarding numerals) the best gross statement we have for the structures referred to. (Other correlates, such as the position of Auxiliaries and Main Verbs are not considered here.)

With these qualifications then, consider the second word order type predicted by the SP and DP. It would be:

(53) a.   VP + Subject
          TVP + Object
          Preposition + DNP
          PossPh + DNP (e.g. the father of John)
     b.   CNP + Adjective
          CNP + Relative Clause
          CNP + Determiner (= Article, Quantifier, or Numeral)

The first two claims in (53a) predict that a language of this type will have VOS as a basic word order. In fact, such languages are rare, although about 12 such cases are known. See Keenan (1978) for a study of their typological properties. On the other hand, though the VOS type is rare, the predictions about word order above are correct (modulo the hedges given above for SOV languages).

But what about the word order types, SVO and VSO, not predicted by the two principles? Not only do they exist, but they are both more widespread than the VOS type, though very significantly less so than the SOV type. (54) summarises the known word order types characterised in terms of the relative order (where fixed) of Subject, Object, and Verb:

(54) SOV > SVO > VSO > VOS > OVS

The list below gives a rough breakdown of the distribution of word order types across the major genetic-areal groupings of languages. A major heading is understood to mark a single genetic group unless indicated otherwise. Subheadings mark genetically coherent subgroups.

Genetic-Areal Distribution of Word Order Types

1. *Australian*
   SOV with much freedom of word order
2. *Indo-Pacific* (6 genetically independent groups)
   SOV
3. *Austro-Tai*
   SVO and VSO both prominent orders. (Some SOV in New Guinea)
4. *Austro-Asiatic*
   4.1   *Munda* — SOV
   4.2   *Mon-Khumen* — SVO
5. *Sino-Tibetan*
   SOV
6. *Dravidian*
   SOV
7. *'Boreo-Oriental'* (possibly four genetically independent subgroups)
   7.1   *Altaic* (Turkic, etc.) — SOV
   7.2   *Uralic* (Samoyedic and Finno-Ugric) — dominantly SOV with some SVO
   7.3   *Japanese, Okinawan, Korean* — SOV
   7.4   *Paleo-Siberian* — dominantly SOV
8. *Indo-European* (extant groups)
   8.1   *Baltic* — SVO
   8.2   *Slavic* — SVO
   8.3   *Germanic* — SVO with traces of SOV
   8.4   *Italic* — SVO with hints of VSO
   8.5   *Indo-Iranian*
         8.5.1 *Iranian* — SOV
         8.5.2 *Indic* — SOV
   8.6   *Dardic* — SOV
   8.7   *Greek* — SVO
   8.8   *Albanian* — SVO
   8.9   *Armenian* (modern) — SOV
   8.10 *Celtic* — VSO

9. *Caucasian* (perhaps 2 genetic groups)
   SOV dominant, scattered SVO
10. *African* (4 genetically independent subgroups)
    10.1   *Khoisan* — SOV
    10.2   *Nilo-Saharan* — VSO, SVO, and SOV all attested
    10.3   *Niger-Kordofanian* — SVO
    10.4   *Afro-Asiatic*
           10.4.1 *Semitic* (modern) — SVO
           10.4.2 *Berber* — VSO
           10.4.3 *Chadic* — SVO
           10.4.4 *Cushitic* — SOV
11. *Amerindian* (13 genetically independent subgroups)
    SOV   probably the dominant order (e.g. Eskimo-Aleut,
           Na-Dene (Athapascan), Hokan, Aztec-Tanoan,
           Andean-Equatorial, Macro-Chibchan)
    VSO   heavily attested (Salish, Wakashan, Penutian,
           Oto-Manguean)
    SVO   is only rarely attested
    OVS   is known in one case (Hixkaryana, a Carib language in
           Brazil, see Derbyshire 1977 for discussion)

It is clear from the table that SOV is clearly the dominant order among the world's languages. The relative proportions of SVO vs VSO are hard to evaluate given that I cannot accurately assess just how widespread it is among the Amerindian languages, though it is clear that it is a dominant order in the genetic groups indicated above. So VSO occurs as a dominant order in several Amerindian phyla, it is one of the dominant orders in Austro-Tai (Polynesian, Philippines, Formosan), and occurs as the dominant order in genetic subgroups of Indo-European (Celtic), Nilo-Saharan (Nilotic), and Afro-Asiatic (Berber). As well it was likely the historical order of older Semitic languages: Classical Arabic, Biblical Hebrew, Babylonian Aramaic. SVO on the other hand, is the dominant order in Europe (ignoring Celtic) though in the phylum as a whole, SOV is a very significant order (Armenian, Dardic, Iranian, Indic). In addition SOV is the dominant order in the extinct IE languages (Hittite) and is the most likely reconstructable order for Proto-IE. SVO is the dominant order in Niger-Kordofanian, a very large group, and occurs as a dominant order in many Austro-Tai language groups (Tai, Indonesian, Javanese). It is the dominant order in Chadic and modern Semitic and occurs sporadically in groups that are otherwise dominantly SOV. I consider it more widespread then than VSO.

VOS only occurs rarely, and then mainly in phyla which independently present Verb Initial as a major order — Austro-Tai and Amerindian. OVS as noted is cited for only one case, though others related to it may have the same order. We shall not further consider this case here.

What about the word order patterns in SVO and VSO languages other than those involving the subject? Essentially they pattern like we predict for the VOS languages, though more 'doubling' (Hawkins 1979a) occurs, especially in SVO languages (e.g., such languages may have both prenominal and postnominal possessors, as English; both prenominal and postnominal adjectives, as French, etc.). Further and large-scale study would be needed to justify the argument that articles and demonstratives occur significantly more frequently postnominally than prenominally, as they are generally considered to do (e.g. Indonesian, Yoruba, Batak, etc.). These observations suggest the following condition:

Subjects Front (SF)

The Subject occurs to the left of other major constituents of Ss. Thus SF is maximally satisfied in both SOV and SVO languages, less satisfied in VSO languages, and still less in VOS and OVS languages. Note further that the SF is a much more specific principle than either the SP or the DP, as the latter quantify over classes of functional expressions, whereas the SF only mentions one specific argument expression — the Subject. If we take then the possible word order types for human language to be those obtained from the set defined by the general principles SP and DP, namely SOV and VOS, and modified in the direction of satisfying Subject Front we obtain (pending of course a more rigorous formulation) a surprising number of correct predictions:

(i) The possible types are SOV, VOS, VSO, and SVO. Just the well-attested cases, with the exception of the one OVS language cited.

Note what a strong prediction (i) in fact is. There are 9 function-argument structures considered and thus in principle $2^9 = 512$ possible word order types. Of which only four are predicted to occur, and they do.

(ii) The principles predict that the SVO, VSO, and VOS languages will evidence the same serialisation in their function-argument structures with the exception of the placement of the Subject. But all the others should be the same, and this is correct.

(iii) The combined effect of the three principles would appear to correctly predict the observed genetic-areal distribution of the word order types.

Thus the rigorous SOV type satisfies all the principles that is in fact the most widely distributed word order type. SVO fully satisfies Subject Front and fails the Serialisation Principle (and the Dissimilation Principle) at just one point: the Subject should follow the VP, that is the TVP + Object. VSO also fails the SP (and thus the DP) at this point, and in addition satisfies Subject Front to a lesser extent than the SVO type and so is less widely distributed. Independently VSO yields a less good correspondence with LF since the TVP + Object does not form a constituent in SF. Finally VOS (and OVS) maximally fail Subject Front and might then be expected to have the least wide distribution.

Despite the logical looseness of prediction (iii) it does seem to me that the approach we have taken to the word order correlates more successfully relates them to function-argument structure than earlier attempts. Vennemann (1972) is perhaps the first (but see note 2) attempt to systematically correlate word order types with function-argument structure. His approach however is not based on an independently justified logic. He takes for example DNPs as functions with VPs and Prepositions as arguments, and their outputs are supposed to somehow have the same category as the argument. But no natural logic treats, for example, *in* and *in the garden* as having the same type of denotation. Further, Vennemann's approach must rule out the Subject-VP relation in principle, so predictions like (iii), however loose, cannot in principle be stated in his framework.

More recently Gil (1979) relates function-argument structures to word order types in the framework of a prosodic theory. His approach assumes our SP and has an analogue of the DP, though much more elaborate. The two approaches are sufficiently different to resist quick comparison, but it is noteworthy that his approach does yield several predictions concerning distinctive prosodic structures in SOV and SVO languages, one of which (greater consonant/vowel ratios in the SOV group) he rigorously supports.

To conclude this section, we might wonder whether the Subject Front principle is anything other than an *ad hoc* device to get the word order types correctly predicted. Is there any independent reason to expect this principle, and is there any independent justification for it? The answer to both questions I feel is yes, although more work than can be presented here would be needed to justify this claim. So briefly:

As regards motivation, the Subject-VP constituent is the major function-argument structure of simple sentences and might well be expected to have more perceptual or cognitive salience than the function-argument structures embedded within either the Subject or the VP. Thus, recall from the Meaning-Form Dependency Principle that how we interpret VPs may vary with the choice of Subject. Thus if the VP preceeds the Subject, hearers will have to suspend an exact interpretation for it until the Subject is enunciated. For example, if English were a VP first language there would be sentences beginning with *is flat ...*, *is strong ...*, etc., where the exact sense of the VP could not be interpreted until we knew whether the speaker was talking about roads, beers, voices, or whatever. Further, the problem would quite obviously be more serious in a VOS language than in a VSO language, since more material in a VOS language would be present before the Subject was enunciated. To say for example in a VOS language that *nobody loves both his father and his mother*, we would begin with, *loves the father of his and the mother of his ...*, without being able to identify the referent of *his*. And if the language allowed sentential objects (the most likely position for complements of verbs of saying) we could begin sentences like *thinks that hurt himself he ...* before the Subject phrase was enunciated, requiring the hearer to 'hold in temporary memory' *himself* and *he* until their referents can be established by the Subject. (See Keenan 1978 for further discussion of the disadvantages of placing the Subject at the end of the sentence.)

The motivation suggested above for presenting Subjects to the left of the other major constituents in a sentence does in fact suggest some independent motivation for Subject Front. In the first place, in those languages which do use a VOS order, we in fact never find that the Object position can be filled in surface by a full sentence. To say in those languages (e.g. Malagasy, Fijian, Toba

Batak, Ineseño Chumash, etc.) things like *John thinks that Fred will win* a variety of alternatives are available, one of which must be used, and all of which present the thinker before the embedded clause. Thus the language (e.g. Malagasy) may simply use a VSO order here, in violation of the normal word order. Or it may passivise (Malagasy, Toba Batak) yielding an order like *thought by John that will win Fred*. Or it may utilise any of various devices (clefting, topicalisation) for presenting the Subject before the VP.

In the second place, all VSO languages and all VOS languages present means of fronting the Subject. Some of these may be clearly marked structures, e.g., a particle may be inserted after the fronted Subject and before the remaining VP, but such options always exist and, in all cases where I have relevant data (Malagasy, Fijian, K'ekchi (Mayan) and Toba Batak) such fronting devices are more commonly used than, for example, the 'backing' devices (e.g. Right Dislocation) in SOV and SVO languages.

In the third place, even in VSO languages, there will be a variety of ways to form complex (intransitive) verb phrases, e.g. by conjoining two independently intransitive verb phrases. The expected order then would be *sing and dance John*. And sometimes this order can be realised (Malagasy, Isthmus Zapotec, Tamazight (Berber)), but in general it seems more common to break open the VP yielding 'dissonant' structures like *sing John and dance*, where we have a surface co-ordination between a VP and a full sentence. And if the VP is a TVP plus Object it is even harder to maintain the VP-Subject order, despite the highly dissonant structures that result. That is, we would expect to get [*kissed Mary and danced*]$_{VP}$ *John*. (And sometimes we do, as in Malagasy.) But the more usual order is [*kissed John Mary*]$_S$ *and danced*.

These cases do then provide independent evidence for *Subject Front* as a constraint in Universal Grammar on the class of possible word order types.

5 Theoretical Significance of Correlations between SF and LF

Why, as linguists, should we be interested in establishing a correlation between the properties of SFs and those of LFs? The answer lies in our goal of trying to represent the linguistic competence of speakers of a language. To know, and thus to learn, a language is to know (learn) much more than simply what the class of grammatical SFs are. Even children from the youngest age do not *randomly* produce approximations to well-formed SFs. Rather they use them with logical (and other) effect. That is, they use them to assert — to make true statements (or statements they intend as true). They use them to deny, and they readily make inferences from what others have said. In other words, in practice, speakers use SFs as LFs. It makes sense to say that what someone has said entails something else, or that it contradicts what someone else has said.

If we represent at least the logical properties of an SF by a set of LFs we may say that what someone knows when he knows a language is a set of pairs $<s,t>$ where s is an SF and t is an LF which represents one of the meanings of s. (So the language will be a very proper subset of SF $\times$ LF.)

(To be sure this idealisation abstracts away from much else we know when we know a language, such as almost everything we might call 'sociolinguistic', but for the moment this abstraction is sufficient for our purpose.)

To know a language in this view then requires that we know what the class of SFs is, what the class of LFs is, and most important that we know which SFs are paired with which LFs. This last claim can be represented by saying that the ideal speaker knows (in the sense of having internalised) a function which associates such SFs with the set T_s of LFs, each of which expresses one of the meanings of s.[3] In fact, one of the explicit goals of current linguistic theory (at least the Revised Extended Standard Theory, EST) is to define such a function, although work specifically on that topic has in fact been rather scant.

Thus, to account for the linguistic competence of the (ideal) native speaker we shall want to characterise the set of SFs, the set of LFs, and the interpreting function which relates the two. And we shall want to use this characterisation to explain what it is that people learn when they learn a language and how it is that children, with a limited and imperfect exposure to the language, none the less learn to identify a substantial subset of the pairs (s,t) which constitute the language.

Part of the explanation for this latter fact within generative grammar has been that humans come biologically equipped with a certain syntactic potential. So the child, or anyone else, is not prepared to accept as a possible set of SFs a very large number of the sets of expressions which can be formally defined. We rightly do not expect that somewhere in the unexplored wilds of New Guinea we will run across a language all of whose sentences have prime length. Thus much work in generative grammar has, rightly to my mind, been concerned to constrain the class of possible grammars the learner can potentially accept. These general constraints would then directly reflect our innate syntactic potential.

Analogous claims hold for the class of possible interpreting functions. We cannot believe that the way humans associate meaning with form, or LFs with SFs, is random. Given a set of SFs for a language, not just any function into a (power) set of LFs is a possible interpreting function for that language. Imagine for example a function F which, for every surface form s, maps s onto a set of LFs none of which mentions any of the LFs which F associates with any of the constituent parts of s. So the LFs which F might associate with *John came early and left late* could be just those that a 'right' interpreting function associated with *Not all unicorns have horns*. Mathematically it is easy to construct such nonadmissible interpreting functions.[4]

So to characterise our competence we want to define the class of possible interpreting functions, and to explain (at least in part) the learnability of human languages, we want to define the class of possible human languages, that is the possible sets of pairs (s,t), as narrowly as possible. Clearly the most constrained class of interpreting functions is the set of identity functions. That is, for any language L, the set of LFs for L would be identical to the set of SFs for L. This would directly explain why speakers can use SFs with logical force (assert, deny, infer, etc.).

Unfortunately this identification does not seem possible in any theory of SF ever propounded. The reason is that, in all theories, at least some SFs will be semantically ambiguous and thus correspond to more than one LF. Note that the objects in which the entailment relation is defined (LFs) cannot be ambiguous in the sense of having more than one truth value in some state of affairs. If p were such a formula then we could argue both that p entails p and that p does not entail p, which is to say that the entailment relation itself is not well defined. (To see this, note that given the existence of a state of affairs in which p is true on one reading but false on another it follows that p does not entail p. On the other hand, 'for any state of affairs M, if p is true in M then p is true in M' is itself trivially true. Which is to say p entails p.)

But how badly *must* the identification of SF with LF fail? Which is to say, how ambiguous are SFs? The question has no *obvious* answer since it depends at least on what SFs our theory defines, and as we have seen, that is a complicated matter. Still, one kind of SF which is semantically ambiguous in all theories is those containing semantically ambiguous lexical items of the same grammatical category and subcategory. Thus *John is a bachelor*, we are told, is four ways ambiguous, according as John is a male seal, a knight's helper, etc. And since it can be true on one reading and false on another, we will need distinct LFs to correspond to each of these readings. Notice however that each of those LFs could be structurally isomorphic to the SF. They might just differ in that within the logic would be four distinct logical common nouns, *bachelor*$_1$, *bachelor*$_2$, etc. This type of ambiguity then, while serious, still permits a very strong form of correspondence between SF and LF. Namely, identity up to lexical disambiguation.

But of course linguists and philosophers have been much concerned with nonlexical ambiguities. Many of these however will be eliminated in a reasonably rich theory of SF. Thus most theories would assign *flying planes can be dangerous* two distinct surface forms. (In one, *flying* would be the head of the Subject, and on the other it would be a modifier. In one the head would be marked + plural, and on the other not, etc.) And it appears that many of the classical structural ambiguities are in fact not ambiguous at a level of SF. Note that even a subcategory difference in a lexical item yields a different labelled node in SF. Thus very possibly *the shooting of the hunters* can be naturally assigned two SFs according as the underlying verb *shoot* is transitive or a derived intransitive.

It is worth noting in this regard that elaborating the base, as by proliferating the number of categories and subcategories, does not seriously complicate the grammar as a whole. That is, the class of context-free or even context-sensitive languages is a very constrained class. If all of English could be given in a context-free (sensitive) form the learnability problem would be solved. On the other hand, the class of languages generable by context-free bases plus length decreasing filters is enormously larger. Thus to constrain the class of grammars we have an interest in enriching the base and limiting as much as possible the filters used.

On the other hand, there are several sorts of 'possible' ambiguity which have been studied by philosophers and linguists alike which are much less likely to be represented by distinct SFs. The major cases known to me are the following: (1) cross-reference ambiguity, as in *John told Bill that he was clever*; (2) quantifier scope ambiguity, as (supposedly) in *Every man loves a woman*; and (3) transparency/opacity ambiguity as in *Suzie wants to marry a Swede* or *John believes that the author of Waverly was the author of Waverly.*

Just how far from isomorphism these cases will force the interpreting function is unclear at the moment. A serious part of the reason is that we have no really clear pretheoretical intuition of what shall count as semantic *ambiguity*.[5] Thus the position that the *he* in *John told Bill that he was clever* is simply freely generated and its interpretation depends on the context of utterance is at least defensible. So in that view the sentence would not be logically ambiguous. Its 'pragmatic' potential would have to be explicated within a theory of pragmatics or speech usage. However, while many are working in this area, there is not yet, to my knowledge, a sufficiently developed body of science here to be called a theory, and the claim that our sentence is only pragmatically one-way rather than logically one-way is only a possibility. Similarly one might want to sweep quantifier scope ambiguity under the rug of pragmatics, and reduce the transparency/opacity ambiguity to one of scope of variable binding operators (an approach which has been reasonably successful for some of the classical opacity cases; but many unsolved problems remain), thus reducing it in effect to the quantifier scope cases.

So it appears thinkable that there could be, at least in principle, something like an isomorphism between an SF and any of its LFs. However, it seems more likely that the mismatch between SF and LF will be greater than that. The ambiguity issue only stated one in-principle condition that required a mismatch. But just because a SF is semantically unambiguous it will not follow that, say, its constituent structure corresponds point for point to that of its LF. And further, in some approaches to SF, many surface forms would be generated which would correspond to the null set of LFs. Examples might be *the man was hitting themselves, John loves each other*, etc. So in this view the interpreting function itself would in effect act as a kind of filter on the SFs.

So it seems to me then that the best assessment of the relation between SF and LF lies somewhere strictly in between isomorphism and randomness. How close to one pole or the other is an open question, but an important one, since our answer to the problem will determine how successfully we can characterise our linguistic (semantic + syntactic) competence. We should, it seems to me, be looking for theories of SF and LF in which the correspondence is as close as possible, while still accommodating the ambiguity 'facts'. For the closer the correspondence the more we have accounted for a speaker's competence in making inferences, denying, etc. Further, a close correspondence theory gives us perhaps an additional means of explaining how children learn quickly with limited exposure. It not only limits the ways the child may attempt to assign meaning to form but it gives an additional reason for the child's quick learning. Namely, we may assume the child is motivated both to express his needs (and in fact his understanding of the world) and also to understand what others say. That is, there is an intense motivation to be able to perform and comprehend 'semantic' acts. So if SFs are directly useful in coding and in decoding meaning the child is motivated (or at least pushed) into learning the semantically significant properties of SFs. In more concrete terms, the child is motivated to learn the grammatical distinctions between common nouns and intransitive verbs if these distinctions are useful in expressing meanings and understanding the meanings others communicate. If, on the other hand, that distinction had no semantic value, the child would be less motivated to learn it, and so presumably slower in acquiring it. The lazy child might relapse into conjugating nouns or putting determiners on verbs. We know in fact from psychology (though the cases studied are not directly comparable to the case we are considering) that people learn meaningful material more quickly than meaningless material. To the extent that SFs can be directly interpreted, that is, treated as LFs, the distinctive properties of SFs are meaningful and can be expected to be learned more quickly than if these properties were meaningless.

6 Conclusion

Unfortunately, it seems to me, much of the post-*Aspects* work in generative grammar has, in different ways in different cases, moved away from a conception of SF in which it is closely related to LF.

The original conception of syntactic theory in *Syntactic structures* however asemantic in conception, lent itself very nicely to a close relationship between LF and syntactic form generally. The kernel sentences in that view represented a *finite* amount of information a language learner had to learn by brute force. The unbounded set of derived structures, however, could naturally have their meanings represented as a function of what they were derived from since the generating functions (the transformations) were in a naive sense semantically interpretable. Thus a child could learn the meaning of Yes-No Question Formation (one of the generating functions) by learning how the meaning of a small sample of questioned kernel sentences differed in meaning from the kernel sentences they were derived from. Then the meaning of any yes-no question can be ascertained relative to the declarative it is formed from simply by recognising that it is, syntactically, a yes-no question. Analogous claims held for most of the major transformations in *Syntactic structures*. A proper semantic theory at this time would have 'simply' faced the task of indicating how the output of a transformation varied in meaning as a function of its input. And this is the sort of thing that logical theories do. Logical derivations by conjunction, disjunction, quantification, and negation do not preserve meaning. Rather we state the meaning of the output as a function of that of the input. Needless to say of course the semantic operations of English would have been at a higher level of complexity than in Classical Logic, but not in principle different.

But as is well known linguistic theory did not develop in this way. By 1964 and 1965 assigning meaning representations to SFs was a recognised goal of the theory, but the theory was reorganised in such a way that only base structures and lexical items were to be semantically interpreted. Taking off from the point, Generative Semantics attempted to argue that the putout of the Base differed very significantly from SFs, and that in fact the base structures (modulo a few differences as regards quantified expressions) resembled the LFs of the classically given first order logic (CL)! This is a terribly negative view of the relation between SF and LF, although that was perhaps not so apparent at the time.

But consider that the entire syntax of LFs in CL can be given in a single paragraph. Here it is: CL has a denumerable set of variables, x_1, x_2, etc. each having the category of Name. It has a set of function symbols each of unique degree $n \geq 0$, and a rule which says that the concatenation of an n-place function symbol with n occurrences of names is a name. The language also has a set of relation symbols each of unique degree $n \geq 1$, and a rule which says that the concatenation of an n-place relation symbol with n names is a formula. And it has two rules for deriving complex formulas. One says that if S and T are formulas then (not S), (S and T), and (S or T) are formulas. And the other says that if S is a formula and x a variable then (for every x, S) and (for some x, S) are formulas. And that's all.

Now the best generative grammars of English we have (Stockwell, Schachter, and Partee 1973) run into hundreds of pages, and they are clearly inadequate. Assuming that the meanings expressible in English can be done in CL or a slight extension thereof, we are saying that almost all of English syntax is needless as regards the expression of (logically representable) meaning. That is, we could have done with a one-paragraph grammar rather than the massive thing we apparently require. And since the diversity of structure present in SFs vastly exceeds the primitive syntax of CL, this view forces a massive correspondence failure between SF and LF. I find this a discouraging view, a kind of modern Babel theory in which Man is punished by God by having to use an absurdly complicated grammar when he could have done with a sleek one-paragraph one.

Nor does this view conform to my experience as one who has been concerned to represent the logical properties of natural language. The more I have looked at natural language the more I have found that almost everything in surface is relevant to the logical interpretation of SFs.

One might expect on the other hand that there would be a more optimistic view of the relation between SF and LF within EST syntax. It is clearly a goal of that theory to map SFs onto LFs, and the closer the correspondence between the two the easier it will be to define the mapping. But I am uneasy about the relation between SF and LF within this theory. On the one hand, in 'Questions of form and interpretation' Chomsky (1974, 16) espouses the view that there is a close relation: '... the thesis of "absolute autonomy formal grammar" ... would not imply that there are no systematic connections between form and meaning. No one, I am sure, has ever doubted that there are highly systematic connections and that a major problem of linguistic theory is to determine them.' On the other hand, Chomsky and Lasnik (1977, 429) assert that they believe, 'There is ... some empirical support for the belief that the syntax of LF is close to that of standard forms of predicate calculus ...' (though that assumption does not appear to me to play an important role in the article).

Given our earlier discussion that an assignment of LFs to natural language expressions is nonobvious in the same sense in which assignment of SFs is, it is certainly unwarranted to assume that LFs have one or another particular shape. To my knowledge no specific attempt has been made within EST syntax to define a function mapping SFs onto descriptively adequate sets of LFs drawn from Classical Logic. We cannot then assess the feasibility of defining such a function nor the demands it would make on the language learner.

I can think of only two reasons why, as generative grammarians, we might want to assume prior to an investigation that the LFs of CL are an appropriate range for an interpreting function for natural language SFs. I shall argue here that these reasons are in fact only apparent.

The first is that according to a certain well-defined metric of logical complexity (the degree of recursive unsolvability of the predicate *logically true*) CL is reasonably simple, though not absurdly so. Thus in CL *logically true* is a recursively enumerable predicate, whereas in second or higher order logics this is not the case. Thus for example in second order logic there can in principle be no complete syntactic characterisation of the entailment relation. So if the child (or whoever) only has to know things of first order difficulty, he has to know less than if he has to know things of second or higher order difficulty. This point is surely correct. To claim that the natural logic for English has the full expressive power of second order logic is to make a stronger claim about our logical competence than to claim that first order logic is sufficient.

However, the order of a logic is not tied to any particular syntactic instantiation, such as that in CL. The order of a logic is strictly determined by the set theoretical type (relative to the universe of discourse) of the variables in the logic. What makes first order logic first order is that we can only quantify over members of the universe of discourse U. In second order logic we can quantify over subsets of U, and so we can say things like 'For every object x there is a property P such that P(x)' and so on. So a logic which only allows quantification over U is first order, and that commits us to very little concerning the class of LFs the logic defines. It only requires that we have variables of a certain type, but otherwise we are free to construct the rules defining the LFs as we please. For example, the extensional logic proposed in *Logical types* is in all essential respects a first order logic. (The range of the variables in that logic appears to be sets of higher types, but in fact they are so constrained as to be in a one-to-one correspondence with the members of U.)

Secondly, the question of close correspondence between SF and LF is in principle independent of the question of autonomy of syntax. I take the autonomy thesis to be essentially that our syntactic capabilities are innately determined up to some level of specificity and that these capabilities are independent of other things, such as the semantic ends we make them serve. In fact construed in this way the autonomy thesis seems to me clearly true. There is to be sure a serious empirical matter as to how much of, say, English syntax is innately determined and how much represents a 'free' choice within the bounds of our innately determined possibilities. But the in-principle question seems clear: only humans use language, so what more natural explanation than that humans differ biologically in this respect from other animals?

But from the autonomy thesis alone nothing *follows* concerning the relation between SF and LF. It certainly does not follow for example that agreement pairs do not correspond to function-argument structures in the way we have claimed in this paper. Nor will it follow that certain function-argument structures are not commonly expressed by SFs which exhibit regular left-right order relations among their parts. Nor will it follow that the interpretation of complex SFs is completely unrelated to the interpretation of their constituent parts.

Whether correspondences exist between SF and their LFs is an empirical matter. To say that there is a massive correspondence failure is to say that man has made very poor use of his syntactic endowment. It is to say that man makes very many syntactic distinctions which are in fact irrelevant to the expression of meaning; and that he fails to code in his syntax distinctions which are semantically relevant. I can believe that we have not made perfectly efficient use of the syntactic instrument we come endowed with; that idioms for example do present meaningful parts whose meaning is (synchronically) irrelevant to the meaning of the entire idiom. And I can believe that there may be certain systematic ambiguities in language, such as the opacity/transparency ones cited earlier, which are not regularly coded in SF.

But I cannot believe that the syntactic elaboration present in each language can be collapsed into the pitiful syntax of CL. How will we represent the voicing systems of the Philippines? The tense systems of Bantu? The switch reference systems of New Guinea and the Americas? Where shall we put the deixis systems present in all languages? Where will imperatives and hortatives go? And subjunctives? And gerunds? What about the rules which most if not all languages have which convert Ss and VPs into NPs and Adjectives? And Adjectives into abstract nouns? Where to put the mass nouns, and noun compounds? And do we really not logically distinguish common nouns from intransitive verbs? And adjectives from adverbs?

Surely if we have all this syntax in our heads we will use it for some semantic effect. It may, to be sure, be difficult to explicate just what the semantic effect is in particular cases, but rather than accept a punishment theory — all that syntax is useless — I would recall the German proverb often cited by Einstein: 'The Lord is subtle but he is not mean.'

Notes

1. Several alternatives for the analysis of PPs are in fact suggested in *Logical types*. The version fully presented there was one in which Prepositions combined with either intransitive verbs (VPs) or transitive verbs (TVPs) to extend the class of DNP arguments they take. The analysis in which this semantics is presented with Prepositions as functions taking DNPs as arguments has been worked out by Faltz (Department of Linguistics, UCLA). For simple DNPs that analysis is equivalent to the one in *Logical types*. If the DNPs are properly quantified there may be relative scope differences between the DNP object of the Preposition and the Direct Object of transitive verbs.

It is interesting to note that perhaps the first scholar to investigate word order correlates, Abel Bergaigne, in 1875, arrives at a very similar analysis: they can be expressed by a 'double formule: le terme qualifiant précède le terme qualifié et le terme régi précède le terme régissant'. The quotation is cited in Holland (1976, 413).

3. We need not require that T_s be the entire set of LFs each of which expresses one of the meanings of s. It is sufficient that T_s be a set of LFs such that any logical form which represents a meaning of s is logically equivalent to one in T_s. T_s then can be expected to be finite for any s.

Note incidentally that whether the set of pairs $<s,T_s>$ is recursive is completely independent of whether an arbitrary, chosen logical form is valid, that is, true in all interpretations of the logic.

4. For example, let I be a correct interpreting function for a set of SFs. So for each SF s, I(s) is the set of descriptively adequate LFs for s. Enumerate the set of SFs (so for each SF we may associate a unique natural number n). Pick any weird numerical function, say the function f which maps each natural number n onto $100 + n^3$. Define a 'wrong' interpreting function I* which maps each surface from s onto I(sf(n)), where n is the number in the enumeration of s, and sp(n) the surface form where number is f(n).

5. For example, as regards entailment we do have a good pretheoretical

intuition. Namely, an (unambiguous) sentence S entails an unambiguous sentence T if T is true in all the cases in which S is true. Model theoretic semantics is an attempt to formalise this notion by formally representing the notion 'true in a state of affairs'.

The best pretheoretical intuition behind the notion 'ambiguity' which I can come up with is at best only a necessary condition for a sentence to be ambiguous. Namely, if S is ambiguous between meanings A and B (however represented) then a speaker on a literal, sincere, etc., use clearly intends either A or B. Thus the speaker cannot respond 'I don't know' to the query 'Do you mean A, or B?' We may attempt to formally represent this intuition by designing an interpreting function for SFs which maps the pretheoretically judged ambiguous ones onto a set containing nonlogically equivalent LFs. But the descriptive adequacy of the mapping is only as good as is our pretheoretical intuition of ambiguity, and that in fact is not very good.

References

Anderson, S.R. (1971) 'On the Role of Deep Structure in Semantic Interpretation', *Foundations of Language* 7, 387-96.

—— (1977) 'On mechanisms by which languages become ergative', in C.N. Li (ed.) *Mechanisms of Syntactic Change*, University of Texas Press, Austin, pp. 317-63.

Capell, A. (1971) 'Arosi Grammar', *Pacific Linguistics* 20 (Series B) The Australian National University, Canberra.

Chomsky, N. (1957) *Syntactic Structures*, Mouton, The Hague.

—— (1974) 'Questions of Form and Interpretation', manuscript, Department of Linguistics, MIT, Cambridge, Massachusetts.

—— and H. Lasnik (1977) 'Filters and control', *Linguistic Inquiry* 8, 425-505.

Comrie, B. (1973) 'The Ergative: Variations on a Theme', *Lingua* 32, 239-53.

—— (1978) 'Ergativity' in Lehmann 1978.

—— and S. Thompson (1978) 'Lexical Nominalisations', manuscript, Department of Linguistics, UCLA.

Derbyshire, D.C. (1977) 'Word Order Universals and the Existence of OVS Languages', *Linguistic Inquiry* 8, 590-99.

Dixon, R.M.W. (1972) *The Dyirbal Language of North Queensland*, Cambridge Univeristy Press, Cambridge.

Gary, J. and E.L. Keenan (1976) 'On Collapsing Grammatical Relations in Universal Grammar', in P. Cole and J. Sadock (eds.) *Syntax and Semantics: Grammatical Relations*, Vol. 8, 63-121, Academic Press, New York.

Gil, D. (1979) 'Prosodic Structure and Linguistic Universals', manuscript, Department of Linguistics, Tel Aviv University.

Hawkins, J. (1979a) 'Implicational Universals as Predictors of Word Order Change', *Language* 55.

—— (1979b) 'Two Types of Word Order Universals: Implicational and Distributional', manuscript, Department of Linguistics, University of Southern California.

Holland, G. (1976) 'The Shift from Postposition to Preposition: Evidence from Early Greek', *Proceedings of the Second Annual Meeting of the Berkeley Linguistics Society*.

Keenan, E.L. (1976) 'The Logical Diversity of Natural Languages', *Annals of the New York Academy of Sciences* 280, 73-92.

—— (1978) 'The Syntax of Subject-final Languages' in Lehmann (1978).

—— and L. Faltz (1978) *Logical Types for Natural Language*, Occasional Papers in Linguistics, No. 3, Department of Linguistics, UCLA.

Kimenyi, A. (1976) *A Relational Grammar of Kinyarwanda*, Ph.D. dissertation, Department of Linguistics, UCLA.

Lehmann, W. (ed.) (1978) *Syntactic Typology*, University of Texas Press, Austin.

Li, C. (ed.) (1975) *Mechanisms of Syntactic Change*, University of Texas Press, Austin.

—— and S. Thompson (1975) 'Subject and Word Order in Wappo', manuscript, Department of Linguistics, UCLA.

Montague, R. (1973) 'The Proper Treatment of Quantification in Ordinary English' in J. Hintikka, J. Moravcsik, and P. Suppes, (eds.) *Approaches to Natural Language: Proceedings of the 1970 Stanford Workshop on Grammar and Semantics*, pp. 221-42. Reidel, Dordrecht.

Moravcsik, E. (1978) 'Ergative and Accusative Patterns', manuscript, Department of Linguistics, University of Wisconsin.

Munro, P. (1976) 'On the Form of Negative Sentences in Kawaiisu', *Proceedings of the Second Annual Meeting of the Berkeley Linguistics Society*, 308-19.

Murane, E. (1974) *Daga grammar*, Summer Institute of Linguistics, Norman, Oklahoma.

Partee, B. (1976) *Montague Grammar*, Academic Press, New York.

Payne, J. (1978) 'Phrasal Conjunction', manuscript, The Typology Project, Department of Linguistics, UCLA.

Reinhart, T. (1976) 'On Understanding Poetic Metaphor', *Poetics* 5, 383-402.

Silverstein, M. (1976) 'Hierarchy of Features and Ergativity', in R.M.W. Dixon (ed.) *Grammatical Categories in Australian Languages*, pp. 112-71. Australian Institute of Aboriginal Studies, Canberra.

Stockwell, R., P. Schachter, and B. Partee (1973) *The Major Syntactic Structures of English*, Holt, Rinehart, and Winston, New York.

Timberlake, A. (1975) 'The Nominative Object in Finnish', *Lingua* 35, 201-30.

—— (1977) 'Reanalysis and Actualisation in Syntactic Change', in Li 1977, 141-77.

Vennemann, T. (1972) 'Analogy in Generative Grammar: The Origin of Word Order', paper read at the Eleventh International Congress of Linguists, Bologna, Italy.

14 THE LOGICAL DIVERSITY OF NATURAL LANGUAGES

Introduction

I will discuss in this paper a conception of language universal which differs from what I'll call the Current View in generative grammar both as regards the methodology for determining universals and as regards the relation between language and mind.

In the Current View, language universals (Us) are conceived of as constraints on the form (and substance) of possible human languages (Ls). These constraints can be represented as overt properties of grammars, given that a L can itself be represented by a grammar. Since each L satisfies the universal constraints, the Us are represented in the grammar of each L and can be determined by studying the grammar of only one L. Properties that vary from L to L are, of course, prima facie not candidates for being Us. And since surface structures of Ls are obviously different, it follows that Us are stated at some abstract, underlying level of structure. At that level Ls are all very similar, if not identical. Finally, Us are explained as direct reflections of our innate linguistic competence, which does not vary across speakers of different Ls.

In the view I am proposing however, Ls are held to be distinct in syntactically and semantically significant ways. Us are not in general representable as overt properties of each grammar, so overt properties of grammars do not in general determine innate mental structures. Rather, Us are determined by the pattern of cross-L variation with respect to a given property. Constancy across Ls is merely the special case of zero variation. Further, the cross-L variation need not be determined at a deep level of analysis; shallow or surface levels are often sufficient. Nonetheless, variation-based Us do determine constraints on the form (and substance) of possible human Ls, and may well be explained in terms of the cognitive similarity of L users, although little concerning the Us I will discuss suggests that that similarity extends to the level of innate linguistic capacity.

Before substantiating my proposal I would like to explain why it is a plausible point of view. It is so because, in my opinion, any particular L greatly underrealises what is universally possible. That is, the constraints on the forms of its structures are normally much stronger than the universally valid ones. To determine the universal constraints, we have to compare the particular constraints of a variety of Ls and then determine what common ground they cover. We will not generally need to state the Us in the grammar of any particular L because the constraints we need anyway will entail the Us and make their statement unnecessary and unmotivated. Advocates of the Current View often assume that the grammar of any particular L will realise to some significant extent what is universally possible.[1] That is why it is plausible, in that view, to consider that it might be possible to 'read off' Us from particular grammars.

I will illustrate my point with two logically different types of examples. In the first, the universal constraint may well occur in the grammars of some Ls, but will not occur in all. Consider e.g. the co-ordinate structure constraint (CSC) proposed in Ross (1967). It says, roughly, that operations that form complex structures from simpler ones by moving elements must be constrained so that an element that occurs within a single member of a co-ordinate structure cannot be moved out of the entire co-ordinate structure. For example, given a sentence like *John saw the man and the boy* we cannot relativise on *boy* yielding *the boy that John saw the man and* since that would involve moving a member of a single conjunct outside the whole conjunction.

However, in many Ls, probably most, the positions that can be relativised as so highly constrained as to make the statement of the CSC on relative-clause formation unnecessary. For example, in many of the Western Malayo-Polynesian Ls such as Tagalog and Malagasy, the language of Madagascar (see Keenan 1972a, 1975a), only subjects of main clauses can be relativised. Now, since no single member of a co-ordinate structure can be the subject of the entire construction in which the co-ordinate structure occurs, it follows that no single member of a co-ordinate structure can be relativised. We are unmotivated, then, to state the CSC for relative-clause formation in these Ls. Furthermore, at least in Malagasy, the other complex structures that are formed by movement are also constrained by the 'subject only' condition (or in some cases a slight weakening of it, but it is still required that a moved constituent bear a major relation to its root S), so there is no motivation at all for the CSC to appear in the grammar of

Malagasy, although Malagasy does, of course, conform to the CSC. To determine that the CSC is (plausibly, at least) a universal constraint on grammars, we need to investigate operations like relative-clause formation in a variety of Ls and then observe that despite the different ways of restricting the relativisable positions in different Ls, it always works out that single members of co-ordinate structures cannot be relativised by a movement process.

The second type of case concerns Us in which it is necessarily the case that each possible L presents a more specific version of the constraint than is universally valid. In this case, then, the U will not appear in the grammar of any L! Examples of such universal constraints are ones that express dependencies between properties of grammars, such as conditional claims of the form: 'If a L (or a grammar) has a property P then it necessarily has some other property Q.' Clearly, such claims constrain the form of possible human Ls, since they rule out Ls that have P but do not have Q. But a given L may satisfy the conditional constraint in any of three mutually exclusive ways: it may have both P and Q, or only Q without P, or else neither P nor Q. Further, any one of these ways is stronger than the conditional universal in the sense that, if generalised to hold of all possible languages, it entails the conditional claim but is not entailed by it. For example, if all languages have both P and Q (or all languages have only Q but not P, etc.), then trivially any language that has P has Q. But the conditional claim itself of course does not entail that all languages have both P and Q (or that all have only Q, etc.).

In general, then, to substantiate a conditional universal we must determine that for a 'fair sample' of possible languages some have both P and Q, others have Q but not P, and others have neither P nor Q. But no language in the sample has P without having Q. So it is clearly the pattern of variation that determines the U here.

I will now support my claims concerning language diversity and variation-based universals, drawing on data from three different subsystems of grammar: the promotion system (e.g. Passives), the cross-reference system, and the relative-clause formation system.

The Promotion System

Among the syntactic operations that form complex structures from simpler ones, Ls may have ways of assigning some NPs the gram-

matical properties of others. Thus in English the Passive transformation (regardless of how it is formally defined) has the effect
of presenting the direct object (DO) of the active sentence as the
subject of the derived sentence. In such cases I will say, without
further attempt at formal definition, that Passive in English
promotes DOs to subjects. English can also promote a few indirect
objects (IOs) to subject. Thus from *John gave the toy to Mary* we
can form *Mary was given the toy by John.* Plausibly, in such cases
the IO *Mary* is first promoted to DO, *John gave Mary the toy,* and
then passivised to subject. This promotion possibility, however, is
quite limited. Only a few common verbs like *give, tell,* and *teach*
allow it. Many verbs that take IOs such as *add, introduce, contribute, dedicate,* etc., cannot promote IOs to DO or to subject.
(*John added a book to the pile,* *John added the pile a book,* *The
pile was added a book by John.*)

Now, Ls vary enormously with regard to which NPs they can
promote to which positions. Many Ls lack such promotion devices
entirely. Thus, many Chadic languages like Hausa (Kraft and Kirk-
Greene 1973), many Kwa languages like Urhobo, and many
Melanesian languages like Arosi (Capell 1971) have no Passive. If
our study of universal grammar were based on only those
languages, it is hard to see how we would be motivated to posit
promotion rules as a possible rule category for human Ls. On the
other hand, many Ls can systematically promote most major (non-
subject) NPs to subject. Thus Malagasy and Philippine languages
usually have from four to eight 'voices' which function to promote
locatives, instrumentals, benefactives, temporal NPs, and so on, to
subject. For example, given the active sentence (1) in Kalagan
(Collins 1970), a typical Philippine language in this respect, all of
the nonsubject NPs can be promoted to subject:

(1) a. kumamang aku   sa tubig na   lata adti balkon
         +active   + nom
         get   I   obj water with can on   porch
         'I'll get the water on the porch with the can'
     b. kamangin ku   ya tubig na   lata adti balkon
         + pass   + agent subj water with can on   porch
         'The water will be got by me on the porch with the can'
     c. pagkamang ku   ya   lata sa tubig adti balkon
         + inst   + agent subj can obj water on   porch
         'The can will be got water with by me on the porch'

    d. kamangan ku   ya balkon sa tubig na   lata
      + loc   + agent subj porch obj water with can
      'The porch will be got water on by me with the can'

Similarly, in many Bantu languages locatives, as well as DOs and IOs, can be promoted to subject.

Chieewa (Bantu: example from Trithart 1975)
(2) a. John a- na- mu-on- a   Mary ku sukulu
       John he-past-she-saw-indic Mary at school
       'John saw Mary at school'
    b. Ku sukulu ku- na- on-edw-a-   ko Mary ndi John
       at school there-past-see-pass-indic loc Mary by John
       'School was seen Mary at by John'

Kinyarwanda (Bantu: example from Gary 1974)
(3) a. Yohani ya- Ø- ic- e   impyisi mu ishyamba
       John   he- past-kill-asp hyena in   forest
       'John killed a hyena in the forest'
    b. Ishyamba ri-Ø ic- iw- e   mo impyisi na Yohani
       forest   it-past-kill-pass-asp-loc hyena by John
       'The forest was killed in a hyena by John'

Note that in each of the promotions illustrated in (1)-(3) the derived subject has the position, case (where marked at all), and verb agreements of a subject, and the verb is marked differently, according as the promoted NP is a DO, instrumental, locative, etc.

Promotion possibilities then vary across Ls, but the variation is not random. Some positions are harder to promote to subject than are others. We have, for example, the following universal constraint: if a L can promote locatives to subject then it can promote DOs to subject, but not conversely. In fact, the available evidence (but more is needed, see Keenan and Comrie (1977), Trithart (1975), and Johnson (1974) for discussion) indicates that the Case Hierarchy below expresses the relative difficulty of promotion to subject (for major NPs of main clauses):

Case Hierarchy

  Subject > DirObject > IndObject > Benefactive > Other Oblique NPs

Thus, if a language can promote a NP low on the hierarchy to subject, then it can promote all intermediate positions to subject; but all the converses fail: some Ls, e.g. French, can subjectivise only DOs; others, e.g. English, can cover some IOs as well. Japanese (Shimizu 1975) and Iban (Keenan and Comrie 1977) can subjectivise DOs, IOs, and Benefactives; and Philippine and Bantu languages as discussed above, can subjectivise almost all major NPs.

The Case Hierarchy also determines the relative difficulty of promotion to DO. Some Ls, like English, can promote IOs to DO. But Bantu is again more generous, frequently allowing instrumentals and some locatives to be promoted to DO.

Luganda
(4) a.   John yatta enkonko na- ekiso
          John killed chicken   with-knife
          'John killed a chicken with a knife'
     b.   John yatt-is- a ekiso enkonko
          John kill- inst- knife chicken
          'John killed-with a knife a chicken'

But if a L can promote oblique NPs to DO then it can promote Benefactives and IOs and DO.

Furthermore, promotion to DO is universally harder than promotion to subject. Thus if a L has rules that promote NPs to DO, then it necessarily has rules which promote NPs to subject.

Note, however, that difficulty of promotion is not directly proportional to the distance between two NPs on the Case Hierarchy. It is not, for example, easier to promote locatives to DO that it is to promote them to subject. (Philippine languages promote them to subject, but not to DO.)

The conditional universals we have stated here clearly determine constraints on the form of possible human languages. They may have certain types of promotion rules only if they have others. Exactly why human grammars should be constrained in this way is not clear. The answer will depend in part on what kind of information is coded in notions like 'subject', 'direct object', etc. (see Keenan 1975b for discussion). So whether the promotion constraints reflect our innate linguistic competence or not is completely open.

The primary purpose of this discussion of promotion systems

has been to establish that L variation is not merely random or accidental. Rather, it is regular and determines constraints on the form human Ls can take, and therefore is a proper object of scientific inquiry. It is tempting, however, to dismiss the variation we have discussed so far as somewhat inessential. After all, if English lost the Passive, the rest of the syntax would not be radically affected. Nor would English suffer a loss of expressive power, since Passives and Actives are more or less paraphrased.

However, the role of promotion systems in other languages is often much more crucial to the rest of the syntax than it is in English. To consider only one example, in Malagasy and the Philippine languages we find that the relative clause (RC) forming system depends crucially on the promotion system. In those Ls only subject NPs can be relativised. Thus we cannot even directly say *the man that John saw*, here *man* functions as the DO of *saw*. To relativise on *man* we must first promote it to subject, and say *the man that was seen by John.*

Malagasy
(5) a. mijery ny olona Rajaona
         see   the person John
         'John sees the person'
     b. jeren-dRajaona ny olona
         seen by-John   the person
         'The person is seen by John'
     c. *ny olona izay mijery Rajaona
         the person that see   John
         'the person that John sees'
     d. ny olona izay jeren-dRajaona
         the person that seen   by-John
         'the person who is seen by John'

These Ls do not use pronouns (relative or other) to mark the position relativised. The semantic role that the head of the RC plays in the restricting clause is coded in the verb voice. If the verb of the restricting clause is passive in form, then the head NP is the underlying DO of the verb, since we must passivise the verb to make the constituent we want relativise a subject. Similarly, if the restricting verb is, for example, instrumental in form, then the head NP is an underlying instrumental, and so on. If we lost the promotion system in these Ls, the means of forming RCs (and Wh-questions, and co-referential deletions, etc. (see Keenan 1975a for discussion), would have to change.

Furthermore, the logical similarity between Actives and Passives is not quite perfect, as Chomsky pointed out some time ago. Thus, to use his example, *everyone in this room speaks two languages* is, it seems to me, vague (not ambiguous), according as it is the same two languages or not. The sentence is simply not explicit on that point. But *two languages are spoken by everyone in this room* has a reading, the preferred or only one for many speakers, in which it clearly does require that we all speak the same two languages. And this fact is no accident. It is universally the case that, other things being equal (and there are very many such other things, see Ioup 1973 for discussion), subjects have wider scope, logically speaking, than nonsubjects. This is even true for those few Ls like Malagasy and Gilbertese (see Keenan 1974 for examples) in which the subject follows the object in the unmarked word order.

Consequently, Ls vary with regard to logically significant operations (although we cannot conclude from this that they vary with regard to basic expressive power, since Ls with limited promotion devices may, and usually do, have other devices for forcing nonsubjects to have wider scope than subjects).

The Cross-Reference System

I should like now to consider a type of cross-language variation in which the prima facie case that Ls differ in logical expressive power is more impressive. The variation concerns the possibilities of stipulating different NP positions as being either *positively co-referential* (i.e., as referring to the same object), or *negatively co-referential* (i.e., as referring to different objects).

If the potentially co-referent NPs occur within the same clause there are, to my knowledge, three possible ways to stipulate their positive co-reference. First, a marked or 'reflexive' form of the verb may be used, as in Russian, Bantu generally, Dyirbal, Blackfoot, Turkish, and many other Ls.

Shona (Bantu)
(6) a.   John akarowa murume
         John struck   the man

   b. John aka*mu*rowa
       John struck-*him* (≠ John)
   c. John aka*zvi*rowa
       John struck-*self*

Second, in a very few cases, notably Eskimo, one of the NPs can simply be omitted.

Eskimo (Woodbury 1975)
(7) a. iNmi-nut tuqup-puq
         self-abl:sg kill-ind:3sg
         'He killed himself'
     b. tuqup-puq
         kill-   ind:3sg
         'He killd himself' or 'He died' or 'He was killed'

And third, a marked form of a pronoun may be used, as in an English sentence like *John hit himself.* The reflexive pronoun forces us to understand that the person hit and the person doing the hitting are the same. By contrast, we infer from sentences like *John hit him* or *John hit Bill* that the hitter and the hittee are different. Note that the logical form of a sentence like *John hit himself* and that of *John hit him* are different, since the conditions under which they are true are not necessarily the same. Some Ls, however, do not syntactically codify this logical distinction. Thus, in many Polynesian languages such as Gilbertese and Tahitian, the same sentence is used in either case, the difference in meaning being left up to context.

Gilbertese (example from Keenan 1973)
(8) E- tara-ia   Teerau
     he-hit- him/himself Teerau
     'Teerau hit him' or 'Teerau hit himself'

Similarly, in some Indo-European Ls this logical distinction is also ignored.

Fering (a N. Frisian dialect: example from K. Ebert, personal communication)

(9)   John hee ham   ferreet
      John has him/himself betrayed
      'John has betrayed him' or 'John has betrayed himself'

Middle English (Chaucer, *The Knight's Tale,* example from Keenan 1973)
(10) a.   He leyde hym, bare the visage, on the beere (v. 2877)
          (He = Theseus, hym = Arcite, as is clear from context)
     b.   At Thebes, in his contree, as I seyde.
          Upon a nyght in sleep as he hym leyde (v. 1384)
          (he = Arcite, hym = Arcite)

These Ls, then, are logically less expressive than contemporary English, since it expresses a logical distinction which they do not.

On the other hand, English does not normally stipulate the co-reference between subjects and possessors of objects. Thus the syntax of *John wrecked his car* allows that it be John's car or that it be someone else's. The reference of *his* depends on context, just as did the reference of the object pronouns in Gilbertese, Fering and Middle English. But many Ls, such as Swedish, Latvian, Russian, Finnish, Japanese, Hindi, and Turkish, distinguish between reflexive and nonreflexive possessors.

Swedish (McClean 1969)
(11) a.   Lars har sin   bok
          Lars has his(= Lars) book
     b.   Lars har hans   bok
          Lars has his(≠ Lars) book

Japanese
(12) a.   Taroo wa zibun   no inu o   butta
          Taroo tpc his(= Taroo) gen dog DO hit
          'Taroo hit his (Taroo's) dog'
     b.   Taroo wa kare   no inu o   butta
          Taroo tpc his(≠ Taroo) gen dog DO hit
          'Taroo hit his (someone else's) dog'

Note that in these examples both positive and negative co-reference is stipulated. In the forms with the reflexive *his* the possessor must be the subject, and in the non-reflexive forms the possessor must be someone other than the subject. English appears to lack this discriminating power, and so is less expressive logically than Swedish, Japanese, and others.

One might argue, however, that although English normally does not stipulate co-reference of subjects and possessors of objects, it can do so, if necessary, by using the form *own*, as done in the glosses above. Thus in *John wrecked his own car* it is clearly John's car that was wrecked, not someone else's. However, the use of *his-own* is not quite equivalent to the reflexive possessives cited above, since *own* forces the meaning of permanent possession rather than temporary possession, and thus contrasts with a mere *his* in contexts like: *the students were given ballpoint pens to write their exams with, but John didn't use his because he preferred to use his own.* Further, even though *his-own* may be used to force positive co-reference in some cases, there seems to be no systematic way of forcing negative co-reference. Clearly the absence of *own* in *John wrecked his car* does not force the nonreflexive reading. What English would need here would be a form like *his-else* corresponding to *his-own*. But English lacks such a form.[2]

Further, when the potentially co-referent positions occur in different clauses, one subordinate to the other, English is even less well adapted to stipulating their co-reference. It has basically two means for doing so. One, it can repeat a full NP, marked perhaps with an anaphoric marker like *the* or *that* as in *While John was explaining the problem to a student, the student was working out a crossword puzzle.* Second, English may delete a positively co-referent NP (triggering perhaps other changes in the sentence as well), as in *John was preparing his lecture while walking in the garden*, where it is clearly John who is doing the walking in contrast to *John was preparing his lecture while he was walking in the garden*, where *he* might refer to John or it might refer to someone else identified in the discourse. A slightly different type of example would be *John expects to be elected*, where clearly John has an expectation about himself, in distinction to *John expected him to be elected*, where the expectation is clearly about someone else. But notice here that the co-referent positions do not occur across clause boundaries in surface, but rather they are the surface subject and object of *expect*. So raising subordinate positions to main clause ones, where co-reference is more naturally stipulated in English, is another option English may use.

Noun marking and deletion are probably universal means of stipulating positive co-reference across clause boundaries, but other strategies are also in common use, and can often apply in cases where the English strategies cannot. I shall discuss three such strategies: *pronoun marking, case marking,* and *switch reference marking.*

Pronoun Marking

English does not systematically stipulate the co-reference of subjects of verbs of thinking and saying and the subjects of their sentential complements. Thus the syntactic form of *John thinks that he will win* allows that *he* refer to John or to someone else already identified in the discourse. But many Ls such as Japanese, Korean, Yoruba (Kwa), and Kera (Chadic) stipulate positive and, generally, negative co-reference of these positions by the use of marked vs unmarked pronominal forms.[3]

Japanese (example from Mat Shibatani, personal communication)
(13) a. Taroo wa zibun ga   katu to   omotte iru
         Taroo tpc self   subj win COMP think   be
         'Taroo thinks that he (= Taroo) is winning'
     b. Taroo wa kare ga   katu to   omotte iru
         Taroo tpc he   subj win COMP think   be
         'Taroo thinks that he (likely ≠ Taroo) is winning'

Yoruba
(14) a. Ojo ro   pe on   mu sasa
         Ojo thinks that he(= Ojo) is   clever
     b. Ojo ro   pe ó   mu sasa
         Ojo thinks that he (≠ Ojo) is   clever

Kera (example from K. Ebert, personal communication)
(15) a. Golsala dig   minti to   bɨ cuuru
         Golsala thinks that   he(= Golsala) is intelligent
     b. Golsala dig   minti wɨ   bɨ cuuru
         Golsala thinks that   he(≠ Golsala) is intelligent

Again, it might be argued that although English does appear to lack the means to stipulate the negative co-reference of these positions, it can stipulate their positive co-reference if necessary. We can, for example, simply mark the embedded subject with a kind of emphatic reflexive, as in *John thinks that he himself should go*. But this use of the reflexive does not in general force co-reference with the matrix subject, as is clear from examples like *The president wanted to send the prime minister to the meeting, but his secretary thought that he himself should go*. Clearly *he himself* here does not refer to *his secretary*. A possibly more general alternative would be to simply repeat, in apposition, the matrix subject, as in *John thinks that he, John, should go*. But this solution will not work when the matrix subject is any of several types of quantified NP. Thus we cannot paraphrase the intended meaning of *everyone thinks that he should go* by anything like *everyone thinks that everyone should go* or *everyone thinks that that person should go*. Similarly, if the subject is *most people, no one*, etc. But the Japanese type languages can stipulate both positive and negative co-reference in these cases. (In fact, the judgement of negative co-reference in sentences with the nonreflexive pronouns is much clearer than in the simpler cases like (13),

Japanese (example from Mat Shibatani, personal communication)
(16) a.   Daremo   ga   zibun ga   katu to   omotte iru
      Everyone subj self   subj win   COMP think   be
      'Everyone thinks that he (himself) is winning'
   b.   Darema   ga   kare   ga   katu to
                                                   omotte iru
      Everyone subj he(definitely = other) subj win   COMP
                                                   think   be
      'Everyone thinks that he (someone previously
      identified) is winning'

So again we have a case where some Ls make a logical distinction that English doesn't.

Case Marking

The possibility of using case marking to stipulate co-reference is perhaps not widely recognised. The following example from Classical Greek, provided by E.J.W. Barber (personal communication) is a magnificent illustration of this strategy.

(17) a. élthōn-Ø
      coming-nom   eis   tēn pólin, ho didáskal-os
   b. élthont-a   édeixe
      coming-acc   into the city   the teacher- nom
                                                   nom
   c. élthont-i   showed
      coming-dat   tón paid-a   tô̂ sōkrát-ē
                       the child-acc the Socrates-dat
   d. élthont-os   acc   dat
      coming-gen
      'Coming into the city, the teacher showed the child to
      Socrates'

The main clause of (17), *the teacher showed the child to Socrates,*
contains three NPs: a nominative, an accusative, and a dative. The
subordinate verb, *come,* which lacks an overt subject, takes the
case marker of whatever NP in the matrix clause is understood to
function as its subject. Thus (17a) means that the person who was
coming into the city was the teacher, (17b) means that it was the
child, and (17c) means it was Socrates. Thus matching of case
markers here forces positive co-reference. English can, perhaps,
also stipulate the positive co-reference in these cases by repeating
full NPs, e.g. *While the teacher was coming into the city the teacher
showed the child to Socrates* (although such a sentence could perhaps be used in a situation in which two different teachers had
been previously identified).

    But Greek affords us an additional possibility — the absolutive
construction illustrated in (17d). Here the use of the genitive case
marker on the subordinate verb stipulates that the subject of that
verb is *not* co-referential with any of the NPs in the matrix, but
must be understood to refer to someone else previously identified.
Thus the condition expressed by the subordinate clause is absolute,
i.e., not dependent on anything in the matrix clause.

    The possibility of stipulating negative co-reference here is, it
seems to us, lacking in English. Notice, however, that many of the
daughter Ls of Indo-European developed absolutive constructions
that functioned to stipulate negative co-reference. In Latin the
absolutive case marker was the ablative (its role in stipulating
negative co-reference is discussed briefly in Winter), in Gothic and
old Slavic it was the dative, and in Sanscrit it was a locative.

    Further, the possibility of stipulating positive co-reference by case marking is not limited to Indo-European Ls. Ken Hale (personal communication) provides the following example from Walbiri, an Australian L:

(18) kudu-ŋku maliki-Ø   paka- nu   wanti-njtja-wanu- lu
     child-erg dog- abs strike-past, fall- inf- COMP-erg
     'The child hit the dog, after falling'

Here the use of the ergative case marker on the subordinate verb *fall* unequivocally indicates that its subject is the ergative NP in the main clause. Thus (18) can only mean that it was the child that fell. If the ergative marker on the verb is replaced by the absolutive marker, Ø, then it is naturally interpreted to mean that it was the dog that fell (although the other interpretation is perhaps also possible, so the co-reference is not unequivocally stipulated in this case, whereas in (18) it is).

Switch Reference

It is characteristic of several language groups that subordinate verbs may carry one of two affixes according to whether their subject is either the same in reference or different in reference from some NP in another clause. This is a typological trait of the Ls of the Eastern New Guinea Highlands Stock (McKaughan 1973) such as Fore (Scott 1973), Kate-Kamano, and Bena-Bena (Young 1971). It is also typologically characteristic of the Hokan phylum of American Indian Ls (see Jacobsen 1967, Winter, and Munro 1974) for discussion) and occurs as well in some Uto-Aztecan Ls e.g. Hopi (Voegelin and Voegelin 1974).

We consider first some cases from American Indian Ls: (in the examples below we use *ds* to abbreviate *different subject*, and *ss* for *same subject.*)

Hopi (example from Pam Munro, personal communication)
(19) a.   pam navoti:ta (pam) mo:titani-q
          he   thinks   (he)   win   -ds
          'He thinks that he (= someone else) will win'
     b.   pam navoti:ta (pam) mo:titani-qua?e
          he   thinks   (he)   win   -ss
          'He thinks that he (himself) will win'

The use of the *different-subject* marker on the subordinate verb in

(19a) clearly means that the subject of *win* is not the same as the subject of *think*, whereas the use of the *same-subject* marker in (19b) clearly means that the subject of *win* is the same as the person doing the thinking. Similar claims hold for the Mojave (Yuman family, Hokan phylum) sentences below, again provided by Pam Munro (personal communication).

(20) ʔi:pa-č̀   su:paw-mpoč piʔipa:-nʸ   iyu: $\begin{cases} \text{-m} \\ \text{-k} \end{cases}$

man- subj know -neg person-dem see- $\begin{cases} \text{-ds} \\ \text{-ss} \end{cases}$

'The man doesn't know who he saw'

If the suffix *-m* is chosen on the subordinate verb *see*, then the subject of *see* must be different from the matrix subject *man*, and thus the man's lack of knowledge concerns someone other than himself. But if the suffix *-k* is chosen, then the subject of *see* is necessarily the same as the subject of *know*. Similarly,

(21) ʔi:pa-nʸ -č   ʔava:-lʸ   nʸa -iyem $\begin{cases} \text{-m} \\ \text{-k} \end{cases}$, yakapit-pč

man- dem-subj house-loc when-come $\begin{cases} \text{-ds} \\ \text{-ss} \end{cases}$, drunk tense

'When the man came to the house, he was drunk'

Again, if the subordinate verb *come* is suffixed with *-m*, then the man who came is different from the person who was drunk. But if the suffix *-k* is chosen, then the man who came and the person who was drunk are the same.

The data from Hopi and Mojave clearly indicate that those Ls can stipulate negative co-reference in a way not possible in English. Furthermore, the use of *ss* markers seems a more effective way of stipulating positive co-reference than the English strategies, since it works as well if the controller NP is quantified. Thus parallel to (21) from Mojave we have:

(22) ʔipač-č   pay nʸa- u:θew   -k yakapi:tč -m
men -subj all when-drink + pl-ss drunk + pl-tns
'When all the men were drinking, they got drunk'

In English however, we cannot generally stipulate positive co-reference in this construction by repeating full NPs. Thus *Everyone got drunk after he returned* is not paraphrasable by *Everyone got drunk after everyone returned.* The deletion strategy may be somewhat more effective, since the sentence *Upon returning, everyone got drunk* seems to imply that the subject of *return* and that of *get drunk* are the same. But even here it can be argued that the subject of *return* is only vaguely specified. Thus, in a context like *Pat and Mickey had had a bloody hard day on the job, so upon returning to their wives, everybody got drunk*, it seems that the subject of return is only *Pat and Mickey*, but the subject of *get drunk* includes their wives as well.

The use of switch reference marking in New Guinea Ls is even more striking in certain respects than in the American Indian Ls. Here it is common in narrative discourse for main clauses to be preceded by up to twenty subordinate clauses (called 'medial' forms in the literature). The subordinate verbs carry different markers according to whether or not their subject is different from that of the main clause in the sequence, regardless of whether the next clause is a main clause or not. Further, the switch reference markers may encode information about the relative times of the actions expressed in the two clauses. And in addition, it often happens that the subordinate verb carries an affix which agrees in person and number with the subject of the following clause, regardless of whether it is the same or different. So subordinate verbs often agree with two subjects: their own, and that of the next clause. (In the examples that follow, matching subscripts indicate sameness of reference, different subscripts different reference.)

Fore (Scott 1973)

(23) a. kana- ogá-   na$_i$ wa-tä- y$_i$- e
        come-ds:3sg:past 3sg go-past-3sg-indic
              coord, act.
        'He came and he went'

    b. kana- nta-   na$_i$ wa-tä- y$_i$- e
        come-ss:3sg:past 3sg go-past-3sg-indic
              coord, act.
        'He came and he went'

In (23a) the use of the *ds* marker unequivocally means that the person who came is not the same as the person who went, whereas these two are the same in (23b).

Kafe-Kamano   (example   from   Harold   Levine,   personal communication)

(24) a.   Ónihava$_j$ joyaf- inti bu-j$_j$- ge-no$_i$ Toiso$_i$ a-   gé- 'n- e
         Onihava$_j$ garden-into go-he$_j$-ds-he$_i$ Toiso$_i$ him-see- past-
                                                                    Emph
         'Onihava went into the garden (and) Toiso saw him'

    b.   Ónihava$_j$ joyaf- inti bu-i$_j$- no$_j$ a- gé- 'n-   e
         Onihava$_j$ garden-into go-he$_j$-he$_j$ him-see-past-Emph
         'Omnihava went into the garden (and) saw him'

Note here that change of subject is overtly marked (24a), but sameness of subject is indicated by the absence of a switch marker. Note also that while both the Fore and Kafe sentences are translated by co-ordinate structures in English, the first clause in each case is clearly marked as being not a main clause by virtue of the anticipatory subject marking. So the first clauses of (23) and (24) cannot stand alone as main clauses.

Some Universals of Co-reference?

Although the diversity of means Ls use to stipulate co-reference makes any generalisations at this point somewhat tentative, the following two 'universals' are largely consistent with the data at my disposal.

A   If co-reference, either positive or negative, can be controlled by any NPs in a language, then, in general, subjects of main clauses may control co-reference.

B   If a language can stipulate the negative co-reference of two positions then it can stipulate their positive co-reference as well.

A states that we cannot have human Ls in which only e.g. direct objects control co-reference.[4] And B states that no L can stipulate only negative co-reference. It appears, then, that, like promotion systems, variation in the cross-reference system of a L is regular, and a proper object of scientific investigation.

Relative Clauses

I want finally to consider certain types of variation found in the relative-clause (RC) forming system across Ls. Ls differ both with regard to the NP positions which can be relativised and with regard to the means (= strategies) used to relativise them. And the two types of variation are not independent: some strategies are more effective than others in that they can relativise positions which the others cannot.

Consider first the *verb-coding* strategy discussed earlier for Malagasy and the Philippine Ls. There, recall, only surface subjects could be relativised. Thus, if the subordinate verb in the RC is, for example, passive, then the position relativised represents an underlying direct object, since it was necessary to passivise the verb to promote it to the relativisable slot. Similarly, if the verb is in a locative form the position relativised is an underlying locative, and so on. So it is the verb form that codes the semantic relation between the head NP and the restricting clause.

But verb-coding strategies are inherently limited, since universally the number of verb voices is less than the number of distinct semantic relations that NPs may bear to verbs. Thus, NPs bearing different semantic relations to the verb will be promoted to subject using the same verb voice, and consequently RCs formed on those subjects will be inherently vague or ambiguous. This is particularly clear when NPs bear different *locative* relations to the verb. Thus the Malagasy sentences (25a) and (25b) differ only in their locative prepositions *on* and *under*.

(25) a. nametraka mofo teo ambony ny latabatra Rabe
        placed   bread there on top of the table   Rabe
        'Rabe placed the bread on top of the table'
     b. nametraka mofo teo ambany ny latabatra Rabe
        placed   bread there under   the table   Rabe
        'Rabe placed bread under the table'

However, when *table* is promoted to subject in either case, the verb goes in the same form, *table* moves to subject position (sentence final) and becomes nominative, losing its preposition. So the derived sentence is the same in both cases:

(26) nametrahan-dRabe mofo ny latabatra
     placed by-   Rabe bread the table
     '?? The table was bread put by Rabe'

So the exact locative relation between *table* and *put* cannot be expressed in this sentence. But this is the only one that *table* can be relativised from. Consequently the RC preserves the vagueness (or ambiguity) of (26).

(27) ny latabatra izay nametrahan-dRabe mofo
     the table   that placed by-   Rabe bread
     'the table where Rabe put the bread'

Thus, in many cases where English has two logically distinct RCs, e.g. *the table under which Rabe put the bread* and *the table on top of which Rabe put the bread*, Malagasy and the Philippine Ls have only one: so English codifies a logical distinction that those Ls don't.

On the other hand, the RC forming strategies used in English are generally less effective than the *noun-coding* strategies characteristic of many Ls in which the surface RC presents a nominal element in the position relativised. The nominal element is a pronoun in Welsh, Czech, Persian, Semitic generally, many Polynesian and Melanesian Ls (Tongan, Fijian), etc. (See Keenan and Comrie 1977 for discussion.)

Hebrew
(28) ha- isha   she- Yon natan la   et   ha- sefer
     the woman that John gave to her DO the book
     'the woman that John gave the book to'

On the other hand, in Ls as diverse as Walbiri and Mabuaig in Australia, Hindi, Kannada, Hittite, medieval Slavic, and Bambara (W. Africa), the position relativised is marked by a full NP. In those Ls a RC can be formed from a sentence simply by adding a morphological marker to the NP which defines the domain of relativisation. Thus from (29a) in Bambara we can form the RC in (29b).

(29) a. ca ye muso ye
       man past woman see
       'The man saw the woman'
   b. cä yé muso min ye
       man past woman rel see
       'the woman that the man saw'

Now noun-coding strategies generally permit the formation of a larger class of RCs than strategies that present no NP in the position relativised (and which I will call for the nonce *deletion* strategies). To take just one example. Ls that use noun-coding strategies can frequently (but not always) relativise into single members of co-ordinate NPs. Thus from (30a) in Hebrew (example from Cole *et al.* 1975) we can form (30b).

(30) a. ha- ish ve- Miriam xaverim tovim
       the-man and-Miriam friends good
       'The man and Miriam are good friends'
   b. ze ha- ish she- hu ve- Miriam xaverim tovim
       this the-man that-he and-Miriam friends good
       'This is the man that he and Miriam are good friends'

And from (31a) in Kannada (example constructed from Cole *et al.* 1975) we can form (31b)

(31) a. sōfa mattu kurciya naduve avaru mējannu ittiddāro
       sofa and chair-gen between they table-acc placed-have
       'They have placed a table between a sofa and a chair'
   b. yāva sōfa mattu kurciya naduve avaru mējannu
                                ittiddāro
       rel sofa and chair-gen between they table-acc
                                placed- have
       adu haleyadu
       that old-is
       'the sofa which they have placed a table between (it) and a chair is old'

Further, many Ls (see Keenan and Comrie 1977 for details) that normally use deletion strategies to form RCs have recourse to noun-coding strategies when relativising 'difficult' positions e.g. possessor NPs, as in *Here comes the student that I can never remember his name,* and NPs in embedded questions, as *This is the road that I don't know where it goes.* For a more detailed analysis of the range of positions that can be relativised by the pronoun-retaining strategies, see Keenan (1974) and Keenan and Comrie (1977). For the noun-retaining strategies see Cole *et al.* (1975) and Keenan and Bimson (1975).

Some Universals of RC Formation

C   If a L can relativise any NPs it can relativise main clause subjects.

D   If a language L uses noun-coding strategies in RC formation to a greater extent that another language L′, then the class of relativisable NPs in L is greater than or equal to that in L′.

D is a way of formulating the intuition that noun-coding strategies yield 'lots' of RCs (relative to the 'norm' for Ls). But it is logically different from the simple conditional universals we have considered up to now. For it says that properties of some Ls are not independent of those of others! That the grammar of one L should be constrained by that of another may seem outlandish, but quite generally, I think, statements of functional equivalence of different syntactic processes will have this comparative quality. Consider for example the oft-cited, and largely correct, claim that case-marking Ls have relatively free word order. Note that both case marking (understood to cover the use of prepositions and postpositions) and word-order freedom are matters of degree. Some Ls (e.g. Machiguenga: Peru, see Snell and Wise 1963) case mark practically no major NPs, whereas others, e.g. Tongan (Polynesia), case mark all major NPs. And in some Ls (Walbiri; Australia) word order is totally free, whereas in others (e.g. French) it is fixed. Given that, we may formulate the trade-off between word-order freedom and case marking as follows: If L case marks to a greater degree than L′, then the word-order freedom of L is greater than or equal to that of L′.

Conclusion: Explaining Variation-Based Universals

The primary purpose of this paper has been to substantiate the claim that Ls vary in interesting ways, that the variation is regular, and that it determines universal constraints on the form of possible human Ls. But we have offered no explanation for this variation. And indeed, an explanation for even a part of it would go beyond our current knowledge. So I would like to close by suggesting a line of research which, if pursued, could in my opinion lead to explanations of some of the variation we have discussed.

The starting point for this research would be the Principle of Autonomous Reference (PAR), which I will define below. The PAR is, at the moment, little more than a personal impression based on work in a variety of Ls. It clearly needs conceptual refinement and systematic empirical corroboration. Further, by itself it does not explain the variation in question, but requires in each case supplementary assumptions concerning the nature of language — assumptions that are, again, in need of conceptual clarification and empirical corroboration.

Principle of Autonomous Reference (PAR)

In the basic sentence types of a L a combination of case marking, position, and verb agreements function to identify exactly one NP as being in principle autonomous in reference.

By *basic sentences* I mean those whose syntactic form is not given as a function of that of other sentences. By *autonomous in reference* I mean an NP used to refer to some object or concept, and whose referent is identifiable to the addressee at the moment of utterance. In other words, in the context of utterance, the information in the NP itself is sufficient to tell the addressee(s) what object or concept is being referred to. Thus the reference of such an NP cannot be made to depend on the reference of some NP that follows it in the discourse. Either it refers directly to some object physically present in the discourse, or it co-refers to an object already identified (or at least known to exist).[5]

Note, of course, that in any given sentence many NPs may, in fact, be autonomous in reference (e.g. in *John loves Mary* both *John* and *Mary* are in fact autonomous in reference). But only one NP in basic sentences *must* be. Others *may* depend on it for their reference (as happens in *John loves himself*, where the identity of the person loved is specified as being the same as that of the one doing the loving).

Now generally speaking, the NPs we identify as subjects of basic sentences are the autonomously referring expressions (AREs) of those sentences. Further, the surface coding properties (case marking, etc.) of basic subjects also identify main clause subjects of complex sentences, and these subjects are AREs as well.

The 'fact' that main clause subjects are AREs might be used in the partial explanation of the variation we have discussed in the following cases:

First, it gives some explanation as to why Ls should have promotion to subject rules. Namely, such rules serve to present NPs as autonomous in reference when they are not necessarily so in basic sentences. It is thus no accident that our judgement of relative scope of quantifier NPs changes when a sentence is passivised. For notice that in an active sentence like *every boy kissed some girl* the 'reference' of *some girl* depends on that of *every boy* in the sense that the truth of the sentence requires that for each boy there be some girl whom he kissed. The choice of girl however, may vary with (that is, depend on) the choice of boy. But, in the passive sentence *some girl was kissed by every boy*, we must identify some girl independently of a choice of a boy, and then establish that every boy kissed that girl. Further, if we could show that DOs fail to have any characteristic semantic or pragmatic property, like autonomous reference, we would have a basis for explaining why it is more usual across Ls to have promotion to subject rules than promotion to object rules.

Second, the 'fact' that subjects are AREs may partially explain why subjects are the easiest NPs to relativise across Ls. For notice that in general, head NPs of RCs are also autonomously referential. That is, the class of objects they specify must be understood independently of the reference of any NP in the restricting clause. Even if the restricting clause precedes the head, the normal order in SOV Ls, we cannot make the reference of the head depend on anything in the restricting clause, e.g. by pronominalising it (see Keenan 1974 for further exemplification and discussion). So when we relativise on a given NP position, we force that position to be autonomously referential. But because subject NPs already have that property, RC formation on subjects changes relatively little our understanding of the way we understand the sentence relativised into. But when objects are relativised, they are forced to have a property they do not necessarily have: autonomous reference. Perhaps RC formation on objects is therefore universally harder than on subjects, since it distorts the meaning of the sentence relativised into more than RC formation of subjects. Further, object RCs have of necessity two AREs in surface: the head NP and the subject of the restricting clause, whereas subject RCs have only one ARE, of necessity. This explains why the pronoun *he* in *the man who he saw* cannot be understood to necessarily co-refer to *man*, for *he* is a subject of a clause of which *man* is an object, and subjects must refer independently of objects. For further discussion of this point see Keenan (1974).

And third, if subjects are generally AREs, it is natural that they should be universally among the controllers of co-reference. For if the reference of a subject is always well defined, then the reference of another NP will also be well defined when it is given as a function of that of a subject.

In conclusion, let me just reiterate that our discussion of the PAR and its role in explaining variation-based universals is intended only as suggestive of further research and is not intended as complete in itself. The primary purpose of this paper has been merely to establish certain patterns of language variation and the constraints they determine on human languages.

Notes

1. For example in Katz (1966, 109) we find: 'That is, each linguistic description has a common part consisting of the set of linguistic universals and a variable part consisting of the generalisations that hold only for the given language.' In discussing the universal part, Katz (p. 110) goes on to say that '... such facts are stated just once in the theory of language as facts about language, thereby making numerous particular statements of them unnecessary'. It appears clear in Katz's view, then, that linguistic universals would appear in the grammars of particular Ls if they were done in isolation. That Katz's view of universals and language variation is different from the one I am proposing is made clear by the final sentence of the paragraph from which the previous quotations were taken (p. 110). 'The farther we thus empirically limit the logically possible diversity in natural languages, the richer the theory of universal structure given in the theory of language.'

2. Of the many ways we might attempt to stipulate negative co-reference, all I have tried seem to me to fail to be equivalent to the Swedish and Japanese type cases. Thus *John wrecked a car which belonged to someone other than him* fails to identify the car and as well leaves the reference of *him* unclear, whereas the Swedish version of *John wrecked his (≠ John's) car* identifies the possessor of the car and makes it clear that it is not John. Similarly, *John wrecked the car, which didn't belong to him*, presupposes that a car has been previously identified and is still vague with regard to the reference of *him*. Another alternative, *John wrecked his, someone else's car* fails for several reasons. First, the reference of *else* is not unequivocally John; we might mean someone else already identified in the discourse. Further, the sentence is pragmatically redundant in a very bizarre way. For the use of *his*, not co-referential with John, presupposes that the speaker and addressee know who is being referred to. And given that the use of proper names like *John* presupposes that the identity of the reference is known to the participants

in the discourse, the added assertion *someone else's* is only redundant. It provides less information than what is already presupposed by the use of *his*. Finally, as per our translation of (12b), *John wrecked his (someone else's) car* fails to paraphrase the intended sentences in Japanese and Swedish because it actually talks, metalinguistically, about some of the words in the sentences namely, the reference of *his*. But the Swedish sentences do not talk about their own words, and so differ in meaning in a very big way from the proposed English translation.

3. Across clause boundaries the use of the *kare* series of pronouns in Japanese may or may not definitely stipulate negative co-reference. In the simple cases like (13b) some speakers find that *kare* can co-refer to the matrix subject. But in cases like (16b) the use of *kare* definitely does stipulate negative co-reference.

4. An interesting potential counterexample here is reported for Angaataha (Huisman 1973), one of the New Guinea Ls. Here the switch reference markers have apparently only a switch location function. One marker indicates that the location of the action of the next clause coming up is the same as that of the clause which carries the marker, and another marker indicates that the location will change in the next clause. But not enough information is available concerning stipulation of co-reference to subjects to allow us to say that Angaataha can stipulate co-reference between locatives but not to subjects.

5. Three weak points in this definition and subsequent claims are: (1) We need operational tests for degree of basicness; (2) the notion of reference is not defined; and (3) the criteria used to determine which NPs are subjects must be established on universal grounds. See Keenan (1975b) for discussion.

References

Capell, A. (1971) 'Arosi Grammar', *Pacific Linguistics* 20 (Series B), the Australian National University, Canberra.

Cole, P.W., S. Harbert, S. Hashimoto, C. Nelson, D. Smietana and S. Sridhar (eds.) (1975) 'Noun Phrase Accessibility and Island Constraints', presented at the Parasession of the Eleventh Regional Meetings of the Chicago Linguistic Society, Chicago, Illinois.

Collins, G. (1970) *Two Views of Kalagan Grammar*, Ph.D. dissertation, Department of Linguistics, Indiana University, Bloominton, Indiana.

Gary, J.O. (1974) 'Promotion Rules in Kinyarwanda', unpublished manuscript, Department of Linguistics, University of California at Los Angeles.

Huisman, R.D. (1973) 'Angaataha Verb Morphology', *Linguistics* 110, 43-54.

Ioup, G. (1973) 'Some Universals of Quantifier Scope', paper presented at the Second Conference on New Ways of Analyzing Variation, Georgetown University, Washington, D.C.

Jacobsen, W.H. (1967) 'Switch-reference in Hokan-Coahuiltecan', in D. Hymes (ed.) *Studies in Southwestern Ethnolinguistics*, Mouton, The Hague.

Johnson, D. (1974) 'Prepaper on Relational Constraints on Grammars', unpublished paper, Mathematical Sciences Department IBM, Thomas J. Watson Research Center, IBM, Yorktown Heights, New York.

Katz, J. (1966) *The Philosophy of Language*, Harper and Row, New York.

Keenan, E.L. (1972a) 'Relative Clause-Formation in Malagasy (and some related and some not so related languages)', in P.M. Peranteau, J.N. Levi, and G.C. Phares (eds.) *The Chicago Which Hunt*, pp. 169-90, Chicago Linguistic Society, Chicago, Illinois.

—— (1972b) On Semantically Based Grammar, *Linguistic Inquiry* 3, 4, 413-61.

—— (1973) 'Logical Expressive Power and Syntactic Variation in Natural language', in E.L. Keenan (ed.) *Formal Semantics of Natural Language*, Cambridge University Press, Cambridge. (Presented at Cambridge Colloquium on Formal Semantics.)

—— (1974) 'The Functional Principle: Generalising the Motion of Subject of', in M.W. LaGaly, R. Fox, and A. Bruck (eds.) *Papers from the Tenth Regional Meetings of the Chicago Linguistic Society*, 298-310.

—— (1975a) 'Remarkable Subjects in Malagasy', in C. Li (ed.) *Subject and Topic*, Academic Press, New York.

—— (1975b) 'Towards a Universal Definition of "Subject of"', in C. Li (ed.) *Subject and Topic*, Academic Press, New York.

—— and K. Bimson (1975) 'Perceptual Complexity and the Cross-language Distribution of Relative Clause and NP-question Types', *Functionalism* 253-60, The Chicago Linguistic Society, Chicago, Illinois.

—— and B. Comrie (1977) 'Noun Phrase Accessibility and Universal Grammar', *Linguistic Inquiry* 8.1.

Kraft, C.H. and A.H.M. Kirk-Greene (1974) *Hausa*, Teach Yourself Books, English Universities Press, Ltd., London.

McClean, R.J. (1969) *Swedish*, Teach Yourself Books, English Universities Press, Ltd., London.

McKaughan, H. (1973) *The Languages of the Eastern Family of the East New Guinea Highland Stock*, Vol. 1, University of Washington Press, Seattle, Washington.

Munro, P. (1974) 'Topics in Mojave Syntax' (unpublished) Ph.D. dissertation, University of California at San Diego.

Ross, J.R. (1967) 'Constraints on Variables in Syntax', Ph.D. dissertation, Department of Linguistics, Massachusetts Institute of Technology, Cambridge, Massachusetts.

Scott, G. (1973) 'Higher Levels of Fore Grammar', *Pacific Linguistics* **23** (Series B), the Australian National University, Canberra, Australia.

Shimizu, M. (1975) 'Relational grammar and Promotion Rules in Japanese', in R.E. Grossman, L.J. San, and T.J. Vance (eds.) *Papers from the Eleventh Regional meeting of the Chicago Linguistic Society*, 529-36, Chicago, Illinois.

Snell, B. and R. Wise (1963) 'Noncontingent Declarative Clauses in Machiguenga (Arawak)', *Studies in Peruvian Indian Languages*, 1, 103-45, Summer Institute of Linguistics, University of Oklahoma, Norman, Oklahoma.

Trithart, L. (1975) Relational Grammar and Chicewa Subjectivisation Rules', in R.E. Grossman, L.J. San, and T.J. Vance (eds.) *Papers from the Eleventh Regional Meetings of the Chicago Linguistic Society*, 615-25, Chicago, Illinois.

Voegelin, C.F. and F.M. Voegelin (1974) 'Some Recent (and not so Recent) Attempts to Interpret Semantics of Native Languages in North America', unpublished paper, Indiana University, Bloomington, Indiana.

Winter, W. no date. *Switch-reference in Yuman Languages*, University of Kiel, Kiel, Germany.

Woodbury, A. (1975) *Ergativity of Grammatical Processes: a Study of Greenlandic Eskimo*, unpublished M.A. essay, Department of Linguistics, University of Chicago, Chicago, Illinois.

Young, R.A. (1971) 'The Verb in Bena-Bena: its Form and Function', *Pacific Linguistics:* **18** (Series B), the Australian National University, Canberra, Australia.

PART FIVE :
SEMANTICS IN UNIVERSAL GRAMMAR

15 FACING THE TRUTH: SOME ADVANTAGES OF DIRECT INTERPRETATION[1]

1. The Problem

Within any model theoretic framework for natural language semantics, we associate with each category C in the language a set of *logically possible denotations* defined in terms of the semantic primitives of the model. We shall refer to this set as the *type* for C (relative to the primitives) and denote it T_C. The problem we are concerned with here is how to specify the interpretations of syntactically simple expressions in a category C where, on the one hand, the expressions are not logical constants, and on the other hand, are not interpretable freely in T_C. Two examples below illustrate the problem.

First, consider that proper nouns (*John, Mary,* etc.) and expressions like *every man, no student, exactly two students,* etc. share a category (NP) in English. Proper nouns are not logical constants and cannot be freely interpreted in T_{NP}. If they could, then the argument in (1) would not be valid, since *John* might denote the same as *no student* or *exactly two students,* and the argument is clearly not valid when *John* is everywhere replaced by any of those NPs.

(1)   John is a vegetarian. All vegetarians are socialists. Therefore, John is a socialist.

How are we to guarantee then that proper noun denotations are to be restricted so that they can never denote the same as *no student,* etc.?

Second, consider (cf. Montague, 1973) that (2) is logically true, and remains so when the adjective *male* is replaced by ones like *tall* and *skilful.*

(2)   Every male thief is a thief.

But replacing *male* by APs like *fake* and *apparent* yields sentences

459

which are not L-true. None of the APs are logical constants, and if all were freely interpreted in T_{AP}, (2) would be L-true for no choice of AP (Montague's option in fact). How then may we constrain the interpretation of APs like *male, tall,* and *skilful* so that sentences like (2) are L-true for those choices?

2. Two Solutions

One approach to this problem, dubbed here *direct interpretation*, assigns the expressions whose interpretations are to be restricted to a subcategory of the category to which they belong; we explicitly define a type for that (sub)category, and freely interpret the expressions in that type. This approach is instantiated in *Logical Types for Natural Language* (Keenan and Faltz, 1978; henceforth KF-78) and is the one I shall argue for here.

A second approach, dubbed here *translation*, is instantiated in PTQ (Montague, 1973). Here we do not enrich our formal English to include subcategories, rather we build an entire language of interpretation (the intensional logic of PTQ) and translate all expressions of formal English into that language. The expressions whose interpretations are to be restricted are translated in either of two ways: (i) as syntactically complex expressions whose denotations (= interpretations) are given compositionally, or (ii) as syntactically simple expressions which indirectly wind up having correct denotations in virtue of constraining the class of acceptable interpreting functions for the language as a whole to satisfy certain meaning postulates, ones which crucially mention the expressions in question.

We illustrate the direct vs translation approach with the example of proper nouns. In the direct approach we enrich our formal English to include a subcategory of NP, call it NP_{prop} for the nonce. We explicitly define the type for NP_{prop}, and freely interpret *John*, etc. in that type. Below we give the definition of that type. For our illustrative purposes it is sufficient to treat NPs extensionally. Thus, the semantic primitives of a model are (i) a set of truth values, say $\{0,1\}$, and (ii) a non-empty universe E of entities. Common nouns (CNs) are interpreted as sets of entities, so T_{CN} is the power set of E, denoted here by E^*. Elements of E^* will be referred to as (extensional) *properties*. Full NPs will denote sets of properties, so T_{NP} will be E^{**}, the power set of T_{CN} ($= E^*$). We then define:

(3)   (a) For all $b \in E$, I_b or *the individual generated by b*,
$$= {}_{\mathrm{df}}\{p \in E^*: b \in p\}$$
  (b) $T_{\mathrm{NP}_{\mathrm{prop}}} = {}_{\mathrm{df}}\{I_b : b \in E\}$

In the translation approach, following (extensionally) PTQ, we define a language of interpretation which includes individual constants (j, m, etc.) interpreted in E. Then *John* is tanslated as $(\lambda P)(Pj)$, which is compositionally interpreted to denote the set of subsets of E containing the interpretation of j as an element.

The two approaches then yield the same denotations for proper nouns, and so, other things being equal, characterise the same valid arguments in which proper nouns figure. They none the less differ in many ways.

Here we shall concentrate on what may appear to be the most innocuous difference: namely, in the direct approach we are obliged to explicitly define the set of possible denotations for proper nouns. In the translation approach we do not define that set; we merely translate (correctly) whatever proper nouns happen to occur. I will argue in this paper that there are many semantic insights concerning English which directly defining types for subcategories naturally leads us to notice. The insights typically concern (semantic) relations between types for certain (sub)categories and those of others. The generalisations expressing these relations then are stated in terms of types for subcategories, and are thus not naturally expressible within the framework of a translation approach, as these types are not defined in that approach. The generalisations do not contradict anything done in that approach; they are simply independent of it. So I am not claiming that the translation approach leads to wrong generalisations, only that it fails to lead to certain right ones — ones which the direct approach does lead to.

I illustrate these claims below with examples from subcategories of NPs, APs and Dets (Determiners). First, however, a somewhat more specific summary of the sorts of advantages to be noted. The summary below is intended for reference, still being rather general, so that in the analysis of specific cases considered we do not have to continually repeat the general advantage being illustrated.

3. Advantages of Direct Interpretation: Summary

(i) A direct approach often gives a more explicit account of the similarities and differences in meaning among expressions in a given category. Thus to define the type for the subcategory of AP to which *male, tall,* and *skilful* (but not *fake* and *apparent*) belong, we explicitly state just what it is about their denotations which makes (2) L-true. The meaning postulate approach here is less explicit. Even taking an appropriately generalised form of (2) as such a postulate, we merely exclude from the set of acceptable interpreting functions for the entire language ones in which that form of (2) is not true. But we have not explicitly said what it is about the meanings of *male,* etc. which allows us to predict the L-truth of (2), nor what it is about the meanings of *fake,* etc. which accounts for its non-L-truth.

(ii) In several respects a direct approach allows us to provide a better account of how the meanings of expressions can be learned and understood in real time. In some cases the type a direct approach associates with a category (e.g. Det) is actually significantly smaller than in a translation approach, whence a language learner has fewer choices to make in learning which of the logically possible denotations to associate with particular Dets in his language.

In other cases we can observe that certain logically possible subcategories of a language are universally empty, whence certain possibilities for associating denotations with surface forms need not be considered by the language learner. We posit a few universals of this sort below (e.g. as regards possible subcategories of AP). We note that they are properly linguistic universals in the sense that the type for the subcategory is not empty, so there is no purely 'logical' reason why languages could not have such subcategories.

In yet more interesting cases we can show that the set of possible denotations we associate with certain categories (NP, Det) is determined (in a sense we make explicit below) by the set we associate with a very proper subcategory of that category. In the case of NP, for example, a linguistic interpretation of this result is that a speaker/learner can in principle figure out the denotation of any NP, provided he knows the denotations of proper nouns and can interpret conjunctions, disjunctions, and negations of NPs, if he knows the interpretations of the conjuncts, disjuncts, etc. So to understand what sorts of things full NPs can denote, it is sufficient to know what proper nouns denote and to understand how to interpret boolean combinations of NPs relative to what they are formed from.

(iii) In several cases, expressed as language universals below, a direct approach yields nonobvious correlations between surface form and semantic structure, thus yielding a more insightful account of how we use surface form to infer meaning. Thus the strong (semantic) similarity between CNs and absolute APs below correlates with certain syntactic similarities between expressions in these (sub)categories. In fact there are certain properties, boolean ones, which almost all types have in common. As these properties are not peculiar to denotations of any particular sort, they are better taken as properties of how we conceive of objects in the world rather than as properties of the objects themselves. That is, they directly reflect as properties of the mind, as George Boole (1854) intended in his *Investigations into the laws of thought.*

(iv) Finally, once types for many (sub)categories are given, we can begin to form a picture of what a possible human semantic system may be. At least we can put certain substantive requirements on such systems by saying that they must include sets of denotations with properties of the sort given below. We refer the reader to Keenan (1982) for much more thorough discussion of this point. We turn now to the study of particular cases — NPs, APs and Dets — which instantiate the claims made in (i)—(iv) above.

4. Proper Nouns and Full NPs

We shall treat NPs extensionally here and accept the definitions of the types for proper nouns and full NPs given in Section 2. (We now use PN for proper noun rather than NP_{prop}.) What kinds of semantically enlightening observations may we make concerning these types? Perhaps the most obvious question to ask is: what portion of the full NP denotations are constituted by the PN ones? The question hardly seems deep, but the answer is perhaps surprising. First note that T_{PN}, the set of individuals, has the same cardinality as the universe E, since the function I sending each $b \in E$ to the individual it generates, I_b, is one-to-one and onto. So in a model with, say, four entities there are four possible PN denotations. Since T_{CN} is the power set of E it has $2^4 = 16$ elements; and since T_{NP} is the power set of T_{CN} it has $2^{16} = 65,536$ elements. So in such a world there are more than 65,000 possible NP denotations, only *four* of which are possible PN denotations!

Semantically then PNs are an incredibly special case of NP; almost nothing that a randomly selected full NP can denote is also a possible proper noun denotation. This is surprising, as philosophers and linguists have often treated PNs as representative of the entire class of NPs. Somewhat more exactly, perhaps, they have treated the class of full NPs as representable (we explicate this point below) by what we may call *individual denoting* NPs. Call an NP *individual denoting* if it is always interpreted either as an individual or as the empty set of properties (CN denotations). So we think here of *the king of France, John's car*, as denoting the empty set of properties in a state of affairs in which France fails to have exactly one king, John fails to have exactly one car, etc. So in a world of four individuals there are five possible denotations for individual denoting NPs — the four individuals and the empty set. This number is still an insignificantly small portion of the more than 65,000 possible full NP denotations in such a world.

Moreover, what holds semantically here holds syntactically as well. 'Most' NPs are not individual denoting. The latter are basically limited to the following: proper nouns, the singular personal pronouns (*I, you* (sg.), *he, she, it*), the singular demonstrative pronouns (*this, that*), and NPs of the form Det + CN where the CN is grammatically singular and the Det is either *the, this, that,* or the possessive form of an individual denoting NP, e.g. *John's, this tall man's,* etc. By contrast, NPs which are not individual denoting include: (i) all NPs of the form Det + CN except those mentioned above (see the list of Dets given in Section 6, for a very large sample); (ii) all boolean combinations of NPs e.g. *John and Mary, either two students or two teachers, John but not Mary,* etc.; (iii) plural personal pronouns (*we, they,* etc.); (iv) the plural demonstratives (*these, those*) and in fact all NPs which are grammatically plural; (v) Partitive NPs (*two of the five students*); (vi) NPs of the form Det + Numeral + CN, e.g. *the five students, John's two cars,* etc.; Exception NPs e.g. *every teacher but Joe*; Comparative NPs, e.g. *more students than teachers,* etc.

Thus individual denoting NPs are not only semantically atypical of NPs in general; they are also syntactically a very limited subset of the full NPs. Yet philosophers (see the eloquent introductory paragraph of Strawson 1959) have often taken such NPs, in particular the PNs, as the primary denoting expressions of a language. And linguists have in recent years taken such NPs as syntactically and semantically representative of full NPs in general. Let us support briefly this last point.

For a considerable period in the history of generative grammar, linguists accepted (despite some well-taken disclaimers by Chomsky 1957) that relation changing rules such as Conjunction Reduction, Passive, Tough Movement, etc., were paraphrastic, as supported by the examples below in which the (a,b) pairs are cognitive paraphrases in the sense of being logically equivalent.

(4) (a) John sang and John danced.
     (b) John both sang and danced.
(5) (a) Mary kissed John.
     (b) John was kissed by Mary.
(6) (a) To read this book is difficult.
     (b) This book is difficult to read.

Note that typical examples of these syntactic transformations used individual denoting NPs. Yet the transformations were defined over the full class of NPs, not just individual denoting ones. And it is embarrassingly easy to find many nonindividual denoting NPs which show these rules to be nonparaphrastic. Replacing *John* everywhere in (4a,b) by *some student* yields a pair in which (4a) clearly does not entail (4b), so they are not paraphrases. Similarly replacing *this book* everywhere in (6a,b) by *every book* results in a (6a) which doesn't entail (6b); it doesn't even entail that any book is difficult to read. As regards the overworked case of Passive, consider that (7a) below does not entail (7b).

(7) (a) Every politician kissed exactly two babies.
     (b) Exactly two babies were kissed by every politician.

Imagine, for example, a state of affairs in which there are just two politicians and four babies; one politician kisses exactly two of the babies, and the other kisses just the other two. Then (7a) is true, but (7b) is false, as in fact no baby was kissed by every politician. So (7a) does not entail (7b). It is equally easy to imagine situations in which (7b) is true and (7a) false, so in fact neither entails the other. Additional examples are easily constructed with decreasing NPs like *no babies, at most ten babies, fewer than ten babies,* etc. as well as other NPs which are neither increasing nor decreasing e.g. *between five and ten babies, every baby but Johnny, exactly two students' babies,* etc.

Given the nonsubtlety of these counterexamples to the paraphrase claims, why should linguists have considered for any length of time at all that relation changing rules like those above were paraphrastic? The answer would appear to be that they were assuming that individual denoting NPs, for which the rules are paraphrastic, were representative of NPs in general. But what was the basis for that assumption? Below we claim to exhibit that basis. We shall do so by examining more closely the relation between T_{NP} and T_{PN}, something we could not do if T_{PN} were not defined.

4.1. The Basicness of Proper Noun Denotations, Individuals

Consider T_{NP}. It is the power set of $T_{CN}(= E^*$, the set of all properties). As such it possesses a rich boolean structure; specifically, it is closed under intersections, unions, and complements relative to E^*. That is, if A and B are sets of properties (subsets of E^*), then so are $A \cap B$, $A \cup B$, and $A'(=_{df} E^* - A)$. As T_{PN} is a subset of T_{NP}, it is reasonable to ask how much of the boolean structure of T_{NP} is possessed by T_{PN}. Is it, for example, closed under intersections? or unions? And the answer is maximally negative.

An intersection of two or more individuals is never an individual. An individual, recall, is the collection of subsets of E which contain a fixed element of E as a member. Thus an individual has exactly one unit set as an element. So the intersection of two or more individuals will have no unit sets and thus not be an individual. Similarly the union of two or more individuals will have two or more unit sets as elements and thus not be an individual. And finally the complement of an individual, the set of properties it fails to have, must contain the empty set ($\emptyset$) of entities as an element, since that set is not an element of any individual as it contains no element of E. So the complement of an individual is not an individual.

Observing that we create sets of properties which are not individuals by taking intersections, unions, and complements of individuals, it is reasonable to wonder just what proportion of the set of NP denotations can be obtained in this way. The answer is that every set of properties can be obtained from the individuals by taking intersections, unions, and complements. We state this below as a theorem, referring the reader to KF-78 for the easy proof:

THEOREM 1

T_{PN} is a set of complete *generators* for T_{NP}. That is, the smallest subset of T_{NP} which includes the individuals and is closed under arbitrary intersections, unions, and complements is T_{NP} itself.

Note that Theorem 1 is a semantic theorem relating proper nouns and full NPs — it claims that a certain relation holds between their sets of possible denotations. Moreover, the theorem has a definite linguistic interest. We may think of it as saying that relative to the boolean operations (intersection, etc.) the entire set of NP denotations is determined by the individuals. To know what NPs in general can denote it is sufficient to know what the individuals are and to understand how to take boolean functions of them. And there is good linguistic evidence that we do know how to take boolean functions of individuals, since we can correctly interpret sentences which contain boolean combinations of individual denoting NPs, e.g. *both John and Mary, either John or Mary, neither John nor Mary, John but not Mary*, etc. (We note without argument that the same motivation which led us to interpret PNs as sets of properties also leads us to interpret a conjunction of PNs as the intersection of the individuals denoted by each conjunct; similarly disjunctions are interpreted by unions, etc.)

Moreover, much more can be said about the relation between T_{PN} and T_{NP}. T_{PN} is not only a set of complete generators for T_{NP}; it is a set with a very special property which we shall call ca-free. We define this algebraic relation below, but we shall not be concerned with the algebraic details. Let us here note the theorem and explicate its linguistically intuitive content.

THEOREM 2

T_{PN} is a set of *ca-free* generators for T_{NP}.

Very roughly, Theorem 2 says that we can say anything we like about individuals, and moreover, anything we can say (in first order) about the more general class of NP denotations is completely determined by what we say about the individuals. Thus the PN denotations not only determine (modulo the boolean operations) what the range of full NP denotations is; they also determine what we can predicate (in first order) about them.

In more detail: consider that a first order n-place predicate may be represented as a function from n-tuples of NP denotations into truth values (differences in representation here will not affect the claims below). But these functions cannot be random ways of assigning truth values to such n-tuples. For example, if the function which interprets the one-place predicate *slept* assigns value false (0) to the individual which *John* denotes, then it must also assign value 0 to the set of properties which *John and every student* denotes. For *John and every student slept* is true just in case both John slept and every student slept. So the *slept* function cannot assign truth values *freely* to the denotation of *John and every student*. Just which sets of properties (if any) can the one-place predicates assign values freely to? The answer is just the individuals, that is, the elements of T_{PN}. (And more generally, the n-tuples of NP denotations which an n-place predicate may assign values freely to are just the n-tuples of individuals.) Moreover, once we have given the values of a one-place predicate on the individuals, its values in all the other sets of properties are uniquely determined. For once we have specified of each individual whether he slept or not, we have intuitively determined whether every individual slept or not, whether some individual slept or not, whether exactly two individuals slept or not, etc. It is in this sense then that what we can say (in first order) about NP denotations is in fact freely and uniquely determined by what we can say about the individuals. And in this more precise sense the individual denoting expressions of a language can be thought of as representing the full class of NPs.

Lest the reader feel dissatisfied with the informality of the above discussion we define below more formally what is meant by a set of *ca-free* generators. The formal details of that definition, however, will play no role in the subsequent discussion, but the definition of a boolean algebra and of homomorphisms should be noted.

4.2. *Boolean Algebra and a Formal Statement of Theorem 2*

A boolean algebra β may be thought of as a set B which has two distinguished elements 0_β and 1_β called the zero and unit elements of β, and in which are defined two binary functions $\wedge_\beta$ and $\vee_\beta$ called *meet* and *join* respectively, and one unary function $'\beta$ called *complement.* These elements and functions are required to satisfy the following conditions: meet and join are both commutative, i.e. for all $x, y \in B$, the element $(x \wedge y)$ and the element $(y \wedge x)$ are the same (we omit the subscript β). Similarly $(x \vee y) = (y \vee x)$. Meets distribute over joins, i.e. $((x \wedge y) \vee z) = (x \vee z) \wedge (y \vee z)$, and joins distribute over meets. The zero and unit are identities with respect to join and meet, i.e. $(x \vee 0) = x$ and $(x \wedge 1) = x$; and the following complement laws hold: $(x \wedge x') = 0$ and $(x \vee x') = 1$. For any boolean algebra β we define a boolean relation $\leqslant_\beta$ as follows: $x \leqslant y$ iff $(x \wedge y) = x$. Provably $0 \leqslant x$ all x in B and $x \leqslant 1$ all $x \in B$ so the zero and unit elements are the minimal and maximal elements, respectively, of the relation $\leqslant$ (provably a partial ordering relation).

Two simple examples of boolean algebras: (i) the power set of a non-empty set E is a boolean algebra, where the zero and unit are Ø (the empty set) and E itself respectively. The meet, join, and complement operations are just the corresponding set theoretic ones (intersection, union, and set theoretic complement relative to the unit). The boolean relation is provably the subset relation. (ii) The set $\{0, 1\}$ is a boolean algebra where meet, join, and complement are defined by the standard truth tables for conjunction, disjunction, and negation respectively; the zero element is 0, the unit 1. The $\leqslant$ relation coincides with the numerical less than or equals relation.

If K is a subset of B and x an element of B, x is said to be a *lower bound* (1b) for K if $x \leqslant k$, all $k \in K$. It is a *greatest lower bound* (glb) iff it is a 1b and for all lower bounds y for K, $y \leqslant x$. In any algebra the element $(x \wedge y)$ is the glb for $\{x, y\}$, and by induction any finite subset of B has a glb — the meet of all its elements. Infinite subsets need not have glb's, however. If every subset of an algebra has a glb, the algebra is called *complete*. Power set algebras are complete. For K a subset of the power set of E, $\cap K$, the collection of all those elements of E which are in each set in K, is provably the glb for K. And all finite algebras are complete, so the algebra $\{0, 1\}$ called henceforth 2 is complete. Similarly y is an *upper bound* (ub) for K if $k \leqslant y$, all $k \in K$. It is the *least upper bound* (lub) if it is $\leqslant$ all other ub's for K.

An atom in a boolean algebra is a smallest non-zero element. That is, x is an atom iff $x \neq 0$ and for all y, if $y \leqslant x$ then either $y = 0$ or $y = x$. An algebra is said to be *atomic* iff for all non-zero elements z there is an atom x such that $x \leqslant z$. Power set algebras are atomic, the unit sets being the atoms. All finite algebras are atomic. And we note the following standard theorem: A boolean algebra is both complete and atomic iff it is isomorphic to the power set of a non-empty set. So in complete and atomic (*ca*) algebras we may always think of the boolean operations as behaving like intersections, unions, and complements.

Finally, if *h* is a function from a boolean algebra *B* into a boolean algebra *D*, we say that *h* is a *homomorphism* iff *h* preserves meet, join, and complement. That is, for all $x, y \in B$, $h(x \wedge y) = h(x) \wedge h(y)$, i.e. *h preserves meets.* Preservation of joins and complements are defined analogously. A homomorphism is called *complete* if it preserves all the glb's. That is, $h(\text{glb}(K)) = \text{glb}(\{h(k) : k \in K\})$. (The glb of a subset *K* of an algebra is normally denoted $\wedge K$.

A subset *K* of an algebra is said to be *closed under meets* (joins, complements) iff $(x \wedge y) \in K$ whenever both *x* and *y* are. It is closed under glb's just in case the glb of every subset of *K* is an element of *K*. Closure under lub's is defined analogously. *K* is said to be a set of *complete generators* for *B* iff the smallest subset of *B* which includes *K* and is closed under complements, glb's, and lub's is *B* itself. We may now define:

DEFINITION

A subset *K* of a complete boolean algebra *B* *is a set of ca-free generators* for *B* iff *K* is a set of complete generators for *B* and any function from *K* into any complete and atomic boolean algebra extends uniquely to a complete homomorphism. *B* itself is said to be *ca-free* if it has a set of *ca-free* generators.

To complete the link between Def and our informal explication of the content of Theorem 2, let us note that the first order one-place predicates are just the complete homomorphisms from T_{NP} to 2. E.g. *slept* must map an intersection of property sets onto the truth value obtained by applying that function separately to each of the sets over which the intersection is taken and taking the meet of the resulting truth values. This is needed to guarantee, for example, that the truth value of *John and every student slept* is identical to the meet of the truth value of *John slept* with that of *every student slept*. Similar reasoning shows that *slept* should preserve joins and complements, so *slept* is a homomorphism. It must preserve all glb's to guarantee that the truth value of *every student slept* is the glb of the set of *slept* (*x*), all individuals *x* with the student property. So we may define a one-place predicate by saying, 'It is that complete homomorphism from T_{NP} into $\{0,1\}$ with the following values on the individuals ...' and then say explicitly, in any way we like (i.e. freely) what those values are. So what we can say about NP denotations in general is determined, in any way we like, by what we can say about individuals, the PN denotations.

4.3. Higher Order Nightmares?

First order extensional one-place predicates (P_1s) must correspond one for one to the sets of individuals. Yet we treat them as elements of a much larger set. $T_{CN} = E^*$ is isomorphic to the power set of the set of individuals; T_{NP} is isomorphic to the power set of that set, and the set of functions from T_{NP} into $\{0,1\}$, the set from which we draw P_1 denotations, is isomorphic to the power set of that set. But only the complete homomorphisms in that set are P_1 denotations. How many are there?

THEOREM 3

The set of complete homomorphisms from T_{NP} into $\{0,1\}$, (the type for P_1) is isomorphic to the power set of the set of individuals.

More generally (KF-78 and to appear), the type for the n-place predicates (P_ns) is isomorphic to the power set of the set of n-tuples of individuals. So such predicates are, up to isomorphism, just what they always were in standard first order logic.

That extensional P_ns denote functions which preserve boolean structure (i.e. homomorphisms) is not explicit on the translation approach in PTQ. Partee and Mats (to appear) argue that certain simple P_2s like *find* will be interpreted by such functions, thanks in part to an extensionalising meaning postulate which mentions *find*. But PTQ does not define types for extensional P_ns and so does not provide a natural way to state generalisations concerning those types. E.g. it is enlightening to note that while APs denote functions from an algebra (T_{CN}) into itself they are essentially never structure-preserving ones (Theorem 7 below). So APs and Predicates differ in a fundamental semantic way.

Similarly we have no way to express the close semantic similarity between extensional 'relational' nouns like *friend* (of), *colleague* (of), etc. and extensional P_2s. Syntactically such 'nouns' combine with full NPs to form complex CNs e.g. *friend of every senator, colleague of a doctor,* etc. Semantically then they may be represented by functions from T_{NP} into T_{CN}. And these functions are in fact c-homomorphisms: An individual has the property expressed by *friend of every senator* iff for every individual I with the senator property he has the property expressed by *friend of I*. Semantically then *friend of* maps a meet (intersection) of individuals onto the meet of the properties obtained by applying the function separately to each of the individuals over which the intersection is taken. I.e. *friend of* preserves meets; similarly it preserves joins and complements, and is thus a complete homomorphism.

And it is easy to see that the type for the extensional relational nouns is isomorphic to that of the extensional P_2s. Extensionally T_{CN} (= E*) is isomorphic to T_{P_1}, the function sending a c-homomorphism h to the property p_h which is in an individual I iff $h(I) = 1$ is an isomorphism; whence the set of c-homomorphisms from T_{NP} into one of these sets will be isomorphic to the set from T_{NP} into the other. Thus the linguistic intuition which calls relational nouns 'transitive' common nouns is well founded semantically.

4.4. A Semantic Generalisation Concerning Argument Categories in English

We have shown that proper nouns bear a very special semantic relation to full NPs in general: namely, T_{PN} ca-free generates T_{NP}. We used this fact to justify the common intuition of linguists and philosophers that proper nouns are the 'basic' NPs in a language. Specifically we showed that PN denotations determine what the full set of NP denotations is, and moreover they determine what can be said of them (in first order).

But we have also shown something very special about T_{NP} itself: Namely, it has a set of ca-free generators. Relatively few boolean algebras do. Those which have this property are characterised in Theorem 4 below (not one of the 'standard' theorems in boolean algebra but one we have proved by standard means).

THEOREM 4

A complete atomic boolean algebra has a set of ca-free generators iff it is isomorphic to the power set of a power set.

Thus by Theorem 4 T_{NP} is always a ca-free algebra, since it is taken as the power set of the power set of the universe E. The other algebras we have informally discussed, however, are not in general ca-free. The set of CN denotations E^* is a power set, but it is not necessarily the power set of a power set and thus does not in general have the semantic property of being ca-free. Similarly the types for the n-place predicates are not in general ca-free algebras. So we have given one completely nonobvious way in which predicates and common nouns are semantically similar and different from full NPs.

Are there other categories of English whose types are ca-free algebras? We might reasonably expect to find such categories among those which behave syntactically like full NPs, namely those which, like NPs, function as arguments of predicates, e.g. categories which may carry case marking, govern verb agreement, and much more generally, be affected by relation-changing rules like Passive, Raising, Tough Movement, etc.

A good candidate here is the category $\bar{S}$. Expressions in this category will include things of the form *that + S*, e.g. *that Fred left* as it occurs in *John knows that Fred left*. But $\bar{S}$ includes much else besides. For example, it will include boolean combinations of $\bar{S}$s. Thus the syntactic objects of *believe* in (8) below are appropriately assigned the category $\bar{S}$.

(8) (a) John believes both that Fred left and that Mary stayed.
    (b) John believes either that Fred left or that Mary stayed.
    (c) John believes that Fred left but not that Mary stayed.

Thus expressions of the form *that + S and that + T*, *that + S or that + T*, etc. are to count as $\bar{S}$s, and probably much else besides, as the object in:

(9) (a) John believes whatever Fred says.
    (b) John proved everything that Fred conjectured.

In any event we clearly want the type for $\bar{S}$ to be a boolean algebra, so as to provide denotations for conjunctions, disjunctions, and negations of $\bar{S}$ denotations. Moreover, for S a sentence we want S and *that +S* to denote differently. The reasons are apparent in the difference in meaning (on preferred readings for those who find them ambiguous) between the sentences in (10) below:

(10) (a) John believes either that Fred left or that Mary left.
     (b) John believes that either Fred left or Mary left.

Syntactically the object of *believe* in (10a) is a disjunction of two
$\bar{S}$s; in (10b) it is an $\bar{S}$ of the form *that* $+S$, where the S in question
is a disjunction of two Ss. Semantically (10a) says that either John
believes that Fred left or he believes that Mary left (and perhaps
both). (That is, *believe* behaves homomorphically in its $\bar{S}$ arguments.) Note that (10a) can be naturally followed in a discourse by 'I
can't remember which', as it asserts that of two things John
believes at least one. (10b) on the other hand does not assert that
of two things John believes at least one. It merely says that he
believes that a certain disjunction holds, but he may have no idea
which disjunct holds. Now if in general S and *that* $+S$ denoted the
same thing, the objects of *believe* in (10a,b) would denote the
same thing and thus the sentences would be logically equivalent,
which is wrong.

One reasonable way to represent these distinct denotations is
given in Keenan (1981). Briefly here, let us enrich the primitives of
a model to include a non-empty set W of possible worlds. Interpret
Ss as *propositions*, that is, as functions from W into 2. Call that set
of functions Prop. It is the type for S and is isomorphic to W^*, the
power set of W, and is thus an arbitrary ca-boolean algebra. Now
if S is a sentence interpreted by a proposition p, let us interpret
that $+S$ by I_p, the set of properties which p has, that is the set of
functions from Prop into 2 which assign p value 1. So I_p is a subset
of 2/Prop, the set of functions from Prop into 2, and is thus an element of the power set of that set of functions. As 2/Prop is isomorphic to Prop*, the power set of Prop, I_p is, up to isomorphism,
an element of Prop**. I_p of course is a denotation in the type for $\bar{S}$,
and since we want that type to be closed under the boolean operations of intersections, etc. to provide denotations for conjunctions, etc. of $\bar{S}$s, it follows that we want the type for $\bar{S}$ to be all of
Prop** (by the same reasoning that we want T_{NP} to be all of E^{**}
— it's the smallest set which includes the individuals and is closed
under arbitrary intersections, unions, and complements).

Thus in this view $T_{\bar{S}}$ is a power set and so by Theorem 4 a ca-
free algebra. Moreover, the ca-free generators are just the I_ps, the
denotations of expressions of the form *that* $+S$.

One further point should be noted here: the treatment of $\bar{S}$s
sketched above preserves one of the fundamental inadequacies of
intensional logic. Namely, it will follow that whenever sentences S
and T express the same proposition, i.e. are true in the same
worlds, then *that* $+S$ and *that* $+T$ will denote the same I_p, and so

the sentences *John believes that S* and *John believes that T* will be true in the same worlds, which is obviously incorrect. We refer the reader here to the treatment of $\bar{S}$s given in Ben-Chorin (1982) where this problem is overcome. And crucially there the type for $\bar{S}$ is still a ca-free algebra, ca-freely generated by the denotations of the *that* + *S*s.

We may take it then that the type for $\bar{S}$ is a ca-free algebra and in that respect has a semantic property in common with T_{NP}. Moreover, the other major argument categories of English also appear ca-free, though their semantics is much less well understood. Two quick examples: let us use $\bar{Q}$ for the category to which *whether Fred left* in *John knows whether Fred left* belongs. Like $\bar{S}$ it is closed under boolean combinations (*John knows either whether Fred will accept or whether Bill will accept, but not both*), and as in $\bar{S}$ we want *whether S or whether T* to be different in denotation from *whether* (*S or T*). So *whether* itself behaves like *that*, mapping question (Q) denotations onto the individuals they generate (the set of properties which hold the denotation of the question). So the type for $\bar{Q}$ will be a ca-free generated algebra, with the denotations of expressions of the form *whether Q* as the generators.

Similarly it is natural to treat expressions like *to swim* in *To swim is healthy* as taking their denotations in a ca-free algebra. Call that category $\bar{P}_1$. Here *to* behaves analogously to *that* and *whether*, mapping P_1 denotations onto the individuals they generate. The type for $\bar{P}_1$ then will be the boolean closure of those individuals, provably (as before) isomorphic to the power set of the power set of the type for P_1. So the type is a ca-free algebra by Theorem 4.

Thus we have found a semantic property which NPs, $\bar{S}$s, $\bar{Q}$s and $\bar{P}_1$s have in common — their types are all ca-free algebras (and the predicates of them behave homomorphically). As these categories have much in common syntactically (they raise, topicalise, trigger predicate agreement, etc.), we have exhibited a most nonobvious correlation between syntactic form and logical form.

5. Subcategories of Adjective Phrases

Intensionally we may represent the type for CN as the set of functions from W, the possible worlds of the model, into E^*, the sets of entities of the model. And as APs combine with CNs to form CNs, we shall take them semantically to be functions from T_{CN} into T_{CN}. Now let us consider some of the properties such functions may have. One such property is *transparency*. A function f from T_{CN} into T_{CN} will be called *transparent* iff for all elements p, q in T_{CN} if p and q have the same extension in a possible world w, i.e. $p(w) = q(w)$ then fp and fq have the same extension in w, i.e. $(fp)(w) = (fq)(w)$. The functions which interpret APs like *male* and *tall* are transparent: if the thieves and doctors are the same in some world, then the male thieves and the male doctors must be the same in that world; ditto for the tall thieves and the tall doctors. However, the functions which can interpret *skilful*, *fake*, and *apparent* need not be transparent. Clearly the thieves and the doctors can be the same without the skilful thieves and the skilful doctors being the same; ditto for the fake and apparent doctors.

Let us begin to build up a set of subcategorisation features for APs. We shall include $+t$ (for transparent) in this set, and subcategories of AP which contain the feature $+t$ will always be interpreted by transparent functions from T_{CN} into T_{CN}. If they have other features, then the functions which interpret them will be required to meet other conditions. If they lack the feature $+t$, then APs of that subcategory will not be required to be interpreted by transparent functions.

Another property which functions from T_{CN} into T_{CN} may have is that of being *restricting*. In general a function f from a boolean algebra into itself is called *restricting* iff for all x in the algebra, $f(x) \leqslant x$. And note that in the intensional framework assumed here for the nonce T_{CN} is a boolean algebra. E^*, the set of (extensional) properties, is straightforwardly a power set boolean algebra. And the set of functions from any non-empty set into a boolean algebra β inherits the structure of β *pointwise*. In the case at hand, if p and q are two functions from W into the algebra E^*, then we define their meet $(p \wedge q)$ to be that function which sends each $w \in W$ to $p(w) \wedge q(w)$, this last meet being taken in E^* since $p(w)$ and $q(w)$ are elements of E^*. Joins and complements of intensional properties (elements of T_{CN}) are defined analogously.

Thus a function f from T_{CN} into T_{CN} is restricting iff for all intensional properties p, $f(p) \leqslant p$. This amounts to saying that for all possible worlds w, $(fp)(w) \leqslant p(w)$, and this in turn amounts to saying that for all worlds w, the set of individuals with $(fp)(w)$ is a subset of those with $p(w)$. Let us add then another subcategorisation feature $+r$ to APs. APs in subcategories with that feature will be required to be interpreted by restricting functions from T_{CN} into T_{CN}. Clearly the subcategories to which *male, tall,* and *skilful* belong must be $+r$ ones since for any world w, the male thieves in w are a subset of the thieves in w; ditto for the tall thieves and the skilful thieves. On the other hand, the subcategories to which *fake* and *apparent* belong will not have the feature $+r$, since fake thieves and apparent ones need not be thieves.

So far we have merely illustrated the direct interpretation approach to the subcategorisation of APs. And at least the following two advantages of that approach may be stated. First, we have stated in semantic terms just what it is about the denotations of *male, tall,* and *skilful* that makes (2) *Every male thief is a thief,* etc. valid and *Every fake/apparent thief is a thief* not valid, and this satisfies one of the primary goals of a semantic theory for a natural language — representing the meanings and meaning differences among natural language expressions.

Second, by studying the types of the subcategories of AP so defined, we are in a position to suggest certain universal constraints on possible AP denotations for natural language. Observe first that with two subcategorisation features we have defined four subcategories of AP: $AP_{+r,+t}$, whose type is the set of functions from T_{CN} into T_{CN} which are both restricting and transparent; AP_{+r}, whose type is the set of restricting functions (not necessarily transparent); AP_{+t}, whose type is the set of transparent functions, and $AP_{\emptyset}$, whose type is all the functions from T_{CN} into T_{CN}. In the first category we shall put APs like *male* and *tall*; in the second we will put APs like *skilful* and indeed most adjectives which naturally compare (*tall* is somewhat unusual in being a restricting AP which is transparent; most degree APs like *rapid, beautiful, good,* etc. are restricting but not necessarily transparent). Finally APs like *fake* and *apparent* will go in the last category, as we have so far not mentioned any conditions their interpretations must satisfy.

Note that we have mentioned no APs which are required to be transparent but not required to be restricting. In fact, despite some serious looking, we have found no such APs. We tentatively suggest as a universal of human language:

UNIVERSAL 1
In all languages transparent APs are also restricting.

And clearly it was an approach that pushed us to explicitly define subcategories of APs and their types, which led us to notice this regularity about human languages.

Obviously further subcategorisation of APs is possible. See KF-78 for some discussion of the difference between *fake* and *apparent*. Here let us concentrate on the difference between *male* and *tall*. They exhibit certain systematic semantic differences. For example, (11a) is valid but (11b) is not.

(11) (a) Every male thief is a male individual.
     (b) Every tall thief is a tall individual.

Thus, if someone is a male anything, he is absolutely male, i.e. a male individual. But a tall something, say a tall thief, need not be a tall individual; he need only be tall relative to the set of thieves; if thieves happen on the average to be short compared to individuals in general, a tall thief might turn out to be a short individual.

We may represent these differences as follows: extensionally we may think of *individual* (or *entity*, or *existent*) as denoting the property which all individuals have, that is, the unit element of E^*. Intensionally then *individual* will be that property mapping each possible world onto the unit in E^*, provably the unit element in the intensional type of CN, 1_{CN}.

Let us define an AP function f to be *absolute*, iff for all intensional properties p, $f(p) = p \wedge f(1_{CN})$. Taking *male*, *female*, etc. to be in a category of AP with the feature $+a$ then guarantees directly that every male thief is a male individual. Not putting *tall* into such a subcategory guarantees that *every tall thief is a tall individual* is not valid, since *tall* may be interpreted by a function which fails to be absolute. Once again then we have stated in terms of denotations what it is that makes APs like *male* different in meaning from ones like *tall* (though there is much more to be said).

Moreover, having defined the type for AP_{+a} to be the absolute functions from T_{CN} into T_{CN}, we may notice some further properties of interest concerning possible subcategories of APs. First, it is obvious that any absolute function f is restricting, since $f(p) = p \wedge f(1) \leqslant p$. What is more surprising, however, is that all absolute functions are also transparent. Let us give a quick proof.

Proof. Let f be absolute and assume $p(w) = q(w)$. We must show that $(fp)(w) = (fq)(w)$.

$$(fp)(w) \quad = (p \wedge f(1))(w) \qquad f \text{ is absolute}$$
$$= p(w) \wedge (f1)(w) \qquad \text{pointwise def of meet in } T_{CN}$$
$$= q(w) \wedge (f1)(w) \qquad q(w) = p(w) \text{ by assumption}$$
$$= (q \wedge f(1))(w) \qquad \text{pointwise def of meet}$$
$$= (fq)(w) \qquad f \text{ is absolute}$$

This is a clear and simple case where we actually learn something about AP denotations by reasoning on the types for their subcategories. We have three subcategorisation features ($+t$, $+r$, and $+a$) so we might expect eight possible subcategories of APs. In fact there are provably only five, since the feature $+a$ entails the features $+t$ and $+r$. (And of the five, AP_{+t} is conjectured to have no members by Universal 1.)

Yet more of interest can be said concerning absolute APs. Observe that two absolute AP functions f and g are identical iff $f(1) = g(1)$, and the value of such a function at the unit element can be any property we like. Thus there are exactly as many absolute AP functions as there are properties. And in fact:

THEOREM 5

The type for the absolute APs is isomorphic to T_{CN}, the function sending any absolute AP f to $f(1)$ being the isomorphism.

Of course for Theorem 5 to make sense we must have defined a boolean structure on $T_{AP_{+a}}$. And this we are independently motivated to do so as to provide denotations for boolean combinations of APs, e.g. *tall and handsome, tall or handsome, tall but not handsome*, etc. And this is easy to do. An individual has the property of being a tall and handsome student iff he has the property of being a tall student and the property of being a handsome student. So meets of restricting (not just absolute) functions are defined pointwise: $(f \wedge g)(p) =_{df} f(p) \wedge g(p)$. Similarly joins are defined pointwise. Complements are a little more interesting. A not very tall student is not simply an individual who fails to be a very tall student; rather, it must be a student who fails to be a very tall student. Thus $(f')(p) = p \wedge (f(p))'$. Note that this algebraic structure is defined on the entire set of restricting functions from T_{CN} into T_{CN}, whence in particular it is defined for the absolute functions. Moreover, the set of absolute functions is provably closed under the meet, join, and complement operations so defined, and thus constitutes a complete subalgebra of the restricting functions.

It is that subalgebra which is isomorphic to T_{CN}.

Of the various categories of APs considered then the absolute ones are more similar to CNs than any others, since the two types are in fact identical up to isomorphism. And this strong semantic similarity (not statable in the absence of a definition for $T_{AP_{+a}}$) is reflected in their syntax. Absolute APs behave syntactically more like CNs than do other APs. For example, in preference they occur closest to their CN heads, e.g. *a tall male thief* but *??a male tall thief*. More interestingly, lexically simple absolute APs may combine directly with determiners to form full NPs. Thus we have:

(12) (a) Two males entered Mario's Pizza Parlour at 6 pm.
      (b) *Two talls entered ... *Two skilfuls entered ...

On the basis of these facts we suggest the following universal:

UNIVERSAL 2
    If a language allows any APs to combine directly with Dets to form full NPs, then lexically simple absolute APs will be among them.

5.1. Similarities Between Adjective Phrases and Other Categories

The boolean structure we have assigned to the restricting and absolute functions on T_{CN} is in no way peculiar to T_{CN}. Given any boolean algebra B, the set of restricting functions from B into B (those functions f such that $f(b) \leqslant b$, all $b \in B$) forms a boolean algebra where meets and joins are defined pointwise and complements are defined as above ($f'(b) = b \wedge (fb)'$). The zero element sends every b in B to the zero element of B, the unit element sends every b in B to itself, i.e. it is the identity function. Anticipating, we may call such algebras *Modifier* algebras. They always have absolute subalgebras isomorphic to B itself.

And not surprisingly other modifier categories of English besides AP have modifier algebras for their types. Consider, for example, *predicate modifiers* such as Adverb Phrases (*slowly*) and PPs (*in the garden*). As they combine with P_1s (among other things) to form complex P_1s we can represent their denotations as functions from the type for P_1 into itself. And characteristically such functions are restricting. Thus *walk rapidly* is booleanly $\leqslant$ *walk*, i.e. in any world w, the individuals who are walking rapidly in *w* are a subset of those who are walking in *w*. In fact, given the extensional isomorphism between T_{CN} and T_{P_1} we may note:

THEOREM 6

The type for the transparent restricting APs is isomorphic to the type for the transparent restricting predicate modifiers.

Moreover, predicate modifiers appear to have a distinguished subset which behaves absolutely (see KF-78 for much discussion), namely the stative locative PPs like *in the garden*. Thus, to *sing in the garden* means basically to sing and to be in the garden. Further the degree predicate modifiers, i.e. ones which compare and have superlatives, like *slowly, rapidly*, etc. are characteristically restricting but not transparent, just like the degree APs.

Given these strong semantic similarities between APs and predicate modifiers, it is not surprising to find them treated similarly in many languages. In languages like German we find little or no difference between lexical APs and lexical adverbs, e.g. we say *he works good* using the same form as the AP in *a good worker*. In English as well this sometimes happens, e.g. *a fast runner/he runs fast*, though in other cases we use some adverbial morphology to form the predicate modifier from the AP, e.g. *rapidly* from *rapid*, etc. Thus by the investigation of types we can justify the traditional grammatical intuition that adjectives are to nouns as adverbs are to verbs.

5.2. *Some Differences Between APs and Other Categories*

Modifiers are syntactically rather different both from Arguments and from Predicates, and these differences are reflected in the nature of their types. Thus Modifier algebras are not in general ca-free, the semantic property which characterises Argument algebras. And second, modifiers are not in general interpreted by homomorphisms, making them distinct from predicates.

The latter point is somewhat interesting in that as modifiers are functions from an algebra into an algebra (itself) they could in principle be homomorphisms. It does not, strictly speaking, follow from the definition of *restricting* that no restricting function is a homomorphism. It does, however, follow that all restricting functions which are homomorphisms are trivial:

THEOREM 7

Any restricting function which preserves complements is the identity function.

Proof.   Let f from B into B restricting and preserve complements $(f(b')) = (fb)')$.
Then f is the identity function, i.e. $f(b) = b$, all $b \in B$.

(a) $f(b) \leqslant b$ since f is restricting.
(b) $b \leqslant f(b)$,   whence $b = f(b)$, as follows:

    $f(b') \leqslant b'$ since f is restricting
    $(fb)' \leqslant b'$ since f preserves complements so $f(b') = (fb)'$
    $b'' \leqslant (fb)''$ $x \leqslant y$ iff $y' \leqslant x'$ in any boolean algebra
    $b \leqslant f(b)$ $x'' = x$ in any boolean algebra

Thus we may say that fundamentally, restricting functions are not the kinds of functions which preserve a boolean structure, there being only one exception, the identity function; thus modifiers are fundamentally different sorts of functions from predicates. Again, such claims are not naturally statable on an approach in which the type for restricting modifiers is not defined.

6. Determiners

Dets are expressions like *every*, *at least ten*, *John's*, etc. which combine with CNs to form full NPs. As we shall only consider extensional (transparent) Dets here, we may represent them as functions from the extensional type for CN, E^*, into the extensional type for NP, E^{**}.

Now just which functions from E^* to E^{**}, that is, just which ways of associating sets of properties with properties, are possible Det denotations in a natural language? That is, what do we want to take for the type for Det?

Note that on a translation approach this question would typically not arise. Most Dets we think of are intuitively logical constants and can simply be adequately represented by translating them as logical constants in the language of interpretation. Similarly for simple Dets which are not logical constants, e.g. we may translate *John's car* as the translation of *the car which John has*.

Yet in fact it is an interesting, even perhaps deep question whether natural languages admit just any way of associating full NP denotations with CN denotations. Below we shall report on work which shows that this is not the case. That is, being a natural language Det imposes very severe constraints on how property sets can be associated with properties. Note that prima facie we expect this to be the case. For if not, then any function from E^* into E^{**} would be a possible Det denotation, and there are unrealistically many of them. For E^* has 2^n elements, where n is the number of individuals of the universe, and E^{**} thus has $2^{(2^n)}$. So the number of functions from E^* into E^{**} is 2^{2^n} raised to the power of 2^n, and thus $2^{(4^n)}$. In a world of only four individuals then there are 2^{256} functions from E^* into E^{**}, a number which is so large as to be inapprehensible to ordinary speakers. So let us show that in fact only a small fraction of this number are acceptable Det denotations.

The work on which the demonstration is based is Keenan and Stavi (to appear; henceforth KS). We refer the reader to that work for much more extensive discussion and all proofs.

The approach taken in KS to defining T_{Det} was as follows: first we drew up a generous and hopefully exhaustive list of all the types of Dets we could think of. We find what denotations we need for them and then define T_{Det} to be the smallest set of functions from E^* into E^{**} we can get our hands on which is large enough to provide the denotations we know we need. The first step then is to specify which English expressions we are to count as Dets. Below we provide a summary of our list. Many questions of a syntactic sort could be raised about elements in the list, but we shall not raise them here. The major point to notice is that we have been generous in what we shall count as a Det. The reason is that we do not want our claim that an adequate T_{Det} is a small subset of E^{**}/E^* to be falsified by the discovery of further Dets whose denotations do not lie in T_{Det} as we define it. If the reader wants to exclude from our list some of the more cumbersome examples, we have no objection, for T_{Det} as we define it will still obviously be large enough to provide denotations for the reduced list, and our claim that it is a small subset of the functions from E^* into E^{**} will remain true.

6.1. *English Determiners Considered*

(The groupings given below are intended for mnemonic reasons;

several expressions arguably belong in more than one group.)

superficially simplex Dets
> every, each, all, both, a, some, one, two, three, ... most, several, a few, the, no, neither, zero, (many), (few), (enough), (this), (these)

strict cardinal Dets
> at least ten, at most ten, more than ten, exactly ten, fewer than ten

adverb + many
> infinitely many, uncountably many, finitely many, (too many)

a + AP + number of
> a prime number of, an even number of, (an undisclosed number of)

possessive Dets
> John's, no student's

bounding Dets
> exactly ten, between five and ten, and Dets of the form: *only +* *Det*: only five, only John's, only finitely many, only SOME (indicates contrastive stress), only the LIBERAL

exception Dets
> all but three, all but finitely many, all but the three smartest, every but John (as it occurs in *every student but John left*)

boolean combinations
> not one, not every, not only John's, neither the dumbest nor the smartest, neither John's nor Mary's, some but not all, at least two and at most ten, either exactly two or exactly ten

comparative Dets
> more than ten, etc., more male than female (as in *more male than female students failed the exam*)

Det + AP
> the tallest, the five tallest, all graduate (as in *all graduate and a few undergraduate students attended*)

determined Dets
> the five, John's five, the five or more

partitive Dets
> most of John's, two of the five, the three tallest of twenty, more than half of John's, more of John's than of Mary's

proportional Dets
> most, half (of) the, every other, every third, five per cent of the, two thirds of the

In addition certain two-place Dets were studied, e.g. *more ...
than ...* as it occurs in *more students than teachers attended, every
... and ...*, etc. We do not report here on such Dets, only noting
that the constraint we impose on T_{Det} for the one-place ones
extends naturally to *n*-place Dets, functions from $(E^*)^n$ into E^{**}.
Items given in parentheses above are ones which for various
reasons cannot be treated strictly extensionally.

Note that our list includes a variety of 'non-logical' elements
among Dets, the simplest being possessives like *John's*. *John's* is
non-logical in the sense that for a given universe *E* there are many
acceptable interpretations for it; how it is interpreted will depend
in part on how the PN *John* is interpreted (any individual will do)
and on which objects we consider that John has (any choice will
do).

Let us now return to the problem of defining T_{Det}. Observe first
that certain Dets form boolean combinations (*some but not all*,
etc.) and their interpretation is straightforwardly pointwise, given
the interpretations of the conjuncts, disjuncts, etc. Thus the properties which *some but not all students* have are the intersection of
the properties which some students have with those that (not all)
students have; and the latter set is clearly the complement of the
set that all students have. We would like then T_{Det} to be a boolean
algebra with the operations defined pointwise, e.g. $(f \wedge g)(p) =
f(p) \wedge g(p)$, etc. so as to provide denotations for boolean com-
binations of Dets. Note further that many Dets are naturally interpreted as boolean functions of others even though they are not
formed from them with *and, or,* or *not*. For example, *fewer than
ten* is naturally interpreted as the complement of *at least ten*; *at
most ten* is the complement of *more than ten*; *exactly ten* is the
meet of *at least ten* with the complement of *more than ten*. Nor are
such boolean interpretations limited to 'logical' Dets: *no student's*
is naturally interpreted as the complement of *some student's*, and
some student's is the join of *x's* taken over all individuals *x* with the
student property. Other examples where we take arbitrary (not just
finite) meets and joins are given by: *infinitely many* — the meet of
at least n taken over all finite *n*, and *a prime number of* — interpreted as the join of *exactly n* taken over all prime *n*.

The observation that T_{Det} is a boolean algebra provides the key
to our definition of T_{Det}. Let us find English Dets whose natural
denotations are not representable (at least obviously) as boolean
functions of those of other Dets. Take such Dets as *basic* and see

what denotations we need for them. Then *define* T_{Det} to be all the functions obtained from these by taking arbitrary meets, joins, and complements defined pointwise. Some examples of Dets which are basic in this sense are: *every*, *a*, *most*, *several*, *John's*, *at least two*, *the two*, etc. And our investigation led us to note two properties which their denotations had in common: they were *increasing* and *weakly conservative*, notions we define below:

DEFINITION
  (a) A subset K of a boolean algebra B is *increasing* iff whenever $x \leqslant y$ and $x \in K$ then y is in K. A function from one boolean algebra into another is *increasing* iff its value at every argument is increasing.
  (b) A function f from an algebra B into its power set algebra B^* is *weakly conservative* iff for all $x, y \in B$, if $x \in f(y)$ then $(x \wedge y) \in f(y)$.

The linguistic intuition behind these definitions is as follows: to say that the denotation of *at least two* is increasing is to say that whenever a property p is in at least two q's (i.e. at least two q's are p's) and $p \leqslant t$ (i.e. all p's are t's) then t must also be in at least two q's. If at least two linguists are vegetarians and all vegetarians are socialists, then clearly at least two linguists are socialists. Similarly the reader can verify intuitively that the denotations of *every*, *a*, *the two*, *John's*, etc. are increasing.

As regards weak conservativity it is clear that if p is in at least two q's, then $(p \wedge q)$, the property of being both a p and a q, must also be in at least two q's. E.g. if at least two linguists are vegetarians, then at least two linguists are both vegetarians and linguists. Similarly the other examples of basic Dets given above are easily shown to be weakly conservative.

Let us take then the denotations of basic Dets to be the functions from E^* into E^{**} which are both increasing and weakly conservative. Call this set *Gen*. We may now formally define T_{Det} as follows:

DEFINITION
  T_{Det} is the smallest[2] subset of the set of functions from E^* into E^{**} which includes Gen and is closed under arbitrary meets, joins, and complements.

We then show that the non-basic Dets in our list take their denotations in T_{Det} as defined. Theorem 8 is useful in that demonstration besides being interesting in its own right:

THEOREM 8

T_{Det} is exactly the set of (strictly) conservative functions: $E^* \to E^{**}$, where we define $f: E^* \to E^{**}$ to be (strictly) *conservative* iff for all $p, q \in E^*$, $p \in f(q)$ iff $(p \wedge q) \in f(q)$.

Theorem 8 is linguistically quite intuitive. Confusing levels, it says that we count as Det denotations just the functions *det* which satisfy the equation below:

(13) det p's are q's iff det p's are both p's and q's

And at a glance it is relatively easy to see intuitively that many of the complex Dets in our list satisfy that equation. E.g. if not only John's car can fly then clearly not only John's car is both a car and can fly, and conversely. If fewer male than female students are vegetarians, then and only then are fewer male than female students both students and vegetarians, etc.

Having established that T_{Det} is large enough to provide denotations for the generous class of Dets we considered, we may proffer the following language universal with some confidence:

UNIVERSAL 3

The transparent (one-place) Dets in any language are interpreted by conservative functions from T_{CN} into T_{NP}.

We should note further (metalinguistic) support for the correctness of constraining T_{Det} to the conservative functions from E^* into E^{**}: namely, Barwise and Cooper (1981) take, without detailed argument, the basic set in which Dets denote to be those functions from E^* into E^{**} which, in their phrase, *live on their arguments*. It is immediate from their definition that f is conservative. Note further that it is quite reasonable to take Det denotations to be functions which satisfy (13), since (13) seems so plausible and no immediate counterexamples come to mind. In KS, however, we did not in fact think out Det denotations in that way, but rather in the way we have indicated here. Thus our approach provides support, in addition to direct intuition and apparent descriptive adequacy, for the correctness of the characterisation of T_{Det}. Namely, we want the increasing and weakly conservative functions in T_{Det} so as to provide denotations for basic Dets. And we want T_{Det} closed under the pointwise defined boolean operations so as to provide denotations for boolean combinations of Dets (as well as others mentioned, e.g. *some student's*, *at most ten*, etc.). Imposing just these conditions on T_{Det} then yields as a theorem that T_{Det} is just the conservative functions, i.e. just those which live on their arguments.

Moreover, the boolean approach we took has several bonuses of interest to this paper. First, we may easily compute the cardinality of T_{Det} so as to determine by just how much the conservativity condition shrinks down the set of all functions from E^* into E^{**}. It is easy to show that T_{Det} as defined is a complete and atomic boolean algebra and thus has cardinality 2^k, where k is the cardinality of the set of atoms of T_{Det}. And it is not hard to compute that $k = 3^n$, where n is the number of individuals of the model. Thus,

THEOREM 9
    The cardinality of T_{Det} is $2^{(3^n)}$, where n is the number of individuals.

Recall that the cardinality of the set of all functions from E^* into E^{**} is $2^{(4^n)}$, massively larger than that of T_{DET} then. For example, in a world of only two individuals there are 2^{16} or more than 65,500 functions from E^* into E^{**}, but only 2^9 or 512 of them are conservative, i.e. in T_{Det}. Thus we see that most functions from E^* into E^{**} are not in fact possible (extensional) Det denotations, and that Universal 3 represents a significant constraint on the class of possible interpreting functions for human languages.

On the other hand, of course, we must acknowledge that 2^{3^n} increases very rapidly with n. Is it at all realistic to think that in a world of only two individuals we can in any sense 'know' 512 ways of associating NP denotations with CN denotations? Perhaps not. But in the definition of T_{Det} proposed we don't have to. It is sufficient to 'know' what the elements of Gen are, that is, the denotations of the Dets we called basic. Any other of the 512 elements of T_{Det} (in our world of two individuals) can be figured out as boolean functions of things we know. So, as with T_{NP}, there is a semantically basic subset of T_{Det} whose elements determine all the elements in T_{Det} relative to boolean operations.

Moreover, we don't even have to know what all the elements in

Gen are, as it is provably bigger than we need to generate T_{Det}. (It is in fact closed under meets and joins, but not complements.) We note:

THEOREM 10

T_{Det} is generated by a subset K of Gen which has cardinality $2^{.n}$, where n is the number of individuals.

There is more than one set K which satisfies Theorem 10, so we cannot pick out uniquely a subset of the basic Dets whose denotations give us all the Det denotations relative to the boolean operations. However, looking through the various subsets of Det which are sufficient in this respect, it is easy to see that T_{Det} as defined is a psycholinguistically realistic set. To generate T_{DET} it is sufficient for example to have a couple of 'logical' Dets (about which more below) such as *some* and *every*, and one general way of forming non-logical Dets, say composition with absolute adjectives. Thus the set of possible denotations of *some male* and *every male* is more than sufficient to generate all of T_{Det}. Such Dets appear somewhat artificial, though presumably they occur in complex Dets like *some male and every female student passed the exam*. None the less, we have no trouble understanding such sentences, whence we may infer that if we know the meanings of *some* and *every* and we can interpret expressions like *some male* and *every male* above, we know enough to figure out any possible determiner denotation.

A second bonus from defining T_{Det} in the way we have is that it naturally gives us interesting subcategories of Dets. Thus we have distinguished a proper subset Gen of T_{Det} and it is reasonable to ask whether the elements of Det which always take their interpretations in Gen are a set we would be motivated to distinguish on syntactic grounds (as is the case for NPs, where the elements of NP which are always interpreted as generators are just the proper nouns). And a partial correlation does exist:

UNIVERSAL 4

Syntactically simple Dets (with the exception of ones translating *no* and *neither* if they are syntactically simple) are always interpreted as elements of Gen.

We note without proof that the elements of Gen are exactly the increasing functions in T_{Det}. As Gen was defined to consist of increasing functions, this just claims that by taking boolean functions of elements of Gen we do not obtain any new increasing functions. So we note then:

THEOREM 11
For all $f \in T_{Det}$, $f \in$ Gen iff f is increasing.

Thus Universal 4 says that syntactically simple Dets other than *no* and *neither* are always interpreted by increasing elements of T_{Det}. If *no* and *neither* are analysed as syntactically simple, then they are counterexamples to the claim, but the only ones as far as we know. Moreover, in English there is a reasonable claim to be made that they are not syntactically simple. On the basis of pairs like *one/none*, *either/neither*, *ever/never*, *or/nor*, *ay(e)/nay*, *aught/naught*, etc. we might argue that *no* and *neither* are both bi-morphemic, consisting of a root and an initial N-morpheme interpreted as negative. This is at least historically correct, the initial *n* in these items deriving ultimately from PIE *ne* '*not*'. Moreover, many languages (e.g. Malagasy, French, and Hebrew) have no single word *no* at all, and in the few other cases we know of where there is a single word *no*, e.g. German *kein* and Danish *ingens*, the form is at least historically polymorphemic.

Further, thinking of Gen as the increasing elements of T_{Det}, another natural subcategory suggests itself: those elements of T_{Det} which are decreasing. They are provably just the complements of elements in Gen. Is the class of expressions in Det which are always interpreted as decreasing in any way syntactically distinguished? Thanks to the insightful work of Ladusaw (1980) and Fauconnier (1979), we have an affirmative answer to this:

UNIVERSAL 5
Dets on subject NPs which trigger negative polarity items in the VP are just the decreasing Dets.

Some examples of decreasing Dets are of course the overt negations of increasing ones, e.g. *not every, not one, not more than ten*, etc. and include as well ones like *at most ten, fewer than ten, no*, etc. They also include non-logical Dets like *no student's, fewer than ten students'*, etc. As can be seen below, they do in fact trigger negative polarity items in the VP:

(14) $\left\{\begin{array}{l}\textit{not one} \text{ student} \\ \textit{at most ten} \text{ students} \\ \textit{no student's} \text{ mother}\end{array}\right\}$ saw *any* deer in the forest

However, if the Dets in (14) are replaced by increasing ones preserving *any* in the VP, the result is ungrammatical (try e.g. *one, more than ten, some student's*, etc.). Further it is generally the case that Dets which are neither increasing nor decreasing fail to trigger negative polarity items: e.g. *exactly three, between five and ten, all but three, more male than female*, etc.

Once again then by examination of the types we associate with subcategories, we have been able to find significant and non-obvious correlations between surface form and semantic structure. Let us now compare T_{Det} with the other sorts of types we have needed in a semantics for natural language.

6.2. Similarities Between Dets and Other Categories

Dets are different from all other categories so far considered, in that they are semantically functions from an algebra into its power set. So there is no other category we know of whose denotations can be conservative.

Notwithstanding T_{Det} does show certain affinities with restricting adjectives. Thus, while T_{Det} is a ca algebra, as is $T_{AP_{+r}}$, neither are ca-free algebras, so Dets and the major APs differ from Argument categories in the same way. Similarly Dets are basically not structure-preserving functions in the same sense in which APs are not: only a few trivial elements in T_{Det} are homomorphisms (see KS for the characterisation of just which elements in T_{Det} are homomorphisms). Third, and most obvious of course, Dets and restricting APs are functions with the same domain. And in one non-obvious respect these functions behave similarly on their arguments. Namely, the possible values of a Det or AP at an argument p increase directly with the number of individuals which have p. For a restricting AP function f we have that $f(p) \leqslant p$, so there are 2^k possible values for such functions at p, where k is the number of individuals with p.

For Det functions, on the other hand, we may show that there are 2^{2k} possible values of such functions at p (as above). In fact the value of a Det function f at p is determined by the properties $q \leqslant p$ which are in $f(p)$. So we may think of elements of T_{Det} as given by functions which associate with each property p a set of properties q, all $\leqslant p$. In this loose sense then we may think of a Det semantically as a kind of higher order restricting AP.

6.3. The Major Difference Between Dets and Other Categories: Its Logical Nature

Almost certainly the most striking difference between Det and other categories is the high percentage of logical constants among the Dets. When we try to think of expressions which are (intuitively still) logical constants in the categories NP, CN, n-place Predicate, or AP, only a handful of cases come to mind. For example, in an extensional logic *exist* is a logical constant among the P_1s, and *be* (the identity function on individuals) is one among the P_2s. Perhaps *individual* (or *existent*, etc.) is among the CNs, etc. But among the Dets most of the expressions we think of initially are logical in nature: *every, some, at least k, all but three*, etc. We would like to know whether this apparent distribution is an accident or not. If we think harder, will we find many more logical expressions among the P_1s? A little trial and error suggests that this is no in the following sense. Any logical element we find among the P_1s (they may be syntactically complex) appears to have the same denotation as *exist* (e.g. *sings or doesn't sing*, etc.) or its complement *not exist* (*is singing and isn't singing*, etc.). Are these apparent facts in any way predictable given the sets of possible denotations we associate with these categories? We show below that basically the answer is yes.

To show this, we must first have some clear idea what logical constants are, and this is a matter of some discussion in the philosophical and logical literature. However, one point on which all theorists would agree is the following:

THESIS
> If an expression e in L is a logical constant then all interpretations of the language relative to a given universe agree on e, i.e. assign it the same denotation.

The logical constants in any category then will be among the expressions which are constantly interpreted in the sense of the Thesis above. Among the Dets, for example *every, at least two, between five and ten*, etc., all meet the condition though one like *John's* do not, since given a universe E, many functions in T_{Det} may interpret *John's* depending on which individual interprets

John and depending on which objects he 'has'. Among the P_1s *exist* and *not exist* are clearly constantly interpreted, but many others, e.g. *sleep, swim*, etc. are not, since given an E, and thus the individuals of the universe, it is arbitrary which ones are *sleeping, swimming*, etc.

We may now, for any category C, look at the elements of the type for C which are the denotations of the constantly interpreted expressions in C. And we may reasonably ask just what proportion of T_C is occupied by the logical elements. But is there any way of identifying these elements except on a case by case basis? Is there not some property they have in common regardless of what category C is chosen? The answer is yes. Consider first the special case of Dets.

Intuitively a 'logical' element of T_{Det} should not be able to discriminate among properties which have the same boolean structure. To make that notion more precise, consider that an isomorphism on an algebra is by definition a function which preserves all of the structures of the algebra. We may think then of two elements p, q in T_{CN} as having the same boolean structure, if there is an isomorphism from T_{CN} onto itself which maps one to the other. (An isomorphism from an algebra onto itself is standardly called an *automorphism*.) So p and q have the same boolean structure iff there is an automorphism i on T_{CN} such that $i(p) = q$. And to say that an element f in T_{Det} cannot discriminate among properties with the same boolean structure is to say that in deciding whether to put p in the set of properties it associates with q, f cannot tell whether it is looking at the pair (p, q) or an automorphic image of such a pair $i(p), i(q)$. Thus,

DEFINITION

$f \in T_{\text{Det}}$ is *automorphism invariant* (AI) iff for all elements p, q $\in T_{\text{CN}}$ and all automorphisms i on T_{CN}, $p \in f(q)$ iff $i(p) \in f(i(q))$.

It is not hard to show that the denotations of *every, at least k*, etc. lie in $T_{\text{Det}_{\text{AI}}}$, the set of automorphism invariant elements of T_{Det}. And it is easy to see that this fails for Dets like *John's*. To see this we note without proof that in a finite universe, two properties are identifiable under an automorphism iff the number of individuals with one is identical to the number with the other. Now consider a finite universe in which there are exactly two cars and two boats, so there is an automorphism i such that $i(\text{car}) = \text{boat}$; John has exactly one car and no boats. Then *John's boat* denotes the empty set of properties and *John's car* the individual with the car property which John has. So car $\in$ John's car but $i(\text{car}) = \text{boat} \notin$ John's $(i(\text{car})) = $ John's (boat), therefore John's is not AI.

Finally we note the following theorem (to be generalised) which holds for all forms of model theoretic semantics for natural language:

THEOREM 12′

For all expressions $d \in$ Det, if d is constantly interpreted as per the Thesis above, then for any universe E and any interpretation m of the language relative to E, $m(d)$ is automorphism invariant.

Thus the set of AI functions in T_{Det} provides a subset of T_{Det} in which the logical constants of Det always take their denotations.

One may query just how big this set is. Again the boolean nature of T_{Det} allows a rather easy answer to this question. First we may easily show that T_{DetAI} is complete and atomic subalgebra of T_{Det} and thus has cardinality 2^k, where k is the cardinality of the set of atoms. In a finite universe with n individuals the number of these atoms may be computed to be $(n + 1)(n + 2)/2$. Thus,

THEOREM 13

In a finite universe with n individuals there are $2^{(n+1)(n+2)/2}$ automorphism invariant functions in T_{Det}.

The absolute figure here is of little interest but two properties it has should be noted. First, it is a fairly small portion of T_{Det} itself. The reader may compute that in a world of two individuals there are, as noted, 512 elements in T_{Det}, only $2^6 = 64$ of which are AI.

The second point to notice is that the cardinality of T_{DetAI} increases with the number of individuals. In this respect we will see that Dets differ from many other categories where typically the number of AI elements in the type has an upper bound which is constant and independent of how many individuals there are. For this claim to make sense, of course, we must define what we mean by a P_1 denotation being AI, etc., as above we gave the definition only for the case of Dets. We sketch the more general definition below. It is in some respects simpler than the special case given above, though it may appear at first to be less intuitive (again see KS for details).

Given a universe E, let us consider all the automorphisms i from E^* $(= T_{CN})$ onto E^*. Each of those automorphisms naturally extends to a function i^* which is an automorphism on every type. That is, for every category C, i^* restricted to T_C is an automorphism from T_C into T_C. For every C, we shall refer to these automorphisms on T_C as the *basic automorphisms* on T_C. We may then define:

DEFINITION

For all categories C and all $x \in T_C$, x is *automorphism invariant* (AI) iff for every basic automorphism i^*, $i^*(x) = x$.

So the AI elements in any type then are just the elements which a basic automorphism must map onto themselves. We show (easily) in KS that this definition coincides with the earlier one on T_{Det}. Further we now have the appropriately general version of Theorem 12:

THEOREM 12

If e in L is constantly interpreted then for all universes E and all interpretations m of L, $m(e)$ is automorphism invariant.

So it now makes sense to talk of the AI elements in the types for the APs, n-place predicates, etc. And when we check what proportion of these types is taken by AI elements, we obtain some interesting results. For example,

THEOREM 14

(a) No element in the type for proper nouns is automorphism invariant.
(b) Exactly two elements in the type for the absolute APs are AI.
(c) Exactly two elements in the types for the P_1s and the CNs are AI.
(d) At most four elements in the type for the P_2s are AI.

Universal 6 is basically a corollary of Theorem 14.

UNIVERSAL 6
 (a) No language has logically constant proper nouns.
 (b) The number of syntactically simple logical constants among
     CNs, the n-place predicates, and absolute APs is small and
     bounded.

Universal 6a is reasonable since by Theorem 14a no element in
T_{PN} is AI, whence by Theorem 12 Universal 6a follows. Theorems
14b,c tell us that there are at most two non-synonymous logical
constants among the absolute APs and the P_1s. So the number of
syntactically simple such constants is limited by whatever constraints limit the number of lexical synonyms in a language and can
be expected to be small. Analogous claims hold regarding
Theorem 14d.

Matters are quite otherwise for Det, however. We saw that in a
world of only two individuals there are 64 AI elements in T_{Det}, so
even a small world can discriminate among many logical constants
among the Dets. And that number increases steadily as the size of
the universe increases. For universes of different sizes we can find
distinct Dets which have the same extension in the smaller but
distinct extensions in the larger one. To take an easy example, in a
world of just seven individuals the Dets *at least eight* and *at least
nine* both denote the zero element of T_{Det}, the function sending
each property p to the empty set. No property q can be in at least
eight (nine) p's since there are at most seven p's. But if we enrich
the world by one individual, then *at least eight* will not denote the
zero Det, though *at least nine* still will, so they have distinct
denotations in a world of eight individuals.

We do then have some reason to expect large numbers, even an
infinite number, of logical constants among the Dets, since for any
number we pick we can always find an E such that T_{Det} provides
distinct denotations for that many distinct constants. Thus the
presence of many logical constants among the Dets is a semantic
possibility in a way in which it isn't for predicates, absolute APs,
common nouns, and proper nouns.

The semantic notion of automorphism invariance turns out to
be interesting in the analysis of English Dets in yet another way.
namely, it allows us, together with other notions, to represent on
the one hand the sense in which certain rather simple Dets like
several and *a few* are 'logical' compared with ones like *John's*,
and yet on the other hand they are less 'determinate' in meaning than

ones like *every*, *at least three*, etc.

To take the latter point first, we clearly want to put *several* in a subcategory of Det which is $+$AI and $+$increasing, thus guaranteeing that it will always be interpreted by an increasing automorphism invariant function. We doubtless want to put other conditions on its interpretation as well, e.g. that it is booleanly $\leqslant$ *at least three*. But these conditions do not uniquely determine the interpretation of *several* in general. That is, for sufficiently large E there will be many functions from E^* into E^{**} satisfying these conditions. So *several* is not a logical constant. Moreover, its interpretation is not determined by the interpretations of other expressions in the language, since *several* is syntactically simple. So in this sense *several* is vague. Within admittedly quite narrow bounds, there is more than one function it might denote, and we have no way of telling which.

On the other hand, *several* is 'logical' compared with e.g. *John's*, since it shares the characteristic property of logical constants — namely it always denotes an AI element of T_{Det}. Note that it is only the AI requirement on *several* which distinguishes it from expressions like *John's*. For example, *John's* itself is increasing. *John's three* is booleanly $\leqslant$ *at least three*, etc.

Thus we can see that explicitly defining the property which the logical constants among the Dets have in common — something we are not motivated to do in a translation approach — has enabled us to represent, at least partially, the meaning differences between certain Dets, including ones which are not themselves logical constants. (We may say that Dets like *several* are logical, but not constant.)

7. Conclusion, and a Last Universal

For the categories we have considered it has generally been the case that expressions in that category took their denotations in a set which possessed a boolean structure, enabling us to interpret them as conjunctions, disjunctions, and negations of expressions in the category. In addition, this boolean structure was used in a variety of more specific ways in defining particular classes of types, e.g. in defining homomorphisms, restricting functions, conservative functions, ca-free generators, etc. The fact that the types for basically all productive categories in English have a boolean structure strongly suggests that the boolean operations, the meanings of *and, or,* and *not,* if you like, are not semantic operations specific to any particular category. E.g. the meaning of *and,* etc. is not that of a function which only applies to sentence meanings, as one might infer by default from the semantics given for standard first order logic. And what this suggests is that the boolean operations, rather than representing properties of objects in the world (denotations), represent properties of the mind, ways we conceive of objects in the world. This assumption allows us to account not only for the syntactic ubiquity of *and, or,* and *not* as illustrated in this paper; it also allows us to account for the naturalness with which we interpret apparent conjunctions, disjunctions, etc. of expressions which we would not normally assign a category to and interpret. Thus we easily interpret such cumbersome expressions as *John bought and Mary cooked the turkey,* even though we do not normally assign an interpretation to expressions like *John bought.* Let us conclude this paper then with a 'Universal' which is not specifically linguistic, though linguistically instantiated by the boolean generalisations about human language we have made in this paper.

UNIVERSAL 7

The boolean operations, expressed by *and, or,* and *not* in English, are operations of the mind.

COROLLARY

The truths of boolean algebra are 'Laws of Thought'.

The 'corollary' is intended to express the indebtedness of this work to the original (in both senses) work of George Boole (1854).

Notes

1. Research for this paper was supported by NSF grant BNS 79-14141.
2. The smallest subset of a set satisfying certain conditions is by definition the intersection of all the subsets which satisfy the conditions.

References

Barwise, J. and R. Cooper (1981) 'Generalised Quantifiers and Natural Languages', *Stanford Working Papers in Semantics* 1, 1-80.

Ben-Chorin, S. (1982) 'Sentence Meanings as a Formal Basis for Intensional Logic', in *Proceedings of the first West Coast Conference on Formal Linguistics*, Stanford.

Boole, G. (1854) *An Investigation into the Laws of Thought*, Cambridge, Cambridge University Press.

Chomsky, N. (1957) *Syntactic Structures*, Mouton, The Hague.

Fauconnier, G. (1979) 'Implication Reversal in Natural Language', in F. Guenthner and S.J. Schmidt (eds.), *Formal Semantics and Pragmatics for Natural Language*, Reidel, Dordrecht.

Keenan, E.L. (1981) 'A Boolean Approach to Semantics', in J.A.G. Groenendink *et al.* (eds.) *Formal Methods in the Study of Language*, Mathematisch Centrum, Amsterdam.

—— (1982) 'Boolean Algebra for Linguists', UCLA Working Papers in Semantics, Vol. 1, Department of Linguistics, UCLA.

—— and L. Faltz (1978) *Logical Types for Natural Language*, UCLA Occasional Papers in Linguistics, No. 3, Department of Linguistics, UCLA.

—— (1978) *Logical Types for Natural Language* (completely revised edition) Reidel, Dordrecht.

—— and J. Stavi (to appear) 'A Semantic Characterisation of Natural Language Determiners', in *Linguistics and Philosophy*.

Ladusaw, W. (1980) *Polarity Sensitivity as Inherent Scope Relations*, Garland Press, New York (also in IULC).

Montague, R. (1973) 'The Proper Treatment of Quantification in ordinary English', in J. Hintikka *et al.* (eds.), *Approaches to Natural Language*, Reidel, Dordrecht.

Partee, B. and R. Mats (to appear) 'Generalised Conjunction and Type Ambiguity', in A. von Stechow *et al.* (eds.) *Meaning, Use and Interpretation*, de Gruyter, Berlin.

Strawson, P.F. (1959) *Individuals: An Essay in descriptive Metaphysics*, Methuen, London.